exotic tropical fishes

EXPANDED EDITION

Dr. Herbert R. Axelrod
Dr. Cliff W. Emmens
Dr. Warren E. Burgess
Mr. Neal Pronek
Mr. Glen S. Axelrod

ISBN 0-87666-537-7 (Looseleaf)
ISBN 0-87666-543-1 (Non-looseleaf)

FIRST REVISED AND EXPANDED EDITION
©1980 by T.F.H. Publications, Inc.
Previous copyrights: ©1962, ©1963, ©1964, ©1965, ©1966,
©1967, ©1968, ©1969, ©1970, ©1971, ©1972, ©1973, ©1974,
©1975, ©1976, ©1977, ©1978, ©1979.

Distributed in the U.S. by T.F.H. Publications, Inc., 211 West Sylvania
Avenue, PO Box 427, Neptune, NJ 07753; in England by T.F.H. (Gt. Britain)
Ltd., 13 Nutley Lane, Reigate, Surrey; in Canada to the pet trade by Rolf C.
Hagen Ltd., 3225 Sartelon Street, Montreal 382, Quebec; in Southeast Asia
by Y.W. Ong, 9 Lorong 36 Geylang, Singapore 14; in Australia and the South
Pacific by Pet Imports Pty. Ltd., P.O. Box 149, Brookvale 2100, N.S.W.
Australia; in South Africa by Valid Agencies, P.O. Box 51901, Randburg 2125
South Africa. Published by T.F.H. Publications, Inc., Ltd, the British Crown
Colony of Hong Kong.

TABLE OF CONTENTS

FISH INTERNATIONAL
NUMBERING SYSTEM   (FINS)

This system is composed of a ten-digit alpha-numeric code which is designed to carry the necessary information to accurately describe the morphological type, origin and size of a given fish species. This system is expandable to carry comparable information for any type of organism, animal or plant. Selected T.F.H. reference books will be likewise coded so that they can be used in conjunction with this system.

1	2	3	4	5	6	7	8	9	0

BOX 1: ORGANISM CODE NUMBER/LETTER

Available: ABCDEFGHJKLMNPQRSTUVWYZ1234567890. (33 characters)

This code number will refer to a particular type of organism.

An example of this breakdown may be:

A = anemones
B = birds
C = cats
D = dogs
E = echinoderms (starfish, etc.)
F = freshwater fishes
H = herptiles
J = invertebrates (other than AENQRW)

K = live foods
M = mammals (other than CD)
N = molluscs
P = plants
Q = corals
R = crustaceans (crabs, etc.)
S = marine fishes
W = worms

BOX 2: ORIGIN/SEX CODE LETTER
Same letters available as in Box 1. (23 characters)

A = wild male
B = wild female
C = wild juvenile
D = wild ? sex
R = wild pair

E = cultivated male
F = cultivated female
G = cultivated juvenile
H = cultivated ? sex
Q = cultivated pair

J = ? origin male
K = ? origin female
M = ? origin juvenile
N = ? origin ? sex
P = ? origin pair

BOXES 3—7: SPECIES CODE NUMBER/LETTER

The same numbers and letters are available as in Box 1. This code will refer to the approximate page in a T.F.H. reference book on the given organism group, using Boxes 3, 4, 5 and 6. Box 7 will contain a letter referring to the supplement (if the organism was added following the original text's publication).

Box 3 will refer to the position on the page.

BOX 3.

T = top
M = middle
B = bottom
R = right
L = left

A = top right
C = top left
D = bottom right
E = bottom left

BOXES 8—10: CONTAINS MORPHOLOGICAL, CHROMATOGENICAL AND SIZE INFORMATION IN A CODE NUMBER/LETTER

The same numbers and letters are available as in Box 1. Different information keys will be available for the different organisms as described in Box 1. Assuming that the organism is a fish (Box 1, F or S), the following would apply:

BOX 8. COLOR VARIETIES:

A = albino	K = black	T = tuxedo
B = blue	M = mixed	U = rainbow
C = chocolate	N = normal	V = variegated
D = gold	P = blotched	W = wagtail
E = white	Q = orange	Y = yellow
G = green	R = red	Z = new
J = lace	S = spotted	

BOX 9. MORPHOLOGICAL DATA:

B = bubblehead	N =normal
E = bearded	R = oranda
F = fantail	S = sailfin
G = bubble-eye	T = split tail, scissors tail
L = lyretail	V = veiltail, long fins
M = mirror	Z = mutant, new

BOX 10. SIZE DATA:

Total length

0	under	2.0 cm		8	"	7.0 & 8.0 cm
1	between	2.0 & 2.5 cm		9	"	8.0 & 9.0 cm
2	"	2.5 & 3.0 cm		A	"	9.0 & 10.0 cm
3	"	3.0 & 3.5 cm		B	"	10.0 & 12.5 cm
4	"	3.5 & 4.0 cm		C	"	12.5 & 15.0 cm
5	"	4.0 & 5.0 cm		D	over	15.0 cm
6	"	5.0 & 6.0 cm		E	unknown	
7	"	6.0 & 7.0 cm				

NOTE: The letter "X" means either not applicable or not important with regard to this entire code system. The following letters are not used as to avoid potential confusion with the numbers: I, O

Introduction

This Expanded Edition of *Exotic Tropical Fishes* represents *the* most important contribution to aquarium literature. The ultimate in freshwater aquarium fish books, this volume covers every important aspect of aquarium management, an evaluation of the most popular aquarium plants, an introduction to breeding tropical aquarium fishes on a commercial basis and, most importantly, a thorough and descriptive catalog of exotic aquarium fishes. Over 800 species and forms of exotic tropical fishes are evaluated, and more than 1000 full-color photographs are used to show all of the fish species covered, making identification a simple matter. In addition, there are color photographs of different aquarium plant species. All of the fish photos in color carry the ten-digit alpha-numeric code for the new Fish International Numbering System **(FINS). FINS** allows exact identification with a minimum of text.

History of This Book

Originally published in 1962, *Exotic Tropical Fishes,* a mammoth volume even then, has been sold to many hundreds-of-thousands of aquarists and scientists throughout the world, has been translated into several languages and is a best seller in every sense. The term *"Expanded Edition,"* however, can only be considered a modest reflection of the updating of this classic tome. Over the years, supplement booklets containing over 800 pages of information on hundreds of aquarium fishes and plants have been published as additional information to the original bound text and as insert material for the looseleaf edition. This new expanded edition contains the original text plus the first 25 supplement booklets, all revised, edited and expanded to over 1300 pages to account for 20 years of growth in the aquarium industry and reflect all changes in scientific nomenclature. Fish descriptions concentrate on the most pertinent and useful information available today, and this volume is fully indexed with both common and scientific names for easy reference.

Two Bindings

Exotic Tropical Fishes, Expanded Edition is available in both permanent hardcover binding and looseleaf binding. Supplement booklets containing additional information will continue to be published as before. These supplements have been, and will continue to be, published as free installments in *Tropical Fish Hobbyist Magazine* and are designed to be removed and inserted into the looseleaf binding. Supplement booklets can also be purchased separately and will be published annually.

About the Authors

The idea of this book and its predecessor was formulated and realized by its senior author, Dr. Herbert R. Axelrod, who is undoubtedly the best known tropical fish expert in the world. As author, university professor, lecturer, publisher, adventurer and scientist, he has already written sixteen definitive texts on ichthyology, published more than twenty-eight smaller books on individual species of fishes for the hobbyist, written hundreds of articles and has discovered about 100 heretofore unknown species, many of which were named after him.

Dr. Axelrod is a graduate of New York University and is a member of the American Society of Ichthyologists and Herpetologists, the Biometric Society, the New York Zoological Society, the New York Academy of Sciences, the National Research Council, National Academy of Sciences, and numerous aquarium societies throughout the United States, England, Germany, Australia and other countries as well. He is also a certified fisheries scientist of the American Fisheries Society.

In March 1977, he received the Smithson Silver Medal from the Smithsonian Institute for his ichthyological endeavors and establishment of the Leonard P. Schultz Fund. In May 1978, he was awarded an honorary Doctor of Science degree by the University of Guelph in Guelph, Ontario, Canada.

Dr. Cliff W. Emmens is presently professor emeritus in the Department of Veterinary Physiology, the University of Sydney. In addition, Dr. Emmens is an avid tropical fish hobbyist and prolific writer. He has authored or co-authored a half-dozen books for T.F.H. Publications alone, including such best sellers as *Catfishes, Exotic Marine Fishes, Fancy Guppies* and the *Guppy Handbook*. Whether it be books for the beginner, advanced aquarist or professional scientist, Dr. Emmens's lucid and informative style makes his works interesting and easy to read. Dr. Emmens was primarily responsible for the *Management* section of this book, and its contents reflect his many years of experience in the aquarium field.

Dr. Warren E. Burgess received his B.S. in zoology and his M.S in marine biology at the University of Miami, Florida. His research dealt with reef fishes and invertebrates and larval marine fishes. He received his Ph.D. at the University of Hawaii, where he continued his studies of reef fishes and completed his dissertation on the butterflyfishes.

He joined the editorial staff of T.F.H. Publications as Senior Editor in 1972, where he has authored numerous books and articles on marine and freshwater fishes as well as marine invertebrates. While at TFH he has worked on aquarium fishes and is undertaking a comprehensive study of cichlid fishes. He has described many new marine and fresh water fishes of interest to the hobbyist.

He is an avid hobbyist as well as a scientist, and he has bred and raised many fishes. Using his expertise, over the past eight years Dr. Burgess has made substantial contributions to the *Tropical Fish* section. This includes, but is not limited to, writing most of the supplement matter published after 1973. Dr. Burgess is a member of several scientific societies, including the American Society of Ichthyologists and Herpetologists, as well as aquarium societies.

Neal Pronek is a world renowned expert in the pet field in general and in the aquarium field in particular. Mr. Pronek joined the T.F.H. Publications editorial staff over twenty years ago and has been Managing Editor for the past ten years. His writings have appeared in dozens of T.F.H. books and he was editor of *Tropical Fish Hobbyist Magazine* for many years prior to taking the helm of the T.F.H. Editorial Department as a whole.

Mr. Pronek's 30 years as a tropical fish aquarist have been used to advantage in this book in that he has made much of his valuable experience available for all to benefit from. Mr. Pronek's primary influence has been in the fish section, although he has made contributions to every section of the book.

Glen S. Axelrod is the relative newcomer to this esteemed group of aquatic experts. He received his B.A. in biology from Rutgers College,R.U., and his M.Sc. in ichthyology from the J.L.B. Smith Institute of Ichthyology, Rhodes University. He is presently working on his Ph.D. in the United States through the J.L.B Smith Institute with the generous assistance and supervision of Professor Karl F. Liem, Museum of Comparative Zoology, Harvard University. Mr. Axelrod's field of research deals with the taxonomic status and ecology of African cichlids, and he spent three years in Africa working on this project.

Mr. Axelrod has been an avid tropical fish hobbyist for almost twenty years. He has several publications, including a book on Rift Lake cichlids, and two scientific publications describing new species that he discovered in Lake Tanganyika. He is a member of several scientific and aquarium societies, including the American Society of Ichthyologists and Herpetologists, and is a Scientific Fellow of the Zoological Society of London.

Mr. Axelrod is a Senior Editor and Assistant to the President at T.F.H. Publications. He supervised the project of revising, editing and expanding *Exotic Tropical Fishes* to its present form.

Using the basic tools of the aquarium hobby, you can create a panorama of natural underwater beauty right in your own livingroom. Photo by R. Zukal.

Principles of Aquarium Management
by Dr. C. W. Emmens

The Tank: Correct selection of a fish tank is the first step in successful aquarium keeping. The rectangular glass tank, either made wholly of glass or with a plastic frame and glass sides and a bottom of glass, slate or other material, is by far the best vessel. The tank will usually contain sand or gravel, plants and decorative rocks or other ornaments, although it is generally felt best to confine the decoration to natural-looking substances. The chief decoration of a furnished freshwater aquarium is the plants. These often contribute more to the attractiveness of the tank than do the fishes themselves.

The tank is usually between 20 and 200 liters in capacity; favorite sizes are 60 x 30 x 30 cm or 60 x 30 x 40 cm, which hold about fifty and seventy liters respectively. Smaller tanks can house neither a decorative selection of the common aquatic plants nor many fishes or any large fishes, while bigger tanks are expensive and somewhat difficult to service. However, tropical fishes can be housed in smaller tanks than coldwater fishes, because they can be crowded more and because many of them do not grow so large. Even a 10- or 20-liter tank can, therefore, contain a selection of the smaller tropicals. With the larger tropicals, a 60-liter tank might comfortably contain a dozen 8 cm barbs but only four or five Goldfish of similar size and only a single pair of fancy Goldfish such as Orandas of the same size.

Tanks are often made with glass which is too thin or with second-hand glass. See that your tank is of unscratched, new glass with a thickness appropriate to its depth, the most important factor because water pressure is dependent only on depth and not on other dimensions. Up to 30 cm depth, use 5 mm sides and a 6.5 mm bottom; between 30 cm and 45 cm, use 6.5 mm plate glass throughout; above 45 cm, use 10 mm plate glass with a 13 mm plate glass bottom; above 60 cm, use 13 mm plate glass throughout.

Fishes and Plants: Fishes breathe oxygen and exhale carbon dioxide, and thus in total they use up oxygen and foul the water with carbon dioxide and excrement. Plants also breathe oxygen, but in sufficiently bright light they manufacture sugar from carbon dioxide taken from their surroundings, whether air or water, and they release oxygen. They also absorb dissolved salts and use these together with carbon dioxide in building up complex organic compounds. Animal excrement, usually known as "mulm," is only available to them after it has been broken down by fungi or bacteria and made soluble. Thus plants in adequate light tend to restore oxygen to the environment and to remove the waste products of animals. In poor light or in darkness they deplete the water or air of oxygen just as do fishes.

From these facts grew the concept of a balanced aquarium, with the waste products of the fishes absorbed by the plants and the oxygen necessary for the fishes provided by the action of the plants in light. This idea must be modified in practice, but the basic principle is nevertheless sound, and a well-planted tank with adequate illumination will usually stay clear and sweet for months or years with little attention.

Biological Cycles: In addition to the above, it has gradually dawned on aquarists that within a fish tank events take place similar to those in a sewerage purification unit or sewerage farm. The extent to which this occurs depends on the particular setup, biological filters which are discussed below giving an optimal effect. In such filters, as in nature, various cycles occur.

The most important of these is the nitrogen cycle, by which excrement, plant debris, uneaten food and even undetected dead fishes are converted to relatively harmless products which can pass off into the atmosphere or be utilized by plants (including algae). Decaying animal or plant material eventually becomes ammonia or one of its salts, then nitrites, then nitrates and, in part, free nitrogen gas. Ammonia and nitrites are poisonous, but nitrates are much less toxic and can be tolerated in large amounts. The exact toxicity of ammonia, a blood poison, depends on pH and temperature, but in general

EXCELLENT.

GOOD.

FAIR.

POOR.

Volume is not the only consideration in choosing which tank is best suited to your needs. The shape of the tank also is important, because shape plays a large part in determining surface area. Drawing by Wilfred L. Whitern.

11

Modern aquaria are made without metal frames or slate bottoms. The sides of the aquarium are held together with a silicone rubber cement. The bottom of the aquarium is usually glass as well.

anything over 0.25 ppm (parts per million) is dangerous. Somewhat more nitrite can be tolerated, but not more than 1 to 2 ppm—better less. Kits are commercially available for checking levels. Nitrates are harmless up to 50 or even 100 ppm, particularly if they accumulate gradually, and proper aquarium maintenance should always keep them well below these levels.

Aquarium Dimensions: Aquaria should be as shallow as possible, since the surface of water exposed to the air is the most important factor in determining the number of fish they can safely hold. However, a very shallow tank is an eyesore, and a compromise is always made between biological and artistic requirements. Many prefer a "double cube" type of construction, with the tank twice as long as it is wide and high, *i.e.,* 60 x 30 x 30 cm as quoted above. This tank is still rather shallow for the full growth of plants and looks better if the height is somewhat increased, so that a common variation is 60 x 30 x 36 cm or even 60 x 30 x 40 cm. Such tanks can hold no more fishes than the first-mentioned; they merely look nicer.

To compute the liter capacity of a tank, multiply the length, width and height in cm together and divide by 1000, thus:

$$\frac{60 \times 30 \times 30}{1000} = \frac{54000}{1000} = 54 \text{ liters}$$

This refers to the actual volume of the tank, and if allowance is to be made for a 2 cm air space on top and 4 cm of sand at the bottom, the actual water volume is only about three-fourths of the calculated volume in this instance. This does not matter when considering fish capacity, however, as we then use the surface area, as explained more fully below.

Fish Capacity: Mention has just been made of the balanced aquarium and of the reciprocal actions of plants and animals. It was believed until recently that the exchange of carbon dioxide and oxygen between fish and plants taking place directly through the water was more important than is really the case. With plants in a good light, and in a crowded tank, this interaction may matter considerably, and the tank is often in a poor state at night. With a tank not unduly crowded, either with fish or plants, the exchange of gases between the air and water is more important than any other factor. This is why the surface area of the tank counts for so much, and why, in practically all circumstances, the influence of plants may be ignored when thinking of fish capacity.

In addition to surface area, surface movement and the circulation of water within a tank are important, and that is why an aerated tank can hold more fish than a still tank. The fact that the movements of the water in aeration are produced by air bubbles is usually of little consequence and is an example of getting the right result for the wrong reason. The old idea behind aeration was to increase the contact of air and water and to "force" oxygen into the water by sending fine bubbles coursing briskly up through the tank. Unless a very heavy spray of very fine bubbles is used, however, the surface of water exposed to air in the bubbles is small and unimportant, and the movement caused at the tank surface is all important.

When we calculate fish capacity by surface area, we may also modify this by including the effects of temperature, water movement and various other factors. The warmer the water, the lower the solubility of oxygen and the lower the fish capacity. However, the following estimates are based on an average temperature of about 24°C (for tropical fishes) without aeration. They are also based on the assumption that young fish and small fish, even though adult, use more oxygen per gram of body weight than do larger fish. This is in line with such scanty experimental reports as are available and also with general experience. The estimates are not based on the "liter" or "cm of fish" rules, which give various figures for the number of centimeters of fish per liter which may be placed in tanks, because this type of computation is clearly wrong and is not in line either with the practice or experience of observant aquarists. It is assumed that, age and activity apart, the same volume or weight of fish uses about the same amount of oxygen per minute whether it comprises a hundred small fish or one big fish. However, small fishes are usually more active and young fishes are still rapidly growing. Therefore they

This is a section of a large tank. As such it can comfortably hold many fish, but its fish-holding capacity would be increased still further by the use of some mechanical aids. Photo by G.J.M. Timmerman.

consume more oxygen, weight-for-weight, and allowance is made for this to the extent that 30 g of one cm fishes is allowed five times the oxygen consumption of 30 g of 5 cm fishes, and at a 15 cm size, each 30 g of fish is allowed rather less oxygen than the 6 cm's. The base line is the 6 cm tropical fish, which is allowed 130 square centimeters of surface area. Fat fishes of the same length are likely to use more oxygen than slimmer fishes, but this fact is fortunately minimized by the greater activity and therefore greater oxygen need of the slimmer, minnow-like types. Estimates should be divided by three for coldwater fishes and by six for fancy Goldfish varieties. The 130 square-centimeter basis for a 6 cm fish is intended to permit further growth and good health. The fishes would not be expected to show distress if their number were doubled, but they would not flourish so well. The estimates are approximate and could be misleading in special cases, but from experience of their application it is felt that they are a much better guide than other common recommendations. One major alteration to the rule applies to the anabantoids (see below) which, when the labyrinth is developed, require only half the surface area per fish otherwise recommended. (The labyrinth is present in all but the very young fry). It is also well known that barbs are in need of more air surface than tetras of the same size.

14

Body length of fishes in cms.	No. of fish per 1000 sq. cm of surface area.	Sq. cms per fish.
1.25	180	5.6
2.0	100	10
2.5	55	18
4.0	20	50
5.0	12	85
6.0	7	140
8.0	5	200
10.0	2	500
12.5	1	1000
15.0	1	1000

The body length excludes the tail fin.

Example 1.

In a 60-liter tank with a surface area of 1900 square cm, the following fishes are to be housed:

8 tetras	each about 4 cm long
10 tetras	each about 5 cm long
6 barbs	each about 5 cm long
6 gouramis	each about 6 cm long
2 cichlids	each about 8 cm long

Are they likely to be overcrowded, or can even more be added?
We have:

$$8 \text{ fishes at } 4 \text{ cm need } \quad 50 \times 8 = 400 \text{ sq. cm}$$
$$10 \text{ fishes at } 5 \text{ cm need } \quad 85 \times 10 = 850 \text{ sq. cm}$$
$$6 \text{ barbs at } 5 \text{ cm need } 170 \times 6 = 1020 \text{ sq. cm}$$
$$6 \text{ gouramis at } 6 \text{ cm need } \quad 70 \times 6 = 420 \text{ sq. cm}$$
$$2 \text{ fishes at } 8 \text{ cm need } 100 \times 2 = 400 \text{ sq. cm}$$
$$\text{Total} = 3090 \text{ sq. cm}$$

CONCLUSION: *The fishes are crowded and cannot be expected to be at their best. Certainly no more should be added, and it would be best to omit a few, especially the barbs.*

Example 2.

What size of tank should be used to house 100 fry at present 1.25 cm in length, with room to grow them to 2 cm before moving them again?

It is the final size of fry that matters, hence the tank must have a surface area of 100×10 sq. cm or 1000 sq. cm. If they were to reach 2.5 cm, then an area of 1800 sq. cm would be needed, i.e., a 60-liter tank.

1

Modern aquaria are available in a wide variety of shapes and sizes. The all glass construction eliminates the metal borders that framed the tank and were used for support. This is no longer necessary because of stronger modern adhesives that safely bind the glass together at the edges.

2

Shown here are: (1) a typical rectangular tank which is available in a wide range of capacities; (2) one of the attractive wooden stands which are available for many aquarium sizes; (3) a double hexagonal aquarium; (4) an octagonal aquarium.

3

4

Factors Affecting Fish Capacity: The best way to increase fish capacity is water movement, usually supplied by aeration. This can double the safety margin, so that up to twice the fish population can be kept in a well-aerated tank, but only if the tank is also well planted and kept clean or if the water is given frequent partial changes to eliminate the accumulation of waste materials. Water movement tends to stir up waste material and aid its more rapid solution in the water, thus adequate provision for purification is needed.

A factor that reduces fish capacity is the presence of waste materials, more especially uneaten food or dead fish and plant material, less so actual excretory products of the fishes. All these substances use oxygen as they decompose, reduce that available to the fishes and cause excess CO_2 production. Another factor is the presence of invertebrate animal life other than airbreathers. Colonial sponges or polyps or an excess of unconsumed living worms or crustaceans may make conditions dangerous for fishes. A final important factor is temperature. Oxygen dissolves more readily the cooler the water, so that at 10°C a liter of water can hold about 7.4 cubic cm of oxygen (or the oxygen from about 37 cubic cm of air) whereas at 26°C, it holds only 5.3 cubic cm, about 25% less. In the average tank, an oxygen content around 2.9 cubic cm per liter is quite adequate for the fishes; some fishes can take down to about 1.2 cubic cm without severe distress. However, at a higher temperature the fishes become considerably more active and their rate of consumption of oxygen rises, with the result that the fish capacity of the tank falls quite rapidly with increased temperature. In tropical tanks, which do not usually experience a wide temperature variation, this is not likely to matter much, but the coldwater tank which undergoes a considerable rise, as on a hotter day than usual, may show severe symptoms.

The question of balance in a fish tank is therefore a relative affair and not as pictured by the average aquarist. The greatest "adjustors" are the fishes themselves, which can vary their respiratory rate about 10-fold and thus cope with a wide range of oxygen availability. This does not mean, however, that they can live in a tenth of the normal oxygen concentration; the rate at which the gills can take it from the water falls sharply with the decrease in concentration, so that the average fish is in distress when a 50% fall occurs, as shown above. That is why some fishes, particularly those used to running water or the open sea, cannot stand ordinary aquarium life, as the oxygen content even at best is below their tolerance.

Aquarium Water: Water from the faucet *may be* perfectly satisfactory for the aquarium immediately after it is drawn, but often it is not. It is likely to contain free chlorine, especially in city areas, and it is possibly under sufficient pressure to contain an excess of other dissolved gases. It may be of the wrong salinity or hardness, and it may be too acidic or too alkaline. However, in most districts tap water is satisfactory after standing for a day or two, a

Mineral blocks are available in a number of shapes and sizes and serve as a buffer for the water. They accomplish this by helping to stabilize the pH at 7 (neutral).

process called "conditioning." This allows for gas exchange between the water and the air, which may be hastened by aeration or by boiling and cooling again, followed by brisk aeration.

Chlorinated water may be rendered safe by the addition of one grain per gallon of sodium thiosulphate (the "hypo" of photographers), *but this does not guarantee its suitability in other ways.* Distilled water or even filtered melted snow may be used; if so, some salts should best be added for the comfort of most fishes, particularly livebearers. A suitable addition to distilled water would be:

> 3 teaspoons (22 ml) of common salt
> 1 teaspoon (7.5 ml) of potassium sulphate
> 1 teaspoon (7.5 ml) of magnesium sulphate

Rain water may need similar treatment, but it is dangerous to use in towns, for on the way down it collects a lot of dirt and harmful chemicals from the air and may be poisonous. Snow is less liable to be polluted, even in towns.

Hard water contains dissolved salts which are largely absent from soft water. Very soft water may have salts added as for distilled water, whereas normally hard water doesn't need them. Typical analyses of sea water, hard water and soft water, in percentages of various important salts, are as follows:

	Sodium chloride	Potassium sulphate	Magnesium sulphate	Calcium carbonate etc.	Total
Sea water	2.8	0.14	0.66	0.10	3.7
Hard water	0.005	0.007	0.007	0.015	0.034
Soft water	0.004	0.000	0.000	0.002	0.006

Hard water is usually alkaline; soft water is usually neutral to acid in reaction. Acidity and alkalinity are measured on a scale which goes from 0 to 14, called the *pH scale*. pH does not stand for "percentage hydrogen," as is often stated, but represents the logarithm of the concentration of hydrogen ions per liter of water. This is a convenient method of expressing the state of affairs in chemistry, but need not worry aquarists further. Neutral water has a pH of 7, acid water has a pH of less than 7, while alkaline water has a pH of more than 7. Strong acids are down in the 1-2 region, strong alkalis up in the 12-13 region. A weak acid like carbonic acid (dissolved carbon dioxide) at full strength has a pH of about 4, and a weak alkali like sodium bicarbonate has a pH of about 9, and this is approximately the range of pH seen in natural waters. Few fishes can stand this entire range, but most can be happy anywhere between 6 and 8, and many do not show distress when well beyond these limits. Most aquarium plants flourish best at a slightly alkaline pH. There was a period of emphasis on pH in fish keeping, when pH differences of 0.1 or 0.2 were thought to matter, but a commonsense view of the problem is now more usual, and few worry about the pH value of ordinary, successfully maintained tanks. When breeding, pH may matter more, as the germ cells or fertilized eggs and fry do not necessarily tolerate as wide a range as the adults, but very little is known in detail on this question. The pH of a tank usually rises during the day, as carbonic acid gas is removed by the plants, and falls at night, when both plants and animals produce it. The extent to which this affects pH readings depends on the degree of aeration, the atmosphere in the room, and the fish and plant density. In a crowded tank in a rather foul room, such as an exhibition tank at a crowded indoor show, the pH may fall alarmingly in a few hours to values of 5.5 or lower.

To measure pH, chemicals called indicators may be used. These are added by drops to a small sample of aquarium water and change color according to the pH. Thus, the commonly used bromthymol blue is yellow when at a mildly acid pH, green when neutral and blue when alkaline, covering a useful range of about pH 6.0 to 7.6. For sufficiently accurate work color charts are supplied in steps of 0.2 or 0.3. Another method is the comparator paper which is dipped straight into the tank and compared with a chart afterwards. These are not always reliable after long storage, and for a really accurate pH measurement, electrometric methods are used.

To adjust pH, when really necessary, acid and alkaline sodium phosphates are best, but sodium bicarbonate may be used on the alkaline side instead. Such adjustments must be made with care along the following lines:

Make a solution of sodium monohydrogen phosphate (Na_2HPO_4, the alkaline phosphate) at a concentration of 1 in 100 (1 gram per 100 ml) and a similar solution of the dihydrogen phosphate (NaH_2PO_4, the acid phosphate). When mixed in equal quantities, these two solutions make up a *buffer* solution

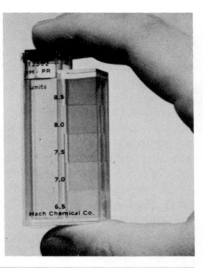

Water test kits are very useful in giving the aquarist the necessary information to help maintain proper water conditions. Test kits are available for pH (acidity and alkalinity), nitrites, hardness and ammonia content. The tests usually involve chemical treatment of a small water sample and then comparison of the sample with a color chart. Chemical test papers are also available; they are less expensive but less accurate.

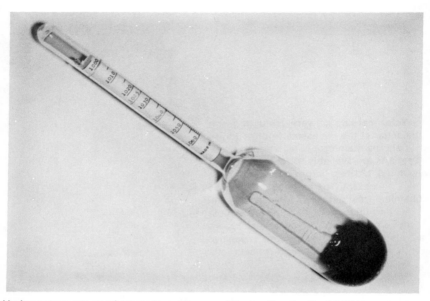

Hydrometers are used to measure the specific gravity of a liquid. This measurement can be used to determine the amount of dissolved minerals in the aquarium water.

with a pH of approximately 6.9 and a capacity for holding its pH against the addition of other salts. Such a buffer solution may be used for holding an aquarium pH steady, but its capacity is not unlimited and the salts are gradually broken down. If so used, not more than about 1 part in 20 of the mixture should be added to aquarium water, which should first be brought to pH 7.0.

To bring a tank to neutral pH or any other desired pH, a sample of the water, a definite quantity such as 500 ml, should be withdrawn. If the pH is too low, *i.e.,* the water is too acid, the alkaline phosphate solution described above is added in small amounts with frequent testing until the desired effect is obtained. Then, by simple proportion, the amount to be added to the whole tank is determined. This addition should be made with constant stirring. If the pH is too high, the acid phsophate solution is used in the same manner. When making such adjustments, do not forget to calculate as accurately as possible the true water volume, making allowance for space occupied by sand, rocks, etc., and for the top level in the tank. Lastly, do not make drastic alterations in pH all at once. Steps of more than about 0.5 per day are to be avoided, and for complete safety it is probably best to make adjustments in steps of not more than 0.2-0.3 at a time. We don't actually know for certain what the safe limits are.

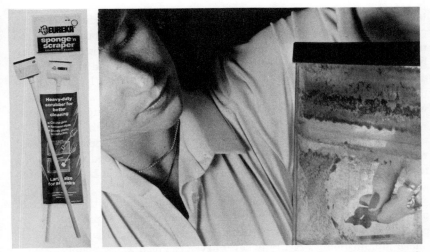

For appearance sake the aquarium glass should be kept free of algal growth. Removal of built up algae can be accomplished using a single edge razor blade. Scrapers with handles are easy to use and it is best to keep your hands and arms out of an aquarium that is full of water and fish. Photo by Glen S. Axlerod.

Changing Water: When the earlier aquarists siphoned off detritus and mulm, they usually filtered the water and returned as much as possible to the tank. As a result, the water gradually acquired a rich wine color and a limpid clarity which is very attractive. It is surprising how yellow or even reddish the water can become without causing comment, unless a sample is compared with fresh, colorless water, when the difference is very obvious.

This "aged" water was supposed to have become more suited to the fishes than freshly conditioned water. The idea is incorrect, but what does occur is that fishes gradually become used to a particular environment—even polluted water if it is not too polluted—and do not like a sudden change—even to much purer water! Thus, it is much the best, even in the presence of adequate biological filtration, to change aquarium water on a gradual, routine basis. About 10% per week is usually quite adequate and may be stretched to say 30% per week, but with never a greater quantity at a time. The new water may be safely added at the right temperature straight from the faucet if only 10% is changed, but larger quantities should be conditioned first. This gradual change keeps nitrates and other relatively harmless pollutants below any critical levels, gets rid of colored waste products that may not be taken up even by a carbon or similar filter and keeps the water in such a condition that newly added fishes will be not be stressed.

Cloudy Water: Water may become cloudy for a number of reasons, some of which demand a complete change with conditioned water, particularly in tanks without filters. The most potentially dangerous condition is green cloudiness due to the presence of green algae. It is usually brought on by too much light in the presence of organic materials in solution. It is fundamentally healthy water, but it spoils the appearance of the tank and is usually not desired, except when raising fry. If it becomes very thick there is a danger that the rapidly growing algae might suddenly die off and foul the water. The first warning sign of this imminent catastrophe is a slight yellowing of the water, which then rapidly turns fetid and is very dangerous to the fishes. The aquarium water should be changed in its entirety without delay or filtered with a power filter of sufficient capacity to clean up the cloudiness within a few hours. A store of spare "aged" water is commonly kept by experienced aquarists for just such an emergency.

Cleanliness, moderate light, no overcrowding of tanks and the presence of plenty of higher plants, especially floating plants, helps to prevent the appearance of green cloudiness. When a tank receives only, or almost only, artificial illumination it practically never develops green water, mainly because it does not receive excessive total illumination. Acidity of the water makes for cleanliness but not for good plant growth, because both the algae and higher plants are discouraged together. It is often said that a partial or nearly complete change of water only serves to stimulate further algal growth; however, this does not always occur, and green water may be cured immediately by siphoning it off—along with any debris in the tank—and replacing it with fresh conditioned water.

Another type of cloudy water, gray cloudiness, may be due to infusoria, bacteria, fungi or just dirt. It often follows on the setting up of a tank, sometimes because the sand was not washed thoroughly but more often because there is a burst of animal life which gets going ahead of the algae. This cloudiness usually disappears in a few days, whether caused by dirt or infusoria, and is not dangerous. Bacterial or fungal cloudiness is a bad sign, usually seen in established tanks which are "going bad." It may be caused by excessive decaying matter, usually dry food, but sometimes by a dead fish, by insufficient light, by overcrowding or by the use of unsuitable gravel or rocks which provide niches and crannies where excreta and food are caught and decay. While attention must be paid to the root causes such as overcrowding, gray cloudiness may often be temporarily corrected by brisk aeration or by the use of a power filter as above. Such filters use porous material or diatomaceous earth, either of which can clean up even bacterial suspensions. Filters in general are dealt with later.

Removal of Mulm and Algae: In the course of replacing some of the water at intervals of one or two weeks as recommended, it is easy to siphon off much of the mulm from the bottom of the tank. A convenient way to do this is with a glass tube of from 6 to 12 mm in diameter, slightly shorter than the aquarium depth if it is left straight or a little longer if the top is given an angle bend. Both are methods for preventing the plastic tubing which is attached to the glass tube from kinking. The end of the glass tube which will be immersed in the water should be softened by heat and then gently pressed onto a flat surface, holding the tube upright so that the entrance is slightly constricted to prevent pebbles, snails and so forth from getting into the tube and clogging it further up. Any foreign matter which enters the tube will be small enough to pass readily through. The end of the plastic tubing should be about 60 or 90 cm below the water level outside the tank so as to give a convenient head of pressure.

A siphon is started by sucking the end of the plastic tubing with the glass tube immersed or, if preferred, by filling it with water by dipping it into the tank. With a little practice, it is possible to start the siphon without getting a mouth full of water. Self-starting siphons are also commercially available. The rate of flow is controlled by pinching the plastic tubing, and the siphon is then run gently over the aquarium bottom like a vacuum cleaner. The end of the glass tube may also be poked well into the gravel, sucking up sample "bores" to see if all is well and that underneath the surface the gravel is not becoming foul and gray with bacteria. If it is, it is wise to go on siphoning the gravel away until the foul patch is removed and to replace it with fresh gravel afterwards. With experience, it is possible to remove much of the bottom of a tank, leaving the plants practically undisturbed, and to replace it by running clean dry gravel down a funnel under the surface of the water. If the gravel is wet, it sticks and must be washed into the tank, or it may be put in by hand and the plants afterwards well brushed to remove grains. The foul gravel may be washed, dried off and left in the sun to be used again.

The base of the siphon may alternatively be flared out like a small funnel, and this if plunged into the gravel does not lift much or any of the actual gravel, but it draws out other matter and helps considerably in preventing the major operation just described. However, a properly set up tank does not often develop serious bottom trouble.

There are a number of aquarium gadgets on the market for the mechanical removal of mulm and other materials. There are little "vacuum cleaners" available for use with an air pump instead of the simple siphon just described. They may be very efficient in clearing the mulm, but their use does not involve the removal of some of the water, and so this should still be done even though little or no visible mulm remains to be siphoned off.

Green algae will cause not only green water, but some types will also coat the inside of the glass if there is too much light. They may be removed with a scraper, essentially a razor blade on a convenient handle, or, more easily, with steel or plastic wool. Wrap a small ball of the wool around the end of a stick and rub the glass over with moderate pressure or use a pad with the hand or

A properly erected, planted and managed aquarium can be a very attractive addition to anyone's home.

Rocks and ornamental pieces of wood can add to an aquarium's beauty and create a natural setting.

fingers immersed in the tank. It usually takes only a couple of minutes to clean a large tank thoroughly. When removing algae at the base of the tank, be careful not to get gravel caught in the wool, as it may scratch the glass.

Under artificial illumination, blue-green algae are more likely to be a nuisance, settling not only on the glass but also on the plants. They may be scraped from the glass as usual, but to remove them from the plants is almost impossible. Cut down the light and hope that the algae disappear or treat the tank with one of the algicidal compounds now available on the market. Copper may also be used if all fishes and invertebrates are first removed and the water is replaced.

Light: Indoor aquaria rarely receive ideal natural illumination, which is daylight coming from directly overhead. If they get sufficient daylight, they usually receive it through a window to one side or at the back. This is satisfactory for most fishes and does not cause undue disturbance to plant growth as long as the tank doesn't get too much oblique light. If it does, the eventual results will be plants growing at an angle or at least with leaves unevenly developed and fishes swimming at an angle, particularly the barbs and some of the characins, which seem to be very sensitive to the direction of lighting.

Large tanks can stand quite a bit of direct sunlight, and if it can be arranged so that this falls more on the back and sides and not much on the front glass, the former will become coated with a lush growth of algae, while the latter can be kept clear with only an occasional wiping. The algae will act as an automatic light screen and usually provide a very pleasant-looking background to other plants, giving a look of maturity and depth to the tank and providing food for the livebearing fishes. Care must be taken to avoid overheating the tank, and it must be recalled that the tank goes on absorbing heat even when the algal coat has formed. A heat-preventing screen should be made of light reflecting material on the face toward the sun. Excellent window screening material intended for sunny rooms is available in the stores.

The prime necessity is adequate light for the plants, as quite dull illumination is sufficient for most fishes. Plants function and flourish only in good light, and many of them need bright light for much of the day to grow properly. Even light of sufficient intensity for comfortable reading may be quite useless for them. The various species of *Cryptocoryne* and *Sagittaria* can take less illumination than the rest and should be used whenever there is any doubt. At the other extreme, plants like *Cabomba* and *Myriophyllum* grow stringy and drab and die off if not in bright light and become a menace instead of an ornament and a help in the tank. Only actively growing plants, and that means adequately illuminated plants, are an asset to the aquarium.

The light utilized by plants in photosynthesis is at the red end of the spectrum, and the growing habit of painting the back of tanks is to be avoided when oblique natural light of borderline intensity will be employed. A significant amount of the useful rays can be removed in this manner but are not removed, of course, when the light comes from overhead and not through the glass. Winter daylight in most parts of the world is not adequate for indoor tanks, and it should be supplemented with artificial lighting.

When there is an excess of light, such as to cause a blanket of green algae over the glass and even the plants and rocks as well, it can always be cut down by shading. This shading is best applied to the windows admitting the light, as heat absorption which is likely to accompany the excessive light is avoided as explained above. If it must be applied to the tank, use treated surfaces so as to reflect as much heat as possible and not to absorb it.

Artificial Light: Artificial light must be bright and close overhead. The light in an ordinary room is very inadequate, even if the tank sits underneath the source of light. Ordinary electric light bulbs may be used, but fluorescent lighting has the advantage of causing little additional heat. Whichever is the choice, it is usual to enclose the overhead tank lights in a reflector. This increases the light thrown into the tank and also prevents dazzle. A reflector decreases the life of the bulbs because they get hotter when hooded over, so that aquarium top-lights need replacements rather frequently when incandescent lights are used.

Overhead lighting may be toward the front or back of the tank, and the general direction of plant growth will differ in the two circumstances. The tank with front lighting has a gloomy back and gives an impression of depth

Artificial aquarium lighting is usually required because the light in an ordinary room is inadequate. Many types of bulbs are made especially for aquaria and produce wavelengths of light that can either stimulate plant growth or inhibit it.

and spaciousness, but the plants at the back may not flourish too well after a period. The tank with back lighting has a fine background growth of plants and looks generally lighter and therefore rather less spacious and intriguing, and the fishes are transilluminated when they swim to the front. This gives an effect which depends on the fish; some look very pleasant and others lose effectiveness. On the whole, back lighting seems to be the less popular, but it is a good idea to use it routinely and to pull the lights forward for exhibition purposes.

With ordinary bulbs, whether frosted or plain, and a reflector of average efficiency, the following are the requirements of various tanks (assuming no help from even weak daylight):

Tank Capacity	Usual Depth	Wattage for a 10-hour day
20 l	22 cm	40
60 l	30 cm	60
120 l	38 cm	75
180 l	45 cm	100
320 l	53 cm	120
500 l	60 cm	150

The figures in the last column show the wattage to employ assuming 10 hours per day of illumination. Thus, a 40-watt bulb turned on for 10 hours over a 20-liter tank is satisfactory, giving 0.4 kilowatt-hours per day.

The difference in plant depth is not doubled because the tank depth is doubled. Plants right down on the sand will be perhaps at about double the distance but not the average plant leaf, which will often be able to reach just as near the bulb whatever the tank depth. In addition, the use of a reflector

Aquarium light reflectors increase the amount of light thrown into the tank and help create even lighting.

modifies the inverse square law and focuses the light into a beam or band, projecting it down into the tank and not allowing it to spread out as much as the light from a naked bulb. It also so happens that even without an overhead reflector, the internal reflection from the inner faces of the glass prevents the escape of much of the light and aids the illumination of the deeper parts of the tank. Thus no simple physical laws apply in calculating the above figures, and those recommended are a mixture of theory and experiment—mostly the latter.

While it would give about the same result to illuminate a 60-liter tank with 120 watts for five hours instead of with 60 watts for 10 hours, it is best to use the weaker light and a longer period, since the fishes do better that way. If, on the other hand, it is desired to illuminate for a longer period, then 40 watts for 15 hours would be quite in order.

Fluorescent Lighting: Fluorescent lighting often looks very attractive, but not all types of fluorescent tubes are suitable. Some give too much light at the blue end of the spectrum and do not benefit the plants. It is therefore best to use those which copy natural daylight most closely or are specially designed to give light best suited to the plants and to bring out the color of the fishes. Many brands are available and a mixture may be used over a large tank. Reports indicate that if so-called "daylight" tubes are used, they must be switched on for longer periods.

Fluorescent lighting is more expensive to install but cheaper to run, and the cost of electricity probably makes it rather less expensive all told. Each watt of fluorescent lighting gives a little over three times the actual light given by one watt of tungsten filament lighting, so that the figures in the above table should be divided by three for fluorescent tubes.

Temperature: Fishes are usually able to stand the temperature variations of their natural surroundings and not much more. If a fish comes from a seasonally variable environment in which it may stew in summer or freeze in winter, like the common carp, it can stand these extremes, but it cannot usually stand a *sudden* change from one to the other. If it comes from rock-pools of the seashore, like many gobies, it may stew in an exposed small pool and then be flushed out by an incoming tide at a temperature 20 to 15°C below that of the pool. The goby can stand this, too. If, like the majority of marine fishes, it comes from a very constant environment and can move about so that even the slow changes in temperature can be avoided if not to its liking, it is likely to be very touchy about the temperature of its surroundings and to be inadaptable.

Freshwater aquarium fishes usually come from fairly still waters which may undergo fairly wide changes in temperature but which do not change suddenly. When these waters are tropical, their temperature does not drop below 18 to 21°C; but it may rise to 32°C, so most tropical fishes can stand this range. In the aquarium, they are less happy at the extremes of their natural tolerance than in the wild and so it is usual to try to keep them within a range of say 22 to 26°C, with as short a period as possible beyond.

The *sudden* exposure to a downward change in temperature of more than 1.5°C is likely to cause shock, followed by disease. Slow changes, taking hours or days, may cover 3 to 6°C. The usual symptoms of chill are a very characteristic slow, weaving motion like slow-motion swimming without getting anywhere, often called "shimmies," and perhaps the development of a disease called "white spot" or "ich." Ich is caused by an organism frequently present in the water but which does not usually gain a hold in healthy fishes. The condition and its cure are described later. Heat shock is also known, but it is not usually seen, even when fishes are suddenly warmed, as when chilled in transport and placed in a warm tank. The signs are gasping respiration, surface hugging and sometimes lack of balance, so that the fish turns slowly on to its side, plunges to an upright position and then repeats the process. The respiratory signs may occur in fishes which simply lack oxygen, whereas after too sudden an increase in temperature they will sometimes occur even in the presence of sufficient oxygen.

The above applies to adult fishes. Their eggs and fry are often much tougher and can stand a greater variability and a wider range of temperature than their parents. As the young fishes grow up, this tolerance is gradually lost. It also applies to involuntary changes which the fishes cannot avoid. In a pool or a tank the water may show quite large differences in temperature from top to bottom. Fishes swim from one layer to another in these conditions without harm, probably because they do not stay long at any one fixed temperature and can tolerate short bouts of immersion in hotter or colder strata. A day-to-night fluctuation in average temperature of 3 to 4°C is also safe for most freshwater fishes but not for many marine or estuarine types. A fluctuation of 6 to 8°C is dangerous and a common cause of unexplained trouble.

Since fluorescent lamps operate at only about 38°C, they do not heat the surface of the water as do filament lamps, and this is a great advantage in hot weather. Another advantage is the spread of light given by the long fluorescent tubes, with resultant even illumination and absence of glare.

Temperature Control: As with lighting, electricity is so much more general and satisfactory for heating aquaria than any other method that gas and oil represent nothing more than auxiliary emergency measures, except when electric current is not available. In fish rooms or houses, steam or hot water may be used. Electric heating has all the advantages—it may be left almost indefinitely without attention, it is clean, odorless, usually cheap and, most important, it does not have to be applied to the bottom of the tank and thus heat the roots of plants.

The heating capacity of an aquarium heater depends upon its consumption of current; the higher the wattage, the more heat produced. Commonly produced heaters rate at 12½, 25, 37½, 50, 75, 125, 150, 175, 200 and 250 watts, but other series are available at 10, 20, 30, 40, 50, 75 and 100 watts, so that it is possible to obtain a ready-made heater of almost any wattage required. This is important when different tanks are to be heated by separate heaters but all controlled by one thermostat. If higher wattages are necessary, more than one heater should be used.

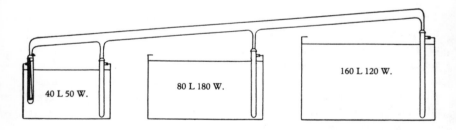

These tanks, each one a different volume and equipped with a heater, are controlled by a single thermostat.

The heat loss from a heated tank depends mainly on the radiating, conducting and evaporating surfaces of the tank and on the difference between the tank and air temperatures. Other things being equal, a small tank requires more heat per liter (more watts per liter) than a large tank, because it loses heat more rapidly. In theory, we should expect the heat loss to be proportional to the surface area, and this is roughly borne out in practice and holds

Aquarists who live in warm climates may not need an aquarium heater.

over a useful range of tank sizes. The rate of heat loss from similar tanks, other things being equal, is also approximately proportional to the square of the air-water temperature difference, thus it takes about four times as much heating to keep a 6°C difference as a 3°C difference from the tank's surroundings. This is because the greatest part of the heat loss does not occur by radiation, which follows a different law, but by convection and, in uncovered tanks, by evaporation. With low differences in temperature between tanks and their surroundings, the rate of heat loss follows much more nearly a square law than anything else, although this is not the relationship to be expected at greater temperature differences.

A covered 60-liter (60 cm) tank requires about one watt per liter, a total of 60 watts, to keep it at 10°C above room temperature. In actual practice a thermostat would be included to cut off the heat at a predetermined point to allow for fluctuations in the room temperature.

The wattage required per liter for tanks of the same general shape but of different sizes, all to be kept at 10°C above their surroundings, is given by:

$$\text{Watts per liter} = \frac{L_{15}}{L_x}$$

where L_{15} = the length of the 60-liter tank (usually 60 cm)

L_x = the length of any other tank.

Thus a 12-liter tank, of 35 cm length, requires not one watt per liter, but $\frac{60}{35}$ or 1.7 watts/liter, a total of approximately 20 watts for the tank to be held 10°C above its surroundings.

The wattage required per liter for the *same* tank, or others nearly identical with it, at different temperatures is given by:

$$\text{Watts per liter} = \left[\frac{T}{11}\right]^2$$

where T is the temperature (°C) difference required.

Thus, a 60-liter tank to be held at 5°C above its surroundings requires $\left[\frac{5}{11}\right]^2$ or 0.21 watts/liter, a total of 12.4 watts.

These formulas may be combined, so that the requirements for similar shaped tanks may be predicted. Tanks which are reasonably alike behave much the same, and almost no rectangular tanks likely to be used by the aquarist will differ enough to matter.

$$\text{Watts per liter} = \frac{L_{15}}{L_x} \times \left[\frac{T}{11}\right]^2$$

where the symbols have the meanings defined above.

From the above we may deduce the wattage of heaters required under different conditions and the relative heater capacities required when one tank acts as a control to the rest, some or all of which are of different gallon capacities.

The following table gives the information for a maximum rise of 11°C above air temperature but not more. The heating capacity needed for greater or lesser differences can be worked out as above. The tanks are assumed to be double cubes (*i.e.*, a 60-liter tank measures 60 x 30 x 30 cm) covered by a sheet of glass. The last column of the table is of particular importance. Being calculated for an 11°C rise, it covers all normal requirements and is therefore a column of the heater wattages to be recommended for different sized tanks, which while being adequate, make it unlikely that the fishes will be "cooked"

34

even if the heater remains on when it should be switched off – either through a thermostatic fault or forgetfulness.

Tank length (cm)	Liter Capacity	Watts per liter	Total Watts
25	4.5	2.4	10.8
30	7.5	2.0	15
35	12	1.7	21
40	18	1.5	27
45	25	1.3	33
50	35	1.2	42
55	46	1.1	51
60	60	1.0	60
65	76	0.92	70
70	96	0.86	82
75	120	0.80	96
80	140	0.75	105
85	168	0.70	117
90	200	0.66	132
106	320	0.57	183
122	480	0.50	240

Heaters and Thermostats: Electric heaters are usually of glass exterior and may be totally submersible or so constructed that their tops must not be placed under the water. Internally, the heater is essentially a heating coil wound on a ceramic or Pyrex glass form. This may be left bare or may be surrounded by a layer of fine sand or asbestos inside the outer tube, which is sealed with a rubber bung or cap through which pass insulated wires. Submergible heaters are watertight; others are not and must stand vertically in the tanks with their tops out of water. The resistance wire, usually of thin Nichrome or similar alloy, heats up as does an electric radiator element, and it is therefore necessary to make sure that the lower part of the upright type of heater is immersed in water, or it will burn out; tanks should never be allowed to fall below ⅔ full when the heater is in use. Care should also be taken not to leave heaters on when emptying tanks or to plug in a dry heater or, worse still, to plunge it into water if it does get hot when dry. Even Pyrex glass may not stand up to that treatment, and soda glass certainly will crack and shatter.

Totally submergible heaters are popular, as they are not conspicuous and also because of the belief that they heat more efficiently. This is not correct, as whether the heater stands upright or lies along the sand, it causes a current of

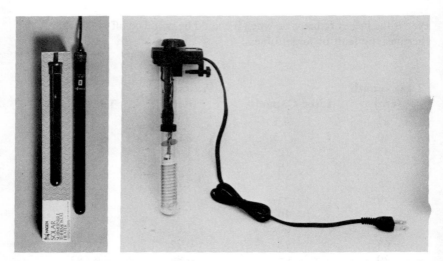

There are many types of heaters available on the market today. Aquarists can rely on their dealers' advice about the type of heater that is best for their requirements.

hot water to rise to the top of the tank and does not heat the water uniformly. The heater should not be buried in the sand; if it is, it may fuse and it may also kill the neighboring plants. As an alternative to the use of conventional heaters, plastic-covered cable is available which may be laid along the base of the tank.

Although a low wattage heater may be safely used without controlling its output, it is usual and much safer to include a thermostat in the circuit. The almost universal type in aquaria is the bimetallic strip made of two types of metal which expand at different rates with a rise in temperature and bend as the temperature changes. The strip carries the electric current, but at the critical temperature the strip breaks contact with one of the terminals in the instrument and the current ceases to flow. As the tank cools again, contact is established, and the current flows once more. The temperature controlled by such a thermostat should remain within about 1°C of that desired; much greater accuracy is not necessary and causes frequent action of the thermostat and tends to burn it out. A good thermostat should have a magnetic "make," which means that the strip, once it gets near to completing the circuit, is snapped over into position by a small magnet which does not allow sparking or arcing. The contacts should be of silver or similar metal to prevent excessive wear, and there should be a condenser or capacitor to prevent radio interference.

The thermostat is usually submergible, but it may not be when it is clipped on to the side of the tank. It has a glass body with the works inside it and a

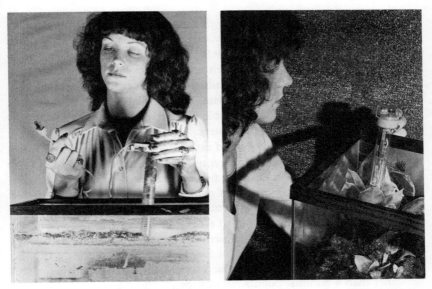

Careful installation of a heater is a very important consideration. Never have the heater plugged into the wall when it is out of the aquarium water. Left photo by Glen S. Axelrod and right photo by Dr. Herbert R. Axelrod.

control which consists usually of a small adjustable screw with a non-conducting portion so that the operator can alter the setting of the bimetallic strip and hence the temperature of the tank. Often a pilot light is included which indicates when the thermostat is operating. There are more expensive models in which the thermostat proper is outside the tank and a temperature "feeler" is placed in the tank like a submersible heater. Combination models of thermostat-plus-heater are commonly used and may be completely submersible. They can only be used in a single tank and hence each combination must be repeated for every additional tank if such a setup is used.

The wattage of a thermostat is the number of watts it can safely control. A usual figure is 500 watts, but anything between 100 and 2,000 is available. A 500-watt thermostat may be used in conjunction with heaters totalling not more than 500 watts. It will often have a multiple plug, allowing several heaters to be plugged directly into it in parallel. Two 100-watt heaters in parallel will mean a current producing 200 watts through the thermostat and so on, but it must be noted that two 100-watt heaters in series means only 50 watts through the thermostat and an output of 25 watts per heater. The normal way of heating several tanks is to plug in suitable heaters to a thermostat placed in the smallest tank if there is any size difference. This is because the smallest volume of water most rapidly loses and gains heat from its surroundings, and if a large tank housed the thermostat a small one might fluctuate too much. This arrangement also has the effect of controlling the temperature of the larger tanks remarkably accurately, and although such an extremely even temperature is not usually desirable, it is better than the alternative of widely varying small tanks. The tanks which are all controlled by the same thermostat must be in reasonably similar situations if it is required that they shall be uniform in temperature. Otherwise, some will be hotter than others, although all may be within a reasonable range. Differences may be offset by the use of varying wattage in the heaters.

Aeration: Something has been said earlier about the relationship between plants and fishes and between the oxygen and carbon dioxide (O_2 and CO_2) content of the water and its effect on fishes. It has been pointed out that the CO_2 content of the water is usually of more significance in an aquarium than is the O_2 content. Fishes suffering from CO_2 in excess gasp at the surface and show exaggerated gill movements, whereas it is alleged that fishes suffering merely from an O_2 deficiency lie quietly on the bottom. If this is true, the usual symptoms seen in a crowded or foul tank certainly indicate a CO_2 excess. This is relieved by aeration, which should always be used when a tank has other than a minimal population of fishes.

Aeration does not force air or oxygen into solution in the water and under usual conditions not much oxygen is absorbed from the bubbles themselves; they merely serve to remove the excess CO_2 from the water. Accounts of the rate at which aeration of different types brings about the solution of oxygen from the air into water differ. The general conclusion seems to be that it is not as efficient as we have been led to believe, some investigators finding that only very brisk bubbling from several aerating stones at once will bring a tank up to 75% saturation within 30 minutes. The normal rate of aeration is a mild trickle from one stone and was found to be ineffective in causing 75% saturation even within several hours. The rate at which carbon dioxide is "blown off" is probably quite small, but the fact remains that quite mild aeration about doubles the fish capacity of a tank, and although brisk, boiling aeration might quadruple it or even much more, as far as air content is concerned, other factors would in any case prevent us from trying to crowd our tanks so much.

The usual method of aeration is to force air through a porous "stone" at the bottom of the tank; such a stone may be made of various substances from fused glass or natural minerals to felt washers on a metal head. Carborundum stones give about the finest bubbles, but they also need the most powerful air pressure, so that only the larger size pumps are satisfactory for their use. All stones tend to clog, especially when used at a low pressure, and should occasionally be removed, baked and replaced. When they are first used or re-used, it is advisable to pass a brisk jet of air through them for a few hours, and when this is turned down a fine spray of bubbles is usually the result.

1

2

3

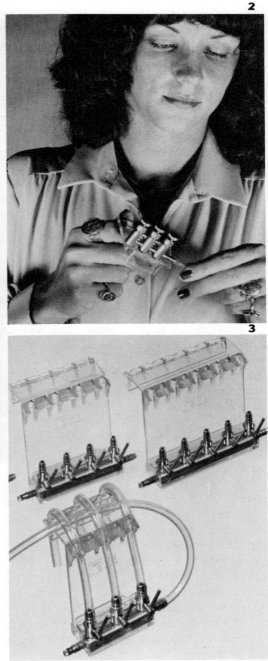

(1) An airstone in operation. Airstones increase both the surface movement of water and the circulation of water within the tank, thus increasing the fish capacity of any given aquarium. Photo by Laurence E. Perkins. (2) Tubing from the airstone can be connected to a gang valve which is used to distribute air to several places. Photo by Glen S. Axelrod. (3) Gang valves are available in several sizes.

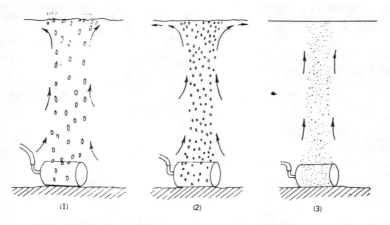

Large bubbles (1) do not stir the water as effectively as the smaller bubbles in (2). A fine spray (3) is also less effective than one of a medium size.

Experience shows that with bubbles of an average diameter of about 1 mm or less, an aerating stone delivering 32 cubic cm of air per minute is adequate in a 60-liter tank. This observation is really of great interest, for it demonstrates the fact that adequate aeration does not work by simple bubble-water interchange, since the surface of the bubbles exposed to the water at any one moment is only about 75 square cm, assuming a bubble diameter of 1 mm and a period of four seconds for a bubble to travel from bottom to top of the tank. A good stone can give bubbles of less than 0.25 mm in diameter when the surface exposed by the bubbles is much greater, as not only is it greater per cubic cm of air but also the bubbles take longer to reach the surface. With 0.25 mm bubbles, which take some 10 to 15 seconds to travel up through the water, the area exposed is some 750-1150 square cm and begins to be an effective factor in gas exchange. With such fine bubbles, the water looks quite cloudy over the stone, for at any one moment something up to one million are suspended in the water. When the bubble diameter is 1 mm, a mere 2,000 are seen at once. However, such very fine bubbles do not move the water much and do not disturb the surface of the water. They thus cause surface interchange to be little affected, and the effects of very fine subdivision of the same volume of air may not be as good as rather coarser subdivision. It is the opinion of some experts that a bubble diameter of about 0.88 mm is the best.

Deep tanks gain relatively more from aeration than do shallower tanks, for not only are they more in need of it, but since the bubbles take longer to rise to the surface they cause more effective stirring of the water and a brisker surface interchange.

The choice of an airpump is dependent on the amount of air that is required. Small tanks will only require a small vibrator pump (1), while larger tanks may require piston pumps or compressors (2).

2

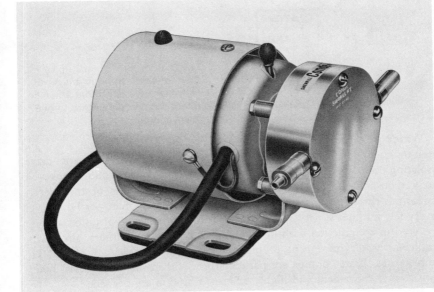

Air Pumps: The usual aerator is an electric air pump. These are usually designed to deliver from about 160 to 3200 cubic cm of air per minute and thus to operate from a few to a hundred stones. The electrical consumption of the most powerful is quite small, no more than about 62 watts, while the smaller pumps take as little as three watts and thus cost relatively little to run.

Pumps for small tanks are usually operated by a vibrating diaphragm, which is preferred by some hobbyists over piston pumps. They do not require oiling and are reasonably silent. They must be placed above the level of water in any tank they supply or water may run back into the pump. On the other hand, they do not reverse, as do some pumps of conventional design, and so cannot actively suck the water into themselves.

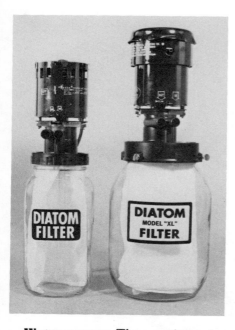

The Diatom filter pumps up to 750 liters of water through a layer of diatomaceous earth that actually filters out particles down to one micron in size.

Water pumps: These are becoming more popular as efficient, silent and non-toxic models have become available. Some have a magnetic drive, isolating the motor from the pumping mechanism. A water pump moves up to a thousand liters per hour, thus pulling the contents of the average aquarium through a filter or other equipment several times per hour, even every few minutes if necessary. This leads to very effective filtration and can be used in conjunction with undergravel or conventional filters, also giving sufficient water movement to make aeration unnecessary in normal circumstances. Water pumps are particularly useful in marine aquaria, where brisk water movement and highly efficient filtration are needed.

Filters: In a filter, an air or water pump shifts water from the tank into a smaller container or from the container back into the tank, the other part of the water-lift being by siphon. A simple filter may be constructed from a plastic container by boring a set of small holes in the base and clipping it onto the side of the tank. Water is then pumped into the container, passes through a bed of filter wool, charcoal or other material and out again into the tank. If water is pumped from the filter back to the tank, the same design can be used, when water will pass up through the holes in the bottom and through the filter. This, however, tends to raise the filtering medium and the water passes more beside it than through it, so the direction of flow is reversed by sucking water from the bottom of the filter, dispensing with a pierced base and siphoning water from the tank into the top of the filter.

Modern outside hanging filters (1) are effective particulate separators that help keep the aquarium water clear and free from excess debris. Corner filters (2) are used in smaller tanks to perform the same purpose. Both filters use a combination of activated charcoal and glass filter wool as a filtering medium.

A more usual type of filter is placed outside the tank, clipped onto the side or even on a separate stand. The siphon which carries aquarium water into the filter is provided with a "starter," which consists of a small rubber ball which when compressed starts the filter without the operator having to suck at the tube or remove it and fill it with water.

It is common practice to place activated charcoal at the base of the filter, then a layer of polyester fiber, through which the water first passes. The fiber traps any grosser debris or particles, and the activated charcoal absorbs small impurities and also actively soaks up some dissolved material as well as actual suspended matter. Both should be replaced at suitable intervals; when this is done, the filter rarely gives trouble. The water intake may be placed at a distance from the filter—perhaps in a front corner with the sand so sloped that waste matter tends to collect there and is transported to the filter. Many filters have adjustable intake siphons to cope with differing aquarium depths and other dimensions. Others have more than one chamber, so that the water first passes through a charcoal bed and then separately through a polyester fiber bed and perhaps a bed of crystals designed to adjust the pH. Filtration is also aeration, as the water is constantly streaming into and out of the filter. In a filtered tank, it may be unnecessary to aerate in addition by any other means, unless with the object of stirring up and removing the mulm.

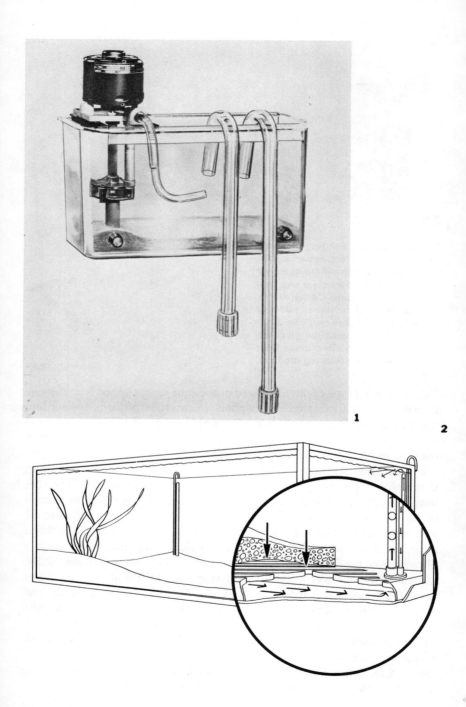

1

2

3

Hanging particulate filters are useful in collecting debris from the aquarium tank water. The filter pictured in (1) collects water from the aquarium with two siphons; the water passes through several layers of glass filter wool and charcoal and is finally drawn from the bottom of the filter tank by a pump and passed back into the aquarium. An undergravel filter (2 and 3) consists of a plastic mesh that is placed under the gravel. Air is pumped down a gravel uplift (see the small tube in 2) and then bubbles up to the surface forcing water with it. The water is drawn through the gravel, passes under the plastic filter and is carried up the gravel uplift exit tube with the air bubbles.

Undergravel filtration: The effectiveness of a filter, other than a power filter by which water is forced through a column of material, depends on its surface area. Public aquaria use very large filter beds and reservoirs so that there is usually more water in the filtering system than in the show tanks. It occurred to aquarists quite early to use the gravel as a filter medium by placing a false bottom in the tanks (perforated to allow water flow) and sucking the water down through the gravel and delivering it back into the tank by a pipe or system of pipes supplied with aeration. This method gives excellent filtration and aeration simultaneously and can move surprisingly large quantities of water – as much as a water pump with a conventional filter. There is only one clear drawback – some plants do not thrive if over an undergravel (sometimes called sub-sand) filter. This may be overcome by turning it off for part of the time, not too long however (for reasons given below), or by placing the filter only under part of the gravel, usually in center front where little or no planting occurs. In a marine tank, it is more imperative to cover the whole base of the tank.

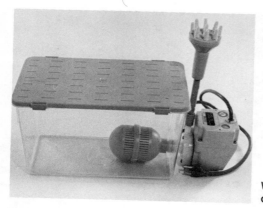

Water pumps are available for outside ponds.

This technique soon revealed an initially unsuspected advantage concerning the nitrogen cycle. Such a filter gradually becomes a biological filter, not merely a mechanical dirt remover. Bacteria cover the grains of gravel or whatever is used and start up the sewerage farm action mentioned earlier. In a new tank, ammonia collects as mulm or other decaying matter accumulates and stimulates the growth of bacteria which convert it to nitrites, which in turn stimulate the growth of other bacteria which convert them to nitrates, relatively non-toxic and useful for plant growth. The whole process takes from several weeks to several months, according to conditions, but it can be hastened by treating with ammonium sulphate before stocking the tank. Kits are available which supply the salts and starter cultures of bacteria to hasten things up.

The serious aquarist does one of two things—he stocks his tank gradually, preferably with "tough" fishes at first, so that the effects of the developing filter bed are not serious, or he uses a starter kit and gets development over before stocking with, if desired, a full complement of fishes. Otherwise he will run into the "new tank syndrome," often serious in a freshwater tank and almost inevitable in a marine one. This is typified by a tank of beautiful new fishes thriving for a week or so and then bursting forth with disease and dying off, sometimes the whole lot. The cause is ammonia accumulating in the water before the bacteria (nitrifying bacteria) which break it down have grown in the gravel in sufficient numbers to cope with it. If some fishes survive the wave of ammonia, they then have to face the nitrites! Tough ones can do it, but those tender, expensive rare tetras or killifishes will go for sure. On the contrary, with an established undergravel filter, ammonia and nitrite levels stay right down without trouble for months on end, and the less the filter is disturbed the better. Only worry if it gets clogged, but a bit of a stir-up and siphoning without removing much of the gravel will usually take care of that problem.

Care in keeping your fishes healthy will often have its rewards in the unexpected spawning of your stock.

Keeping Fishes Healthy

Setting Up A Tank: A good start is essential in the keeping of healthy fishes, and for this the first consideration is the location of the fish tank. The control of plant growth and the suppression of green water or other unwanted algae is much easier if the tank receives only artificial light. Drafty locations must be avoided and so must the tops of radiators, which heat the base of the tank, cause the plants to wilt and can overheat the tank far too easily. Thus, the popular window location over a radiator is not to be recommended.

The second consideration is the furnishing of the tank with sand or gravel, rocks and plants. The purpose of the gravel is to hold down rooted plants and to provide decoration. A sand which is fine packs tightly and prevents plant roots from penetrating; it also promotes the growth of anaerobic bacteria—those which thrive in oxygen-free surroundings and which turn the sand gray or black. If it is too coarse a gravel, the plants get little grip and ride free; unconsumed food and other detritus can get down into the gravel and are not easily removed. The finer the grains, the more surface area they have for bacterial growth, which we have seen is essential in an undergravel filter. This gives another reason for a compromise.

Fairly coarse gravel averaging 5 mm in diameter is considered best for most aquaria.

These facts show that the best type of medium is fairly coarse gravel averaging about 5 mm in diameter, preferably with a variable grain size for pleasant appearance. It should be laid deep enough to provide adequate root space for the plants, so that in all but the smallest tank 5 cm at the back and less in front is about right, but it may be banked up much more than this if desired for decorative effects. Since a great depth is likely sooner or later to become foul, it is best to avoid it or to pack the deeper areas with rock beneath the sand, unless it is used as a filter.

The placing of deep gravel at the back automatically provides for three things. First, it looks pleasant, giving the aquarium base a gentle forward slope which best exhibits the content. Secondly, it provides for the largest plants to be sited at the back, where they are usually required. Thirdly, it encourages the mulm to collect toward the front of the tank, where it is easily removed.

Gravel must be thoroughly washed before use. Even if supplied as "washed," it will normally require some further washing. Really dirty material may need 20 or 30 swirlings in fresh buckets of water or half an hour's thorough hosing in a shallow container. Failure to do this may cause cloudy water for weeks or more serious trouble.

European aquarists sometimes use peat, loam or earth beneath the gravel or in pockets of rock to nourish the plants. General experience is, however, that such materials sooner or later cause trouble; either they get stirred up and make a mess of the water or they turn bad and have to be removed. If one is interested primarily in growing fine plants it is possible to take care and to use these substances, but they are hardly to be recommended for the amateur.

The plant growth that results is from the material supplied beneath the gravel, and the plants may not, therefore, be performing their essential function of removing much of the waste products of the fishes as well as they otherwise would. This is a point which hasn't been clarified, and further research and observation are needed.

As a rule, the fishes are more colorful in an aquarium with dark, even black, gravel on the bottom.

Stones and Rocks: The placement and choice of stones and rocks in the tank is a matter for personal taste, *except* when they are used for shelter or for breeding. There are various theories about the relationship between stones and the sand they lie in and the direction of rock strata, which may influence judges in shows when furnished aquaria are being considered, but they are of little practical importance.

Ornaments such as treasure chests, divers, seashells and mermaids are popular but hardly natural looking. It is again a matter of personal choice. Seashells or shell grit (sometimes used instead of gravel) are in place in the marine tank, but they will make a freshwater tank too alkaline, even if their appearance can be tolerated.

Only hard, insoluble rocks must be used in an aquarium. Rocks with a soluble mineral content may kill fishes and plants in a few weeks.

Planting: A tank should be set up with young, healthy-looking plants which have been disinfected or quarantined before use. If you wish to use them immediately, a rapid wash in salt water (1½ teaspoons to the liter) or sea water of not more than 15 seconds duration followed by a thorough wash in fresh water will probably rid them of most pests. If possible, they should preferably be left for two or three days in a solution of potassium permanganate at a strength of 3.2 mg to the liter (3 parts per million). A longer period should not be used or degeneration may set in. A quick and easy method for sterilizing plants is to soak them for five minutes in a solution of alum (1 tablespoon per liter of water), and then rinse them thoroughly in gently running tepid tap water.

It is best to make a diagram of the desired planting scheme before going about the job, or it may turn out very different from that hoped for by the inexperienced. The higher-growing and larger plants look best at the back and sides, particularly the long, grass-like plants and the long-stemmed plants like *Cabomba* and *Myriophyllum*. Then, perhaps in relationship to rocks or stones, may come groups of other plants such as *Cryptocoryne*, *Echinodorus* or *Ludwigia*. These are best placed in groups of one type, not mixed up. Some of the smaller grasses or dwarf varieties of other plants may be used in front, but it is customary to leave a free swimming space in the center front. A particularly fine plant, such as an *Echinodorus*, is often used as a centerpiece in the larger tanks.

1

Gravel must be thoroughly washed before use. It can then be poured into the aquarium (1) and spread on the bottom (2). Plants and other objects, such as wooden ornaments (3), can be inserted into the gravel before the water is added to the tank. Colorful tank backgrounds are also available (4) to help enhance the beauty of the aquarium. Photos by Dr. Herbert R. Axelrod.

2

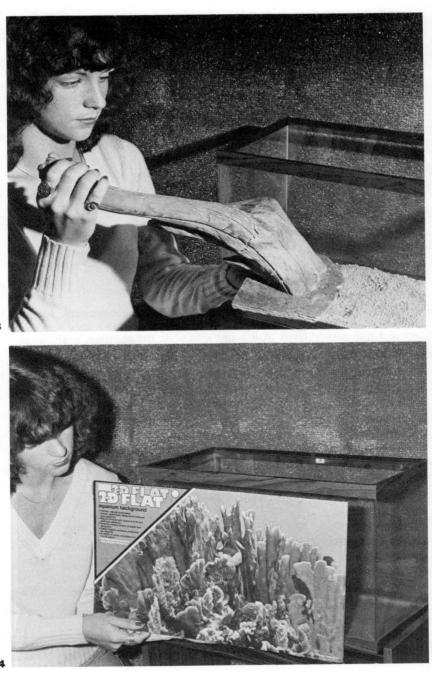

3

4

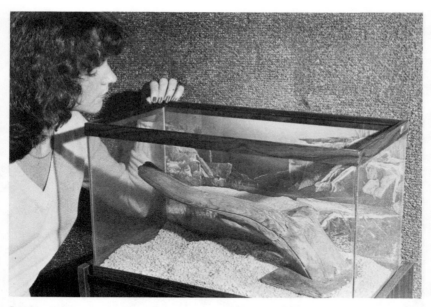

Setting up an aquarium involves the imagination of an interior decorator. Patience plus a good eye for arrangement are both advantageous. It is a good idea to experiment with several types of arrangements when the aquarium is still empty. Photos by Dr. Herbert R. Axelrod.

First place about 4 cm of level gravel in the tank and smooth it back and to the sides in the desired formation, placing any rocks or stones in position at this stage. Next place a large cup or jar in the front of the tank and gently pour water into it so that it slowly overflows and fills the tank for a depth of 15 to 20 cm, which is most convenient for planting. Meanwhile, keep the plants wet; a short period of drying may kill or set them back severely. Cut back the roots of all plants to a length of 3 to 5 cm, according to size, and anchor them by pushing them into the gravel about 3 cm forward of their eventual site, then drag them backwards or sideways through it into their final position. This makes a slight mess of the arrangements but is easier than trying to push them into place in the usual way with sticks or tongs. It is useless to worry about spreading the roots nicely, as they decay and are replaced by new growth in most cases.

Some plants, like the grasses and *Cryptocoryne*, have a crown above the roots and must be carefully planted so as to leave the crown exposed or they may wither and die. Others may be thrust into the gravel with less care, but it is best not to submerge too much of the stem and leaves or these may decay and foul the tank. Leave small spaces between plants, about 1 to 2 cm at least with grasses and tall, thin plants, and much more with bushy plants, so as to budget for subsequent filling-out by growth and the striking of new plants. A typical 60-liter tank, with a floor area of 1000 square cm, will need about three dozen back and side plants and a dozen central plants.

53

Planting sticks, long sticks with a notch in one end and perhaps a sharp, chisel-like blade at the other end, are useful for second thoughts when the rest of the plants are in place and for resetting plants which have floated up before becoming firmly rooted.

Planting trays are sometimes used. These are flat trays, usually of such dimensions that two or three of them fill the base of the tank. They are an advantage when it is required to empty the tank frequently, as for exhibition or breeding purposes, but require careful camouflage if they are not to be too obvious. Smaller trays may be used with advantage if set unobtrusively in the sand or behind rocks and may house prize plants or varieties needing particular care or which are wanted from time to time in different tanks. It is best to use trays made of plastic, china or earthenware, not of metal.

When planting is complete the tank should be filled. If the recommended 15 to 20 cm of water is already present and the tank is new, leave it for a day and then complete the filling, just in case of leaks. These are more likely to occur in framed aquaria than in all-glass tanks, but can happen in either.

Filling after planting must be done gently, so as not to disturb the bottom. Continue to pour into a jar up to 25 to 30 cm, but if the tank is deeper than this, the rest can be poured in from a few cm above the water level as long as the inflowing water creates a mass of bubbles, which breaks its force and prevents it from sweeping down onto the bottom. Fill to about 3 cm from the top—the tank usually looks best if the waterline is just hidden under the top in a framed tank.

It is best not to fill a new framed tank and empty it again before planting to clean it or test for leaks. This may result in springing a leak when the tank is emptied, which then becomes apparent on refilling. It also helps to cause more cement to be pushed out from between the frame and the glass than is desirable if the tank has not fully hardened. It is generally unwise to empty completely any new tank within a few months of first filling it, particularly a large tank, unless Silastic is used.

Accessories: Every independently heated tank should have a thermometer. There are various types, some floating and some fixed, and most of them liable to be off as much as 3°C either way. They should be checked at say, 21°C and 27°C against a standard mercury thermometer. Your local druggist will probably be prepared to do this for you if you have no reliable thermometer of your own.

The newer strip thermometers which are stuck onto the outside of the tank and change colors with temperature changes are most attractive.

There is often a considerable top-to-bottom temperature difference in tropical tanks. This is no cause for worry, as it mimics conditions in nature, where the heat of the sun frequently raises the top water temperature well above that of the lower strata and the fishes just stay down.

Lighting other than daylight is supplied from on top as already indicated.

A good aquarium hood will slow down water evaporation and also prevent the fish from jumping out of the tank.

Side lighting may give interesting effects, but it causes some fishes to swim lopsidedly and may eventually upset them. Also the plants will grow toward the light and may look very odd when obliquely illuminated for any length of time.

In addition to the cover afforded by a reflector, the top of the aquarium is best completely enclosed in some fashion. Glass is popular, and it is necessary when light must enter through the cover. Otherwise, any material which is water-resistant may be used, and some of the modern plastics are commonly used.

Covers serve a number of purposes. They prevent fishes from jumping out and prevent other creatures, from beetles to cats, from getting in. Covers also prevent airborne contaminants from fouling the water, and they help keep the tank warmer and prevent rapid evaporation. A tight-fitting cover which encloses about 3 cm of air space over the water does not suffocate the fishes, which obtain plenty of oxygen from the air enclosed, even if the cover is really airtight, and it usually isn't. The removal of the cover or part of it once or more a day for feeding admits enough fresh air. A cover is convenient if made in two pieces so that either a strip along the front or a corner-piece can be lifted for feeding or servicing without removing the whole. In modern all-glass tanks, the cover of the hood rests on a lip built into the top so that condensation drippings are directed back into the tank rather than over the frame and down the outside of the glass. Some hoods and covers have metal parts.

They should be built so that direct contact between those parts and water condensation is avoided, otherwise drippings of condensation from those parts could poison the aquarium water and kill the fishes. Stainless steel parts are fairly durable and will not cause any poisons to drip into the aquarium.

Plant Varieties: A very large number of varieties of water plants are now available to the aquarist. For present purposes, these plants may be divided into the rooted plants, which are placed in the sand or gravel, the rootless plants, which may, nevertheless, be anchored in the gravel, and the floating plants, which have roots hanging freely down into the water.

Among the rooted plants, the various grass-like plants such as *Vallisneria, Sagittaria* and *Eleocharis* may be obtained in many forms, from giants with strap-like leaves which may grow to a meter in length to tiny dwarf varieties only a couple of centimeters or so in height. Such plants reproduce by runners which lie along the surface of the sand or a little beneath it and put out buds at frequent intervals. They put forth surface flowers, which unfortunately wither in the reflector of the usual tank but which may look very attractive in a tank with daylight illumination and no top cover. The larger types of grass-like plants are usually placed at the back and sides of the tank.

Other rooted plants form fine centerpieces or plants which may be arranged in clumps to good effect. Centerpieces include the Amazon sword plants (*Echinodorus* species), the Madagascar sword plants and the Madagascar lace plant (*Aponogeton madagascariensis*), a much-prized beauty which is still highly priced in most parts of the world. The Amazon sword plants reproduce by runners which ride up into the water. New plants occurring on these runners may be carefully broken off and planted separately when they have produced sufficient roots to look ready for it. The *Aponogeton* have bulbs which may bud off new ones or may be propagated from seeds from surface flowers.

Still further rooted plants which may be used as centerpieces in smaller tanks or for side decoration in others include various species of *Cryptocoryne*, which also propagate by runners. These are slow-growing plants which look very decorative and can thrive with weaker lighting than most others. Some, such as *C. becketti*, *C. axelrodi* and *C. cordata*, grow only several centimeters high, while others, such as *C. griffithi* or *C. ciliata*, grow nearly 30 cm in height. The various varieties of water fern (*Ceratopteris*) are in contrast fast-growing and need frequent attention. *Hygrophila, Myriophyllum* and *Limnophila* are fine-looking when planted in bunches and will strike roots from odd pieces thrust into the sand. *Cabomba* is another very attractive plant which needs rather more light than most, but it will also root from pieces pushed into the sand. *Ludwigia* is a bog plant with attractive red undersides to the leaves in one variety; it survives well completely immersed. *Elodea* puts out roots all over the place and grows very rapidly.

Rootless plants include *Ceratophyllum* (hornwort) and *Nitella,* which grow in profusion in a good light and may be artificially anchored in bunches with fine effect. These are both particularly useful plants for spawning or for providing a hiding place for young livebearers.

Floating plants may also be used to give refuge for young fishes or to cut down the amount of light entering the surface of the water. *Salvinia* has fairly large, hairy leaves – which are green in ordinary conditions but turn red in bright sunlight – and long hairy roots. It does best out of doors but will propagate in a good indoor light. *Lemna* (duckweed) is a smaller green floating plant with a single root which propagates rapidly in all normal circumstances and can be a nuisance. *Riccia* (crystalwort) floats beneath the surface of the water and together with *Lemna* is a favorite food for some fishes. It also provides perhaps the best cover for newborn livebearers, but it does not flourish in poor light.

Introducing the Fishes: After a tank has been set up with the plants in place it is best left for several days before fishes are placed into it. During this period there is a chance to check that all is well, that no leaks have started and that the temperature control is satisfactory. Nothing is more disheartening than to set up a tank and place the fishes in it and then have to dismantle everything hurriedly and find an emergency home for them. This rest period also allows the plants to become settled in and to start functioning, which they will do fully only after a week or two; more importantly, it also gives some of the most troublesome fish diseases and parasites a chance to die off if they have been introduced by accident into the tank. This is particularly important with the parasite known as ich or "white spot," which does not live long without the presence of fishes and which is the most widespread of all tropical diseases.

If an undergravel filter is used, give it time to mature as described above. A few fishes may be introduced after a short time, but the tank will only accommodate its full complement (which is greater than if no undergravel filter is employed) after the bacterial population has been fully established. These considerations are not so critical in the freshwater aquarium as they are in marine tanks, but they are still important. Proper attention to them will help to avoid many a disease problem that would otherwise occur.

Look over all new fishes very carefully before placing them in the tank. If they seem all right, there is no reason why they should not all be put into the new tank together, taking special care not to chill them or to subject them to a large pH change. The best way to avoid this is to float the plastic bag or jar in which they have probably arrived in the water in the new tank until they are at about the same temperature and then gradually mix the waters together. Do not overstock the tank; it is much better to understock it for the first few weeks. Once the tank has a fish population, do not introduce new fishes

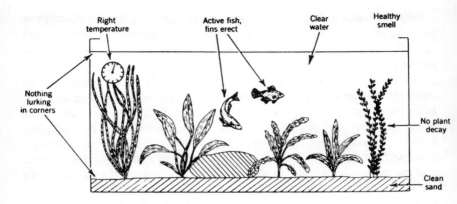

Things to check when looking over the state of an aquarium.

without quarantine unless you know for certain that they have been in a disease-free tank for at least a week and know for certain that they have not been chilled on their way to you or subjected to any other risks. If they have travelled for more than a few hours, you can rarely know this. Otherwise, they should be given two weeks of quarantine in a special tank, even if they look perfectly well. It is impossible for the owner of only a single community tank to do this, but at least he may as well realize that he takes a risk every time he introduces strangers to the tank and may think twice about adding any fishes which are in any way subject to suspicion. The same applies to new plants. The new fishes can be floated in the main tank in a jar or bowl of generous size, care being taken to see that they are given enough room and air surface and that they don't jump into the tank.

If you have no spare isolation tank and have other fishes already in a tank to which you have decided to introduce new ones, probably the best thing to do is absolutely nothing, except to keep a close watch on all the inhabitants for several weeks and be ready to give immediate treatment for any malady which may turn up. It is best not to dose the tank with antibiotics as this may engender disease resistance. Instead, treat prophylactically with a bland disinfectant such as methylene blue or acriflavine.

If, after all, a new fish does develop disease, don't always blame the previous owner or the dealer. Disease may be present in your tank and the new fish may have caught it from your own stock, which may not be showing it actively. Or the new fish may be weakened in transit and fall sick after its arrival. Subsequently, the whole tank may be affected, as it is quite common for a latent disease to start up on a new rampage once it has been given a start by the presence of a susceptible host. From him it can spread back to the rest in heightened form.

Handling Fishes: The best advice about handling fishes is *don't*, unless necessary! Nets for catching adult fishes in small tanks should be as large as possible and not very deep. They should not come to a point anywhere, either like a dunce's cap or in pointed corners, but instead should be gently rounded so as to give a minimum risk of injury to the fishes. They may be made of mosquito netting or other suitable fabric with a reasonably wide mesh so as to offer small resistance to the water. Synthetics are popular, as they dry with a shake and can last for a long time without rotting. It is also worthwhile to make or purchase nets with plastic-coated frames, as the fabric does not then rot at the edges so readily. Nets for catching fry should be quite shallow, so that they do not cause the fry to "ball up," but when in use they must be carefully watched as fry usually jump.

If your fishes have the common habit of rushing to the top of the tank to be fed, they may often be caught practically all together with a single well-directed sweep of the net. If you fail at the first attempt it is not usually so easy to repeat the maneuver with any success, so try again later. Most fishes can otherwise be caught without much fuss if you are not in a hurry, but once the necessary self-control is lost a tank is easily wrecked. It is a good idea to try stealth first—gently approach the fish with a good-sized net and try to slip it under the fish and lift it cleanly out without causing any panic. If this or your patience fails, you may chase more actively, usually with little success. When this stage is reached, it is best to stop and try again in a few minutes; but if you are in a great hurry, then place the net at one end, well ballooned out into the darkest part of the tank, and chase the fishes into it with a free hand or another net. Then, unless you want to remove the lot, lift the net and rest it on the frame of the tank with the fishes in water but still trapped. Finally, remove the specimens wanted with a small tumbler or cup. Never actually handle small fishes if you can avoid it. Large fishes, including Goldfish, are often best caught and removed gently by hand, if possible, as they struggle in a net and may injure themselves more that way than if gently handled. If you are not in a hurry, it often pays to wait until the tank has been in darkness for about half an hour, when, if the lights are switched on, the great majority of fishes will remain stationary in the water for a few minutes. During this period they may be located and netted out without fuss as long as they are not alarmed by sudden and violent movements.

Do not move fishes any more than is absolutely necessary, particularly when they have been established in one tank for a long time. Sometimes a transfer to an apparently perfectly suitable tank with water from the same original source is fatal. This does not mean that most fishes cannot be safely moved—they can—but don't do it unnecessarily, just to try the look of them here and there in different tanks. Remember also that it is quite difficult to catch a fish without doing it some slight injury and that all such abrasions are likely to be the site of an infection which may spread not only on the individual but also throughout a whole tank.

When the tank is finally established and seems to be a happily running concern, you must still be vigilant. Take a purposeful look at your tank at least once a day—for instance, when you feed the fishes. Even after much experience the aquarist may miss the early signs of trouble if he doesn't look carefully for specific symptoms. He must learn to look at the component parts of the setup and to notice anything that may spell trouble so that corrective action may be taken at the most effective stage.

Points to remember are:

The *smell* of a healthy tank is earthy and pleasant. Look for the cause of any departure from this.

The *plants* should be of good color and not decaying in part or whole. Remove any large decaying leaves, stems or roots and test the pH if decay continues.

The *water* should be clear or very mildly green; its surface should be clean and without a film of dust, oily material or bacteria.

The *gravel* should be clean, loose and not gray below the surface. If it is disturbed no bubbles should rise from it.

The *fishes* should look alert and well, with fins clear and held away from the body. "Clamped" fins or peculiar swimming motions mean impending trouble. The fishes should have no strings of excreta hanging from them for any length of time.

The *corners* of the tank and hidden crannies should be searched for dead fish or sick fish hiding away.

The *temperature* should be checked as a daily routine in tropical tanks.

Foods and Feeding: Most research on fish foods has been done by commercial fish farms and used as a guide for the aquarium trade. Fishes are very good utilizers of food and convert about twice as much into their own body weight as do most domestic animals, as long as the food is high in protein. This requirement is particularly high in young fishes, which should receive at least 50% protein by dry weight in their diet. Adults still need at least 40%. They need the usual amino acids of higher vertebrates and can digest some fat, up to 20-30% in their diet, as long as choline and general vitamin intake are adequate. Starch needs to be hydrolyzed.

The water-soluble vitamins (notably C and the B group) are needed as in other vertebrates, and vitamin C requirements are related to stress and rates of protein synthesis (*e.g.*, wound healing). Less is known about fat-soluble vitamin requirements (notably A and D). Vitamin D, although stored in the liver of some fishes, is not required for normal growth and function in salmonid fishes unless the water is soft. Little is known of trace mineral needs.

The natural food of brook trout has been shown to be made up as follows, with an analysis of its overall contents:

Constituent	% in Diet
Insects	88.8
Crustaceans	8.2
Fishes	2.5
Molluscs	0.3
Other	0.2

% Dry Food Content	
Protein	48.8
Fat	15.0
Carbohydrates, etc.	25.9
Ash	9.9

Natural Foods: Nearly all fry feed on plankton, which consists of single-celled organisms (infusoria), the young stages of insects, crustaceans, worms and other water creatures. Very small fish fry such as those of the anabantoids (labyrinth fishes) consume small single-celled algae or infusoria, later eating large single-celled or multi-celled creatures.

When the fishes grow up, their diet is more varied in nature, but many show a preference for an animal or vegetable diet. Animal diets are preferred by characoids (tetras), cyprinodonts (killifishes) and many of the larger fishes which eat insects, worms, crustaceans, snails and other fishes. Vegetable diets are preferred by many livebearers, by the *Scatophagus* tribe and by odd members of the tetras and gouramis, such as the Kissing Gourami and *Metynnis* and *Leporinus* species. Almost all fishes will accustom themselves to an unusual diet in time, but some will only eat live foods. These are fortunately rarities but include *Badis badis, Belonesox* and some of the sticklebacks. Even these are said to with training eat fish roe.

Live Food: An occasional feeding with live food is helpful to ensure the health of fishes and desirable for breeding many species. However, the present availability of frozen, freeze-dried or canned fish foods is such that live food can usually be dispensed with except in rare cases. Much effort has gone into the production of first-class fish food over the last few years. Such foods are usually fortified with vitamins and minerals, even though we are not sure if some of them are really needed. Thus, entirely live diets are quite unnecessary except in the few instances where the fishes won't eat prepared food. This is rarely the case, with the plethora of good prepared foods now commercially available, and a little training will often solve the problem.

Worms are often an excellent food source for larger fish.

Earthworms: The earthworm is a fine fish-food, given whole to the big fishes, chopped to the smaller fishes and shredded to the very small ones. If you are sensitive, the worms can be killed immediately before use by plunging them into hot water. Unfortunately, fishes seem to prefer them uncooked. Earthworms may be stored in leaf-mold, in urban shrub boxes or window boxes, or may be coaxed from the lawn by pouring a solution of potassium permanganate at a strength of about ¼ gram per liter onto the surface. They emerge in a few minutes. Avoid the dung worm, which is yellow, smelly and not good for fishes.

Insect Larvae: Insect larvae are another fine live food. Those of various species of mosquitoes and gnats may be netted by the thousands in warm weather from stagnant water. They may also be cultivated by leaving suitable receptacles in the garden, but avoid increasing the adult mosquito population if you do this. In cultivation it is important to have smelly stagnant and dirty water, as clean water offers little food and does not attract the female mosquito.

The female mosquito lays egg rafts, small sooty-looking floating masses of up to 300 eggs, which hatch out into a swarm of minute "wrigglers." Typical species develop through the next eight or nine days before pupating and offer during this period a nice range of sizes of fish food. The larvae grow steadily and molt several times, finally turning into pupae, which are comma-shaped, and soon develop into adults. The larvae and pupae are air-breathers and may be fed freely to the fishes without fear of crowding them out but with a possibility of them developing into adults if given in excess.

When collecting larvae or pupae, it is best to catch them as cleanly as possible with a fine net and then, if necessary, to sort them for size by letting them wriggle down through a sieve or series of sieves made from various meshes of wire screening. If they are stored in a refrigerator they keep longer without metamorphosis and also keep sweeter. It is advisable to wash catches thoroughly and to feed the bigger ones only to fishes large enough to clean them up quickly. Care must of course be taken to exclude any sizeable insect larvae, such as those of the dragonfly, which are likely to escape being eaten and grow to dangerous proportions.

Chironomid larvae or "bloodworms" are rather similar but are blood-red. Their parents are also gnats, so the creatures are not really worms but insect larvae. They stay down in the water more than any other gnat or mosquito larvae and must be separated from the mud after collection. This is best done by sieving as with the others, choosing a mesh so that the mud escapes and the larvae are retained. *Chaoborus* larvae (glass worms) are like bloodless chironomid larvae but are found in cold weather and swim freely in the water. Sometimes they may be collected in quantity, and they keep well in crowded conditions.

Daphnids: These are small crustaceans about the size of a small flea or smaller. They appear in warm but not hot weather in stagnant pools and may be almost colorless, green or red, depending on the variety and also on their food. Different types also vary considerably in size.

When really plentiful, daphnia (also called water fleas) occur in large swarms and may be netted out in thick clumps, so thick that an improperly shaped net will ball them up together and injure them. The right net is fairly shallow and does not come to a point but is rounded in section. The daphnia will suffocate if not given fair room in transporting them and should also be kept cool.

Daphnia are regarded by many as the very best food for fishes. They are not actually very good in food value, as they have a high water content and a hard tough shell, and fishes fed exclusively on daphnia do not thrive as a rule. They should be used in moderation for most tropical fishes but may be fed more liberally to Goldfish. Daphnia are available in dried form but are rather expensive this way, except for the fact that the dried eggs in the bodies of the females will sometimes hatch out and can be used to start a live daphnia culture. These are the winter eggs, which normally last over winter and hatch out the following spring.

The artificial cultivation of daphnia is possible if large pools are available, and on a worthwhile scale it is possible even in tubs or old tanks. Daphnia normally live on unicellular algae and other organisms, and it is these which must be supplied in bulk. They are cultured by enriching the water in the pool or tub with decaying vegetable matter or manure. Sheep manure is said

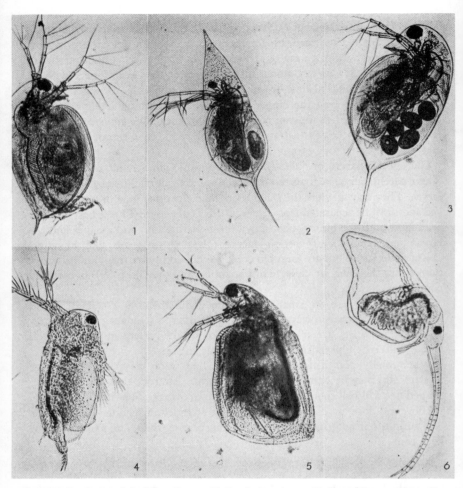

Several *Daphnia* related Crustacea: (1) *Daphnia magna.* (2) *Daphnia cucullata.* (3) *Daphnia-longispina.* (4) *Syda cristallina.* (5) *Simocephalus vetulus.* (6) *Bosmina coregoni.*

to be the best. An appropriate pool would be about 1.5 x 3 m in area and .6 m deep. After seeding it liberally with refuse and waiting for it to turn cloudy or green, the daphnia are introduced and should breed well. Such a pool might yield enough daphnia for a regular feeding two or three times a week to several hundred small fishes, but don't expect too much. Such pools are smelly, and yeast or wheat flour may be used indoors as the source of nourishment. If kept well aerated, these have little or no smell.

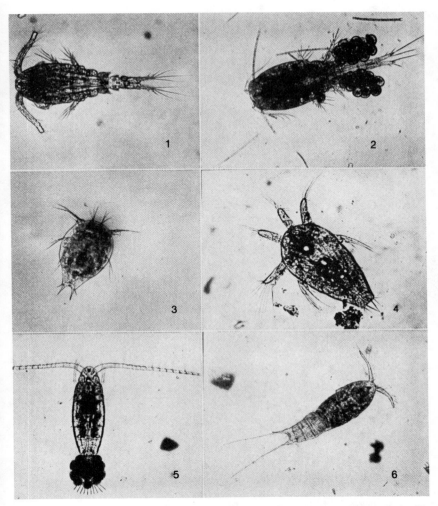

Several copepod-related Crustacea: (1) *Cyclops* species. (2) *Cyclops* species with egg sacs. (3) *Cyclops* species larva. (4) *Cyclops* species during development. (5) *Diaptomus* species. (6) *Canthocamptus* species.

Other Crustaceans: *Moina, Cyclops, Diaptomus* and other less important crustaceans are found with daphnia and can also be cultivated. They are not usually as abundant or as palatable to all fishes as daphnia, but they are small and easily cultivated and are welcome to growing fry. Some cyclops unfortunately seem to be feeders on the unhatched eggs of tropical fishes and should be excluded from breeding tanks at the initial stage.

Gammarus (an amphipod or scud) and *Asellus* (an isopod or water sowbug)

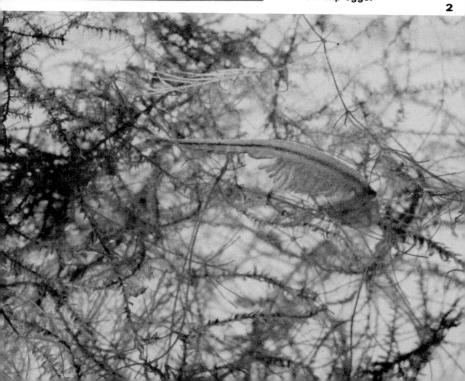

(1) A fully grown, mature brine shrimp. (2) A mature shrimp in an aquarium. (3) Brine shrimp eggs.

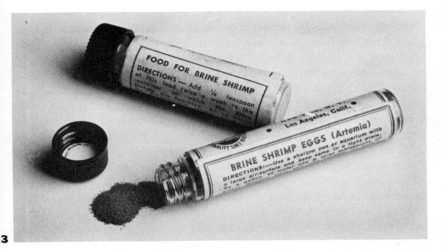

3

are two common shrimp-like larger crustaceans. They are both about .5 to 1 cm in length and both can be cultured in aquaria with rotting leaves for food. They are caught in the roots of plants and rushes and often occur in ditches. They are eagerly taken by the larger fishes and their younger stages are eaten by smaller species. They have also the advantage that they survive for an appreciable period in salt water and so may be fed to marine fishes. Uneaten specimens—and it is surprising how long *Gammarus,* in particular, sometimes manages to escape—are excellent scavengers. In the eastern United States *Gammarus* is largely replaced by the common *Hyalella* and other genera, but the fishes don't mind.

Brine Shrimp: The brine shrimp, *Artemia salina,* is also a crustacean, but it merits a heading to itself. It is a live food of great importance, as without it thousands of young fishes would never reach maturity. The genus *Artemia* is composed of small shrimps which live in very salty water, such as the Great Salt Lake in Utah, and whose eggs can withstand drying up completely for many years. Hence it is very important, for these eggs are collected commercially and made available to aquarists all over the world. They can be stored for over a decade if necessary, as long as they are kept dry and at an even temperature. More remarkable still, they can be dried out again, even after they have become moist, and they will still retain their hatching capacity.

The eggs look like a fine brown powder and are minute. About the smallest pinch you can take contains several hundred, and it is customary to hatch many thousands at a time. They are not used until they are hatched—it is the living young shrimp that are of importance in feeding baby fishes and even adults of the smaller species. There are two methods of hatching, in shallow pans or in deep cultures with aeration. Much better hatching results are usually obtained by the aeration method.

The eggs hatch only in *salt* water, but oddly enough they hatch more quickly and more evenly in weaker salt water than is needed by the adults. They thrive beautifully in sea water, although the adults do not. Thus, for hatching, use 6 heaped tablespoons of salt to 4 liters of tap water (approximately 42 g to the liter or a 4.2% salt solution). The eggs will float on the surface and should be sprinkled onto the water and left there, using not more than 1 teaspoon of eggs per 8 liters of water. The eggs will hatch in about a day at temperatures of over 27°C, but they will take a week or more at less than 21°C. Even at 27°C some of the eggs will take a couple of days to hatch out. If more eggs than recommended above are used, relatively fewer will hatch.

The empty eggshells will continue to float if undisturbed, whereas the shrimp swim with a jerky motion. They also collect in the lightest part of the vessel and will congregate so thickly that they will suffocate in a spot that is really bright in contrast to the rest. They may be siphoned off free of eggshells if the last few teaspoons of water are left behind and drained on an old handkerchief or other cloth. They should then be rinsed in fresh water to avoid introducing gradual doses of unwanted salt into the freshwater tank and fed with an eyedropper or by rinsing the cloth in the tank.

By the alternative method of hatching, four-liter jars, or even larger vessels, are two-thirds filled with the same salt water as above and subjected to brisk aeration. One or two teaspoons of eggs may then be used for every 4 liters, and the eggs are whirled around in the water until they hatch. To collect the shrimp, the aeration is turned off and the eggshells allowed to settle; this they usually do partly on the bottom and partly on the top. The shrimp may then be siphoned off with few or no eggshells. There are also special outfits on the market for the deep hatching of brine shrimp, with convenient taps running off from the base of the culture vessels. A shell-less brine shrimp egg preparation has recently been introduced and promises to simplify production of this important food.

Brine shrimp grow to about one centimeter in length and are a meaty meal at that stage. They need a different brine from that used in hatching, so that newly hatched shrimp should be transferred within a day or two to a brine made by taking a breakfast cup (300 grams) of salt, two heaped tablespoons (60 grams) of Epsom salts and one tablespoon of baking soda to 4 liters of tap water. This brine is about twice the strength of sea water and much more alkaline.

The young shrimp (nauplii) feed naturally on algae, etc., but baker's yeast may be substituted—about ¼ teaspoon per 4 liters, well stirred up. Into 4 liters of brine plus yeast, preferably in a shallow tub or tray, put just a few shrimp—not more than a few hundred, unless you intend to use them only partially grown, in which case thousands can be reared. Feed yeast again when the brine clears, which may be in a day or week, according to

Tubificid worms in a ball.

temperature and the number of shrimp. Cover to prevent too much evaporation. The shrimp reach maturity in about six weeks, sooner if kept really warm, and they will feed on yeast throughout the period and reproduce readily. If undisturbed, the culture will soon contain both young and older shrimps, but do not expect it to yield an indefinite supply—you will still need to buy more eggs. Siphon off and wash the adults as you would the young before using them.

Brine shrimp eggs from different sources may need different types of brine for hatching. Look on the label for any particular recommendations.

Tubificid Worms: The mud worms or sludge worms, *Tubifex rivulorum* and other similar *Tubifex* or *Limnodrilus* species, are excellent food, but they are found in very dirty surroundings and must be carefully washed before use. These worms absorb waste material from slow-moving polluted streams, being rarely found in quantity in stagnant water. They live at the bottom or sides of streams and wave their tails in the water, retiring promptly into a tube in the mud when disturbed. They are reddish in color and vary from threadlike creatures a couple centimeters long to solid worms eight or ten centimeters in length. They may establish themselves in an aquarium and be hard to eliminate *(Corydoras* will dig them up) and whether they are regarded as an acquisition or a nuisance depends on the beholder.

Collecting tubifex is usually a filthy task. If they are present in worthwhile amounts they will be seen as a reddish wriggling carpet or in separate red patches which jerk into the mud when a shadow or footfall disturbs them. Dig well under the mud where a patch was seen—or if you are lucky it will be so thick that even when retracted it is still visible—and put mud and all into a

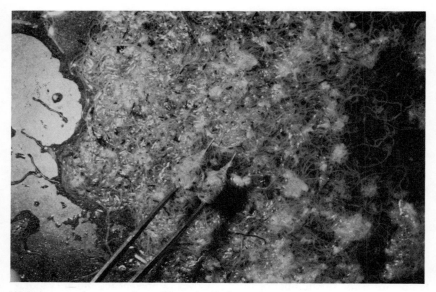
White worms from a culture. Photo by E. Stansburg.

large bucket. When the bucket is nearly full, leave it until lack of oxygen forces the worms to collect at the surface, when they may be removed with some mud still adhering to them. If they must be left for long, run a gentle drip of water into the bucket or they will die and be useless. Most of the worms can be removed within a day or two and must be well washed under a brisk stream of water to remove the residual mud, when they will aggregate into balls and may be stored for a long time, even a month, if placed in large vessels of water under a constant drip from a tap or hose, with a suitable overflow arrangement. They also store well in a refrigerator if placed in preferably airtight containers with no water at all. Stored masses should occasionally be stirred up and washed more briskly to remove the dead and feces, and should not be fed to fishes for at least the first day.

White Worms: White worms (enchytrae) are relatives of tubifex and of earthworms. They are small worms about 2 cm in length which are commonly found in cool, moist surroundings where there is plenty of humus or other decaying matter for them to use as food. The underside of trash cans when on soil is a favorite spot, but the worms are practically never collected from such sites now, as they may be purchased from dealers to start a culture. The common species is *Enchytraeus albidus.* White worms may be cultured in wooden boxes of rich soil with added humus and oatmeal. These are stored in cool places such as cellars, and further oatmeal, mashed potatoes, cheese, bread

A microworm culture.

and milk or a variety of other things that will suggest themselves are placed on the soil or into small holes in it at intervals of a few days. The whole is tightly covered, preferably by a sheet of glass in contact with the top of the soil, mainly to exclude ants and other predators (even mice), but also to keep the soil in a damp state—not wet, just damp. When needed, the worms may be scraped off the glass or collected from the food pockets. A culture usually needs about six weeks before harvesting can commence.

On a smaller scale, the worms may be cultured between milk-soaked crusts of bread stored in tightly covered tins or other vessels. It is advisable to boil the milk and to pour it on the crusts while hot, as this helps to sterilize them and prevents early souring of the culture. This method nevertheless requires frequent sub-culturing, as the bread slices rapidly go sour and moldy.

There is usually little trouble in separating white worms from their food, but if it is encountered, place the mass of half-cleaned worms on a rather hot surface and they will rapidly crawl to the top. These worms may be inadvisable as a frequent food, as they are said to cause fatty degeneration of the reproductive organs.

Microworms: A group of minute nematode worms (roundworms) of the genus *Anguillula* supplies the familiar vinegar eel, *A. aceti*, and the paste eel, *A. glutinus*. Another, *A. silusiae*, is found in soil, and it is assumed that this is the species usually called the microworm. It is a very small livebearing worm,

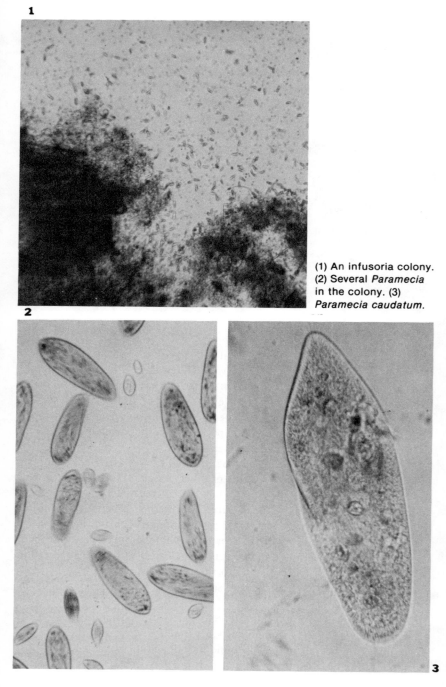

(1) An infusoria colony.
(2) Several *Paramecia*
in the colony. (3)
Paramecia caudatum.

at a maximum about 2.5 mm long, with young very much smaller.

Microworms are easy to culture. This is best done in shallow vessels with tight covers. In the base of each vessel is placed about a 3 mm layer of any of the quick-cooking powdered breakfast oatmeals or wheatmeals. The use of wheat germ is said to give superior results to other meals. The meal is moistened with about its own volume of water and is then inoculated with a little baker's yeast and some microworms. The yeast may be omitted if unavailable. Growth is rapid and the worms form a seething mass in a few days. If small pieces of wood, watersoaked beforehand, are placed crisscross over the meal so that the top ones are clear of it, the worms crawl up and collect free of cereal on the top-most pieces. If the sides of the vessel are roughened, as can be done with plastic containers, the worms will crawl up them and can be scraped off. It is not usually worthwhile to feed cultures once established, but it is best to keep a series going so that the worms are always ready for use. Each culture will last for up to two weeks. The worms thrive best in warmth up to 26°C.

Microworms withstand desiccation, so that a dried-up culture can be restarted merely by wetting it.

Grindal Worms: Another white worm, intermediate in size between the usual one and the microworm, was first cultivated by Mrs. Morten Grindal, a Swedish aquarist whose name has become attached to the worm. It was isolated from ordinary white worm cultures and prefers more heat than the usual enchytrae. It is at most one centimeter in length and slimmer in proportion than white worms.

Cultures are maintained as with white worms, except for a higher temperature—21°C or a little more seems best. Growth is very rapid.

Infusoria: It is still common practice to advocate the use of cultures of infusoria for certain newly hatched fishes, despite the fact that newer methods of fry feeding make these practically obsolete.

Infusoria are any minute living creatures in water needing a microscope for identification. The term includes plants and animals. A "culture" may be started with suitable pond water or from a previous culture. The best method is to boil up some lettuce or other vegetable matter in a liter of water, allow it to cool and then inoculate with the infusoria-containing material. Even if left to itself, the culture will start up, but not necessarily with the desired types of infusoria. Aeration is advisable, as it both increases the yield and keeps down smell. A medium light is also best; too strong a light may result in an excess of green algae.

Infusoria tablets may be purchased which are merely placed in water and result, or should result, in a rich culture of organisms within a few days. The culture will usually need feeding with vegetable infusion as described above. Water from a flower-vase is often rich in infusoria.

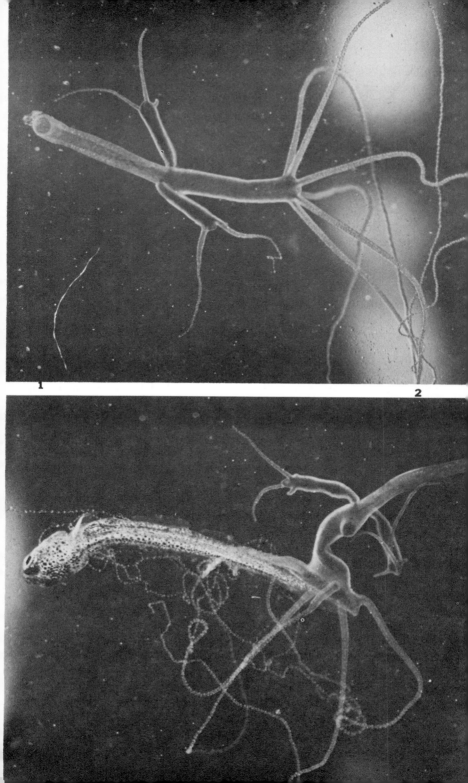

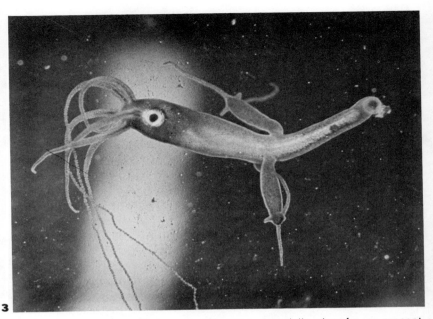

3

Hydra are not recommended as a food source, especially when fry are present. The sequence of photos one through three shows a Hydra eating a small fry. Photos by Klaus Brauner.

Prepared Foods: The term *prepared food* is used to denote any non-living food made up by the aquarist or bought ready-made for the consumption of his fishes. There is a wide variety of satisfactory commercial preparations on the market, some of which may be used as a staple food with the addition of such live food as proves possible from time to time. A good deal of rubbish is talked about the need of variety in food, but this is only needed in our present state of knowledge because any single food may be lacking in some factor or another which may, if we are lucky, be supplied by a different food. Otherwise there is nothing against supposing that an unvaried constant diet could prove as completely satisfactory for fishes as it does in the laboratory for many animals. The better foods have the higher protein content.

If you make up your own dry food, which is likely to be much cheaper than buying it if you keep a large number of fishes, there is no need to make the complex cookery exercise out of it that many books advise. Take about equal parts by volume of shredded dry shrimp, liver meal and a fairly finely divided breakfast cereal — preferably one made from wheat germ, and mix thoroughly. The best particle size to select depends on the size of your fishes. If you want to feed very small ones, then select a very fine grade of shrimp and cereal. It is not usually necessary to add any salt or other mineral to the mixture.

1

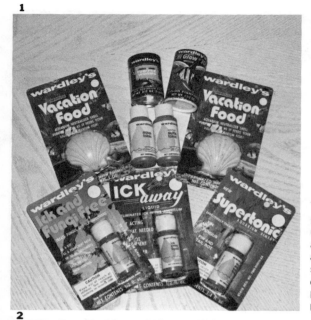

There are many prepared foods and medications (1) available to the aquarist. Ask your pet store dealer (2) which ones he recommends. Photos by Dr. Herbert R. Axelrod.

2

A food for large-scale feeding, recommended by the late Myron Gordon, is made from:

Liver of beef	5 kg.
Pablum	14 kg.
Shrimp shell meal	6 kg.
Shrimp meat shredded	3 kg.
Spinach	3 kg.

The raw beef liver is cut into 5 cm pieces and boiled for 15 minutes and removed; the same water is used for boiling the other ingredients. The boiled liver is ground or chopped and returned to the mixture for a further 15-minute boiling. The paste is dried and ground for storage.

Finer grades of prepared food for fry feeding may be made from coarser supplies by grinding them in a pepper mill or crushing them between flat tiles and then sieving carefully. Such food for young fishes may preferably contain more animal material and may be made from 100% dried shrimp or crab.

A feeding ring may be floated on the surface of the water when using dried food. This is a small ring of hollow glass or plastic which confines the food to a portion of the tank and makes it easier to remove unconsumed portions.

Most fishes like the various baby foods made for human consumption, but preferably with a little dried shrimp mixed in with it. Serve it in small soggy lumps, but expect to have to clear up the tank afterward unless you gauge the fishes' appetite very precisely.

Various non-spiced canned foods are much appreciated, such as canned crab or lobster, fish roe or canned spinach. The coldwater fishes, mostly heavy eaters, are particularly fond of chopped canned foods of this description.

Egg in various forms is also good for fishes—as an omelet, boiled and chopped up, or poured into boiling water and beaten as it solidifies. Meat is readily taken, particularly minced heart or liver, but this should only occasionally be fed, as it seems to produce intestinal troubles if used much, resulting in thin fishes and fouled tanks. Large fishes may be fed almost anything from the kitchen that is not spiced or oily—the latter because the oil spreads as a film over the water rather than because it is indigestible or otherwise harmful, but any food must be fresh and suitably sized.

How to Feed: Most tropical fishes should be fed frequently. The warmer the water, up to about 26°C, the better the appetite of the fishes. Thus Goldfish need almost no feeding in the depth of winter and in normal cold weather should be fed only two or three times a week. In summer, however, twice daily is not too often. Tropicals are never so torpid as the coldwater varieties at the lower end of their temperature range, but they have in general only poor appetites at below 21°C. At 24°C they are good eaters and should be preferably lightly fed two or three times daily. At 26°C they are ravenous and will eat practically as often as you give it to them. Even so, they will not starve if fed only once per day or even every other day, particularly if fed on live food, but it is difficult to gauge the amount to give if it is given too seldom.

The feeding of prepared food requires careful handling, and the tendency of the beginner is to give far too much at a time. It is therefore very important indeed that the following rule be strictly adhered to at all times. It is a rule originally stated by Innes:

Feed only enough prepared food at one time so that practically ALL of it is consumed within five minutes.

Then siphon off any that remains.

An aquarist can go round his tanks dumping in the right amounts of dry food without looking to see the result only after very long experience. Each time you feed, see that the fishes eat it and see that they are well and alert and eating normally. Feed dry foods slowly and give them time to swell up with water inside the fishes before offering too much. Some aquarists soak food first, but the fishes do not eat so readily when this is done. Feed little and often whenever this is possible. It comes as rather a surprise to most to hear that about 30 grams of prepared food such as wheat germ and shrimp mixture will last 100 average tropical aquarium fishes for about two weeks with no other feeding at 24°C.

As long as they are usually well fed, adult tropical fishes can be starved without trouble for several days. Even starvation for a couple of weeks is feasible, as long as the temperature is about 21°C. Coldwater fishes can take starvation easier as long as they too are reasonably cool—say below 15°C. Longer periods may be survived, but the tropicals at least will be pretty thin at the end of them. The importance of this is that in a normal vacation of not more than two weeks it is possible to forget adult fishes but not young fry. This may be preferable to getting a friend to feed them, unless he is also an aquarium keeper. Other people far too often make mistakes in fish keeping, the most common being gross over-feeding and pollution. If a non-fancier must be asked to undertake the task, it is vitally necessary to give him a few lessons or to make up separate packages of food, one per feeding, with strict instructions not to supplement them with anything else whatever. The only food which can be given in mild excess to tide the fishes over a period is mosquito larvae. These do not consume dissolved oxygen to any appreciable extent and will survive some time if uneaten before turning into pupae and then adults. A tight cover over the tank will prevent the escape of any that manage to reach maturity. A further exception is the recently introduced blocks of dry food which disintegrate gradually without fouling the water. These are well worth a trial. Mechanical dispensers are costly and do not seem to have caught on.

This tetra is diseased with ichthyophthiriasis, commonly called either "ich" or white spot. Photo by R. Zukal.

Diseases and Parasites

Fishes suffer from a series of diseases resembling those of higher animals, but those about which we know most and can often successfully treat are the external diseases with symptoms visible to the aquarist. Until recently, very few effective treatments were available, but the cheapening of antibiotics for veterinary use and the discovery of some other methods of cure for a few of the common diseases have now made their treatment much more feasible. Some good commercial cures are now available, but if you wish to try your own remedies, the following should help.

Various conditions will be taken in approximate order of importance to the tropical fish-keeper, not classified by symptoms or by the nature of their causative organisms. Some of the most important diseases of tropical fishes are caused by protozoans, tiny one-celled animals which parasitize the skin or gills or in some cases penetrate further. This is in contrast to human diseases, the majority of which are caused by viruses and bacteria. Antibiotics such as penicillin are not effective against most protozoa, hence they are not much used in fish medicine. The wide-spectrum antibiotics like aureomycin or chloromycetin, however, are spectacularly successful in some instances and are used less than they might be only because of their adverse effects on undergravel filters and the danger of creating resistant bacterial disease strains.

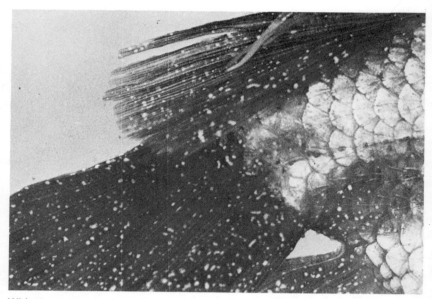

White spot can be seen most readily on darkly colored fishes. The disease is very contagious and should be treated immediately. Photo by Dr. G. Schubert.

Since it is often necessary to treat the whole aquarium, remedies such as methylene blue and potassium permanganate are not recommended because they color the water and stain plants and decorations to such an extent as to spoil things fairly completely. Equally effective but colorless or nearly colorless treatments are preferred instead, so that you can see what is happening and don't have to clean the tank up afterwards. Malachite green or brilliant green usually becomes decolorized rapidly, although it may give a deep color initially, and does not stain rocks or plants objectionably.

White Spot: White spot, "ich" or ichthyophthiriasis was until two decades ago the commonest scourge of tropical fishes, but it has recently been rivalled by velvet disease, described below. It can attack coldwater fishes and tropical fishes. It is caused by a protozoan which imbeds itself in the skin of the fish and causes a small white blister to form. This blister enlarges in a few days and then bursts; the adult parasite drops to the bottom of the tank and forms a cyst which then produces up to 2,000 young in its interior. These become free-swimming and start the cycle once more. At 21 to 26°C the whole process takes only eight or 10 days, but at lower temperatures it may last many weeks.

The symptoms of white spot are, at first, the fish scrubbing itself on plants and other suitable objects, then visible white spots which grow up to about 1 mm across. These are usually first visible on the fins (but actually infect the gills at the earliest stage, causing heavy breathing and itching), but later and in heavy attacks are seen all over the body. Some species are more susceptible than others, but susceptibility varies with condition and past history. The Guppy *(Poecilia reticulata)*, Head and Tail Light Tetra *(Hemigrammus ocellifer)* and Ruby Barb *(Puntius nigrofasciatus)* are examples of particularly susceptible fishes.

White spot is very contagious, so every care must be taken not to infect other tanks. It is fortunately only transferred by wet objects and does not live in the completely dry state. It may, however, be transferred on plants, even if they are washed. All nets and other implements must be thoroughly washed in boiling water or in disinfectant after use in the affected tank and splashing scrupulously avoided. The hands should also be washed after handling the affected tank. Attacks are brought on by direct infection from a case of the disease or by chilling a tank which has organisms present in dormant form. As the *Ichthyophthirius* parasite can occur in tap water in certain areas, although not when it is heavily chlorinated, white spot can seem to come on spontaneously with no apparent cause. However, to show the disease, a fish usually has either to be attacked fairly heavily by masses of parasites or to be in poor health, when it may succumb to a light attack.

It is stated that the free-living stage must find a host within a few days or perish. A tank void of fishes should therefore cure itself of white spot quite rapidly, so that if all fishes are removed for treatment, the tank itself should need no disinfection. Unfortunately, the experiences of many aquarists lead us to believe that something may be wrong with this story, for white spot disease does not behave so obligingly and is extremely difficult to eradicate completely without thorough disinfection of tanks, plants and fishes.

The disease organisms are susceptible to treatment while they are in the free-swimming stage, but existing spots on the fish are resistant to most forms of therapy. There are several chemical treatments that are effective against ich. The effectiveness of these treatments may be enhanced considerably by elevating the temperature of the water to about 30°C. Not only does the heat hasten the life cycle of the parasite, but it also directly kills the free-swimming young parasites. This high temperature can only be used if aeration is continued and even increased, for at 30°C water cannot hold very much dissolved oxygen. The increased aeration helps keep the water adequately oxygenated.

MALACHITE GREEN: The most widely used chemical treatment for ich is malachite green. This is the major ingredient in most commercially manufactured and packaged ich cures. Different manufacturers may package the chemical in different strengths, so it is best to explicitly follow the manufacturer's directions. Most malachite green ich cures may be used repeatedly, within recommended limits, of course, until the disease is eradicated. Certain small fishes such as some of the characoids (especially small tetras) are quite sensitive to malachite green. With these fishes only half the recommended dosage should be used.

What is most important for this or any other ich treatment is that the therapy be continued for 10 days. This is the only way to be relatively certain that all free-swimming parasites are exposed to the treatment, for the free-swimmers that emerge from the last spot to fall off the fish may not appear until several days later. Furthermore, a few resistant individuals may survive the treatment on the first round, but the chances of their offspring surviving the treatment are even less.

QUININE: Another effective chemical treatment is quinine, which can be administered as a hydrochloride or as a sulphate. This, too, is packaged commercially for aquarium use but be sure to use it in dosages recommended by the manufacturers.

ANTIBIOTICS: Antibiotics can, in some cases, be used as a treatment against ich, but they are not usually very effective against this disease. Furthermore, most antibiotics are not very selective in the pathogens they kill, and their use in an established aquarium will destroy the beneficial bacteria that flourish in the gravel and break down fish wastes. In addition, certain individual bacteria of almost any kind are more resistant to antibiotics than others. Some of these may be disease pathogens, and when antibiotics are really needed to fight a bacterial infection, the strain may have become totally immune to the drug. Antibiotics should not be used indiscriminantly in the aquarium.

Velvet or Rust Disease: With this disease, the skin of the fish looks as if it has been dusted with golden or yellowish powder. At the beginning there will be a few dots of yellow; later the fish may be covered with them. The difference from white spot is that the spots are *yellower* and *smaller*. This disease is especially fatal to young fishes and must be treated immediately when it is seen. Adults often carry it without showing distress, but if they are used for breeding the fry will succumb to the disease.

The cause of the disease is another kind of protozoan, a dinoflagellate called *Oodinium limneticum*. It attaches itself to its victim, and then grows more deeply into the fish's body by penetrating the skin with pseudopods. At maturity, as with ich, the adult parasite drops off the fish and at the bottom of the tank encysts and begins to divide internally, producing within a day or two as many as 200 new free-swimming dinoflagellates. Treatment may be as follows:

ACRIFLAVINE: is one of the most effective chemicals for killing *Oodinium*. Its use, however, should be restricted to as short a time as possible (usually about 10 days), for prolonged use of acriflavine has been associated with certain reproductive problems in some fishes. The effectiveness of acriflavine against velvet may be enhanced by increasing the water temperature to 27°C and adding one teaspoon of salt to each four liters of water.

For aquarium use, acriflavine is packaged either in its pure crystalline form, in a pure liquid form (diluted with water) or in a mixture of other chemicals which also help cure velvet. Correct dosage instructions are given on the label by each manufacturer.

COPPER: Copper salts such as copper sulphate are toxic to velvet, but also to fishes, and a balance has to be struck where the disease organisms are killed without killing the fishes. Turn off all carbon filters and add five drops per four liters of a 1% solution of copper sulphate (available as a commercial preparation and sold by tropical fish shops); repeat after three days. About half this amount of copper citrate may be used if available, but it is not always easy to obtain (some commercial cures contain it as one of the ingredients). When the carbon filter is turned on again, it will remove much of the copper rapidly, and the small amount that remains is harmless in a freshwater tank. The free-swimming parasites are killed directly by the copper. Do not introduce new fishes to the copper-treated water, as it may kill them. If, during the treatment, the fishes cease feeding, start to gasp at the surface or show any other distress symptoms, remove the copper at once by carbon filtration.

COMBINATION CURES of copper plus acriflavine may be used in combating this resistant and dangerous disease. After any cure has apparently been successful, keep watch for a recurrence, since velvet is very hard to eradicate completely. The dreaded Red Sea *Oodinium* of marine fishes usually needs such a combined attack.

Hole-in-the-Head Disease: This disease seems to strike mostly larger fishes, especially cichlids like discus and oscars. It may well strike smaller fishes, but, because of their small size, the pits or depressions in the head may be more difficult to detect. The disease has been associated with a flagellate called *Hexamita*. These protozoan parasites apparently enter the fish's bloodstream through the gut and eventually cause festering sores or holes to appear on and around the skull. In addition to the sores, the victim shows lethargy and loss of appetite.

The best treatment for the disease is a drug called Flagyl®. Unfortunately, for the drug to be effective it must be given to the fish internally; this is indeed a problem, since usually by the time the symptoms are noticed the fish has already lost its appetite, so mixing the drug with the food will be of no avail. Another problem with this treatment is that the drug is not available commercially except by prescription.

Dylox® has been used effectively in treating hole-in-the-head disease by external application as in a bath. Dylox® is available only in powdered form, as once it is mixed with water it degenerates in about three days. Aquarium medication manufacturers package it in a vial containing a measured amount

The *Hemigrammus caudovittatus* in this photo have fungal infections that should have been treated before this advanced stage. Photo by G. J. M. Timmerman.

of powder. The aquarist simply fills the vial with water to dissolve the powder and pours the solution into the appropriate amount of aquarium water. The treatment should be repeated after three days.

Fungus: Various fungi of the genera *Saprolegnia* and *Achyla* attack fishes which have been wounded or are in a poor state of resistance. The spores of such fungi are universal and cannot be eradicated as they float into the tank from the air. The affected fish appears to have whitish fuzzy areas which may be like a slimy surfacing only or have a brush of fungus filaments projecting from them. If not treated, the fungus may spread and destroy much of the tissues of the fish, finally causing death. The disease therefore has to be treated as it occurs and is not to be regarded as infectious in the ordinary sense of the word, so that a fish while under treatment may be returned to a community tank as long as none of the other fishes in the tank are stressed or injured. Treatment may be as follows:

MALACHITE GREEN OR BRILLIANT GREEN (zinc-free): The affected fishes are taken from the tank and immersed for 30 seconds *only* in a solution of dye at 60 mg per liter or 1 in 15,000, and the fish is replaced in its tank. The fungus is colored by the dye and usually disappears by the next day. If not, repeat treatments may be given. An alternate dying treatment is to hold the fish in a wet net and, using a cotton swab, coat the affected area with Mercurochrome® or Argyrol®. This may be repeated several times a day until the fungus is gone.

84

The older treatment for fungus is the progressive salt treatment, which must be given in a bare receptacle. It is usually effective but is much more trouble. With the fishes in the bare tank, salt is added gradually over a day or two (best to add a solution of salt in water, not the dry salt) or marine water is added. A final concentration of about 0.5% is usually advocated; some fishes can take more. This may be achieved by adding a small volume of water containing a level teaspoon of salt for every 4 liters in the tank at intervals of a few hours until five teaspoons have been added. When a cure occurs, gradually reduce the salt concentration.

Fungus on the *eye* is dangerous and may be given special treatment by touching with a cotton swab dipped in a 1% solution of silver nitrate, followed by a 1% solution of potassium dichromate. A red precipitate forms which restricts the silver nitrate to the outside of the eye.

If a group of fishes is infected with fungus, treatment of the whole tank is indicated. Malachite green may be tried, but only at a concentration of one-half drop of a 1% solution per liter; this is not so effective as in a bath and is not generally advocated. Instead a newer drug, phenoxethol (2-phenoxyethanol), is better.

Add 10 ml phenoxethol per liter of a 1% solution in distilled water to the tank, to be repeated once only in a few days' time if necessary. Phenoxethol is an oil, sparingly soluble in water, hence the large dosage volume. Do *not* use para-chlorophenoxethol, recommended by some authorities, as experience has shown it to be toxic to fishes.

Mouth Fungus: This is a condition which looks like fungus but is confined to the mouth. It is actually caused by a bacterium, *Chondrococcus columnaris*. It is a killer, and once it breaks out in a tank it is liable to spread very rapidly. The characteristic appearance is a white line around the lips of the fish; when this is seen, do not delay treatment.

The disease is cured by penicillin, 10,000-25,000 units per liter, or by other wider-spectrum antibiotics. Penicillin is particularly harmless and easy to use, and it may be placed in the tank and left. It does not deteriorate very rapidly and there is no need for repeated frequent dosing. If a cure is not effected, the dosage may safely be increased to 50,000 units per liter. At this strength it is clearly more economical to remove the affected fishes and treat in a small receptacle, in which a cure may be expected within four or five days.

FIN and TAIL ROT: This is a bacterial disease characterized by ragged, opaque-looking fins and tail, and even by bloody streaks in the fin. Fry are prone to be affected if they are overcrowded, as may adult fishes too.

The treatment is better conditions and aeration, combined with up to 1% chloromycetin in the food for one week. Mix powder from a capsule with dry or prepared food and feed sparingly so that the fishes gobble it up quickly. Enough gets into the gut to act from within.

This *Haplochromis burtoni* has a severe case of tail rot. Photo by R. Zukal.

Antibiotic treatment is often very effective if administered orally (with the food), but if there are feeding or other difficulties use acriflavine as for velvet disease. A combination of the two treatments may be best of all. The advantages of antibiotic feeding are cheapness, as little as needed can be given, and the avoidance of a heavy dosage in the water which may cause the emergence of resistant strains as discussed above. Penicillin, advocated for mouth fungus, is not of much use against most other bacterial infections because it only affects Gram-positive organisms; most bacteria responsible for fish diseases are Gram-negative. However, some new relatives of penicillin *are* effective against the latter, are colorless and may prove useful. The author has tried Ampicillin successfully, but it has the drawback of being an irritant to fishes while curing them, so that as long as it is present they go on scratching against plants and rocks.

Dropsy: "Dropsy" occurs in two forms—a general swelling of a fish which may become severe enough to cause the protrusion of scales, so that the fish looks like a porcupine fish, or a local or general protrusion of scales without body swelling. Only the former is true dropsy; the latter merely resembles it. Dropsy is usually caused by *Aeromonas punctata*, a bacterial infection which attacks kidneys and other internal organs and upsets the water balance. Phenoxethol may be given at a dose of 10-20 ml of a 1% stock solution per liter gradually added over 24 hours.

This *Rivulus cylindraceus* has an advanced case of dropsy and it is doubtful that the specimen will recover from this late stage. Malawi Bloat has a very similar appearance. Photo by R. Zukal.

This *Macropodus opercularis* has an obvious case of exophthalmia, or pop-eye, in one eye. Photo by R. Zukal.

In severe cases of dropsy, surgical treatment by puncture of the fish and attempted withdrawal of the fluid has been advocated, but it is a rather heroic procedure in the hands of any but an expert.

Exophthalmia (pop-eye): This appears to be of bacterial origin, sometimes perhaps following an injury, and particularly affects Angelfish. It is also stated that it may be caused by gas bubbles behind the eye. The progressive salt treatment as applied for fungus or a reduction in temperature may help to reduce pressure, but no specific treatment is known.

Ichthyosporidium: *Ichthyosporidium* is caused by a fungus-like organism (*I. hoferi* and others) which attacks the fish internally, starting with infected food and water taken into the stomach. From this organ the parasites penetrate into the blood and reproduce all over the body. The disease cannot usefully be treated, therefore, by the common external baths.

The disease is manifested as multiple cysts containing yellow, brown or black granules which sometimes break the surface of the body and may be ulcerated. The ovaries are commonly attacked and sterility results. Other symptoms will depend on the sites of worst attack, and signs of liver, circulatory or other disease may be seen.

Treatment was ineffective until about 20 years ago when the following cure was suggested. Phenoxethol in a 1% solution is added to the food and effects a cure in about four days.

Swim Bladder Disease: Sometimes a fish hops about in the water at an angle rather than swims and may eventually become completely incapacitated by the condition. It may float helplessly on the surface, belly-up, or be unable to rise from the bottom. The condition is said to be caused by chilling, as during transport, or may arise without obvious cause. It is due to the inability of the swim-bladder to control its air content, so that the fish is too light, too heavy or ill-balanced. The condition is rarely fatal unless extreme, and no effective treatment is known.

Skin Slime: A slimy condition of the skin, often with faded colors and clamped fins, may be caused by a variety of infections. Common ones are *Cyclochaeta domerguei, Chilodon cyprini* or *C. hexastichus,* and *Costia necatrix.* All are protozoans. Treatment is best with quinine hydrochloride.

Tuberculosis: This disease causes emaciation and may be due to a variety of organisms, of which some may actually be related to a human tuberculosis. There is, however, no chance of infection. There is no known cure. Two light yellow spots on the caudal peduncle of tetras is a symptom of tuberculosis.

Neon Tetra Disease: Neons affected by this disease show fading of the blue-green line and eventually lose the color almost entirely. The disease is not confined to this species and may affect glowlight tetras, zebra danios or other small fishes. The disease has been ascribed to various organisms, usually sporozoans, either *Glugea* or *Plistophora,* and has no known cure.

Malawi Bloat: Termed "Malawi bloat" because of its initial recognition in (and possible restriction to) Lake Malawi cichlids, this disease seems to affect a fish's ability to control its osmotic regulation. The fish stops eating, becomes lethargic and bloats with fluid before death. Little is yet known about this highly contagious disease, but it often responds to treatment with Furanace and/or Chloramphenicol.

Flukes: The commonest flukes, which may attack both coldwater and tropical fishes, are monogenetic; they have only one host and do not require snails or some other creature as an intermediate host. That is why they thrive in aquaria, whereas the digenetic flukes, requiring an intermediate host, usually do not. These flukes, or flatworms, can be a considerable bother and are responsible for many deaths, particularly in fry. They infect the skin and gills, holding on by an organ known as the haptor, which has hooks.

When attacked by flukes, fishes may dash around and rub themselves, eventually ceasing through sheer exhaustion. Flukes are hard to get rid of, and several treatments of fair to good efficiency are the best that can be offered.

Gyrodactylus can be seen on the gills, fins or skin with a hand lens, as little waving white threads. It lives all the year round in both cold and tropical tanks and bears living young. The following treatment may be tried.

Place fish in an external bath of 1 ml of DFD (difluorodiphenyltrichloromethylmethane) per 9½ liters of water for two minutes. Do not introduce the drug into the tank.

A carp with Furunculosis yielding open wounds.

Dactylogyrus affects only the gills, but looks much the same on inspection with the hand lens. It may be differentiated from *Gyrodactylus* by having four head organs instead of two. It is a much tougher brute, and the above treatment has no effect on it. Luckily it is more seasonal, at any rate in coldwater tanks, and lays eggs. It is usual for any outbreak to be confined to early summer.

The best available cure is potassium permanganate, approximately 2 parts per million. This is 2 mg per liter. The fishes should be left in for several hours and in fact can stand twice the concentration without severe distress. The whole aquarium may be treated and at least half the water siphoned off from the bottom to remove flukes which have let go and sunk down.

Other treatments recommended for flukes of undefined species are a bath for 20 seconds in 1 part of glacial acetic acid in 500 of water, repeated in three days, or 5 drops of formaldehyde per liter for 5 to 10 minutes or until exhaustion.

Fish Lice and Anchor Worms: These are larger parasites rather than diseases, and they burrow into the flesh of the fishes. Both are rare in tanks. Goldfish sometimes bring them in from ponds, where they often abound. The fish louse (*Argulus*) is about 5 mm in size and looks like a mite or small spider. It is flat and colorless and clings to the fish, biting its way into the flesh. The anchor worm digs in with a large foot, from which it gets its name, with a thread-like body up to 1 cm long hanging free. Both may be treated with the permanganate treatment as for *Dactylogyrus,* but Dylox® at a strength of 1 ppm is a quicker and more effective cure.

Shimmies: This condition is usually caused by chilling or by foul conditions and is characterized by "swimming on the spot." The fish swims without getting anywhere. Treatment is by heat, up to 29°C, and improvement in general conditions. Livebearers are most frequently affected.

WEIGHTS AND MEASURES

The following comparison tables and conversion tables for weights and measurements are given to assist those who are not familiar with the metric system on which this book is based.

Linear measurements:

10 millimeters (mm)	= 1 centimeter (cm)	= 0.394 inches
100 centimeters	= 1 meter (m)	= 39.4 inches
1000 meters	= 1 kilometer (km)	= 0.621 miles
1 inch		= 2.54 centimeters
12 inches	= 1 foot	= 0.305 meters

Square measurements:

100 sq. millimeters	= 1 sq. centimeter	= 0.155 sq. inches
10,000 sq. centimeters	= 1 sq. meter	= 1,550 sq. inches
1,000,000 sq. meters	= 1 sq. kilometer	= 0.386 sq. miles
1 sq. inch		= 6.45 sq. centimeters
144 sq. inches	= 1 sq. foot	= 929 sq. centimeters

Cubic measurements:

1000 cubic millimeters	= 1 cubic centimeter	= 0.0610 cubic inches
1,000,000 cu. centimeters	= 1 cubic meter	= 35.3 cubic feet
1 cubic inch		= 16.4 cubic centimeters
1728 cubic inches	= 1 cubic foot	= 0.0283 cubic meters

Capacity measurements:

10 milliliters (ml)	= 1 centiliter (cl)	= 0.338 fluid ounce
100 centiliters	= 1 liter (l)	= 1.06 liquid quarts
1 fluid ounce		= 0.0296 liters
32 fluid ounces	= 1 quart	= 0.946 liters
4 quarts	= 1 gallon	= 3.79 liters
20 gallons		= 75.8 liters

Weights:

1000 milligrams (mg)	= 1 gram (g)	= 15.4 grains
10 grams	= 1 decagram (dg)	= 0.3527 ounces
1000 grams	= 1 kilogram (kg)	= 2.20 pounds
1 grain		= 0.0648 grams
437 grains	= 1 ounce	= 28.3 grams
16 ounces	= 1 pound	= 454 grams

Temperature:

degrees centigrade (Celsius) = °C and degrees Fahrenheit = ° F

$°C = (F°/1.8) — 17.8$ $°F = (°C + 17.8) \times 1.8$

It is best to get solutions of drugs made up professionally. These often need diluting for use, however, and the following tables give sufficiently accurate indications for doing so. The table of weights is only for common salt solutions, not other substances.

Home Measure (fluid)	Metric System	Fluid Measures U.S. Fluid Measure
1 drop (eyedropper)	1/20 cc (or ml)	1/60 fluid oz.
1 teaspoon	4 cc	1/8 fluid oz.
1 dessertspoon	10 cc	1/3 fluid oz.
1 tablespoon	20 cc	2/3 fluid oz.
1 teacup	180 cc	6 fluid oz.
1 breakfast cup	295 cc	10 fluid oz.
1 pint	480 cc	16 fluid oz.

Table for Salt Solutions

Home Measure (salt)	Weight (Apoth.)	Metric Weight
1 level teaspoon	5 grams	75 grains
1 heaped teaspoon	8 grams	125 grains
1 level dessertspoon	10 grams	150 grains
1 heaped dessertspoon	16 grams	250 grains
1 level tablespoon	20 grams	300 grains
1 heaped tablespoon	33 grams	500 grains
1 teacup	220 grams	7 oz.
1 breakfast cup	370 grams	12 oz.

When thinking in percentages or parts per million, it is easiest to use the metric system. One cubic centimeter (1 cc) or milliliter (1 ml) of water weighs 1 gram. A 1% salt solution is therefore 1 gram of salt in 100 ml. of water approximately. To make a gallon of 1% salt solution we must know that one gallon equals 4 liters approximately, or 4000 ml, and so we need 40 grams of salt. This is best measured as 8 level teaspoons of salt to the gallon. A British gallon is 4½ liters.

STOCK SOLUTIONS

The aquarist with many tanks is wise to keep by him stocks of all the commonly needed drugs and salts, preferably already made up for use. A suitable drug supply would be:

Substance	Concentration	Stock Quantity
Quinine hydrochloride	19 mg/l	500 ml
Methylene blue	44 mg/l	300 ml
Malachite green	44 mg/l	300 ml
Potassium permanganate	2 mg/l	300 ml
Penicillin	— — —	1 million units
Chloromycetin	— — —	10 capsules, 250 mg.

Cichlasoma nigrofasciatum, a substrate spawner, watching over and fanning the eggs in an aquarium. Photo by R. Zukal.

Breeding Fishes

The sexes in fishes are always separate, and in the few cases in which it has been studied, sex determination is genetic and determined by the spermatozoa, as in most other vertebrates; but unlike most other vertebrates, the genetic sex may sometimes alter spontaneously, particularly in livebearers. When this occurs, the transformation is apparently always from female to male.

Fertilization usually takes place at the moment of spawning (except in livebearers, of course). Fish spermatozoa do not live long once they have been ejected into the water. Some aquarium fishes are community spawners, an outstanding example being *Rasbora heteromorpha,* but the majority of species will spawn in single pairs, even though in nature they may spawn communally. The livebearing fishes were thought to have true internal fertilization, but this is more doubtful since in some instances it has apparently been shown that the male does not place sperm in the oviduct but merely shoots packets of them in the right general direction through the water.

The fertilized eggs usually hatch rapidly. Those of many characins hatch within 24 hours at about 24 to 27°C, most barbs within 40 hours, Goldfish in about three days at 27°C but as long as a week at 16°C. Many species of cyprinodonts lay eggs which take 10 to 14 days to hatch, while some of those

Poecilia reticulata, the guppy, is a livebearer and is shown here releasing her young. Photos by Chvojka Milan.

of this group may take several months, as in the genera *Cynolebias* and *Nothobranchius*. The young are usually very small and require careful and special feeding. Typical numbers of eggs per spawning are 100 to 1,000 in aquarium species, most of which should be fertile. Livebearers drop anything from half a dozen to 200 young, the latter only from older females.

Livebearers: The livebearing fishes (Poeciliidae) breed naturally in the aquarium without special attention, as long as they are well fed and cared for. The only problem is saving the young from being eaten by their parents. A deficiency of either light or warmth can arrest reproduction completely, as also can acid water. Within the temperature range 20 to 27°C, the only influence of heat is to shorten the period of gestation.

The differentiation of sexes is easy, fortunately, in most fishes of this family. The males characteristically possess a *gonopodium*, an organ of copulation which is formed from the modified anal fin. There is often a large difference in the size of the sexes, males being the smaller. This is particularly obvious in the Guppy, in which the male is also colored and may have long and variously shaped decorative fins, while the female is drab. Recent strains of Guppy have quite colorful females, however.

The males of *Poecilia vivipara, Quintana atrizona, Phallichthys amates, Pseudoxiphophorus bimaculatus, Heterandria formosa* and *Gambusia affinis* are much smaller than the females, while in most other aquarium livebearer species the males are only slightly smaller. In the swordtails, platies and mollies, both sexes show a variety of colors and are almost the same size. In *Xiphophorus variatus*, however, the females are often not as brightly colored as the males.

Much more is known about the inheritance of color and color variations in the platies, swordtails and Guppies than in most other species, with the result that strains have been established in some of them for the early recognition of sex in the newly dropped young. This is done by color linkage, so that before the gonopodium develops it is still possible to tell the males from the females, all of one sex being a particular color or spotted with black.

Fertilization and Development: Young livebearing females can be fertilized at a very early stage if mature males are present, in the case of platies some eight days or so after birth. Even when they are fertilized very early, the females do not bear young for many weeks, and Guppies, platies and swordtails may be expected to drop their first brood not earlier than 10 to 12 weeks. Males take no notice of whether a female is already gravid or even about to drop young, but pay court to all and sundry, including other immature males. They hover around the female or chase her about the tank, often with a spreading of fins and, particularly in the swordtails, a backward swimming motion which is very characteristic. The female seems indifferent to all of this, and the male simply darts in and ejects his sperm when the chance presents itself. The sperm are stored in the female reproductive tract and fertilize successive crops of eggs for the next five or six months. If fertilization continues to occur, as it does in a mixed tank, the new sperm certainly fertilize some of the eggs, but the extent to which the original insemination can be superseded by later ones has never been fully worked out.

In the Guppy, platy, swordtail, mollie and *Gambusia,* successive crops of eggs occur in batches so that one lot of young all of the same age is produced, followed about a month later by another batch. At an average temperature of about 24°C, the actual development of the young from the time of fertilization to birth takes about 24 days, while the brood interval is about 30 days. The extra week is taken up by the development of the next crop of eggs prior to their actually being fertilized. Most livebearers produce young at about 22-day intervals when kept near to 27°C and in a bright light. At 20°C and still in a bright light, the interval lengthens to some 35 days or more. In a dull light it also lengthens, and as remarked above, cool conditions plus dullness will stop reproduction.

In *Heterandria, Poeciliopsis* and some of their relatives, the eggs ripen and are fertilized at much more frequent intervals, batches being produced every few days and young being born at similar intervals, so that there are always young at different stages present in the mother and a few are dropped at a time.

The embryos developing within the female poeciliid possess a yolk-sac, a bag containing nourishment present in the egg when fertilization takes place, and during embryonic development use up the food stored within it. The young fishes develop in a folded position, head to tail, and are often born with this fold still present. They may sink to the bottom for a short period but are usually able to fend for themselves either immediately or within a couple of hours. An average length for the newly born swordtail or platy would be about ½ cm. Some mollies can be as long as 1 cm at birth. The first brood from a young female may number only six; later broods may rise to 200. Mollies, however, rarely exceed 30 or 40, and a typical swordtail, Guppy or platy birth is around 60 to 80.

The pregnant mother swells unmistakably in most livebearers and also presents the "gravid spot," which is a dark spot near the base of the anal fin caused by the stretching of the peritoneal wall. Moving the mother, particularly in mollies, is likely to cause premature birth. She is best moved either early or very late, so that the young are in no danger or so ready for birth that they come to no harm. The young swim toward the light and if the tank is heavily stocked with fine-leaved plants, they will swarm into them and be safe from cannibalism.

Breeding Traps: The oldest breeding trap for saving young livebearers was a cut-off funnel in a jar; the mother could not swim through the small

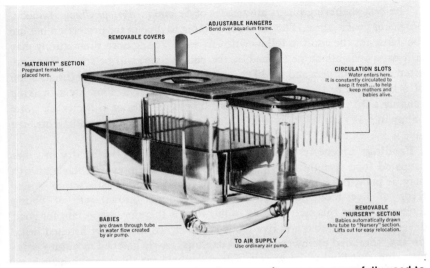

ADJUSTABLE HANGERS
Bend over aquarium frame.

REMOVABLE COVERS

"MATERNITY" SECTION
Pregnant females
placed here.

CIRCULATION SLOTS
Water enters here.
It is constantly circulated to
keep it fresh...to help
keep mothers and
babies alive.

REMOVABLE
"NURSERY" SECTION
Babies automatically drawn
thru tube to "Nursery" section.
Lifts out for easy relocation.

BABIES
are drawn through tube
in water flow created
by air pump.

TO AIR SUPPLY
Use ordinary air pump.

Breeding traps, like this circulating hatchery, are often very successfully used to separate the young fry from the mother and thereby prevent possible cannibalism.

hole, but the young could escape and survive. Such an arrangement does not suit many females, who dash around and injure themselves, and it is more frequently the practice to use a small aquarium with a cage suspended in it with walls of such material that the young can escape but the mother cannot. A cage or barrier of glass rods or plastic material is satisfactory but tedious to make and rather expensive to buy. Perhaps the most satisfactory arrangement is a screen of mosquito netting, best made of plastic, which can be wedged across the darkest part of the tank so as to confine the female to one end while allowing the young to pass to the lighted end. Even a loose-fitting dividing glass is fairly good, as the young seem to find the slots at the edges quite rapidly and make their way past.

However, most breeders seem to prefer the more natural method of plants in abundance to provide shelter for the young, with removal of the mother at the earliest chance. If the mother is supplied with more live food than she can eat, she is unlikely to account for many of her own young, so mosquito larvae or daphnia are added. If the young have to be moved, siphon them off as gently as possible or, better still, ladle them out with a soup ladle or teacup. Do not use a net. Mollies will usually not eat their young unless they are very hungry, so that a well-fed tank of this species has young present in plenty without further precautions.

The best sheltering plants are masses of *Salvinia, Myriophyllum, Ambulia, Nitella* or coarse algae. They allow the young to dive in for protection but are too dense for the adult to follow with any ease. Young born prematurely may still have a visible bulge formed by the yolk-sac and will be small. They are often poor swimmers and are likely to die off rapidly. Sometimes the addition of a little salt to the water helps, about a teaspoon to four liters, making roughly a 0.1% solution, or even more. Young mollies or Guppies are quite happy in a 1% salt solution and, if bred from marine-acclimated parents, can take a 3% solution.

Feeding: Livebearer young are quite large and can be fed dry or other prepared food straight away. If they are given only prepared food, growth may be poor, but a mixture of live and dry foods is quite satisfactory. A few feeds of live food much affect the subsequent growth-rate of young livebearers, and this early feeding of live food is therefore important for good development. Suitable first live foods are microworms, newly hatched brine shrimp, shredded earthworms, sifted daphnia, newly hatched mosquito wrigglers and shredded white worms. Sifted daphnia are those which have been passed through a mesh to exclude the larger sizes. However, if adult daphnia are used in reasonable numbers—not so as to overcrowd the tank and compete seriously for oxygen—their young are a continual source of food. Suitable dry foods include any fine powdered food, such as dried shrimp, fine cereals and liver or egg powder. Frozen plankton is also a suitable first food, and tubes such as "Livefry" containing large globules of food mix are readily available.

The young livebearers should be fed several times daily and kept at not lower than 24°C. Young livebearing fishes can take high temperatures and thrive in them. They do well with their bellies full and should go around looking like a fish stuck onto a small football for the first few weeks. They will not overeat, even though it may look like it. If much dry food is used, and of course it must be suitably small in size, scavengers should be present. Snails are the easiest to install, but *Corydoras* will not eat the young fishes as long as they have leftovers to clear up.

A week or so later larger live foods and coarser prepared foods can be fed, although the smaller sizes will still be eaten. Tubifex worms, larger larvae of various species and medium sized daphnia are now suitable. The young of mollies should be fed up to six or eight times a day when this is possible.

Purity of Strains: There are many color and other strains of platies, swordtails and mollies. The first two species cross readily and it is doubtful whether the great majority of so-called platies and swords are pure species at all, but are instead hybrids of one type or another.

Some of the hereditary factors (genes) concerned in the size, color or configuration of these fishes have been studied in detail, while others have not. Some characters are clear-cut, present or absent, whereas others are the result of the combined action of several genes and exist in all sorts of grades and shades. Thus red and green in the swordtail are mutually incompatible colors—typically a fish is either red or it is green, and excellent examples of both may be produced by the same parents in the same brood. Moreover, the redness of the red or the greenness of the green is not necessarily affected by the fact that it has come from a parent of another color. It may be affected by other factors, some genetic and some environmental, and it may be true that a really good red swordtail can only be bred from red stock, because only then could factors tending to intensify the redness be properly concentrated and observed. However, this is all conjecture, and observation on the point is needed.

In general, therefore, fine specimens and really worthwhile strains, whether for color or other features, must be kept separate. The fishes themselves do not distinguish between differences of that sort, and any platy will mate with any other platy of opposite sex.

Hybrids and General Breeding: Platies and swordtails mate together readily, and most hybrids are fertile. Other species, such as the mollie and Guppy, do not produce hybrids nearly so readily, and it is with platy-swordtail crosses that the aquarist is mainly concerned.

When placed with a mixture of platies and swordtails, a fish usually but not always tends to mate only with its own kind, but if it has no choice, it will mate with the other species. Thus, for hybridizing it is best to place a mature male of one species with developing young of the other, whereupon the females will be impregnated by the adult male before their brothers have a chance. These young males are also removed as they become detectable, as they will interfere later on if left.

First-cross hybrids of the platy-swordtail varieties are large, fine-looking fishes. They are much more uniform than later generations, and if they come from a mating of fairly pure lines of parents, they will be very uniform. They usually grow bigger than either parent, exhibiting a phenomenon called "hybrid vigor" seen in many such crosses. They are deep bodied, with short swords in the males. When mated back to either parent stock, fish of any desired degree of platy or swordtail "blood" can be produced.

If livebearers are being bred for particular qualities and colors, they must therefore be separated very early from potential sources of cross-breeding. The scheme will vary according to circumstances, but if an adult male of the desired type is not placed with the young so as to catch the females early, they must be separated as soon as it is possible to tell their sex, and a careful watch must be kept for the development of male characters in any of them. By this method, the stock can be housed in two tanks, one with males and the other with females and undeveloped males.

As soon as those young which are of the best quality can be selected, the rest are discarded and the desired matings are made. Sometimes the best parents are not the best lookers, and a fine strain of fish may have grandparents of only second-rate appearance. It is thus best to keep several pairs and to progeny-test them—*i.e.*, keep them and their offspring until you can see which line of fishes you want, and then go on breeding from the parents, discarding the others of the same generation.

EGG-SCATTERERS

The egg-scatterers include the majority of aquarium fishes—the Characidae, Cyprinidae and Cyprinodontidae. Most of them lay adhesive eggs which stick to plants, and some lay non-adhesive eggs which fall to the bottom. Nearly all eat their eggs if they are given a chance. A typical spawning routine is a chase of the female by the male, accompanied by spasms of egg-laying and simultaneous fertilization. Activity may continue for from an hour to several days, but a few hours at a time is the more general rule.

When the eggs of an egg-laying fish have been deposited, the problems of the breeder may be regarded as just having started, for the eggs must be preserved from predators and disease, must hatch and the young must then be protected, fed and raised. It is very unusual for any young of an egg-scattering species to survive in a community tank and somewhat unusual for them to survive if left with their parents, except in some cyprinodonts. The care of the eggs and young usually includes special preparations for spawning and removal of the parents at an appropriate early stage.

It is therefore necessary to describe a number of general principles which are fairly clearly established, to indicate how improvements may be made in the future and, above all, to recommend an experimental approach by all concerned. Perhaps the best general advice is that few species turn out to be as particular in the conditions they demand for successful spawning as most people think and that cleanliness, healthy fish and proper feeding are often more important than pH, temperature, light and shade. The most important factor in some cases is, however, the hardness of the water. Soft water is sometimes essential for success and it is rarely other than an advantage. The series of books by Dr. Axelrod and others on breeding particular species should be consulted for details applicable to individual fishes.

Telling Sex: The majority of the egg-scatterers have distinguishable sexes, even out of the breeding time, while nearly all can be told apart quite easily as the female fills with roe. Details of the various ways in which sex can be told are given when discussing individual fishes. When these do not help as much as they might, it pays to remember that the male is often the slimmer and rather smaller fish and is often more brightly colored. In the Characidae he

Courtship is a very important aspect of breeding for most fish. Here and on the following two pages *Brachydanio rerio* court as the male chases the female around the tank, pushes up against her side and wraps his fins around her. Photos by J. Elias.

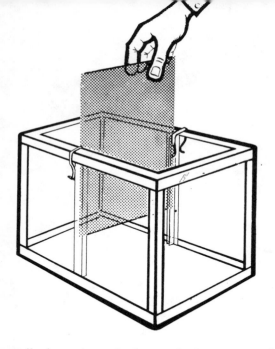

Tank dividers are a convenient way to separate pairs of fish that are not yet ready to breed.

usually has minute hooks on the lower part of the anal fin. These may sometimes be seen as a marking on the fin, or they may actually catch in a fine net and leave him hanging from the mesh. In the Cyprinidae, the breeding males often develop small white pearly dots on some part or other, as on the gill-covers of Goldfish. Most of the barbs have color differences between the sexes and are very easy to sex for that reason. In the Cyprinodontidae, color differences are again the rule, which once more makes matters fairly easy as long as you are certain that some of each sex are present. The technique for breeding these fishes differs from that usual for egg-scatterers and they will be dealt with separately.

Preparation for Spawning: The egg-scatterers are best bred in specially prepared tanks, using no gravel, no plants and specially treated water. The importance of the latter varies with the species, but it is never a mistake to use it with freshwater aquarium varieties. Gravel is substituted by *peat*, plants by *nylon mops* or other readily disinfected material, and the tank water should be *soft* and *acid* in pH. These factors are the key to successful fish breeding in the great majority of cases.

The peat for lining the tank should be used whether nylon mops are employed or not, as it catches stray eggs and also gives an opaque base to the tank, which is best for many fishes. It is never used new but must be prepared by soaking in water for some time before use. It is often possible to use peat from the setup employed in preparing the water to be used in the tank. The nylon mops may be bought commercially or made from nylon wool. They may be sterilized in hot water and used again and again.

The water should be softened and acidified in a suitable filter system in a tank or reservoir set aside for the purpose. The filter contains an ion-exchange resin, such as Zeocarb 225 (Permutit Co.), which removes hardness from the water and substitutes sodium for heavier metals. Water-conditioning filter materials of various kinds are available commercially. In districts with very hard water, the amount of sodium salts left in the water may be excessive, and these may in turn be removed by a suitable resin, which leaves the water equivalent to distilled water, except for sterility. Distilled water may of course be used from the start, but it is expensive and must be *glass* distilled or it may contain a harmful amount of copper. If it is used, a small amount of sodium chloride should be added, about one teaspoon per 40 liters.

It is not usually feasible to include enough peat in such a filter to acidify the water with the so-called "humic" acids that seem so beneficial to fishes. Instead it is best to layer the base of the tank with about 2.5 cm of previously washed peat and gradually to replace the peat as it is used in the spawning tanks. The resultant water is then soft and acid (a suitable pH is 6.0 to 6.5) and of an amber color. Too long a soaking in peat will give it a very brown appearance, but this does not matter as long as the pH is correct.

The measurement of pH has already been discussed. Hardness may be measured with one of the several commercial testing kits, which give full instructions to the purchaser. A reliable method is by noting the point at which a standard soap solution produces suds. The solution is added by drops to a measured amount of water, and the bottle is shaken at frequent intervals, the end-point being when suds occur. A formula for converting drops of standard solution to parts per million hardness is given by the supplier. Another method is to use a titrating solution which causes a color change as the end-point is reached. Kits are available that utilize this method.

The size of tank depends largely on the size of the fishes to be spawned. Most small fishes to a 5 cm size can be spawned in 10- to 20-liter tanks, with a mop or two weighted down in the center of the tank, which is lined by about ½ cm of *used* peat.

The medium barbs, like *Puntius conchonius* or *P. ticto*, should have rather large, say 20- to 40-liter, tanks otherwise similarly arranged. This size is suitable for the danios, although those which scatter non-adhesive eggs require a different setup. Only really large fishes like the Goldfish require big tanks.

A dividing glass with rubber-covered edges is useful for some varieties. This is used for separating the fishes before spawning is required. Adequate illumination must be provided, and many fishes like a well-lit spawning area. It is now the custom of some European aquarists to use a spotlight, illuminating only an area of the tank over the mops in which the fishes will come and spawn. Tanks should also have individual temperature control as it

Hyphessobrycon flammeus male nudges the belly of the female (1) and pushes up against her as she lays her eggs (2). The eggs (3) are scattered about the tank. Photos by R. Zukal.

will sometimes be necessary to raise or lower it to produce the required results.

Tanks prepared for fishes which normally lay their eggs on floating weeds, such as the panchax group, are similar to those above, but the nylon mop is floated by cork floats.

Spawning: If the fishes are kept at an average temperature of 24°C, the majority will spawn without a further rise in temperature. All that is necessary is to place a full female and a male into the tank with as little disturbance as possible. The pair of fishes placed in the breeding tank must be ready to spawn. For this they are best conditioned for a week or so beforehand with live food, but many species do not require this as an imperative procedure. The female should be full of spawn, bulging, but not left too long, or the eggs may not be fertile and she may become egg-bound and die. A thin female will sometimes spawn but usually gives few eggs, for if she has a normal quota, she won't be thin. The male should look pert and well colored. He may become pale on being moved, but he should rapidly regain his form, even within a few minutes. Young males may not fertilize all of the eggs and young females will not give a very large number of eggs, but there is no reason otherwise why they should not be spawned. Spawn early and spawn regularly for the best results. Often a female will be ready every 10 to 14 days or even more frequently.

The fishes may spawn immediately or they may wait for several days. It is best to watch the whole process and to take them out as soon as spawning is over, for they must be removed as soon as possible or there may be few eggs left uneaten. Even flooding the tank with live food does not always prevent egg-eating, although it may help. However, the use of peat helps to preserve more eggs than would otherwise be saved, as they fall into the peat and are less readily eaten, but those on the mops are still in danger. Spawning may take from an hour or two to a couple of days, but the shorter period is fortunately more typical.

If the fishes do not spawn within a few hours, they may do so early the next morning, so be up within two hours of dawn or cover the tank so that it will stay dark and daylight may be admitted at your convenience. Alternatively, place the glass divider in position with one fish on each side of it and let them contemplate each other for a spell. This often helps, so much so that some breeders use the device regularly for a few hours or days before allowing the pair to come together.

If they have not spawned within two days, gradually raise the temperature by 2° or 3°C. This often stimulates spawning quite promptly, but wait for another day or so if nothing happens. If spawning has still not occurred within three or four days, it is usually best to remove the pair, separate them or place them in a large community tank and try again a few days later. If they are kept in the spawning tank for more than two days, they should be given live food in moderation.

Variations on the above procedure include the routine placing of breeders in the tank after dark to induce spawning next morning, placing the female in about half a day ahead of the male or placing two males with one female. The latter is thought to increase the percentage of fertilized eggs, but it is a rather doubtful procedure, as the males often spend more time chasing each other than chasing the female.

The spawning action varies with species. Most of them indulge in the typical chase of the female by the male, but some start with the reverse procedure, and the female chases the male. This is often seen in *Hemigrammus ocellifer* (Head and Tail Light Tetra). Finally, however, it is the male who chases, and he takes up a position beside the female in or over the spawning mops and with a quivering motion the eggs and milt are released. Some species have spectacular habits at the moment of spawning. The Glowlight Tetra *(Hemigrammus erythrozonus)* pair does a complete barrel-roll, the Giant Danio *(Danio malabaricus)* female whirls around several times in a horizontal plane, and the female *Rasbora heteromorpha* loops the loop vertically, depositing her eggs on the underside of flat-leaved plants as she does so (and thus cannot be spawned by the mop technique).

The above account covers many of the egg-scatterers which lay adhesive eggs. A few lay non-adhesive eggs, outstanding among which is *Brachydanio rerio* (Zebra Fish). With this fish and with the related *B. nigrofasciatus* (Spotted Danio) and *B. albolineatus* (Pearl Danio), it is necessary to catch the eggs to prevent their being eaten. This used to be done by covering the bottom with small marbles or pebbles, sometimes interlaced with plants, or by means of a grid of glass rods or other material which allows the eggs to fall beneath and prevent the parents from following. Fairly shallow water, not above 15 cm, is also to be recommended as it prevents the adults from having too long a time in which to chase and eat the falling eggs, as they tend to spawn near to the surface. A peat-strewn tank is all that is necessary, as the eggs fall into the peat, which is stirred up a little as the fishes swim, and remain uneaten.

Copella arnoldi lays adhesive eggs above the water line and should be given a sheet of sanded glass or similar material projecting several inches into the air and slanting at an angle of about 45°. The fish leap into the air and deposit the eggs some 5 cm above the top of the water; these are guarded by the male from some distance off, and at frequent intervals he dashes over and splashes them with water. Luckily for him, they hatch in about 24 hours.

The Bloodfin *(Aphyocharax anisitsi)* also leaps out of the water when spawning, but the eggs fall back into the water and, being non-adhesive, sink to the bottom as with *Brachydanio*. The Croaking Tetras *(Coelurichthys* and *Glandulocauda)* were a puzzle to breeders for a long time until it was found that a normal-appearing courtship is not followed immediately by egg-laying. This occurs a day or so later, in the absence of the male, when the female deposits fertile eggs singly on the leaves of plants. These fishes get their name from the noise made by males.

A number of fishes are community breeders, spawning in nature in large groups of mixed sexes. This happens with some of the barbs, such as *P. conchonius* and *P. ticto,* but they are also able to spawn in pairs if put to it. Some of the *Rasbora* are much more choosy and very rarely spawn except in communities. *Rasbora heteromorpha* will spawn fairly readily when at least 8 or 12 fish are present and very readily in communities of larger size, when unfortunately the eggs are nearly all consumed on the spot by the onlookers. The best results so far have been reported with smaller groups placed in planted tanks so that their habit of depositing eggs on the underside of growing plants can be practiced. Breeders are removed as soon as activity ceases or as soon as the eggs are being eaten by any of the fishes present.

Incubation of the Eggs: The great majority of aquarium-fish eggs hatch in one day or rather less at 24 to 26°C. It is best to keep the temperature at the same level as when spawning occurred. The same is true of young fry. There are many reports of characin eggs taking two to three days to hatch, and while some are undoubtedly correct, it still remains true that the majority of young are hatched within the first day. They are often hard to see and it may be two or three days before they hang on to the side of the tank and become easier to see, and thus it is simple to get the impression that they have not hatched out for longer than is the case.

After spawning is complete, eggs should be sought in the tank. They may be attached to the mops and also be in the peat on the bottom, appearing like small glass beads, usually very small indeed. They should remain clear, and the development of the embryo should be watched to check that all is well. Infertile eggs quickly become opaque and fungused, looking like a powder-puff with white filaments of fungus sprouting in all directions. Fertile eggs lying

1

Aequidens itanyi cleans the spawning surface (1) soon before spawning. The female lays the eggs on the rock (2) as the male hovers nearby. Photos by R. Zukal.

next to a mass of fungus-covered infertiles may be attacked, but they usually remain unaffected.

If you cannot see the eggs, don't despair; they are hard to see, particularly when peat is used. Once you have observed those of a particular species, it will be much easier to see them the next time.

Hatching: When the eggs hatch, the young fry still have a yolk-sac containing the remnants of the nourishment in the eggs. They live on this for a short time, sometimes only one or two days, sometimes as long as five days, before taking other food. For the first 12 to 24 hours they often remain still at the bottom of the tank in the peat and in some species they take flea-like hops up into the water, sinking back again afterwards. In practically all species they then attach themselves to the glass or to mops or plants (if present), hanging motionless for a further one or two days, still not feeding. They may also hang under the surface film of the water and frequently start on the glass and then transfer to the surface film. Finally, the yolk-sac is absorbed and they swim freely in the water, hugging the bottom in daylight and spreading all over the tank at night or in the dark.

At the stage when the fry cling to the glass, it is easy to see them in the right light, which is preferably from behind or the side. They cling head-upward and are visible as a little glass splinter with a fat tummy (the yolk-sac) and two very large eyes. Watch the yolk-sac go down, for when it does the time to feed is near. In the later, free-swimming stage, they are less easily seen, and at night is the best time. Use a flashlight and send a beam across the tank from one side, and the fry will be seen swimming in mid-water. They may be counted with fair accuracy at this stage or at the clinging stage before it. The best way to count is to choose a typical section of the tank and count it fairly carefully, then multiply by the relative sizes of section to tank as a whole. It is good practice to make this count so as to check what is happening later on and to estimate food requirements.

ANABANTOIDS AND CICHLIDS

The anabantoids build bubblenests with their mouths; usually the male builds the nest and guards the young on its own. The eggs are floated in the bubblenest until they hatch, and the fry remain in the nest for some time after this. The male is usually fierce at this stage and may kill the female if she remains in the tank. Many cichlids lay eggs on   rocks or plant leaves, and both parents take care of them and of the young. The eggs are fanned, and when the young hatch out they are mouthed about, even moved from place to place, and are finally shepherded around in a flock with watchful, savage parents on guard all the time. Some cichlids brood the eggs in the mouth of a parent.

Telling Sex: Both anabantoids and cichlids show well-marked sexual differences in the adult, but some are very difficult to tell, in particular the

Angelfish *(Pterophyllum scalare)* and the Discus *(Symphysodon discus)*. Apart from color differences, the males tend to have longer and more pointed dorsal and anal fins. In the breeding season they are brilliant, and even out of the breeding season they are usually bright. An anabantoid female full of roe is usually very plump, but cichlids may show little or nothing.

As he begins to be ready for breeding, the male anabantoid blows bubbles, sticky with secretion, at the surface of the water. It is easy to see how this has evolved from the habit of these labyrinth fishes of breathing air at the surface of foul water; their air-breathing habits enable them to use surface nests to an advantage. The chosen site is often under a leaf or floating plant or at the edge of a mass of duckweed or algae.

The cichlids like to choose their own mates and may kill one selected for them. It is therefore best to keep young fish together until some pair off and can be separated for breeding. The other method is to introduce pairs to each other and to watch and be prepared to remove one of the pair before it is injured or even killed. The loser is not always the female.

Suitable Tanks: There is no need for disinfected or bare tanks when breeding these fishes, and since the fry of anabantoids are small and need the finest live food at the start, they are best supplied with this by the presence of mulm and decaying material in the spawning tank. This can, however, be supplied after hatching if a clean tank is used, so it does not seriously matter. In fact, many anabantoid breeders prefer to use a bare tank which makes it easier for the male to find all the newly fertilized eggs for placement in the bubblenest. The cichlid young are quite large, so the tank can be clean or dirty; the parents will keep the eggs spotless whichever is the case. If cichlid eggs are to be hatched in the absence of the parents, however, they must be removed to a very clean tank and particular care taken of them.

Both families should be supplied with large tanks for spawning, the anabantoids because they are in need of infusorial food in plenty and because they usually produce many young, and the cichlids because they are usually big fishes. For the anabantoids, the tank should be well planted and not too deep, up to 25 cm at most, and preferably tightly covered to protect the surface nest. Most cichlids tear up plants, so it is superfluous to have them present, but it doesn't really matter, at least not to the fishes. Both like a temperature around 26°C, and many species will not spawn at much below it. Even if the cichlids are given no plants, there should be a good layer of sand, as this is used in nest-making.

Anabantoid Courtship and Spawning: When the male anabantoid's nest is ready, spreading several centimeters across the water with a central depth of perhaps one centimeter if he is a big fish, the female may be introduced. The male is often bad-tempered, particularly the male Siamese Fighting Fish *(Betta splendens)*, and he must be watched to see that all goes

Betta splendens in a spawning embrace under their bubblenest. Photo by R. Zukal.

well. The female is often bullied, but she should not be removed again unless she is really badly treated.

The male will eventually persuade or drive the female below the bubblenest, circling her with a display of erect fins and distended gill-covers in the case of Fighters. The female responds with a "submissive" behavior pattern which inhibits the male from attacking her further.

As they swim below the nest, the male encircles the female in an embrace in which his head meets his tail and they sink slowly downward, with the release of a number of eggs. The male then dives down and catches them, placing them in the bubblenest with his mouth. Further embraces and spawning follow at intervals for perhaps several hours. An interesting variation of the above occurs when the female remains in a corner of the tank and the male remains under the nest; the female dashes up at intervals to indulge in the nuptial embrace and as soon as it is over, she rushes back to her corner until the next time.

When spawning is over, the male takes complete charge and the female may be removed, particularly if he is too fierce. Otherwise her presence is said to make him take better care of the eggs. He continues to blow bubbles and to restore any falling eggs to the nest, but subsequent behavior varies with species. The male should remain with the nest until the eggs hatch, as he performs a useful function in keeping them afloat and healthy. With most, it is best to remove the male at hatching, which occurs two or three days after spawning, and even the best of fathers is likely to start eating the young at the end of the first week.

3

Colisa lalia in a spawning sequence below their bubblenest. The nest includes bubbles and pieces of plants. (1 and 2) Embracing under the nest. (3 and 4) Releasing the eggs. Photos by R. Zukal.

4

Cichlid Courtship and Spawning: Cichlid fishes also take care of their eggs and of their young. The extent of this care differs with different species. Linked with this development is a strong tendency to a savage disposition toward other fishes of the same or different species. An established pair of cichlids may be left to their own devices, and sooner or later they will probably spawn. It is only when trying out new pairs that the aquarist must exercise care and be ready to remove one or the other. If spawning has taken place and anything goes wrong, or if all of the young are suddenly removed, the pair may quarrel, as if they suspected each other of disposing of the young.

Courtship in the cichlids is worth watching for its own sake. At first, approaches are made with spreading fins and the body quivers, but often the fishes take each other by the mouth and start to wrestle. They roll over and over, twisting and tugging vigorously, and woe betide the fish that tires too quickly. For this reason, some attempt at matching size when introducing new pairs to each other is often made, but there are many very unequal-sized pairs which get along quite well.

The pair will finally start to clear a place for spawning, and it is given a very thorough cleaning, sometimes for several days. Large stones are favorite spots, but in their absence a patch of the glass side of the tank may be cleaned. Light-colored objects are said to be preferred, and so marble or other light-colored stone is often offered. As spawning approaches, a breeding tube appears from the vent of both sexes. When it is first visible it means that spawning will occur soon, and within a day or two the tube lengthens to perhaps 7 mm and spawning takes place.

The female (of substrate-spawning cichlids) deposits a few eggs at a time on the chosen surface and is followed by the male who fertilizes them. They are often laid row upon row, until in the course of several hours up to 2,000 may be deposited and fertilized. From then on a constant guard is maintained and the eggs are frequently fanned and inspected. Opinions differ as to whether the primary function of this fanning is aeration or the prevention of disease. Aeration seems most likely as the fishes also clean the eggs and eat any which become fungused. The incubation period lasts three to four days; at this period the parents dig pits in the sand. Often several pits are dug, and as the young hatch they are moved to one of them. Both parents participate in this, often dashing from the spawning area to the sand pit in lightning dashes, one with a mouthful of young being transferred, the other to take up the vacated position. Transfers from pit to pit then continue until the young are free-swimming, which may not be for another three or four days. Each time they are moved to a new pit, they are mouthed over and spat into the pit. Since the object of the move can hardly be to guard them, as the parents could presumably do this without shifting them around, it has again been suggested that the process is one of cleaning. Moving them from one pit to another is

Cichlasoma meeki extends the membrane under its buccal cavity in an effort to defend its spawning area and scare off intruders. This brightly colored membrane makes the fish look larger than it actually is during a frontal attack. Photo by G. Marcuse.

thought to ensure that every one is well mouthed and cleaned, but there is no evidence that this is necessary, and we do not know why the frequent moves are made.

During this period the young live on the yolk-sac, looking at first like a mass of quivering jelly which gradually resolves into wriggling and hopping individuals which finally swim up into the water. The parents guard them carefully and herd them together, spitting any which stray too far back into the swarm. They are quite large and should now be fed small live foods. The parents will continue to guard them for weeks if allowed to do so, but during this period they will not lay further eggs. If frequent breeding is desired, the young should be removed or the eggs hatched artificially from the start.

The Angelfish *(Pterophyllum scalare)* lays its eggs on large plant leaves, preferably giant *Sagittaria* or *Echinodorus*. Alternatively, the fish will accept upright slate, opaque glass bars, rods or even the aquarium glass itself. They do not dig pits, but move the young from one leaf to another until they are free-swimming, when they guard them as usual. They are particularly liable to eat their spawn, so it is commercial practice to remove the leaf or rod on which it has been deposited to a clean tank with a gentle trickle of aeration to replace the parents' fanning. Four drops of 5% methylene blue per liter are added to inhibit fungus growth on the eggs.

Discus *(Symphysodon)* must be left with their young, which feed on secretions on the sides of their parents for the first week or more.

117

Cichlasoma meeki (1)
spawning in a bottomless
flowerpot and (2) guarding
the eggs. (3) The young fry
school together. Photo by
R. Zukal.

3

Some cichlids have moved a stage further in the care of their young; they incubate the eggs and fry in the mouth. During this time, the parent that guards the young starves, gets very thin and, as he or she has a large head to begin with, assumes a somewhat emaciated appearance. The young swim out to feed, but they return to the parental mouth if alarmed and only learn to fend for themselves when they get too large for all of them to get back again.

African Lake Cichlids: The pre-spawning activities of the African lake cichlids involve elaborate rituals of courtship, including recognition signs such as color exhibition. The males often build nest areas, and territories are established. These fishes have been traditionally divided into two groups, substrate-spawners and mouthbrooders, on the basis of their breeding behavior. Mouthbrooders incubate their fertilized eggs within their oral cavities, and substrate-spawners have their fertilized eggs develop on external surfaces. The substrate-spawners guard their eggs and developing fry. As some egg-guarders lay their eggs in open areas while others lay them in partially enclosed areas (*e.g.*, stone caves), the terms "open brooders" and "hole brooders" may be applied. While substrate-spawners are divided into these two categories, all mouthbrooders are considered to be in the "hole brooder" category. It has been suggested that the substrate "hole brooders" have a closer relationship to the mouthbrooders than to the substrate "open brooders," as the mouthbrooders and substrate "hole brooders" hide their eggs and offspring.

119

Male and female *Aphyosemion* *australe* (1) press up against each other, (2) dive into a clump of plants that acts as a spawning medium and (3) swim together during spawning courtship. Photos by R. Zukal.

CYPRINODONTS

The killifishes, family Cyprinodontidae, include the various types of "panchax," *Aphyosemion*, pearlfishes (*Cynolebias* species) and other related fishes which lay eggs taking some time to hatch. The panchax group and some of the *Aphyosemion* spawn at the surface on nylon mops and are allowed to do this for up to about 10 days at a stretch, when the parents or the mops are removed to another tank. Hatching occurs in 12 to 14 days or longer, and the young must be sorted for size or they will eat one another. Each female lays up to 20 eggs per day, and it is common practice to mate one male with two females.

Other *Aphyosemion* spawn into peat at the bottom of the tank. The *Aphyosemion* eggs will hatch out if left long enough, but they may be collected together with the peat and dried out for a period before being replaced in soft prepared water, when most of the eggs will hatch out all together and give an even batch of fry. This technique is very useful and prevents the difficulties of sorting otherwise encountered. The best period for drying varies with species from two or three weeks to over a month. It is essential not to dry completely or the eggs are killed, but drying should be carried to an advanced stage for best results, so that the peat feels like tobacco.

Cynolebias, *Nothobranchius* and other types which naturally undergo a period of drying are also treated in the same manner but need an even longer period of treatment. It is usual to allow spawning for about a month, followed by drying for about 12 weeks with *Nothobranchius* species and 12 to 24 weeks for *Cynolebias* species. When the peat containing the eggs is replaced in water, a little dry food added to the water may help hatching.

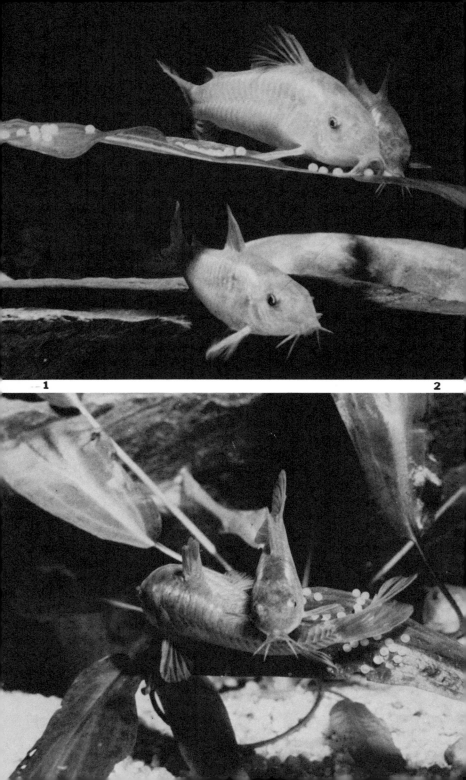

3

Corydoras aeneus individuals (1-3) stay in groups as they hover about their eggs soon after spawning. The eggs adhere to a plant leaf. Photos by R. Zukal.

OTHER TYPES OF FISHES

Various other aquarium fishes are bred, some very occasionally and others with regularity. Details are given under the various species later in the text, but a few general remarks will be made here. Again, specialist books should be consulted for details of particular species.

The *Corydoras* of various species (South American armored catfishes) breed well in captivity, particularly *C. aeneus* and *C. paleatus*. They breed best in communities and lay eggs on plants or on the glass and do not harm either them or the young. The eggs hatch in three or four days, and the young feed heavily on live or prepared food from the start. In *C. paleatus* courtship is brief, with the males swimming over the females. Finally, with a male underneath, a male and female take up a crossed position and the female swims up with four eggs clasped in her ventral fins. These she deposits on a leaf or elsewhere, and the process is repeated. It is not yet clear where the eggs are fertilized; some observers allege that the female takes sperm into her mouth and sprays it over the eggs, but others deny this. In *C. aeneus*, it is also said that the male spreads sperm on the glass and that the female follows and lays her eggs.

Carassius auratus spawning in a clump of plants. Photos by R. Zukal.

Loaches of various species have also been known to breed in the aquarium, but rarely to order. *Acanthophthalmus kuhli* (Kuhli Loach) was once thought by some to be a livebearer, but this is not true. Their eggs are green.

Some of the nandids are easy to breed. *Badis badis* spawns rather like cichlids and guards the young for a time, and so do the leaf fishes *(Polycentrus schomburgki* and *Monocirrhus polyacanthus). Polycentropsis abbreviata,* on the other hand, builds a bubblenest. The male guards the young as in the anabantoids. Other nest-builders include the sunfishes (Centrarchidae). The male of the Pygmy Sunfish *(Elassoma evergladei)* builds a nest at the bottom of the tank and guards the eggs and so do the males of various sticklebacks (Gasterosteidae). The males of bumblebee gobies *(Brachygobius)* also guard the young but do not build a nest.

With all of these fishes it is merely necessary to have them in a tank together, except perhaps the *Corydoras*, with which orthodox spawning techniques may be used. Naturally, if you wish to breed them you will provide plenty of shelter, place only the desired species in the tank and feed plenty of live food.

In the Medaka or Rice Fish *(Oryzias latipes),* pairing takes place as usual in the egg-scatterers; the eggs stick to the female's vent in a cluster, later to be brushed off at random onto plants. This is one of the few fishes which, although it does not take care of its young, doesn't eat them either. The White Cloud Mountain Minnow *(Tanichthys albonubes)* is fairly safe with its parents also. Some of the pencilfishes *(Nannostomus)* guard the area in which eggs have been laid, although this is not the general habit in the characins, to which they belong.

Raising Fry: Before the advent of microworms and brine shrimp, and before the use of artificial preparations to replace infusoria, the feeding of young fry was a much more difficult task than it is now. In the opinion of the author, it is now very rarely necessary to prepare infusoria at all, as these may be substituted by egg-yolk suspensions, live yeasts or young microworms together with the material in which they thrive. In addition, many species of fish produce fry which can eat adult microworms or newly hatched brine shrimp straight away and do not need infusoria or substitutes for them. It is usually safe to feed a mixture of microworms and the culture medium in moderate quantities, which between them rarely fails to provide adequate nourishment even for the smallest fry. The size of the fry is furthermore not always the deciding factor so much as their willingness or capacity to eat certain types of food.

It is always easy to check whether fry are eating, particularly with brine shrimp, because their bellies become red and swollen. With microworms they become milky and swollen. Sometimes it will be noted that only some of the batch are able to take the food offered. Either microworms or brine shrimp are

Cichlasoma nigrofasciatum fry stay together near the bottom of the aquarium soon after hatching. Photo by G. Marcuse.

a completely satisfactory food, and either alone is sufficient for the first few weeks of life without any other food, as long as it is eaten.

FOOD SIZES

Grade 1 (suitable as a start for all fry but livebearers and some of the larger fry such as cichlids): One-celled algae, baker's yeast, some infusoria, infusions made by shaking a small piece of the yolk of a hard-boiled egg in a little water vigorously, microworm culture medium containing young and various commercial fry foods. The algae and infusoria may be fed as green water, which is a great help for many anabantoid fry at the start. Microworm culture medium has the advantage of containing moving food, which may be necessary for some types of fry. The movement may be simulated with foods like yeast or egg suspension by gentle aeration that is not vigorous enough to swirl the fry around.

Grade 2 (suitable for many fry as a start and for others within a week): Daphnia, newly hatched brine shrimp, finely ground dry food and finely shredded tubifex or other worms. Gentle aeration helps to keep foods moving and prevents even live food such as microworms from collecting too readily at the bottom of the tank. If any appreciable amount of dry or shredded food is

126

used, aeration is essential and the introduction of small snails should be considered.

Grade 3 (suitable for all fry at two to four weeks and for newly born livebearers): All Grade 2 foods, plus large size daphnia, small mosquito larvae, Grindal worms, chopped white worms, chopped tubifex or other worms, "fine" grades of dry food, deep frozen plankton and commercial fry foods.

Grade 4 (suitable for half-grown and adult fishes): All Grade 3 foods, plus fully grown daphnia, mosquito larvae, white worms, tubifex, chopped earthworms and ordinary grades of dry food. It is still possible to feed microworms and newly hatched brine shrimp to small adult fishes, but they need a generous allowance.

Infusorial Feeding: Although we have stated that infusoria are rarely necessary for feeding fry, sometimes they are needed either because the fry are very small or because other foods are not available. The need for a continuous supply of live food or of moving suspended food particles in the early days of the life of the fry may be supplied by drip feeding. Many successful breeders never use it, but some feel happier if they supply it.

When a spawning is planned and infusoria are to be used, a culture should be on the way in case it is needed. But if it doesn't come along well, use an egg or yeast suspension instead. To feed by drip, it is necessary to siphon the culture very slowly over into the tank. It is not usually necessary to supply a drain for overflow as not all that much water will be run in.

The main difficulty in drip feeding is to get a slow enough drip, but this is achieved very easily by means of a simple device. A 1.5 mm internal diameter glass tube is bent four times and inserted into a cork or other float. This diameter tubing fills itself by capillary action and will drip at 1 drop per minute (3 ml per hour) or faster, as long as the delivery end of the tubing is bent upward. If it faces downward a minimum speed of about 40 drops per minute is the best it can do, and that is too fast for most cultures. The rate is controlled by raising or lowering the tube in the float, and very slow drip rates are best prevented from stopping (because of surface tension effects) by slipping a piece of tubular tape, wick or shoelace over the dripping end. A 1.5 mm siphon is also self-starting and can be used in the tank as an overflow drip of similar design.

An alternative drip feed is a wick or piece of cloth, but this may filter off too much of the culture, leaving behind a rich medium and delivering a thin one. Actively feeding fry will eat continuously at the rate of several small infusoria per minute, so a tank of, say, 200 fry needs a delivery of some 60,000 organisms per hour. A rich culture may supply one or two hundred very small organisms per drop, hence a drip rate of about 300 per hour or five per minute might be right, but only experience and rough counting of both culture and fry numbers can suffice as a guide.

The number of infusoria needed per day can be dumped into the tank in two or more doses and will not overpopulate the tank while being eaten, as long as the fry are not extremely overcrowded. That is why drip feeding is rarely necessary, but the dumping has to be done with reasonable foresight and careful checks on the condition of the tank. Watch the fry, see that they are eating and estimate even if only roughly the proper amount of culture to feed. Not very much is needed at the start, but the rate at which the fry require food is always increasing as they grow, so larger amounts must be supplied.

Later Feeding: After a start has been made if necessary on a Grade 1 food, try after a few days to substitute a Grade 2 food. Give some and watch what happens with a hand lens. See if it is taken and try to estimate if all the fry are taking it. If not, keep both foods up together for a day or two and make the changeover gradually. Do exactly the same when attempting to move from any food to any other food of larger size, and do not starve your smaller fishes. Runts are produced by neglecting this point.

By this method, most if not all of the fry can be brought along as an even batch. The exception is with Goldfish, among which so variable a spawning may result that all sorts of fry sizes and quality may be encountered despite the most careful feeding. But with tropicals, which breed true, 1% of runts is as much as should be expected. The rest will vary in size a bit, but they should not show the enormous variation so often seen, to the extent that the largest fry finally eat the smallest and so even things up a bit. This is due to inadequate or inappropriate feeding, or both, and can be avoided.

As the fry grow, even if they have been raised entirely on live food for the first few weeks, it is quite in order to start substituting a proportion of prepared food. Keep to live food all the time if you can, but do not starve them by trying to supply live food when there isn't enough available. As with full-grown fishes, fry after the first few weeks do very well on about 50% of live food and quite well on only 25 to 30% if really necessary. Deep frozen and canned foods can even substitute completely.

Growth: Very young fry tolerate surprising degrees of crowding. Even at one centimeter in length the fry of many species can be kept at some 8 to 10 to the liter. An outstanding exception is the Goldfish, in which fry need good space after the first few weeks for adequate growth and must be sorted out fairly early. The fry of nearly all tropicals can if necessary be kept in the small 12- to 20-liter breeding tank advocated here for the first four to six weeks unless the spawning is over 250 per tank, when they will do better if given more room after the first four weeks. Experimentation will determine the fish capacity of tanks to be used in later stages of fry raising, and remember that *it is never a fault to give more room than necessary.*

It is difficult to adequately express in words the beauty of a properly planted aquarium.

Aquarium Plants and Their Cultivation

The interest in aquatic plants has undoubtedly increased over the last fifty years to the extent that aquarists not only regard them as necessary adjuncts to the decorative aquarium but also cultivate them for their own attraction and biological peculiarities. The reason for this growing interest is two-fold; firstly, the importation of exotic marsh and water plants has, as a result of more frequent collecting trips throughout every continent, brought desirable new and often very rare species into commercial supply in America and western Europe and hence into the hands of aquarium plant connoisseurs. Secondly, since Dr. James W. Atz first pointed out the balanced aquarium myth, most aquarists have abandoned the naive assumption that the purpose of a few specimens of *Elodea* and *Vallisneria* in an aquarium is to establish the gaseous exchanges which complement those of the fishes' respiration. Consequently plants have been regarded more as objects with which to decorate the aquarium, creating not only a pleasant visual effect but also a more natural habitat for the fishes. Of course the basic principle of the complementary respiratory exchanges of fishes and plants within a container is sound, but it was long ago grossly exaggerated in the idea of the balanced aquarium.

Despite the new enthusiasm shown in aquarium plant culture, there are still many aquarists who make little attempt to lay out rockwork and plants in imaginative designs or to cultivate and propagate their plants. These two aspects of plant culture are quite distinct. The layout of an aquarium is largely determined by the aquarist's imagination, patience and concepts of pleasing visual effects. In creating an attractive design the important theme is one of contrast, between high and low, light and shade, erect and horizontal, entire leaves and dissected leaves, smooth leaves and ruffled leaves and so on. In an aquascape created by the imaginative aquarist the illusion of depth, the interest at all levels of the water and the apparently natural growth of the plants will be conspicuous features. Though improvements in aquarium layout usually accrue from practice and experience, aquascaping is an individual ability and no hard and fast rules exist to discipline the beginner. The other aspect of aquarium plant culture, the actual propagation and manipulation of the plants, deserves a more comprehensive discussion. Two natural methods of reproduction, sexual and vegetative, occur among plants. Sexual reproduction may involve the formation, dispersal and germination of seeds, as in the flowering plants, or the union of sex cells formed by a separate plant body derived from minute spores, as in the ferns and other flowerless plants. The first type of sexual reproduction is mentioned later in relation to the propagation of the rarer flowering aquatic plants. The second type is referred to in the section devoted to the interesting aquarium plants which belong to the lower groups of the plant kingdom. Natural methods of vegetative propagation are discussed throughout wherever they are relevant to the needs of the aquarist. I shall now discuss the manipulation of some familiar aquarium species.

Manipulation is usually understood as gardening. Pruning, for example, is employed to improve the appearance of underwater foliage. Of the gardening methods, we may first distinguish the cutting back of premature floating leaves which tend to replace the submerged leaves on vigorous specimens of *Aponogeton, Echinodorus, Nymphaea* and other large heterophyllous plants. This is usually progressive pruning designed solely to impair the vigor of the plant, thus delaying the climax of its cycle.

Manipulative pruning of species of aquarium plants often yields the finest bushes of foliage in the underwater scene. The principle of this pruning is that removal of the stem apex eliminates the inhibition of the dormant axillary buds by hormones from the apical bud. This principle is an important feature of the growth habit of many terrestrial plants, though the precise details of the physico-chemical mechanism whereby the inhibition is maintained or removed are unknown. Some species, such as *Hygrophila polysperma*, have a branching habit without removal of the apical bud, and lateral shoots develop freely once the plant is established. Extremely accommodating as regards compost, temperature and pH value of the water, this post-war introduction

There is a wide variety of plants available to the aquarist. Aquarium horticulture can be as challenging as keeping the aquarium fish themselves. Upper photo by Dr. D. Sculthorpe; lower photo by R. Zukal.

Cardamine lyrata (broad-leaved plant). Photo by Dr. D. Sculthorpe.

from India was the first truly aquatic species of its genus to become popular in the aquarium hobby. Its bushy habit renders it useful for masking the sides and corners of tanks, and its bright pale green leaves in pairs along the stems contrast with the fine-leaved bushy species of *Cabomba*, *Limnophila* and *Myriophyllum*. The beautiful rich green sprays of the related giant species *Hygrophila corymbosa* are, with their bold lanceolate leaves, more strikingly handsome but less easy to trim to the desired shape.

A popular species equally decorative and equally accommodating as *Hygrophila polysperma* is *Cardamine lyrata*, whose stems branch freely if the apical buds are nipped from time to time. Its fast-growing but delicate stems bear rounded lobed leaves of a brilliant fresh green; these leaves adjust themselves so that they are exposed to the maximum light intensity and the plant thus forms a fine bush which looks admirable in front of tall, dark rock formations. Another round-leaved species superficially similar to *Cardamine lyrata* is *Lysimachia nummularia*, a plant frequently inhabiting moist garden soil but easily acclimated to submerged life in coldwater or tropical aquaria.

Like *Hygrophila* and *Cardamine,* it readily forms adventitious roots from the lower nodes and after removal of the apical buds soon forms a dense bush of rich green foliage. *Bacopa caroliniana* is a familiar round- to oval-leaved aquarium plant which was known in England for a while, due to a dealer's error, as *Macuillamia rotundifolia.* Its stout, fleshy, ridged stem is extremely buoyant, and roots develop slowly from the nodes; despite these disadvantages this unusual species is often seen in aquaria. It is a difficult plant to model, for it is easily twisted out of shape and does not branch as freely as other species planted as cuttings. Its stems and leaves are unusually hairy, and out of water the plant has a pronounced fragrance. A fourth, and rare, round-leaved species is *Hemianthus orbiculatum,* whose thin, frail-looking stems bear tiny round, slightly folded leaves which quickly respond to the direction of light.

Production of bushes of foliage is also possible with fine-leaved species by nipping out apical buds. The three main genera of aquarium plants with dissected leaves, *Myriophyllum, Cabomba* and *Limnophila,* all respond to this treatment by growing many lateral shoots. There are many species of *Myriophyllum* native to the United States and to the countries of western Europe; a less common species suitable for tropical aquaria is *M. elatinoides,* with whorls of delicate shining green leaves divided into hair-like segments. All the species of *Cabomba* commonly available to aquarists are suited to water at all temperatures from 10°C to about 27°C. The two most frequent species are *Cabomba caroliniana* and *C. aquatica,* the former being distinguished by the formation of narrow floating leaves prior to the flowering phase. Its pretty white flowers are insect-pollinated and develop into small fruits borne downward in the water within the dying remains of the petals. A rosy-hued variety of *C. caroliniana* is sometimes available, as is *C. furcata,* a species which has the leaves set closely together on the stems. The leaves of *Limnophila sessiliflora* are more finely divided than those of *Cabomba* and are whorled, not paired.

The water wisteria, *Hygrophila difformis,* introduced to aquarists in 1954, is a splendid fast-growing species with a wide range of leaf shapes from entire, smooth-margined, oval leaves to deeply divided, toothed leaves superficially resembling those of the Indian fern, *Ceratopteris thalictroides.* The leaves are borne close together on the stout erect stem and from their axils arise lateral shoots; these are encouraged by removal of the apical bud and the plant very quickly forms a luxuriant bush of bright green foliage. The species tolerates a wide range of water conditions and will thrive in a compost of barren gravel, sand or any of the sand/soil mixtures.

Of course, there are a few species used by aquarists which grow naturally in a habit which displays their foliage to remarkable advantage. Well-known examples are species of *Sagittaria,* such as *S. latifolia* and *S. subulata,* both of

Acorus gramineus. Photo by Dr. D. Sculthorpe.

which spread their long fleshy leaves from the crown in a conspicuous manner quite unlike the habit of species of *Vallisneria*, with which they are often confused by novices. *Acorus gramineus* var. *pusillus,* the dwarf rush, and *Acorus gramineus* and its variegated form are even better examples. Their narrow flattened tapering leaves spread out in the form of a fan as they mature and are replaced by younger ones. The fan arises from the almost horizontal rhizome and the dwarf habit, unusual appearance and shallow root run all contribute toward the value of these species in the foreground of an aquarium, where they require nothing of the manipulation necessary to control the more rampant species of aquarium plants.

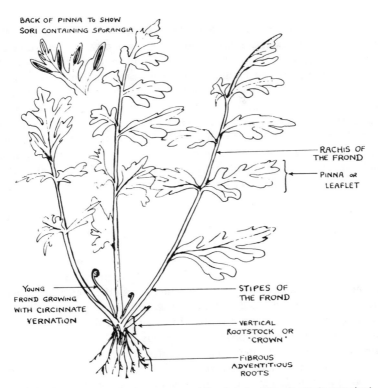

BACK OF PINNA TO SHOW
SORI CONTAINING SPORANGIA

RACHIS OF
THE FROND

PINNA or
LEAFLET

YOUNG
FROND GROWING
WITH CIRCINNATE
VERNATION

STIPES OF
THE FROND

VERTICAL
ROOTSTOCK OR
"CROWN"

FIBROUS
ADVENTITIOUS
ROOTS

A typical flowerless aquatic plant and its details (*Ceratopteris* species).

Flowerless Aquatic Plants

Most aquarium plants are prevented from flowering by the culture methods used to maintain their decorative submerged foliage. Even so, they have the ability to flower and set seed. A few of the most interesting and attractive plants used by aquarists never produce flowers, and they belong to groups lower in the plant kingdom which reproduce, not by flowers, but by inconspicuous spores. The methods the plant uses to produce and disperse these spores are often complicated and only visible under the microscope; since spores are seldom seen they need not concern us here, for these plants rarely reproduce themselves sexually, even in nature. Instead, as is characteristic of almost all water plants, they multiply vegetatively, either by baby plants produced viviparously on the parent or by fragmentation, which in floating species often occurs at a prodigious rate.

135

Ceratopteris thalictroides (from *keras* and *pteris*, the Greek words meaning *horn* and *fern*), the Indian fern or water sprite, is a popular aquarium plant which may be grown floating or submerged. Indigenous to tropical America, Asia, the East Indies and China, it grows in stagnant pools, rooted in the mud, and is often collected as fresh food. A French botanist distinguishes two varieties, one from Sumatra with finely dissected fronds, the other from tropical America as far north as Florida with broad, only slightly indented fronds. This distinction is not really justified as the shape of frond produced depends on the age of the plant and the depth of water in which it is growing. Fronds which are mature or from deep water are twice divided, while fronds which are juvenile or from shallower water are usually smaller, broader and less divided, with oblong pinnae. Fronds of all sizes and shapes may often occur on one good plant. Only sterile fronds are produced by rooted submerged plants, the pinnae unfolding as the fleshy quadrangular stem grows from the crown, at first horizontally and then straightening up to the light. Floating specimens have profuse branching roots with dense root-hairs, while the sterile fronds recline on the surface, forming a rosette of up to 75 cm in diameter. Erect fertile fronds may be produced from the crown to a height of 70 cm; they are finely divided with linear segments bearing longitudinal lines of sporangia which contain the spores. In aquaria, fertile fronds are uncommon, but the plants readily produce viviparous youngsters at the notches of the fronds. These are best detached and floated at the surface until they have strong enough roots to be planted. The bright yellowish green fronds of *Ceratopteris thalictroides* are unlike any other aquarium plant and contrast excellently with the dark green foliage of many species of *Cryptocoryne*.

Ceratopteris thalictroides. Photo by Dr. D. Sculthorpe.

Ceratopteris siliquosa. Photo by R. Zukal.

The rapid spread of *Ceratopteris* is characteristic of two other genera of water ferns, *Salvinia* and *Azolla.* The first of these, which was dedicated to Antonio Mario Salvini, a Florentine professor of the seventeenth century, is a cosmopolitan genus inhabiting lakes, pools and stagnant ditches. From the horizontal stem of the large form of *Salvinia auriculata* arise two rows of rounded pea-green surface leaves, clothed beneath with brownish hairs, the upper surfaces glistening with a dense covering of curious looped white hairs which repel any drops of water falling on the plant. Beneath each pair of leaves hangs a cluster of finely branched, rust-colored submerged leaflets; these are not roots as is often thought. The small form of *S. auriculata* has leaves 6 mm long but is otherwise very similar. Once introduced to an aquarium, these plants soon cover the surface by rapid vegetative multiplication and they need rigorous control. They thrive under the bright lights of an aquarium hood or the diffuse light of a tropical pool and, though preferring warm water, may be acclimated to cold water.

Azolla filiculoides. Photo by Dr. D. Sculthorpe.

Species of *Azolla* (from the Greek *a* — without, and *zoe* — life, alluding to the rapidity with which the plant dries up) are just as adapted to the floating habit as *Salvinia,* their covering of short hairs imprisoning air and preventing them from being submerged. *Azolla nilotica,* a much-branched species, grows to 15 cm long and, with *Salvinia* and *Ceratopteris,* is important as a constituent of the sudd, the dense floating masses of vegetation which block slow-moving rivers in flat open country, for example the Nile and the Ganges. *Azolla mexicana* is a smaller purplish species from the irrigation ditches of Mexico and the southern United States. The two most widely distributed species are the smallest and the two most well known to aquarists. These are *Azolla caroliniana* and *Azolla filiculoides,* which have in the last ninety years demonstrated the efficiency of their vegetative reproduction and dispersal by spreading all over Europe from their origin in western North America, Central and South America. Both seem to have been introduced into Europe via botanic gardens. *A. caroliniana* reached Europe in 1872, spreading through France by 1879, to England in 1883 and to Italy in 1886. It is rare in England, *A. filiculoides* being confused with it.

138

Azolla filiculoides was introduced to France by a Bordeaux botanist in 1879 and 1880. In England in 1888, a teacher is said to have procured some from Glasgow and put it in a ditch at a village on the Norfolk Broads. Heavy floods in August, 1912 carried it up the main rivers and spread it all over the Broads. Now locally common in England, particularly in the warmer humid counties of the southeast and southwest, it is prevented from spreading to the northwest by hard winter frosts.

Identical to the naked eye, both species have a branched stem with thin pendulous roots and overlapping leaves above in two rows alternating right and left. Each leaf has two lobes; the upper floats and possesses chlorophyll and a symbiotic blue-green alga, while the lower is submerged and colorless. The hairs on the upper surface of the leaves of *A. filiculoides* are unicellular, while those of *A. caroliniana* are bicellular. The overall bluish green tint of the two species becomes purplish red in strong sunlight, particularly in late summer.

Ceratopteris cornuta. Photo by Dr. D. Sculthorpe.

The plants reproduce by fragmentation and spread rapidly until the whole aquarium or pool surface is covered by the tufted mass.

While the fern *Azolla* appears more like a leafy liverwort, another flowerless aquarium plant, *Riccia*, actually is a liverwort. The plant is a simple flat thallus which branches dichotomously. *Riccia fluitans*, a cosmopolitan species dedicated to Ricci, an Italian botanist, is common in aquaria, bright green tangled masses floating just beneath the surface. It is just as attractive when pegged to the gravel and allowed to grow into a dense carpet.

Ricciocarpus natans is a related floating species which is much rarer, but like *Riccia* species, it is found in ponds and ditches rich in mineral and organic matter. It is quite similar to the common duckweed, having lobed thalli about 5 mm in diameter, each lobe being bright green and bearing shaggy purple scales beneath.

The freshwater moss *Fontinalis antipyretica* is an attractive aquarium plant growing naturally in rapid hill streams. Its specific name alludes to its water-holding capacity and its supposed use in bandaging burns; its common name is willow moss. In general appearance it is very similar to its terrestrial relatives with its thin, wiry, brownish stems clothed with alternate triangular leaves of a deep translucent green. Underwater it forms thickets and is useful as a spawning and decorative plant, but it is only suitable for coldwater aquaria. A finer leaved variety, light green in color, *Fontinalis antipyretica* var. *gracilis* is suitable for warm water.

Riccia fluitans.

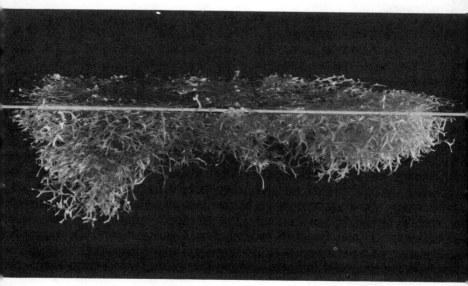

140

Marsilea quadrifolia. Photo by R. Zukal.

Among the dwarf plants so popular nowadays in front of rocks in an aquarium waterscape are species of the genus *Marsilea.* These ferns from shallow waters and mud flats in temperate and tropical regions of the world are named in honor of an eighteenth century Italian botanist, Fernando Conte Marsigli. In growth habit *Marsilea* has rhizomes creeping in the mud or sand, sending up erect stalks alternately on each side which bear four pinnae rather like a four-leaved clover. The pinnae unfold from the coiled bud when the stalk reaches its prescribed height, which varies from 2 to 12 cm. Many species are available to the aquarist: *M. quadrifolia,* from central Europe and Japan; *M. drummondii,* from Australia; *M. vestita,* from the Pacific coast of America; and *M. mucronata,* from the high plains, Rocky Mountains and southwestern states, are probably the most common. Being amphibious plants, they all show a distressing tendency to form floating and aerial leaves; these may be prevented by judicious pruning and planting in water of more than 15 cm.

Very closely related to *Marsilea* is the peculiarly named tropical fern *Regnellidium,* of similar habit but usually larger and with leaves of only two light green pinnae. It may be rooted or left floating with the rhizome just beneath the surface, the roots hanging below. When *Marsilea* and *Regnellidium* are grown as marsh plants they form spores within stony bean-shaped sporocarps borne singly near the base of the leaf stalks. Mature sporocarps germinate readily in water if they are first cracked. They imbibe water and after a few minutes a strange worm-like structure emerges and slowly swells until it disintegrates, releasing the spores.

Another relative of *Marsilea* is similar to hair grass; this is *Pilularia globulifera,* the pillwort, from temperate regions of Europe. A plant of shallow pond margins, its slender creeping rhizome may be rooted or free-floating. Narrow cylindrical leaves grow alternately from each side of the rhizome to 8 to 10 cm tall. They are fresh green and circinately coiled like those of *Marsilea.* A common but easily overlooked plant of Great Britain and the U.S.A., it is more frequent in the west than in the east. It may be gathered wild and used as a dwarf carpet plant in the coldwater aquarium.

The last flowerless aquarium plants of interest are not true ferns; they are the strange plants of the genus *Isoëtes* (from the Greek, *isos*—equal, and *etos* year, referring to the evergreen nature of the plants). Known popularly as the quillworts, most species inhabit the stony beds of bleak, barren, mountain lakes in the cold and temperate regions of the world. *Isoëtes lacustris,* native to northern Europe, has a tuft of spikey green leaves with transverse white markings and profuse roots growing from a stout rootstock. The leaves usually bear spores in cavities on the inside of the wide leaf base. When planted in small groups, this handsome species has a striking appearance in a coldwater aquarium. Other species, such as *I. garnierii,* introduced into France from the Sudan in 1947, and *I. bolanderii,* native to the southern United States, are suitable for warm water.

None of the species of aquatic ferns, mosses and liverworts just described are demanding in their culture requirements. All thrive under a wide range of light intensities, though the floating species enjoy the higher intensities more than submerged species. Gravel, coarse sand or a sand/soil mixture suits all the rooted species, sand giving a closer root hold to *Marsilea* and *Pilularia,* which sometimes tend to be disturbed by bottom-feeding fishes. *Isoëtes, Pilularia* and to a certain extent *Fontinalis,* coming from lakes and streams poor in dissolved salts, are lime-hating and must be given non-calcareous gravel or sand and rather acid water.

Echinodorus paniculatus. Photo by R. Zukal.

Large Tropical Aquatic Plants

Gone are the days when Amazon swordplants were rarities in aquaria. Many of the thirty or so species of *Echinodorus* from the American continent, such as the Amazon swordplant, *E. paniculatus,* and the chain swordplant, *E. grisebachii,* have variable growth forms. All species of *Echinodorus,* however, produce bushes of bold foliage and are therefore eminently suitable as centerpieces and specimen plants. Their leaf stalks are short and they will not produce floating and aerial leaves unless the light intensity is too high. Most species are now commercially plentiful, including the unusual *E. berteroi,* the cellophane plant, which grows through a series of leaf forms, and *E. tenellus,* the pygmy chain swordplant, still erroneously shown in some aquarium books as *Sagittaria microfolia.*

A few species are still rare and have not been introduced to some European countries. *Echinodorus maior,* the ruffled swordplant from Brazil, with its spectacular furled strap-shaped leaves up to half a meter tall, and *E. grandiflorus,* the Amazon spearplant from tropical America, with its large spearshaped leaves, are examples of such plants.

The water orchid is a rare specimen plant; it is often erroneously named *Spiranthes odorata*, a species which will not survive under water. The form usually grown in aquaria is probably a variety of *Spiranthes latifolia*, a bog species readily adaptable to continued submerged growth. From the fleshy tuberous roots, essential for the plant's survival, grow spreading emerald green lanceolate leaves. Growth is slow, but if the plant is in shallow water under bright light it will produce an aerial stem bearing pale yellow flowers.

Two very rare species of *Barclaya* were introduced in 1958 by Dr. Herbert R. Axelrod; both come from Thailand and belong to the same family as *Cabomba* and the water lilies, the Nymphaeaceae. *Barclaya longifolia* forms a bush of tapering wavy leaves which are prettily veined and olive to mid-brown in color. *B. motleyi*, the other species, produces spreading leathery leaves about 7.5 cm wide, whose young pinkish red color matures to a shade of coppery brown.

The genus *Aponogeton* has been much exploited by aquarists, and most of the available species have erect undulating and twisting foliage arising from a tuberous rootstock. Contrary to popular opinion, *A. crispus* is not synonymous with *A. undulatus;* it is a distinct and uncommon species originating in Sri Lanka and India. *A. cordatus* is also uncommon, coming from Southeast Asia and therefore, with *A. undulatus*, producing the undivided flower spike of Asian species which contrasts with the U-shaped double flower spike of African species such as *A. ulvaceus*. *A. crispus* may be recognized when young by its short petioles which bear the narrow lanceolate leaves in an erect attitude; when mature the species has narrower leaves than either *A. undulatus* or *A. cordatus*. The leaves of *A. undulatus* are smoothly undulating and of a conspicuous bronze-green tint whereas those of *A. cordatus*, the loveliest species of the three, are very closely crinkled at the margins, deep rich green in color and though not fully translucent, show the longitudinal and transverse veins as a molded lattice. *A. natans* quickly forms floating leaves, though its submerged foliage of broad, bright yellowish green, slightly wavy leaves may be maintained by ruthless cutting of the leaves which push toward the surface.

The species of *Aponogeton* about which most has been written is of course *A. madagascariensis*, the Madagascar lace plant. The leaves, which may attain a length of 20 to 25 cm, are borne on slender brittle petioles arising from a tuberous rootstock and are at first reddish bronze, later assuming a deep green hue. The blade of each leaf consists of seven parallel veins joined transversely by short minor veins, forming a regular lace-like network with almost no cellular tissue. Though of fragile appearance, these skeletal blades are comparatively tough and strong. The species produces an aerial inflorescence which consists of a twin spike bearing the white flowers. On numerous occasions *A. madagascariensis* has been found to produce submerged inflorescences, as frequently happens in the hardy pool species *A. distachyus,* the Cape water hawthorn. Self-fertilization occurs before the inflorescence opens and seedlings slowly develop while still attached to the bud. The lace plant occurs in Madagascar between 100 and 900 meters above sea level, rooted in non-calcareous sand in the crevices between stones in semi-shaded slow-moving water.

The submerged leaves of species of *Aponogeton* show an interesting structural series. Those of *A. natans* and *A. distachyus* are the least translucent and have the least conspicuous veins; those of *A. crispus, A. undulatus* and *A. cordatus* are more translucent with the veins in relief, while *A. ulvaceus* has fully translucent foliage. In the rare Madagascan species *A. bernierianus,* the cellular interstices of the leaf partially degenerate, but the lace network is not as fully apparent as in the related *A. madagascariensis.*

There is considerable confusion over names in the genus *Cryptocoryne,* too. That usually offered for sale as *C. cordata,* with elongated, tapering, olive to bronze leaves, is really *C. beckettii;* the commercial species of that name, with pointed smooth bright green leaves, is the small growth form of *C. nevillii. C. haerteliana* was a temporary name derived from the surname of the German who imported the then unknown plants at the end of the thirties. Later they were identified as plants of *C. affinis,* the correct name which dates from 1893. The plant offered as *C. axelrodii* very closely resembles the species *C. undulata.* The true *C. cordata* is a rare and only occasionally imported plant. It is a dark green species growing to about 30 cm tall, with rounded, mottled leaves resembling those of *C. griffithii.* A distinctive species of comparatively recent introduction from Thailand is *C. balansae,* whose spreading leaves are bright shining green with a deeply crinkled surface. Of an equally bright shade of green are the leaves of *C. johorensis;* they are broad and pointed and have recurved basal lobes.

A delightful Sinhalese species, *C. thweitesii,* is little known to aquarists; it is a most desirable plant for the connoisseur. Discovered by Kendrick Thweites, a director of the Peradenyia botanic garden from 1857 to 1880, it is a slow-growing species with finely serrated, delicately marked leaves up to 6 cm long and dark green in color. In deep water its leaves tend to lengthen and become tinted with yellow and brown. This rare species produces very few stolons, and its lilac and blue aroid inflorescence has been seen by only one or two people.

During the second half of the nineteenth century the Italian explorer Odoardo Beccari brought to Europe many extensive collections of tropical Asiatic plants, among which was *Cryptocoryne ferruginea,* from Borneo. This is a large handsome species growing to a height of 40 cm, with broad rich green leaves borne on sturdy stalks. The shape of the leaf varies, a feature common to most species of *Cryptocoryne,* but the surface is nearly always

Cryptocoryne versteegii. Photo by F. Driessens.

deeply crinkled and the margin is waved. Specimens grow well in dim electric light and should not be exposed to direct sunlight; they must be given ample space in which to spread their foliage.

C. versteegii is one of the only two species of *Cryptocoryne* at present known to occur in New Guinea, where G. M. Versteeg discovered it in 1907 on the Lorentz River. It is a dwarf plant suitable for the aquarium foreground, where its rigid triangular green leaves make a conspicuous display. The upper surface is glossy and is never mottled with areas of anthocyanin pigmentation. The rate of growth of this species is variable; there are numerous reports of it never producing a new leaf for many months. When conditions suit it, however, subterranean stolons are formed in abundance and its inflorescence is not uncommon.

Introduced to European aquarists in 1954 by an Amsterdam importer, *Cryptocoryne walkeri* resembles *C. beckettii*, though it does not usually reach a comparable size. It also differs in having shorter and broader leaves which do not usually curl back and which may be slightly ribbed at their margins. It lacks the distinctive olive-green hue of *C. beckettii*. *C. ciliata* is one of the large and fairly common species which grow consistently when submerged in tropical aquaria. The tapering pale green leaves are usually gently furled and borne erect on stout stalks to an overall height of 40 to 50 cm.

The beautifully colored inflorescences of species of *Cryptocoryne* are seldom formed when the plants are growing submerged; for some species to bloom is rare indeed, whatever the growth conditions. Plants seem to bloom more readily if they are rooted in a rich compost of about three parts leaf mold, two parts peat and one part coarse sand contained in closed tanks or glass jars and kept at a temperature of 24°C. At first the plants should be just submerged, the water level being gradually reduced until the foliage is growing in humid air at a temperature of 20 to 21°C. Some species such as *C. ferruginea* and *C. retrospiralis* are unfortunately less amenable to this treatment and must be kept partially submerged.

Cryptocoryne walkeri. Photo by F. Driessens.

C. retrospiralis is an unusually slender species with wavy mid-green leaves only 3 to 6 mm wide. Other *Cryptocoryne* have been introduced but most of them are unidentified and not in supply. One species, probably from Indonesia, has attractive tapering and undulating leaves about 2.5 cm across at their widest point. When young they are a bright yellowish green, but within a couple of weeks the color has passed through olive to rich brown. The newest introduction is a very beautiful species with oval to spade-shaped leaves, reddish with dark brown markings above and mahogany red underneath. This superb specimen plant, which grows to a height of 38 cm or more, has been described as *Cryptocoryne siamensis*.

Stenospermation popayanense var. *aquatica*, an unusual aroid introduced to Europe in 1950 by a Frenchman, is native to Colombia and thrives in an aquarium temperature of 15 to 27°C. When transplanted it does not lose any leaves as *Cryptocoryne* often does, and during the course of a year it forms many clusters of leaves. The plant slightly resembles *Cryptocoryne ciliata*, and its firm lanceolate pointed leaves have conspicuous veins. The flowers are surrounded by a typically aroid spathe that is pure white in color.

Even more exploited than the Aponogetonaceae, the Araceae have yielded all the species of *Cryptocoryne, Anubias, Acorus, Stenospermation* and *Pistia* which may be used in aquaria. About twenty years ago, two species of another aroid genus, *Lagenandra,* appeared in commercial supply in England. One of them, *Lagenandra ovata,* had been previously cultivated in aquaria as *Aglaonema simplex* until it was correctly identified. Both the species of *Lagenandra* are indigenous to the coastal regions of southern India and Sri Lanka, where they grow in brackish water as well as in fresh water. Leaves are continuously produced along the creeping rootstock and there is consequently a fine display of young and mature foliage in all levels of water. Each leaf emerges from the sheath of the preceding one and the unrolling blade is borne on a stout petiole. Mature leaves have blades of about 25 cm in length and an approximate overall length of 40 to 45 cm. *Lagenandra ovata* has dark green petioles which bear lighter green blades with rather wavy margins. *L. lancifolia* is one of the half dozen or so species of aquatic plants which have variegated foliage; its dark green blades have a marginal silver band and are borne on reddish petioles.

All the plants discussed make superb specimens in decorative aquaria, but as most of them are bog species, they must be given a rich non-calcareous soil. They are most conveniently grown in a compost of garden soil, peat moss and sand confined within a small plant-pot and covered with gravel to prevent clouding of the water. Species of *Aponogeton* appreciate more sand and less humus. Plants may be propagated by division of the rootstock or by germination of fertile seed. Young seedlings of *Lagenandra* and young plants from the stolons of *Cryptocoryne* and *Stenospermation* should be grown as bog plants in

Lagenandra lancifolia. Photo by R. Zukal.

a peaty soil at a temperature of 18 to 22° C. With some of the less vigorous species of *Cryptocoryne*, such as *C. thweitesii,* care is needed to avoid removing stoloniferous young plants from the parent plant before they are sufficiently robust. Some aroids such as the *Lagenandra* and *Cryptocoryne* species prefer the more shaded sites in the aquarium and so contrast with species of *Aponogeton,* which must be bathed in bright overhead light and must be given ample room if they are to display their undulating foliage. The tendency of species of *Echinodorus* and *Aponogeton* to produce floating leaves is discouraged by pruning, a process which sets back the life cycle and at the same time discourages the formation of flowers. Of course, some species such as *Aponogeton cordatus* retain their submerged foliage more easily than others and still flower even when drastically pruned. Some species mentioned may lose a few leaves after transplanting, but when once established they produce leaves throughout the year, rarely showing any annual rest period and indeed often flowering out of their natural season.

Utricularia sp. Photo by R. Zukal.

Flowering Plants With a Floating Habit

Floating plants are put to various uses by aquarists: when distributed evenly over the surface of the water, they reduce the intensity of light reaching the submerged plants; in masses they are of use to many spawning fishes, and they provide a sheltered habitat for fry; they have a decorative value; and for such fishes as *Leporinus* they are food. Their use results primarily from their habits of growth; some species are small and much-branched, forming a dense network of vegetation, while others have conspicuous aerial foliage and profuse submerged roots. In an earlier section I discussed species of the genera *Ceratopteris, Salvinia, Azolla, Riccia* and *Ricciocarpus,* all of which had floating habits; now I shall consider six genera of flowering plants.

Bladderworts, of the genus *Utricularia*, when not in flower live completely submerged just below the surface of the water; the plants are rootless and have branched axes bearing finely divided segments from which arise small utricles or bladders. The usual botanical concepts of stem, root and leaf are of little value in describing species of *Utricularia*; some authors have regarded the whole plant body as a root system, while others have tried to differentiate between stems and leaves, interpreting the bladders as modified leaflets. Whichever interpretation is accepted, the structure is certainly anomalous and shows the plasticity so characteristic of aquatic plants. The family Lentibulariaceae, to which the bladderworts belong, contains mainly marsh plants, and Goebel suggested in 1891 that the aquatic *Utricularia* are descendants of marsh forms which have become more and more involved in aquatic life. Species such as *U. minor* and *U. intermedia* are capable of producing terrestrial forms, though these do not flower.

Each bladder has a thin translucent wall usually two cells thick and is filled with water and bubbles of air; several long multicellular bristles surround the truncated entrance from which a colorless flexible valve slopes into the cavity of the bladder. There is no doubt that minute animals, particularly crustaceans such as *Daphnia* spp., *Cypris* spp. and *Cyclops* spp., are trapped within the bladders where they die slowly, possibly by asphyxiation; bacterial decay reduces the bodies to a soluble form appearing as a murky fluid which is probably absorbed by the hair-like glands in the lining wall of the bladders. Their ability to trap newly hatched fry is unquestionable.

In shallow water some species of *Utricularia* form "earth-shoots" which have sparse segments; these anchor the plant very firmly in the mud or sand. Another modification, known as an "air-shoot," is produced by *U. vulgaris* and *U. neglecta*; it seems to be a reduced inflorescence, thread-like, white and bearing stomata through which gaseous exchange occurs between the atmosphere and the internal tissue.

The yellow flowers of most species of *Utricularia* are borne on an aerial shoot which is maintained erect by a whorl of much-divided segments just beneath the water surface. Bladderworts reproduce vegetatively by fragmentation and, in species inhabiting temperate regions, by turions or "winter buds." In *Utricularia vulgaris*, for example, the apical region of each shoot forms, between August and November, a tight cluster of sturdy reduced leaves which is covered by a layer of mucilage. Such turions may remain attached to the parent plant throughout the winter, or they may break off and rise to the surface where the foliage opens and growth recommences in the early spring. In natural conditions turions are only formed in the fall, but they can be induced at any other time of the year by conditions of poor nutrition.

Few aquatic plants have caused serious economic problems; three which do possess this singular distinction are well-known floating species, *Pistia*

Eichhornia crassipes. Photo by L. E. Perkins.

stratiotes, the water lettuce, *Eichhornia crassipes,* the water hyacinth or devil's lilac, and *Salvinia auriculata.* *Salvinia auriculata* has been stimulated into an explosive phase of reproduction by conditions associated with the rising flood waters of the Zambesi. *Pistia stratiotes* forms rosettes of pale green spatulate leaves whose upper and lower surfaces are covered with minute water-repellent hairs. Over seventy per cent of the volume of each leaf is occupied by air, and when the plant is free-floating, a spongy air-filled tissue develops near the base of the leaf; this tissue, which seems to give the plant extra buoyancy, is not formed when the rosettes are stranded on mud. In the bottom of a groove at the tip of each leaf is a small pore through which drops of water are actively extruded, usually in the early morning. Such water pores are also to be found at the apices of the leaves of most species of *Eichhornia.* During periods of bright illumination the leaves of *Pistia* spread out almost horizontally, from which position they move vertically, closing together during the night.

Pistia stratiotes reproduces itself vegetatively by proliferating young rosettes, each of which is borne away from the parent by a cylindrical fleshy stolon just beneath the water surface. When such reproduction occurs rapidly, the rosettes, stolons and profuse white roots become entangled and form a surface network which rapidly colonizes creeks, backwaters and shallow river margins. As a result *Pistia* often constitutes a great hindrance on the rivers of equatorial Africa, such as the Ogowé and the tributaries of the Congo. In her book *Travels in West Africa,* published in 1897, M. H. Kingsley wrote, "It is very like a nicely grown cabbage lettuce, and it is very charming when you look down a creek full of it, for the beautiful tender green makes a perfect picture against the dark forest that rises from the banks of the creek. If you are in a canoe, it gives you little apprehension to know you have got to go through it, but if you are in a small steam launch, every atom of pleasure in its beauty goes, the moment you lay eye on the thing. You dash into it as fast as you can go, with a sort of geyser of lettuce flying up from the screw; but not for long, for this interesting vegetable grows after the manner of couch-grass . . . and winds those roots round your propeller."

The vegetative reproduction of species of *Eichhornia* is very similar to that of *Pistia stratiotes;* young rosettes arise from the leaf axils of the parent and are borne out along the water surface by stout stolons. The two most frequent species, *Eichhornia crassipes* and *E. azurea,* are native to the swamps and water meadows of Brazil but have been introduced to many other countries during the last hundred and fifty years. First introduced to the Old World about 1829, *E. crassipes* had become a serious hindrance on the waterways of Java and Singapore sixty years later. In 1896, after high winds and storms had swept Florida, it blocked the St. John's River for twenty-five miles, although it was only six years before that it had been accidentally introduced there. It also flourished in Australia and Cambodia, causing similar problems for local industries which used the inland waterways for transport. It has now spread over the African continent, colonizing the headwaters and upper reaches of the Nile River.

The size and shape of the leaves of *Eichhornia crassipes* vary at different stages of development and in different external conditions; this feature of the plant habit is known as heterophylly. Young leaves are very slender and have small circular blades; in succeeding leaves the relative proportions of the blade and stalk change, until the mature form with its ragged transparent sheath, swollen air-filled stalk and thin orbicular blade is attained. The anatomy of the leaves suggests that the blade and stalk are not equivalent to the lamina and petiole of the leaves of other aquatic plants such as *Nymphaea* spp. and *Nuphar* spp.; they probably correspond only to the petiole, the tip of which becomes flattened and widened to produce the blade. Bright light and a low temperature seem to induce more prominently swollen, air-filled tissue in

Hydrocharis morsus-ranae. Photo by Dr. D. Sculthorpe.

the stalk than do high temperatures and poor illumination. The swelling is considerably reduced in leaves formed while a plant is stranded on mud or on marshy ground.

As aquarium plants, both *Eichhornia crassipes* and *Pistia stratiotes* flourish in a humid atmosphere and with natural illumination, but they do not grow very satisfactorily in artificial light. Their range of temperature tolerance is from about 18 to 29 or 32°C, though these are not absolute limits. *Eichhornia crassipes* produces a short-lived aerial spike of large clawed flowers, violet-blue in color and often speckled with yellow. *E. azurea* is distinguished by its erect oval leaves and sessile pale blue flowers. After its introduction to Singapore, *E. crassipes* was cultivated by the Chinese, who sold its flowers in the streets. *Pistia stratiotes* produces insignificant flowers from which develop berries containing large numbers of minute seeds. It is also cultivated in China for hog food, though it must first be chopped and boiled.

The roots of both *Eichhornia* and *Pistia* form convenient natural spawning mops; those of *Pistia stratiotes* are usually white or brown, while mature roots of *Eichhornia crassipes* bear dense rows of lateral roots, in all of which there develops a purplish magenta pigment.

The family Hydrocharitaceae, whose members are all aquatic, contains three genera of floating plants known to aquarists: *Hydrocharis*, *Limnobium* and *Stratiotes*. The frog-bit, *Hydrocharis morsus-ranae*, forms a rosette of bronzed pale green leaves, from the base of which hang long unbranched roots densely clothed with root-hairs. From the nodes of long slender stolons which grow horizontally, just below the surface of the water, from each parent rosette, young rosettes arise throughout the summer. In autumn, or during adverse conditions, these stolons form terminal turions, each of which is enclosed by two scale leaves. When these turions break off, they usually sink to the substratum where they remain dormant until the following spring; the center of gravity of each turion is in the basal stalked end and so they remain morphologically upright. A minimum limiting intensity of light, especially at the yellow and red end of the spectrum, is required for germination to occur; then the bud scales open, the young leaves develop air-filled lacunae and the growing plant rises to the surface.

The aerial male and female flowers of the frog-bit are borne on the same plant though at different nodes; the female flowers are solitary whereas the male flowers arise in groups of two or three enclosed within a spathe. Whether male or female, each flower has three obovate white petals which are marked with yellow at their base and which usually appear ragged and crumpled. Flowers only appear if the plants are brightly illuminated almost daily throughout late spring and early summer.

Hydrocharis morsus-ranae is a widespread inhabitant of pools, small lakes and stagnant water; though it grows more successfully in cold water, it can be acclimated to a tropical aquarium. A more suitable species for warm water is the American frog-bit, *Limnobium stoloniferum* – also known as *Trianea bogotensis* – which differs from *Hydrocharis* in the structure of its leaves, which are thick, fleshy and cordate in shape.

Stratiotes aloides, the water soldier or water aloe, is a curious semi-floating species whose affinities with *Hydrocharis morsus-ranae* are revealed by the similar structure and arrangement of its flowers. The petals are larger and, in England at least, the fruit is rarely, if ever, produced. The species occurs all over Europe and northwestern Asia; in the northern region the plants are female while in the south they are nearly all male. A few hermaphrodite plants have been recorded from time to time, but this is to be expected since the flowers of most members of the family Hydrocharitaceae have rudimentary male and female organs.

The stiff but brittle leaves of the water soldier sometimes grow as long as 50 cm and are usually covered with small spines, particularly at their margins.

The young leaves of the offsets which are produced in the autumn are a bright rich green in color, though this becomes dark and brown as the plant matures. Each plant forms only a few roots, but these are fast-growing, increasing at an average rate of 6 to 8 cm per twenty-four hours, short-lived and quickly replaced by new ones. That plants are often unbalanced when any of these roots are experimentally destroyed suggests that their function is primarily to maintain the equilibrium of the surface rosette.

The famous rising and sinking of *Stratiotes aloides* was thought by the first observers to occur twice within each year; it is now known that the plant rises in the spring, flowers during the early summer and in late summer sinks back to the bottom of the water, where it forms offsets. The mechanism of these movements is probably a chemical one; during the summer an incrustation of crystalline calcium carbonate is deposited on the aerial leaves by the evaporation of a very dilute solution of that compound which seems to be secreted on the leaf surface by certain cells. This process, together with the waterlogging of old decaying leaves in late summer, increases the specific gravity of the plant, and it sinks. While the plant is submerged, the calcium carbonate is slowly redissolved in the water, and in spring the rapid growth of young succulent leaves probably decreases the specific gravity of the plant, which then floats up to the surface.

Though rather a large species for a coldwater aquarium, the water soldier is a fascinating plant for the outdoor pool, and there is commercially available a smaller variety, growing to about 15 cm in diameter, which flourishes in a tropical aquarium, though it does not show the same regular cycle of movements.

Trapa natans, the water chestnut, is an equally curious species with a floating habit. It occurs in many European localities and in Siberia, the Caucasus and the Far East, but it is rarely in commercial supply. It is now extinct in many places where fossil deposits have shown that it once occurred, for example Belgium, Holland, Sweden, Scotland and the lowlands of Switzerland. It is an annual species, developing from a dark brown sculptured nut, the horns of which seem to anchor the young seedling in the substratum. When the nut germinates, the first structure to emerge is the hypocotyl, which bears the two rudimentary shoots and the root. One of the two shoots is dormant while the other grows upward, producing small narrow leaves which quickly die and are replaced by adventitious roots. At the surface this shoot forms a symmetrical rosette of triangular serrated green leaves; these have glossy, waxed, upper surfaces and dilated petioles. The root does not respond to the force of gravity and grows upward at an angle of about 45 degrees to the vertical; it later produces many lateral roots which soon grow downward to the substratum. Though occurring naturally in temperate as well as tropical regions of the world, this species thrives in tropical aquaria.

Isolepis setacea. Photo by Dr. D. Sculthorpe.

Dwarf Aquarium Plants

There is a considerable demand from aquarists for low-growing and dwarf species suitable for the foreground of an aquarium. I have already mentioned aquatic ferns of the genera *Marsilea* and *Pilularia* and fern allies such as *Isoëtes*, and these together with dwarf aroids of the genus *Cryptocoryne* and miscellaneous plants such as *Spiranthes latifolia* have growth habits which render them useful to the aquarist. There are a number of other genera containing species with a striking appearance and a rosette or branching form of growth, all of which are admirable plants for cultivating in front of strata rockwork.

Hair grass, *Eleocharis acicularis,* forms thickets of very narrow cylindrical leaves and grows to a height of about 14 to 20 cm. New plants are produced at the nodes of slender stolons which creep along or just below the surface of the substratum; the species spreads very rapidly in clear water and a fine compost. When first planted in an aquarium, it should be given a sandy compost in which the sparse frail roots can easily anchor themselves, for in a coarse gravel medium it is apt to be uprooted by bottom-feeding fishes. The predominantly vertical growth of the plant gives it great value in relieving the horizontal lines of rock strata.

Elodea nutalli and *E. minor* are both subtropical species which thrive in tropical aquaria under a wide range of light intensities. *E. nutalli* will grow to a height of 30 or more centimeters, but if the apical bud of each stem is removed lateral branches readily develop and the plant can be induced to form a dense bush. Native to the Argentine, *E. nutalli* is distinguished from the widespread species of temperate regions, *E. canadensis*, the Canadian water weed or water thyme, by its paler green, twisted leaves, each of which has a bright red or brownish base. It may also be distinguished during the flowering phase; both *E. canadensis* and *E. nutalli* have inconspicuous male and female flowers on separate plants, but whereas the male flowers of *E. canadensis* break away from the tubular spathes borne in the leaf axils and rise to the surface, those of *E. nutalli* are carried up to the surface solitarily on thread-like stalks. The female flowers of both species are borne up to the surface solitarily by an elongated floral tube; at the surface the flower opens and exposes its three receptive stigmas. Pollination is effected by the buoyant pollen grains liberated by the explosive rupture of the male flowers floating by chance onto these stigmas.

Elodea minor is a much smaller species, though it has a similar growth habit to that of *E. nutalli*; the pale green fragile stems bear tiny narrow yellowish green leaves which are recurved, similar to those of *Lagarosiphon major*, a species also known, erroneously, as *Elodea crispa*. Unlike those of other species of *Elodea*, the leaves of *E. minor* are not arranged in whorls on the stem. Both *E. minor* and *E. nutalli* grow very quickly in any compost of sand or gravel, producing adventitious roots from the lower nodes of the stems once they have become established.

A foreground plant of unusual appearance which, though it grows naturally in peat bogs and acidic soils in the cooler regions of Europe and Africa, is adaptable to water at a temperature of 13 to 24°C is *Hydrocotyle vulgaris*, the pennywort. A creeping rhizome produces from each node one simple leaf consisting of a horizontal, slightly lobed lamina borne on a slender petiole. The length of the petiole is extremely variable; when the plant is only partially submerged the petiole may be as short as 2 cm; but in an aquarium the petioles tend to elongate, and unless this tendency is controlled by judicious pruning the plant loses its attraction. Flowers are formed in the leaf axils when the species is growing out of water or only partially submerged; these are inconspicuous and develop into bilobed fruits which are about two millimeters in diameter. Another pennywort, *Hydrocotyle verticillata*, occurring in the Atlantic Coast regions of North America, is very similar in structure to *H. vulgaris* and is equally useful in aquaria.

Most species of the genera *Nymphaea*, *Nymphoides* and *Nuphar*, all usually known as water lilies, are too large for either coldwater or tropical aquaria, but the species *Nuphar pumilum*, also known as *N. minimum*, is sufficiently small

Samolus floribundus. Photo by Dr. D. Sculthorpe.

to be useful in the foreground of an aquarium. Growing from a stout rootstock, the leaves spread out so that their blades are exposed to the maximum illumination; the edges of the leaves are often furled, and the color is a rich translucent green. This plant has a wide temperature range and often grows only slowly, reaching a height of 10 to 15 cm after about a year.

Samolus floribundus, known as water rose, is another dwarf plant which withstands a similarly wide range of temperatures. It produces compact rosettes of oval, pale green leaves which are prominently veined; flowers are only formed when the plants are growing in boggy soil with most of their foliage out of the water. They grow profusely in a compost of sand or gravel and reproduce themselves under water by offsets arising close to the crown of the parent rosettes.

Lobelia dortmanna, the water lobelia, is a curious plant of Europe and parts of America; it inhabits the shallow margins of lakes with soft, rather acid water. From the short vertical stem there arise stout linear dark green leaves which bend horizontally at the tip; each leaf contains two large longitudinal air canals which give the plant buoyancy. The profuse simple white roots are frequently spirally coiled. Under natural illumination the species flowers in early summer, producing from each rosette a single scaly aerial stem bearing several bell-shaped flowers which vary in color from a very pale pink to a rich lilac. A related plant, known by the horticultural name of *Lobelia cardinalis* var. *cardinalis* and originating in South Carolina, is more suitable for tropical aquaria, *L. dortmanna* being acclimated to water temperatures above 18°C only with difficulty. This plant has stout stems bearing oblong to lanceolate leaves and readily forms axillary branches after the removal of the apical buds. When grown in aquaria these two water lobelias should be rooted in a sandy medium. They thrive in any intensity of artificial light—which, however, does not encourage the formation of flowers.

Lobelia cardinalis var. *cardinalis.* Photo by Dr. D. Sculthorpe.

Lobelia dortmanna flowering stems emerging above the surface of the water. Photo by Dr. D. Sculthorpe.

Subtropical and Temperate Plants

Several plants cultivated in tropical aquaria occur naturally, not in the tropics, but in subtropical and temperate regions, and their ability to grow in water at temperatures from 10 to 27°C seems to be due to the fact that they have a much more extensive range of temperature tolerance than do genuine tropical species. The aquarist is able to acclimate them to almost any desired range of water temperature; such species are exemplified by some of the most well-known aquarium plants, *Vallisneria spiralis*, *Egeria densa*, *Lagarosiphon major* and a few species of the genus *Myriophyllum*.

The genus *Vallisneria*, which belongs to Hydrocharitaceae, contains many plants of use to the aquarist. *Vallisneria gigantea* is native to the Philippines and New Guinea and has linear leaves growing to over a yard in length, brilliant translucent green in color and sometimes gently undulated. Its size restricts its use to large aquaria and tropical pools, but it has a wide temperature range, from about 12 to 27°C. *Vallisneria spiralis* is a smaller plant from temperate waters in every continent, and it thrives equally well in coldwater and tropical aquaria. It has linear tapering leaves produced from the short vertical stem, or crown, and reproduces vegetatively by runners

161

above the surface of the substratum which form young plants at the nodes. The leaves of *V. americana* are spirally twisted while those of *V. spiralis* forma *rubriformis* are suffused with a reddish anthocyanin pigment which sometimes slowly disappears under artificial light and is more successfully maintained when the plants are grown in natural illumination and in water at a temperature lower than 21°C.

The pollination mechanism of *Vallisneria spiralis* is an elaboration of that of *Elodea canadensis*. Male and female flowers are borne on separate plants; the solitary female flowers grow up to the surface on the elongated stalks of their spathes. Hundreds of male flowers, each containing two stamens and a small bubble of air, are formed within a spathe near the crown of the plant. When the spathe breaks open, the flowers are released to the surface where each one is ruptured. A man named Scott, the Director of the Calcutta Botanic Gardens, in 1869 reported "seeing under a noonday sun the innumerable florets freed from their spathes and ascending like tiny air-globules till they reach the surface of the water, where the calyx quickly bursts – the two larger and opposite sepals reflex, forming tiny rudders, with the third and smaller recurved as a miniature sail, conjointly facilitating in an admirable manner the florets' mission to those of the emerging females." The heavy female flowers depress the surface film and the males are blown to them, sliding down the slope and rubbing the sticky pollen from the dehiscing stamens onto the stigmas. The developing fruit then sinks through the water, partly due to its own weight and partly to the spiral contraction of the stalk.

The members of Hydrocharitaceae thus show an interesting range of floral structure. Most of the genera have unisexual flowers, but it is only in *Hydrocharis* and *Limnobium* that both sexes occur on the same plant. These two genera, together with *Stratiotes*, have conspicuous aerial flowers pollinated by insects. Other genera such as *Elodea* and *Vallisneria* have male and female flowers on separate plants and effect pollination at the water surface; in a related marine genus, *Halophila*, pollination takes place under water. Only in *Ottelia* do hermaphroditic flowers occur regularly; one species of this genus, *Ottelia ulvaefolia*, is occasionally available to aquarists. It comes from Madagascar and tropical areas of Africa and has translucent furled leaves similar to those of *Aponogeton ulvaceus* but with conspicuous carmine-tinted veins. It is a fragile plant though it has a temperature range of 18 to 32°C and will grow in fine sand or gravel.

Egeria densa, also referred to as *Elodea densa*, is an Argentinian species which adapts itself to tropical or coldwater aquaria or to ornamental pools. Luxuriance of foliage is encouraged by natural illumination; in a tropical aquarium under artificial light the stems grow very rapidly and the leaves are smaller and paler green. Whereas the leaves of *Egeria densa* are arranged on the stem in whorls of four, those of *Lagarosiphon major*, previously known as

Elodea crispa, are not whorled and usually bear short stiff hairs. Although it grows in North Africa in water at a temperature of 24 to 29°C, *Lagarosiphon major* is not as easily acclimated to warm water as is *Egeria densa.*

A large number of species and varieties of *Ludwigia* are known to aquarists. *Ludwigia natans,* originating from the temperate regions of Europe, Asia and North America, is a fast-growing species with a temperature range of 15 to 27°C. Its stout stems bear oval bright green leaves in pairs and it forms branched adventitious roots from the lower nodes. The solitary greenish flowers are formed in the leaf axils only when the plant is growing out of water in damp soil. This species, and the related *L. arcuata,* are easily propagated by cuttings. *L. arcuata* is a less common species with slender stems bearing very narrow tapering leaves of a bronze-green color and with a more restricted temperature range.

There are three genera of aquatic plants with a bushy growth habit and divided leaves occurring naturally in the cool waters of Europe and North America, yet possessing the ability to grow in water at higher temperatures. The genus *Hottonia* contains two species, *H. palustris,* the water violet, and *H. inflata,* a North American plant, which resemble each other in structure, culture requirements and tolerance of temperatures from about 10 to 21°C. The whorled pale green leaves of *H. palustris* are divided into narrower linear flattened segments, and from the apex of the shoot axillary inflorescences grow up into the air under natural illumination in early summer. Each inflorescence bears whitish pink or lilac flowers and is kept erect by a symmetrical whorl of large leaves just below the water surface. The species does not produce any perennating organs; young branches arise from the base of the inflorescence and develop into new plants in the following spring. Both species of *Hottonia* will grow as floating plants or rooted in a sandy, loamy compost.

The hornwort, *Ceratophyllum demersum,* is an interesting pool or aquarium plant of unusual appearance, though the plumes of foliage are rarely as luxuriant in an aquarium as they are out-of-doors when the plant receives sunlight. The species does not form roots and, unless it is desired as a floating plant, should just be anchored in the aquarium gravel. Although the plant is brittle, young bright green leaves are hardened by a covering of cutin. In natural habitats, flowering and pollination frequently occur, but fruits rarely develop, as they require a water temperature of 27 to 32°C to attain maturity, and the plant reproduces mainly by fragmentation and by the production in late summer of dense shoot apices which remain dormant throughout the winter.

Two species of water milfoil, *Myriophyllum verticillatum* and *M. spicatum,* are widely distributed throughout Europe and North America and will thrive in aquaria at temperatures of less than 21°C. From the rhizomes of both species there arise erect branching stems bearing whorls of finely divided leaves, each with about fifteen to thirty segments, and in the summer months aerial spikes carrying male and female flowers which are wind-pollinated. The leaves of *M. verticillatum* are a deep rich green in color and are arranged in whorls of four whereas those of *M. spicatum* are bronze-green and are arranged in whorls of three or five. Toward the end of summer *M. verticillatum* forms club-shaped dark green turions at the apices of axillary branches. The leaves which constitute these turions are small and contain a high concentration of starch and other food reserves; in the spring the turions germinate, forming young plants anchored in the substratum by adventitious spirally coiled roots. Although naturally perennating organs, turions are formed by the plant in conditions of reduced light intensity, lowered temperature and reduced supplies of soluble nutrients.

Myriophyllum spicatum. Photo by R. Zukal.

Myriophyllum spicatum. Photo by R. Zukal.

A Brazilian species of *Myriophyllum, M. proserpinacoides* – the parrot's feather – has become naturalized in parts of North America and is one of the most beautiful aquatic plants. Its growth habit is really semi-aquatic as even when it is rooted its stems grow upward to produce whorls of finely divided bluish green leaves above the water. The leaves show diurnal movements, opening out in bright light and then closing up tightly round the shoot apex as the light fades; this habit is also shown by *Hygrophila corymbosa, Hygrophila difformis, Limnophila sessiliflora* and young plants of *Myriophyllum verticillatum.* As a result of its producing aerial foliage the parrot's feather is more suitable for the tropical or warm pool than for aquaria.

A common feature of aquatic plants is the tendency to produce pigmented foliage under certain conditions. The pigment is usually red or purple and, except in numerous horticultural varieties of water lily of the genera *Nym-*

phaea and *Nuphar,* seems to be formed only in the superficial tissues of the leaves and stems. Species which often develop such pigment include *Bacopa caroliniana, Cabomba caroliniana, Azolla caroliniana* and *A. filiculoides,* several species of *Cryptocoryne* and *Echinodorus, Hydrocharis morsus-ranae, Vallisneria spiralis,* several species of *Ludwigia* and *Myriophyllum spicatum.* There is evidence, though it is sparse, that pigment formation is more conspicuous in plants grown in water at a temperature lower than is normal and subject to intense illumination, but a systematic investigation of the chemistry of these particular pigments and their distribution in aquatic plants is needed.

Vallisneria spiralis. Photo by R. Zukal.

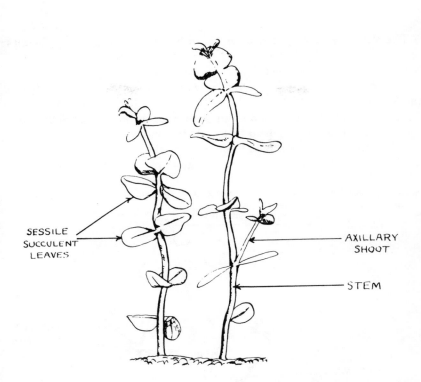

SESSILE
SUCCULENT
LEAVES

AXILLARY
SHOOT

STEM

An example of a fleshy leaved plant propagated by cuttings (*Bacopa* species).

How To Grow Aquarium Plants

The difficulties experienced by many aquarists in cultivating plants are worsened by there being few clear-cut rules or techniques. This is partly because of inadequate experimental data on the influence of physical and chemical factors on the growth of different species and partly because the cultivation of aquatic plants is still based, to some extent, on the myths and misconceptions of the early aquarists. I have previously mentioned techniques of cultivation relevant to the particular species which I described, but it may be useful to discuss these techniques more fully. This survey is neither free from imperfections nor does it present any basically new techniques or ideas, but it does attempt to dispel some of the uncritical and often fantastic notions which, if their prevalence in the aquarium literature is any criterion, still influence aquarists.

167

The structure of a species determines the method of planting. Species which are obtained as cuttings, *e.g.*, species of *Hygrophila, Cabomba, Limnophila, Ludwigia, Hottonia, Myriophyllum, Ceratophyllum, Cardamine, Lysimachia, Bacopa, Elodea, Egeria* and *Lagarosiphon*, should be planted in the following way:

    (i) The leaves should be stripped from the lowermost nodes.

    (ii) The shoots should be loosely tied in groups.

    (iii) Each group should be pressed into the gravel or anchored on the surface of the gravel by attaching a pebble or a piece of lead foil.

A cutting plant with leaves composed of petiole and lamina, and showing palmate venation *(Cardamine* species).

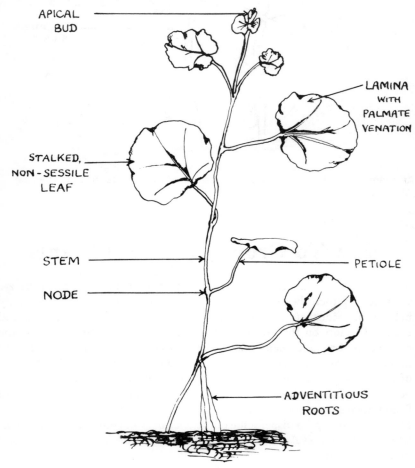

Cardamine bulbosa. Photo by G. Wolfsheimer.

Species of *Fontinalis* may be gathered from their natural habitats with the wiry stems attached to water-worn stones.

Species which are obtained as intact plants should be established as follows:

(i) Species of *Marsilea, Regnellidium, Pilularia, Acorus* and *Hydrocotyle* should have all their roots covered and their creeping rhizomes just beneath the surface of the gravel.

(ii) Species of *Gymnopteris* should also have their roots buried but their rhizomes creeping over the gravel.

(iii) Species of *Sagittaria, Vallisneria, Ceratopteris* and *Lagenandra* should have their roots buried and their short swollen stems, or "crowns," just above the surface of the gravel.

(iv) Species of *Isoëtes, Aponogeton, Nymphaea* and *Nuphar* should have their stout tuberous or corm-like rootstocks just covered by the gravel.

(v) Species of *Echinodorus, Spiranthes, Barclaya, Cryptocoryne, Lobelia* and *Samolus* should have all their roots buried and the leaf bases at or just above the surface of the gravel.

Most aquarium plants have fragile organs, especially genuine aquatic species, the stems and leaves of which possess few strengthening elements and much spongy air-filled tissue, and care is needed in using wooden or metal planting sticks. Planting by hand, being less severe, is to be preferred. The

169

texture of the rooting medium and the nature of the root system affect the efficiency of the planting method. For a species to become speedily established it is essential that it should have the most suitable rooting medium, particularly if the aquarium contains disturbing bottom-feeding fishes.

(i) Many species have deep vigorous root systems and grow well in fine or coarse gravel or very coarse sand.

(ii) Cuttings which have no adventitious roots require a fine gravel, which packs round and weighs down the plant better and facilitates the anchorage of young roots more than does coarse gravel.

(iii) A fine densely packing gravel is also useful for very buoyant species, such as *Lobelia dortmanna.*

(iv) Species which have shallow root systems, *e.g., Eleocharis acicularis,* require a medium to coarse sand.

Roots are never formed by a few species, such as *Ceratophyllum demersum,* and are not induced to form by administering to the plant hormones of the beta-indolyl carboxylic acid series.

Lobelia cardinalis var. *cryptofolia.* Photo by Dr. D. Sculthorpe.

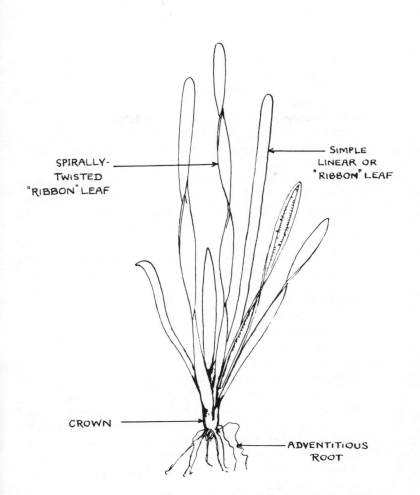

SPIRALLY-
TWISTED
"RIBBON" LEAF

SIMPLE
LINEAR OR
"RIBBON" LEAF

CROWN

ADVENTITIOUS
ROOT

A linear-leaved rooted plant *(Sagittaria* or *Vallisneria* species).

The possible advantages and disadvantages of mixing peat or soil with sand or gravel in the rooting medium have been debated at unnecessary length in the literature and I mention only these points:

    (i) It is not fully known which substances different species absorb from the substratum in which they are rooted and which substances they absorb from the surrounding water. From observations of the thin permeable epidermis of the stems and leaves and the poorly developed roots, several pioneer plant physiologists assumed that aquatic plants absorbed all the necessary inorganic and organic substances directly from the surrounding water. There is no reason to suppose that all species require the same proportions of the different substances or that they all absorb similar relative amounts from the water and the substratum. It is reasonable to assume that aquarium plants which are bog species, growing naturally in rich organic soils, will benefit from the addition of loam to their rooting medium.

(ii) To sterilize loam before using it in an aquarium destroys its value by killing most, if not all, of the microscopic bacteria, protozoa and fungi which convert the organic debris in the soil into a form which can be absorbed by the plants' root-hairs.

(iii) Peat alone is a useless addition since it contains no substances of great value to the plants. It will reduce the pH value of the water and if mixed with soil it will create a more open and less dense compost.

(iv) Sterilized gravel is not completely devoid of inorganic salts useful to the plants.

(v) The decaying leaves and feces which accumulate in the gravel probably supply many of the substances required by the plants.

(vi) An extensive layer of loam beneath the gravel of a large aquarium creates more problems than benefits. Since an undergravel filter cannot then be used, water does not circulate through the rooting medium, which therefore becomes foul and soon needs cleaning out. An undergravel filter normally causes water to circulate through the interstices of the gravel, removing noxious gases such as hydrogen sulphide which are by-products of bacterial action, and it incidentally draws the organic debris down to the roots of the plants.

(vii) Loam may be given to specimen plants grown in pots or to plants which are cultivated in separate aquaria without causing serious problems.

Of the many other factors affecting the growth of aquatic plants, the pH value of the water, light intensity and water movement are often discussed. As many species which are cultivated in nurseries and dealers' aquaria thrive in waters of a wide pH range it may be concluded that the hydrogen ion concentration of the water is not, for them, of prime importance. But the aquarist must not expect plants from temperate waters of extreme pH value either to acclimate themselves to or reach the climax of their life cycle in aquarium water of opposite pH value. For example, specimens of *Lobelia dortmanna* obtained from lakes in which the water may be pH 4 to pH 5 rarely thrive in aquarium water of pH greater than 7.

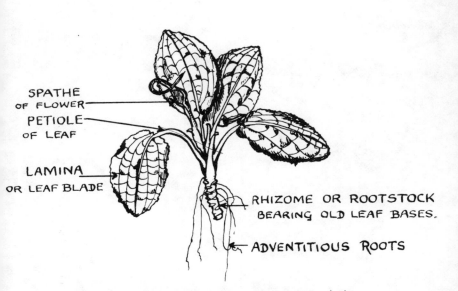

SPATHE
OF FLOWER
PETIOLE
OF LEAF

LAMINA
OR LEAF BLADE

RHIZOME OR ROOTSTOCK
BEARING OLD LEAF BASES.

ADVENTITIOUS ROOTS

Diagram of an aroid species *(Cryptocoryne* species).

With an aquarium containing a variety of species of plants the aquarist attempts to provide an intensity of light which will be conducive to the growth of all the species but which, in fact, may not be the optimum for any one of them. In providing his plants with natural or artificial illumination the aquarist is involved in a conflict between:

    (i) the different optimum intensities of light for different species,

    (ii) the unknown intensity of light which will ensure healthy growth of the majority of species,

    (iii) the rampant growth of filamentous and free-swimming green algae, colonial blue-green algae and diatoms which occurs in intense illumination, and

    (iv) the etiolation of fast-growing species, such as *Egeria densa* and *Lagarosiphon major,* which occurs in poor illumination.

It is important to remember that the intensity of light decreases with increasing depth of water because of reflection from the water surface and absorption by particles in suspension. Floating plants and vigorous submerged plants usually require the brightest illumination. Few species reach the climax of their life cycle, the flowering phase, without some natural illumination.

Cryptocoryne cordata. Photo by R. Zukal.

It has been said that circulation of the water in aquaria is beneficial to plants which occur naturally in flowing waters. Examples of such plants are species of the genera *Myriophyllum, Ceratophyllum, Hottonia, Cabomba, Limnophila* and *Ceratopteris,* all of which have dissected leaves, and *Aponogeton.* Since the character of their foliage does not change in still water, movement of the aquarium water should not be considered essential for their successful cultivation.

Many aquatic plants, especially species of *Cryptocoryne,* lose some or all of their leaves soon after they have been introduced to an aquarium. The cause of this frequently reported phenomenon is not really known, but it has been vaguely suggested that the mechanical shock of transplantation, a difference in water temperature or pH value, or chilling prior to planting could be responsible.

Techniques used for the maintenance of aquarium plants are of three types:
- (i) The trimming of plants.
- (ii) Methods for vegetative propagation.
- (iii) Methods for propagation by seed.

Trimming the foliage of aquatic plants is desirable for:
- (i) Tidiness, but it should not be indiscriminate cutting; rather it should be a systematic removal of old or deformed leaves and shoots.
- (ii) The stimulation of branching, by removing the apical bud of a shoot, so partially eliminating the inhibition of growth of the axillary buds.
- (iii) The prevention of the floating habit in species which are desired for the decorative value of their juvenile, submerged foliage.

Vegetative propagation may be accomplished by two principal methods:
- (i) By taking cuttings from established plants and by dividing rootstocks.
- (ii) By cultivating natural reproductive structures produced by the plants.

Myriophyllum verticillatum. Photo by Dr. D. Sculthorpe.

Gymnopteris species. Photo by Dr. D. Sculthorpe.

Turions and dormant apices of species such as *Myriophyllum verticillatum, Ceratophyllum demersum, Utricularia vulgaris* and *Hydrocharis morsus-ranae* may be collected from wild habitats, ornamental pools or coldwater aquaria later in the year and induced to germinate in water at a temperature of 10 to 12°C. Offsets produced by rosette plants, *e.g., Samolus floribundus,* may be detached from their parents and grown in a sandy compost in shallow water. Young plants produced by stoloniferous species, *e.g., Cryptocoryne* spp. and *Vallisneria* spp., may similarly be detached from their parents and grown in the recommended compost. Plants produced viviparously by *Ceratopteris thalictroides* should be carefully removed from the parent and allowed to float until they have developed strong root systems. Fronds of *Gymnopteris* spp. which are bearing young plants should be left intact and pegged down horizontally on the surface of the gravel so that the offspring may take root without being disturbed. It is important in cultivating rare and slow-growing species, such as *Cryptocoryne thweitesii*, that stolons and offsets should not be detached from the parent until the young plants are sturdy and almost independent.

Propagation by seed is often a long and tedious procedure. The difficulties of obtaining seeds from flowering aquatic plants are several:

    (i) Sexual reproduction is remarkably uncommon in truly aquatic species, particularly those living in deep water, although they are capable of developing the necessary organs.

  (ii) With dioecious species, there may not be available in the aquarium both male and female plants.

 (iii) Natural methods of pollination, by insects, wind, etc., will probably not occur in aquaria, though they probably will occur in outdoor pools.

 (iv) Artificial pollination is not easily accomplished with the small delicate flowers of many species and with the heterostylic condition of a species such as *Hottonia palustris*.

  (v) Even if pollination and fertilization are successful the seeds may not mature.

Aquarium plants are encouraged to flower by raising the temperature of the water, by allowing them sunlight during the later stages of growth and by refraining from pruning those species which naturally form mature floating or aerial leaves. Flowers may not be formed even after the aquarist has made all these three adjustments, or they may arise without him making any of them. Seeds are often formed by self-fertilizing species of *Echinodorus* and by species of *Lagenandra*, *Aponogeton* and *Ottelia*. If the aquarist is lucky enough to have male and female flowers produced simultaneously by a species which has hydrophilous pollination, *e.g.*, *Vallisneria spiralis*, he may also get seeds produced.

Few hybrid aquarium plants have ever been obtained, though over three dozen natural hybrids occur in the pondweed genus *Potamogeton*. The rarity of inter-specific hybrids among aquatic plants is mainly due to:

    (i) The practical difficulties of effecting pollination and fertilization which were mentioned above.

  (ii) The species having different flowering seasons or structurally different flowers which hinder or prevent cross-pollination.

 (iii) The species possessing some physiological incompatibility mechanism which prevents cross-fertilization.

 (iv) The hybrid embryo being inviable or later infertile.

Since those species in which sexual reproduction is rare usually propagate themselves rapidly by vegetative reproduction, the need for the aquarist to attempt to propagate them by seed is questionable.

Further Notes on Aquatic Plants

The following section gives additional information on the genera and species of a number of popular and/or interesting aquatic plants. Many of the genera and species discussed are illustrated in color photos.

ANUBIAS SPECIES / *Water Aspidistras*

The water aspidistras are undoubtedly connoisseurs' plants; they are highly decorative in larger tropical aquaria, but their very slow rate of growth and propagation ensures that commercial supplies are limited and never cheap. The species known to aquarists are few and belong to the small genus *Anubias,* an aroid group related to *Cryptocoryne* and *Lagenandra,* which includes about twelve species in all. They are perennial rhizomatous plants from the bogs, marshes and shaded river banks of rain forests in tropical Africa. For most of the year in their natural habitats they grow above the surface of the water, being submerged for short periods during the rainy season. Yet despite this normal aerial habit they all survive for long periods when submerged in aquaria, though their growth is considerably retarded. This slow growth may be an advantage in large community aquaria, since it obviates the need for frequent pruning, assuring the aquarist of a splendid display of foliage.

The rhizome of *Anubias* is stout and branching, and since fertile seeds are difficult to obtain on the rare occasions of flowering, division of the rhizome provides the principal method of propagation. The rhizome creeps slowly along at or just below the surface of the compost, and care must be taken not to bury it too deeply when specimens are planted in the aquarium. The leaf bases should be just level with the surface of the compost. From the nodes of the rhizome there develop strong adventitious roots which branch profusely within the compost. Specimens rooted only in the shallow barren gravel of the aquarium bed show poor growth; for such sturdy plants a deep root run and an abundant supply of nutrients are essential. It is therefore recommended that specimens should be planted in pots at least 10 cm in diameter and in depth, containing a mixture of equal parts coarse sand, peat and old clay or garden soil, this compost being covered with gravel. In planting, the tough roots should be spread out in the compost, not bunched together, and the specimen should be firmly pressed down, a lighter layer of compost, then gravel, being sprinkled over the rhizome and around the leaf bases.

Species of *Anubias* thrive in soft water of a slightly acid or neutral reaction. The temperature of the water should be above 21°C for most of the year; indeed, these plants will tolerate temperatures as high as 30 to 32°C. For a short period of relative dormancy it is preferable, though not essential, to reduce

A vegetative specimen of *Anubias nana*.

the temperature to within the range of 18 to 19°C. Intensity of illumination appears not to be an important factor in the cultivation of these plants, and they will thrive under artificial lights, even if these are on for only a few hours per day. Strong lighting seems to have no intrinsically harmful effects, though it does lead to the formation of thick "skins" of colonial blue-green algae on the foliage.

If sufficient tank space is available, cultivation of species of *Anubias* under bog conditions is strongly recommended, especially if the specimens purchased from dealers are comparatively young. Under such conditions, mature size and dense foliage are more rapidly achieved, and the resulting specimens may then be submerged in decorative aquaria. Sudden immersion after a prolonged period of aerial growth very rarely causes the disconcerting loss of foliage characteristic of many species of *Cryptocoryne*. Bog conditions may be simulated by keeping the plants potted in a rich compost of the type described above in a fairly deep tank in which the water is approximately level with the tops of the pots. In this culture technique humidity is probably the most important physical factor; the tank must be covered and the atmosphere within as nearly saturated with water vapor as possible, a condition which is readily

Anubias lanceolata. Photo by F. Driessens.

Anubias nana. Photo by R. Zukal.

achieved by passing a vigorous air stream through the water for a few hours each day. Though some authorities state that both air and water temperatures should be as high as 25 to 30°C, I have found that these plants thrive in such tanks if the water is about 23 to 26°C, with the air temperature varying between 20 and 23°C. Under such bog conditions mature plants may reach the climax of the life cycle and produce their inflorescences. Each inflorescence has the characteristic aroid structure, with a spadix bearing the actual flowers surrounded by a fleshy sheath-like spathe. Successful fertilization is followed by the development of small fruits which have a succulent wall and resemble berries.

Only four species are usually available to aquarists, and of these *Anubias lanceolata* is most frequently in commercial supply. It is a handsome plant reaching a height of 38 to 45 cm in cultivation, though wild plants often exceed this size. The lanceolate leaves are rich dark green in color, and each has a prominent midrib and many visible lateral veins. The leaf stalk is often tinted with reddish brown and the leaf blade sometimes curls back slightly along the margins.

Two rare small species, *A. nana* and *A. afzelii*, are admirable specimen plants for smaller aquaria or as foreground plants in larger tanks. Both bear considerable similarities in appearance to species of *Lagenandra*. They vary in height from 10 cm to 20 cm and have strikingly dark green leaves, the blades of which are often borne in a conspicuous horizontal attitude in *A. nana*.

Unlike many amphibious plants, species of *Anubias* show little variation in vegetative structure between aerial and submerged forms; the aerial leaves are slightly thicker, tougher and larger, and their surface has a more conspicuous waxy gloss.

APONOGETON SPECIES / *The Madagascan Aponogetons*

The species of *Aponogeton* which are strictly endemic to the island of Madagascar and a few neighboring smaller islands constitute a remarkable group of aquatic plants. Some of them, such as *A. madagascariensis* and *A. ulvaceus,* have been known to aquarists for many years; others, such as *A. bernierianus, A. henkelianus* and *A. guilotti,* are less familiar. Why these plants should occur only in such a confined range is a problem which has intrigued plant geographers for considerable time.

These species all resemble others of the genus in that they produce their foliage and inflorescences from a tuberous rootstock growing in the substratum. They are suitable for only tropical aquaria and should be cultivated for most of the year in water at a temperature within the range of 18 to 29°C; when the foliage begins to die down the temperature should preferably be reduced to about 13 to 16°C. Available reports suggest that in their natural ranges all the species occur in a wide variety of substrata, from

Leaf form in *Aponogeton:* (1) A very young leaf showing narrow lamina with the whole of the tissue complete. (2) Older leaf with broader lamina and partly fenestrated tissue. (3 and 4) Leaves of a mature plant showing more or less complete fenestration of the tissue.

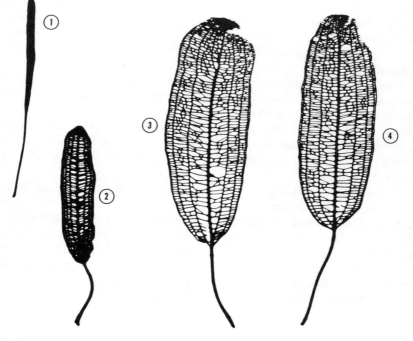

thick organic mud to sand and pebbles. In the aquarium, each specimen should be planted in a flowerpot of 8 to 10 cm diameter which contains a compost of equal parts of coarse sand or gravel and loam or clay. The tuberous rootstock should be firmly buried with its growing point at, and the leaf bases just above, the surface of the compost. There are no reliable data on the influence of the pH value and the hardness of the water upon the growth of these species. The foliage is exclusively submerged, and growth is strong even if the illumination is of low intensity. Adequate space must be afforded, because the large leaves spread outward from the rootstock and soon become tangled and damaged if they are unduly restricted. Given ample space, these and other species of *Aponogeton* provide some of the most magnificent plants available to aquarists.

The general features of the lace plant, *A. madagascariensis*, were described earlier, and it only remains to add that there appear to be at least two forms of this species. The leaves of the most common form seen in aquaria rarely exceed a total length of 30 to 38 cm, the skeletal lamina being from 25 to 30 cm long and the slender petiole from 10 to 12 cm. A less common form has rather longer and much wider leaves with 8 to 12 principal veins, and the midrib of each leaf is sometimes inconspicuous. A third form bears leaves which may attain a length of 30 to 35 cm but a width of only 4 to 5 cm; these leaves are sometimes bluish green in contrast to the more usual olive-green or reddish green color. These different plants, which may be no more than growth forms developed in different prevailing physical conditions, all have the characteristic fenestration of the mature leaves; juvenile leaves, however, often show laminas in which only parts of the interstitial tissue have been lost, giving an irregular "lace" effect. *Aponogeton madagascariensis* occurs principally in Madagascar, but it also occurs in the smaller islands of Sainte Marie and Nossi-Bé.

Aponogeton henkelianus, found in the vicinity of the rivers Betsiboka and Ikopa in the regions of Ankasobe and Antsatrana on Madagascar itself, and *A. guilotti* both resemble *A. madagascariensis* in having skeletal leaves at maturity. *A. bernierianus,* however, resembles the juvenile specimens of *A. madagascariensis* because the leaves show an irregular "lace" effect, much of the interstitial tissue remaining even at maturity. The apex of each leaf is conspicuously pointed.

The fenestration of the leaves of these four species of *Aponogeton* has been the subject of much conjecture and is still not adequately explained. It has been suggested that this structural feature increases the surface area of the leaf available for gaseous exchange in photosynthesis and respiration and that it decreases the resistance of the leaf to the current of flowing water.

The fifth species, *Aponogeton ulvaceus,* occurs as a ricefield weed in central Madagascar; it is nevertheless one of the most beautiful of the genus. The leaves show no fenestration but are membranous and fully translucent. When the plant is mature, each leaf may reach a length of 45 cm or more and a width of up to 15 cm. Its shape is oblong-elliptical and its margins are deeply undulate; indeed, the whole leaf may be spirally twisted. Although the laminas are fragile and easily torn, the petioles on which they are borne are sturdy and fleshy, and the plant as a whole provides a strong and handsome specimen ideal as a centerpiece in a large tropical aquarium.

If allowed to develop to maturity, species of *Aponogeton* bloom quite readily under artificial illumination. The inflorescence of all species is typically aerial and first appears as a greenish elongated cone-shaped structure on a short stalk near the leaf bases. This stalk grows rapidly upward and on reaching the surface of the water it grows horizontally for a short distance before breaking through the surface; the horizontal part of the stalk is wider and more spongy and its buoyancy probably helps to maintain the aerial inflorescence erect. Above the water, the cone-shaped protective hood is shed and the inflorescence itself elongates, the flowers maturing in succession from base to apex. The African (including Madagascan) species of *Aponogeton* differ from others in having an inflorescence which is forked, the two arms diverging like the arms of a lyre. The flowers are often densely crowded on all sides of each arm, each flower usually possessing three petal-like segments, three pistils and six stamens. Among the various species, the flowers are most frequently white, those of *A. madagascariensis* having a pale yellowish tint and those of *A. henkelianus* being pale pinkish violet.

When the aerial inflorescence is produced, as in normal growth, natural pollination does not occur in aquaria and viable seeds are not formed. Occasionally some species, such as *A. madagascariensis,* produce inflorescences whose growth is apparently retarded, so that the stalk remains submerged. Self-fertilization takes place while the flowers are still enclosed in the protective hood. The resulting development of seeds is usually manifest as a swelling of the inflorescence, and the hood is thereby ruptured and shed. The seeds germinate rapidly, even while still attached to the remains of the inflorescence; sooner or later they fall to the substratum and there become rooted. Indeed, the appearance of several dozen tiny seedlings beneath the parent may be the first sign of this whole process that the unsuspecting aquarist notices.

The seedlings are very fragile and sensitive and often die at an age of four to five weeks unless they are carefully transplanted to a more suitable rooting medium. A mixture of equal parts of medium-grain sand and fine loam is recommended; a proprietary brand of good seed compost may also be used. The compost should be spread to a depth of 2 cm in a glass jar or small aquarium and covered with water from the aquarium in which the seedlings have developed. The water should be shallow at first, *i.e.*, about 2 to 4 cm deep, and the depth should be increased gradually as the seedlings develop. The seedlings must be transferred to this container as rapidly as possible; they should be spaced about 2 to 5 cm apart, and the roots of each one should be lightly compressed into the compost. The temperature of the water should be varied as little as possible and should be within the range of 18 to 24°C. When the young plants have reached a height of about 6 to 8 cm they may be transplanted to 5 cm diameter pots.

Although considerable care and patience are essential, the cultivation of such seedlings provides a relatively easy method of propagating these valuable plants. Propagation is otherwise possible only on the rare occasions that a secondary growing point arises on the rootstock, which may be divided when the younger plant has reached a height of from 8 to 13 cm and become vigorous and sturdy.

APONOGETON SPECIES / *The Sinhalese Species*

The genus *Aponogeton* is distributed throughout tropical and subtropical Africa, Asia and Australia, and species from each of these areas have been introduced to aquaria and ornamental pools during the last two decades. Just as one group of species occurs only in Madagascar and its associated islands, so another group appears to be restricted in its natural distribution to Sri Lanka. Three of these species, *A. crispus, A. undulatus* and *A. natans,* are familiar to most aquarists. The cultivation of these and other species is in all respects similar to that of the Madagascan species.

The mature foliage of *Aponogeton crispus* consists of a thick rosette of narrow leaves arising from the terminal growing point of the stout tuberous rootstock. It is, however, one of the smaller species of the genus, and the leaves do not normally exceed a height of 30 cm; hence, the species is of great value in small and medium tropical aquaria. A group of three or four of these plants, spaced about 5 to 8 cm apart, provides a bold and striking feature. The elongated lanceolate leaves are usually bright green and have tightly crinkled margins and finely tapering apices.

Aponogeton undulatus is rather more variable in habit and generally taller at maturity, reaching a height of 50 to 60 cm. The foliage varies in color from pale green to dark green, olive or even bronze. Each leaf is lanceolate, the lamina tapering at its apex and narrowing gradually to the petiole at its base. In contrast to *A. crispus,* the margin of the lamina is gently furrowed, so that the leaf appears to be smoothly undulate rather than crinkled. The lamina is usually between 20 and 40 cm long and from 1 to 5 cm wide at its widest point. In texture it is often more or less translucent. At maturity, and usually prior to flowering, *A. undulatus* produces long-petioled floating leaves which are pale green in color and narrowly lanceolate in shape, reaching a length of 5 to 13 cm and a width of 1 to 3 cm. The inflorescence arises in a manner similar to that of the Madagascan species: when the stalk emerges from the water, the inflorescence itself, which is then about 1 to 2 cm long and hooded, begins to grow, the lowermost flowers opening first. Within three to four days the inflorescence is mature and from 8 to 13 cm long. It resembles the inflorescence of other non-African species of *Aponogeton* in that it is comprised of but a single spike of flowers, which, in *A. undulatus,* are white.

In the early stages of growth, *Aponogeton natans* closely resembles the less common Madagascan *A. ulvaceus* and is, indeed, sold as such by Sinhalese shippers and many aquarium dealers. The earliest leaves are broadly lanceolate to elliptical in shape and quite flat. Later they become more nearly oblong with deeply undulate margins. At the approach of maturity, the submerged leaves are from 20 to 25 cm long and 5 to 8 cm wide. These leaves are borne on stout petioles that are up to 20 cm long. Throughout growth the submerged foliage is pale green and membranous, though rather less translucent than that of *A. ulvaceus.* A fully mature plant also possesses long-petioled floating leaves which are oblong-elliptical in shape and have a rounded tip and abrupt base. They are from 5 to 15 cm long.

The Dutch authority H. W. E. van Bruggen has described a species of *Aponogeton* found in a consignment of plants imported to Amsterdam from the Atweltota in southern Sri Lanka. The species possesses a dark creeping rhizome thickly clothed with fibrous roots. The laminas are borne on angular petioles from 20 to 35 cm long. The lamina, the most notable character of which is its rigidity, which suggested the name *Aponogeton rigidifolius,* is from 25 to 50 cm long, 2 to 2.5 cm wide, narrowly lanceolate in shape and tapering very gradually to the petiole at the base. The texture of the leaves is non-translucent, the color is dark green, and the margins may be flat or shallowly undulate. The inflorescence consists of a single spike about 15 cm long and densely clothed with white flowers.

OTHER APONOGETON

Most of the species of *Aponogeton* that are admired and used by aquarists are strictly tropical and are of no value in cooler aquaria or ornamental pools out-of-doors, unless these are in warm humid localities. There are, however, several species of the genus with a natural distribution extending through subtropical and temperate regions of Africa and Australia, and these show greater tolerance of temperature fluctuations.

The Australian species *Aponogeton loriae* is suitable for cultivation in water

186

at temperatures from 10 to 27°C and may, therefore, be grown either in tropical or in cool aquaria. Its tuberous corm-like rootstock should be firmly anchored in a compost (of equal parts of coarse sand and loam) contained within a flowerpot 8 cm in diameter. It will also grow satisfactorily if it is merely rooted in the bottom gravel of the aquarium, provided that this is no shallower than 6 cm in order not to restrict the profuse adventitious roots which develop from among the leaf bases and grow to a considerable length. The bright yellowish green foliage is almost entirely submerged and arises as a rosette from the growing point of the rootstock. At maturity the overall height of the leaves is from 45 to 55 cm. Each lamina is from 24 to 40 cm long and is borne more or less erect on a sturdy petiole. Apart from their color and rougher texture, the leaves bear a marked resemblance to those of *Aponogeton undulatus*, being lanceolate in shape and having undulating margins. At the time of flowering a few floating leaves may arise. These leaves are borne on long thin petioles and are from 5 to 8 cm long and oblong-elliptical in shape. The aerial inflorescence is from 5 to 10 cm tall and consists of a solitary spike of yellow flowers. As has previously been noted for other species of *Aponogeton*, the inflorescence is produced in aquaria even if the illumination is only artificial. *A. loriae* also resembles other species in requiring adequate space to spread its submerged foliage and in becoming depauperate or incompletely developed if cramped.

One species which is eminently suited to cultivation in heated pools or in pools out-of-doors in temperate countries in summer is *Aponogeton desertorum*, the dog-with-two-tails, which was formerly known as *A. kraussianus* and is distributed in Africa northward from Cape Province to Angola, Ethiopia and Eritrea. Its tuberous rootstock grows in mud and produces long-petioled, leathery floating leaves, each of which is from 8 to 15 cm long, 5 to 8 cm wide, oblong in shape and rounded at both base and apex. In common with other African species, *A. desertorum* produces a twin-spiked inflorescence. The inflorescence stands about 15 cm above the surface of the water, and each arm bears many sweetly scented sulphur-yellow flowers. In southern Africa, together with species of *Nymphaea*, *Aponogeton desertorum* is important as a rampant weed of irrigation dams. It is occasionally imported with other aquatics into the western world and there cultivated in horticultural nurseries. Its cultivation is relatively easy. It should be rooted in an ample volume of a compost of equal parts of loam and clay, to which a little sand and organic manure has been added, contained within a large pot or wire basket and submerged at a depth of not more than about 60 cm. Frost and ice usually kill the rootstock, so it is recommended that the plant be lifted before the winter if it is out-of-doors and stored in damp moss or soil until the following April.

The Cape water hawthorn, *Aponogeton distachyus*, which is native to South

Africa, has been used as an ornamental aquatic for many years and, probably by periodic escape, has become more or less naturalized in numerous localities in western Europe and the U.S.A. Except in very harsh winters, because it is a hardy plant, it need not be removed from an outdoor pool. Its tuberous rootstock is edible, and each spring it produces many floating leaves which quickly spread over the available water surface if conditions are good. Each leaf is about 15 cm long by 4.5 cm wide, oblong-elliptical in shape and rounded at both base and apex. The two arms of the inflorescence sometimes float on the water or stand about 5 cm above it. On each arm there are usually about ten fragrant white flowers, each of which possesses just one petal-like segment and from 6 to 18 jet-black anthers. The petal-like segments are unusually large and stand out laterally from the spike so that each arm of the inflorescence appears much wider in proportion to its length than is typical for other species of *Aponogeton*.

The Cape water hawthorn should be cultivated in a manner similar to that described for *A. desertorum*, and it thrives equally well if it is rooted merely in clay. Its tolerance of different rooting media and of a wide range of temperatures renders it one of the most versatile plants for pools. Another related plant, the blue water hawthorn, *Aponogeton leptostachyus lilacinus*, resembles *A. distachyus* in general structure, differing only in its bluish violet flowers and in not being completely hardy. It may be grown out-of-doors in summer but must be lifted inside with the approach of cooler water. Aquarists possessing large cool or heated tanks may cultivate both water hawthorns as aquarium plants, but some natural illumination is usually necessary to induce flowering, and the specimens must be pruned annually to prevent growth becoming too rampant.

Aponogeton desertorum. Photo by Dr. D. Sculthorpe.

Bacopa amplexicaulis.
Photo by R. Zukal.

BACOPA AMPLEXICAULIS

This plant of the family Scrophulariaceae comes from the southeastern United States and from Central America. In its natural habitat it is found as both an emerged and amphibious plant.

The emerged form has a stem with a diameter of 2 to 4 mm. It grows creepingly, is weakly fuzzy and reaches lengths up to 1 meter in nature. The upper surface of the oval leaves is shiny green, while the underside shows a slight fuzz. The flowers are dark blue. On submerged specimens dark veins stand out on the leaves. The leaves are slightly wavy. The stems may be partly recumbent, so that under good conditions they soon cover a large part of the surface of the tank. Otherwise the plant also reproduces by means of cuttings from parts of the stalks.

Bacopa amplexicaulis is a good aquarium plant, but it needs acid water. Temperatures are of little importance. Direct sunlight is unfavorable, and the species thrives best in shadowy locations. Artificial lighting usually makes it grow up vertically. In order to give it the correct lighting conditions it is advisable to place some floating plants *(Ceratopteris, Salvinia)* on the surface. Growth is not especially quick, but even older leaves keep fresh for long periods. *Bacopa* should be protected against algae infestations; leaves covered with algae quickly rot and drop off. This is one reason why the plant should not be subjected to continuous bright light.

A close relative of the described plant is *Bacopa monniera*. But even a quick glance shows us the difference between the two species. *Bacopa monniera* has very small leaves without clear veins. In tall tanks the stalk may reach the same length as that of *B. amplexicaulis,* but then it loses its lower leaves. Also, it is richly branched out.

Lush stands of *B. amplexicaulis* are very ornamental and impressive. It is good advice not to meddle too much with the plant by moving it from place to place. The species is advisable for hobbyists with some experience.

189

CABOMBA SPECIES / *Fanworts*

The genus *Cabomba* comprises several species of beautiful submerged aquarium plants, some familiar to hobbyists, some new. All the species possess finely divided submerged leaves arranged in opposite pairs or in whorls, and prior to flowering they produce small floating leaves which are undivided and resemble, in miniature, those of water lilies of the genus *Nymphaea*, to which plants the *Cabomba* species are in fact related. Although they are perennial plants tolerating a wide range of temperatures, they are sensitive to harsh changes of conditions and must be cultivated with considerable care.

One of the most frequently grown species, *Cabomba caroliniana*, exists in several varieties, each differing in details of vegetative structure. The submerged foliage of all the varieties varies in color from a purplish brown to a bright green, the purple tints being developed more conspicuously in cooler water under good sunlight. The submerged leaves are paired and divided into segments which have spatulate tips. The most common form in aquaria is *C. caroliniana* var. *paucipartita*, which has comparatively few segments in each leaf, whereas var. *multipartita* when mature has huge leaves divided into many dense segments, each leaf reaching a diameter of 5 to 6 cm. The floating leaves of *C. caroliniana* are narrowly lanceolate; the flowers are white, with a yellowish center.

The submerged leaves of *C. aquatica* are finely divided and paired; the floating leaves differ from those of *C. caroliniana* in being rounded, and the flowers are rich yellow.

In addition to the above *Cabomba* species, three other species have become available to aquarists. *C. australis*, from the Argentine, Chile and Uruguay, has submerged leaves which are very finely divided into many hair-like segments which are bright green, sometimes tinted red on the underside at their tips. The basal segments usually grow at right angles to the petiole, giving the leaf as a whole a semi-circular shape. The floating leaves of this species are ovate to elliptical, and the flowers are white.

From the Caribbean region and South America comes *C. piauhyensis*,

Cabomba species. Photo by Dr. D. Sculthorpe.

which is a more slender and graceful plant than the other species. The submerged leaves are sparsely divided into numerous fine segments which are pale green in color at most temperatures but often suffused with reddish brown in cool water. The flowers are a striking deep mauve, and the floating leaves formed during the flowering phase are linear-lanceolate and acutely pointed.

Whereas most species of *Cabomba* have paired submerged leaves, *C. warmingii* commonly has whorls of three leaves at each node of the stem. The leaves are comparatively small and irregularly divided into many short segments; the color is commonly brownish green, and young growing shoots are brilliant mahogany red.

It is scarcely possible to give details of the overall size of species of *Cabomba*, because they readily adapt themselves to a particular depth of water and may grow to enormous lengths just under the surface. As a result of their habit of growth they are all easily propagated by cuttings taken from the long stems; the formation of adventitious roots from the lower nodes is quite rapid but may be further hastened by stripping off the lowermost leaves before planting the specimen. Once established, the plants may be induced to form bushes of foliage useful for background or side decoration in the aquarium by carefully removing the apical bud of each of the more vigorous shoots.

All the species appreciate a rich compost of equal amounts of coarse sand and clay or loamy garden soil; they do not tolerate very acid water, and they should be left to establish themselves and disturbed as little as possible. Frequent transplanting ruins their growth. In their natural geographical range most of the species extend into subtropical and warm temperate regions and tolerate quite low temperatures, at least during the winter months. Their growth is substantially improved if they are maintained in water at 18 to 25°C for about eight months of the year and at lower temperatures of 10 to 15°C for the remaining time. The more tropical species, such as *C. aquatica*, will of course stand higher temperatures and should not be grown in water at less than about 15 to 17°C. Artificial illumination should be bright; growth becomes more luxuriant if the plants are exposed to some sunlight, at least during the summer months. The finely divided foliage is unfortunately liable to infestation with algae and fine sediment, and care must be taken to prevent this from spreading as soon as it appears. If the water is soft, not above 6 DH, the growth of algae is less troublesome.

Under natural illumination, and occasionally under intense artificial lights, the floating leaves and aerial flowers are produced, even in quite small tanks. The flower stalks show conspicuous post-floral movements, bending over, becoming submerged and eventually pointing vertically downward; this is a common adaptation for dispersal of the fruits, though it frequently occurs even when the flowers have not been pollinated.

CRYPTOCORYNE SPECIES

Many species of *Cryptocoryne* are not easy to cultivate, but the three to be described here, *C. affinis*, *C. becketti* and *C. axelrodii*, have long been known to aquarists, and their sturdy growth in a relatively wide variety of conditions recommends them as suitable for novices. All species of *Cryptocoryne* must be handled with care. They should be potted in a compost containing soil or clay, peat and sand with the growing point of the rhizome at the surface of the compost. Their foliage must not be harshly cut back, and the plants must be left undisturbed, as they are rather slow in establishing themselves. The

The structure of the inflorescence of *Cryptocoryne:* A. Anterior view of the inflorescence: 1. Limb, or "flag", of the spathe. 2. Collar. 3. Throat. 4. Entrance to spathe. 5. Tube or duct of spathe. 6. Pod, or "kettle." 7. Peduncle, or "stalk." B. Posterior view of the inflorescence: 1. Limb, or "flag." 2. Tube, or duct. 3. Pod, or "kettle." 4. Peduncle, or stalk. C. Vertical section through the pod: 1. Opening from tube. 2. Flap covering entrance to pod. 3. Stamens. 4. Wall of pod. 5. Ovaries. 6. Peduncle, or stalk.

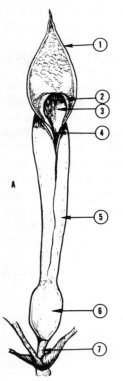
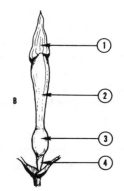
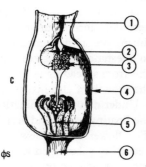

temperature of the water should normally be between 20 and 27°C; the illumination should be of low to medium intensity.

Cryptocoryne affinis, which reached Europe over forty years ago through the German importer Haertel, is one of the few species particularly suited to submerged growth; indeed, it usually deteriorates if its foliage is exposed above the water. From the creeping rhizome arise handsome lanceolate leaves to a height of 25 to 30 cm. The petiole is approximately equal in length to the lamina and is usually brownish red. The lamina, the margin of which is often slightly undulated, has a rich bluish green upper surface which frequently shows a silken sheen; the midrib and principal lateral veins are conspicuously pale, sometimes almost white. The leaves of mature specimens display a dark reddish purple lower surface, but this pigmentation is incomplete or is absent from young plants. The inflorescence of this species is usually produced on specimens growing in shallow water; its spathe normally opens just above the water surface, rarely while still submerged. The flag of the spathe is dark red and has a long tapering tip. The growth of *C. affinis* tends to be suppressed by intense illumination and is most luxuriant in shade; the species is therefore particularly suitable for the foreground, where it is likely to be overshadowed by taller specimens. In such positions it rapidly covers all the available area by forming many stolons which grow horizontally through the bottom gravel, rooting and forming young rosettes of foliage at their nodes.

The Sinhalese species *C. beckettii* reaches a mature height of 10 to 12 cm when growing submerged. The robust rhizome, which may grow more or less erect, produces a dense cluster of leaves which seem to attain greater size and better color in slightly acid water and diffuse illumination. The petiole of each leaf is brownish and bears an elongated lanceolate to elliptical lamina, the upper surface of which is always olive-green to greenish brown, whereas the lower surface is often brownish purple. As was noted for *C. affinis*, these purplish and brownish tints become deeper with increasing age. The margin of the lamina is usually widely furrowed and partly folded back, and the principal veins are sometimes purplish on the upper surface. *C. beckettii* is also one of the easiest species to grow in bog conditions. Its aerial leaves are notably shorter and broader than the submerged ones. The species very rarely blooms when it is growing submerged; inflorescences may, however, appear on emergent plants growing in natural light or good artificial light for several hours each day. The flag of the spathe is greenish to ochre yellow, whereas its throat is at first dark chocolate brown and after two to three days more reddish brown. When the spathe opens, the flag, the left margin of which has irregular indentations, stands erect, but toward the end of the blooming period it bends over backward.

Cryptocoryne axelrodii is one of the most freely available and least expensive species of the genus. In coloring and habit its foliage is somewhat variable,

Anubias nana   [Dr. D. Terver]

194

Bacopa amplexicaulis   [R. Zukal]

199

velvety purple. This coloration goes down to the widest point of the kettle, from whence it proceeds downward in the form of thin long stripes consisting of light red to purple dots disposed in regular rows. The tube of the inflorescence has the same width as the upper part of the kettle, which makes *C. pontederifolia* an exception within its genus. The spathe is opened vertically, very short, and shows a striking warty wine-red. The mouth of the tube is dark purple, also warty. The sheath is extended into a long erect little tail-like appendage which grows ever longer when the other parts of the flower are together. The walls of the kettle as well as of the tube are fleshy, very thick and brittle. The inflorescence is very attractive and interesting due to its huge size, and its many-colored hues reinforce this impression.

Reproduction is mostly achieved from emergedly cultivated plants. *C. pontederifolia* is one of the species on which the young do not grow directly out of the rootstock but come from offshoots. Out of its roots one parent plant **generally puts forth two or three shoots, on each of which originates a new** plant at a distance of 8 to 12 cm. Sometimes such offshoots continue growing further on, so that one single branching-out gives origin to two or three plants which in turn are able to grow independently and to divide into new specimens. Considering the fact that the species is sensitive and relatively rare, it is not advisable to cultivate it emergedly in the terrarium but rather to propagate it in special tanks in its emerged form. This is the only way of getting it to reproduce quickly.

When cultivated in the aquarium, *C. pontederifolia* should be kept in very clear soft water at temperatures of 20 to 25°C, with a pH of 5 to 6.5 and under diffused lighting. The plant makes a very decorative centerpiece if planted in groups of three to five specimens. In winter it is advisable to adjust the supplementary lighting in a manner that the plants receive twelve hours of light each day. Otherwise during these shortened days it tends to lose its leaves, stops growing and only revives in spring—if the relatively little-branched rootstock has not died in a tank with insufficient lighting.

CRYPTOCORYNE SPIRALIS

Usually considered a slow grower and not much of a plant to look at, even though it is a member of the popular plant genus *Cryptocoryne*, *Cryptocoryne spiralis* is not a truly popular aquarium plant, although it finds its way into the tanks of specialists from time to time. In some ways the long tapering leaves make the plant look more like a *Vallisneria* species than a *Cryptocoryne* species; the flower and spathe form, of course, make it unquestionably a *Cryptocoryne* despite its superficial resemblance to plants of other genera; the flowering apparatus of *C. spiralis* is, as a matter of fact, among the most eye-pleasing of all *Cryptocoryne* species, providing the small bit of distinction that the plant has. It is native to India, where it grows mostly in swamps that are only occasionally flooded.

The rootstock of *C. spiralis* is very strong and richly equipped with branches that bear five to 10 relatively long leaves. The leaves and stems are up to 35 cm long; the green leaves are elongatedly elliptical, often nearly in the shape of ribbons, measuring 10 to 20 cm in length by 1 cm to 2.5 cm in width. Both sides of the leaves show a fresh green, the lower side being of a slightly lighter hue, and the leaves have a strikingly protruding central vein, while the lateral veins are nearly indistinguishable. The leaves taper at both ends, gradually melding into the leaf stalk at the basal end.

In fish tanks *C. spiralis* grows very slowly. It demands good illumination, preferably locations that receive direct sunlight during part of the day at least. If placed at darker or shaded spots it develops thin leaves and does not resemble the other species of the genus at all. It needs slightly acid to neutral water and temperatures above 20°C.

Specimens that are chosen to preserve and reproduce the species are best kept in an aquarium that is covered with a glass pane or a sheet of clear plastic. A fit substratum is peat moss fertilized with the usual plant foods, which should not contain any calcium derivatives. The plant is fertilized by means of an admixture of mineral solutions to the water according to the manufacturer's instructions. Under such conditions *C. spiralis* develops quite well; within a year a single parent plant may produce five to 10 offspring, which always grow from offshoots of the roots. These descendants only come directly from the rootstock. The offshoots often grow to a distance of up to 40 cm from the parent plant, and each of them puts forth one or (rarely) two new offshoots and plants.

If cultivated in this way, *C. spiralis* blooms easily and the plant gives origin to new inflorescences at intervals of three to six weeks. The flowers contain aromatic bodies that smell like roses.

ECHINODORUS SPECIES / *Amazon Swordplants*

The species of *Echinodorus* whose habit of growth and leaf shape place them within the popular designation of Amazon swordplants may be divided on the basis of overall size into two groups: the larger specimen types and the dwarf types. The larger species, including *E. paniculatus, E. amazonicus* and *E. berteroi,* reach a mature height of 25 cm or more and so are suited only to larger aquaria. The dwarf types, including *E. grisebachii, E. tenellus* and the newest introduction, *E. andrieuxii,* are suitable for all tropical aquaria and are particularly useful in the foreground, where they quickly form a carpet-like thicket of foliage.

Cryptocoryne nevillii [R. Zukal]
Cryptocoryne pontederifolia sarawacensis [T. J. Horeman]

Cryptocoryne siamensis var. *ewansii*   [R. Zukal]
Cryptocoryne spiralis   [R. Zukal]

Many species of *Echinodorus* are heterophyllous; this habit is notably illustrated by *E. berteroi*, which is sometimes known as the cellophane plant in allusion to its translucent foliage. This species occurs as a perennial swamp plant in the central and southern United States, the West Indies and Central America. It has a compact rootstock which may be split quite easily, and when submerged it first produces linear then lanceolate leaves, each with a short petiole and growing to a length of 20 to 30 cm. With increasing age the petiole becomes comparatively longer and the lamina shorter and broader until the mature cordate shape is attained in floating and aerial leaves. At maturity the inflorescence, composed of small white flowers, may be produced in good illumination; if this is kept submerged young plants often develop on it. The species produces no runners and should be rooted in a rich compost of coarse sand, soil and some peat: it tolerates temperatures above about 19 to 20°C and thrives in light of high intensity.

E. paniculatus is the species to which the popular name of Amazon swordplant was probably originally applied. The pale green lanceolate leaves have pointed tips, and the tissue of the lamina runs along part of the petiole at the base. The leaves are usually arched so that the plant forms a striking large rosette of foliage. Submerged specimens very rarely produce an inflorescence; if this does form, the flowers usually fail to mature, and young plants arise at intervals along the stalk, which may therefore be anchored to the aquarium gravel until the plants have become established. The species is widely distributed as an amphibious plant throughout much of the tropics and subtropics of South America. Two varieties of the normal species are commonly available to aquarists: *E. paniculatus* var. *rangeri* and *E. paniculatus* var. *gracilis*. *E. paniculatus* var. *rangeri* has noticeably broader leaves, whereas var. *gracilis* has linear to linear-lanceolate leaves. Specimens of all three attain a mature height of 40 to 50 cm and should be planted in 10 cm pots containing a compost of sand, clay or loam, and a little peat. In correspondence with their normal geographical range, these plants tolerate a wide range of temperatures, from about 18 to 32°C. Illumination need not be of high intensity.

The Amazon swordplant *E. amazonicus*, occurring in Brazil, is a smaller species which reaches a height of 25 to 38 cm. It is otherwise structurally similar to *E. paniculatus*, with pointed lanceolate leaves when it is growing in water. The aerial leaves have longer petioles and shorter, broader laminas with the venation in conspicuous relief on the lower surface. When the plant is partly or wholly above the water it produces a sturdy inflorescence as much as 60 cm in height. Submerged, its habit resembles that of *E. paniculatus*, since young plants are frequently formed on the flower stalks; its culture is also similar.

The three dwarf species of swordplant reproduce vegetatively by forming young rosettes at the nodes of fast-growing runners, several of which may be produced from the compact rootstock of a single parent. Indeed, once they are established these species often spread with embarrassing profusion, even if they are rooted only in gravel or coarse sand. Because of this tolerance of a less rich rooting medium it is unnecessary to pot specimens. However, they grow to greater size if the rooting medium is enriched by some soil or clay. All three species thrive as foreground plants even if they are overshadowed by taller plants and the light they receive is of very low intensity. They appear to be equally tolerant of different degrees of hardness in the water.

E. grisebachii is a perennial bog species from Central America; growing above water in natural habitats, it reaches a height of 15 to 20 cm, the leaves being dark green, pointed and elliptical to lanceolate. Submerged in aquaria, it rarely attains this size and its leaves are more commonly narrower; the shape is nevertheless variable, and broad-leaved and narrow-leaved forms are frequent. The temperature of the water should be between 21 and 29°C.

E. andrieuxii is also a vigorous grower, quickly forming numerous runners. The bright green sessile leaves are linear and spiky in young specimens, broader and arched in more mature ones. Young plants arising at the nodes of runners form many adventitious roots and soon establish themselves.

Often referred to as the pygmy chain swordplant, *E. tenellus* has been known to aquarists for many years; it has a vast geographical range, being distributed throughout much of North, Central and South America. In natural habitats the species rarely grows taller than 10 cm, and in tropical aquaria its height is most commonly 2.5 to 5 cm. The pale green narrow pointed leaves grow densely in arched rosettes, and by vegetative reproduction the species rapidly weaves a thick carpet over the compost. In the different regions of its natural range annual coldwater and perennial tropical forms probably occur; as a consequence of the extension of its distribution through temperate as well as tropical habitats, it tolerates a wide range of temperatures in aquaria and will grow well in water as cool as 7 to 10°C.

Although numerous species of *Echinodorus* have been cultivated extensively, *E. muricatus*, the Amazon spearplant, and *E. maior*, the ruffled swordplant, are still comparatively rare in commercial supplies, especially in European countries. Both species are large and produce superb rosettes of foliage, and they are consequently highly prized specimen plants for tropical aquaria. In both habit and general structure they differ markedly from other members of the genus; they do, however, resemble other species in being perennial and in producing their foliage from a stout rootstock. They both adapt themselves readily to submerged growth and usually thrive in aquaria if they are given a rich deep rooting medium and illumination of medium to high intensity.

The popular name of *Echinodorus muricatus* indicates the shape of its mature leaves, each of which may attain a height of 35 to 40 cm. The petiole, which is stout and fleshy, varies in length from 15 to 25 cm and the lamina

Echinodorus parviflorus

[R. Zukal]

Echinodorus andrieuxi　　　　　　　　　　　　　　　　[R. Zukal]
Echinodorus andrieuxi　　　　　　　　　　　　　　　　[R. Zukal]

from 12 to 20 cm, the petiole normally being more or less erect and bearing the lamina at an inclined angle or even in a horizontal position. The vivid green lamina is shaped like the blade of a spear, with a finely tapering apex and an abrupt slightly rounded base; the only variation is in its width, juvenile leaves being relatively narrower than mature ones. There are from five to eleven principal lateral veins departing from the midrib at the base of each lamina. When fully established, the plant spreads its leaves to receive the maximum light and so forms a bold and handsome specimen ideal for central siting in the aquarium.

The ruffled swordplant, *Echinodorus maior,* bears a certain superficial resemblance to *Aponogeton undulatus,* from which its foliage may easily be distinguished by the blunter tips and the venation of the leaves. Each leaf is narrowly lanceolate, almost strap-like, and may attain a height in mature specimens of 40 to 50 cm and a width of from 3 to 5.5 cm. The lamina is usually eight to ten times longer than the petiole, which rarely exceeds 8 cm. The leaf tissue is somewhat translucent, especially in newly formed leaves, but this appearance is likely to be misleading, because both the lamina and petiole are characteristically tough and not easily broken. Other than the shape of the mature leaves, the feature which most clearly distinguishes this species from others of the genus is the beautifully furled margin of the lamina, to which the popular name of the plant alludes.

Both *E. muricatus,* which is native to northern regions of South America, and *E. maior,* which is indigenous to Brazil, tolerate a relatively wide range of temperatures in aquaria, provided these vary toward greater rather than less heat, *i.e.,* from about 21-22°C to 30-32°C. Probably the most important aspect of their cultivation is the nature of the compost, which must be rich in organic and inorganic nutrients because a dearth of these results in depauperate specimens. A compost of two parts weathered clay or good garden soil, one part coarse sand and one part peat moss, well mixed to give a good crumb structure, is recommended for both species. The compost should be contained within a pot, the size of which depends largely on the age of the specimen when it is obtained. Young plants 5 to 13 cm tall may be planted in 5 to 6 cm diameter pots, but they will need transplanting to larger pots after about three months. Older and mature specimens must be in pots 5 cm or more in diameter, and the depth of the compost must not be less than 5 cm, because both species produce many strong adventitious roots which grow to a considerable length and soon become pot-bound. Propagation of both *E. muricatus* and *E. maior* is extremely difficult because flowers are produced only very rarely, even in good conditions in aquaria receiving natural light. Young plants will develop adventively on the stalk of the inflorescence if this is kept submerged; even if flowers develop, viable seeds are rarely formed, and although they germinate very quickly the seedlings themselves grow slowly and take over eighteen months to reach a height of 4 to 5 cm. Occasionally the rootstock branches and a young rosette is formed at the side of the parent; should this occur, the young plant must not be removed until it has reached a height of 5 cm or more. If the roostock is divided before this time, the young plant would be insufficiently vigorous to establish itself, and the health of the parent would also possibly be impaired. Since these two species are rare and valuable, the aquarist attempting to propagate them should exercise great patience and care.

THREE LARGE SPECIES OF ECHINODORUS

Upon seeing in their natural habitats mature specimens of the species of *Echinodorus* they cultivate in their tropical tanks, most aquarists would express considerable amazement at the remarkable differences of size and sometimes vegetative structure. Most species of this genus are perennial swamp plants growing with most of their foliage above the waterline. When they are cultivated as entirely submerged specimens, their leaves often become more slender and their maximum height often as little as one-half to two-thirds that which they attain in natural habitats. Nowhere is this overall difference in size between submerged and bog specimens more clearly seen than in three uncommon species, *Echinodorus macrophyllus*, *E. grandiflorus* and *E. argentinensis*, which are occasionally available to aquarists and are ideal for either the larger aquaria of the connoisseur or aquaterraria and garden pools.

The general technique for the cultivation of these three species is identical to that recommended for *Echinodorus maior* and *E. muricatus*. The need for both adequate space in which the foliage may spread and adequate depth for the unrestricted development of the root system cannot be over-emphasized. When submerged, all three species reach a height of 40 to 50 cm and to attempt to stunt specimens to a smaller size in order to keep them in aquaria of small and average dimensions often leads to a serious deterioration of the plants and, therefore, is not recommended. Illumination should be of high intensity and should preferably be supplemented with some sunlight, at least during the season of active vegetative growth. In garden pools in warm districts all three species may flower, producing aerial stalks bearing small blooms which may give rise to viable seed. The inflorescence of *E. grandiflorus* is particularly notable. It grows to a height of 1.5 m or more. In aquaria flowering is very rare, and even if an inflorescence is produced, seeds only occasionally develop. Plantlets are frequently produced, however, if the stalk of the inflorescence is submerged; these plantlets should either be allowed to develop to about 4 to 5 cm tall and then separated and planted, or they should be pegged down to the aquarium gravel from the time that they

Echinodorus maior [R. Zukal]
Echinodorus maior [R. Zukal]

Echinodorus grandiflorus
Echinodorus grandiflorus

[H. Schultz]
[T. J. Horeman]

appear. Very infrequently, the rootstock of these species forms a short lateral branch at the growing point of which a young rosette of foliage arises. The temperature of the water in which these three species are grown should be within the range 21 to 29°C, and it is beneficial, though not essential, for the natural rhythm of growth of the plant if this is reduced to 18 to 21°C for about three months annually.

The South American *Echinodorus grandiflorus* reaches a height of about 45 cm under water, though considerably more when it is emersed. It has a very stout rootstock from which arises a rosette of tough, handsome leaves of a rich mid-green color. There is little variation of leaf shape, the juvenile leaves being slightly narrower. The petiole is usually rather longer than the lamina, which is flat, oval to elliptical, and bears nine to fifteen prominent veins in relief on the lower surface.

Young specimens of the Brazilian *Echinodorus macrophyllus* bear a superficial resemblance to *E. muricatus* by virtue of the elongated elliptical or spear-shaped leaves. As the plant matures, however, the basal half of each leaf becomes proportionately wider so that the shape becomes more nearly cordate or even sagittate. The margin of the lamina is sometimes slightly furled and the basal part of each side of the lamina frequently stands out at an angle from the rest of the leaf. In addition to the midrib there are from eight to twelve principal lateral veins on each lamina and these are very conspicuous on the lower surface. The color of the leaves varies from pale to vivid green.

Echinodorus argentinensis, also native to Brazil, differs from other species in having very long petioles, a habit which may be of advantage in aquaria possessing a thick carpet of vegetation. Above water the petiole may attain a length of 50 cm, bearing a lamina some 18 to 23 cm long, but when the plant is submerged the overall length of the leaf rarely exceeds 38 to 45 cm. Juvenile leaves usually possess narrowly elliptical laminas, tapering very gradually at both base and apex; at maturity, the lamina is relatively wider, being broadly elliptical or roughly melon-shaped.

ECHINODORUS LATIFOLIUS

This plant, native to Central and South America, is a member of the family Alismataceae. Europeans have known this species for a long time under the erroneous name of *Echinodorus magdalensis. Echinodorus latifolius* is numbered among the smaller species of its genus, and certain stages of its development are very similar to those of other related species, such as *E. tenellus, E. austroamericanus* and *E. quadricostatus.* In its emerged form it is very suitable for stocking the larger and more compact parts of aquaterraria. Each plant develops 10 to 15 leaves which are disposed as rosettes. These leaves reach lengths of 10 to 15 cm and widths of 5 to 10 mm. Sometimes they are nearly stalkless, while on other occasions they change over slowly into shorter or longer leaf stalks.

Echinodorus latifolius is one of the ornamental plants which is most easily kept in our tanks. It will grow in very poor soil; that is, in pure washed sand, where it thrives reasonably well but reproduces very slowly. On the other hand, it is not affected by excesses of organic matter, which means that you can cultivate it in tanks with abundant nutrients and a large detritus content. It is not a typically tropical plant either, adapting quite well to the shorter days of the Temperate Zone. This also includes it in the group of those plants whose submerged forms develop quite well in winter without receiving additional lighting, meaning at spots where the duration of daylight is not extended artificially. *E. latifolius* is even more ornamental in winter than in summer, when it generally shows shorter leaves and reproduces abundantly.

Like that of all the smaller species of the genus, the reproduction of *E. latifolius* takes place by means of offshoots of the roots in the same manner as the reproduction of *Vallisneria*. Each of these shoots gives rise to from 10 to 20 new plants which may be cut off so that they grow a root system of their own.

Echinodorus latifolius is very suitable for stocking the front and central parts of fish tanks. It is advisable, though, to fence off its location with rocks in order to avoid excessive proliferation with the consequent spreading out to other spots in the aquarium intended to be occupied by other plants. If such spots are not fenced off, *E. latifolius* can be counted on to spread over the whole tank, especially in summer time, and you will only be able to hold it in bounds by means of the systematic elimination of its offspring.

This swordplant multiplies most quickly at temperatures that range from 25 to 30°C, but it also withstands lowerings of the thermometer down to 15°C without being harmed. Water chemistry is an absolutely secondary matter, and the intensity of the lighting is not important either. But under extensive lighting or at locations which receive direct sunlight, the submerged forms remain shorter than those growing at shadowy places. Contrarily, plants that are cultivated in emerged form in aquaterraria do quite well with plenty of light.

ELODEA DENSA

This widely distributed aquatic plant belongs to the family Hydrocharitaceae, which includes among others the genus *Vallisneria*, despite the fact that the external disposition of the plant body differs considerably from that of *Vallisneria*. *Elodea densa*, the best-known plant in the genus,

Echinodorus latifolius   [R. Zukal]
Echinodorus latifolius   [R. Zukal]

Echinodorus macrophyllus
Echinodorus macrophyllus

Elodea densa. Photo by R. Zukal.

ranges from the southeastern United States to Argentina. It is found over almost all the subtropical and tropical areas of the New World.

It is the largest representative of its genus. The stalk with its fork-like branchings generally is richly and densely covered with leaves and reaches lengths up to 3 m. From the spots where it branches out, the stalk sends out unbranched white roots which serve either to attach it to the bottom or to absorb nutritional substances directly from its aquatic surroundings.

The deep green leaves generally are disposed in whorls of five. They are narrow-lanceolate and, depending on the conditions under which they grow, reach lengths of 16 to 35 mm, with widths of 3 to 5 cm. At first glance the edges seem apparently smooth, and only if you examine them under a magnifier or hold them up against the light will you see that they are slightly serrated.

Elodea densa shows the rare capacity to absorb nutrition through its whole surface, but especially through the leaves. The real function of the roots is only that of anchoring the plant to the bottom. This means that you can keep the plant in your tanks as a floating plant or as one that is rooted down. Both free-floating and rooted specimens send the most densely leaf-covered parts of their shoots upward, where they stay just below the surface. There they form a dense thicket which serves as a hiding place for newly born fry of livebearers, while at the same time it represents a very convenient spawning medium for many species of fishes. Even anabantoids like to seek out these dense entanglements in order to build their bubblenests there.

Elodea densa rarely blooms in a tank, and it is quite probable that very few aquarists ever come to see its flowers. In larger tanks in hothouses, the plant blooms from May to August. The 23 to 35 mm flower stems grow out of the leaf insertions and end in a single male flower with three white crown leaves, in the center of which one notices yellow pollen leaves. The flowers have an average diameter of 10 to 23 mm and float on the surface of the water, out of which they grow occasionally to heights of 10 to 23 mm above the water. According to present experience, female flowers have never grown under artificial cultivation in tanks.

Elodea densa is able to withstand extremely hard water and has a reputation for being able to soften hard water in which it is kept, supposedly because of the plant's capacity to extract calcium salts from the water. The closely related *Elodea canadensis*, incidentally, was long used in Europe as a water purifier, especially a decalcifier, and planted in pools formed by run-off from paper mills and distilleries. Both *E. densa* and *E. canadensis* therefore are well suited as decorative plants in hard-water tanks.

There is a considerable difference in leaf coloration between *E. densa* specimens grown in soft water and those grown in hard water, the hard-water plants being a much deeper green. Soft-water plants are more yellowish green than deep green. The texture of the plant varies according to its water also, soft-water plants (both leaves and stems) being much more brittle.

Elodea densa is much less tolerant of bad lighting conditions than it is of widely fluctuating temperatures. It will take cold water very well, but it will not take poor lighting. For good growth, it must have sufficient illumination.

Elodea nutalli

Heteranthera reniformis
Heteranthera reniformis

[T. J. Horeman]
[R. Zukal]

HETERANTHERA SPECIES

Fast-growing plants which may be manipulated to produce thickets of foliage and propagated rapidly by cuttings are of great value in aquaria. Starting from relatively few and inexpensive specimens, the aquarist may soon obtain a vast stock of plants which may be arranged in groves to conceal the background and sides of the aquarium and to provide a decorative curtain against which other large solitary plants may be seen to better advantage. Among the more common examples of such versatile aquarium plants are species of *Hygrophila, Ludwigia, Bacopa, Myriophyllum* and *Limnophila,* but there are two less well-known species of *Heteranthera* which may be used to similar effect.

The genus *Heteranthera,* which belongs to the same family as the water hyacinths and pickerel weeds, the Pontederiaceae, comprises some ten tropical and subtropical amphibious plants inhabiting swamps and temporarily flooded areas in parts of the American and African continents. Just two of these ten species, *Heteranthera zosterifolia* and *H. dubia,* are in frequent supply. Both have a wide range of temperature tolerance and may be grown in temperate as well as tropical aquaria (*i.e.,* in water at temperatures from about 17 to 32°C). They are able to withstand lower temperatures for short periods, but in general their growth is more consistent in warmer water so that they are popularly regarded as tropical species.

Naturally rhizomatous plants, they are normally obtained in the form of cuttings taken from the vigorous erect shoots. To accelerate the formation of adventitious roots, the lowermost five or six leaves should be carefully removed from each cutting. Groups of three or four cuttings should then be pressed gently but firmly into a compost of equal parts of coarse sand and loamy soil contained within 5 cm diameter pots and covered with a thin layer of aquarium gravel or coarse sand. Establishment of the plants is fairly rapid under most conditions, but it is preferable that this early cultivation be in water at a temperature of from 21 to 24°C and in bright illumination. The origin of lateral shoots from the nodes near the surface of the compost soon follows, and it may be induced elsewhere along the active ascending stems by nipping the apical bud. Once the plants have begun to thrive, they may be transplanted to their permanent positions or, alternatively, used as a source of further cuttings.

For the long-term cultivation of both species in established aquaria, the compost of sand and soil is recommended as a rooting medium. Both species will, however, grow well when they are rooted in coarse sand or gravel, particularly if this contains organic detritus, as indeed it would on the bed of an aquarium which has not been overhauled for some time. Illumination should be bright to intense; some sunlight encourages more luxuriant growth, but

Heteranthera zosterifolia. Photo by Dr. D. Sculthorpe.

flowering often occurs under artificial light alone. If the species are to be used in cool water, the temperature of the water must be lowered gradually, for although both species are fairly hardy and less sensitive than many aquatic plants, a sudden drop in temperature has an adverse effect on the photosynthesis, respiration and other metabolic processes of the plant.

Heteranthera zosterifolia, the water stargrass indigenous to Bolivia and Brazil, is the slower growing of the two species. Submerged, its stems are rather brittle and the internodes are short, so that the opposite or alternate leaves are closely arranged. Each leaf is sessile, linear to narrowly lanceolate, and pale yellowish green in color. It attains a length of 5 to 8 cm and a width of up to 6 mm. Unless arrested the stems continue to strive upward through the water, eventually growing horizontally beneath the surface and producing small stalked orbicular leaves which float on the surface and help to maintain the rather inconspicuous pale blue flowers in the air above. When the plant is grown with its foliage above the water-line, the leaves are glossy, shorter and darker green, and their tips are rounded instead of pointed. The popular name "stargrass" alludes to the appearance of the apex of the shoot viewed from above.

Heteranthera dubia is more nearly a genuine aquatic. It may be grown above the water-line only with difficulty. Its stems are stouter than those of *H. zosterifolia,* and the internodes are relatively longer so that numerous cuttings must be planted together to avoid a straggly appearance. The leaves are linear, sessile, often reflexed, from 5 to 13 cm long and up to 6 mm wide. Both leaves and stems vary in color from a pale, almost translucent green through olive-green to coppery bronze. Whereas the adventitious roots from the nodes of *H. zosterifolia* are branched and usually in tufts, those of *H. dubia* are solitary and unbranched. The shoots of *H. dubia* reach tremendous lengths, hugging the surface of the water and producing golden yellow aerial star-shaped flowers. This species thrives even when it is densely planted, and it is particularly recommended for the back and corners of the aquarium.

221

Heteranthera limosa
Heteranthera reniformis

[Dr. Jiri Stodola]
[Dr. Jiri Stodola]

222

Hydrocleis nymphoides

HYDROCLEIS NYMPHOIDES / *Water Poppy*

Most of the submerged aquatic plants cultivated by aquarists produce flowers only rarely under artificial illumination, and even these rare occasions are liable to be anticlimactic because the flowers are often inconspicuous and uninteresting. With the exception of several dwarf species of *Nuphar, Nymphaea* and *Nymphoides,* nearly all the aquatic plants which do produce splendid blooms are too large to be cultivated in aquaria. The water poppy, *Hydrocleis nymphoides,* is one of the very few plants whose size, habit of growth and readiness to bloom are all amenable to cultivation in tropical aquaria, and it is a great pity that the species is uncommon in the stocks of many commercial suppliers. The requirements for its growth are more straightforward than for numerous popular aquarium species, and any aquarist who encounters it will be amply repaid by its beauty and propagation, even if the initial cost of the specimen is high.

The water poppy is indigenous to standing and slow-flowing waters in Central and tropical South America, where it often forms dominant colonies in shallow flood pools and littoral regions. Closely resembling the water lilies in its habit of growth, it is a glabrous herbaceous plant which roots in the muddy substratum and produces floating leaves. The stems are long, creeping horizontally through the mud and rooting at the nodes. The leaves occur in clusters, each being borne on a slender petiole varying in length from 8 to 25 cm or even more, depending upon the depth of the water. The lamina reaches a length of 5 cm and a width of 2 to 4.5 cm; in shape it is broadly oval to orbicular, with an obtuse apex and slightly cordate base. The margin is entire, and on each side of the thickened spongy midrib are three principal lateral veins. The upper surface of the floating lamina is shining green and sometimes bears faint brownish markings, while the lower surface is of a paler color. Prior to flowering, the plant forms a long shoot which is often branched and ascends to the surface. From this shoot arise the aerial flowers which may be solitary or in clusters of two or three. Each flower may be as large as 5 cm in diameter and has three petals which are bright yellow with a rusty tint on the inner surface. The flower's several anthers are purplish.

Perhaps the most important point to be remembered in cultivating *Hydrocleis nymphoides* is that its growth soon becomes rampant if its rooting medium is very rich in nutrients and if it has no competitors at the surface of the water. The best technique is to establish the original specimen in a small pot containing a compost of two parts coarse sand to one part loam. Be sure that the roots are well spread and firmly anchored. Subsequently formed shoots may then be allowed to root in the gravel of the aquarium bed, where the concentration of nutrients is unlikely to be very high. There is some evidence that growth is more luxurious in soft water, but the species appears

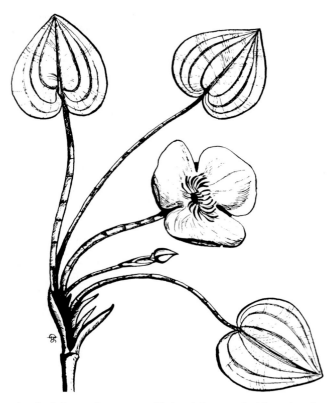

The apex of a shoot of the water poppy, *Hydrocleis nymphoides,* showing the form of the floating leaves and two flowers—one open, the other in bud.

generally to be tolerant of a wide range of water conditions. The temperature of the water should be maintained, for most of the year, between 15 and 29°C. After flowering, the rate of growth slows down, and during this period the water may be cooled to a temperature between 10 and 15°C. Blooming is induced more effectively if the plant receives some sunlight, but flowers have developed on several specimens of mine which have received only bright artificial light. Propagation of the species is very easy since strong lateral shoots arise frequently at the nodes of the main creeping shoots, and these develop rapidly if they are carefully detached, complete with roots, and planted in the compost mentioned above. Should the increase of the plant in the aquarium be too profuse, one or two of the shoots should be cut back. It is recommended that this technique be followed as a normal part of the cultivation of the plant, rather than let the growth become rampant and then drastically cut back most of the shoots, a practice which usually results in the loss of the specimen.

Hygrophila polysperma   [T. J. Horeman]
Hygrophila corymbosa   [T. J. Horeman]

Ludwigia palustris   [R. Zukal]
Ludwigia natans   [T. J. Horeman]

LUDWIGIA PALUSTRIS

The genus *Ludwigia* is a member of the family Oenotheraceae, being practically the only genus of the family whose many species may be cultivated under water. Hobbyist literature mentions quite a series of species which, allegedly, are fit for growing in fish tanks. One of the names thus mentioned, for example, is that of *Ludwigia alternifolia,* a plant that in its natural habitat is subjected to only short floodings and therefore cannot be cultivated under water permanently by any means. One species, though, which is well adapted for aquaristic purposes is *Ludwigia palustris,* especially the American variety.

Ludwigia palustris grows in Europe, Asia and the northern part of Africa. It has a creeping stalk which roots down at any spot where it grows leaves. The leaves are nearly without petioles, measuring 2 to 2.5 cm and showing a striking pattern of veins. The upper face of the leaves is a vivid green with a velvety luster, while the lower face may be bright green, olive or, if cultivated in dimly lit locations, sometimes a reddish brown. This plant is by far less colorful and ornamental than the American variety. It comes from temperate and subtropical zones of the Old World and generally dies off in winter when kept in an aquarium. This does not make it very fit for keeping in fish tanks, its use being restricted mainly to the terrarium, where it conquers its place in damp but cool and unheated installations.

In the southern states of the United States, *Ludwigia palustris* var. *americana* grows in shallow waters. The hobby generally knows it under the widespread but erroneous name of *Ludwigia natans.* This kind also develops a creeping stalk, and in its emerged form it is fit for both cold and warm terraria. It develops a dense low growth with shiny dark green leaves which differ from those of the European form because they do not possess the protruding veins and are considerably wider.

The stalks of the submerged form sometimes creep along the bottom, while at other times they grow vertically from the roots toward the surface of the water. The leaves on the stems are inserted in pairs on opposite sides of the stalk. They are broadly lanceolate or oval, the upper face a dark and shiny green, and with the lower face only rarely greenish, generally reddish brown to purple-red. They measure 2 to 3 cm in length and 2 cm in width.

The most beautiful form of this species is *Ludwigia palustris* var. *americana* forma *elongata.* The hobby has long known this form under the commercial name *Ludwigia mullerti.* Its leaves reach lengths up to 4 cm. The edges are slightly undulated, and the lower face of the leaves is always red or purple.

Ludwigia palustris blossoms only in its emerged form. The flowers develop in the leaf insertions and have long green cups that are grown together and drawn out into tips. Between these tips grow only a few minute yellow leaves. The flowers are self-pollinating and easily develop minute seeds which ger-

232

Ludwigia palustris. Photo by R. Zukal.

minate immediately. However, reproducing *Ludwigia palustris* by means of seeds does not pay, as it is much easier and quicker to reproduce the plant by sticking cut-off tips into the soil. If you want to get a really beautiful *Ludwigia*, the thing to do is to plant three to five specimens together, cutting off their tips regularly whenever they grow longer than 10 to 20 cm. This causes the stems to branch out in forks, which in turn makes the plant develop into a large, densely leaved and branched bush which shows a lively pageant of shiny green and vivid purplish red colors, with the upper and lower faces of the leaves alternating as you look at them.

This is the reason why one should cultivate only plants of American origin

Ludwigia brevipes [R. Zukal]
Ludwigia brevipes [R. Zukal]

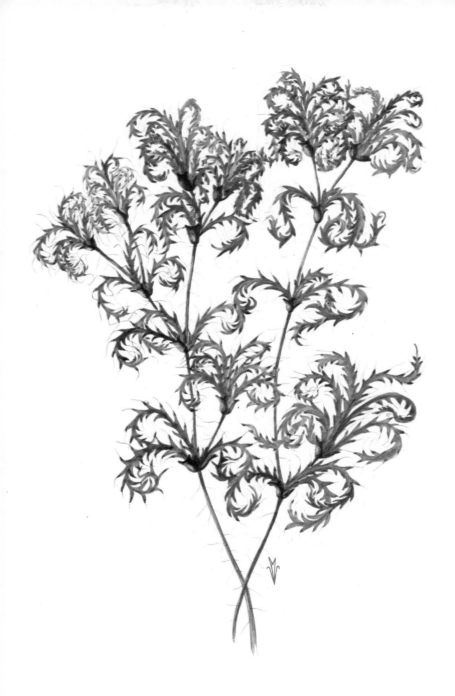

Najas minor

235

which winter easily in well-illuminated tanks and are undemanding as to temperatures and also as to the chemical composition of the water. The plant does quite well when standing in pure sand and hard water. The best surroundings for the species are found in water with a neutral to slightly alkaline reaction.

Ludwigia demands abundant light and prospers if afforded direct sunlight during at least part of the day. Temperatures from 15°C up are sufficient, which makes our plant better for coldwater tanks than for heated ones.

NAJAS SPECIES / *The Nymphworts*

The genus *Najas* comprises some 35 species, all of which are slender, submerged, fresh or brackish water plants inhabiting temperate and tropical regions. Many members of the genus resemble *Ceratophyllum demersum,* the hornwort, in having extremely brittle foliage and in succeeding equally well as floating submerged plants or as plants anchored in the substratum. The stem of most species is much branched and roots at the lower nodes while the narrow leaves are oppositely arranged or in whorls. The base of each leaf forms a tiny sheath around the stem and within each sheath are two minute scales. The inconspicuous unisexual flowers are usually hidden in the leaf axils. Each male flower is enclosed in a spathe and possesses just a single stamen; each female flower is naked and gives rise, after pollination and fertilization, to a single oval or elliptical fruit.

By virtue of their dense clusters of attractive translucent foliage, a few species of *Najas* may be recommended for use in aquaria, where they may prove of additional value for fishes that deposit their eggs in plant thickets and also as food for some species. Indeed, the introduction of the vegetarian *Sarotherodon melanopleura* is employed as a control measure in some areas of Africa where species of *Najas* occasionally infest dams and irrigation channels. However, aquarists growing these plants must remember their fragility and cultivate them in tanks containing no very active or vegetarian fishes.

The cultivation of species of *Najas* presents no serious problems. If it is desired that they should be rooted, cuttings should have the few lowermost leaves carefully removed and then be pressed gently into a compost of four parts coarse sand and one part garden soil covered by a thin layer of sand or gravel. The enrichment of the rooting medium with soil is not absolutely necessary, and some species will grow almost as luxuriantly when they are anchored in gravel alone. All the species branch profusely, so pruning to stimulate the formation of axillary shoots is unnecessary. A wide range of intensities of illumination is tolerated, but a very high intensity is not recommended as it frequently results in infestation of the dense foliage by filamentous and gelatinous colonies of green and blue-green algae.

236

Three species, *Najas horrida*, *N. indica* and *N. microdon*, are commonly available to aquarists. Others, some of which are difficult to identify with certainty, are less frequently seen in commercial supplies. *Najas horrida*, which is indigenous to most regions of the African continent including Madagascar, and *N. indica*, which is a native of Malaysia and Indonesia, are both tropical and subtropical species which may be cultivated in aquaria at temperatures of 17 to 29°C. The translucent bright green leaves of *N. indica* are arranged in close whorls along the slender but not too brittle stem. Each leaf is sessile, linear to narrowly lanceolate and reaches a length of 2.5 to 5.5 cm and a width of up to 6 mm. The margin of the leaf is deeply serrated. The leaves of *N. horrida* are relatively longer and narrower and are frequently reflexed; toward the base of established plants they are often whorled, whereas they are arranged in an opposite manner on younger growing stems. The leaf has an extremely coarsely toothed margin and varies in color from pale green to olive-green and even brown. The species resembles *N. indica* in being stronger and more wiry than most other species of the genus.

Najas microdon is a slender brittle plant of annual habit. Its smooth stems reach a length of about 30 cm and bear whorls of three leaves in the older parts, pairs of opposite leaves in the young regions. Each leaf reaches a length of 2.0 to 2.5 cm, is a pale translucent green and has a margin which is sparsely and minutely toothed. The natural distribution of this species has interested plant geographers for many years because of its asymmetrical range on either side of the Atlantic Ocean; in North America the species is distributed throughout both the Atlantic and Pacific regions from about 30°N to about 50°N, whereas its European range is much less extensive and more northerly (from about 51°N to about 62°N). In Europe the species occurs only in scattered localities on the northwest seaboards of the British Isles and Scandinavia. Fossil discoveries of the plant suggest that its range has become very restricted in post-glacial time, and a further interesting feature is that although the species has withdrawn from eastern and central Ireland to its present northern and western localities, the retreat in Scandinavia was southeasterly, toward the shores of the Baltic.

In aquaria, *Najas microdon* appreciates rather lower temperatures than the two species described above, from about 10 to 22°C. It may be of interest to note here that another aquatic plant, *Elodea nutalli*, shows a similar native distribution and marked structural resemblances to *Najas microdon*. The linear-lanceolate pale green leaves occur in whorls of three to five on slender branching stems. Each leaf is translucent and its margin has tiny projecting teeth. *E. nutalli* resembles other species of *Elodea* in temperate countries in forming winter buds. In aquaria it requires a temperature similar to that recommended for *Najas microdon* and its rooting medium should be composed of equal parts of clay and coarse sand.

Nuphar luteum   [R. Zukal]
Nuphar luteum   [R. Zukal]

Nymphaea "Isabella Pring" [P. Stetson]
Nymphaea "Castaliflora" [P. Stetson]

NUPHAR AND NYMPHAEA SPECIES / *Aquarium Lilies*

Water lilies are normally regarded as pool plants, yet there are a few species of *Nuphar* and *Nymphaea* which are naturally dwarf plants and are eminently suitable for cultivation in tropical aquaria. Some of these are natural forms, whereas others are plants which have been developed and cultivated in horticultural nurseries. All have the same general habit of growth and accordingly demand similar conditions. From the stout creeping rootstock there develop submerged juvenile leaves, followed sooner or later by floating leaves and aerial or floating flowers. Species of *Nuphar* are cultivated particularly for their submerged foliage, which is usually translucent and attractively furled. Water lilies must be planted in pots, which are much more convenient for subsequent handling of the specimens and for containing the necessary rooting medium. The compost should be a rich heavy fibrous loam; these plants will not grow successfully for long periods in barren gravel or sand. Some dealers offer rootstock cuttings of lilies all too frequently; such specimens must be avoided, as bacterial decay quickly starts at the cut end. Young thriving seedlings or established rootstocks should be obtained wherever possible. Most lilies are fast-growing plants, and care is needed to prevent them from becoming pot-bound; initially 5 cm or 8 cm diameter pots are adequate for species of *Nuphar* and 8 cm or 10 cm ones for species of *Nymphaea,* but after about twelve months specimens usually need transplanting to larger pots. Apart from this treatment, however, the plants should not be disturbed, and excessive pruning is not recommended, as it frequently leads to a deterioration of the stock.

The commonest aquarium species of *Nuphar* is the spatterdock, *N. pumilum,* a small plant with rich green translucent leaves and bright yellow flowers, which in its submerged phase provides a good foreground plant.

The wild European species, *Nuphar luteum,* is naturally a cool temperate plant; young specimens may be used in tropical aquaria for a limited period, though their rapid growth in the warmer water often produces ungainly plants. The leaves are pale green and reach a width of 20 to 25 cm.

The Cape Fear spatterdock, *Nuphar sagittifolia,* is probably the most useful and decorative species, useful by virtue of its producing only submerged leaves and decorative on account of the shape and translucence of these leaves. A mature specimen may attain a height of 30 cm or more, the leaves spreading out in a dense bush from the rootstock. Each leaf is sagittate, bright green in color and borne on a short petiole; the undivided margins of the leaf are usually curled back at intervals, giving a wavy outline. The species will thrive within the temperature range 15 to 27°C.

Two wild species of *Nymphaea* are suited to life in tropical aquaria. These are *N. tetragona,* from Asia and North America, and *N. maculata,* a common aquatic weed of tropical Africa. The former is well known as the pygmy water lily; its leaves reach a diameter of 5 to 8 cm, its white flowers 2.5 to 4 cm. Its growth in aquaria at temperatures of 21 to 26°C tends to be rapid, and it will tolerate much cooler water, down to 7 to 10°C. The floating leaves of *N. maculata* are even smaller, reaching a diameter of 3 to 4.5 cm. Cordate in shape, they have a glossy dark green surface attractively mottled with bluish red tints. The submerged leaves arising from the stout rounded rootstock are olive and sometimes bear similar mottled patterns. Under sustained good light this species forms white surface flowers about 4.5 to 5.5 cm in diameter with acutely pointed petals.

Nearly all species of *Nuphar* and *Nymphaea* require a high light intensity, preferably with some daily sunlight, at least during the growing season, though exceptions are afforded by *N. daubenyana*, which flowers freely in artificial light, and by *Nuphar sagittifolia*, which, in being exclusively submerged, tolerates lower intensities. If species with floating leaves are grown in aquaria under artificial lights, a sheet of glass should be placed between the lamps and the water surface to minimize the effects of heat on the leaves, thereby preventing scorching.

NYMPHOIDES SPECIES / *Banana Plants* and their relatives

The banana plant, which has attracted the interest of aquarists for many years, and its lesser-known relatives are all species of *Nymphoides*, a genus of some twenty tropical and subtropical plants. Despite their similarities of structure and growth habit, these plants belong not to the Nymphaeaceae, or water lily family, but to an unrelated family, the Menyanthaceae. Their vegetative resemblances to the water lilies provide a fine example of convergent evolution, the organs of these unrelated plants having become similarly adapted to a particular set of environmental factors, those prevailing in and at the surface of stationary or slow-moving water which fluctuates in depth.

The banana plant itself, *Nymphoides aquatica*, is native to southern North America and is an interesting specimen for aquaria within the temperature ange 18 to 27°C. It will grow equally well as a floating or as a submerged rooted plant. The rootstock is short and compact, and below it hangs a cluster of curved tuberous roots closely resembling a stalk of bananas. Exposed to light, these roots develop photosynthetic pigments and appear green; buried in the compost, they are usually brownish white. When the specimen is planted, unmodified adventitious roots develop from the rootstock, anchoring the plant. If it is desired as a submerged specimen, the plant should be potted in a compost of equal parts sand and garden soil covered with gravel, and it should be so anchored that most of the tuberous roots are just above the sur-

Nymphaea species

[Dr. Herbert R. Axelrod]

Nymphoides aquatica

243

face of the compost, though these will have to be buried initially if the specimen has no other roots. Pots 5 to 8 cm in diameter are quite adequate for this species, and it is not absolutely essential to have a compost of soil, as the plants will thrive for long periods in ordinary gravel or coarse sand. Growth is more luxuriant, however, in the presence of additional inorganic and organic nutrients. When established, the species produces submerged leaves quite rapidly. These are usually few in number unless the water is deeper than 38 cm; they are roughly cordate, rather irregular in outline, somewhat crinkled, mid-green in color and borne on petioles varying from 2 to 15 cm in length, the leaves themselves reaching a diameter of 6 cm or more. Sooner or later, long petioles grow rapidly upward bearing cordate floating leaves which do not open until they reach the surface. The petioles continue to elongate for some time, so the leaves are carried away from the plant to some distance. This may be interpreted as an adaptation to possible sudden increases in water depth, the extra length of the petiole enabling the leaf to remain floating. These floating leaves reach a diameter of 5 cm.

The best known relative of the banana plant is the fringed water lily, *Nymphoides peltata,* native to central and southern Europe, northern and western Asia and now naturalized in parts of the United States. It does especially well in water at temperatures from about 10 to 21°C but will grow quite successfully at higher temperatures. Reported failures with this species in tropical aquaria are almost certainly due not to the warmth of the water but to the restricted surface area available to the plant. It has an extensively creeping rhizome which forms adventitious roots profusely at the nodes and from which develop long-petioled floating leaves. These leaves are orbicular, deeply cordate at the base, up to 10 cm in diameter, sinuate in outline, purplish below and mottled with purple on the glossy green upper surface. Long floating stems with opposite leaves are eventually produced, and from the axils of some of these leaves aerial stalks bear clusters of four or five flowers to a height of 5 to 8 cm above the water. The flowers open in succession and last only for two or three days; each is about 4 cm in diameter and has five bright yellow petals which are lobed and have shaggy margins. This species is well worth cultivating, though its habit of growth demands a large aquarium, 90 cm or more long, or a heated pool. It will also grow well in outside pools but is likely to suffer in hard winters. When first obtained it should be rooted in a rich loam; roots produced subsequently from the creeping rhizome will anchor themselves in the aquarium gravel or pool bed. In aquaria or indoor pools intense illumination is required, preferably with some sunlight if flowering is to be induced.

A similar habit of growth is shown by *Nymphoides indica,* which is indigenous to Southeast Asia and parts of Australia and is sometimes available to aquarists. It differs from the previous species in only one aspect of cultivation: it is suitable only for warm water at temperatures of 21 to 30°C, though it may be cooled for a rest period each year at 15 to 18°C.

RORIPPA AQUATICA / *The Water Nasturtium*

Easily propagated plants with finely divided foliage are understandably popular with aquarists. One species which possesses these attributes and yet is somewhat uncommon in either tropical or coldwater aquaria is the water nasturtium, *Rorippa aquatica.* That it has not achieved the popularity enjoyed by, for example, the water wisteria, *Hygrophila difformis,* or the Indian fern, *Ceratopteris thalictroides,* is surprising, the more so because it is a common native or introduced member of the flora of lowland ditches, streams and rivers throughout many parts of Europe and the U.S.A. Aquarists wishing to procure it with minimum labor may do so by visiting the nearest retailer of fresh salad vegetables, for *Rorippa aquatica* is known to most people as the familiar watercress!

The water nasturtium is a perennial herbaceous plant with smooth hollow shoots varying in length from 10 to 60 cm. In the shallow water of their natural habitat their stems are often procumbent (trailing along the ground) near their bases, where they develop tufts of fine adventitious roots from the lowermost nodes. The free portions of the stem either float near the surface of the water or grow erect under the water and above it. The leaves and stems are an even mid-green in color while those of a related and very similar species, *Rorippa microphylla,* are green for most of the year, becoming tinted strongly with purplish brown in late summer or whenever the water becomes unusually cool.

The water nasturtium is hardy, tolerating temperatures from about 4 to 27°C, and is therefore suitable for coldwater aquaria and garden pools in addition to tropical aquaria. In warm water, under light of a low intensity, the foliage sometimes becomes spindly and yellowish green; to prevent this etiolation, it is recommended that the illumination be as bright as possible. Once established, the plant grows rapidly and will form numerous lateral shoots of its own accord. Branching may be further stimulated by carefully pruning the apical bud of the main shoot. With remarkably little attention the water nasturtium soon develops into a magnificent bush of fine crisp foliage which looks exceptionally good in front of red or brown sandstone rocks.

SAGITTARIA SUBULATA

The home range of this plant is the eastern states of the U.S.A., where it grows in shallow waters and swamps. Emerged specimens have a lanceolate

Rorippa aquatica

[R. Zukal]

Sagittaria subulata gracillima

[R. Zukal]

leaf surface on a stem that is about four times as long as the leaf. The leaf shows an oval, cylindrical shape. The submerged leaves change into a kind of phyllode, meaning a flattened, widened leaf stem. There are three subspecies of *Sagittaria subulata,* all cultivated by hobbyists under erroneous names.

One subspecies is *Sagittaria subulata subulata,* often mistakenly called *Sagittaria pusilla.* This is the smallest form, the submerged leaves of which reach lengths of 5 to 10 cm with a width smaller than 6 mm. The leaves are light green, and the plant does not bloom in depths over 15 cm. The only flowers it produces come forth in shallow water or from emerged forms.

Another subspecies is *S. subulata gracillima,* the submerged leaves of which grow to lengths of 20 to 40 cm; this plant is sometimes erroneously called *S. subulata f. natans.* Sometimes the leaves of this plant grow so long that they twist and fold below the surface of the water. This is dependent upon the conditions the plant is given. The inflorescence grows to lengths of 90 cm, the female and male flowers being white with sizes of 10 cm to 12 mm.

The most beautiful but least known of the three subspecies is *S. subulata kurziana,* the phyllodia of which reach lengths of 30 to 40 cm, sometimes strikingly spread out at the top. In tanks it blooms only rarely and resembles the *Vallisneria* species. All three subspecies often form lawns in the aquarium, the short forms of which are hard to differentiate.

The species as such thrives in neutral to slightly alkaline water. The temperature in the tank may vary between 17 and 24°C. The plant is very undemanding and presents no problems with regard to the composition of the soil. Lighting should be fairly heavy; best results are achieved when illumination corresponds to the duration of daylight under natural conditions. Floating plants placed above the *Sagittaria* species make them tend to develop rich roots.

S. subulata propagates very quickly and is not sensitive to algae. Since it often grows on the front side of the tank, very heavy growths often have to be torn out and replanted, because a dense growth would obscure the view into the tank. Under optimal conditions all three subspecies will form dense lawns in the aquarium.

Partial changes of water have a beneficial effect on the growth pattern of *Sagittaria subulata.* It has been noticed that plants that have reached a plateau in growth suddenly put on a spurt of new growth after part of their water was changed.

VALLISNERIA GIGANTEA

Vallisneria gigantea, of the family Hydrocharitaceae, is the largest representative of its genus. In its native range (Philippines and New Guinea) it is found in permanent waters one to two meters deep, where it covers large areas of the bottom with dense thickets.

The plant has a bulbous rootstock, out of which grow short but numerous bunches of roots. From the stalks originate ten to fifteen ribbon-like leaves that are 2 to 3.5 cm wide and 1 to 2 m long. These are vivid to pale green and usually show fifteen elongated nervures which are mutually interconnected in slanted irregular lines. In shallower waters, with depths around 50 cm, the huge leaves reach the surface, winding in spirals that form a dense thicket. These spots are sought out by fishes that need hiding places in the upper reaches of the water.

Like many other *Vallisneria* species, *Vallisneria gigantea* is dioeceous, meaning that there are male and female specimens, but sexes cannot be differentiated except during the blooming period. The female flowers grow on long and thin, often spirally twisted, stems on the surface of the water. On the tip of the stem sits an about 1 cm-long chalix, out of which grow three tongue-shaped stigmata, from which in turn grows a tough, wart-like, yellow-white tissue. The male flowers form an inverted inflorescence near the bottom. At first this inflorescence is hidden with a filmy covering. Later on the covering opens, and the pollen sacs come loose and float up to the surface. There the pollen meets the female flowers, fertilizing them.

In aquaria female plants are the most prevalent, recognized by the very long thread-like stalks and the female blooms which float on the surface. The relatively rare male plants' flowers, which are hidden within the thicket of leaves near the bottom, are likely to escape notice. Their presence is detected only when the pollen comes free and floats on the surface, forming green circles of light green grains which are about 1 millimeter in size. So far it has not been possible to observe pollination and development of fruits under artificial conditions.

V. gigantea demands a roomy tank but above all a sufficiently high column of water. Practically, it is only suitable for tanks that are at least 50 cm deep, so that it has sufficient space for development. Planted in bunches of two or three individual plants, it will soon fill out the tank with its solid and extraordinarily long leaves.

The plant is undemanding as to soil conditions and the composition of the water. It grows to sufficient size in clean gravel. Its best development is reached in slightly acid water, a fact that makes it especially fit for larger and deeper aquaria which are stocked with *Cryptocoryne*. *Vallisneria gigantea* is sufficiently adaptable, however, to be kept in neutral or lightly alkaline waters too, together with larger or smaller species of *Echinodorus, Cabomba, Myriophyllum* and the like. Angelfish love to spawn on the solid leaves. With regard to temperature, the plant demands a minimum of 20°C but tolerates up to 30°C. Reproduction takes place vegetatively but nowhere near so quick-

Vallisneria gigantea   [R. Zukal]

Vallisneria portugalensis   [R. Zukal]

ly as that of the smaller *Vallisneria* species. The young plants originate from offshoots out of the rootstock, but each rootstock comes to the end of its growth with the development of a new plant. Each parent plant sends forth only two or three offshoots, which give rise to two to five descendants, after which reproduction stops. If you want a large number of young plants, separate them as soon as their leaves have reached a length of about 20 cm, transplanting them at this point. Two or three weeks after being moved, the new specimens put forth new offshoots.

Commercial reproduction of *V. gigantea* consists of setting the plants into 15 to 20 cm deep dishes. Half of each dish is filled with peat moss, while the remaining space is filled up with clean gravel. The dishes with the plants are placed on the bottom of a garden pond with soft water, where they are left during the whole summer at a temperature of 14 to 20°C. Under such conditions *V. gigantea* reaches lengths of only 15 to 30 cm, but in compensation it reproduces vegetatively in large numbers, and from May to August each parent plant in a dish gives birth to quite a number of new plants, often with leaves that measure only 5 cm. The harvest that is reaped in this manner is transferred to hothouses, where it is kept at temperatures between 20 and 23°C. During daytime the plants receive twelve hours of supplementary lighting. Under such conditions the short, stunted young that were developed in the pond during the summer reach lengths of around 40 to 62 cm and are then completely fit for transfer into fish tanks.

Vallisneria gigantea. Photo by R. Zukal.

GLOSSARY

Adventitious root: a root which develops from the node of a stem or similar organ, such as rhizome, stolon or runner.

Apical bud: the principal growing point of the stem.

Axillary bud: a bud, capable of developing into a lateral shoot, present in the angle between a leaf and the stem on which it is borne.

Dichotomous: dividing into two equal branches.

Dioecious: having male or female flowers on separate plants.

Etiolation: the formation of weak, spindly foliage deficient in chlorophyll; usually occurs in light of too low an intensity.

Heterophyllous: having leaves of different forms on the one plant.

Heterostylic: having flowers which differ in the relative length of their styles and stamens, such that any one flower is very rarely, if ever, self-pollinated.

Hydrophilous pollination: the transference of pollen from the anthers of the stamens to the stigmas on the surface of the water or under water.

Hypocotyl: that part of the stem of a seedling below the cotyledons.

Lamina: that part of a leaf which is flattened, to a greater or lesser degree, as the "leaf-blade."

Node: that part of the stem from which one or more leaves arise.

Petiole: the stalk of a leaf.

Physiological incompatibility: the existence of some chemical or physical factor in the reproductive organs of a plant which prevents fertilization.

Pinna: a part of the leaf of a fern, corresponding to a leaflet in some flowering plants.

Rachis: the continuation of the stipes in a fern leaf which is divided.

Rhizome: a stem growing more or less horizontally near the surface of the soil or gravel and sometimes appearing above it.

Rootstock: a very short, but often thick, stem growing vertically at or just above the surface of the soil or gravel; often referred to as the 'crown' of the plant.

Runner: a horizontal stem growing just above the surface of the soil or gravel and rooting at its nodes.

Sessile: a term used to describe a leaf which has no petiole.

Stipes: the stalk of a fern leaf; corresponding to the petiole in flowering plants.

Stolon: a horizontal stem growing just beneath the surface of the soil or gravel, as in numerous species of *Cryptocoryne*.

Stomata: minute pores in the surface of leaves and herbaceous stems through which exchange of gases with the atmosphere occurs.

Thallus: the body of a plant which is not differentiated into stem, root and leaf.

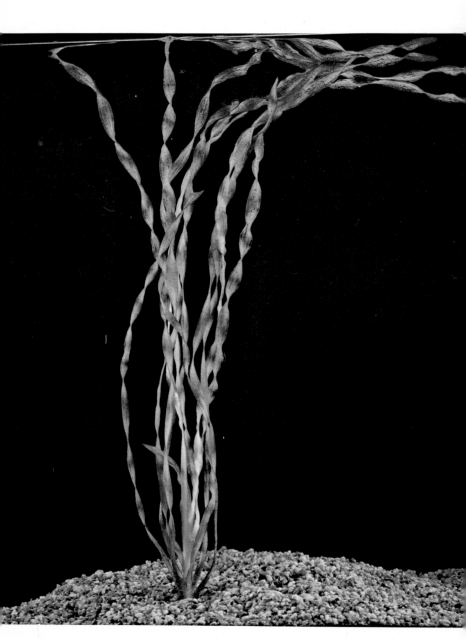

Vallisneria tortissima

[R. Zukal]

Vallisneria americana [T. J. Horeman]
Vallisneria gigantea [T. J. Horeman]

Turion: a modified bud, the leaves of which contain abundant storage reserves, by means of which the plant survives winter and renews its growth in spring.

Venation: the arrangement of veins in a leaf.

Vernation: the manner in which a leaf, or the parts of a leaf, are rolled up in the bud; also applied to the manner in which the frond of a fern unrolls.

Viviparous: bearing young plants on vegetative organs, such as leaves.

Whorl: a group of more than two organs of the same kind, for example leaves, arising at the same level.

ABRAMIS BRAMA (Linnaeus) / *Bream*

Range: Europe and northern Asia.
Habits: Peaceful; a bottom-feeding species which will help clean up food which has been left uneaten by other fishes.
Water Conditions: Not critical.
Size: Up to 30 cm.
Food Requirements: Will thrive on almost any food.

The Bream occurs in small schools in ponds and sluggish streams in European and northern Asiatic waters, where it is often caught by anglers. Sexes can only be distinguished in fairly large specimens, when the females become heavy with roe. This fish is not a very popular aquarium inhabitant, but young specimens may be kept with other coldwater species such as Goldfish. There are numerous species of this genus and all have similar appearance and habits. They are members of the family Cyprinidae, the carp-like fishes. Capturing young specimens for aquarium use should be a fairly simple matter. The best time to catch them is early summer, when the fry which have hatched in the spring have begun to grow. The best net is a seine dragged along the bottom near the shore.

ABRAMITES HYPSELONOTUS (Günther) / *Headstander*

Range: Upper Peruvian Amazon, Paraguay, Venezuela.
Habits: May be aggressive, also nibble plants.
Water Conditions: Water should be soft and slightly acid. Temperature 23 to 25°C.
Size: About 12.5 cm; usually smaller specimens are sold.
Food Requirements: Living foods are eagerly accepted, and the fish are fond of nibbling algae or a lettuce leaf.

Abramites hypselonotus has been known in the aquarium for 40 years, but Günther first published an account of it in 1868. *Abramites microcephalus,* which had not become known until 1926, has proven itself to be nothing more than a form of *A. hypselonotus* and was therefore placed in synonymy with it. This is an interesting and active species and needs plenty of tank room to swim about. This species is not a good community fish as it may often become very aggressive. *A. hypselonotus* is very fond of nibbling plants and will sometimes continue this activity on its fellow tankmates, nibbling away at their fins and scales. Fully grown Headstanders may make enemies among their own kind and nip each other to death. If you are daring or foolish enough to keep this species, they should be given a tank with tough-leaved plants and a leaf of lettuce to nibble on if there is not enough algae present. Chances are that if they find algae or a lettuce leaf, the plants and maybe the tankmates will be left alone.

Abramis brama F D X 2 5 7 X N N E
Abramites hypselonotus F D X 2 5 8 X N N E
[R. Zukal]

Acanthodoras spinosissimus F D X 2 5 9 X N N E

Acanthophthalmus javanicus F D X 2 6 0 X N N 6

ACANTHODORAS SPINOSISSIMUS (Eigenmann & Eigenmann)
Spiny Catfish, Talking Catfish

Range: Middle Amazon region.
Habits: Mostly nocturnal; will not molest any fish it cannot swallow.
Water Conditions: Not critical. Temperatures should range between 24 and 28°C.
Size: Maximum 15 cm; matures at 10 cm.
Food Requirements: Prefers living foods, especially daphnia, tubifex or enchytrae. Earthworms should be chopped if fed.

As the popular names indicate, this is a spiny fish capable of emitting a sound. This is a faint croak, which you would have to listen very attentively to hear. As with many of the catfishes, they are mostly nocturnal by habit, shunning bright light. For this reason they should be provided with adequate hiding places, such as flat rocks under which they can dig. We can find no record of their spawning in captivity, but it is thought by some authorities that it is probably a nest-builder which exercises a certain amount of parental care. There are no known external sexual characteristics. Great care should be exercised in handling this fish; the first spine of the dorsal and pectoral fins is very stiff and sharp and can inflict a painful wound. This is a fish which one could have in a large tank for months at a time without ever seeing it. Not only does it prefer to remain hidden below rocks, but it also has a habit of burying itself in the gravel, in which case it is very likely to uproot some plants.

ACANTHOPHTHALMUS JAVANICUS Bleeker / *Javanese Loach*

Range: Java and Sumatra.
Habits: Peaceful and able to slither into almost inaccessible places and pick up food other fishes cannot reach.
Water Conditions: Clean water. Temperature about 24 to 28°C.
Size: About 8 cm.
Food Requirements: They pick up most uneaten foods but are very fond of tubifex and white worms.

As their common name indicates, they come mostly from Java, but some are also recorded from Sumatra. Their tank should not be only well planted but also have some flat rocks beneath which the fish can dig. Sexes can be told only when the females become heavy with eggs, but the problem there is whether the ones that do not fill up with eggs are males or not. The best way is to keep several pairs in the same tank, as this genus is not averse to "community spawning." The young frequently remain hidden for a week or more after hatching and are easily raised on crushed worms or the like. The parents should be removed when it is seen that they have spawned. Other fishes in the same tank, which would mistake the youngsters for tiny worms, should also be removed.

ACANTHOPHTHALMUS KUHLI (Cuvier & Valenciennes)
Coolie Loach, Leopard Eel

Range: Northeastern Bengal, Assam, Malaysia, Burma, Java, Sumatra, Borneo, Singapore and Malacca.
Habits: A peaceful little fish found on muddy bottoms in its native water. Hides from bright light and becomes active at night.
Water Conditions: They prefer clean, clear water with a temperature of 24 to 28°C. The use of coarse gravel should be avoided.
Size: 8 cm; matures at 7 cm.
Food Requirements: A good scavenger which can be counted on to pick up much of the food other fishes leave uneaten.

The Coolie Loach has long been a favorite among aquarists. It has the ability to slither into almost inaccessible places and eat any food which would otherwise die there and foul the water. The trouble is that most aquarists think that it can subsist only on "leftovers." This is far from the truth, and enough living foods should be fed to insure a good supply for the "Coolies." These fish have a protective tough transparent skin over the eyes which enables them to dig into the sand without injuring themselves. If the sand is too coarse and has sharp edges, however, the nose and mouth can be injured, resulting in a wound which often becomes covered with fungus and may easily cause death if not caught early enough.

ACANTHOPHTHALMUS MYERSI Harry / Slimy Myersi

Range: Southeastern Thailand.
Habits: A nocturnal swimmer; prefers hiding during the day, so wholesalers use inverted, split coconut shells in their aquaria.
Water Conditions: Prefers soft, acid water with a pH of 6.2. Temperature 26 to 28°C.
Size: Less than 7.5 cm.
Food Requirements: Worms, frozen brine shrimp and anything that will fall to the bottom and not require teeth to chew.

The Slimy Myersi is so-called because it seems to have a slimier skin than the other loaches and is thinner. When a few hundred are kept together in a tank, they "ball up" and are very sensitive to light, preferring to remain hidden in the sand or in a dark corner. They are not to be recommended for the community aquarium, as you will never see them . . . except at night, and then the slightest shadow will send them darting back into hiding. Not much is known about its breeding habits, but it can be assumed to be a difficult fish to induce to spawn.

Acanthophthalmus kuhli ⬚F ⬚D ⬚X ⬚2 ⬚6 ⬚1 ⬚X ⬚N ⬚N ⬚E [A. van den Nieuwenhuizen]
Acanthophthalmus myersi ⬚F ⬚R ⬚X ⬚2 ⬚6 ⬚2 ⬚X ⬚N ⬚N ⬚E [Dr. Herbert R. Axelrod]

1. *Acanthophthalmus semicinctus* F D T 2 6 3 X N N E
2. *Acanthophthalmus semicinctus* var. F H M 2 6 3 X A N E

Acanthophthalmus shelfordi F D X 2 6 4 X N N E   [Dr. Herbert R. Axelrod]

ACANTHOPHTHALMUS SEMICINCTUS Fraser-Brunner
Half-Banded Loach

Range: Sunda Islands.
Habits: Peaceful; often remains hidden when the light is bright and comes out at night.
Water Conditions: Clean, clear water with a temperature of 24 to 27°C. Do not give them a bottom with coarse gravel.
Size: A little over 7.5 cm.
Food Requirements: An excellent scavenger which will pick up uneaten food, but should get its share of live food, too.

This species has often been confused with the so-called "Kuhli" or "Coolie" Loach, which it resembles very closely. Probably many hobbyists who think they have *Acanthophthalmus kuhli* actually have this species, and vice versa. In any case, both species are very attractive as well as useful. Their activities, which are largely nocturnal, include a very thorough cleaning of the bottom gravel, and much food is eaten which would have been out of reach of the other fishes. Coming as they do from streams with muddy bottoms, their mouths are quite soft and coarse gravel will easily cause severe injury if the hungry fish pushes its mouth against it. For this reason the use of a finer gravel is recommended in a tank with these fish.

1. *Acanthophthalmus semicinctus* (p263) shows a close resemblance to the Coolie Loach, *A. kuhli* (p262).
2. This is an albino variety of *A. semicinctus* (p263).

ACANTHOPHTHALMUS SHELFORDI Popta / *Shelford's Loach*

Range: Borneo.
Habits: Peaceful. Usually remains hidden during the day and comes out at night. When feeding time arrives it may come out even though it is light.
Water Conditions: Although quite tolerant of varied conditions, optimum would be medium soft (about 5 DH) and slightly acid to neutral pH. Temperature should be 21 to 24°C.
Size: To about 8 cm.
Food Requirements: Not critical. Foods that sink to the bottom, like worms, can be used.

In view of their nocturnal habits, suitable hiding places must be furnished. Therefore their aquarium must include rocks, slate or other material that creates caves or dark niches for the loaches. The water should be medium soft (about 5 DH or less) and with a pH of about neutral to slightly acid although they are very tolerant and can exist with a pH as high as 7.6 or as low as 6.4. The temperature should not be too high as they seem to show discomfort at temperatures as high as 26°C; 21 to about 24°C will do. The water should be kept as clean as possible, and changes of up to 25% of the volume of their tank should be made every two to three weeks.

ACANTHOPSIS CHOIRORHYNCHUS (Bleeker) / *Long-Nosed Loach*

Range: Southeastern Asia, Sumatra, Borneo, Java; occurs in fresh water only.
Habits: Mostly nocturnal; in the daylight hours it usually remains buried in the gravel with only its eyes showing.
Water Conditions: Neutral to slightly acid water. Temperature between 24 and 30°C.
Size: Wild specimens attain a length of 18 cm; in captivity they remain smaller.
Food Requirements: Living foods only: tubifex worms, white worms, daphnia, etc.

Although this fish likes to dig in the sand, don't count on it to clean up and eat leftover foods. It may do this when very hungry, but its preference is worms, and they should be wriggling. This species is one for which you must search frequently, and then often without success. Most of the daylight hours are spent buried in the sand, right up to the eyes. For this reason you must provide a fine grade of gravel or injuries may result when they dig in. Small fishes are perfectly safe with *Acanthopsis choirorhynchus;* they are seldom molested. One thing to be remembered if small specimens are purchased is that they will grow, and space will soon be a problem. So many people forget this or have the attitude that they will cross this bridge when they come to it when buying the young of large fishes. It is better to be prepared before this happens or to stick to fish species which stay small.

ACARICHTHYS HECKELI Müller and Troschel / *Elusive Cichlid*

Range: Throughout central Brazil and all the Amazonian tributaries.
Habits: A large, beautiful fish which is rarely imported but which exists in quantity in nature. It should have a large aquarium.
Water Conditions: Not sensitive to water conditions, but is in best color when it is kept in soft, slightly acid water at a temperature of about 24°C.
Size: To about 15 cm.
Food Requirements: As with most cichlids, they prefer large, bulky live foods such as small garden worms, but they eagerly take pelletized fish foods and frozen foods.

While fishing in the Rio Urubu about 32 km north of Itacoatiara, in 1959, the author (HRA) collected this beautiful specimen. In a few hours it was in a photo tank and had its beautiful form recorded for history! This was one of the few fishes, from the thousands the author collected, that really impressed him. After spending several hours looking for a likely female of the species, the author gave up in vain. In the next river, he caught hundreds of them and shipped them back to the United States alive. They were not the "smash hit" he thought they would be, and that was the end of what could have been a very interesting addition to the aquarium field. No one was able to breed them even though some of the finest fish breeders in Florida tried it.

They probably breed as a mouthbrooder, but there is no direct evidence to support this supposition. No young were ever collected, so it's quite possible that the young look nondescript.

Acanthopsis choirorhynchus [F][D][X][2][6][5][X][N] [N][E]
Acarichthys heckelii [F][A][X][2][6][6][X][N][N][C]   [Dr. Herbert R. Axelrod]

Acaronia nassa Ⓕ Ⓐ Ⓧ ② ⑥ ⑦ Ⓧ Ⓝ Ⓝ ⑧   [Dr. Herbert R. Axelrod]
Acestrorhynchus microlepis Ⓕ Ⓓ Ⓧ ② ⑥ ⑧ Ⓧ Ⓝ Ⓝ Ⓔ   [Harald Schultz]

ACARONIA NASSA (Heckel) / *Big-Eyed Cichlid*

Range: Northern Amazon Region.
Habit: Nasty, greedy and pugnacious; cannot be trusted in the company of fishes smaller than itself.
Water Conditions: Not critical. Temperature about 24°C.
Size: Up to 20 cm.
Food Requirements: A heavy feeder; likes food in large chunks. Cut-up earthworms, pieces of raw fish or smaller whole fish are consumed eagerly.

This is one of those species which sometimes gets mixed up into a shipment of other fishes when small, about 2.5 cm in length. At that size they are quite attractive with their big eyes and dark horizontal stripe which tilts upward somewhat like that of *Cichlasoma festivum,* and the dealer who gets them has little trouble selling them. His trouble comes a few months later when the customer brings back some big nasty cichlids with the complaint that they ate everything in sight, including some valuable fish. The writer recalls getting two little ones when they came in a shipment of mixed dwarf cichlids. They were small, and their unfriendly attitude towards the others was soon noted and they were given an 80-liter tank of their own. Here they were given large chunks of whatever food was available: pieces of shrimp cut to fit their large mouths, raw fish, fish which had become sick or crippled, and even dog food from cans! Everything went down their capacious gullets, and they got bigger and sassier until a friend expressed the desire to take them over, and they were gratefully given to him. They were about 12.5 cm long at the time.

ACESTRORHYNCHUS MICROLEPIS (Schomburgk) / *Pike Characin*

Range: Northern South America.
Habits: Will eat or damage any other fish put with it.
Water Conditions: Requires much room and a good deal of heat, 26 to 28°C.
Size: About 30 cm.
Food Requirements: Will take only living foods, preferably smaller fishes.

One look at the torpedo-shaped body, the hungry eyes and barracuda-like teeth of this fellow identifies it as a predatory species of the worst kind. Unlike the pike, which lies quietly half-concealed or cruises along almost motionless like a twig in the water, *Acestrorhynchus microlepis* prefers to pursue its prey, and it is seldom that it cannot overtake it. It is the bane of fish collectors, who get a great many fish damaged or eaten whenever their catch includes one of these. What is more, they must be picked up with caution, or those needle-sharp teeth will tear into the fisherman's hand. Natives where this fish exists seek it for food, and its flesh is supposed to be very delicate in flavor. When captured the tiny scales are easily damaged, leaving the fish a prey to disease.

ACHIRUS ERRANS Miranda-Ribeiro / *Brazilian Freshwater Sole*

Range: Originally described from the Amazon and the Rio Paraguay, also ranges into the Rio Araguaia, near Aruana, Brazil.

Habits: A slow, lazy swimmer, it waits on the bottom until food swims by and then it lunges savagely and its huge mouth opens to engulf whatever it attacks.

Water Conditions: They prefer a sandy bottom so they can lie partially imbedded in the sand camouflaged from view. They are not the scavengers they are supposed to be. They require warm, soft, acid water. Prefer a temperature of 26°C.

Size: To 10 cm.

Food Requirements: They prefer live, moving foods such as baby Guppies, but as they grow they take larger foods. They also take tubifex.

Freshwater soles are not rare. Even the common eastern American sole, *Achirus fasciatus*, comes into the freshwater rivers that empty into the ocean, but they never live long in an aquarium. No one has ever imported the true freshwater Brazilian Sole. This fish lives very well in the home aquarium and spends its entire life in fresh water. The author (HRA) collected thousands of this species deep in the Brazilian jungle. Additional Brazilian soles include *Achirus achirus* (Linnaeus), which ranges from Florida's Gulf of Mexico down to Argentina on the east and Peru on the west; *Achirus garmani* (Jordan); *Achirus jenysi* (Günther); *Achirus mentalis; Achirus microphthalmus;* and *Achirus punctifer.*

These fish are very interesting aquarium subjects, but they must be kept with fishes that are larger than themselves.

ACIPENSER RUTHENUS Linnaeus / *Sterlet*

Range: Eastern Europe.

Habits: A peaceful fish much given to ceaseless cruising over the bottom.

Water Conditions: Not critical.

Size: In nature to one meter. Aquarium specimens seldom exceed 30 cm.

Food Requirements: Earthworms, snails, tubifex are preferred. Will also accept frozen foods.

Color Variations: Back and sides blue-gray, underside pale yellow. Fins dark.

The sturgeons are a widely distributed group, ranging throughout Europe and North America. None are suitable for the aquarium when mature, since they attain gigantic proportions (some species up to 4 meters), but young fishes make good aquarium subjects if the aquarium is kept cool. The Sterlet is an extremely graceful fish whose ease of movement is a source of wonder to all who behold it. This species is a bottom-feeder. Unfortunately, it is not a voracious feeder and other fishes in the aquarium may consume all the food before the Sterlet finds it. Chances of spawning this species are relatively small. The spawning season in nature is from May through June. The parents deposit the eggs over gravel in rivers. The young are similar to young tadpoles and are black in color.

Achirus errans ⬚F ⬚D ⬚X ⬚2⬚6⬚9 ⬚X ⬚N ⬚N ⬚E
Acipenser ruthenus ⬚F ⬚C ⬚X ⬚2⬚7⬚0 ⬚X ⬚N ⬚N ⬚E

[Dr. Herbert R. Axelrod]
[J. Kassanyi]

Acipenser sp. ⬚F⬚C⬚X⬚2⬚7⬚1⬚X⬚N⬚N⬚E
Adinia xenica ⬚F⬚A⬚X⬚2⬚7⬚2⬚X⬚N⬚N⬚5

[Dr. Herbert R. Axelrod]
[Aaron Norman]

ADINIA XENICA (Jordan & Gilbert) / *Diamond Killifish*

Range: Southeastern Florida to central Texas along the Gulf Coast; mostly in estuarine, brackish, salt marsh areas.

Habits: Relatively peaceful. Males may become rough during courtship. Does well with other small brackish water fishes that are not too aggressive.

Water Conditions: Prefers brackish water. Can be adapted to pure fresh water, but for full color and vitality they should have salt added to their water.

Size: About 5 cm.

Food Requirements: Accepts almost any high quality flake food as well as frozen and freeze-dried foods. Should be offered algae or other vegetable matter such as cooked spinach. The Diamond Killifish is especially fond of mosquito larvae.

Color Variations: Males dark green above, lighter grayish green below. Sides with a series of dark vertical bars alternating with 10-14 pearl-colored bars. Belly yellow; jaw orange. Dorsal and anal fins greenish covered with light (pale blue) spots. Females rather plain.

This small Gulf Coast killifish has not attained the popularity it deserves. It is handsome and hardy and not difficult to breed in typical killifish fashion. Males and females mature at about the same size (20 mm) though males grow to a much larger size. With the approach of spawning season males become more strikingly colored, and there is an elongation of the dorsal and anal fins. "Contact organs" appear on and in the vicinity of the anal fin of the male.

During spawning the pair swim about together, with the male above and slightly behind the female. At an appropriate spawning site (the female may clean the stalks of some aquatic plants or an inside filter) the female flexes her body and deposits a single egg. The male at the same time clasps her, wrapping his dorsal, anal and caudal fins around her. The pair separate and swim rapidly around the area for a few seconds. The spawning act is repeated many times although an egg is not produced every time.

In nature males generally outnumber the females, in some cases as much as two to one. Often there are battles when two rather evenly matched males try and court the same female. They will chase each other with fins spread, and, if neither withdraws from the fray, actual contact will be made. When a larger male approaches a courting male, the smaller one may be driven away and replaced by the larger one.

The 2 mm-diameter eggs hatch in about two weeks at 25.5°C. The young mature and are ready to spawn in about ten months.

For best results give them plenty of room and use about 25% to 50% salt water. This can be obtained by mixing ¼ to ½ as much marine aquarium mix as recommended for full-strength sea water. Any type of fish food is readily accepted, even by newly collected individuals. Algae or cooked spinach should be added occasionally, or try one of the commercial foods which have vegetable matter included.

AEQUIDENS CURVICEPS (Ahl) (incorrectly **Acara thayeri**)
Flag Cichlid, Thayer's Cichlid

Range: Amazon River and its tributaries.
Habits: Peaceful except when spawning; does not dig and uproot plants as much as most cichlids. Can be safely kept in community aquaria.
Water Conditions: Water should be soft and about neutral to slightly acid. Temperature about 24°C; for breeding, 28°C.
Size: 7.5 cm; breeds at 6.5 cm.
Food Requirements: Live foods such as tubifex worms, enchytrae, daphnia, mosquito larvae, etc. If earthworms are fed, they should be chopped.
Color Variations: Back brownish green, sides silvery gray shading to blue posteriorly. Anal and caudal fins have bright blue spots.

This is probably the most peaceful member of the genus *Aequidens*, with the possible exception of *A. maroni*. Because of their comparatively small size, they can be bred in aquaria as small as 40 liters, but of course a larger aquarium gives the fry a better start. The male, easily distinguished by his longer, more pointed dorsal and anal fins, will signify his intentions to spawn by taking possession of a particular spot and cleaning off a rock or section of the glass. He then half drives, half coaxes a female to the spot. Finally, after a few false starts she pastes row after row of eggs on the surface which was prepared, closely followed by the male who fertilizes them. They then guard the eggs and fan them with their tails. They also frequently pick at them to remove any foreign matter. In 4 days the eggs hatch. After the fry are free-swimming they should be fed with infusoria and very fine dried food, later with newly hatched brine shrimp.

1. *Aequidens curviceps* (p274) spawning on a stone in an aquarium.
2. *A. curviceps* male (p274) with his spawning coloration.

Aequidens curviceps female fanning her eggs with her fins. Photo by R. Zukal.

1. *Aequidens curviceps* F Q X 2 7 3 X N N 5   [H. J. Richter]
2. *Aequidens curviceps* ♂ F E X 2 7 4 X N N 5   [H. J. Richter]

1. *Aequidens itanyi* ♂ ⟨F⟩⟨A⟩⟨X⟩⟨2⟩⟨7⟩⟨5⟩⟨X⟩⟨N⟩⟨N⟩⟨B⟩ [R. Zukal]

2. *Aequidens itanyi* ⟨F⟩⟨R⟩⟨X⟩⟨2⟩⟨7⟩⟨6⟩⟨X⟩⟨N⟩⟨N⟩⟨B⟩ [R. Zukal]

AEQUIDENS ITANYI Puyo / *Dolphin Cichlid*

Range: Northeastern South America, especially French Guiana.

Habits: Very peaceful for a middle-sized cichlid but destructive of plants.

Water Conditions: Prefers hard and alkaline waters, but will live and spawn in softer, more acid water. Temperature 23 to 28°C.

Size: Male to 14 cm; female slightly smaller.

Food Requirements: Not fussy; accepts all live, freeze-dried and frozen foods.

Color Variations: Body greenish brown, with black blotchy line extending from just behind the eye to just below posterior portion of dorsal fin. Black spot at upper base of tail; black line from mouth through eye.

The first specimens of *Aequidens itanyi* to make an appearance on the aquarium scene were collected in the Itanyi River in French Guiana and transported to Dresden, Germany; the fish was an immediate hit with European aquarists, who appreciated it as much for its peaceful temperament toward other species as for its subdued, yet attractive coloration. Unfortunately, the lack of aggression showed with other species by *A. itanyi* is not so well evident in its disposition to members of its own species. Smaller, weaker specimens kept with older and stronger Dolphin Cichlids are often bullied and kept cowed. *A. itanyi* spawns by laying strings of slightly elliptical eggs on a flat surface, usually a smooth rock, although other surfaces have been pressed into service on occasion. Up to 500 eggs may be laid and fertilized, the male and female alternately performing their duties until the spawning has been completed. The eggs hatch in about 48 hours at a temperature of 26°C. Some breeders have reported good success in rearing the young by leaving the eggs and later the fry with the parents until the young are free-swimming, but most aquarists eliminate the danger of egg-eating by hatching eggs artificially.

1. *Aequidens itanyi* male (p275) preparing to spawn.
2. *A. itanyi* female (p275) laying eggs on a stone while spawning in a home aquarium.

Aequidens itanyi pair with their eggs soon after spawning. Photo by R. Zukal.

AEQUIDENS MARIAE Eigenmann / *Maria's Cichlid*

Range: Upper Amazon, Peru and Colombia.
Habits: Fairly peaceful with fishes its own size. A bit dangerous when spawning.
Water Conditions: Not too sensitive to water conditions. Does best in water from 24-28°C, with a pH of 6.8 and as soft as possible.
Size: To 12.5 cm.
Food Requirements: Prefers live foods such as tubifex worms, earthworms and small fishes. Willingly accepts frozen brine shrimp, dried foods, especially those which are pelletized, and bits of beef.

This is a fish which can easily be imported in great quantity because it has such a large range in areas where a considerable amount of fish collecting goes on anyway. This fish is found in the same waters as the Neon Tetra. According to scientific reports, this species is found in Barrigoon, Curnaral, Cano, Caruiceria, Villavicencio, Bogota, Quebrada and Cramalote, Colombia, and from Yarinacocha, Rio Morona, Iquitos and Yurimaguas, Peru. In Brazil it is found in the upper Amazon, the part they call Solimoes, which runs from near Manaus to Benjamin Constant. It is a very colorful cichlid with interesting spawning habits if offered the proper environment. Set up a 60- or 80-liter aquarium in which the water has been darkened a little with tea. Be careful that the pH doesn't go below 6.8. Since this fish likes dark water, use black gravel on the bottom to make the aquarium even darker and let the top grow thick with floating plants. This is the water in which the fish will become extremely colorful and active.

AEQUIDENS MARONI (Steindachner) / *Keyhole Cichlid*

Range: Surinam, Demarara River, Guyana.
Habits: Very peaceful; has been known to breed in community aquaria without molesting the other fishes. Seldom uproots plants.
Water Conditions: Clean water, neutral to slightly acid. Temperatures should be a bit higher than for other *Aequidens*, about 28 to 30°C.
Size: 9 cm; begins to breed at 6.5 cm.
Food Requirements: Live foods of all kinds, but not too large.

This is a beautiful, highly desirable cichlid; the only thing which can be said against it is that it is not very easy to spawn. Sexes are not easy to distinguish, as both develop long filaments on the dorsal and anal fins. However, when they are ready to spawn and the little tube begins to project from the vent, it will be noticed that the female's tube is heavier. A well-mated pair will spawn in the usual cichlid manner: a smooth surface is cleaned off and the eggs are placed there and fertilized. Both fish usually take turns fanning and mouthing the eggs, which can number up to 300 but are usually less. Hatching takes place in 5 days, and the parents usually take excellent care of their offspring, but of course there is a possibility for exceptions.

Aequidens mariae FDX277XNN6
Aequidens maroni FAX278XNN9

[Dr. Herbert R. Axelrod]
[Wolfgang Bechtle]

1. *Aequidens portalegrensis* ♂ F E X 2 7 9 X N N B
2. *Aequidens portalegrensis* F Q X 2 8 0 X N N B

AEQUIDENS PORTALEGRENSIS (Hensel) / *Port Acara, Black Acara*

Range: Santa Catarina, Rio Grande do Sul, Bolivia, Paraguay, Rio Uruguay.
Habits: Moderately peaceful, but should not be kept with smaller fishes. Will do some digging, and some plants may be uprooted.
Water Conditions: Not critical. Temperature 22 to 24°C. Large aquaria are recommended because spawns are often large.
Size: 12.5 cm; attains maturity at 7.5 cm.
Food Requirements: Has a robust appetite, and to the usual menu of live foods may be added such items as chopped beef heart, canned dog food, etc.
Color Variations: Body greenish brown; each scale has a dark border. Dorsal, anal and caudal fins have a reticulated pattern.

A popular cichlid species, one of the easiest to breed. Because of their size and the fact that they generally produce many young, a large aquarium should be given them. This will obviate the necessity for transferring some of the young to other aquaria while they are still small to prevent crowding. Sexes are fairly easy to distinguish. Females are slightly smaller, and males have long, flowing dorsal and anal fins. This species is likely to do some digging, and therefore plants with a firm root-stock, such as the *Cryptocoryne* species or *Sagittaria,* should be preferred. A rock with a flat surface should also be provided. When the parents are ready to spawn, and with a healthy pair this will be quite often, they will clean off this rock and deposit on it a great many eggs. Parental care is usually very tender, and a family of these fish is an intriguing thing to watch. Young hatch in four to five days, as is usual with cichlids, after which time the parents dig a number of shallow depressions in the bottom gravel. The fry are moved from one to the other of these depressions, and any youngster with the temerity to try to swim away is promptly gobbled up by the parent and spat back into the protection of the depression.

1. *Aequidens portalegrensis* male (p279) with his spawning coloration.
2. *A. portalegrensis* (p279) spawning on a stone in an aquarium.

Aequidens portalegrensis pair in an aquarium. Photo by L. E. Perkins.

AEQUIDENS PULCHER (Gill) (formerly **A. latifrons**) / *Blue Acara*

Range: Panama, Colombia, Venezuela and Trinidad.
Habits: Is very apt to bully smaller fishes; should be kept only with their own kind or larger fishes.
Water Conditions: Not critical; water should be kept well filtered, because the fish are likely to stir up the bottom by digging. Temperature 21 to 26°C.
Size: 15 cm; will begin to breed at 10 cm.
Food Requirements: All kinds of live foods, supplemented by chopped beef heart, earthworms, etc.

The Blue Acara may be easily distinguished from the other acara species by its unusually broad forehead. It is more apt to be troublesome to keep than the other species, but it has to its credit the fact that it is one of the easiest to breed and also one of the least likely to eat its own eggs and fry. It is probably the most robust of all the acaras, and if given the proper attention it will outlive many other aquarium fishes. Spawns like the others, but loves to dig and can be expected to uproot many plants. When replacing plants, do not put them back where they came from, or they will be uprooted again. Sometimes this fish, instead of cleaning off a flat surface, will dig down until the bottom is reached and will spawn on the surface thus afforded. Preliminaries are apt to be a bit more boisterous than with the others. A pair will sometimes seem to be getting ready to tear each other to pieces by locking their jaws together and kicking up a tremendous commotion all over the aquarium, and then they wind up by settling down to a very affectionate spawning.

AEQUIDENS RIVULATUS (Günther) / *Green Terror*

Range: Peru.
Habits: A vicious fish; will fight with all other fishes, including members of its own species.
Water Conditions: Not critical. Temperature 21 to 26°C.
Size: Up to 23 cm.
Food Requirments: Will take all standard aquarium fare for large cichlids.

The fishes of the genus *Aequidens* that have become well known among aquarium hobbyists range widely in size, from *A. curviceps* on the small end to *A. portalegrensis* among the large species. But until recently all of the fishes of the genus were considered to be characterized by a sameness in temperament; they were not the most peaceful of fishes, but for cichlids they were not bad actors at all. The introduction of *Aequidens rivulatus* in 1970 changed that opinion, because here was an *Aequidens* species that was downright mean. *A. rivulatus* is an attractive fish, but there simply is no escape from the fact that it is vicious. It will not hesitate to attack both other species and members of its own species. It is not satisfied merely to attack and warn off intruders into its own territory; if it can kill them, it will.

Aequidens pulcher ⬚F⬚⬚Q⬚⬚X⬚⬚2⬚⬚8⬚⬚1⬚⬚X⬚⬚N⬚⬚N⬚⬚B⬚   [R. Zukal]
Aequidens rivulatus ⬚F⬚⬚A⬚⬚X⬚⬚2⬚⬚8⬚⬚2⬚⬚X⬚⬚N⬚⬚N⬚⬚D⬚   [R. Brewer]

Aequidens tetramerus ☐F☐ ☐A☐ ☐X☐ ☐2☐☐8☐☐3☐ ☐X☐ ☐N☐ ☐N☐ ☐E☐

[Harald Schultz]

Amblyodoras hancocki ☐F☐ ☐D☐ ☐X☐ ☐2☐☐8☐☐4☐ ☐X☐ ☐N☐ ☐N☐ ☐E☐

[R. Zukal]

AEQUIDENS TETRAMERUS (Heckel) / *Pishuna*

Range: Found throughout northern South America from Guyana and throughout Brazil as far south as Rio de Janeiro.
Habits: A typical cichlid with typical cichlid behavior.
Water Conditions: Insensitive to minor water changes. Appreciates warm water but does well in water from 18 to 30°C. pH of 6.0-7.4; water up to 10 DH.
Size: 15 cm; becomes mature at 10 cm.
Food Requirements: Eats all types of bulky foods, whether living or not. Prefers frozen brine shrimp and tubifex.

So far has this fish ranged that it has been known under a number of different names from different places. Heckel first described this fish in 1840 as *Acara tetramerus* from the Rio Branco of Brazil. Eigenmann and Bray in 1894 used this species to establish the genus *Aequidens*. In 1891 Eigenmann and Eigenmann called this fish *Astronotus tetramerus* from the Amazon. Linnaeus called the fish *Labrus punctatus* in 1758, though there is a question about whether this was exactly the fish he meant or not.

AMBLYDORAS HANCOCKI (Cuvier & Valenciennes)
Hancock's Amblydoras

Range: Peruvian and Bolivian Amazon and tributaries, and the Guianas.
Habits: Mostly nocturnal; prefers a well-shaded tank. Will seldom uproot plants, and does not harm other fishes they cannot swallow.
Water Conditions: Temperatures between 24 to 26°C. Water about neutral to slightly alkaline.
Size: To 15 cm.
Food Requirements: Small live foods are preferred, such as daphnia, tubifex or white worms.

This attractive catfish is often confused with and sold as *Acanthodoras spinosissimus*. Although it is also spiny, *Amblydoras hancocki* is not in a class with its cousin. It is more peaceful and can be trusted in a community aquarium. When frightened it has the capability of burying itself in the sand with only its large eyes looking out. It can do this so skillfully that the bottom is not roiled, and seldom is there ever a plant uprooted. Sexes may be distinguished quite easily: males have spotted bellies and females do not. Secondarily, females have a narrower white band on the sides and the whiskers are not as distinctly ringed. Also, the pectoral and dorsal spines are more strongly hooked in the male than in the female. *Amblydoras hancocki* has not so far been bred in captivity, but in their native waters they have been observed to build nests from leaves, deposit their eggs in these and then guard eggs and young until the young are able to fend for themselves. A Dutch firm, Hanselmann, was the first to import this fish, in 1950. It was about this time that the first ones found their way into the United States as well.

AMIA CALVA Linnaeus / *Bowfin, Mudfish, Dogfish*

Range: Found in the United States from Vermont to the Dakotas, from Florida to Texas.
Habits: A vicious, voracious fish, not to be kept with any fish smaller than itself.
Water Conditions: Capable of living in any water which is not poisoned, though it prefers warm water from 21 to 30°C.
Size: Males grow to 50 cm; females to 75 cm.
Food Requirements: This is a fish which will only eat live foods. Small earthworms are acceptable. Larger specimens can be taught to accept beef heart and other meat products.

Here is a truly interesting fish. The illustration shows a baby not more than 5 cm long. He has a lot of growing to do, and in two years he will be about 45 cm long. The fish *Amia calva* is of great interest to zoologists becase of its relation to many prehistoric forms. The adult coloration is blackish olive with green reticulations on the sides. The lower side of the head has dark spots. The male has a black ocellus (eye-spot) edged with orange at the upper base of the caudal fin. You can see the spot clearly in this young male. The fish is very common in Florida, especially in the lowland swamps and the larger, still pools. The young are very interesting and they poise like snakes above their prey and strike with a fast darting action. They are always moving. They can live for hours out of water, and the author has successfully shipped them by air for 30 hours packed only in damp moss.

The jaws are equipped with an outer series of conical teeth, behind which is a row of rasp-like teeth. They have small teeth on the vomer, palatines and pterygoids. This fish is best kept alone or with fishes as large or larger than itself. It makes a fine pet and learns to eat from your hand. Try keeping one in an unheated 200-liter aquarium. They do very well if kept at room temperature and fed well.

ANABAS TESTUDINEUS (Bloch) / *Climbing Perch*

Range: India, Sri Lanka, Burma, Southeast Asia, southern China, Philippine Islands and Malaysia.
Habits: Aggressive; should be kept by themselves. Large aquarium should be provided and kept covered.
Water Conditions: Not critical. Has a wide temperature tolerance, 18 to 30°C.
Size: Up to 25 cm; becomes mature at 10 cm.
Food Requirements: Eats almost anything; in the absence of live foods, canned dog food with a high beef content is an acceptable substitute.
Color Variations: Dirty gray to greenish, with a dark spot at the caudal base and another just behind the gill plate.

The Climbing Perch, which incidentally is not a perch, has long been a great curiosity, and it used to be that a show which featured aquarium fishes

Amia calva ⬚F⬚ ⬚C⬚ ⬚X⬚ ⬚2⬚ ⬚8⬚ ⬚5⬚ ⬚X⬚ ⬚N⬚ ⬚N⬚ ⬚6⬚   [Dr. Herbert R. Axelrod]
1. *Anabas testudineus* ⬚F⬚ ⬚D⬚ ⬚X⬚ ⬚2⬚ ⬚8⬚ ⬚6⬚ ⬚X⬚ ⬚N⬚ ⬚N⬚ ⬚E⬚   [H. J. Richter]

2. *Anabas testudineus* [F][D][X][2][8][7][X][N][N][D]
3. *Anabas testudineus* var. [F][D][X][2][8][8][X][Y][N][B]

[Dr. Herbert R. Axelrod]
[Earl Kennedy]

counted on the antics of this fish to attract many people. A board was placed above an aquarium and one of these fish was netted out and placed on it. It would waddle the length of the board and plop back into the water, to the tireless amusement of the audience. In its native haunts the fish inhabits swampy places where, when the water begins to dry out, it must make its way from puddle to puddle across dry land until it finds another body of water. They are used as food fish, and the natives pack them in baskets with a little wet grass, keeping them alive in this way. It seldom spawns in the aquarium; males may be distinguished by their darker colors. The floating eggs receive no attention whatsoever and hatch in slightly less than two days. Spawns may be very large, and it may be necessary to distribute the fry among several aquaria to prevent crowding. Copious feeding should be provided as soon as the youngsters begin to swim, and the only problem thereafter will be what to do with them all.

1. *Anabas testudineus* in a home aquarium (p286).
2. This group of large *A. testudineus* requires a sizable aquarium (p287).
3. This is the xanthistic form of *A. testudineus* (p 287).

Anabas testudineus, the climbing perch, displaying its interesting skill of "walking" on land. In nature it uses this skill to move from pool to pool as its habitat dries out, thus surviving the dry season.

ANABLEPS ANABLEPS Linnaeus / *Four-Eyes*

Range: Northern South America from the Guianas and Venezuela to the Amazon in Brazil.
Habits: Surface fish spending most of their time on the surface of the water with their bulging eyes exposed to the air. In nature they move quickly over the surface of the water.
Water Conditions: They prefer very hard, warm water. Their natural habitat is usually brackish water canals. They are not found in large rivers or fast moving streams. Temperature 22-26°C.
Size: To about 30 cm in length.
Food Requirements: They prefer live food such as small fishes, worms and insects, but they can be tempted to take frozen brine shrimp and bits of beef heart on occasion.

The Four-Eyes is a large fish and has eyes in elevated sockets which give it the ability to see in air as well as water. The pupil is divided by a horizontal cross-partition. This is a livebearing species and gives birth to its young in small non-uniform batches. The young are about 5 cm long when born. The sexes are left- and right-handed, with a right-handed male mating with a left-handed female. Sexes are easy to ascertain as the male has a gonopodium-like adaptation on his anal fin which is a scaly tube. There is a great preponderance of females in this species. The author (HRA) once collected some 200 *Anableps anableps* in Guyana by laying a net in water less than 5 cm deep. The fish were "herded" onto this shallow bed and the net swiftly lifted. Of the 200 fish collected, only three males were apparent.

1. *Anableps anableps* (p290), swimming near the surface of the water, peers into the air.
2. The bulging eyes of *A. anableps* (p290) are in elevated sockets which give it the ability to see into the air.

ANCISTRUS HOPLOGENYS (Günther) / *Pearl Sucker*

Range: Widely dispersed over South America from Guyana to the Rio Paraguay which separates Paraguay from Brazil.
Habits: A nocturnal fish which clings to the glass but prefers "nightwork."
Water Conditions: A very hardy species which does well in any type of water as long as it is not too salty. It can be safely maintained in water at a temperature of 19-30°C.
Size: The usual size is under 12.5 cm.
Food Requirements: Eats every type of food usually offered aquarium fishes. Should be offered live foods on occasion.

The family Loricariidae contains such familiar fishes as *Plecostomus, Xenocara, Farlowella* and *Loricaria,* as well as *Ancistrus. Ancistrus* is closely related to *Xenocara.*

This species is one of the most colorful in the genus and though it has a very wide range, it is found in each area in very limited numbers. This should be a very simple fish to spawn as it rarely gets larger than 10 or 12.5 cm. Males have more and longer tentacles than females.

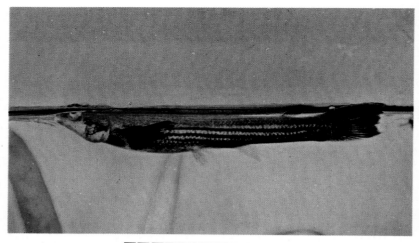

1. *Anableps anableps* F D T 2 8 9 X N N E   [Dr. Herbert R. Axelrod]
2. *Anableps anableps* F D M 2 8 9 X N N E   [W. A. Tomey]

Ancistrus hoplogenys F D X 2 9 0 X N N E   [Dr. Herbert R. Axelrod]

Ancistrus lineolatus F D X 2 9 1 X N N E   [Harald Schultz]

Ancistrus temmincki F D X 2 9 2 X N N E   [Harald Schultz]

ANCISTRUS LINEOLATUS Fowler / *Bristle-Nose*

Range: Upper Amazon, Colombia.
Habits: Does not attack other fishes, but two males of the same species would be likely to fight. A nocturnal feeder.
Water Conditions: Clean, roomy tank in not too bright a location. As these come from far inland, no salt should be added to the water. Temperature 22 to 26°C.
Size: About 15 cm.
Food Requirements: Should get some vegetable as well as animal nourishment; tubifex worms, daphnia, brine shrimp and chopped spinach.

There are quite a few species of this freakish-appearing genus, but they come in so seldom that the name "Bristle-Nose" is applied to all of them. A look at these always reminds one of the picture of the dog which has just made the mistake of attempting to bite a porcupine. A number of bristles, some of them branched, cover the upper part of the head and mouth, standing out in all directions. The size and thickness of these odd growths vary at different times of the year, and it is thought that they attain their greatest vigor and luxuriance during breeding season. This fish prefers a heavily planted tank, for this gives it a chance to get out of the bright light. Chances are you will seldom see it, as it will come out into the light only when driven by hunger. This is one of those fish that is so ugly that people are attracted to it because of its sheer ugliness. As with other fish which are equipped by nature with "whiskers," these are sensitive tactile and olfactory accessory organs. They permit the fish to feel its way around in the darkness and smell whatever food particles there are to be found on the bottom.

ANCISTRUS TEMMINCKI (Valenciennes) / *Temminck's Bristle-Nose*

Range: Upper Amazon, Peru, the Guianas and Surinam.
Habits: Generally peaceful toward other fishes, but two individuals cannot always be trusted to get along peacefully.
Water Conditions: Clean, well-oxygenated water is essential. Once established in a tank, they should be moved as little as possible. Temperature 21 to 26°C.
Size: About 15 cm.
Food Requirements: All small live foods are readily accepted, and an occasional meal of chopped spinach is beneficial.

This species differs from *Ancistrus lineolatus* in that the snout is not so broad and the body has more spots on it. Although the bristles on the fish in the picture are rather small, don't let that fool you! At other times of the year, they can be so bristly that you may wonder how it gets any food through them. In order to insure that they get their fair share of the feedings, it is well to put in some food before turning out the light. Then the others would not gobble it up before the Bristle-Nose gets it. Care must be taken not to overfeed, though.

292

ANCISTRUS TRIRADIATUS Eigenmann / *Branched Bristle-Nose*

Range: Colombia and adjacent Venezuela.
Habits: Nocturnal; shy and peaceful. Must have plenty of hiding places.
Water Conditions: Requires clean, heavily aerated water. Temperature 21 to 26°C.
Size: 12.5 cm.
Food Requirements: Vegetable matter plus additional live food.

Ancistrus belongs to the section of the family Loricariidae which has an unarmored ventral surface. *Stoneiella, Xenocara,* and *Plecostomus* also belong to this section. *Farlowella, Otocinclus,* and *Loricaria* all have armor plating on the belly and in addition lack an adipose fin. Loricariid catfishes are distinct from all other fishes in having an iris-lobe which expands or contracts to cover or expose the pupil of the eye. Other animals have muscles in the pupil of the eye which contract or expand to control the amount of light entering the eyes. The advantage of an iris-lobe in loricariids is unknown—perhaps it is just a unique development which has no actual advantage over a contractable pupil.

So far this species, like other *Ancistrus,* has not been spawned in the aquarium. Probably it would spawn in much the same fashion as *Xenocara.*

ANOSTOMUS ANOSTOMUS (Linnaeus) / *Striped Headstander*

Range: Guyana; Amazon River above Manaus.
Habits: Mostly peaceful; prefers large aquaria which are well-planted. Likes to nibble algae.
Water Conditions: Fairly soft water is preferable, neutral to slightly acid. Temperature 24-25.5°C.
Size: 18 cm; usually collected and sold at 8 to 10 cm.
Food Requirements: All living foods are preferred, but dried or frozen foods are also taken. Diet should be supplemented with green foods.

A small, pointed head with a mouth which points upwards characterizes this handsome fish. It is a partial vegetarian and occasional feedings of boiled spinach (chopped and sold in little jars as baby food) are eagerly consumed and very beneficial. All efforts at breeding this fish have so far been unsuccessful. Some conditions cannot be duplicated in the aquarium; for instance, a fish may be able to spawn only at greater depths than any aquarium can offer, or it may require more swimming space than it can get in the largest aquaria. Again, there may be an item on its native diet which will bring the fish to spawning ripeness and which we cannot supply or duplicate. Even though the fish has been known to aquarists since 1924, we are still very much in the dark with this one. Once one of the "difficult" species is bred successfully in the aquarium, it is very likely that succeeding generations of the fish will be comparatively easy to propagate. This has been the case with the Angelfish and later the Neon Tetra.

Ancistrus triradiatus FAX293XNNE

Anostomus anostomus FNX294XNNE

[Dr. Herbert R. Axelrod]

[R. Zukal]

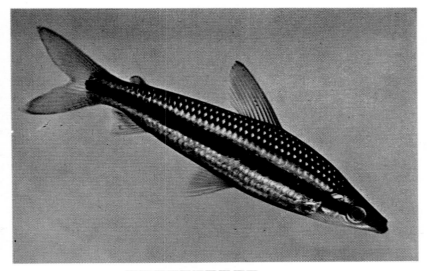

Anostomus taeniatus F D X 2 9 5 X N N E [Harald Schultz]
Anostomus trimaculatus F R X 2 9 6 X N N E [H. Hansen, Aquarium Berlin]

ANOSTOMUS TAENIATUS (Kner) / *Lisa*

Range: The Amazon from Brazil to the upper Amazon in Colombia and Peru.
Habits: Jumps at the slightest provocation. Its tiny mouth indicates it must have small particled food.
Size: To 12.5 cm.
Water Conditions: Prefers warm, soft, slightly acid water. Temperature 25°C.
Food Requirements: Small particles of dry food and tiny worms are accepted. Frozen brine shrimp is a favorite food.

This species has been known under nearly every genus in the family! Kner called it *Schizodon taeniatus* in 1859, representing its range as the Rio Guaporé, Barra do Rio Negro and Mato Grosso; Cope in 1878 called it *Laemolyta taeniata* and said it came from Pebas, Peru; Günther, in 1864, called the fish *Anostomus taeniatus;* while Fowler in 1950 uses *Laemolyta* as the proper genus. Because of the mouth's being subcircular in cross-section and because its behavior in an aquarium is absolutely *Anostomus*-like (with upside-down feeding, high jumping and sensitivity to shadows), the author decided to stick to the Günther categorization.

ANOSTOMUS TRIMACULATUS (Kner) / *Three-Spotted Headstander*

Range: Amazon Basin, the Guianas and Surinam.
Habits: Moderately peaceful; may be kept safely with fairly large fishes.
Water Conditions: Soft and slightly acid water. Temperature 25 to 26°C.
Size: 20 cm; specimens are usually sold at about 10 cm.
Food Requirements: Live foods and dried foods, with the addition of occasional feedings of green foods such as chopped spinach.

This fish is a bit large for the average aquarium, but it is quite peaceful. It is wise with this type of fish to provide an aquarium which is in a bright location, to encourage a growth of algae, which will be nibbled. With a species like this one, it is also advisable to provide plants which have strong stalks such as *Sagittaria, Cryptocoryne* and the like. These plants will be well cleaned of algae but not chewed, as the tender leaves of water sprite or some other soft-leaved plant would be. As with *Anostomus anostomus,* we are still waiting to hear of this species being successfully spawned. This species may prove to be even more difficult, as it becomes still larger. Sexes are not distinguishable to our knowledge, and it possible that the females have roe which never actually ripen in the close confines of captivity. This is a fish which if given conditions it likes may live to a ripe old age in the aquarium. Young specimens when they first arrive have a rosy-pink tail which seems to fade when the fish becomes older. The head-down swimming position which is typical of the genus is also evident here.

APELTES QUADRACUS (Mitchill) / *Fourspine Stickleback*

Range: Brackish and salt water from Labrador to Virginia.
Habits: Cannot be kept with other species; very scrappy.
Water Conditions: Prefers water to which some salt has been added, about a tablespoonful to every 4 liters. Aquarium should be unheated.
Size: 5 cm; breeds at a slightly smaller size.
Food Requirements: Live foods only; brine shrimp or daphnia preferred.

When the weather begins to get warm in the spring and early summer, the males develop their breeding colors and the females become heavy with roe. Males tear off bits of plants and build a nest among the weeds, cementing the stuff together with a sticky salivary secretion. The nest is a ball about the size of a walnut, with a tunnel through the middle. The female is coaxed into the nest, and her head and tail protrude from each end. The male joins her and a mighty quivering takes place which almost threatens to tear the nest apart. About a dozen eggs are expelled, after which the fish swim out and recuperate; then the process is repeated. When she has completed her duties, the female is driven off and should be removed to prevent bloodshed. The male is usually an excellent parent and the young are soon able to tear up newly hatched brine shrimp.

APHANIUS DISPAR (Rüppell) / *Long-Finned Arabian Minnow*

Range: From northern India westward through Iran, Saudi Arabia, Ethiopia, Israel, Jordan. It not only inhabits both sides of the Red Sea but also has apparently has penetrated into the Mediterranean Sea.
Habits: Very active, fast fishes. Probably should be kept by themselves because they do better in a brackish water environment.
Water Conditions: Prefer brackish water 3-6‰. Temperature 20 to 28°C.
Size: Attains a length of about 8 cm.
Food Requirements: The preference is for live foods of all kinds although some vegetable matter in the form of algae, cooked spinach, etc. should be added.
Color Variation: Male and female differ in color. The male is greenish gray or greenish brown with many bluish white spots; the dorsal, anal and pelvic fins are patterned with stripes and spots of similar colors and the caudal fin is yellowish with 2-4 vertical bands. The female is greenish or grayish yellow with a number of vertical dark bars.

The male has large, colorful dorsal and anal fins in contrast with the female's, which are much smaller and not very colorful at all. Spawning is no problem, as left by themselves in an aquarium they will breed by themselves. If you are a more serious breeder, keep the sexes apart until you are ready to have them spawn. Prepare the spawning tank with fine-leaved plants or a suitable synthetic substitute in which the eggs can be caught. Place the spawners together in this tank (female first so she can become acclimated) after about a week of conditioning on live foods. The spawning will take place (hopefully) on the fine-leaved plants put there for that purpose. After spawning, the parents should be removed.

Apeltes quadracus 🄵🄳🅇297🅇 Ⓝ Ⓝ🄻

Aphanius dispar 🄵🅁🅇298🅇 Ⓝ Ⓝ🄫

[Aaron Norman]
[Dr. Gerald R. Allen]

1. *Aphanius iberus* ♀
F B C 2 9 9 X N N 5

2. *Aphanius iberus* ♂
F A A 2 9 9 X N N 5

Aphanius mento F R X 3 0 0 X N N 5

APHANIUS IBERUS Cuvier & Valenciennes / *Spanish Minnow*

Range: Spain and Algeria.
Habits: Peaceful and very active. Best kept two females to one male.
Water Conditions: Neutral to slightly alkaline fresh water. Temperature 22 to 24°C.
Size: To 5 cm.
Food Requirements: Should be given live foods whenever possible. Other foods are eaten unwillingly or ignored.
Color Variations: Body greenish blue, with about 15 light blue bars. Tail blue with light edge. Females have much less color and colorless fins.

The Spanish Minnow has the distinction of being one of the few aquarium fishes native to Spain. Feeding them is a bit of a problem, because they are not easily accustomed to prepared or frozen foods. It is best to have a ratio of two females to each male, as the males are exceptionally vigorous drivers. Eggs are laid near the surface in bushy plants and are not eaten by the parents unless they are driven by hunger. Of course, their safety is assured if they are taken out. Hatching takes place in 6 to 8 days.

1. *Aphanius iberus* female (p299).
2. *Aphanius iberus* male (p299).

APHANIUS MENTO (Heckel) / *Persian Minnow*

Range: Iran, Syria, Asia Minor, in strongly brackish to fresh waters.
Habits: Will not annoy other fishes, but best kept with only their own kind with similar water requirements.
Water Conditions: Slightly hard, alkaline water with 1 teaspoonful of salt to every 4 liters of water.
Size: To 5 cm.
Food Requirements: Live foods with some vegetable matter added.

The Persian Minnow, often confused with the look-alike but morphologically different *A. sophiae* from the same general region, is among the most handsome and the most popular of the little-known *Aphanius* group. Their range is much more limited than that of their close relative *Aphanius fasciatus*, but they are reputed to be quite numerous where they occur. The upper fish (the female) in the picture looks distinctly pinchbellied, but this may be a sign that she has recently gotten rid of her eggs rather than a sign of ill-health. The difference in coloration for the sexes is very much apparent here. Note how the male has brighter, more sparkling colors and, most of all, more than double the amount of blue spots on the sides. Persian Minnows are easy to breed, but if possible two or more females should be used for one male. Otherwise he will drive her tirelessly until she no longer has any eggs left and then keep right on until her fins are in tatters. Eggs are large and easily seen. They can be picked out with tweezers by tearing away the bit of leaf on which they hang and placing the eggs in a hatching tank by themselves. They hatch in 10 to 14 days and the hardy fry are easily raised.

300

APHREDODERUS SAYANUS (Gilliams) / *Pirate Perch*

Range: Atlantic coast of the U.S. from New York to Texas; Mississippi Basin to Michigan.
Habits: Nocturnal predator. Will hunt for food at night and will eat any smaller fishes in the aquarium.
Water Conditions: Not critical.
Size: Attains a length of about 12.5 cm.
Food Requirements: Usually spurns anything but live foods, with minnows its favorites.

The Pirate Perch is an anatomical curiosity. Although it superficially looks quite normal, on closer inspection it is discovered that the vent is not where the vent should be! In juveniles the vent is placed normally (just anterior to the anal fin), but then it migrates anteriorly as the fish grows and winds up beneath the throat just behind the gill openings. Aside from the misplaced vent, the Pirate Perch has two anal spines (most fish have three) and three dorsal fin spines. It is brownish in color, with some darker brown markings on the head.

In an aquarium the Pirate Perch is found during the day reclining among the decorations (rocks or plants) at rather odd angles, perhaps an attempt to keep its head away from the bright lights.

APHYOCHARAX ANISITSI Eigenmann & Kennedy / *Bloodfin*

Range: Argentina, Rio Parana.
Habits: Active, peaceful species which likes to travel in schools and may be trusted in the community aquarium.
Water Conditions: Requires clean, well-aerated water which is neutral to slightly acid. Temperature should average about 24°C.
Size: 5 cm; begins to breed when slightly smaller.
Food Requirements: Not fussy, as long as there is enough; has tremendous energy and therefore requires frequent feedings.

One of the old favorites, and rightfully so. A small school of these lovely fish disporting themselves in an aquarium is a pretty sight. They are not very sensitive to lower temperatures, but when kept cool most of the color fades out. To breed this fish, prepare an aquarium of about 40-liters capacity with a layer of marbles, about 4 deep, on the bottom. Pour in water from the tank in which they were kept, to which is added one-third fresh tap water of the same temperature until it comes about 15 cm above the marbles. Select the heaviest female and the most active male and place them in this aquarium. A vigorous driving soon takes place which is punctuated by frequent stops, usually over the same spot. The pair assumes a side-by-side position and with a great deal of quivering a few eggs are expelled and fertilized. These eggs are non-adhesive and sink to the bottom among the marbles. When the female has become depleted and the pair begins to hunt for eggs, they should be removed. The eggs are very small and hatch after only 30 hours.

Aphredoderus sayanus [F][D][X][3][0][1][X][N][N][8]   [Aaron Norman]
Aphyocharax anisitsi [F][Q][X][3][0][2][X][N][N][E]   [Dr. Herbert R. Axelrod]

Aphyosemion australe ⬚F⬚E⬚X⬚3⬚0⬚7⬚X⬚N⬚N⬚4

Aphyosemion bertholdi ⬚F⬚E⬚X⬚3⬚0⬚8⬚X⬚N⬚N⬚4

APHYOSEMION AUSTRALE (Rachow) / *Lyretail, Lyretailed Panchax*

Range: Southern Cameroon to Gabon.
Habits: Peaceful; will not bother other fishes, but will do better if kept by themselves.
Water Conditions: Soft, well-aged acid water.
Size: 5 cm; will begin breeding at 2.5 cm.
Food Requirements: Daphnia, tubifex worms, enchytrae, brine shrimp, etc.

Probably the most popular of the so-called "panchax" species, which includes genera like *Epiplatys, Aphyosemion, Aplocheilus, Pachypanchax* and *Aplocheilichthys.* Even while very young, males can be distinguished by their beautiful lyre-shaped tail. Females are comparatively drab brown, with rounded fins and only a few red spots for color. A very easy breeder. Males drive almost ceaselessly, and it is better to use several females for each male. Floating plants may be used to receive the eggs, which hang from the leaves by a sticky thread. Eggs are not eaten. There are several ways to hatch the eggs. One of the easiest is to let the fish spawn for a week or so and then remove either the plants or the fish. Another is to remove the eggs by feeling the plants for hard little lumps which look like glass beads. The eggs hatch in 10 to 15 days, depending upon temperature. Strangely, eggs kept at a lower temperature (about 21°C) will hatch more quickly than those kept warmer.

APHYOSEMION BERTHOLDI Roloff / *Berthold's Killie*

Range: Liberia.
Habits: Not aggressive, but they are best kept in their own tank to keep them at their ease.
Water Conditions: Very soft water. Temperature about 23.5°C.
Size: About 5 cm.
Food Requirements: Small live or freeze-dried foods.

We can always depend on a great number of brilliantly colored fishes in the *Aphyosemion* group. Here we have *Aphyosemion bertholdi,* found in Totoba, Liberia by E. Roloff of Karlsruhe, Germany. Mr. Roloff discovered many of our most attractive killies. Like the rest of the *Aphyosemion* group, there are variations in body color with this species. The predominating color of the species is blue, but in other specimens it is much more green. Still others have a great deal of yellow in the head. As with most of the *Aphyosemion* species, the females lack almost all of the colors so generously bestowed upon the males. They are a muddy reddish brown in color and have only a few small spots in the fin and tail. Eggs are buried in the bottom and hatch in 2 to 3 weeks. The fry are not particularly hard to raise.

APHYOSEMION BIVITTATUM (Lönnberg) / *Two-Striped Aphyosemion*

Range: Cameroon and Niger Basins, in small streams and swampy areas.
Habits: Peaceful, but does better if kept with its own kind.
Water Conditions: Well-aged acid water. Temperature about 25°C.
Size: 6 cm; breeds at 4 cm.
Food Requirements: Live foods such as daphnia, tubifex worms, enchytrae, brine shrimp, etc.
Color Variations: Body color reddish brown, almost white on the belly. Two dark horizontal stripes. Long red dorsal and lyre-shaped tail fin.

This beautiful *Aphyosemion* species likes a tank of its own which is not too brightly lighted and is well planted. Once it has established itself, it will do quite well and give its owner much pleasure. It deposits its eggs on fine-leaved plants near the surface, but we have also observed that occasionally an egg is buried in the bottom sediment. For this reason, no matter how thoroughly the plants are gone over for eggs, an occasional youngster shows up, seemingly from nowhere. *Aphyosemion* eggs are quite firm, even hard to the touch, and may be handled with little danger of breaking them. However, if hatching time is close at hand, it has been known to happen that an occasional youngster pops out from its shell. There is some danger of the parents eating their young after they hatch; the trick is to keep them well-fed. The young also learn very early in life that it behooves them to stay away from anything larger than they are. Any fish which does not learn this early in life does not live very long. As with the others, hatching time is 10 to 15 days and the young grow well if started on newly hatched brine shrimp.

Aphyosemion species which do not bury their eggs may be spawned successfully in small aquaria, about four to eight liters. Using these reduces the area in which the eggs may be laid and makes them easier to find. Occurring as they do in small ditches and pools in their native haunts, they do not feel as cramped as a more active fish might. Do not let their leisurely movements fool you, however; they can move rapidly if the occasion demands and are lively jumpers. Never come to the conclusion that because the water level is a bit low they cannot jump out of an uncovered aquarium. Many a good fish has been found on the floor dried up because someone thought they couldn't jump out. A sheet of glass is a small investment and will keep your valuable fish where they belong.

1. This *Aphyosemion bivittatum* (p310) specimen was the product of a mating between parents from two different locations, one from east Nigeria and one from southeast Nigeria.
2. Two *A. bivittatum* male hybrids (p310) fighting. Both are sterile.

1. *Aphyosemion bivittatum* ⬚F⬚E⬚X⬚3⬚0⬚9⬚X⬚N⬚N⬚5   [Col. J.J. Scheel]

2. *Aphyosemion bivittatum* ⬚F⬚E⬚X⬚3⬚1⬚0⬚X⬚N⬚N⬚5   [Col. J.J. Scheel]

1. *Aphyosemion bualanum* ⬚F⬚E⬚X⬚3⬚1⬚1⬚X⬚N⬚N⬚5 .   [Col. J.J. Scheel]

2. *Aphyosemion bualanum* ⬚F⬚E⬚X⬚3⬚1⬚2⬚X⬚N⬚N⬚5   [Col. J.J. Scheel]

311

APHYOSEMION BUALANUM (Ahl) / *African Swamp Killie*

Range: Eastern Cameroon and the Central African Republic.
Habits: Peaceful when kept with fish its own size.
Water Condition: Varies from soft acid water to hard alkaline water.
Size: To 6 cm; females slightly smaller.
Food Requirements: Readily accepts live or prepared foods.
Color Variations: Green on the back, grading to light blue on the flanks with vertical red bars along the body extending to the end of the caudal fin. Blue marginal bands on the caudal fin.

Aphyosemion bualanum has been found in a wide variety of habitat types ranging from cool swift mountain streams of eastern Cameroon eastward to warm stagnant marshes on the plains of the Central African Republic. Accordingly, there are some color variations between populations, some having more intense blue than others. Both blue and red forms are known in the trade.

The long, pointed snout and the lyre-shaped caudal fin with its long, filamentous tips give the fish a more slender appearance than most of the other *Aphyosemion* species. Because of the wide range of habitats in which *A. bualanum* is found, the fish adapts well to nearly any reasonable pH and DH in which they are kept. However, if they are kept in relatively cool (25°C) well-shaded aquariums, their colors appear much richer. This species spawns in plant thickets or near the top in floating nylon mops. They are not as prolific as the majority of their congenerics and under favorable conditions will produce only two to three dozen eggs in a week of spawning activity. The eggs should be water-incubated and will hatch in about 14 days. The fry are able to eat newly hatched brine shrimp nauplii as their first food. Unlike most other *Aphyosemion* species, the fry grow rather slowly at first and will not reach sexual maturity until they are about four months old. Although there are some negative factors surrounding the propagation of *Aphyosemion bualanum,* these negatives are more than compensated for by this fish's enchanting beauty.

1. *Aphyosemion bualanum* male (p311).
2. This fish (p311) is a hybrid resulting from the cross between *A. bualanum* species and *A. exiguum* species. This specimen is fertile and has most of the characteristics of *A. bualanum*.

APHYOSEMION CALLIURUM (Boulenger) / *Blue Calliurum*

Range: Liberia to northern Angola.
Habits: Peaceful in mixed company, but they are happier with just their own kind.
Water Conditions: Soft, slightly acid water. For spawning, pH value should be about 6.5. Temperature 23 to 25.5°C.
Size: To 6 cm.
Food Requirements: Live foods; frozen or dried foods are taken reluctantly.

It is a good policy for those who own both *Aphyosemion ahli* and *A. calliurum* to be careful to avoid mixing up the females. Results, if any, of a mating between a male of one variety and a female of another could result in a hybrid which is far inferior in color to either variety, as well as a fish which might easily be sterile. Spawning, of course, is the same as in the other egg-hanging species. Eggs are deposited singly near the water's surface in plants or any reasonable plant substitutes given them by their owner. Eggs hatch in 12 to 15 days and the fry begin eating at once. They are hardy and grow rapidly.

APHYOSEMION CHAYTORI (Roloff) / *Chaytor's Killie*

Range: Sierra Leone.
Habits: Typical mop-spawning African killifish; generally peaceful, although males will fight with one another.
Water Conditions: Soft, slightly acidic water best.
Size: Both males and females to about 5 cm.
Food Requirements: Prefers small live foods but accepts meaty frozen foods; dry foods not always accepted.

There is a great deal of understandable confusion concerning the taxonomic status of many of the killifish species of West Africa, especially as regards the differentiation among species of the genus *Aphyosemion*. This is especially true of those species discovered and described subsequent to the publication of Jorgen Scheel's masterful definitive treatise on African killifishes, *Rivulins of the Old World*.

In its native Sierra Leone, *Aphyosemion chaytori* lives in small, fairly fast-flowing waters that are surrounded by heavy jungle vegetation; these waters range from between 23 to 25°C in temperature and are soft and acidic.

There are two distinct races of this species. In the race found in the Kasewe Forest, the males are more intensely marked with blue; fish of the race found around the vicinity of Rokupr are more plainly colored, although they are still very attractive.

313

Aphyosemion calliurum F E X 3 1 3 X N N 5
Aphyosemion chaytori F Q X 3 1 4 X N N 4

[Col. J.J. Scheel]
[V. Elek]

Aphyosemion christyi 🄵🄴🗵③①⑤🗵🄽🄽④   [Col. J.J. Scheel]

Aphyosemion cinnamomeum 🄵🄴🗵③①⑥🗵🄽🄽④   [Col. J.J. Scheel]

APHYOSEMION CHRISTYI (Boulenger) / *Christy's Lyretail*

Range: Central Congo drainage.
Habits: Completely peaceful, but does best in the company of other killies.
Water Conditions: For general care old, moderately hard water is preferred. Water for breeding and hatching should be soft and slightly acid.
Size: About 5 cm.
Food Requirements: Live or frozen brine shrimp, daphnia, mosquito larvae, etc.

This is one of the species of the genus *Aphyosemion* which develops distinct projections on the dorsal and ventral edges of the caudal fin. The length of these extensions varies greatly from strain to strain, with some showing very little extension while others, such as those from the Kinshasa area of Zaire, develop elegant extensions. A second form, characterized by a large number of red spots on the sides and fins, has been called *A. cognatum,* which is a completely different species. The various color strains and geographical races of *A. christyi* cross readily, but the young are often sterile. This is due in part to the fact that the different populations differ in chromosome numbers. The aquarist interested in propagating this species is urged to use peat moss on the bottom in the place of sand. In addition to slightly acidifying the water, the peat moss seems to put a number of beneficial substances into the water which stimulate spawning. The moss should be boiled for about an hour and carefully rinsed before being placed in the aquarium. Christy's Lyretail is a plant-spawner whose eggs hatch in about 8 days. The fry require infusoria for two or three days and live baby brine shrimp thereafter.

APHYOSEMION CINNAMOMEUM Clausen / *Cinnamon Killie*

Range: Western Cameroon, Africa.
Habits: Should be kept in a tank of their own.
Water Conditions: Slightly acid water about 6 DH. Keep them at about 24°C; spawn at 24 to 25.5°C.
Size: About 5 cm; females slightly smaller.
Food Requirements: Live or freeze-dried foods.

Females are a grayish brown all over and are a little smaller than males. This species belongs to the bottom-spawning group. Their spawning tank should have about 2.5 cm of peat moss on the bottom. When the fish begin to spawn into this, the peat moss is removed with the eggs, carefully pressed out and then placed in a glass jar which is loosely covered and stored for a month. Then fresh water is poured on the peat moss, and the fry hatch out in a few hours.

APHYOSEMION COGNATUM Meinken / *Red-Spotted Aphyosemion*

Range: Lower Congo River, in the vicinity of Kinshasa.
Habits: Peaceful, but best kept by themselves.
Water Conditions: Soft, acid, well-aged water.
Size: 6 cm; breeds at 4 cm.
Food Requirements: Live foods; daphnia, tubifex worms, enchytrae, etc.

Males have an oddly-shaped dorsal fin which has the longest rays toward the tail, making it look as if it had been stuck on backwards. Although this species will not take as much abuse as *A. australe* and some of the others, it is fairly hardy and easily bred. It is not a new fish to the hobby, having made its first appearance in 1950 in Germany, where it was identified by the well-known expert Hermann Meinken. This is one of the top-spawning species. A small aquarium is provided which contains some floating fine-leaved plants or a substitute such as a bundle of nylon yarn which has been tied to a cork. The fish readily accept this substitute and spawn into it. After a few days this mop is removed and the strands separated. Eggs are seen stuck to the threads with a fine sticky string. They may be lifted off by this string with a pair of tweezers to be placed in a jar where they will hatch in about 14 days. Young may be fed on newly hatched brine shrimp.

APHYOSEMION FILAMENTOSUM (Meinken) / *Togo Lyretail*

Range: Tropical West Africa.
Habits: Peaceful in the community aquarium, but better kept with their own kind or similar species.
Water Conditions: Water should be soft and slightly acid. Temperature about 24°C. A well-planted or well-shaded aquarium is best.
Size: Males about 5.7 cm; females about 4.5 cm.
Food Requirements: Live foods essential; will eat frozen or dried foods.

Do not judge *Aphyosemion filamentosum* by the illustration; this is a male that has just reached full size and is only beginning to get his adult finnage. This consists of two long white tips at the upper and lower points of the tail and a number of longer rays in the anal fin which give the fin a fringed appearance. Therefore the name *filamentosum*, meaning filamentous. With most *Aphyosemion* species, the female is about the same size, but here the female is considerably smaller and has far more modest coloration and finnage. Her tail is round, her anal fin is not fringed, and she has only a few red spots on her body. This is one of the top-spawning species, and the male is a very active driver. For this reason it is best if possible to give him two or three females so that he can divide his attentions between them rather than run one ragged. Eggs are laid a few each day in the plant thickets near the surface, and hatching time may vary from two weeks to a month.

Aphyosemion cognatum ⬚F⬚E⬚X⬚3⬚1⬚7⬚X⬚N⬚N⬚5   [Col. J.J. Scheel]

Aphyosemion filamentosum ⬚F⬚E⬚X⬚3⬚1⬚8⬚X⬚N⬚N⬚5   [Col. J.J. Scheel]

318

1. *Aphyosemion gardneri* 🄵🄴🄧③①⑨🄧🄝🄝⑤   [Col. J.J. Scheel]

2. *Aphyosemion gardneri* 🄵🄴🄧③②⓪🄧🄝🄝⑤   [Col. J.J. Scheel]

APHYOSEMION GARDNERI (Boulenger) / *Steel-Blue Aphyosemion*

Range: Coast of Nigeria to the Republic of Congo, where it occurs in small bodies of water.
Habits: Should be kept by themselves; males will fight and tear fins if two are kept together.
Water Conditions: Well-aged, soft, acid water.
Size: 6 cm; will begin spawning at 4 cm.
Food Requirements: Living foods such as daphnia, tubifex worms, enchytrae, etc.
Color Variations: Males are a greenish blue which shades to a deep steel-blue toward the tail. There are many purple dots and markings. Caudal with blue or yellow edges.

This is another of the bottom-spawners; an aquarium for spawning them may be prepared by putting a layer of peat moss about 1 cm thick on the bottom of a 20-liter aquarium. The peat moss must be well boiled to remove any excess acidity. Soft water is then poured in and when the peat moss settles, the pair of fish is introduced. Some cover such as floating plants and a few rocks may also be added to provide an occasional refuge for the female when she is chased too hard. Spawning takes place in the loose peat moss, and close observation will show the preferred locations. The eggs are removed by gently stirring up the peat moss and siphoning them out with an eyedropper. Once the preferred spawning sites are established, much work can be avoided by placing a shallow glass dish filled with peat moss or silicate sand in these spots, then gently lifting out the dish to remove the eggs. Eggs are stored in darkened jars in soft water to which has been added a little methylene blue. Eggs hatch in 6 weeks.

1. *Aphyosemion gardneri* male, the blue finned form (p319).
2. *Aphyosemion gardneri* male, the yellow finned form (p319).

Aphyosemion gardneri mating pair with the male above. Photo by Milan Chvojka.

APHYOSEMION GERYI Lambert / *Gery's Aphyosemion*

Range: Sierra Leone.
Habits: Peaceful, but better kept in pairs in a small aquarium.
Water Conditions: Acid, pH 6.5 to 6.8 and well aged. Temperature 23 to 26°C. Small tanks of 8 to 20 liters capacity seem to be preferred.
Size: Males about 7.5 cm; females about 6.5 cm.
Food Requirements: Live foods preferred, but will accept freeze-dried foods.

Gery's Aphyosemion is an extremely hardy species that can tolerate a wide range and extremes in water conditions. Furthermore, they are not susceptible to many diseases. This, together with the male's bright red coloration (especially during breeding periods), makes this species an excellent aquarium fish. *A. geryi* is not a retiring species and will readily display itself if raised in a well-lit aquarium with open spaces. In nature this fish inhabits pools and slow-moving streams in shaded forest areas. The areas in which they are normally found are usually densely vegetated.

Aphyosemion geryi is best kept in a ratio of one male to two or three females. If kept in pairs, the male may hurt or kill the female in his attempt to spawn with her. This species is an easy one to spawn, and the young are not difficult to raise. After spawning in a typical killifish manner, the eggs are deposited on the bottom of the aquarium in either plants or non-floating mops. Depending on the temperature, the eggs will hatch in about fourteen days. Because the fry are small, they should initially be given infusoria. After three or four days the infusoria may be replaced with newly hatched brine shrimp.

1. *Aphyosemion geryi* male, the yellow-tailed form (p322).
2. *Aphyosemion geryi* male, the blue-tailed form (p322).

Sierra Leone, Africa. African fishermen with nets collect *Aphyosemion* species which will be used in taxonomic studies. Photo by Dr. Herbert R. Axelrod.

321

1. *Aphyosemion geryi* ꎎ ꍗ ꌩ ③ ② ① ꌩ ꌧ ꌧ ⑥   [Col. J.J. Scheel]

2. *Aphyosemion geryi* var. ꎎ ꍗ ꌩ ③ ② ② ꌩ ꌧ ꌧ ⑥   [Col. J.J. Scheel]

322

Aphyosemion guineense Ⓕ Ⓔ Ⓧ ③ ② ③ Ⓧ Ⓝ Ⓝ ⑨   [Col. J.J. Scheel]

Aphyosemion labarrei Ⓕ Ⓔ Ⓧ ③ ② ④ Ⓧ Ⓝ Ⓝ ④   [Col. J.J. Scheel]

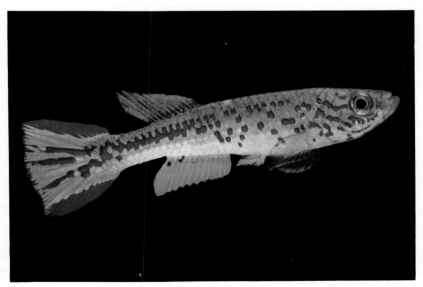

APHYOSEMION GUINEENSE Daget / *Guinean Killie*

Range: Sierra Leone, Upper Niger drainage of Guinea.
Habits: Peaceful, but should have an aquarium of its own.
Water Conditions: Neutral to slightly acid. Temperature 23-26°C. An addition of salt, one quarter teaspoon per liter, may prove beneficial.
Size: Attains a length of 10 cm or more.
Food Requirements: Live foods are preferred, but will eventually accept prepared foods.

Although similar in appearance to most annuals, this species is not an annual. It requires only about two weeks for complete egg development. *A. guineense* can be spawned using standard mops or peat moss. The pair seem to be sporadic spawners, sometimes dropping only a few eggs per week and at other times up to 50 or more per day. The mop or peat can be removed weekly if the pair are left in the tank continuously or, if they are separated before spawning, removed immediately after spawning. The eggs develop and hatch without delay according to Scheel. Hatching may be delayed for up to 3 or 4 weeks if the medium is stored in plastic bags or jars, but if the temperature is too high (26.5°C or higher) they will hatch out prematurely and perish. Upon reimmersion they should hatch out normally.

APHYOSEMION LABARREI Poll / *Labarre's Aphyosemion*

Range: Congo River and tributaries, near the mouth.
Habits: Peaceful, inclined to be shy. They jump, and their tanks should be kept covered.
Water Conditions: Neutral to slightly acid water. Temperature 23 to 26°C.
Size: To 5 cm; females 0.5 cm smaller.
Food Requirements: Small live foods; frozen or dried foods accepted reluctantly.

This beautiful *Aphyosemion* species naturally inhabits rain-forest streams which are slow-moving and dense with vegetation. Soft, slightly acid water with a temperature between 23 and 26°C is preferred in the aquarium as it is in nature. This fish does not do well in colder temperatures. The water should be kept clean and clear, and partial water changes should be made weekly. When healthy and content with its environment, this fish will have a very good appetite.

Aphyosemion labarrei will readily breed in a ten-liter aquarium and will prefer temperatures in the lower end of its recommended range. After the typical killifish spawning ritual, this species lays large clear eggs, 1.7 to 1.8 mm in diameter, which adhere to floating plants or artificial spawning mops. As with many other killifish, it is a good idea to have two or three females for every male. This will divide the male's attention so that the females will not be worn-out by his constant sexual pursuits. It is also important to note that females are especially sensitive to the water conditions. After a successful spawning, the fry will hatch in about two weeks. The large fry grow slowly but can take newly hatched brine shrimp.

APHYOSEMION LIBERIENSE (Boulenger) / *Liberian Killie*

Range: Liberia.
Habits: Not scrappy, but should have their own aquarium.
Water Conditions: Soft and slightly acid. Temperature 22 to 26°C.
Size: About 5 cm.
Food Requirements: Live, frozen or freeze-dried foods.

Aphyosemion liberiense shows off its beautiful colors best when it is provided with a relatively large tank of 20 to 40 liters capacity, the bottom of which is covered with black (or some other dark color) gravel. A few plants, such as *Cryptocoryne*, are good, and dim lighting will complete the setup. The light should come from overhead for best results.

This fish will spawn without too much trouble when two or three females are put with one male. The pre-spawning behavior is in typical killifish fashion. Some hobbyists consider this species as a sort of halfway mark between the egg-laying and egg-burying fishes. Given a tank where they have the opportunity of hanging their eggs in bushy plants, they will do so, but when given the opportunity of burying their eggs, they will do this too. It has been observed that eggs left in the breeding aquarium do not hatch on time. Instead of the usual 10 to 12 days, the eggs hatch in upwards of 30 days. It should be noted that if the water in the aquarium is kept clean and free of dirt or peat, the eggs will not exhibit annual characteristics common in killifishes.

APHYOSEMION OCCIDENTALIS Clausen / *Golden Pheasant*

Range: Sherboro Island and Sierra Leone along the coastal lowlands.
Habits: Better kept by themselves. This is not a fish for a community aquarium.
Water Conditions: Soft, acid water. Temperature 24 to 26°C.
Size: To 10 cm.
Food Requirements: Prefers live or fresh foods such as brine shrimp, mosquito larvae or beef heart; will reluctantly adapt to prepared dry foods.

Although this fish has been in the hobby for many years, it was only first recognized as a distinct species in 1966. The first account of this fish was on June 9th, 1908. Grote, a German aquarist from Hamburg who was serving on a ship returning from West Africa, caught three specimens of this species on Sherboro Island near Sierra Leone. At the time, these specimens were thought to be in the genus *Fundulus.*

Aphyosemion occidentalis is an annual rivulin species. During mating, the male uses his dorsal and anal fins to grasp the female while fertilizing the eggs. After fertilization, the eggs are deposited about one cm below the substrate. The eggs usually need over ten weeks to incubate. It should be noted that peat moss makes a very good substrate medium. After hatching, the fry grow very quickly. The entire cycle of egg-laying, hatching, maturing and mating of the offspring takes roughly 8 months.

Aphyosemion liberiense F E X 3 2 5 X N N 4 [Col. J.J. Scheel]

Aphyosemion occidentalis F E X 3 2 6 X N N 8 [Col. J.J. Scheel]

Aphyosemion petersi F Q X 3 2 7 X N N 5   [G. Wolfsheimer]

Aphyosemion seymouri F E X 3 2 8 X N N 4   [H. J. Richter]

APHYOSEMION PETERSI (Sauvage) / *Yellow-Edged Aphyosemion*

Range: Ghana, Ivory Coast and Togo.
Habit: Peaceful; does better when kept by itself, but may be kept in community aquaria.
Water Conditions: Well-aged water of about 8 degrees of hardness.
Size: 6 cm; females 5 cm.
Food Requirements: Live foods such as daphnia, tubifex worms, enchytrae.

This fish was first discovered in 1882 and came into prominence again in 1952 when some were brought in to be sold to aquarists in this country and Germany. It is a peaceful species, and the writer recalls keeping a number of them in a community tank for some time. They do not have the gaudy beauty found in many of the *Aphyosemion* species, but rather a quiet charm all their own. This is another top-spawning species; eggs are laid near the surface in bundles of floating plants or their substitutes. Here is another plant substitute which may be used, besides those already given: tie a bundle of Spanish moss (which was previously well boiled) to a cork to keep it near the surface. If you do not care to pick out the eggs and want to save time, simply leave the bundle with the breeders for about 10 days, take it out, snip off the cork and tie it onto another bundle. Eggs hatch in 10 to 15 days like the others, and the youngsters are quite easy to raise.

APHYOSEMION SEYMOURI Loiselle & Blair / *Seymour's Killifish*

Range: Ghana, primarily around the city of Accra.
Habits: Males aggressive among themselves and can be hard on females; other species of comparable size generally ignored.
Water Conditions: Not critical as to hardness and alkalinity levels. Temperature range of 23 to 26°C.
Size: About 5 cm in captivity; much larger in nature.
Food Requirements: Live foods preferred above all others, but meaty prepared foods (especially frozen brine shrimp) accepted.

Aphyosemion seymouri is one of the killifishes that has not achieved any great degree of popularity in the fish hobby, even among specialists in the keeping of rivulin species. It is a good-looking fish, but it is a very slow grower and a very poor producer. The great German aquarist Erhard Roloff, for example, related that from 40 eggs that were produced by the first pair he kept only six hatched, and they were all belly-sliders. These results were obtained by keeping the eggs in water rather than in damp peat moss; when the peat moss method was used (six to seven weeks is the best length of time to keep the eggs in the peat moss), results were much better but still nowhere near comparable with the number of eggs and fry of many other *Aphyosemion* species. *Aphyosemion seymouri* will spawn at the age of about four months but has an active life span of only about seven months.

APHYOSEMION SJOESTEDTI (Lönnberg) / *Blue Gularis*

Range: Guinea to Cameroon.
Habits: Better kept by themselves; definitely not a fish for the community aquarium.
Water Conditions: Soft, acid water. Temperature 24 to 27°C.
Size: To 9 cm.
Food Requirements: Live foods of all kinds.

Here is a fish to try anyone's patience to a breaking point! The Blue Gularis comes from a region in which the dry seasons are exceptionally long. This means that eggs are laid before the waters recede completely and then the eggs which have been buried in the mud go into a sort of resting period from which they are released when months later the rains begin to fall and the areas where the eggs were laid again begin to fill with water. Hatching follows very quickly and the fry grow at a furious rate until they become mature and lay their own eggs in the few months before the evaporating waters leave them stranded. Of all the West African "annuals," this one has the longest incubational period: 3 to 6 months. In the aquarium a pair is allowed to spawn in a 2-cm layer of peat moss on the bottom for several weeks, until the female has become depleted. The peat moss with the eggs in it is then removed and placed in a covered container where it is kept damp but not wet. Here is where the patience comes in: 3 months at least must go by, and then if the eggs do not hatch the peat moss is dried again and further attempts are made until success is achieved.

APHYOSEMION STRIATUM (Boulenger) / *Five-Lined Killie*

Range: Coastal lowlands of Gabon and Equatorial Guinea.
Habits: Not scrappy if kept with fish their own size or a bit larger.
Water Conditions: Does well in soft slightly acid water but adapts well to harder, more alkaline conditions. Temperature 19 to 23°C.

Size: 5 to 6 cm; females slightly smaller.
Food Requirements: Prefers live or fresh foods such as brine shrimp, mosquito larvae or beef heart, but will adapt to prepared dried foods.

Aphyosemion striatum is a typical plant-spawner that will lay its eggs in either clumps of vegetation or in floating nylon spawning mops. The eggs should be water-incubated and will hatch in 12 to 16 days. The fry are large enough to take newly hatched brine shrimp nauplii as a first food. They grow quickly and will begin spawning in about three months. Like many of the other African killifish species, the fry are particularly susceptible to velvet disease, *Oodinium*. This can be easily avoided by giving them frequent partial water changes and by adding about ½ to 1 teaspoon of non-iodized salt to every 4 liters of their water.

Aphyosemion sjoestedti F E X 3 2 9 X N N 8 [Col. J.J. Scheel]

Aphyosemion striatum F Q X 3 3 0 X N N 5 [H. J. Richter]

Aphyosemion walkeri ⬚F⬚E⬚X⬚3⬚3⬚1⬚X⬚N⬚N⬚7 [V. Elek]

Apistogramma agassizi ⬚F⬚Q⬚X⬚3⬚3⬚2⬚X⬚N⬚N⬚7 [R. Zukal]

APHYOSEMION WALKERI (Boulenger) / *Walker's Killifish*

Range: Ghana.
Habits: Non-aggressive.
Water Conditions: Not critical as long as extremes are avoided. Temperature 23 to 26°C.
Size: Males to about 7.5 cm; females 6 cm.
Food Requirements: Prefers live foods and prepared meaty foods; will take flake foods but usually not finely granulated dry foods.

Originally distributed within the aquarium trade in both Europe and the United States and Canada as *Aphyosemion spurrelli,* this fish is more correctly known by its older name, under which it was described in the early part of this century. It shares with many of the African killifish species good looks and a high degree of colorful charm, and it is relatively hardy. As with most other *Aphyosemion* species, adult males are very easy to distinguish from adult females, as the females are much less ornately adorned with color and have less elaborate finnage. Female *A. walkeri,* however, are more liberally sprinkled with red dots than most other *Aphyosemion* females. This is a bottom-spawning species in which the eggs should be stored in peat moss for a comparatively long period before they are ready to hatch; they may alternatively be left in water rather than stored in peat moss, but under such conditions many more eggs will fungus, as the peat moss has a better preservative effect on them. Whether kept in water or peat moss, the eggs take about a month to a month and a half to develop sufficiently for hatching. Male *A. walkeri* are often rough with the females, especially females that cannot be readily coaxed into spawning.

APISTOGRAMMA AGASSIZI (Steindachner) / *Agassiz's Dwarf Cichlid*

Range: Middle Amazon region.
Habits: Fairly peaceful except when spawning.
Water Conditions: Fairly soft, almost neutral water. Temperature 23 to 25°C.
Size: 7.5 cm; begins breeding at 5 cm.
Food Requirements: Live foods, enchytrae and tubifex worms preferred.

Apistogramma agassizi is a very popular fish. One of the big advantages with dwarf cichlids is that they do not require a large aquarium for breeding. Forty liters is ample with this one. Some retreats should be provided, such as a flowerpot laid on its side and a few rocks. The pair should be carefully fed in advance and be in the best of condition. They will soon inspect one particular spot and begin by cleaning it carefully. The female then lays row after row of eggs, which the male fertilizes. Then the female suddenly takes over. She drives away the male and guards the eggs, which hatch in 4 days. The male should be removed when he is done with spawning, to prevent bloodshed.

332

APISTOGRAMMA AMBLOPLITOIDES Fowler
Peruvian Dwarf Cichlid

Range: Rio Ucayali, Peru.
Habits: Usually peaceful, but may get slightly aggressive when spawning.
Water Conditions: Soft, slightly acid water. Temperature 24 to 27°C.
Size: About 10 cm.
Food Requirements: Live or frozen foods.

As we follow that most tremendous of all rivers, the Amazon, into Peru we note that it splits into three main streams, the Tigre, the Marañon and the Ucayali. From these streams come some of our most beautiful aquarium fishes, most of which are shipped by air from the attractive and fairly modern little city of Iquitos. From the Rio Ucayali comes this modest little *Apistogramma* species, which is shorter and blunter of body than most species of the genus. The vertical bars are not always in evidence and are sometimes replaced by a diagonal stripe, at which time the black spot in the upper center of the body becomes very prominent and the diagonal stripe passes through it from the gill-cover behind the eye to the base of the soft rays of the dorsal fin.

APISTOGRAMMA BORELLI (Regan) / *Umbrella Dwarf Cichlid*

Range: Central and southern regions of South America.
Habits: Males play at being fierce toward other members of the tank. Best kept in a tank of their own.
Water Conditions: Water hardness shouldn't exceed 12 DH. Also the pH should remain within the range of 6.0 and 6.5. Temperature between 21 and 25°C.
Size: Up to 7 cm.
Food Requirements: Freeze-dried brine shrimp is relished. Will also accept certain dry foods. Must vary their diet, which should include live foods, especially at spawning time.

When individuals of this species wear their spawning colors, they are truly beautiful. The male is transformed into one of the most eye-catching of the dwarf cichlids. *Apistogramma borelli* is not too difficult to spawn. At least you are able to recognize that a spawning is going to take place in your tank: the female meticulously begins cleaning the site she has picked for depositing her eggs. Just before the actual spawning time, you will see the female's small nipple-like projection, the ovipositor. With this species the female is the one who takes the initiative in courtship; she gets the male interested by swimming alongside him, and with her body slighlty tilted, she beats him lightly with her tail. With this movement the edges of her tail caress the belly region of the male, exciting him and creating within him the desire to spawn. He then hypnotically follows her to the selected spawning spot, which is usually the upper part of a cave or flowerpot, if it has been thoughtfully included by the aquarist within the tank setup. The aquarist will easily recognize the eggs, for they are oval and colored red!

Apistogramma ambloplitoides [F][A][X][3][3][3][X][N][N][6] [Dr. Herbert R. Axelrod]
Apistogramma borelli [F][A][X][3][3][4][X][N][N][6] [Dr. Herbert R. Axelrod]

Apistogramma cacatuoides F P X 3 3 5 X N N 5

Apistogramma corumbae F A X 3 3 6 X N N 4

APISTOGRAMMA CACATUOIDES Hoedeman / *Cockatoo Dwarf Cichlid*

Range: Guyana and Surinam.
Habits: Peaceful, but better kept by themselves.
Water Conditions: Soft, slighly acid water. Temperature 24 to 27°C.
Size: Slightly over 5 cm; females about 1 cm smaller.
Food Requirements: Live or frozen foods.

This dwarf cichlid was known to hobbyists for many years simply as "Apistogramma U2," a name which came to us from Germany. "U" in this case stood for *"unbekannt"* or "unknown." What the "2" stood for and if there ever was a "U1" was never explained. The fish itself, on the other hand, became well known even if its specific name was not yet given. It finally fell to Dr. Hoedeman to identify and name it. The Cockatoo Dwarf Cichlid is a perky little fellow whose aggressive manner is mostly bluff. Given a number of hiding places, several pairs have been known to spawn at the same time and raise the young to the free-swimming stage. Once the female is guarding eggs she develops a bright yellow color and has a mean disposition toward her mate. He becomes a very worried and harassed individual until removed to another tank, and if the female has to rush from her duties with the eggs to keep the male at a proper distance she is likely to get so excited that she will eat her eggs.

APISTOGRAMMA CORUMBAE (Regan) / *Apistogramma commbrae* or *Corumba Dwarf Cichlid*

Range: Upper Parana and Rio Meta region, northwestern South America.
Habits: Peaceful except when spawning.
Water Conditions: Prefers older, well-established tanks which are well planted and offer some hiding places. Temperature 24 to 26°C.
Size: Males 5 cm; females 4 cm.
Food Requirements: Diversified live foods when conditioning for spawning; otherwise, some dried foods may also be given.

When the *Apistogramma* species first became popular in this country, dealers would demonstrate their ease of spawning by putting a pair in an 8-liter aquarium and letting them breed there. This procedure, while it is often effective, is not the safest way. They spawn on a rock, in or on a flower-pot, or in a corner of the aquarium. Immediately after spawning is completed, the otherwise docile little female becomes a little tigress and will furiously drive away the male every time he approaches the eggs. Using a smaller aquarium gives the male less chance for escape, and there is an excellent chance that he will be killed. On the other hand, a male which is ready to spawn might easily damage a female which has not reached the point of ripeness where she is ready to release eggs. A heavily planted aquarium of at least 20 liters is recommended.

APISTOGRAMMA KLAUSEWITZI Meinken
Klausewitz's Dwarf Cichlid

Range: Central Amazon region.
Habits: Peaceful, but better kept by themselves.
Water Conditions: Soft, slightly acid water. Temperature 24 to 27°C.
Size: About 5 cm; female slightly smaller.
Food Requirements: Live and frozen foods.

Klausewitz's Dwarf Cichlid is not a very well-known fish in the aquarium hobby even though it was first introduced in 1962. Named in honor of Dr. Wolfgang Klausewitz, the famous German ichthyologist, this species was found by Harald Schultz while on an expedition to the central Amazon

Although this species is generally peaceful, *Apistogramma* males are known to occupy large territories and will have a tendency to fight among themselves if crowded. Males can be easily distinguished from the females by their high, jagged dorsal fin, which increases in size as the fish gets older. Males also have a considerable elongation of the first ray of the ventral fins which makes the fins almost long enough to reach the base of the tail. This fish will spawn most readily only if the female is gravid and the conditions are within the above prescribed limits. Able and ready males will often pester females that are not yet ready to spawn. This should be avoided, even at the expense of separating the sexes until they are both ready to spawn.

APISTOGRAMMA KLEEI Meinken / Banded Dwarf Cichlid

Range: Central Amazon region.
Habits: Usually peaceful, except when spawning; better kept by themselves.
Water Conditions: Water quality is important over the long run, especially for spawning. Water hardness should be 8 German degrees or less; the pH should be slightly on the acid side of neutral. Temperature should be about 28°C.
Size: Up to 9 cm; males up to 6.5 cm.
Food Requirements: Prefers live or frozen foods.

The Banded Dwarf Cichlid is one of the largest members of the genus *Apistogramma*. A common characteristic of *A. kleei* males is a row of rust colored scales from the posterior edge of the eye to the caudal base, running above the lateral line.

This species is more difficult to breed than most of the other *Apistogramma* species. The pair perform a breeding ritual which culminates in the female laying eggs that stick to a wall or ceiling of a cave. The egg number varies between 60 and 100, depending upon the age of the fish and the spawning conditions. Furthermore, the eggs vary in color, the color depending upon the diet of the female before spawning. Fry hatch in three days and become free-swimming four to five days after hatching. The fry can eat newly hatched brine shrimp. The fry reach sexual maturity in six months.

Apistogramma klausewitzi F A X 3 3 7 X N N 4
Apistogramma kleei F E X 3 3 8 X N N 8

[Harald Schultz]
[H. J. Richter]

gramma ortmanni [F] [J] [X] [3] [3] [9] [X] [N] [N] [7]
gramma pertense [F] [A] [X] [3] [4] [0] [X] [N] [N] [4]

[K. Paysan]
[H. J. Richter]

APISTOGRAMMA ORTMANNI (Eigenmann) / *Ortmann's Dwarf Cichlid*

Range: Guyana and the middle Amazon region.
Habits: Peaceful and may be kept in the community aquarium, but should be taken out when they show signs of wanting to spawn.
Water Conditions: Well-aged slightly acid water. Temperature 24 to 25.5°C.
Size: 7.5 cm for males; 5 cm for females. Will spawn when two-thirds grown.
Food Requirements: Diversified live foods, alternated with frozen or dried foods.

A peculiarity of the *Apistogramma* species is the wide variability of form in the tail fins of the males. *A. agassizi* has a tail which comes to a single point, *A. corumbae's* is round and *A. ortmanni* has a square tail in which the top and bottom rays are slightly elongated in some specimens. This species does not have the brilliant colors of some of the other members of the genus, but it has the saving grace that it is easy to breed and the parents do not often eat their eggs or young. As with the other members of the genus, the female becomes very "bossy" after the eggs are laid, and while the male might be damaged somewhat, he is usually just driven away and not hurt unless he really gets "nosey." To make life easier for the otherwise very busy female, it is recommended that he be removed after the spawning is completed. Usually the first inkling that the parents have spawned is the bright yellow finnage of the female and the way she bustles back and forth to a particular spot where the eggs may be found on closer examination. Eggs hatch in 4 to 5 days, and the fry are able to eat brine shrimp when they swim.

APISTOGRAMMA PERTENSE (Haseman) / *Amazon Dwarf Cichlid*

Range: Central Amazon region.
Habits: Peaceful in mixed company, but best kept by themselves.
Water Conditions: Soft, slightly acid water. Temperature 24 to 27°C.
Size: Males to 5 cm; females somewhat smaller.
Food Requirements: Live or frozen foods.

Although this not unattractive little dwarf cichlid does not have many of the frills of its cousins, it is nevertheless a desirable fish; for one thing, these are probably the best parents of all the dwarf cichlids. They seldom eat their eggs and do not seem to go in for all the hysterical histrionics the others resort to when they imagine their precious eggs are threatened. Even the female does not become quite the tigress that most females of the *Apistogramma* species develop into once there are eggs to be guarded. If the tank where they spawn is not too small she will sometimes tolerate the presence nearby of her mate, and pairs have been known to raise their young in perfect harmony. This is a risky proposition at best, however, and if the safety of the fry is to be assured it is much better to leave them with the mother or, better yet, to allow the eggs to hatch artificially with a gentle stream of air flowing past them.

340

APISTOGRAMMA RAMIREZI Myers & Harry
Ram, Ramirez's Dwarf Cichlid, Butterfly Cichlid

Range: Rio Orinoco basin, Venezuela and Colombia.
Habits: Timid, very peaceful. Should have their own well-planted, well-heated (27°C) aquarium.
Water Conditions: Aged water, slightly acid. Tank should be placed so that some sunlight falls in every day for several hours. Temperature 27-29°C.
Size: 5 to 5.5 cm; females only slightly smaller.
Food Requirements: Live foods, preferably enchytrae or tubifex worms. Dried foods are taken with hesitation.

Breeding this fish is not an impossible job. A pair which eats eggs and fry consistently should be separated from their eggs and artificial hatching resorted to if offspring are desired. German breeders use a system by which they raise many *A. ramirezi*. A number of small stones are provided, of which the parents choose one upon which to spawn. When spawning is over, the stone is lifted very carefully and placed into a jar which is hung under the outlet tube of an outside filter. That is to say, the tube which returns the clean water to the aquarium. The clean, flowing water running over the eggs keeps them free of sediment and provides the same action which the female gives when she fans them with her fins. Fry will hatch in 60 to 72 hours, and eggs which have turned white should be removed with an eyedropper. Fry will swim out with the overflowing water when they are able to swim, at which time feeding begins with infusoria.

APISTOGRAMMA REITZIGI Ahl / *Reitzig's Dwarf Cichlid*

Range: Central Rio Paraguay region.
Habits: Peaceful. Does better by itself, but may be kept in community aquaria.
Water Conditions: Clean, aged water, neutral to slightly acid. Temperature 24.5 to 25.5°C.
Size: Males 5 cm; females 4 cm.
Food Requirements: Diversified live foods which are small enough for such a small fish. Dried foods may be fed occasionally.

This is one of the smallest known cichlids. The outstanding characteristic of the males is the long, flowing dorsal and anal fins, both of which reach almost to the tip of the tail. This species has been known to use a broad plant leaf instead of a rock surface for spawning. One of the signs of approaching spawning has been described by some breeders: females will begin to herd a swarm of live daphnia as they would a school of their young. Another is the heightened coloring, especially of the yellow in the belly region. Usually the female takes no part in the preparation of the spawning site and shows no interest until the male finally coaxes her there. It is comical to see the male, after spawning is completed, attempt to help with the eggs. The female will have no part of it, however, and keeps driving him away with vim and vigor.

341

Apistogramma ramirezi F E X 3 4 1 X N N 6   [H. J. Richter]
Apistogramma reitzigi F E X 3 4 2 X N N 5   [Aaron Norman]

Apistogramma steindachneri [F][E][X][3][4][3][X][N][N][7]   [H. J. Richter]
Apistogramma trifasciatum [F][E][X][3][4][4][X][N][N][6]   [H. J. Richter]

APISTOGRAMMA STEINDACHNERI (Regan)
Steindachner's Dwarf Cichlid

Range: North-central South America.

Habits: Quarrelsome among members of its own species and with other cichlids, but peaceful with most other fishes, especially those that swim at mid-water and top-water levels.

Water Conditions: Not critical, except that partial water changes should be made even more frequently than with most other species, as being constantly maintained in "old" water has a pronouncedly bad effect on this fish. Temperature 22 to 26°C.

Size: Males to about 7.5 cm; females slightly smaller.

Food Requirements: Takes all standard aquarium foods; especially relishes frozen blood-worms.

This good-looking dwarf cichlid, close in requirements to other *Apistogramma* species, is a dependable breeder and parent, and it is as prolific as well. Breeds in typical *Apistogramma* fashion.

APISTOGRAMMA TRIFASCIATUM (Eigenmann & Kennedy)
Blue Apistogramma

Range: Central Amazon region.

Habits: Peaceful except when spawning. Best kept in their own tank.

Water Conditions: Water hardness should be about 6 to 10 DH. Temperature 22°C. Raise to about 24°C for spawning.

Size: Males to 6 cm; females slightly under 5 cm.

Food Requirements: Live or freeze-dried foods. Will take dried foods only when very hungry.

This is a fish in the so-called *"cacatuoides"* group, distinguished by an elongation of the second and third rays in the dorsal fins of the males. The species was imported in the early 1960's and is still among the rare dwarf cichlids, not because it is difficult to breed, but because of a scarcity of breeding stock. It is recommended that a tank of about 40 liters in capacity be used with a number of rocks, an empty flowerpot on its side and other retreats. This dwarf cichlid is not very needful of high temperatures, doing quite well at about 22°C. When the female is prepared to spawn she takes on a body color of gleaming yellow. A few hours before spawning begins, the female's ovipositor, or breeding tube, becomes plainly visible, and she gives her undivided attention to the spot which has been chosen for her eggs. The male waits patiently until she begins to plaster down row after row of reddish colored eggs, and he follows, fertilizing them. Then the usual *Apistogramma* drama unfolds: the female, once the male has completed his fertilizing duties, becomes a veritable tyrant and viciously drives away the male. Take him out; the female takes over from there.

APLOCHEILICHTHYS FLAVIPINNIS Meinken / *Yellowfinned Lampeye*

Range: Lagos, Nigeria.
Habits: Peaceful; best kept in group of at least a dozen. Because of their small size, they should be given their own quarters.
Water Conditions: Soft, slightly acid water is the best. Temperature 23 to 26°C.
Size: About 3 cm.
Food Requirements: Small live foods only are accepted.

These little beauties from Africa have the additional feature of being very easy to breed. If a number of them are put together, males and females pair off and in a short time a small cluster of eggs is seen hanging from the vent of some of the females, in a manner similar to that of *Oryzias javanicus*. The eggs are soon brushed off when the female swims through some plants, and in 12 to 18 days the very small fry hatch. Here the writer might be taken to task for the statement that they are easy to breed. They are, but the tiny fry are a problem to feed. Only the smallest infusoria can be handled, and growth is extremely slow. Once they have been brought to a size where they can eat newly hatched brine shrimp, then things become more normal and growth is speeded up greatly. All it takes is a lot of patience, which is eventually well rewarded. These fish have a short life span, usually not much over a year. Remember this if you wish to have them constantly in your aquaria, and always have some growing up. It should also be noted that these fish are active jumpers and their aquarium should be covered at all times.

APLOCHEILICHTHYS KATANGAE (Boulenger) / *Katanga Lampeye*

Range: Katanga, Zaire.
Habits: Peaceful; best kept in a group of at least a dozen. Should not be kept with large fish.
Water Conditions: Soft, slightly acid water. Temperature 23 to 25.5°C.
Size: About 4.5 cm.
Food Requirements: Small live foods exclusively.

Like the others of the genus, this one also has a short life span, which should serve as a warning not to wait too long before letting them spawn. This is best done by giving them a bundle of *Nitella* or *Riccia,* where the eggs are found clinging singly or in small clusters. As with the *Aphyosemion* species which spawn near the surface, there are three choices of procedure if the eggs are to be allowed to hatch: remove the eggs by tearing off a bit of the plant on which they hang and place them in a hatching tank; take out the parent fish and allow the eggs to remain where they are; or remove the entire plant bundle, eggs and all, and place it in a hatching tank. There is another method which was not mentioned because an occasional fish might be eaten: don't disturb anything, and catch the fry when you see them swimming near the surface. Eggs are quite large and take about 3 weeks to hatch.

Aplocheilichthys flavipinnis F R X 3 4 5 X N N 2   [K. Paysan]
Aplocheilichthys katangae F A X 3 4 6 X N N 3   [Dr. Herbert R. Axelrod]

Aplocheilichthys loemensis ⬚Ⓕ⬚Ⓓ⬚Ⓧ⬚③⬚④⬚⑦⬚Ⓧ⬚Ⓝ⬚Ⓝ⑤
Aplocheilichthys macrophthalmus ⬚Ⓕ⬚Ⓡ⬚Ⓧ⬚③⬚④⬚⑧⬚Ⓧ⬚Ⓝ⬚Ⓝ③   [Dr. Karl Knaack]

APLOCHEILICHTHYS LOEMENSIS (Pellegrin) / *Loëmé Lampeye*

Range: Coastal streams of southern Chad to northern Angola.
Habits: Stays hidden unless kept in schools of 6 or more. Otherwise peaceful.
Water Conditions: Neutral to slightly alkaline water with a slight salt addition (1 teaspoonful for 4 liters). Temperature 24 to 26°C.
Size: 5 cm.
Food Requirements: Live foods of all kinds, preferably those which remain near the surface.

The Loëmé Lampeye is still a very rare thing among hobbyists. So rare is it that it took a lot of researching to get any data on it. According to Dr. Max Poll's notes published by the Musée du Congo Belge in 1952, this fish appears in the coastal streams of southern Chad to northern Angola. This species attains a length of 5 cm and is one of the larger members of the genus. Like the others, *Aplocheilichthys loemensis* is a schooling fish and is not happy when only one or two specimens are kept. In their natural waters they appear in large schools and their large, almost luminous eyes give the appearance of tiny insects moving through the water. Doubtless this is an effective sort of camouflage, and a guess would be that it protects them from fishing birds and other predators. The fact that they appear in tidal waters may be an indication that the presence of a little salt in the water would be helpful.

APLOCHEILICHTHYS MACROPHTHALMUS (Meinken)
Bigeye Lampeye

Range: Nigeria, near the coast, where they occur in small freshwater streams, swimming against the current.
Habits: Peaceful, but should never be kept with large fishes, because of their small size.
Water Conditions: Water should be soft and about neutral. Temperature 24 to 25.5°C.
Size: 4 cm; spawns at about 2.5 cm.
Food Requirements: Small living foods, as well as dried foods.

Spawning them presents little difficulty. When the female is ready, and this can be seen by the eggs which are clearly visible through her body wall, she may be placed with a male which is lively and shows good color in a tank of about 20 liters capacity. A bundle of *Nitella* or a few strands of *Myriophyllum* are placed with them. Temperature should be about 24.5°C. After a great deal of driving, the pair come together in a plant thicket and after a great deal of quivering, an egg is expelled. The egg is amazingly large when compared to the size of the female. Spawnings are small and may last over a period of several days. Eggs hatch in 8 to 10 days, and the fry must be carefully fed on very fine dried food after a week on infusoria. Growth is extremely slow, and full size is not attained until after at least a year has passed.

APLOCHEILICHTHYS MYERSI Poll / *Myers' Lampeye*

Range: Kinshasa, Zaire.
Habits: Peaceful, but because of their tiny size they cannot be put in community aquaria with any other fishes. Happiest in a school of 12 or more.
Water Conditions: Soft, slightly acid water. Temperature 23 to 25°C.
Size: 2.5 cm or slightly less.
Food Requirements: Small live foods exclusively.

Myers' Lampeye is a brilliantly colored little fish which moves in a darting manner. This led the Germans to nickname it the "hummingbird fish." These fragile fish are most happy in the company of their own kind and tend to school.

The spawning period can last up to several weeks and is highlighted by interesting courtship behavior on the part of both sexes. The eggs are placed onto fine-leaved plants where they will hatch in about two weeks, depending upon the temperature. The female, who places the eggs on the plants, can be distinguished from the male by her stockier body. Although she has a similar color pattern, her fins are usually colorless, while the male's are pigmented. It is not essential to remove either parent fish after the eggs hatch. If the fish are well fed, there is little cannibalism and many of the young ones can be raised right with the parents. The newly hatched fry are minute and should be given infusoria as a first food. They are hardy but grow slowly at first.

APLOCHEILICHTHYS PUMILUS (Boulenger) / *Tanganyika Lampeye*

Range: Lakes Edward, Kivu, Victoria and Tanganyika and their affluents.
Habits: Peaceful; prefer to be kept in a school instead of singly or in pairs.
Water Conditions: Water should exceed 10 degrees of hardness; alkalinity about 7.5 pH. Temperature 22 to 25°C.
Size: About 4.5 cm.
Food Requirements: Living foods preferred, but it is possible that they may be trained to take frozen or prepared foods.

Contrary to the places where most *Aplocheilichthys* species are found, this one is native to the large lakes of Africa and the streams flowing into them. The waters in this area of the African continent are mostly strongly alkaline, and in the aquarium we must attempt to duplicate these conditions. Even with the best of care these fishes have only a short life span, and an individual that passes the ripe old age of one year is unusual.

The conditions recommended above are also required for spawning. The spawning ritual is characterized by interesting courtship behavior and culminates in the production of small clusters of eggs. These clusters are fertilized by the male and then placed on fine-leaved water plants by the female. The eggs hatch in 12 to 14 days, depending upon the temperature, and the fry should be cared for in the same manner as *A. myersi.*

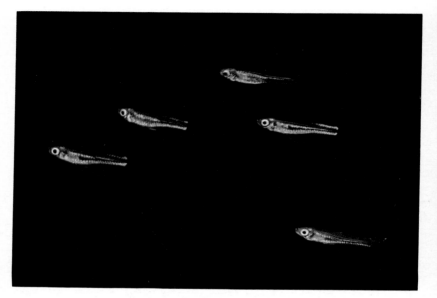

Aplocheilichthys myersi [F][D][X][3][4][9][X][N][N][1]   [Mervin F. Roberts]
Aplocheilichthys pumilis [F][R][X][3][5][0][X][N][N][3]   [P. Brichard]

Aplocheilichthys schoelleri [F][R][X][3][5][1][X][N][N][4]
Aplocheilus blocki [F][J][X][3][5][2][X][N][N][5]

[Dr. Herbert R. Axelrod]
[Col. J.J. Scheel]

351

APLOCHEILICHTHYS SCHOELLERI (Boulenger) / *Egyptian Lampeye*

Range: Egypt.
Habits: Peaceful; being a bit larger they must be kept with other peaceful species of approximately the same size. Happiest in a group of 12 or more.
Water Conditions: Soft, slightly acid water. Temperature 23 to 25.5°C.
Size: 5 cm.
Food Requirements: Small live foods exclusively.

This Egyptian member of the lampeye group is seldom available to hobbyists. The Nile is not as productive of small, colorful fishes as for instance the Congo, and there is not as much profit for a collector to look for aquarium fishes here. Still, the Nile is a huge body of water and there may be many species which so far have gotten little attention from natives because they are too small to eat but which would elicit a joyful gasp from even a hardened aquarist. As has happened in many other parts of the world, transportation is always becoming faster and taking people to more and more previously unattainable places. These places are sometimes rich in fish life and provide the treasured "newcomers" to our hobby.

APLOCHEILUS BLOCKI (Arnold)
Dwarf Panchax, Green Panchax, Panchax from Madras

Range: Madras, India.
Habits: Peaceful, but should not be kept with large fishes.
Water Conditions: Well-aged water which is soft and slightly acid. Temperature 21 to 25°C.
Size: Males 5 cm; females slightly smaller.
Food Requirements: Will eat dried foods, but this *must* be supplemented with live foods.

Aplocheilus blocki is the smallest species of the genus. It was named after a Captain Block of Hamburg, Germany, who brought in a great many Bettas around 1909 and included this fish in one of his importations. The fish has never achieved a very great popularity, possibly because it does not possess the flashing colors of some of the other members of this family. Nevertheless it has a quiet beauty and does not grow so large that it endangers the smaller members of a community aquarium. It prefers the upper reaches of the water. Because of its small size, it can be spawned in a limited space. An 8-liter aquarium will accommodate a pair comfortably, and eggs will be found among the surface plants with a fair amount of regularity. These will hatch in about 2 weeks, but the young will be found to be rather small. Infusoria must therefore be fed at first, but the young will soon be large enough for newly hatched brine shrimp. From here on raising them is easy. Like other members of the group, this species is an accomplished jumper, and the aquarium in which they are kept should be kept covered with a pane of glass.

APLOCHEILUS DAYI (Steindachner) / *Day's Panchax, Singhalese Panchax*

Range: Sri Lanka.
Habits: Will not annoy anything it cannot swallow. May be kept in company with larger fishes.
Water Conditions: Neutral to slightly acid. Temperature 24.5 to 25.5°C.
Size: 8.5 cm; females only a little smaller.
Food Requirements: Dried food will be taken, but live food should be supplemented at least occasionally.

Unlike *A. blocki,* this fish needs a bit more room in which to spawn, but this is not to say a large tank. One of about 20 liters capacity is enough for spawning purposes; keep it covered. Of course, they may be kept in larger quarters at other times. This fish is a top-spawner, and its eggs will be found at fairly regular intervals in the plants near the surface. There will never be a large spawning at any one time; with this family of fishes only a few eggs ripen each day, and these are the ones which will be laid. They will not be eaten and may be allowed to accumulate for several days before gathering.

APLOCHEILUS LINEATUS (Cuvier & Valenciennes)
Panchax Lineatus, Striped Panchax

Range: Malabar and Madras, India, and Sri Lanka.
Habits: Best kept by themselves; although usually peaceful except with small fishes, they sometimes harass other fishes.
Water Conditions: Neutral to slightly acid soft water. Temperature 24 to 27°C.
Size: 10 cm; will begin to spawn at 6 cm.
Food Requirements: Live foods such as daphnia, tubifex worms, enchytrae and grown-up brine shrimp. Dried foods may be fed occasionally.

Aplocheilus lineatus are best kept in an aquarium of their own, where they will show off to excellent advantage. Fully grown specimens if kept in a community aquarium may swallow fishes as large as male Guppies or White Clouds; besides this they may take a violent dislike to another member of the aquarium and drive him around unmercifully. Its beauty, when fully grown, makes it worthy of its own aquarium. Several pairs may be kept in a 60-liter aquarium. When spawning is desired, separate females and feed them until they become well-rounded. Then select the best male and put them together in an aquarium of about 20 liters capacity, using two females to each male. Provide plenty of floating bushy plants; in a few days they will be festooned with eggs which hang from them by a thread, like balls from a Christmas tree. Then return the breeders to their original aquarium. In 10 to 15 days the good-sized fry will be seen swimming around just below the surface, where they will feed greedily on newly hatched brine shrimp and grow rapidly.

Aplocheilus dayi F A X 3 5 3 X N N 7
Aplocheilus lineatus F R X 3 5 4 X N N 7

[H. Hansen, Aquarium Berlin]
[Wardley Products Co.]

Aplocheilus panchax  [R. Zukal]
Apteronotus albifrons [Dr. Herbert R. Axelrod]

APLOCHEILUS PANCHAX (Hamilton-Buchanan)
Panchax Panchax, Blue Panchax

Range: India, Burma, Malay Peninsula, Thailand, Indonesia.
Habits: Will not bother anything they cannot swallow, and may be kept in community aquaria which do not contain small fishes.
Water Conditions: Soft, slightly acid water, preferably well aged. Temperature 24 to 26°C.
Size: 6 to 8 cm; will begin spawning when three-fourths grown.
Food Requirements: Mostly living foods such as daphnia, enchytrae or tubifex worms. Frozen or dried foods may be given occasionally.

Coming as they do from a wide range, it is to be expected that this fish would show a variety of body colors. This it does to such an extent that it was once thought to be several species, and older literature lists the same fish under a number of names. For a time it was confused with *Aplocheilus dayi*, until it was established that *A. panchax* does not occur in Sri Lanka, although it covers most of the rest of the range for the genus. The Blue Panchax spawns like the other species, among floating plants or substitutes such as nylon mops, bundles of nylon fibers or Spanish moss. A temperature of about 26°C works best for spawning. If eggs are removed for hatching, they may be handled with the fingers; if tweezers are used, do not grasp the eggs directly with the tweezer points. The concentrated pressure can easily damage the shells. Close the points under the egg and then lift them up. Eggs hatch in 12 to 15 days.

APTERONOTUS ALBIFRONS (Linnaeus) / *Black Ghost*

Range: Amazon River and Surinam.
Habits: A peaceful, friendly fish.
Water Conditions: Soft, slightly acid water best, but this is not too important, as variations in water composition are taken in stride.
Size: Up to 47 cm.
Food Requirements: Not a fussy eater; will take dry, frozen and live foods. Tubifex eagerly accepted.

The Black Ghost is different from the other knifefishes; it is a completely peaceful fish and will not disturb others. What's more, it can be tamed and accustomed to taking food directly from the hand of its owner, like some of the larger cichlids. In a fish as large as *Apteronotus*, this can be a very impressive sight. This, coupled with the fish's very prepossessing appearance, makes the Black Ghost a distinctive attraction, well worth the high price that is asked for the specimens that are occasionally available. Some of the South American Indians, no doubt themselves impressed with the fish's appearance, have endowed *Apteronotus* with a spiritual quality. They believe that the ghosts of the departed take up residence in *Apteronotus*, and they refuse to molest it.

356

ARAPAIMA GIGAS (Cuvier) / *Arapaima, Pirarucu*

Range: Entire tropical South American region, usually in the deeper, larger streams.
Habits: Because of their size, any more than one to a large tank would be unthinkable.
Water Conditions: Water conditions are not particularly important with this species. Temperature 24 to 27°C.
Size: To about 4.5 m in the open; captive specimens seldom over 60 cm.
Food Requirements: In captivity they will eat nothing but small living fishes.

Arapaima gigas belongs to the family Osteoglossidae, which comprises some of the largest freshwater fishes in the world. This family is also known for its many primitive characteristics. For example, *A. gigas* is covered with heavy, bony scales which form a mosaic pattern across its body. This can be very impressive looking when one sees a large specimen, which incidently can weigh in excess of 200 kg.

The Pirarucu can only be kept in very large aquaria of 200 liters or more. It is important that the tank be well covered as this fish tends to jump. This species is the largest of the South American freshwater fishes and probably the most important food fish for the natives who live along the Amazon and its larger tributaries.

ARNOLDICHTHYS SPILOPTERUS (Boulenger)
Arnold's Characin, Red-Eyed Characin

Range: Tropical West Africa, especially the Lagos region and the Niger Delta.
Habits: A peaceful species which is usually out in front.
Water Conditions: Soft, neutral to slightly acid water. Temperature 26 to 28°C.
Size: Seldom exceeds 6 cm.
Food Requirements: Has a good appetite and will eat dried food as well as live foods; some live foods should be provided, however.

Arnold's Characin is one of the most common of the African tetras. The large iridescent scales are most attractive when seen with the light behind the viewer. There is a faint horizontal line which also reflects all the colors of the rainbow. Although it has been known to aquarists since 1907, it has never been reported as having been bred in captivity. A clue could be taken from its life habits: it is known to swim in large schools near the surface of open waters. Maybe this fish is one of those which prefer to spawn in more or less large numbers, and it would be necessary to keep a school of them together in a large aquarium before results could be looked for. Unfortunately, we are not likely to see a large number of these fish at any one time. They are lively swimmers, and any time the collectors get them into the seine, they have the exasperating habit of playfully leaping over the top of it. This species is also sensitive to water changes and should not be moved from one tank to another more than can be helped.

Arapaima gigas ⎡F⎤⎡D⎤⎡X⎤⎡3⎤⎡5⎤⎡7⎤⎡X⎤⎡N⎤ ⎡N⎤⎡D⎤   [Dr. Herbert R. Axelrod]
Arnoldichthys spilopterus ⎡F⎤⎡D⎤⎡X⎤⎡3⎤⎡5⎤⎡8⎤⎡X⎤⎡N⎤ ⎡N⎤⎡E⎤   [S. Frank]

Asiphonichthys sp. ⬚F⬚D⬚T⬚3⬚5⬚9⬚X⬚N⬚NE⬚ [Dr. Herbert R. Axelrod]
Aspidoras pauciradiatus ⬚F⬚D⬚M⬚3⬚6⬚0⬚X⬚N⬚NE⬚ [Dr. Herbert R. Axelrod]

Aspidoras poecilus ⬚F⬚D⬚B⬚3⬚6⬚0⬚X⬚N⬚NE⬚ [Dr. Herbert R. Axelrod]

ASIPHONICHTHYS SP. / *Transparent Tetra*

Range: Guyana.
Habit: Peaceful toward other fishes and plants.
Water Conditions: Soft, slightly acid water. Temperature 22 to 26°C.
Size: About 4.5 cm.
Food Requirements: Not known, but will probably eat just about everything.
Color Variations: Body greenish and very transparent; scales have an opalescent sparkle and each has a tiny black dot. Large black spot at tail base.

This fish comes from the savannah country around Lethem, Guyana. Although it is very hardy, it was never imported into Europe or the United States in any quantity, so little information about its behavior or requirements is known. The tiny scales of this fish have an opalescent sparkle and the body is very transparent. It proved to be very peaceful when kept with other fishes.

ASPIDORAS SPP.

Range: Central South America.
Habits: Peaceful; useful in that they feed off the bottom and get much food left by other fishes.
Water Conditions: Neutral to slightly acid water, soft and low in salt content. Temperature 22 to 28°C.
Size: 4 cm.
Food Requirements: Although these fish will do a good clean-up on the bottom of the aquarium, they should be fed with prepared flake food. They really thrive on live foods.

This genus is closely related to *Corydoras* and many research workers believe that it should be included in the latter. Most of the species included in this genus can be considered dwarf fishes. Unfortunately, many of these species have not been imported into this country in sufficient numbers to attract hobbyist interest. Thus, little is known about their breeding habits or general behavior.

ASTRONOTUS OCELLATUS (Cuvier)
Oscar, Peacock Cichlid, Velvet Cichlid

Range: Eastern Venezuela, Guyana, Amazon Basin to Paraguay.
Habits: Only very small specimens may be kept with other fishes; when bigger, they will attack and swallow smaller fishes.
Water Conditions: Not critical. Temperature 22 to 28°C. Breeds at 26°C.
Size: 30 cm; spawns at half that size.

Food Requirements: A very greedy eater which prefers its food in large chunks. Live fish, snails, dog food, raw beef heart, etc.

Color Variations: Dark brown with light brown to yellow mottled markings. Youngsters go through various color changes. Red ocellated spot at tail base. Males have red markings on body.

Many breeders have a pair of Oscars which they use as a "garbage can." Any fishes which are crippled, ill or dead are thrown to the Oscars, much as the Christian martyrs were thrown to the lions. They make short work of them and are usually looking for more. A pair will generally get along quite well, but sometimes battles occur. A separation of several days by placing a pane of glass between them will sometimes calm them down. Usually they are excellent parents, guarding their eggs and fry, but as so often happens with cichlids, eggs might be eaten. If this is done frequently, the parents or eggs should be removed and the eggs hatched artificially by placing an air-stone near them, causing a gentle circulation. Spawns are generally large and may number as high as 1,000 eggs. Young hatch in 3 to 4 days and grow rapidly if fed generously. First food should be newly hatched brine shrimp, graduating to larger foods as the fish grow. Parents should have a large aquarium, and if there are any plants, they are likely to be uprooted. Provide some large, smooth rocks and deep gravel; they like to dig.

1. *Astronotus ocellatus* mature male, normal form (p362).
2. *Astronotus ocellatus* form with colored ocelli that are not bilaterally symmetrical (p362).
3. *Astronotus ocellatus* juvenile 2 cm in length (p363).
4. *Astronotus ocellatus* mature male, red form (p363).

Astronotus ocellatus pair fanning their newly laid eggs. Photo by J. Jarvi.

1. *Astronotus ocellatus* F E X 3 6 1 X N N D   [K. Paysan]
2. *Astronotus ocellatus* F D X 3 6 2 X N N D   [Dr. Herbert R. Axelrod]

3. *Astronotus ocellatus*  [Dr. Herbert R. Axelrod]
4. *Astronotus ocellatus* var. ⟨F⟩⟨H⟩⟨X⟩⟨3⟩⟨6⟩⟨4⟩⟨X⟩⟨R⟩⟨N⟩⟨D⟩ [Dr. Herbert R. Axelrod]

In late 1969, when the forerunners of the fish that was later to become solidly entrenched in popularity in the hobby as the Red Oscar were first introduced to the American aquarium market, there was much speculation as to the origin of the fish. No one knew exactly how the fish came to be, and some surmised that it was sufficiently different from normal *Astronotus ocellatus* to be a completely different species. The mystery surrounding the fish wasn't dispelled entirely until mid-1970, when Dr. Herbert R. Axelrod's article about the development of the strain ("The Origin of the Red Oscar," *Tropical Fish Hobbyist,* May, 1970) was published. Red Oscars and their offshoots, Tiger Red Oscars, were the results of breeding work done by Charoen Pattabongse of Bangkok, Thailand, who had produced reddish Oscars as early as 1966. By continual culling of the offspring, Pattabongse was able to purify the strain to the point where the Red Oscars bred completely true. When fish farmers and other commercial breeders began to import the fish in quantity, their perpetuation in good supply on the aquarium market was assured. Red Oscars breed the same as regular *Astronotus ocellatus* and are just as prolific; some breeders maintain that young Red Oscars grow more quickly than non-red Oscars, but this opinion is not shared by everyone.

Astronotus ocellatus—mature male with red ocellated spot on the tail. Photo by G. Marcuse.

ASTYANAX BIMACULATUS (Linnaeus) / *Two-Spotted Astyanax*

Range: Northeastern and eastern South America south to the La Plata Basin.
Habits: Peaceful if kept with other fishes of about the same size.
Water Conditions: Water characteristics are not important, if clean. Temperatures 21 to 25°C are optimum.
Size: To 15 cm; in captivity usually half that size.
Food Requirements: Live or frozen foods preferred, but prepared food also taken if hungry.

This is one of the fishes which are generally discarded by collectors because they have no bright colors and are generally too large to ship economically for the price they would bring. They are very hardy and once they have become accustomed to a large, well-planted tank will prove to be very attractive, especially if a number of them are kept together. They should not be kept with other species which are considerably smaller than themselves, or the usual condition of bullying will take place. Sexes are quite difficult to distinguish with any amount of certainty until the females develop eggs, at which time their rounder contours provide the only certain method of sexing. If it is desired to spawn them, a pair should be given their own tank of at least 60 liters capacity. At a temperature of about 25°C, active driving by the males takes place and soon a great number of eggs are dropped among the plants and haphazardly about the tank. Hatching takes place in 24 to 36 hours, and after 5 days the yolk-sac is absorbed and the fry become free-swimming. Raising them is easy; newly hatched brine shrimp can be fed at once. Growth is rapid.

ASTYANAX DAGUAE Eigenmann / *Plain-Tailed Astyanax*

Range: Colombia.
Habits: Should not be kept with smaller fishes which it may attack.
Water Conditions: Soft, slightly acid water. Temperature 24 to 27°C.
Size: About 8 cm.
Food Requirements: Will accept most foods.

Astyanax daguae is an active and hardy *Astyanax* species which does best in a large aquarium that affords a good amount of space for movement. Moderate planting in an aquarium with soft to medium-hard water is best. Live foods are preferred, but this fish will usually accept freeze-dried and flake foods as well. The Plain-Tailed Astyanax is a generally peaceful species and will make a good community aquarium fish providing that it is not placed with other fishes that are less than half of its size.

Astyanax daguae is an easy fish to breed and will do so providing the conditions in the aquarium approximate those outlined above. The species is an active driver. After courtship, mildly adhesive eggs are laid among the plants and in open water. Hatching occurs in 24 to 48 hours and the fry are free-swimming in 4 to 6 days. The fry are easy to raise.

Astyanax bimaculatus ☐F☐D☐X☐3☐6☐5☐X☐N☐N☐E   [Dr. Herbert R. Axelrod]

Astyanax daguae ☐F☐D☐X☐3☐6☐6☐X☐N☐N☐E   [Dr. Herbert R. Axelrod]

Astyanax fasciatus fasciatus F Q X 3 6 7 X N N 7   [H. J. Richter]
Astyanax fasciatus mexicanus ("Anoptichthys jordani") F Q X 3 6 8 X A N E

ASTYANAX FASCIATUS (Cuvier) / *Silvery Tetra, Mexican Tetra, Blind Cave Tetra*

Range: Texas to Argentina.
Habits: Will get along with other fishes of its size; very likely to eat plants.
Water Conditions: Not at all critical, but slightly alkaline water is best. Temperature 21 to 24°C.
Size: To 9 cm.
Food Requirements: All foods accepted, but there should be some vegetable substances included, such as lettuce or spinach leaves.

The only characin which can be collected in United States waters is *Astyanax fasciatus*. It is the northernmost representative of a widespread genus which comprises about 75 species all the way down to Argentina. The subspecies *mexicanus* occurs from Panama up to the Rio Grande and can be found in Texas streams which empty into this river. A very hardy fish, they require a generous amount of space and are not averse to sunlight. An unfortunate habit of nibbling at plants makes them unlikely ever to win a popularity contest among hobbyists. This habit can be curbed somewhat by giving them fresh lettuce leaves to nibble on. Spawning is very similar to that of most tetra species. The male drives the female through the plants, and eggs are scattered in all directions. The eggs are not very sticky and many fall to the bottom. Once the pair has finished, an egg-hunt is begun, and if they are not removed most of the eggs will be eaten. Hatching takes place in 24 to 36 hours, but it is not until 5 days later that the fry absorb their yolk-sacs and begin to swim freely. They are able to tear up newly hatched brine shrimp at once and are easily raised.

One of the most interesting examples of natural adaption is the Blind Cave Tetra, an evolutionary variety of *Astyanax fasciatus mexicanus* formerly called *Anoptichthys jordani*. Here we have a fish which has lived for countless generations in total darkness; over the years the eyes have gradually been lost. To compensate for this it has a strange sense which prevents it from bumping into things and hurting itself. The sense of smell is also very keen, and it can find food every bit as well as sighted fishes. To spawn this fish, it is advisable to give them an aquarium of about 40 to 60 liters capacity, with a double layer of pebbles or marbles on the bottom. Eggs are expelled in a more or less haphazard fashion, and if there is no means of keeping the parents away from them, they will be gobbled up almost as quickly as they are laid. Immediately after egg-laying has been completed and the breeders show no more interest in each other, they should be removed. Hatching takes place in three to four days, and on the sixth or seventh day the fry become free-swimming. Feedings of infusoria may be supplemented with very fine dried food, and growth is very rapid. In about a week newly hatched brine shrimp may be substituted as a diet, followed by other larger foods.

AULONOCARA NYASSAE Regan / *African Peacock Cichlid*

Range: Lake Malawi, Africa.
Habits: Relatively peaceful for an African cichlid.
Water Conditions: Hard, alkaline water preferred. Temperature 22 to 26°C.
Size: Up to around 15 cm in the aquarium.
Food Requirements: Takes all standard aquarium foods; relishes regular feedings of live foods.
Color Variations: Males vary in the intensity of the basic blue body coloring and the extent of rusty-orange blotches on body.

Referred to in the United States as the African Peacock Cichlid and in Germany as the Emperor Cichlid, *Aulonocara nyassae* made an immediate hit for itself in both countries. Adult males of this species are among the most brightly colored of all Rift Lake fishes, and they aren't killers. Adult males may go through a lot of bluffing and scare-tactic display threats, but they don't usually really hurt one another unless kept in very cramped quarters. If you give them enough room to allow the establishment of discrete territories, they'll leave each other alone.

Sex differences in fully adult fish of the species are very easy to spot: the male becomes a deep shiny blue with rusty patches spread over the forward portion of his body, and the female stays mostly a plain brown or brownish gray with vertical bars along the side of her body; she can also show rusty patches around her head. The male has the vertical bars also, but on him they are subdued by the blue and show less prominently. Juvenile *Aulonocara nyassae* show the color pattern of the adult female. The first signs of sexual differentiation in color pattern begin to emerge on juveniles when the males begin to show a lightening in the far edge of the dorsal fin; the intensification of blue follows, and the emergence of the rusty area usually comes last.

A. nyassae is a maternal mouthbrooder; eggs—not many in each clutch, as this is not a prolific species—are laid on a hard substrate and picked up by the female, who broods them in her mouth for up to four weeks. Temperature of the water in the tank housing the brooding female plays a large part in determining the length of time it takes for the fry to emerge from their mother's mouth; at 26°C they usually are released in three weeks. The fry are large and easy to feed when they start to swim free, with newly hatched brine shrimp, preferably live, being the food of first choice.

1. *Aulonocara nyassae* mature males (p370) are peacock blue in breeding color.
2. *Aulonocara nyassae* females or juveniles (p370) exhibit a striped pattern.

1. *Aulonocara nyassae* ⬚F⬚E⬚X⬚3⬚6⬚9⬚X⬚N⬚N⬚C [G. Meola, African Fish Imports]
2. *Aulonocara nyassae* ⬚F⬚F⬚X⬚3⬚7⬚0⬚X⬚N⬚N⬚8 [Dr. Warren E. Burgess]

Austrofundulus dolichopterus FRX371XNNE [H. J. Richter]

AUSTROFUNDULUS DOLICHOPTERUS Weitzman and Wourms
Sicklefin Killie, Saberfin

Range: Venezuela.

Habits: Timid, easily spooked.

Water Conditions: Soft, acid water best for breeding, but neutral to slightly alkaline water suitable. Temperature 20 to 23°C.

Food Requirements: Live foods preferred.

Size: 4-6 cm.

Color Variations: Females much less spotted than males, especially on fins. Bluish sheen that overlies belly area (and sometimes fins) of male entirely lacking in female.

This pleasingly marked and easily cared for species, one of the smallest of the South American annual fishes, attracted much attention when it was introduced to the aquarium hobbyists in the late 1960's, but since that time it has been more or less eclipsed in popularity by species that offer more in the way of brilliancy of coloration. The major charm of the species, or at least the male, is the way in which both anal and dorsal fins are drawn out into long, streamer-like filaments; on a good specimen the length of the leading edge of the anal fin might be equal to two-thirds of the entire body length. The tips of the caudal fin are also drawn out, but less markedly so than the anal and dorsal fins. Being a dweller of impermanent water holes that are dry for roughly half of each year, *A. dolichopterus* is fairly resistant to changes in water composition, although most of the bodies of water in which it lives in nature contain a good deal of decaying organic matter that provides the basis for making the water acidic. Like other annual species, *A. dolichopterus* doesn't need a large tank for spawning purposes; a 10-liter tank or large drum bowl is sufficient. The eggs, kept in peat moss, should be stored from four to six months before an attempt to hatch them out is made. Considering the small size of the adults, the fry are relatively large and are able to eat newly hatched brine shrimp immediately. It is important that all leftover food be removed from the tanks of both growing fry and adults as soon as it is noticed. This is a fairly timid species that does best if provided with a refuge from bright light; the fish should not be kept in a glare. If they are maintained in small aquaria, their quarters should be covered to prevent jumping caused by fright. (As this book goes to press, we learn that *dolichopterus* has been placed in the new genus *Terranatos,* a placement its long fins and small size would seem to require.)

AUSTROFUNDULUS MYERSI Dahl / *Myers' Killifish*

Range: Northern Colombia.
Habits: Apt to be nasty to other fishes; best kept with their own kind.
Water Conditions: Soft and slightly acid. Temperature 24 to 26°C.
Size: Slightly over 12 cm.
Food Requirements: All sorts of living foods peferred; if not available, frozen foods or beef heart.

Like the Guppy breeders, the aquarium hobby has given birth to another highly specialized group, the killifish breeders. These people make a specialty of keeping and propagating cyprinodonts. There are about 25 genera in this group, the species of some of which can be divided into two general spawning groups: the plant-spawners and the egg-buriers. Our *Austrofundulus myersi* is a member of the latter, the egg-burying class. It occurs in ditches and small bodies of water in northern Colombia, and collectors who want mature fish must hunt for them when the waters have receded considerably. At this time they spawn and bury their eggs in the soft bottom mud. Eventually the water dries up, leaving the parent fish stranded and gasping, shortly to die. The eggs live on in an almost-dry state until the downpours of the rainy season fill the bodies of water once more and the eggs hatch.

AUSTROFUNDULUS TRANSILIS Myers / *Venezuelan Killifish*

Range: Venezuela.
Habits: Aggressive; should not be kept in tanks with other fishes. Males should not be kept together.
Water Conditions: Hard water should be avoided, as should temperatures below 21°C or above 26°C. Prefers neutral to slightly acid water.
Size: Reaches 8 cm; female smaller than male.
Food Requirements: Needs live foods such as insect larvae, worms or small Guppies. Will also eat frozen foods, scraped beef and beef heart mixtures.

A. transilis is an aggressive, voracious fish which should not be kept with fish small enough for it to nip at or swallow. Two males should never be put in the same tank, nor should only one female be put with a male. If trios (two females and a male) are used for spawning, there is much less chance of the females being injured or killed. Venezuelan Killies spawn like other bottom killies, and their eggs and fry should be treated as one would treat those of *Cynolebias*.

Although this species only lives 7 or 8 months in nature, it can be maintained for up to 2 years in the aquarium. This difference is probably caused by the simple fact that aquaria do not dry out and ponds do. Pearlfishes, in contrast, die *in the aquaria* by the end of their first year, whether the tank dries or not.

Austrofundulus myersi F A X 3 7 3 X N N E [Dr. Herbert R. Axelrod]
Austrofundulus transilis F R X 3 7 4 X N N 7 [H. J. Richter]

Axelródia riesei Ⓕ Ⓓ Ⓧ ③ ⑦ ⑤ Ⓧ Ⓝ Ⓝ ⓪
Badis badis badis Ⓕ Ⓓ Ⓧ ③ ⑦ ⑥ Ⓧ Ⓝ Ⓝ ⑥

[Dr. Herbert R. Axelrod]
[H. Hansen, Aquarium Berlin]

375

AXELRODIA RIESEI Gery / *Ruby Tetra*

Range: Rio Meta, Colombia.
Habits: Excellent aquarium fish. Pert, lively, but not at all aggressive. Shouldn't be kept with large fish that will take advantage and keep it in constant hiding.
Water Conditions: Especially clean water conditions are necessary. Best colors will appear when water is on the soft side with a pH slightly on the acid side, about 6.5. Temperature 22 to 26°C.
Size: Up to 2 cm.
Food Requirements: Will accept freeze-dried feedings. Certain flake foods are also willingly taken. Live foods should be included in their diet.

A Colombian expedition turned up this prize discovery. Dr. Herbert R. Axelrod and Mr. William Riese, after whom the species is named, were the lucky gentlemen who first collected this South American fish. Everyone on this expedition was astonished at finding such an incredibly tiny species. *A. riesei* will undoubtedly prove to be one of the smallest aquarium fishes on record. But regardless of its diminutive proportions, it is still an eye-opener; its ruby-red color rivals the red of the Cardinal Tetra, *Cheirodon axelrodi*. *Axelrodia riesei's* eye coloring is also most unusual, ruby-red above, golden with blue iridescence below. This species is also characterized by a short anal fin and a conspicuous, asymmetrically set, black spot on the caudal fin. It is difficult to keep alive in captivity.

BADIS BADIS BADIS (Hamilton-Buchanan)
Badis, Dwarf Chameleon Fish

Range: India.
Habits: Peaceful, but will hide a great deal when kept in a community aquarium.
Water Conditions: Not critical; a well-planted aquarium should be provided, with several small flowerpots laid on their sides.
Size: Up to 8 cm; will begin breeding at 5 cm.
Food Requirements: Live foods only, in sizes tiny enough for their small mouths.

This interesting little nandid has all the characteristics of the dwarf cichlids. It will find life a bit frightening in the community aquarium, unless it has an adequate number of places in which it can hide if danger threatens. When kept by themselves in a small aquarium, they breed readily. A rock or leaf surface, or the inside of a flowerpot if one has been provided, will be cleaned scrupulously by the male. The female is then coaxed to the spot and, if she is ready to spawn, will hang 50 to 60 eggs on the surface. Sometimes a plant leaf or the corner of the aquarium is selected. Unlike the dwarf cichlids, the female does not take complete charge of the eggs and fry but shares it with her mate. Eggs hatch in 2 to 3 days, and the fry are very small and helpless at first. Not until 2 weeks have passed do the youngsters become independent of their parents. Infusoria should be fed initially, and when the fry become large enough to handle newly hatched brine shrimp, growth becomes rapid.

BADIS BADIS BURMANICUS (Ahl) / *Burmese Badis*

Range: Burma.
Habits: Peaceful, but will hide a great deal if kept in the community aquarium.
Water Conditions: Not critical; should have a well-planted aquarium with a number of hiding places.
Size: About 6 cm.
Food Requirements: Small live foods only.

Think this subspecies of *Badis badis* is a new one? Well, you're wrong by more than 50 years! The late Johann Paul Arnold, the well-known authority on aquarium fishes, mentioned in his book *Fremdländische Süsswasserfische* that he first acquired and bred this fish in 1920, but that since it did not find much favor in Germany, it died out, not to reappear until 1934 when another shipment arrived from Rangoon. It was finally established as a subspecies in 1936 by Dr. Ernst Ahl. In body form it resembles *Badis badis,* but the colors differ considerably. The sides are covered with numerous rows of red dots, interspersed in the upper half with blue ones. At times there are 6 to 9 dark bars which extend halfway down the sides. Colors do not make such drastic and startling changes as with *Badis badis,* but spawning procedure is exactly the same for both. The female Burmese Badis carries the same colors as her mate, but they are not as bright.

BALANTIOCHEILOS MELANOPTERUS (Bleeker) / *Bala Shark*

Range: Thailand, Sumatra, Borneo and Malaysia.
Habits: Active and peaceful. A skilled jumper which requires a covered tank.
Water Conditions: Neutral to slightly alkaline. Temperature 24 to 26°C.
Size: To 36 cm; in the aquarium it seldoms exceeds 13 cm.
Food Requirements: All sorts of live foods are preferred. Also fond of boiled oatmeal.

There have been frequent importations of the Bala Shark in the last few years, and although they have commanded a high price the demand is still greater than the supply. Do not let the popular name "Shark" fool you into thinking that this is a ferocious, predatory fish. The sole reason for the name is a superficial resemblance of the dorsal fin's shape to that of the oceanic marauder. This is a perfectly peaceful fish which minds its business at all times. It goes over the bottom frequently and thoroughly, picking up bits of food that were overlooked by the others. This is done without a great deal of stirring up of the gravel and sediment. Add to this useful trait the facts that it is attractively colored and easily fed, and you have the reasons for its popularity. Only one thing can be said in its disfavor; it may grow too large for the home aquarium. It is said to grow to 36 cm in Borneo and Sumatra, but specimens from Thailand attain only 20 cm. Of course, these sizes are greatly curbed in the aquarium, and it is seldom that we see one more than 13 cm long. Not yet bred in captivity.

Badis badis burmanicus  [Dr. Herbert R. Axelrod]

Balantiocheilos melanopterus F D X 3 7 8 X N N C [Dr. Herbert R. Axelrod]

Barbodes binotatus 🄵🄳🆇③⑦⑨🆇🄽🄽⑦   [Dr. Herbert R. Axelrod]

Barbodes callipterus 🄵🅁🆇③⑧⓪🆇🄽🄽⑥   [Dr. Herbert R. Axelrod]

BARBODES BINOTATUS (Cuvier & Valenciennes) / *Spotted Barb*

Range: Thailand, Malaysia, parts of East Indies.
Habits: Will not molest species of its own size, but is best kept apart from smaller species to avoid nipping and bullying.
Water Conditions: Soft, slightly acid water. Should have large tank. Temperature 24 to 26°C.
Size: Up to 16.5 cm; usually seen much smaller.
Food Requirements: Takes almost all live, frozen and dried foods.

Getting this fish to spawn is not difficult, considering its size, but a large tank is necessary, for the fish is very active during pre-spawning maneuvers. The Spotted Barb lays adhesive eggs in thickets of plants, and it does not at first try to eat them. If the eggs are not removed promptly enough, however, the fish, spurred on by a very hearty appetite, will seek out and devour them. Eggs hatch within 48 hours at a temperature of 26°C; when free-swimming, the fry should immediately be fed plenty of newly hatched brine shrimp. Fry grow quickly, but they require a large tank for best growth. The Spotted Barb is often accused of being an uprooter of plants; where this tendency is noted, anchor firmly.

BARBODES CALLIPTERUS (Boulenger) / *Clipper Barb*

Range: Niger River and Cameroon, West Africa.
Habits: Usually peaceful, but some specimens are fin nippers.
Water Conditions: Soft, slightly acid water preferred. Temperature 21 to 30°C.
Size: Up to 8 cm.
Food Requirements: Live foods are preferred, but dry foods and frozen foods are accepted if not fed exclusively.

This barb is not often seen in the fish shops, and it has not really been missed much, although it was fairly popular many years ago. In comparison with some of the other barbs, it has little to offer in the way of attraction, although barb specialists would welcome the fish for at least one reason: it is tough to breed, and it therefore offers a challenge to their ingenuity. One difficulty in breeding the Clipper Barb is the fish's insistence on spawning under different conditions at different times. One time it may spawn in water which is pH 6.6 and DH 6, whereas at some other time of the year it will reject these conditions and force the breeder to work out alternative water compositions. Like many of its relatives, the Clipper Barb likes a well-planted tank; some of the plants should be of the soft variety, which will enable the fish to add some vegetable matter to its diet. *Nitella* is good for this purpose, but *Nitella* is in many localities too expensive to be used as a diet supplement, so some other plant must be offered. If another plant is used, it should be a fine-leaved variety, because in this case the same plant can also serve as a spawning medium into which the fish may lay its eggs.

380

BARBODES DORSIMACULATUS (Ahl) / *Blackline Barb*

Range: Sumatra.
Habits: Active and peaceful.
Water Conditions: Soft, slightly acid water. Temperature 21 to 30°C.
Size: 3.5 cm.
Food Requirements: Accepts all foods, small living crustaceans being preferred.

Although the physical characteristic made mention of in this fish's specific name would ordinarily lead hobbyists to choose a name such as "Spotted Dorsal" for the popular name of this species, this is not the case, probably because there are many other barbs that would qualify under the same name, thus adding to the confusion that already exists in both the popular and scientific terminology applied to these cyprinid fishes. In any event, the thin black line along the side of the fish serves hobbyists as more of a distinguishing characteristic than the black markings in the dorsal. Aside from these markings, there is little to keep the species from being completely neglected as a plainly colored not-too-desirable aquarium inhabitant. About the best thing that can be said about the color pattern is that the fish would provide a nice contrast to more brightly colored fishes. To the best of our knowledge, this fish has not yet been bred in the home aquarium. This, plus its relative drabness, makes it a fish which is not seen too often.

BARBODES EUTAENIA (Boulenger) / *African Red-Finned Barb*

Range: Tropical West Africa.
Habits: Peaceful when small, but inclined to aggressiveness when older.
Water Conditions: Soft, slighlty acid water. Temperature 24 to 30°C.
Size: Up to 18 cm; usually seen much smaller.
Food Requirements: Accepts all foods.

Unlike some of its relatives within the genus *Barbodes*, *B. eutaenia* needs to be kept warm, an ideal temperature for successful maintenance being 26°C. This is because it is a more strictly tropical species than some of the other *Barbodes*, many of which come from waters in which temperatures never get very high, usually keeping at the 15 to 21°C level. Many hobbyists automatically assume that a fish which comes from Africa is bound to need very warm water, but this is definitely not the case. For example, many African fishes are found in swiftly moving mountain water, waters which are necessarily cool. *Barbodes eutaenia* is a pretty little barb which breeds in standard barb fashion. If a spawning attempt is made, there would be little difficulty in telling the sexes apart, as the male ventral and anal fins are considerably more red than those of the female, whose predominant finnage coloration is yellow.

Barbodes dorsimaculatus F D X 3 8 1 X N N 3   [Dr. Herbert R. Axelrod]

Barbodes eutaenia F R X 3 8 2 X N N 5   [Dr. Herbert R. Axelrod]

Barbodes everetti ⬚F⬚R⬚X⬚3⬚8⬚3⬚X⬚N⬚ ⬚N⬚E⬚   [G. J. M. Timmerman]
Barbodes fasciolatus ⬚F⬚R⬚X⬚3⬚8⬚4⬚X⬚N⬚ ⬚N⬚E⬚   [Dr. Herbert R. Axelrod]

BARBODES EVERETTI (Boulenger) / *Clown Barb*

Range: Malaysia, Sarawak, Borneo.
Habits: Requires a large tank; should not be kept with small fishes.
Water Conditions: Water should be fairly soft and neutral. Temperature about 25°C.
Size: About 13 cm.
Food Requirements: Healthy eaters; will extend their appetites to plants in the aquarium.

Although this is one of the most attractive barbs that you can put into your aquarium, this very hardy fish has one typical barb drawback, it cannot be trusted with plants and will nibble at any that are placed in the aquarium.

This is not an easy barb to spawn in the aquarium. It is important that the sexes be separated for up to three weeks before spawning. In general, the female has a paler over-all coloration than the male. During their period of separation, the fish should be fed on live foods such as midge larvae and tubifex worms, as well as a healthy diet of vegetable matter such as mentioned above. A large tank is required for spawning, with a temperature of about 27°C. If possible, position the tank so that it can receive the morning sunshine.

BARBODES FASCIOLATUS (Günther) / *African Banded Barb*

Range: Zimbabwe (Rhodesia) area.
Habits: Active and fairly peaceful.
Water Conditions: Neutral to slightly acid water. Hardness not too important, as long as extremes are avoided. Temperature 21 to 30°C.
Size: 6 cm.
Food Requirements: Takes all foods, but live foods are accepted much more readily.

This West African barb is prettier than some of its barb cousins from Africa, but it will certainly never rival the popular Asiatic barbs in the favor of hobbyists. First of all, it has none of the brilliant coloring of such Asiatic species as the Tiger Barb; secondly, it is very seldom seen, because no commercial efforts have been made to breed this species and also because it is very seldom imported.

The females of this species are noticeably more robust than the slimmer males and their lateral stripes are much paler. This easily managed species is very active and has been bred with little difficulty. The spawning substrate should consist of fine-leaved plants. The water should be mature and slightly acidic (pH about 6 or 6.5). The addition of fresh water will sometimes help to stimulate spawning. The spawning tank should be positioned so that it will catch the morning sunlight. If the mating pair is placed in the breeding tank in the evening, there is a good chance that they will spawn the following morning. After a period of active driving, adhesive eggs are produced that stick to the plants and also fall to the bottom of the aquarium. The eggs will hatch in one or two days depending upon the temperature of the water.

BARBODES HEXAZONA (Weber & de Beaufort)
Belted Barb, Six-Banded Barb

Range: Malay Peninsula, Sumatra.
Habits: Active, peaceful.
Water Conditions: Soft, slightly acid water. Temperature 24-27°C.
Size: 5 to 6 cm.
Food Requirements: Takes all foods.

A great deal of confusion has resulted from the close resemblance of many of the barbs to one another. Such is the case with a number of fishes within the genus *Barbodes*. An illustration of the difficulty of categorizing these fishes correctly comes up when we make a comparison between two such fishes as *Barbodes hexazona* and *Barbodes pentazona*, the Six-Banded Barb and the Five-Banded Barb. Both look very much alike, and both are almost identical in the matter of scale and fin counts, two of the most important considerations in cataloguing species within a given genus. About the only difference which makes itself immediately obvious is the black bar running from the front of the dorsal fin. This bar is short in *Barbodes hexazona* but long in *Barbodes pentazona*. In markings and form *B. hexazona* resembles *Capoeta tetrazona*, the Tiger Barb, but the former is much less colorful and at its best is only a pale imitation of its more popular cousin. The Six-Banded Barb breeds in typical barb fashion, scattering its eggs into plant thickets, but it does not spawn readily.

BARBODES HOLOTAENIA (Boulenger) / *Spot-Scale Barb*

Range: Tributaries of the central Congo River.
Habits: Peaceful and active.
Water Conditions: Soft, slightly acid water. Temperature 21 to 29°C.
Size: Up to 12 cm.
Food Requirements: Accepts all foods.

This big barb breeds readily, but the young are not easy to raise; they are quite small for a fish of this size. Although the Spot-Scale Barb has little to recommend it in the way of coloring, the crescent marking which appears in each scale gives the fish at least an interesting appearance, even if it is not of enough importance to create a real demand for the fish. One color note is introduced into the over-all drab pattern by the eyes, the upper portion of which is a light red. Oddly, this characteristic does not appear in all *Barbodes holotaenia;* some specimens have the half-red eyes, but others do not. When the fish was first imported it was believed that the presence or absence of red coloration in the rim of the eye was indicative of sex, but later developments showed that this was incorrect, for sometimes two fishes with colored eyes would spawn successfully, and at other times two fishes without any red color to their eyes would also spawn successfully.

Barbodes hexazona [F][Q][X][3][8][5][X][N][N][5] [Dr. Herbert R. Axelrod]
Barbodes holotaenia [F][D][X][3][8][6][X][N][N][E] [Dr. Herbert R. Axelrod]

Barbodes lateristriga ⬚F⬚H⬚X⬚3⬚8⬚7⬚X⬚N⬚NE   [Dr. Herbert R. Axelrod]

Barbodes pentazona ⬚F⬚D⬚X⬚3⬚8⬚8⬚X⬚N⬚N⬚4   [R. Zukal]

BARBODES LATERISTRIGA (Cuvier and Valenciennes)
T-Barb, Spanner Barb

Range: Java, Borneo, Sumatra, Thailand, Malay Peninsula.
Habits: Peaceful at smaller sizes, but inclined to bully smaller fishes when it reaches full size.
Water Conditions: Soft, slightly acid water. Temperature 21 to 29°C.
Size: 20 cm, but usually seen much smaller.
Food Requirements: Takes all foods, particularly live foods.

One thing that can be said in favor of *Barbodes lateristriga* is that it moves more slowly than many of its relatives within the family Cyprinidae; unlike some of the other barbs, the T-Barb is not given to the swift back and forth pacing that is so characteristic of the smaller barbs. It can be assumed in general that the larger barbs are less darting than their relatives, but this does not always hold true; for example, *B. fasciatus,* the Striped Barb, also reaches a good size, but it is a quick mover nevertheless. The T-Barb is no longer considered one of the really common aquarium fishes, but it still has a following with hobbyists who like to maintain at least one tank of large fishes; it is well suited to this use. As is to be expected with so large a fish, many eggs are laid. These eggs are scattered in and around plant thickets, and the parents, although not averse to eating their eggs, are not to be counted within the ranks of the really avid egg-eaters.

BARBODES PENTAZONA Boulenger / *Banded Barb, Five-Banded Barb*

Range: Malay Peninsula, Borneo.
Habits: Active and fairly peaceful.
Water Conditions: Soft, slightly acid water. Temperature 23 to 26°C.
Size: 5 cm.
Food Requirements: Accepts all foods, especially small live foods.

This pretty fish, of which *Barbodes hexazona* is considered by some authorities to be at the most a variety, is more colorful than its six-banded relative. Aside from that and the fact that *B. pentazona* is considered to be easier to coax into spawning, there is little difference between the two. Neither of these two fishes has attained any degree of popularity, partly because they are imported so seldom and partly because they are unable to compete with the colorful beauty of the Tiger Barb, which they resemble in markings. Still and all, they are attractive, and in a sunny, well-planted tank they make a nice display. Oddly enough, *Barbodes pentazona* is as easy to spawn as *Barbodes hexazona* is difficult. *B. pentazona* spawns in the customary barb manner, but the mating act is accompanied by more "dancing" and less chasing from one end of the tank to the other than with its relatives. Sexing adult specimens is not difficult, as the female is fuller in form and is less colorful; in the female the pectoral fins are clear.

BARBODES SCHWANENFELDI (Bleeker) / *Tinfoil Barb*

Range: Sumatra, Borneo, Malacca, Thailand.
Habits: Peaceful and very active; a very good jumper and a plant eater.
Water Conditions: Soft, slightly acid water; sediment should be kept to a minimum. Temperature 23 to 26°C.
Size: Up to 35 cm.
Food Requirements: Takes all foods, but should have plenty of vegetable matter in its diet.

Usually offered for sale at a size of about 5 cm, this fish grows rapidly and is soon too big for all but the largest tanks. As it grows older the body continues to deepen, and what the hobbyist had originally bought as a small, streamlined barb is now a fat giant. Even at its full size, however, the Tinfoil Barb does not lose all of its attractiveness, for the orange coloring of the fins is heightened with age, which is the reverse of the usual procedure, as most fishes lose their bright colors as they increase in age and size. This fish has not been bred in the U.S. yet, but it is presumed that the general spawning pattern of large barbs would be adhered to. Sex differences have not been noted, but the male is probably the more colorful of the pair, as is true with other cyprinids. The Tinfoil Barb, while not disdaining meaty foods, needs a lot of vegetable matter.

BARBODES UNITAENIATUS (Günther) / *Red-Finned Barb*

Range: Southwest Africa, Angola.
Habits: Peaceful at all but the largest sizes.
Water Conditions: Neutral, slightly soft water. Temperature 24 to 31°C.
Size: About 7.5 cm.
Food Requirements: Accepts all foods.

The popular name of this species might lead to the supposition that the fish has a very distinct and attractive color pattern to recommend it to hobbyists, but this is not so. The red coloration in the Red-Finned Barb is more of a subdued pink; indeed, if the fish is not kept in proper condition, this color fails to show at all. It certainly never approaches the brilliant red coloring so obvious on the fins of the Bloodfin, *Aphyocharax anisitsi*. Still and all, it does have a slight rosy tint, and this is sufficient to make it desirable for some of the more enthusiastic barb fanciers. Coming as it does from Africa, *Barbodes unitaeniatus* was never in good supply, and, since it didn't excite the hobby very much when it was offered for sale, it seems that it will be seen more and more infrequently as time goes on. Perhaps it will at some future date disappear from the aquarium scene altogether. If the Red-Finned Barb is to be maintained in a community aquarium, it should be kept with the fishes which like warm water, because *B. unitaeniatus* has a decided preference for high temperatures and it cannot exist comfortably in cool water.

Barbodes schwanenfeldi F Q X 3 8 9 X N ND
Barbodes unitaeniatus F D X 3 9 0 X N N E

[Dr. Eugene Balon]

Barbodes usambarae ⬚F⬚D⬚X⬚3⬚9⬚1⬚X⬚N⬚ ⬚N⬚E [Dr. Herbert R. Axelrod]
Barbodes viviparus ⬚F⬚R⬚X⬚3⬚9⬚2⬚X⬚N⬚ ⬚N⬚5 [Dr. Herbert R. Axelrod]

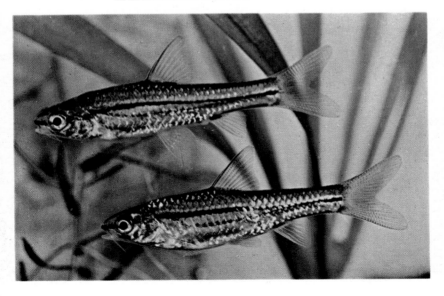

BARBODES USAMBARAE (Lönnberg) / *Peppered Barb*

Range: This fish is only known from one locality, a large pool near Tanga, Tanzania.
Habits: Peaceful and very active; a good jumper.
Water Conditions: Neutral to slightly acid water. Temperature 25 to 29°C.
Size: About 9 cm.
Food requirements: Accepts all foods.

Although *Barbodes usambarae* is a very drab African species, it managed to become popular for a short while. This species has a very restricted range which most likely accounts for its scarcity. It was originally described in 1907 from only one specimen (holotype) which has since dried out and become valueless for taxonomic work.

This barb, like most others, is a fairly hardy aquarium fish. It requires a good deal of space because it is an active fish and a hearty oxygen user. The Peppered Barb does best in a planted environment with plenty of light. Although this species will accept most prepared foods, live food is preferred, especially if the hobbyist is interested in breeding them. In general, it is a good idea to equip a barb tank with extra aerators. The temperature should not be allowed to fall below 22°C. Remember, these fish come from a very warm, shallow, tropical pool near the equator.

BARBODES VIVIPARUS Weber / *Viviparous Barb*

Range: Southeast Africa.
Habits: Peaceful and very active; a good jumper.
Water Conditions: Soft, slightly acid water. Temperature 23 to 26°C.
Size: To 6 cm.
Food requirements: Accepts all foods, but prefers live or frozen food.

The lack of body depth in this African barb, *Barbodes viviparus*, makes it look much like a *Rasbora* species. Its coloration is not very bold, but a specimen in good condition is still an eye-catcher. It has an overall silvery color and the upperside is olive with two longitudinal black stripes. A dark blotch can sometimes be seen on the anal fin base.

Little is presently known about the reproduction of this species as it is not a widespread fish in the hobby. Weber, the describer of this fish, named it *"viviparus"* because he thought it was a livebearing fish. He came to this conclusion through dissection of specimens and never actually saw the fish spawn in the wild or captivity.

When feeding this fish, any good prepared aquarium food can form the basis of their diet. It is a good idea, however, to offer some live foods once or twice a week. In general, barbs are heavy eaters and one can see their abdomens swell if they are given too much food. It is well to remember that dried food swells in water and amounts to much more than the dried flakes that are added to the water.

BARBODES SP.

Range: Lower Zambesi River and branches.
Habits: Peaceful and very active; a very good jumper and a plant nibbler.
Water Conditions: Soft, slightly acid water. Temperature 24 to 27°C.
Size: 6 cm.
Food Requirements: Takes all foods; does best with a combination of live and dried flake food.

This attractive little fish probably is *Barbodes radiatus*, but admittedly, many African barbs are difficult to identify. *Radiatus* and a few other African species are sometimes placed in the genus or subgenus *Beirabarbus*, a name seldom used by aquarists.

Little is known of this fish in the aquarium hobby as it is not widely kept. It was usually imported along with other similar species and "just went along for the ride." There are literally hundreds of African barbs now known to science. Unfortunately, less than 70 of the estimated 800 + species have ever entered the aquarium hobby. It is doubtful that you can walk into any aquarium shop and find more than three or four different African species at any one time. For this reason, many barbs, including this one, are not well known and probably will not be in the immediate future.

BARILIUS CHRISTYI Boulenger / *Copper-Nose Minnow*

Range: Lower Congo River and its tributaries.
Habits: An active fish which can only be trusted with others which are as large or larger.
Water Conditions: Slightly acid, clean, well aerated water. Temperature 22 to 25°C.
Size: Up to 15 cm.
Food Requirements: Has a healthy appetite and will take dried as well as living foods. Is particularly fond of insects which have been thrown on the surface.

Judging from the way it carries itself, *Barilius christyi* is a fish which comes from moving streams. The author (HRA) verified this on his 1957 African expedition. It should therefore be given a roomy aquarium with clean water and some aeration. Here it shows its attractive, metallic colors. If possible, it is best to keep it in a small school of about 6 or more. They are very active and will almost surely jump out if their aquarium is left uncovered. Females can only be distinguished when fully grown. At this time they show a deeper belly while the males are more slender and also more highly colored. We have only one account of their spawning, and that a sketchy one; they spawn in the same manner as *Danio malabaricus*. A tank of at least 60 liters is provided, and a layer of pebbles or glass marbles is placed on the bottom. A ripe pair or, better yet, several pairs are placed here. The water should not be more than 25 cm above the layer of pebbles or marbles. If all goes well, the fish will pursue each other in a lively manner, dropping eggs at intervals; these fall between the pebbles.

Barbodes sp. [F][D][X][3][9][3][X][N][N][6]
Barilius christyi [F][D][X][3][9][4][X][N][N][E]

[Dr. Herbert R. Axelrod]
[Dr. Herbert R. Axelrod]

Bario steindachneri  [Harald Schultz]
Bedotia geayi [H. J. Richter]

BARIO STEINDACHNERI (Eigenmann) / *Blotch-Tailed Bario*

Range: Peruvian Amazon.
Habits: Peaceful toward fishes of comparable size.
Water Conditions: Prefers slightly acid, clean, soft water. Temperature 24 to 27°C.
Size: Specimens of 10 cm have been known.
Food requirements: Eats all kinds of foods, but is especially fond of frozen brine shrimp. Live foods should be offered once a week.

Bario steindachneri is a rather large Amazonian fish which is closely related to *Moenkhausia*. Although this species is not very well known in the hobby, its spawning has been reported. The mating itself is quite simple. An active male and a female heavy with eggs are placed into a clean aquarium with several plant thickets. The water should be fairly soft, about 5 German DH; the temperature should be brought to 27°C. Eggs are laid among plant thickets, and the pair should be removed as soon as they lose interest in each other. Depending upon the temperature and other conditions, hatching will take two or three days. Fry are easily raised and will accept newly hatched brine shrimp or finely crushed flake food.

BEDOTIA GEAYI Pellegrin / *Madagascar Rainbow*

Range: Madagascar.
Habits: Peaceful and active; never molest their tankmates.
Water Conditions: Somewhat alkaline water required, about pH 7.3 or 7.4. Temperature 24 to 26°C.
Size: 6 to 7 cm.
Food Requirements: Not a fussy eater; will eat dried foods readily, but should get live food occasionally.
Color Variations: Body greenish with a dark stripe running from the eye to the caudal base. Dorsal, anal and caudal have dark edges.

This fish usually makes an immediate hit with all who see it for the first time. While it is not as gorgeous as some of our outstanding beauties, it has a quiet charm and alert liveliness which make it desirable, and we venture to predict that someday when it becomes more obtainable it will be one of the more popular favorites. Some of the males which have been more blessed by Mother Nature have an added attraction: the ends of both caudal lobes are tipped with a bright red. This is also seen in some of the females to a lesser extent. The double dorsal fin identifies it as a close relative of the well-known Australian Rainbowfish and the Celebes Rainbowfish. These species have the characteristic that they prefer alkaline water, and *Bedotia geayi* is not at all happy when placed in the slightly acid water to which most egg-laying species are usually relegated. Given water which ranges from neutral to slightly alkaline, however, they soon feel very much at home. They spawn near the surface in closely-bunched plants, only a few brown eggs every day. Eggs and fry are not usually eaten, and the youngsters are easily raised on brine shrimp.

BELONESOX BELIZANUS Kner / *Pike Top Minnow, Pike Livebearer*

Range: Southern Mexico, Honduras to Costa Rica, Nicaragua and Guatamala.
Habits: Very vicious; cannot even be trusted with smaller members of their own family.
Water Conditions: Roomy tank which has been heavily planted is ideal. Water should have an addition of salt, 1 tablespoonful for every 4 liters.
Size: Males about 15 cm; females about 20 cm.
Color Variations: Sides are grayish to olive-green, with numerous tiny black dots on the sides.

If you like your fish nasty, this one is for you. This would be an ideal species for a Guppy-breeder who has to keep weeding out the undesirable specimens to make way for the good ones and therefore has a constant supply of unwanted fish. The Pike Livebearer is very similar in habits to his namesake the pike: always hungry, ever ready to sneak up on some unsuspecting prey and gobble it up. One look at the pointed snout and sharp teeth will confirm this. The small, needle-pointed teeth are not designed for slashing and chewing, but are grasping teeth which enable it to hold its prey and prevent its escape. This it cannot do unless its captor opens its mouth, and *Belonesox* will only do this to get it further down his throat and swallow it. Females which are ready to deliver young, as their swollen bellies would indicate, should be placed in their well-planted quarters at a temperature of about 29°C. The youngsters are quite touchy at first and must also be protected from their greedy mother. Daphnia is a good food for them to start out with, followed by fully grown brine shrimp or baby Guppies. Keeping this fish fed is the greatest problem.

1. *Belonesox belizanus* (p398) female (above) and male (below).
2. This species has a large, well equipped mouth (p398).

Belonesox belizanus mating pair. Photo by Milan Chvojka.

1. *Belonesox belizanus* F R X 3 9 7 X N N A   [H. J. Richter]
2. *Belonesox belizanus* F D X 3 9 8 X N N E   [H. J. Richter]

1. *Belontia hasselti* ♂ F A X 3 9 9 X N N A   [Aaron Norman]
2. *Belontia hasselti* ♀ F B X 4 0 0 X N N E   [S. Frank]

BELONTIA HASSELTI (Cuvier & Valenciennes) / *Java Combtail*

Range: Java, Bali, Borneo, Sumatra.
Habits: Peaceful for a large anabantoid.
Water Conditions: Composition of water not critical, but temperature is; the temperature should not be allowed to fall below 24°C.
Size: Up to 10 cm in the aquarium; probably larger in the wild.
Food Requirements: Accepts all standard aquarium foods.
Color Variations: The spot at the base of the rear of the dorsal fin on males varies in size and intensity from fish to fish; over-all body color ranges from golden to light brown.

With the exception of bettas and gouramis, few anabantoid fishes have found much favor with aquarium hobbyists. Continental European aquarists give much attention to the African *Ctenopoma* species, but hobbyists in English-speaking countries generally neglect them, and nobody pays much attention at all to the bulk of the Asiatic anabantoids. *Belontia signata*, the Combtail, is an example: the fish has been known to hobbyists and available at least sporadically for many years, but it has never become established within the aquarium trade. *Belontia hasselti* is much newer to the aquarium scene, even though it has been known to science since 1831, but even though it is a very attractively marked fish it probably will never achieve a great degree of popularity. Much more deep-bodied and less aggressive than *Belontia signata*, *B. hasselti* has a subdued appeal. It is not colorful, but the lacy effect achieved by the markings in the tail, dorsal and anal fins of the male is very pleasing. *Belontia hasselti* spawns like *B. signata* by blowing a very sketchy bubblenest to hold the floating eggs together. Males and females are easily differentiable; the females do not have the dark spot at the rear of the body below the dorsal, nor do they have the lacy markings in the fins.

1. *Belontia hasselti* male (p399).
2. *Belontia hasselti* female (p399)

A lake in Java where the Java Combtail was collected. Photo by Dr. Herbert R. Axelrod.

BELONTIA SIGNATA (Günther) / *Combtail*

Range: Sri Lanka.
Habits: Vicious toward smaller fishes; should be kept only with those which are able to take care of themselves.
Water Conditions: Large tank is required. Water not critical. Temperature should be at least 25°C.
Size: 12.5 cm.
Food Requirements: Very greedy; will take coarse dried foods, but prefers chunks such as pieces of earthworms or lean raw beef.
Color Variations: Sides are a reddish brown, lighter in the belly region; outer edge of the tail is fringed.

This species is very similar to the Paradise Fish, *Macropodus opercularis,* not only in appearance but also in habits. As in the other anabantoids, the male may be distinguished by his longer, more pointed fins and slightly brighter colors. Like the Paradise Fish to which it is related, it is a very heavy eater, and it may be a bit difficult to keep a tank in which a number of them are quartered spotlessly clean. In the winter months when live foods are not so easy to come by, other foods may be substituted such as pieces of shrimp, chunks of clam or crab meat, or pieces of lean beef. This fish builds a bubblenest in which a great number of eggs are placed. Sometimes a pair will share parental duties in guarding the eggs and fry, but more often one or the other will be constantly driven away. If this happens, take out the fish which is being chased. When they become free-swimming, the youngsters have no further need of parental attention. There is always the chance that the appetite of the parents might overcome their affection, and they should also be removed. This is not a fish for the community aquarium.

1. *Belontia signata* (p402).
2.-5. *Belontia signata* spawning (p402).

Belontia signata pair in aquarium. Photo by G. J. M. Timmerman.

1. *Belontia signata* 2. *Belontia signata*

[H. J. Richter]

Betta bellica F A X 4 0 3 X N N E
Betta brederi F R X 4 0 4 X N N 8

[Dr. Herbert R. Axelrod]
[E. Roloff]

BETTA BELLICA Sauvage / *Slender Betta*

Range: Perak, in Malaysia.
Habits: Not a good fish for the community tank. Although there is not the aggressiveness between males as with *B. splendens,* they are best kept alone.
Water Conditions: Not critical, but a high temperature (25 to 30°C) must be maintained.
Size: About 10 cm.
Food Requirements: Should get living foods, with occasional supplements of dried foods.

Looking at this species and comparing it with a wild specimen of *Betta splendens,* one cannot help but wonder what the result would have been if the breeders had bestowed as much care and time on *B. bellica* as they did on *B. splendens.* Perhaps the result would have been even more beautiful than the gorgeous *B. splendens* one sees today. But *B. bellica* is more beautiful than the wild *B. splendens.* Would aquarium-bred specimens have yielded the wide variety of colors and huge fins that *B. splendens* has? All these are interesting speculations, but we will not know the answer for a long time to come. This attractive fish is longer and more slender in the body than *B. splendens,* and the males can be distinguished by their longer ventral fins. Unfortunately they have proven not to be quite as active as their illustrious cousins. They spawn by building bubblenests.

BETTA BREDERI Myers / *Breder's Betta*

Range: Java and Sumatra.
Habits: Although they are not vicious, it is best to keep this species by themselves.
Water Conditions: Not critical, as long as the tank is clean. Temperature about 25°C.
Size: To 8 cm.
Food Requirements: Live foods exclusively.

This species is not a bubblenest builder like most of the other labyrinth fishes; but it is a mouthbrooder. After the nuptial embrace, the male catches the large eggs in his folded anal fin and fertilizes them. Then the female picks them up from there in her mouth and offers them to her mate by spitting them toward him. Sometimes he refuses one or two and she has to pick them up again and spit them at him once more. This little game goes on until all of the eggs are safely lodged in the brood-pouch of the male, which extends from his mouth to his throat. The eggs hatch in about 40 hours, but the fry continue to be carried about until they are capable of swimming and hunting for their own food. Raising them is not difficult, and their aquarium should be kept covered for two reasons: first, to prevent them from gulping chilled air, and second, to prevent a scum from forming on the surface which would interfere with the youngsters coming up to breathe the atmospheric air.

BETTA IMBELLIS Ladiges / *Peaceful Betta, Crescent Betta*

Range: Malaysia.
Habits: Peaceful among themselves or other species.
Water Conditions: Neutral water of moderate hardness. Temperature 23 to 27°C.
Size: About 5 cm.
Food Requirements: Will take a variety of live, frozen or prepared foods.
Color Variations: Males dark brown with a bright orange border along the posterior edge of
the caudal fin and on the distal tips of the anal and pelvic fins. Females are a dull mottled
brown with orange pelvic fin tips and a less intense orange border on the caudal fin.

In nature, *Betta imbellis* is found in shady habitats in thickets of vegetation or under submerged roots. In captivity it is also predisposed toward dwelling in dark or shady places. Therefore, the fish will show its best colors by providing it with plants having large overhanging leaves or floating vegetation such as *Riccia* or water sprite.

It breeds in the fashion of a typical bubblenest builder with the male offering all of the parental care. E. Roloff, who successfully bred this fish, recommends a water change to stimulate it into breeding. Once the spawning is complete, the female should be removed. The offspring, which are quite small at first, are kept in the bubblenest by the male until such time as their labyrinth organs begin to develop and the young fish are able to fend for themselves. At this time the male should be removed.

BETTA SMARAGDINA Ladiges / *Peaceful Betta*

Range: Korat, near Laotian border.
Habits: Peaceful for a *Betta* species; males do not attack one another except when vying for attention of females.
Water Conditions: Neutral, soft water suitable. Temperature should be kept from 22 to 27°C.
Size: To about 6 cm for both males and females.
Food Requirements: Takes all prepared and frozen meaty foods and all regular live foods; especially relishes tubifex worms.

Betta smaragdina does not have the extensive finnage development of cultivated male bettas, but there appears to be little doubt that experienced breeders will be able to produce long-finned mutations as time goes by. If they are as successful as they hope to be, *Betta smaragdina* might someday replace *Betta splendens* as the most commercially important *Betta* species. In addition to its less combative nature, it also is able to withstand maintenance at slightly cooler water temperatures, and the fry are easier to raise than Siamese Fighting Fish fry. Males do not fight.

405

Betta imbellis F Q X 4 0 5 X N N 5   [E. Roloff]
Betta smaragdina F A X 4 0 6 X N N 6   [E. Roloff]

1. *Betta splendens* F F X 4 0 7 X R N 6 [Al Liebetrau]
2. *Betta splendens* F E X 4 0 8 X B N 7 [Al Liebetrau]

BETTA SPLENDENS Regan / *Betta, Siamese Fighting Fish*

Range: Thailand, Malaysia, Southeast Asia.

Habits: Usually peaceful with other fishes of its own size, but two males in the same aquarium will fight until one retreats.

Water Conditions: Not critical; breathing atmospheric air as they do, they can be kept in very small containers. Temperature should not go below 25°C.

Size: 5 to 6 cm.

Food Requirements: Will take dried foods, but should get an occasional meal of live foods.

Color Variations: Many colors have been developed: red, green, blue and combinations of these colors.

Next to the ubiquitous Guppy and Goldfish, this is probably the most popular of all aquarium fishes. Their brilliant colors are a monument to the fish-breeder's art and have been developed by selective breeding from a rather nondescript greenish, short-finned fish which is still bred in Thailand today for fish-fighting. Fish-fighting is as much of a sport in Thailand as cock-fighting is in many other parts of the world. The procedure is simple: two males are placed in a small aquarium and wagers are made and taken as to the outcome. The fish tear away at each other furiously until one or the other is overcome by exhaustion or weakness. The vanquished is then fished out by its owner, who either disposes of it or nurses it back to health, and the winner's owner collects his money. *Betta splendens* is easily bred.

1. *Betta splendens* female (p407).
2. *Betta splendens* male (p407).

Betta splendens are known for their beautiful long finnage as well as their fighting instincts. The variety shown here is called the butterfly betta. Mr. Tutweiler developed this strain over 20 years ago. Photo by Dr. Herbert R. Axelrod.

BETTA SPLENDENS Regan / *Libby Betta*

Habits: Males viciously attack each other and cannot be kept in the same aquarium. Females and individual males may be kept in the community tank. Some individuals may kill smaller fishes.
Water Conditions: Not critical.
Size: Up to 10 cm.
Food Requirements: Live, frozen or dried foods accepted.
Color Variations: Available in all standard Betta colors including red, black, green, blue and Cambodia.

The Libby Betta carries at least two mutations for extended fin length. The first of these mutations appeared in this country in fish imported from Cambodia in the 1920's, and it is the mutation most commonly available. The second mutation appeared in the 1960's and was fixed into a commecial strain by Warren and Libby Young. It is through the interaction of both these mutations that the unusually long fins of the Libby strain develop. The Libby mutation is easily detected even in relatively young males by the development of a unique lengthening of the rays of the pectoral fin, especially on the dorsal edge. Unfortunately not all the fish sold under this name are representative of the strain. The first specimens made available were red, green or blue, but the mutation was later extended into the Cambodia series. There is also a split-tail strain of Libby Bettas available. The Libby characteristic is easily lost and for this reason the strain should not be outcrossed to another strain for two consecutive generations. The Libby strain is subject to two problems which hinder it in competition. First is a condition which is referred to as "cranial hump," which is the doming of the top of the head. The second is a pronounced tendency for the rays of the dorsal portion of the tail fin to turn upward rather than follow the normal contour of the fin. Both of these conditions are hereditary and can be controlled by careful breeding.

BETTA SPLENDENS Regan / *Split-Tailed Betta, Double-Tailed Betta*

Habits: Males are not well suited to the community aquarium because of their slow movements.
Water Conditions: Not critical.
Size: Up to 7.5 cm.
Food Requirements: Accepts any animal-based food.
Color Variations: Available in all standard Betta colors.

It is not known exactly how long the Betta has been under cultivation, but it probably ranks only second to the Goldfish in length of domestication. Two distinct breeds have evolved, fighting Bettas and display Bettas. The former are seen only in the Orient, where they are raised for their pugnacity, which is much more pronounced than in their wild ancestors. It was probably from fighting strains that the long-finned mutations arose. Much more recently an

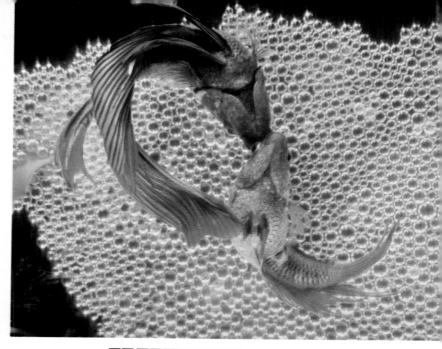

1. *Betta splendens* F Q X 4 0 9 X M N 7   [Al Liebetrau]
2. *Betta splendens* F E X 4 1 0 X B N 7   [H. Hansen, Aquarium Berlin]

3. *Betta splendens* [F][Q][X][4][1][1][X][M][N][7] [Al Liebetrau]
4. *Betta splendens* [F][E][X][4][1][2][X][B][T][7] [Al Liebetrau]

interesting mutation appeared in a strain of short-finned Bettas bred for fighting. This mutation has two pronounced effects on the fish. First, the caudal fin is split into two distinct lobes. Second, the number of rays in the dorsal fin is enormously increased. This results in a fin which is nearly a mirror image of the anal fin. This mutation was transferred to long-finned Bettas by Oriental breeders, and it is this form which is seen by aquarists. The split-tail gene *(S)* is a semi-lethal, dominant gene. Thus a fish which carries one dose out of a possible two *(Ss)* shows the characteristic, while individuals with two doses *(SS)* die in the egg. The split-tail strain does not breed true. When two Bettas showing the characteristic are mated, two-thirds of the offspring show the characteristic while one-third do not. When a split-tail is mated to a normal tail, half of the fry show the characteristic and half do not.

1. *Betta splendens* mating below a bubble nest (p410).
2. A handsome male *Betta splendens* (p410).
3. The male *Betta splendens* is chasing the female (p411).
4. A Double-Tailed *Betta splendens* male (p411).

Betta splendens in the aquarium. Photo by Dr. Herbert R. Axelrod.

BIOTODOMA CUPIDO (Heckel) / *Cupid Cichlid*

Range: Middle Amazon Basin and western Guyana.
Habits: Extremely quarrelsome.
Water Conditions: Not critical.
Size: About 12.5 cm.
Food Requirements: Like most other large cichlids, this species requires large amounts of animal-based foods.

The Cupid Cichlid does not appear to be a species destined for great popularity except with the most dedicated cichlid enthusiasts. This species is suitable for community aquariums only when its companions are as large or larger, with temperaments that match that of *B. cupido*. *B. cupido* has one of the most objectionable cichlid habits, that of constantly grubbing about in the sand. Not only does this tend to up root plants, but it also keeps the water in a constant state of turbidity. Those who are interested in keeping the larger cichlids are generally content to do without rooted plants, or they may use plastic plants or achieve a degree of success by putting plants in individual pots and covering the area around the crown of the plants with stones to prevent digging. When plants are not used, there is a good chance that waste materials will build up in the aquarium to the degree that a cottony growth of fungus may cover the glass and bottom. This can be prevented by vacuuming the sand each week and replacing about one fourth of the water. A power filter is extremely useful in removing suspended matter from the water. This species is reported to be a mouthbrooder, but it is seldom bred. Any aquarium used for breeding this species should be large and have ample hiding places. The pair should be watched carefully and separated if love-making becomes too rough.

BIOTOECUS OPERCULARIS (Steindachner) / *Green Dwarf Cichlid*

Range: The Amazon River system of Brazil.
Habits: Typically nocturnal; hugs the bottom of the aquarium and hides among plants and any other nook it can find.
Water Conditions: Not very sensitive to water conditions as long as the temperature is between 21 and 29°C and not too acid or alkaline. Tolerates a pH of 6.0 to 8.0.
Size: Under 10 cm.
Food Requirements: Prefers worms to anything else, but eagerly takes frozen brine shrimp and beef heart.

The fish spawns rather easily if properly fed on live foods such as small garden worms, tubifex worms and frozen brine shrimp. The pair seeks seclusion, sometimes even going into a darkened flowerpot, where about 60 eggs are laid in a small circle. They exercise extreme parental care and zealously guard their young until a week after they are free-swimming. It is advisable to remove the parents as soon as the young are free-swimming and able to take freshly hatched brine shrimp.

Biotodoma cupido ⒻⒹⓍ④①③ⓍⓃⓃⒷ   [Aaron Norman]
Biotoecus opercularis ⒻⒹⓍ④①④ⓍⓃⓃ⑦   [Dr. Herbert R. Axelrod]

Boehlkea fredcochui ⬚F ⬚Q ⬚X ⬚4 ⬚1 ⬚5 ⬚X ⬚N ⬚N ⬚5   [A. Kochetov]
Boleophthalmus pectinirostris ⬚F ⬚A ⬚X ⬚4 ⬚1 ⬚6 ⬚X ⬚N ⬚N ⬚C   [Aaron Norman]

BOEHLKEA FREDCOCHUI Gery / *Cochu's Blue Tetra*

Range: Peruvian Amazon region, near Leticia, Colombia
Habits: Peaceful but very sensitive; best kept with other fishes with similar characteristics.
Water Conditions: Soft, slightly acid water is highly important with this species. The addition of acid peat moss in the filter is benefieial. Temperature 23 to 26°C.
Size: Up to 5 cm.
Food Requirements: Live or frozen foods; dried foods only when there is nothing else at hand.

Like many of the tetras from the Upper Amazon region, Cochu's Blue Tetra is not seen at its best unless it has water which is to its liking. At this point of the huge river the water has very little mineral content and there is an influx from the other streams where the humic acid content is high, plus a great deal of rain water at certain times of the year, so we must approach these conditions by using water which is soft and has a certain amount of acidity. The most beautiful specimens of this fish ever seen by the author (HRA) were in a large aquarium in the lobby of a hotel in Iquitos, Peru.

BOLEOPHTHALMUS PECTINIROSTRIS (Linnaeus)
Comb-Toothed Mudskipper

Range: Japan and China to Malaysia, the East Indies and Burma.
Habits: Rather territorial, requiring roomy, specialized aquarium with bottom that slopes from a water depth of not over 15 cm to dry land to allow the fish to leave the water. Rocks and pieces of driftwood should be provided for resting places.
Water Conditions: Water should be brackish. Salinity should range from a tablespoon of sea salt for every 4 liters of fresh water to a mixture of half fresh water and half sea water. Tank must be covered tightly and kept warm to maintain high humidity. Temperature 25 to 28°C.
Size: Up to 20 cm in nature.
Food Requirements: Small worms, *Drosophila* (fruit flies), other insects or live foods. Substitutes such as small pieces of beef heart sometimes accepted.

Among the truly unusual fishes of the world are the large gobies known as mudskippers. Obviously so-named because of their habit of springing or "hopping" over the tropical mudflats where they live, seeming almost more like insects than fishes, in some cases they even seem to prefer jumping away from an enemy to swimming away. The Comb-Toothed Mudskipper, like others, has "bugged" eyes which are perfectly adapted to aerial vision. This is unusual, since most fishes' eyes would be no more useful out of water than ours are under water without the aid of a face mask. Mudskippers are quite intelligent and under good conditions become very tame. It is important that high humidity be maintained in the aquarium

BOTIA BEAUFORTI Smith / *Beaufort's Loach*

Range: Thailand.
Habits: Generally peaceful toward other fishes; mostly nocturnal. Will remain mostly in the darker portions of the aquarium.
Water Conditions: Soft, slightly acid water, well-aerated. Tank should have a number of hiding places and be dimly lighted. Temperature 23 to 26°C.
Size: 20 cm.
Food Requirements: Live foods, especially tubifex or white worms preferred; frozen and prepared foods also eaten, and food left by other fishes.

Don't try to keep *Botia beauforti* unless you have a large tank. The 20 cm size given is a maximum, but 15 cm specimens are not at all unusual. One of the distinguishing marks of this species is the lack of taper in the body toward the caudal base, which is almost as wide at this point as it is at the middle of the body under the dorsal fin. The snout is not as underslung as in most of the other species, sticking almost straight out. This species has a double spine under the eye. *B. beauforti* should not be kept singly, but rather in a group. If kept singly, they may develop a nasty attitude toward their tankmates; on the other hand, if kept in a group a sort of "pecking order" is established among themselves, and they should be provided with a number of hiding places for the protection of the weaker ones.

BOTIA BERDMOREI Blyth / *Berdmore's Loach*

Range: Burma.
Habits: Peaceful toward other fishes if kept in a group; mostly nocturnal.
Water Conditions: Soft, slightly acid water, well-aerated. Tank should have a number of hiding places and be dimly lighted. Temperature 23 to 25°C.
Size: To 8 cm.
Food Requirements: Live foods, especially tubifex and white worms, preferred; frozen and prepared foods also eaten, and food left by other fishes.

BOTIA HORAE Smith / *Hora's Loach*

Range: Thailand.
Habits: Peaceful, mostly nocturnal. Will remain mostly in the darker portions of the aquarium.
Water Conditions: Soft, slightly acid water, well-aerated. Tank should have a number of hiding places and not be brightly lighted. Temperature 23 to 25°C.
Size: To 10 cm; usually smaller.
Food Requirements: Live foods, especially tubifex or white worms, preferred; frozen and prepared foods also eaten, and food left by other fishes.

The *Botia* species all have a protective device which is shared by a few other fishes. There is an erectile spine, sometimes two, under each eye. This inflicts a painful but non-poisonous sting when the fish is handled. This has proven to be the downfall of many a bird or larger fish which caught a *Botia* and did not spit it out quickly enough, to have it lodge in its throat and choke on it.

Botia beauforti ⬚F⬚A⬚T⬚4⬚1⬚7⬚X⬚N⬚N⬚B   [B. Kahl]

Botia berdmorei ⬚F⬚R⬚M⬚4⬚1⬚8⬚X⬚N⬚N⬚8   [G. Wolfsheimer]
Botia horae ⬚F⬚D⬚B⬚4⬚1⬚8⬚X⬚N⬚N⬚E   [Dr. Herbert R. Axelrod]

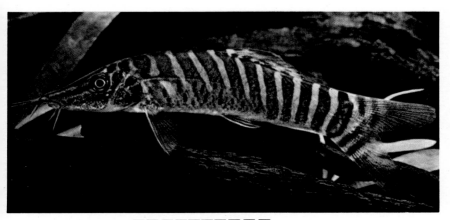

Botia hymenophysa ⬛Ⓕ⬛Ⓓ⬛Ⓧ⬛④⬛①⬛⑨⬛Ⓧ⬛Ⓝ⬛Ⓝ⬛Ⓑ   [B. Kahl]

1. *Botia lohachata* Ⓕ⬛Ⓒ⬛Ⓜ⬛④⬛②⬛⓪⬛Ⓧ⬛Ⓝ⬛Ⓝ⬛①   [S. Sane]

2. *Botia lohachata* Ⓕ⬛Ⓓ⬛Ⓑ⬛④⬛②⬛⓪⬛Ⓧ⬛Ⓝ⬛Ⓝ⬛⑦   [Dr. Herbert R. Axelrod]

BOTIA HYMENOPHYSA (Bleeker) / *Banded Loach*

Range: Malaysia, Thailand, Singapore, Java, Sumatra and Borneo.
Habits: Occurs in flowing streams of fresh water. Mostly nocturnal; shuns light and stays in the darker portions of the aquarium.
Water Conditions: Should be given clean, well-oxygenated water. Temperature 24 to 27°C.
Size: In captivity about 15 cm; wild specimens are said to attain 30 cm.
Food Requirements: Will take any living foods, including small fishes. Will also rummage around the bottom for uneaten leftovers.

This attractive loach is a useful addition to an aquarium of larger fishes, but it should not be trusted with smaller ones which could be swallowed. It is nocturnal in habits to a great extent and should be provided with a number of retreats such as rock caves. Care must be taken to place the rocks for these caves on a firm foundation or they will be undermined and fall on the fish which is doing the digging. This loach is found in flowing streams, so it is best provided with clean, well-filtered and well-aerated water. For some unexplained reason, they will sometimes dash madly from one end of the aquarium to the other, stirring up the bottom sediment and anything else which is loose. Perhaps this is sheer playfulness. Sex differences have never been fully determined, and if they have ever spawned in captivity it has never been observed or reported.

BOTIA LOHACHATA Chaudhuri / *Pakistani Loach*

Range: India and Pakistan.
Habits: A typical loach with bottom-dwelling habits.
Water Conditions: Prefers very soft, slightly acid water with high temperatures in the high 20's (°C).
Size: Seldom larger than 10 cm in length.
Food Requirements: This species often starves in an aquarium, for they must have worms in their diet, preferably tubifex.

The Pakistani Loach is famous only because it is one of the very few fishes from Pakistan which have made aquarium history. The Pakistani people are very active in the aquarium field and their aquarium in Karachi must be applauded as a major contribution to "living museums of the world." This loach has never been exported from Pakistan in commercial quantities only because there are so few exporters in the small country. But shipments arrive regularly from India, especially Bombay, where they are collected in large quantities. The Indian variety is probably a subspecies, if not a separate species, as it is very much lighter in color and is much smaller, but there is so much variability from population to population that it is impossible to determine the differences between the two varieties without a statistical analysis of the validity of certain meristic differences.

1. *Botia lohachata*, a 2 cm juvenile (p419).
2. *Botia lohachata*, a 7 cm mature fish (p419).

BOTIA MACRACANTHA (Bleeker) / *Clown Loach*

Range: Sumatra, Borneo and the Sunda Islands.
Habits: Peaceful, not quite as nocturnal as some of the other species.
Water Conditions: Clean, well-aerated water. Temperature should not exceed 24°C.
Size: 30 cm maximum, but most specimens do not exceed 10 cm.
Food Requirements: They like to grub for leftover morsels at the bottom, but should also get some living foods.

The Clown Loach is the most popular and colorful member of the genus. It does not appear to be quite as sensitive to light as the others, and therefore it has the added attraction of being more apt to stay in sight. However, there should also be places provided where they can get into a shady spot to rest their eyes. This is a very active species that often swims up and down the glass sides of the aquarium for no apparent reason. To the best of our knowledge there have been no successful spawnings observed in the aquarium, probably due to the fact that conditions which are present in their natural environments are missing in the aquarium. For instance, the fish may spawn in soft mud, which would never be permitted by an aquarist who wants to see his fish and plants. Some day some fortunate aquarist will be successful, and a very desirable aquarium fish will become more available at a lower price. At the present time it is also not known what the external sex diferences are, and it is impossible to tell the males from the females without killing them. Some day we may also hear from some observant Asiatic naturalist who studies the life habits of this fish in its native environment.

BOTIA MODESTA Bleeker / *Orange-Finned Loach*

Range: Thailand, Vietnam, Malaysia.
Habits: Peaceful; a community aquarium fish. Nocturnal.
Water Conditions: Does best in water at a pH of 6.6 in very soft water. Prefers high temperatures of about 28°C.
Size: To 10 cm.
Food Requirements: Prefers tubifex worms, but as a scavenger it probes the bottom for almost any kind of food.
Color Variations: The orange fins may become yellow if they do not have insects or shrimp in their diet.

This is a rarely imported loach that frequently accompanies shipments from Thai (Siamese) exporters. The fish is very sensitive to chemicals and it should not be treated with dyes such as malachite green or methylene blue unless the fish is dipped into a bath and quickly removed. They prefer a place to hide during the day and should be given a half coconut shell under which they can escape bright light.

Botia macracantha [F][D][X][4][2][1][X][N][N][9] [Dr. Herbert R. Axelrod]
Botia modesta [F][D][X][4][2][2][X][N][N][E] [Dr. Herbert R. Axelrod]

Botia sidthimunki ⬚F⬚ ⬚R⬚ ⬚X⬚ ⬚4⬚ ⬚2⬚ ⬚3⬚ ⬚X⬚ ⬚N⬚ ⬚N⬚⬚4⬚ [Dr. Herbert R. Axelrod]
Brachydanio albolineatus ⬚F⬚ ⬚E⬚ ⬚X⬚ ⬚4⬚ ⬚2⬚ ⬚4⬚ ⬚X⬚ ⬚N⬚ ⬚N⬚⬚6⬚ [Dr. Herbert R. Axelrod]

BOTIA SIDTHIMUNKI Klausewitz / *Dwarf Loach*

Range: Thailand.
Habits: Peaceful, playful, seem to be less nocturnal than the other species.
Water Conditions: Soft, alkaline water, well-aerated. Temperature 23 to 25°C.
Size: 4 cm.
Food Requirements: Small live foods preferred; other foods accepted.

Although it is a *Botia*, it has none of the faults found among other members of the genus. They aren't always hiding and do not seem to have the dislike for the lighter spots that the others have. *B. sidthimunki* is the smallest known member of a group in which some species get rather big. The writer had some which were not yet full-grown when he got them. They were about 2 cm in length. One day there was only one when there were formerly three. After a thorough search it was found that the other two had squeezed into the intake tube of the outside filter, where they were found happily grubbing around in the glass-wool. It was some time before they became too large to squeeze through the narrow openings, and they frequently had to be netted out of the filter. It is doubtless the most active and playful of the *Botia*.

BRACHYDANIO ALBOLINEATUS (Blyth)
Pearl Danio (golden variety known as Gold Danio)

Range: Moulmein Region of India, Burma, Thailand, Malacca and Sumatra.
Habits: Very active swimmer; likes sunny tanks with clean, well-aerated water. Likes to swim in schools with others of its own kind.
Water Conditions: pH and hardness not critical. Aquaria need not be large, but should provide a good amount of open space for swimming. Temperature 22 to 25°C.
Size: 6 cm.
Food Requirements: A good eater like most active fishes. Will thrive on dry as well as living foods, but some living foods should be included occasionally.

This little fish has all the attributes of a good aquarium inhabitant. It is above all peaceful; it does not outgrow a small aquarium; it eats all foods and besides is one of the most easily bred egglayers. A small school of these fish with the sun playing on them in a well-planted aquarium is a very pretty sight. This is the only fish which the writer has had spawn for him in the dark of a paper pint container on the way home from the store. The approved way of spawning them is to place them in a long aquarium with about 10 cm of half fresh and half aged aquarium water. The bottom should be covered with several layers of large pebbles or glass marbles. The pair (some breeders use two males to one female) should be healthy and in good condition, which the female shows by her increased girth. They begin driving almost at once, dropping eggs which are non-adhesive and fall among the pebbles or marbles. Temperature should be 23 to 25°C. When the female has become depleted, the fish are netted out. Fry hatch in 36 to 48 hours.

BRACHYDANIO FRANKEI Meinken / *Leopard Danio*

Range: Not definitely known, probably India.
Habits: Peaceful and very active. Prefers to swim in small schools.
Water Conditions: Not critical, as long as the water is clean and well aerated. Temperatures 24 to 26°C.
Size: About 6 cm; females slightly larger.
Food Requirements: A good eater, accepting prepared as well as live or frozen foods.

There is, of course, a gold variety of the Pearl Danio, but these spotted ones are very different. Herr Franke wrote an article in an East German magazine which published a picture as well. Doubt was expressed as to whether this was a new species or a hybrid. Herr Franke expressed the opinion that this was a genuine newcomer, which was confirmed by Hermann Meinken, who named it in Franke's honor. The *Brachydanios* have long been very popular because of their attractive colors, ceaseless activity, small size and the ease with which they are bred. The Leopard Danio spawns in the same manner as the Zebra Danio by laying non-adhesive eggs, but the female does not become depleted in one spawning; eggs are laid daily until there are as many as 1,000. Hatching time is the same, and the fry are easily raised on brine shrimp.

BRACHYDANIO KERRI (Smith) / *Kerr's Danio*

Range: Koh Yao Yai and Koh Yao Noi Islands, Thailand.
Habits: Peaceful, active, best kept in a group.
Water Conditions: Not critical; water should be clean and well-aerated.
Size: 4 cm.
Food Requirements: Small live foods preferred; frozen and prepared foods also taken willingly.

This is one of the lesser-known species of a popular genus. Why it has not "caught on" is one of those mysteries. It is every bit as peaceful, active and hardy as the Zebra or Pearl Danio, and its colors are certainly far from unattractive. It is as easy to breed as the others, and raising the young presents no problems either. Maybe some day some breeder will make a great "discovery" and suddenly everybody will wonder why they have been passing them up all these years. Like the other danios, the best way to keep them is in a school of about a dozen, with enough swimming space to suit their active nature. They will not interfere with any other fishes in the tank with them, unless their tankmates are fishes which are made nervous by their constant activity. This species has been known to science since 1931 and was first introduced to hobbyists in Germany in 1956. Strangely enough, this species is not very popular among European hobbyists either. The European hobbyist seems to prefer species which present a little difficulty and as a rule avoids the livebearer and "easy" egglayers.

Brachydanio frankei F Q X 4 2 5 X N N6   [Dr. Herbert R. Axelrod]

Brachydanio kerri F E X 4 2 6 X N N 4

Brachydanio nigrofasciatus ⬚F⬚ ⬚Q⬚ ⬚X⬚ ⬚4⬚ ⬚2⬚ ⬚7⬚ ⬚X⬚ ⬚N⬚ ⬚N⬚ ⬚5⬚ [S. Frank]

Brachydanio rerio ⬚F⬚ ⬚Q⬚ ⬚X⬚ ⬚4⬚ ⬚2⬚ ⬚8⬚ ⬚X⬚ ⬚N⬚ ⬚N⬚ ⬚5⬚ [S. Frank]

BRACHYDANIO NIGROFASCIATUS (Day) / *Spotted Danio*

Range: Upper Burma to Rangoon and the Moulmein region.
Habits: Active swimmer; does not require a large aquarium, but some open space should be provided.
Water Conditions: Clean, well-aerated water; pH and hardness not critical. Temperature should be between 22 to 25°C.
Size: Slightly under 5 cm.
Food Requirements: Dried and frozen foods as well as living foods are eagerly eaten, but should not be too coarse.

Like the other *Brachydanio* species, *B. nigrofasciatus* is an active, peaceful and hardy fish. This fish was once known as *Brachydanio analipunctatus,* but it got its present name back in 1869. Being a smaller and not quite as strikingly colored fish, we do not see it as often as *B. rerio* or *B. albolineatus,* but it is every bit as satisfactory in the aquarium. Rather than keep it in pairs, it is better to put about 6 to 12 together, as they like to congregate in schools. Both sexes are very similar in coloration, but the females may be distinguished by their fuller, heavier bodies. Like the other *Brachydanio* species, this one lays non-adhesive eggs which should be allowed to fall betweeen layers of pebbles or glass marbles to prevent their being eaten by the parents.

BRACHYDANIO RERIO (Hamilton-Buchanan)
Zebra, Zebra Danio, Striped Danio

Range: Coromandel Coast of India, from Calcutta to Masulipatam.
Habits: Peaceful, active, likes to travel in schools.
Water Conditions: pH and hardness not critical. Prefers clean, well aerated water, being native to flowing streams.
Size: About 5 cm.
Food Requirements: A heavy eater, like all active fishes. All foods are accepted, but some live foods should be included.

This is probably the most popular among the egglaying fishes, and for good reasons. The Zebra Danio is hardy, always active, and will never attack any of its tankmates. Besides, it is easily bred, easily fed, and will withstand much abuse without serious consequences, making it just about the perfect aquarium fish. Many advanced breeders remember it as the first egglayer they ever spawned, and in almost all cases many of the fry were raised successfully. There are many methods of breeding the Zebra Danio, which, like the other *Brachydanio* species, lays a non-adhesive egg. All of these methods have the same purpose, to keep the parents from eating their spawn. Of course, the layer of pebbles or marbles technique described for the other *Brachydanio* species is still the most popular, because it gives the breeders the most swimming area. Another is a bag of nylon mesh, wide enough to let through the eggs but not the breeders, which is suspended in the breeding aquarium.

BRACHYGOBIUS AGGREGATUS Herre / *Philippine Bumblebee Goby*

Range: Philippine Islands.
Habits: A typical goby that spends most of its time "hopping" from one spot to another, often attaching itself to the glass with modified ventral fins.
Water Conditions: Hard, alkaline water is preferred, with very high temperatures in the 20's (°C) being necessary.
Size: Under 5 cm.
Food Requirements: Live food is a necessity; small worms are best.

This is a bottom fish which should be kept in mildly brackish water. They will not be difficult to care for under these conditions, but they are very delicate when kept in soft freshwater.

Brachygobius aggregatus can sometimes be induced to spawn with partial water changes. A varied diet and an abundant amount of live foods are also important considerations. Relatively large eggs are laid under flowerpots or stones and number between 75 and 140. Depending upon the temperature of the water, the young will hatch in 4 to 5 days. They will be guarded by the male for at least one week.

BRACHYGOBIUS DORIAE (Günther) / *Doria's Bumblebee Goby*

Range: Borneo and the Malayan Archipelago.
Habits: Should be kept by themselves in a small aquarium. Hiding places should be provided.
Water Conditions: Water should have an addition of one heaping teaspoonful of table salt per 4 liters. Temperature 24 to 26°C.
Size: Up to 2.5 cm.
Food Requirements: Small live foods exclusively.

These interesting little fish come from partly brackish waters, and for this reason their water should have an addition of table salt, one heaping teaspoonful per 4 liters. Like most of the goby group, the ventral fins are joined and form an efficient sucking disc, by means of which they can attach themselves to stones or any other flat surface. Because of this they do not have to battle against any current which comes along. When the pull is too strong to swim against with its little fins, the fish merely attaches itself to a stone or any other firm object which happens to be handy until things quiet down. *Brachygobius doriae* spawns in a very similar manner to many of the cichlids. The male cleans off a patch in a secluded spot, such as the inside of a flowerpot. The eggs are laid here and then the male guards them. Hatching time varies greatly from one egg to the other, but at the end of 5 days the fry should all be out. Two days later they are free-swimming. All this time the male is guarding them fiercely, but there is no point in leaving him there when the young are able to take care of themselves, and they could be eaten.

1. *Brachygobius doriae* female (p430).
2. *Brachygobius doriae* male (p430).

Brachygobius aggregatus [F][D][X][4][2][9][X][N][N][4]   [Dr. Herbert R. Axelrod]

1. *Brachygobius doriae* ♀ [F][F][M][4][3][0][X][N][N][5]   [H. J. Richter]
2. *Brachygobius doriae* ♂ [F][E][B][4][3][0][X][N][N][5]   [H. J. Richter]

Brachyrhaphis terrabensis [F][R][X][4][3][1][X][N][N][1] [Dr. Martin R. Brittan]

Brochis splendens [F][D][X][4][3][2][X][N][N][6]   [Dr. Herbert R. Axelrod]

431

BRACHYRHAPHIS TERRABENSIS (Regan) / *Upland Livebearer*

Range: Pacific slope of southern Costa Rica and western Panama, at higher elevations.
Habits: Fairly peaceful, but females are antagonistic toward males.
Water Condition: Not important. Temperature 16 to 24°C.
Size: Males 2.5 cm; females 3 cm.
Food Requirements: Accepts dried food.

There are at least 20 genera of livebearing fishes, but most are rarely seen in the aquarium. For the most part, these livebearers are drab fishes with few markings and little or no color. A substantial number, such as the Upland Livebearer, are attractively but modestly colored. Even at their best, however, these livebearers are drab when compared to platies, swordtails and mollies. Because of this, species like *Brachyrhaphis terrabensis* are rarely imported. This is unfortunate when one considers that wild platies and swordtails have little color and that domesticated ones have acquired their bright colors and vivid patterns as the result of mutation and selective breeding. There can be no doubt that the same could be true of dozens of species of livebearers, such as the Upland Livebearer. *Brachyrhaphis terrabensis* is by no means unattractive. The basic olive-gray shades to a pearly white on the belly. Along the sides is a string of black blotches overlaid with black crosshatching. Metallic scales in the same area complete the complex pattern. All unpaired fins are margined with yellow and the dorsal is attractively checkered with white and black. There is a black blotch above the anal fin.

BROCHIS SPLENDENS (Castelnau) / *Short-Bodied Catfish*

Range: Upper Amazon; also in the Ambiyacu River, a tributary in Peru.
Habits: Peaceful, feeds on the bottom, where it is useful in picking up uneaten foods left by other fishes. Seldom uproots plants.
Water Conditions: Not critical; sensitive to only one thing: there must be no salt in the water.
Size: About 6 cm.
Food Requirements: Eats any kind of prepared foods, but should get an occasional feeding of tubifex worms, of which it is very fond.

At first sight, this fish looks like a stubby *Corydoras aeneus,* but there are enough important anatomical differences to put it into another genus. The body is much higher and more compressed; the adipose fin is considerably larger and has one ray which is spiny and gives the fin a pointed appearance; the armor plates on the head also extend onto the snout. There are no known external sex differences, with the possible exception that the armor plates in female specimens may not meet as closely as in the males, which would probably be more noticeable in females with eggs.

BRYCINUS CHAPERI (Sauvage) / *Chaper's Characin*

Range: West Africa, Upper Guinea, Gold Coast to the Niger River.
Habits: Peaceful if kept with fishes of its own size.
Water Conditions: Water should be soft and slightly acid. Temperature 24 to 26°C.
Size: Attains a length of 9 cm.
Food Requirements: Dried food is taken when hungry, but any kind of live food is preferable.

This is one of the African characins which we do not see very often, but due to increased facilities from that area we may see it a bit more frequently and also get better acquainted with it. Although it was first introduced into Germany in 1911, nobody can yet tell with certainty which are males and which are females without first dissecting them. How they breed has also not been determined. Some illustrations picture this fish as bright green; this is not so. The large scales are opalescent and gleam with a light green tint. The short stripe which begins at the caudal base and passes through the middle caudal rays varies with age; in younger specimens there is a dark diamond-shaped marking behind the gill-plate which then becomes a thin stripe and widens into a heavier stripe about three-quarters down the body. Dorsal fin and tail are brick-red. The upper part of the dorsal and the tips of the caudal lobes are greenish. This is one of the fishes which give the collector many a headache: they get a whole lot of them rounded up into a net, and suddenly all of them jump out!

BRYCINUS LONGIPINNIS (Günther) / *Long-Finned African Tetra*

Range: Tropical West Africa, Sierra Leone to Zaire.
Habits: Timid; an active swimmer which remains in the middle reaches of the aquarium.
Water Conditions: Water should be soft and slightly acid, preferably filtered through peat moss. Temperature 24 to 26°C.
Size: To 12.5 cm.
Food Requirements: Larger sized live foods; can be accustomed to frozen foods or beef heart.

Sexes can be distinguished by the shape of the anal fin, rounded in the male and with a straight edge in the female. Besides, the male has a high, pointed dorsal fin while that of the female is considerably smaller and round. Both sexes have a horizontal stripe which begins in the middle of the body at a point above the end of the anal fin and is carried by the middle rays through the fork of the tail. The eye is another attractive feature, a bright red. Like *B. nurse*, this is a timid fish which is likely to hide if kept with more boisterous fishes. There should be enough plants to allow them to take cover if necessary and at the same time enough open space that they will not feel hemmed in. Avoid using a lot of rocks and keep their water clean and well aerated. First introduced to the hobby about 1928.

Brycinus chaperi ⬚F ⬚D ⬚X ⬚4 ⬚3 ⬚3 ⬚X ⬚N ⬚N⬚E   [Dr. Karl Knaack]
Brycinus longipinnis ⬚F ⬚Q ⬚X ⬚4 ⬚3 ⬚4 ⬚X ⬚N ⬚N ⬚B   [J. Elias]

Brycinus nurse ⬚F⬚D⬚X⬚4⬚3⬚5⬚X⬚N⬚N⬚E [Dr. Herbert R. Axelrod]

Brycinus taeniurus ⬚F⬚D⬚X⬚4⬚3⬚6⬚X⬚N⬚N⬚A [Dr. J. Gery]

435

BRYCINUS NURSE (Rüppel) / *Nurse Tetra*

Range: Widely distributed in tropical African waters, Nile to Senegal.
Habits: Somewhat shy, very active. Prefer to swim in groups in the middle reaches of the aquarium.
Water Conditions: Water should be soft and slightly acid, preferably filtered through peat moss. Temperature 24 to 26°C.
Size: To 25 cm; usually offered for sale at 8 to 10 cm.
Food Requirements: Large live foods such as cut-up earthworms or fully grown brine shrimp; can be accustomed to frozen foods.

It is extremely unlikely that an average hobbyist will ever raise these fish to their full size in a home aquarium. The colors are far from spectacular, although the young specimens usually sold have pink to reddish fins, a characteristic which is lost as the fish grows older. One thing which can be said for them is that they are active, graceful swimmers and are well suited to a large aquarium where a constant activity rather than brilliant colors is desired. Probably because of their large size and active nature, there have been no recorded spawnings in captivity, although their wide distribution in African water indicates an active as well as prolific nature. Sexes can be easily distinguished even while they are young. The females have an anal fin which is straight at the edge, while the males have one with a rounded edge. These fish do not take very well to prepared foods. Best bet of course are the large-sized live foods such as cut-up earthworms, but they can also be won over to lean raw chopped beef or chopped beef heart. They no doubt can also be taught to accept frozen mature brine shrimp. Swatted flies and small beetles are taken greedily.

BRYCINUS TAENIURUS (Günther) / *Narrow-Lined African Tetra*

Range: Central Africa.
Habits: Peaceful and active; may be a fin nipper due to its teeth. Relatively unknown.
Water Conditions: Soft, acid water with a pH close to 6.0 or even lower. Temperatures should be above 24°C.
Size: Up to 10 cm; may grow larger if properly cared for.
Food Requirements: Accepts all live foods; better fed freeze-dried tubifex worms, especially those worms with added daphnia, chlorella algae, etc.

Dr. Jacques Gery, one of the world's leading experts on characins, collected, photographed and identified this specimen for us. Previously, we only knew this fish from small ones which were shipped in intermingled with other fishes as this is not a recognized aquarium species.

Chances are that it would be difficult to spawn, as are most African tetras, because they are so badly handled prior to reaching our aquariums. Even this beautiful specimen, collected and photographed in Africa, lost a few scales during handling, as can be seen above the vent.

BRYCONOPS CAUDOMACULATUS (Günther) / *Red Cross Tetra*

Range: Guianas and the central Amazon region.
Habits: Active and quarrelsome; should be kept only with their own kind.
Water Conditions: Soft, slightly acid water. Temperature 24 to 26°C.
Size: To 13 cm.
Food Requirements: All kinds of live foods; live baby fishes preferred.

There are certain fish species which a collector almost always ignores for fear that he will be "stuck" with them and not be able to dispose of them even at a low price. The *Bryconops* species are a perfect example. The collector will go out and try to load up with the desirable species, discarding those which lack color or have some other undesirable traits such as being nasty toward other fishes, eating plants, growing too big, etc. But sometimes things don't go too well and at the end of a hard day's work there are still many unfilled cans. The answer of course is to load up with some of the fish he has been discarding rather than return with a light load. *Bryconops caudomaculatus* is not such a "bad actor," but it is not advisable to try keeping them with other species. Even among themselves there are sometimes some pretty vigorous scraps. Otherwise it is not an unattractive fish, and a tankful swimming back and forth might even evoke an occasional second look. They should have a large tank with generous planting at the sides and back and plenty of swimming space in the center.

BRYCONOPS MELANURUS (Bloch) / *Jumping Anchovy*

Range: Upper Amazon, Peru and Guyana.
Habits: A school fish which jumps from the waters to catch flying insects. Very peaceful but requires a large tank with a great deal of swimming space.
Water Conditions: Prefers moving water or water that is heavily agitated. Temperature should be 25°C and the softer the better. A pH of 6.6 is best.
Size: Up to 13 cm.
Food Requirements: Prefers live food such as the wingless *Drosophila* flies which can be sprinkled onto the surface of the tank, but they do well on dried foods and frozen brine shrimp.

The Jumping Anchovy is a delicate species which is difficult to keep in the aquarium. Possibly for this reason, *Bryconops melanurus* is seldom seen in the aquarium hobby. This species prefers slightly acid water with warm temperatures between 25 and 28°C. The tank must be very well covered because, as its common name states, this fish likes to jump. It is best kept in its own company of a dozen or so tankmates and will school almost continuously. Because of this activity, a large aquarium is required. Live food is preferred. In nature, this fish jumps from the water to catch passing insects.

Bryconops caudomaculatus 🄵🄳🆇4️⃣3️⃣7️⃣🆇🄽🄽8️⃣   [Dr. Herbert R. Axelrod]
Bryconops melanurus 🄵🆁🆇4️⃣3️⃣8️⃣🆇🄽🄽8️⃣   [Dr. Herbert R. Axelrod]

Bunocephalus coracoideus F D X 4 3 9 X N N C [Harald Schultz]
Butis butis F D X 4 4 0 X N N B [Noel Gray]

BUNOCEPHALUS CORACOIDEUS (Cope) / *Two-Colored Banjo Catfish*

Range: Throughout Brazil and as far west as Ecuador and south to Uruguay.
Habits: A bottom-dwelling catfish that is nocturnal in habit and ugly in appearance.
Water Conditions: Tolerant of any water with a pH of from 5.0 to 8.0 and a temperature between 16 and 29°C.
Size: About 15 cm.
Food Requirements: A true scavenger which ingests everything to be found at the bottom of the aquarium whether or not it is digestible.

Some fish are famous for their beauty . . . some for their ugliness . . . and the Banjo Catfish happens to be the latter case. This fish is so unfishlike that it is hard to tell where its eyes are or where its mouth opens. Its lack of beauty is more than balanced by its interesting reproductive habits and the ease with which it spawns in home aquaria. Sex is easily distinguished because females are much fatter and fuller than males. After selecting an active pair, place them in an aquarium all by themselves and feed them heavily on tubifex or small earthworms. Spawning usually is easier in the spring. If you have the pair well conditioned after a month on live foods, you can induce spawning by changing 50 % of their water with *fresh* tap water of the same temperature. In 48 hours the pair will spawn. Sometimes they spawn under a fallen leaf, but other times they spawn on a large rock and incubate their eggs like a chicken . . . by sitting on them!

BUTIS BUTIS (Hamilton-Buchanan) / *Crazy Fish, Ca Bong*

Range: Found from India to the Solomon Islands.
Habits: A typical goby which clings upside down to plants and rocks and swims upside down as well.
Water Conditions: Not very particular about water conditions, but since it is found in some brackish water areas, it is assumed that it has a tolerance for hard water.
Size: About 15 cm.
Food Requirements: Prefers live foods, but is an active scavenger and cleans rocks and plants of algal growths incessantly.

The author (HRA) entered the aquarium depot of Lee Chin Eng in Djakarta, Indonesia in 1959 and was greeted with the exclamation: "Dr. Axelrod, I've discovered a new fish!" The author quickly investigated the fish and remarked, "I doubt that it's new, but it sure is acting crazy." That night Lee wrote a letter to a German importer and said he had "Axelrod's new Crazy Fish." The name stuck in Europe and in the United States, and the Crazy Fish became a very popular scavenger. The Crazy Fish, even with its big mouth, doesn't seem to be too dangerous to smaller fishes, but this may have been because it was so well fed. The ones kept by the author worked 24 hours a day working over every rock and plant leaf sucking in whatever there is to suck from such surfaces. Their bellies were always full and the fish were always healthy.

CALAMOICHTHYS CALABARICUS Smith / *Rope Fish*

Range: Niger Delta, Cameroon.
Habits: Largely nocturnal; spends most of its time on the bottom. Best kept only with its own kind.
Water Conditions: Not critical; is not dependent upon the oxygen content of the water for breathing.
Size: Up to 40 cm; tank-raised specimens do not attain this size.
Food Requirements: All living foods which are not too large to be swallowed are accepted; also strips of lean beef, beef heart or earthworms.

This interesting fish sometimes is included in African shipments. It looks more like a snake, an illusion which is further enhanced by its motions. In its habitat it occurs in pools which sometimes dry out in the dry season. Like the lungfishes, it is capable of burying itself in the mud and leaving only a tiny hole for breathing. The dorsal fin of this fish is interesting: it is broken up into a series of small finlets like those found on the mackerel family in ocean waters. The air-bladder is paired, with one much larger than the other. This acts as an accessory breathing organ. This fish, like some of the others, is also said to be occasionally found at night out of the water, traveling through the wet grass from one pool to another. It propels itself not only in a snakelike manner, but also with the help of its long, powerful pectoral fins.

CALLICHTHYS CALLICHTHYS (Linnaeus) / *Slender Armored Catfish*

Range: Eastern Venezuela, Trinidad to Buenos Aires.
Habits: Quite active for a catfish; in its native waters it prefers quiet water and a muddy bottom.
Water Conditions: Not critical. Temperatures should not exceed 24°C. Well-rooted plants should be used lest they be uprooted.
Size: 18 cm; tank-raised specimens do not usually exceed 13 cm.
Food Requirements: A very greedy eater. Prefers living foods, up to and including small fish.

This catfish is not uncommonly imported, and a certain number of them are usually available to aquarists. The armor plates on the sides form a herringbone pattern, and there are even plates protecting the head. This fish has a huge appetite and should not be trusted with small fishes or his appetite will extend to them. If kept in a large aquarium which is to their liking, they live to a ripe old age. If it is desired to spawn this fish, a very large aquarium is required. In the summer months a pool might be given them, although we have not heard of this procedure being used. Sex differences are very slight, but the females have slightly duller colors and a deeper, more rounded body. The male is said to build a bubblenest in which he keeps and guards a huge number of eggs.

441

Calamoichthys calabaricus F D X 4 4 1 X N N D [K. Paysan]

Callichthys callichthys F D X 4 4 2 X N N E [Aaron Norman]

Callochromis pleurospilus [F][A][X][4][4][3][X][N][N][9]   [Dr. Herbert R. Axelrod]

Campylomormyrus tamandua [F][D][X][4][4][4][X][N][N][C]   [Dr. Herbert R. Axelrod]

CALLOCHROMIS PLEUROSPILUS (Boulenger) / *Pastel Cichlid*

Range: Lake Tanganyika, Africa.
Habits: Not exceptionally quarrelsome, but will eat fish that they can swallow.
Water Conditions: Hard alkaline water. The addition of one teaspoon of non-iodized salt per 4 liters of water is beneficial. Temperature 24 to 27°C.
Size: Rarely exceeds 9 cm.
Food Requirements: Not a picky eater. Easily adapts to dry food or tubifex worms.

Recent first-hand observations of some of the breeding techniques of lacustrine (lake-dwelling) cichlids in nature have revealed that there are apparently a number of different breeding schemes followed by different species, most resulting in maternal mouthbrooding. One such scheme, used by *Callochromis pleurospilus,* is group spawning. These fish dwell over sandy habitats in fairly well-formed schools. Nesting arenas are dug in the sand by the males while the females school over the area. The males rise toward the school of females, each choosing a mate, then the pairs drop down to the nest where spawning begins. When a female leaves the nesting arena, another is brought in, until all the females in the school have spawned. There is some adaptive significance to this seemingly disordered confusion. Since the fish dwell in open sandy areas and all of the females in the school have spawned at about the same time, the fry which are all released at about the same time derive mutual protection by virtue of their large numbers, being able to rapidly exchange signal stimuli when danger threatens.

CAMPYLOMORMYRUS TAMANDUA (Günther)
Worm-Jawed Mormyrid

Range: Congo River in the vicinity of the Stanley Pool.
Habits: Inhabits quiet pools which have bottoms covered with fallen logs and trees. This is a very sensitive fish which prefers privacy, quiet and darkness.
Water Conditions: Prefers warm water at a temperature of about 26°C with a pH of 7.2 and as soft as possible.
Size: Aquarium specimens are under 20 cm.
Food Requirements: A true bottom-feeding scavenger which eats worms, pelletized dry foods and frozen brine shrimp.

Go to any small lake or pool in Africa and find yourself a pile of logs, rocks or fallen branches and you are almost certain to find one of the mormyrids. There are at least one hundred different members of this very interesting family. All have highly specialized mouths and most have dorsal and anal fins which are set back on the last third of the body. Most have a thin caudal peduncle and have the general body shape of a submarine. They are very delicate fish and do best in an aquarium which has been set up and designed especially for them. Their aquarium requires a minimum of light and a maximum of privacy.

CAPOETA ARULIUS (Jerdon) / *Longfin Barb*

Range: India.
Habits: Peaceful, especially when kept with barbs of an equal size. Very lively.
Water Conditions: Soft, slightly acid water; tank should be placed so as to receive occasional sunshine. Temperature 24 to 26°C.
Size: Up to 12 cm.
Food Requirements: Live foods of all types; frozen foods of small size, such as frozen daphnia, should not be fed often. Accepts dry foods.

Here is one of the frequent barb importations which comes into the country, enjoys favor for a while and is then more or less forgotten in favor of more colorful or interesting fishes. The Longfin Barb's main claim to beauty lies in the attenuated middle rays of the male's dorsal fin, although under proper lighting the fish takes on a decidedly pleasing metallic overcast. In the tanks of dealers they do not show up well, particularly if they are offered for sale while still young, before the male has gained his distinctive feature. The Longfin Barb is peaceful; about the only time the fish evidences animosity to others is during spawning time, when one male may threaten his brothers to keep them away from the females. Spawning takes place in thick bundles of floating plants after much energetic driving by the male. The eggs, which are adhesive and stick to the plants, are eaten eagerly by the parents.

CAPOETA CHOLA (Hamilton-Buchanan) / *Swamp Barb*

Range: Burma, eastern India.
Habits: Peaceful and active; when confined to small tanks, becomes less active.
Water Conditions: Soft, slightly acid water. Temperature 21 to 27°C.
Size: Up to 12 cm.
Food Requirements: Accepts all live and frozen foods and most dry foods.

The Swamp Barb is so named because in its home waters in Asia it is encountered most often in low-lying, swampy areas with much small vegetation. It is frequently found in land given over to rice culture, and this would almost lead one to the conclusion that the fish likes, or is at least able to stand for long periods, dirty water. This is definitely not so! Like most of its relatives, the Swamp Barb, despite its name, feels best in large, clean, well-filtered tanks; when not provided with surroundings of its preference, *Capoeta chola* soon declines and loses whatever faint traces of color it possessed when kept in water more to its liking. The colors spoken of here are definite, even though they are not pronounced enough to make the fish desirable for its looks alone. When the Swamp Barb is in good condition, the red coloration of the operculum is very evident, and it makes a nice contrast to the circular black blotch at the peduncle. Out of condition, however, this red color is subdued, in some cases vanishing almost completely. The Swamp Barb is not difficult to breed, as it quite readily scatters its eggs among the plants.

Capoeta arulius ⬚F⬚ ⬚E⬚ ⬚X⬚ ⬚4⬚⬚4⬚⬚5⬚ ⬚X⬚ ⬚N⬚ ⬚N⬚ ⬚B⬚
Capoeta chola ⬚F⬚ ⬚D⬚ ⬚X⬚ ⬚4⬚⬚4⬚⬚6⬚ ⬚X⬚ ⬚N⬚ ⬚N⬚ ⬚E⬚

[H. J. Richter]
[Dr. Herbert R. Axelrod]

446

Capoeta hulstaerti 🄵🄰🅇🄴🄴🄷🅇🄽🄽🄵   [Aaron Norman]
Capoeta melanampyx 🄵🅀🅇🄴🄴🄶🅇🄽🄽🄶   [Dr. E. Schmidt]

447

CAPOETA HULSTAERTI (Poll) / *Butterfly Barb*

Range: Central Zaire region.
Habits: Peaceful, almost shy; should be kept only in company with very small fishes or their own kind.
Water Conditions: Soft, clean, highly acid water. Temperature about 26°C. Should be moved from tank to tank as little as possible.
Size: 2.5 cm; mostly a little smaller.
Food Requirements: Small live foods preferred.

Original shipments were only males, which are easily distinguished by their yellow dorsal, anal and ventral fins. These are bright yellow with black tips. Females have very little color at all in these fins. It was amusing at first when the males came in by the hundreds that everybody had a different way to find "females" by looking for some tiny difference. As the specimens at hand died and were dissected, the truth finally dawned and African shippers began to collect females as well as males and ship them out. Nevertheless, although the fish has been with us for many years now, it is seldom bred. The few successful breeders tell us that it breeds like the other barbs by depositing its eggs in bushy plants. The fry are tiny, and spawnings are small. Raising them is quite a task. Perhaps some day a breeder will discover the magic formula and will be able to turn them out in quantity.

CAPOETA MELANAMPYX (Day) / *Ember Barb*

Range: India.
Habits: Peaceful and active; a good jumper.
Water Conditions: Soft, slightly acid water. Temperature 23 to 26°C.
Size: 8 cm.
Food Requirements: Takes both live and prepared foods.

The Ember Barb is one of the most colorful barbs to be brought to the attention of hobbyists in a long time. The male, when in condition, takes on a beautiful red color accentuated by the dusky black of the fins. Luckily, the red coloring is kept throughout the year, even outside spawning time, but it is most bright during the spawning period. The female, normally plain in color, also takes on a red hue at this time, but she is never as intensely colored as the male. The Ember Barb spawns in the usual barb manner, but the males are very hard drivers, and harm might come to the females if sufficient hiding space is not provided. Dense masses of floating plants provide good hiding places, but even caves can be used to provide refuge. Eggs hatch in two days at a temperature of 24°C, which is the correct spawning temperature. Fry are ready for newly hatched brine shrimp as soon as they have absorbed their yolk-sacs they grow quickly, but only if given enough room. Crowding will stunt young of this species very much, as will poor feeding within the first few weeks.

CAPOETA OLIGOLEPIS Bleeker / *Checker Barb*

Range: Sumatra.
Habits: Peaceful and active.
Water Conditions: Soft, slightly acid water is desirable, but small variations in water composition are easily withstood. Temperature 23 to 26°C.
Size: About 5 cm.
Food Requirements: Takes all foods.

Definitely one of the most desirable of all the barbs, the Checker Barb has much to recommend it. It is small, hardy, peaceful, easy to breed and active; also, although by no means brilliant, it is an attractive fish. In prime condition, the male of the species takes on a pleasing red-orange hue to his fins, and the coloring of the upper portion of his body becomes darker, providing a handsome contrast. When in good condition, it is very easy to tell the sexes apart, but even when the male has not assumed his courting dress there is little difficulty, for the female is fuller and the black edging of her dorsal fin is less pronounced. For so small a species, the scales are quite large and distinct, which adds to the attractiveness of the fish. The Checker Barb spawns in typical barb fashion, but the newly hatched young, which emerge from the eggs in about 2½ days, are very small and require very tiny first foods.

CAPOETA PUCKELLI (Boulenger) / *Two-Spot African Barb*

Range: Congo River near Kinshasa.
Habits: Peaceful; may be combined with other peaceful species.
Water Conditions: Soft, slightly acid water. Temperature 23 to 26°C.
Size: Females 6 cm; males 5 cm.
Food Requirements: Prepared and frozen foods taken just as eagerly as live foods.

The Two-Spot African Barb is an active and peaceful fish. Because of its active nature, this species should only be kept in medium to large aquaria of at least 50 liters. Soft, slightly acid water is best. The bottom soil should be dark to help show off this fish's coloration. Although plants are an attractive idea, they should not be so dense as to restrict the swimming area. This fish prefers to occupy the middle to lower water layers of the aquarium. Weekly water changes of up to 20% of the aquarium water are recommended. *Capoeta puckelli* makes an excellent community aquarium fish. Feeding is easy, and almost all types of aquarium food will be accepted.

Breeding is not a difficult task with this fish. Several fine-leaved plants are suitable for the spawning substrate. Although soft, slightly acid, mature water is preferred during spawning time, courtship is often stimulated by the addition of fresh, neutral water. The female often initiates the driving courtship. The fertilized eggs are adhesive and will stick to the plants or fall to the bottom of the aquarium. The young hatch in one to two days depending upon the temperature of the water. The parents should be removed from the spawning tank directly after the spawning has taken place.

Capoeta oligolepis F Q X 4 4 9 X N N 5
Capoeta puckelli F R X 4 5 0 X N N 4

[H. J. Richter]
[Dr. Herbert R. Axelrod]

Capoeta semifasciolatus ⬚F⬚R⬚X⬚4⬚5⬚1⬚X⬚N⬚N⬚5   [R. Zukal]
Capoeta titteya ⬚F⬚Q⬚X⬚4⬚5⬚2⬚X⬚N⬚N⬚5   [H. J. Richter]

CAPOETA SEMIFASCIOLATUS (Günther) / *Half-Striped Barb*

Range: Southern China.
Habits: Peaceful.
Water Conditions: Soft, slightly acid water; tank should be densely planted. Temperature 21 to 27°C.
Size: 7 cm.
Food Requirements: Takes live, frozen and dry foods.

The Half-Striped Barb prefers a medium to large aquarium (larger than 50 liters) which is placed in a sunny position. Although it will stand temperatures in the range given above, 22 to 24°C is ideal. The tank should contain some plants but not enough to cramp the overall swimming area. This fish can stand up to both low temperatures of about 20°C and also low oxygen levels. Aquarium aeration is not required.

The male *Capoeta semifasciolatus* is slimmer than the female and more colorful. This is most noticeable around spawning time. During the pre-spawning courtship the male approaches the female with his dancing body in an oblique position. He tries to coax her into the plants where the eggs will be laid. The yellow to cream eggs hatch in 24 to 36 hours depending upon the temperature of the water.

CAPOETA TITTEYA (Deraniyagala) / *Cherry Barb*

Range: Sri Lanka.
Habits: Peaceful; a good community fish.
Water Conditions: Soft, slightly acid water; well planted tank. Temperature 22 to 28°C.
Size: 5 cm.
Food Requirements: Accepts both live and prepared foods; particularly likes small living crustaceans.

Of the five or six barbs that have gained lasting popularity in this country, the Cherry Barb ranks right near the top. Small, peaceful and undemanding, it has been around for a long time and will stay around for many years to come. For the beginning barb enthusiast perhaps no other barb, with the possible exception of the Checkered Barb, has so much to recommend it. In coloring, prior to spawning, it is particularly attractive, with the body suffused with a rich reddish brown sheen. During the actual spawning act this color is intensified to an oxblood hue, and although the deepness of the color at this time is not of long duration (it loses much of its dark, rich quality after spawning) the fish is still nicely colored if maintained under proper conditions. Inducing the species to spawn is not too difficult if they have been well treated during their period of acclimatization; eggs are scattered into plant thickets, where they are eagerly sought out and eaten by the parents, who should be removed as soon as possible. The fry, which are very small, emerge from the eggs within 1½ days at a temperature of 26°C, and when they become free-swimming they need the very smallest of live foods.

Capoeta partipentazona, the Banded Barb, is a very active and fast-swimming fish. Photo by G.J.M. Timmerman.

CAPOETA PARTIPENTAZONA (Fowler) / *Banded Barb*

Range: Malay Peninsula.
Habits: Active; a fast swimmer inclined to nip fins of slower fishes.
Water Conditions: Soft, slightly acid water; tank should be well planted and receive good light. Temperature 22 to 28°C
Size: 5 cm.
Food Requirements: Accepts all foods, especially small live foods.
Color Variations: Yellowish body with five vertical bands, one band running through dorsal fin onto top portion of back. Fins reddish.

Here is another barb of the "banded barb" grouping, similar to *Capoeta tetrazona, Barbodes hexazona* and *Barbodes pentazona.* These barbs are much alike in coloring and general markings, but, since *Capoeta tetrazona,* the Tiger Barb, is so much more crisply marked the others have lost favor during the years and are seldom seen any more. Indeed, it appears that they will rarely ever be brought back into the country in large numbers because the Tiger Barb is now so cheap and plentiful that the others would be hard put to give it a battle in the popularity race. *Capoeta partipentazona* has one advantage over the Tiger Barb, however: although it is a nippy fish, it seldom carries its harassment of a victim to the same extreme as the Tiger Barb, contenting itself with occasional passes at the object of its misplaced attentions, whereas the Tiger Barb will often hound its victim so persistently that the fish jumps clear out of the tank to avoid pursuit, even if it is a fish ordinarily thought of as being a non-jumper. Oddly enough, *Capoeta partipentazona* and *Capoeta tetrazona* usually get along well together when kept in the same tank, members of both species forming little schools of their own.

1. *Capoeta tetrazona* ⬚F⬚ ⬚H⬚ ⬚X⬚ ⬚4⬚ ⬚5⬚ ⬚3⬚ ⬚X⬚ ⬚N⬚ ⬚N⬚ ⬚5⬚   [G.J.M. Timmerman]
2. *Capoeta tetrazona* var. ⬚F⬚ ⬚H⬚ ⬚X⬚ ⬚4⬚ ⬚5⬚ ⬚4⬚ ⬚X⬚ ⬚A⬚ ⬚N⬚ ⬚5⬚   [H. J. Richter]

3. *Capoeta tetrazona* var. [F][H][X][4][5][5][X][G][N][5]   [H. J. Franke]

4. *Capoeta tetrazona* var. [F][E][X][4][5][6][X][G][N][5]   [H. J. Richter]

CAPOETA TETRAZONA (Bleeker) / *Tiger Barb, Sumatra Barb*

Range: Sumatra, Borneo.

Habits: A very active fish and a fast swimmer; inclined to nip the fins of slower species.

Water Conditions: Soft, slightly acid water. Temperature 21 to 29°C.

Size: Up to 8 cm.

Food Requirements: Takes both live and prepared foods. Should also have vegetable matter included in diet.

Color Variations: Sides yellow, interrupted by four wide black stripes. Bottom portion of dorsal fin black. Upper portion of dorsal fin trimmed in red; upper and lower lobes of tail and ventral fins red; snout red. An albino variation is also available.

The Tiger Barb has much to recommend it. It is flashily colorful, hardy, easy to breed and usually in good supply. About the only drawback the fish has is that it is inclined to nip its tankmates; long-finned fishes are usually the victims in these cases, but the Tiger Barb is not particular in its choice, and other fishes are also pursued. Oddly enough, some schools of Tiger Barbs are kept in a community tank without ever doing any damage; in this regard, one or two *tetrazona* are likely to do more fin nipping than six or seven, presumably because the barbs in the larger group are so busy chasing each other that they don't have time to bother other species. For spawning *C. tetrazona,* which spawns in typical barb fashion, use water which is softer than the water in which they are customarily maintained. For example, if their regular tank water is 8 DH, they will spawn more readily in water of 6 DH. The fry are small at first but grow rapidly, especially if given plenty of room; if kept in small tanks they will not attain their full size.

The always popular Tiger Barb has long been known to aquarists. It has become such a standard favorite that it would be hard to find a hobbyist who has not kept it at one time or another. The introduction of an albino Tiger Barb some years back was met with mixed emotions—some loved it; others thought it looked terrible. Recently new color varieties have appeared and have been becoming more and more available to the average aquarist. Among these are the blue, moss-green and a black-eyed "albino."

Spawning these new varieties usually presents no problems, and they can be treated in the same manner as the normal Tiger Barbs. The black-eyed albino, called the Red Barb in Germany, appears to be stronger and more aggressive than the true albino strain. Optimum temperatures for breeding seem to be between 23° and 27°C, the pH 6.6 to 6.7, and a hardness of about 6 DH.

1. *Capoeta tetrazona*, normal variety (p454).
2. *Capoeta tetrazona*, albinistic fish from the moss-green line (p454).
3. *Capoeta tetrazona*, scaleless fish from the moss-green line (p455).
4. *Capoeta tetrazona*, an almost unicolor moss-green male (p455).

CARASSIUS AURATUS (Linnaeus) / *Goldfish*

Range: Originally from China, now introduced into temperate waters the world over.
Habits: Peaceful; large-finned specimens should not be kept with other fishes which might nip the fins.
Water Conditions: Water characteristics not critical, but should be clean and well aerated. Best temperatures 10 to 21°C.
Size: Sizes vary with breeds. Average size in the aquarium 8 to 10 cm.
Food Requirements: Prepared and frozen foods taken just as eagerly as live foods.
Color Variations: Has been bred into various colors and color combinations of red, black, white, yellow, etc.

The hobby of fish-keeping owes its popularity more than anything else to the Goldfish. They are mentioned as early as 970 A.D. by the Chinese, and in the sixteenth century their care and breeding, which were at first playthings of the nobility, became commonplace and a number of fancy breeds were developed. Because of their innate love for beauty and living things, the Chinese and Japanese have remained the world leaders in the development and production of the many fancy breeds of Goldfish available today. We see such freakish fish as the Lionhead, Pompom, Telescope, Celestial, Eggfish and many others too numerous for this small space. There are fish with short single fins and others with long flowing fins. Some breeds have double fins; some have large, sail-like dorsal fins; and others have no dorsal fin at all. Some are pure white; others are midnight black. Still others vary from light yellow to deep red, and some are peppered with red, white, black, yellow and even blue. Goldfish have a wide temperature tolerance, and fish which have been kept outdoors can live under a layer of ice for quite a time. They are also kept successfully in the tropics.

FANCY GOLDFISH VARIETIES

It seems that the lessened popularity of the common Goldfish has come about as a result of the recognition on the part of hobby newcomers of the advantages the true tropical fishes have over Goldfish. However, warm-water fish tanks within the home have not greatly affected the interest in fancy Goldfish varieties. Really good Goldfish of the hard-to-get varieties are eagerly sought after and command high prices. Unfortunately, not enough hobbyists ever get a chance to see some of the fancier varieties; the excellent Goldfish photos shown here will help to make these products of patient and skillful breeding programs more familiar to everyone.

1. *Carassius auratus*, common form (p458).
2. *Carassius auratus*, Oranda (p458).
3. *Carassius auratus*, Fantail (p459).
4. *Carassius auratus*, Red-cap Fantail Oranda (p459).
5. *Carassius auratus*, Chocolate (p462).
6. *Carassius auratus*, Bubble-Eye (p462).
7. *Carassius auratus*, Bearded Goldfish (p463).

1. *Carassius auratus* F H X 4 5 7 X D N C [A. Roth]
2. *Carassius auratus* var. F H X 4 5 8 X D R C [Dr. Herbert R. Axelrod]

3. *Carassius auratus* var. ⬚F⬚H⬚X⬚4⬚5⬚9⬚X⬚D⬚V⬚C   [A. Roth]
4. *Carassius auratus* var. ⬚F⬚H⬚X⬚4⬚6⬚0⬚X⬚M⬚R⬚C

Carassius auratus has many different body and color morphs. Above is the Fantail Calico Goldfish, photo by R. Zukal, and below is the Fantail Pearlscale Goldfish, photo by G. Marcuse.

The popular Bubble-Eye Goldfish (above) has a thin, fluid-filled sac under each eye, forcing the eyes into an almost dorsal position (photo by G. Marcuse). The Solid Fantail Goldfish (below) is another popular variety (photo by Milan Chvojka.)

5. *Carassius auratus* var.  F H X 4 6 1 X C N B   [Dr. Herbert R. Axelrod]
6. *Carassius auratus* var. F H X 4 6 2 X D G D   [S. Kochetov]

7. *Carassius auratus* var. F H X 4 6 3 X E V C [Dr. Herbert R. Axelrod]

Above is a Metallic-scale Goldfish with exceptionally fine finnage (photo by L.E. Perkins). Below is a Veiltail Goldfish (photo by Dr. Herbert R. Axelrod).

CARNEGIELLA MARTHAE Myers / *Black-Winged Hatchetfish*

Range: Venezuela, Peru, the Brazilian Amazon, Rio Negro and the Orinoco.
Habits: Active jumpers; have to be kept in a covered tank, preferably a long one. Peaceful; may be kept with other non-aggressive species.
Water Conditions: Soft, slightly acid water. Temperature 24 to 27°C.
Size: 4 cm; usually a bit smaller.
Food Requirements: Floating prepared foods eaten when very hungry, but live foods like mosquito larvae or wingless fruitflies are best.

The Black-Winged Hatchetfish is the smallest known member of the genus *Carnegiella*. The name *marthae* was given to this species in 1927 by Dr. George S. Myers because they were favorites of his wife Martha. They are easily distinguished from the other hatchetfishes not only by a black edge on the keel of the belly back to the caudal base, but also by a black area inside the long pectoral fins. These pectoral fins are called "wings" because their length and size give them that appearance, but they are not wings in the sense that the fish can fly with them, any more than the well-known marine flyingfishes fly with theirs. These pectoral fins are actuated by the most powerful muscles the fish has and give it enough impetus to leave the water and glide for a considerable distance along its surface. Insects which congregate in this area are efficiently snapped up on these "flights." This fact gives us a clue as to why the hatchetfishes are not the easiest to keep and feed and why they seldom spawn in captivity. This is where the ingenuity of their owner comes into the picture, figuring out how to feed them live insects without having them escape into the room.

CARNEGIELLA STRIGATA STRIGATA (Günther)
Marbled Hatchetfish

Range: Guyana, middle and upper Amazon region, especially in jungle streams.
Habits: Occurs in schools near the surface. In the aquarium they are peaceful, but are likely to jump if a cover is not provided.
Water Conditions: Soft, slightly acid water. Temperature about 26°C.
Size: About 8 cm.
Food Requirements: Will readily accept dried foods which float on the surface, but anything which falls to the bottom cannot be picked up.

This is one of the most attractive of the hatchetfishes, first introduced to aquarists in 1912. Most works say that it has never been bred, but the fact is that it has happened, but only rarely. The sexes can be distinguished by looking at the fish from above; the females are slightly wider in the body. The rare descriptions of the spawning say that tiny eggs are laid in plant clusters at the surface, and to the best of our recollection very few if any of the fry were hatched and raised. One of the obvious assumptions as to why the fish will not spawn readily is that there is some food, possibly winged, which the fish will devour in their natural habitat and which the aquarist cannot duplicate.

Carnegiella marthae ⬚F ⬚D ⬚X ⬚4 ⬚6 ⬚5 ⬚X ⬚N ⬚N ⬚3   [Dr. Herbert R. Axelrod]
Carnegiella strigata strigata ⬚F ⬚D ⬚X ⬚4 ⬚6 ⬚6 ⬚X ⬚N ⬚N ⬚5

Carnegiella strigata fasciata ⬚F⬚D⬚X⬚4⬚6⬚7⬚X⬚N⬚N⬚5 [Harald Schultz]
Catoprion mento ⬚F⬚D⬚X⬚4⬚6⬚8⬚X⬚N⬚N⬚A [Harald Schultz]

CARNEGIELLA STRIGATA FASCIATA (Garman)
Marbled Hatchetfish

Range: Guyana.

Habits: Found in shaded pools where it leaps from the water for insects flying very close to the surface.

Water Conditions: Very sensitive to temperature and water changes. Prefers very soft, slightly acid water. Temperature 23 to 26°C.

Size: Under 8 cm.

Food Requirements: This species must have small live food. Dropping wingless *Drosophila* flies onto the surface of the water is an ideal way to feed this species. They also take small amounts of floating foods containing brine shrimp.

It is generally accepted that the hatchetfishes of the subfamily Gasteropelecinae are the only true "flyingfish" which move their pectoral fins to aid in their flight. The other so-called flyingfishes, such as the marine Exocoetidae and the freshwater African *Pantodon,* do not voluntarily move their pectorals in flight but probably use them for stabilization while in "flight." Probably the best food would be mosquito larvae, because these spend a great deal of time at the surface and, being insects, would be the food most relished by a fish which gets its food at the surface. Another insect food which is good is *Drosophila,* the wingless fruitfly.

CATOPRION MENTO (Cuvier) / *Wimple Piranha*

Range: Lower Amazon, Bolivia, Guianas.

Habits: Peaceful, but will attack small fishes.

Water Conditions: Soft, slightly acid water in a well-planted tank. Temperature 23 to 26°C.

Size: About 10 cm.

Food Requirements: Larger live foods are best. Otherwise, frozen foods or bits of fish, shrimp, clams or oysters.

Catoprion mento has all the ferocious appearance of a true piranha as well as an attractive set of colors of its own, which makes it an interesting aquarium fish capable of being kept in a community tank without danger to its tankmates, unless they are small. They resemble a piranha so convincingly that even the natives who collect them are sometimes fooled. The writer recalls netting pencilfishes and other small characins with a few native helpers in a small stream in Guyana. One of the natives yelled "perai" when the net came up and a Wimple Piranha flopped about in it. They warned me not to touch it or I might lose a finger, and they did not calm down until I picked it up, pried its mouth open and told them "Look, no teeth!" Strangely enough, a little while later we fished a different spot in the same stream and came up with some *real* piranhas, and then it was my turn to warn the natives to be careful, because these fellows *had* teeth. Although the Wimple Piranha cannot compete with the real piranhas in dental equipment, they *do* have small teeth which they will not hesitate to use on something as small as a Guppy or Neon Tetra. In nature the fish is a scale-eater.

468

CENTRARCHUS MACROPTERUS (Lacépède) / *Flier*

Range: Southern United States; Texas to Virginia and Mississippi Valley.
Habits: An aggressive territorial fish that is best kept with other fishes of equal size or larger.
Water Conditions: Neutral to alkaline water of moderate hardness. Temperature 15 to 22 °C.
Size: To 18 cm in nature but rarely exceeds 10 cm in captivity.
Food Requirements: Earthworms, crickets and small crayfish, but will accept guppies and small chunks of beef.

At least partly because of its smaller size, the Flier readily adapts to a captive existence. It should, however, be kept only with other temperate species, as it does not adapt well to warmer water that most tropical species are kept in. The Flier can usually be found in weedy ponds or near weed beds along the sandy shores of lakes and rivers. It is best to start with young fish about 3 cm in length, as the young ones will more readily adapt to aquarium foods.

Being a temperate-water fish, *Centrarchus macropterus* spawns on a seasonal basis, usually once in the spring and often again in the late summer. It should be kept fairly cool between spawnings, as the cooler water will amplify its coloration.

There may be local regulations prohibiting the taking of this species for maintenance in aquariums. Therefore, as with all other native American fishes, one should check with the local fish commission before capturing it.

CHACA CHACA (Hamilton-Buchanan) / *Frogmouth Catfish*

Range: India and the Indo-Malayan Archipelago.
Habits: Nocturnal, sedentary. Should not be kept with smaller fishes.
Water Conditions: Not critical. Temperatures around 24°C are best.
Size: Reaches 20 cm.
Food Requirements: Will eat almost any living or frozen food, but prefers earthworms.

This bizarre catfish is the only member of its family, the Chacidae. The tough skin, numerous barbels and fleshy processes on the head, broad mouth and tadpole-like shape combine to make this a unique fish. Flattened fish are usually found on the bottom, and *Chaca* is no exception.

The Frogmouth is a nocturnal catfish, coming out to feed only at night. It requires a heavily shaded aquarium with many plants or caves in which to hide during the day. The gigantic mouth enables it to swallow large fish, so it should never be put in a tank with smaller fishes. Although the Frogmouth is so sluggish that it *probably* couldn't catch your prize dwarf cichlid, one can never predict what will happen after the lights go out. Take no chances!

Centrarchus macropterus F D X 4 6 9 X N N 9   [Aaron Norman]
Chaca chaca F D X 4 7 0 X N N D   [H. Hansen, Aquarium Berlin]

Chaetobranchus bitaeniatus 🄵🄳🆇4️⃣7️⃣1️⃣🆇🄽🄽9️⃣ [Harald Schultz]

Chalceus macrolepidotus 🄵🄳🆇4️⃣7️⃣2️⃣🆇🄽🄽🄰 [Dr. Herbert R. Axelrod]

471

CHAETOBRANCHUS BITAENIATUS (Ahl) / *Two-Striped Cichlid*

Range: Middle Amazon basin.
Habits: Said to be peaceful and not grub up the bottom.
Water Conditions: Not critical. Temperature 24 to 27°C.
Size: To 12 cm.
Food Requirements: Seem to prefer the larger live foods, but can be acclimated to chunks of beef heart.

This is a fish which is rarely collected, but a few young specimens sometimes come in masquerading as either "unknown" species or something else. When mature, most of them get such a ragged appearance on the anal fin that they look as if they came out second best in a battle. This is a normal characteristic, however, and actually the species is said to be quite peaceful in the few accounts we get. Personally the author is of the opinion that Mother Nature did not give them such a big mouth for nothing and would hesitate to put one in mixed company or with a number of others unless the tank were heavily planted and contained a number of hiding places.

CHALCEUS MACROLEPIDOTUS Cuvier / *Pink-Tailed Chalceus*

Range: Guyana, Surinam and French Guiana.
Habits: Peaceful if kept in a school with no small fishes in the same tank.
Water Conditions: Not critical; best temperature about 25°C. Once they have become established, they should be moved as little as possible.
Size: To 25 cm.
Food Requirements: Generous feedings are necessary, using earthworms, tubifex worms or chopped beef heart.

This is another fish which is often offered by dealers while it is still very young, and it grows and grows until it has become too big for all available tanks. If given an aquarium of at least 200 liters capacity which is well planted and aerated, a group of about a half-dozen *Chalceus macrolepidotus* makes a very attractive picture. They are active and always on the move, and their big scales have a highly metallic gleam. When in particularly good condition, the fins as well as the tail become bright red. They are excellent jumpers, and when being seined in their native Guyana waters most of them will leap nimbly over the net rather than let themselves be caught. A glass cover on their aquarium is therefore essential if one does not want to find them on the floor some morning. When in Guyana, the author noticed that the Indians were always quick to pounce upon these fish when their large size made it advisable to discard them. They considered them a delicacy which they seldom got otherwise, because their slender shape and active habits made it difficult to shoot them with a bow and arrow, the Indians' accepted method of catching fish.

CHALINOCHROMIS BRICHARDI Poll / *Brichardi*

Range: Lake Tanganyika, Africa.
Habits: Not especially vicious. A good aquarium fish when kept with species of the same size.
Water Conditions: Hard alkaline water. DH 10 to 20; pH 7.5 to 9.0. Temperature 24 to 26°C.
Size: 15 cm in nature; slightly smaller in the aquarium.
Food Requirements: An omnivorous feeder requiring some vegetable matter in its diet. Will readily take frozen and prepared dry foods.

C. brichardi has unusually thick lips that are covered by many papillae. These papillae may function as tactile sensory organs in feeding and mating behavior, since this species grazes on algae-covered rocks and is a substrate-spawner.

Sexing is not easy with this species, since they show little sexual dimorphism. As is typical among cichlids lacking sexual dimorphism, *C. brichardi* tends to form strong bond pairs. Some fights may ensue during pair formation. To ensure having a breeding pair, it is best to purchase five or six juveniles and allow them to mature together so that they will pair off naturally.

Although these fish are substrate-spawners, they do not lay their eggs out in the open, as do some of their susbstrate-spawning relatives. Rather, they prefer to spawn in the dark recesses of caves and crevices. Accordingly, they should be provided with plenty of rocks or inverted clay flowerpots with small openings cut in them. Once they have spawned, usually one parent at a time performs the brooding duties, while the other stands guard outside the spawning areas. Since the eggs are concealed, it is not known exactly how long it takes them to hatch. The fry make their first appearance at about one cm in length when the parents guide them out of the cave for their first foraging experience. They are usually abandoned by their parents when they reach two cm in length.

These fish go through several color phases as they mature, and observers can easily mistake juveniles for some other species. Initially, the young have several dark longitudinal bands along the body and the dorsal fin base, as well as bands across the head and through the eye. As the fish mature the longitudinal bands break up into rows of dark spots. By the time the fish reach sexual maturity, there remains but one spot at the posterior of the dorsal fin, and even this one eventually disappears. They do, however, retain the dark bands across the head and snout.

1. *Chalinochromis brichardi*, normal form (p474).
2. *Chalinochromis brichardi*, dashed form (p474).

1. *Chalinochromis brichardi* F D X 4 7 3 X N N B [P. Brichard]

2. *Chalinochromis brichardi* var.
F D X 4 7 4 X S N B [G. Meola - African Fish Imports]

Chanda baculis ⃞F ⃞D ⃞X ⃞4 ⃞7 ⃞5 ⃞X ⃞N ⃞N ⃞5
Chanda buruensis ⃞F ⃞D ⃞X ⃞4 ⃞7 ⃞6 ⃞X ⃞N ⃞N ⃞6

[Dr. Herbert R. Axelrod]
[G.J.M. Timmerman]

CHANDA BACULIS Hamilton-Buchanan
Pla Kameo or *Burmese Glassfish*

Range: Burma, India and Thailand in the Sikuk River, in the headwaters of the Menam Chao Phya, in the lower Menam Nan and in the Bung Borapet.
Habits: A dainty but beautiful small fish; peaceful.
Water Conditions: Strictly a freshwater species which prefers the higher temperatures in the upper 20's °C.
Size: The smallest of the large genus *Chanda*. Rarely larger than 5 cm.
Food Requirements: Prefers live foods, but accepts frozen brine shrimp and some dry foods in pellet form. Requires copious amounts of live food such as microworms and daphnia.

Chanda baculis is a member of the glassfish family Ambassidae. This family is widely distributed throughout the world, being found in such far away places as in the waters surrounding some Pacific islands and in East Africa. There are only a few freshwater species in this family; only fishes of the genera *Chanda* and *Ambassis* are seen in the aquarium hobby.

This species does best in relatively warm, mature aquarium water. The aquarium should be heavily planted with dark gravel and should be given plenty of sunlight. The Burmese Glassfish is very peaceful and should only be kept with fishes that have a similar nature. Spawning produces 150 or more eggs which hatch in one to two days depending upon the temperature of the water. The fry are very small and should be fed infusoria.

CHANDA BURUENSIS (Bleeker) / *Siamese Glassfish*

Range: Thailand, Malaysia, Sumatra, Celebes and the Philippines.
Habits: Best kept by themselves. Even then, two males in the same tank might pick on each other.
Water Conditions: Native to brackish waters, which must be duplicated in the aquarium by adding 2 tablespoons of salt to every 4 liters of water. Temperature about 26°C.
Size: To 7 cm. Aquarium-raised specimens usually under 5 cm.
Food Requirements: Small living foods such as newly hatched brine shrimp and small worms. Dry foods taken only when starving.

Because of its lack of bright colors we do not often see this glassfish among importations. *Chanda buruensis* is longer in the body than its better-known cousin *Chanda ranga*. The males do not sport a blue edge on the second dorsal and anal fins, but there is a good deal of black in these fins, and in the first dorsal as well. Males are likely to have little disagreements, and for this reason a tank which affords some opportunity for concealment is recommended, where the defeated ones can escape the bullying of their victors. They spawn readily, but the resulting fry are very small and getting them to a size where they can handle larger foods is a real problem. A good rotifer culture would be the answer, but these are not always very easy to come by. Once they are large enough to take newly hatched brine shrimp, the battle can be considered won.

CHANDA RANGA Hamilton-Buchanan / *Glassfish, Glass Perch*

Range: Northern India, Bengal to Burma.
Habits: Very numerous in rice paddies and other shallow bodies of water in their habitat; peaceful in the aquarium.
Water Conditions: Requires somewhat hard water with a light salt content. Once established in an aquarium, they should be moved as little as possible. Temperature about 26°C.
Size: 5 cm; in nature they become slightly larger.
Food Requirements: Some prepared foods are unwillingly accepted, but the bulk of foods given should be alive.
Color Variations: Body light amber with a glassy transparency. In the males, the soft dorsal fin and the anal fin have a bright blue edge.

Here we have one of the old favorites, known to the aquatic world since 1905. As for the scientific world, Hamilton-Buchanan first identified and described it in 1822. It is interesting to note that this fish is so numerous in India that farmers often use it for fertilizer. In the aquarium it is not so prolific; at first it was considered one of the difficult ones, but the truth is that the fish breeds quite readily, but the fry are so small that they usually die of starvation before they become large enough to eat foods like newly hatched brine shrimp. An annoying trait the fry also have is that they do not hunt for food, but they will snap at it when it swims near them. Males are distinguished by the bright blue edge on the soft dorsal and anal fins, of which there is only a trace on the females. A 20-liter aquarium is of sufficient size for spawning, and eggs are deposited in a clump of floating plants like *Riccia* or *Nitella*. The aquarium should be placed in a sunny location and the fish disturbed as little as possible. Best temperature is about 25°C. Eggs hatch in one day, and when they begin to swim, fry should be provided with the smallest infusoria.

CHANNA MICROPELTES (Cuvier and Valenciennes) / *Red Snakehead*

Range: Southeast Asia, into India.
Habits: A voracious, greedy species, but not everything that it kills is destined to serve as food, as it often kills without eating the fishes it has destroyed.
Water Conditions: Not critical; this is a very hardy and adaptable fish.
Size: Up to 1 meter; usually offered for sale at 8 to 10 cm.
Food Requirements: Eats most meaty (living and non-living) foods when young; in larger sizes, prefers live fishes and amphibians but will take large chunks of meat.
Color Variations: As the fish grows older the red stripe becomes much less intense, gradually fading to a muddy tan or into blotches instead of an uninterrupted stripe.

Channa micropeltes, formerly called *Ophiocephalus micropeltes,* has been offered in the aquarium hobby more frequently over the last few years than it has been in the past, even though it has been known to aquarists for a long

Chanda ranga ⬚F⬚ ⬚H⬚ ⬚X⬚ ⬚4⬚⬚7⬚⬚7⬚ ⬚X⬚ ⬚N⬚ ⬚N⬚ ⬚5⬚   [H. J. Richter]
Channa micropeltes ⬚F⬚ ⬚C⬚ ⬚X⬚ ⬚4⬚⬚7⬚⬚8⬚ ⬚X⬚ ⬚N⬚ ⬚N⬚ ⬚7⬚   [Aaron Norman]

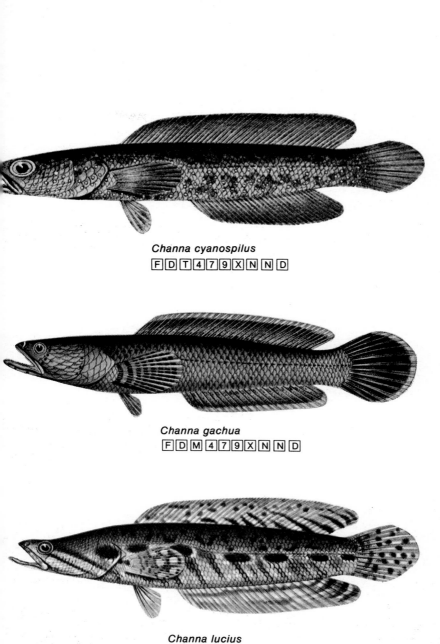

Channa cyanospilus
F D T 4 7 9 X N N D

Channa gachua
F D M 4 7 9 X N N D

Channa lucius
F D B 4 7 9 X N N D

time from sporadic importations. In one way at least it is a very satisfactory aquarium fish, because it is one of the most hardy known. Possessed of an auxiliary breathing apparatus, it is capable of withstanding exceedingly foul water conditions in its aquarium, being sensitive on only one point of aquarium management, water temperature; the species is highly susceptible to bad effects caused by chilling. Despite its hardiness and the obviously colorful appearance of young specimens, however, the Red Snakehead definitely is a fish to avoid for someone with limited facilities, for it is one of the greatest killers known among aquarium fishes. If its habit of destruction were reserved only for fishes that are intended to serve as food, the situation wouldn't be as bad, but the fact is that the Red Snakehead often kills and just ignores its victim, leaving it lying around the tank to rot. In its smaller sizes the fish is necessarily less destructive than when it has begun to put on real growth, but many a community tank of small fishes has been quickly wiped out after the tank's unsuspecting owner had innocently introduced a seemingly harmless and attractive Red Snakehead. As the fish grows it becomes a menace to just about everything that can get within its reach, and it is entirely willing and capable of literally biting the hand that feeds it. In its home waters in Asia fully grown meter-long individuals guarding their young have been known to attack people entering the water.

Channa micropeltes is not a very active fish, except at feeding time, but large specimens can jump or snake their way out of the tank, and for this reason the tank should be covered.

Channa micropeltes, the Red Snakehead, in an aquarium. Photo by G.J.M. Timmerman.

An unidentified *Channa* species (above) moves freely in an aquarium (photo by G. Senfft). *Channa asiatica* (below) has a greedy look about it which one should not underestimate (photo by J. Harrington).

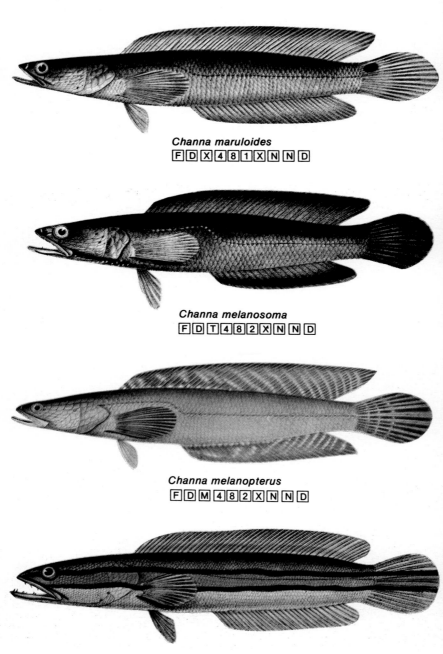

Channa maruloides
F D X 4 8 1 X N N D

Channa melanosoma
F D T 4 8 2 X N N D

Channa melanopterus
F D M 4 8 2 X N N D

Channa micropeltes
F D B 4 8 2 X N N D

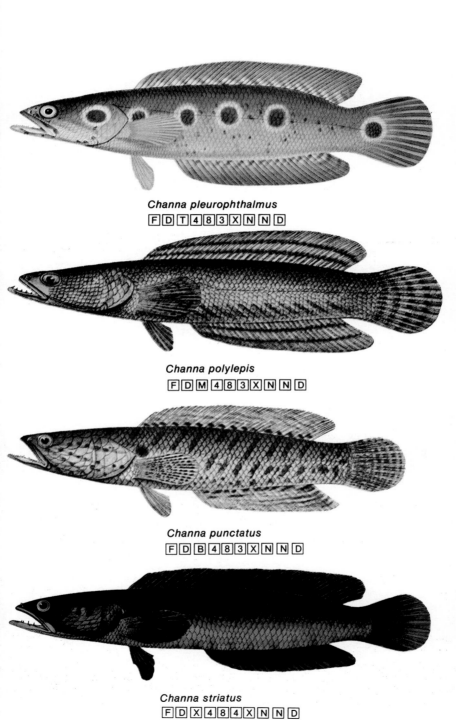

Channa pleurophthalmus
F D T 4 8 3 X N N D

Channa polylepis
F D M 4 8 3 X N N D

Channa punctatus
F D B 4 8 3 X N N D

Channa striatus
F D X 4 8 4 X N N D

483

Channa species are vicious fish that seem to kill just for the sake of killing. They have a voracious and greedy appetite, but even when that is satisfied they will continue to kill. Above are young *Channa punctatus* (photo by G. Senfft) and below are young *Channa asiatica*.

CHANNALLABES APUS (Günther) / *Eel Catfish*

Range: Zaire and Angola regions.
Habits: Mostly nocturnal. Young specimens will not bother the other fishes, but it is best to keep larger ones by themselves.
Water Conditions: Not critical. Temperature 21 to 24°C.
Size: Up to 30 cm.
Food Requirements: Greedy eaters which will consume great amounts of tubifex worms. Other foods may be substituted, such as beef heart or pieces of fish.

Channallabes apus resembles nothing as much as a young eel with whiskers. The body is compressed laterally and the dorsal, caudal and anal fins form an unbroken line from the back to the anus. The ventral fins are missing completely. The head is very small and at first sight one might be led to believe that a large brown worm had somehow gotten into the aquarium. They are very hardy and long-lived, and because of an accessory breathing organ they are not dependent upon the oxygen in their aquarium water. They are greedy eaters and their diet of tubifex and white worms may be augmented by pieces of beef heart, raw shrimp or fish cut into small pieces. They get to be about 30 cm long and have never to our knowledge been spawned in captivity. There is little likelihood that anyone will ever try it, either; such a venture would undoubtedly be a scientific achievement, but commercially the result would merely be a lot of wormlike catfish which nobody would want.

CHARACIDIUM FASCIATUM Reinhardt / *Banded Characidium*

Range: South America, Orinoco region in the north to La Plata region in the south.
Habits: Comes from streams where there is some current; therefore requires fresh, clean water in an uncrowded aquarium.
Water Conditions: Clean, well-oxygenated water, about neutral. Temperature should not exceed 24°C.
Size: 6 cm.
Food Requirements: Not a fussy eater, but prefers living foods.

Because of its lack of bright colors and rather retiring habits, this fish does not very often find itself in the tanks of aquarists. It stays mostly in the lower reaches of the aquarium and often digs into the gravel for bits of food. Males are recognizable by their larger fins, which are yellowish in color. Spawning is accomplished in the lower parts of the tank, and as many as 150 eggs may result. The very tiny eggs hatch in 30 to 40 hours, and the fry begin to swim in 3 days. Remaining near the bottom as they do, they often remain undetected until they have grown considerably. Fine infusorian food is of course indicated for a short time, until they have grown a bit and their small mouths can handle such morsels as newly hatched brine shrimp. Because they can pick food from the bottom, some of the infusoria substitutes could probably be used with success, but of course living infusoria is preferable.

Channallabes apus ⬚F⬚D ⬚X⬚ ⬚4⬚⬚8⬚⬚5⬚ ⬚X⬚ ⬚N⬚ ⬚N⬚ ⬚D⬚
Characidium fasciatum ⬚F⬚⬚D⬚ ⬚X⬚ ⬚4⬚⬚8⬚⬚6⬚⬚X⬚ ⬚N⬚ ⬚N⬚ ⬚6⬚

[G. Wolfsheimer]
[Aaron Norman]

Charax gibbosus ⬚F⬚ ⬚D⬚ ⬚X⬚ ⬚4⬚ ⬚8⬚ ⬚7⬚ ⬚X⬚ ⬚N⬚ ⬚N⬚ ⬚B⬚   [Dr. Herbert R. Axelrod]

Cheirodon kriegi   ⬚F⬚ ⬚R⬚ ⬚X⬚ ⬚4⬚ ⬚8⬚ ⬚8⬚ ⬚X⬚ ⬚N⬚ ⬚N⬚ ⬚5⬚   [Harald Schultz]

CHARAX GIBBOSUS (Linnaeus) / *Glass Headstander*

Range: Guianas, lower and middle Amazon region and Rio Paraguay.
Habits: Perfectly peaceful and harmless.
Water Conditions: Not critical. Temperature should average about 24°C.
Size: 15 cm; aquarium specimens are usually much smaller.
Food Requirements: Prefers live foods, but dried foods may be fed when others are not available.

Here we have a fish which looks fierce but actually is a "shrinking violet." As the name describes, it has a *gibbous* or *humpbacked* appearance. The head is small in contrast to the body, and the mouth large. A strange characteristic is that the head is at an angle to the body, and when the fish swims in its characteristically downward tilted position the head is practically straight. Because of its lack of colors, this is a fish which is not often imported and still more seldom bred. Males are slightly smaller than their mates and have a more slender build. Because of their size, a large aquarium is required if spawning is desired. Some bundles of bushy plants are provided, and the fish soon lose much of their accustomed sluggishness when courtship begins. Eggs are released among the plants, and the spawning is apt to be quite large. Incubation period is 30 hours, and the resulting fry are very small. The first days are critical, and an abundance of infusoria is essential. Once they begin growing and larger foods can be provided, they will be found to be very hardy.

CHEIRODON KRIEGI Schindler / *Three-Spot Tetra*

Range: Upper Guaporé River, Brazil.
Habits: Perfectly peaceful and not a bit shy.
Water Conditions: Not critical; best is slightly acid, soft water. Temperature 24 to 27°C.
Size: 5 cm.
Food Requirements: Not a fussy eater; dried foods are accepted equally as well as live or frozen fare.

Cheirodon kriegi is not one of the really glamorous species like *Cheirodon axelrodi,* but the fish has a quiet charm which is difficult to describe. In a tank of mixed species it quickly makes itself at home, and I have never seen one attack another fish. In the photograph the lower fish is the male and the upper the female. The fact that there is a black spot in the same place as the "gravid spot" of the livebearing species is no indication that the fish is ready to spawn, and if there have ever been any spawnings we have not heard of them. This is not a very popular aquarium fish, and there have been few importations of them into the United States or Europe.

CHEIRODON AXELRODI Schultz / *Cardinal Tetra*

Range: Upper Rio Negro and Colombian waterways.
Habits: Perfectly peaceful and active. Likes to swim in schools, and therefore it is best to keep at least 6 of them together.
Water Conditions: Water should be soft, clean and on the acid side, about pH 6.5 or lower, in order to show the fish in its brightest colors. Temperature 21 to 24°C.
Size: 5 cm.
Food Requirements: All foods, either live or prepared, should be given with their small size in mind. Not a fussy eater.
Color Variations: Back is brown on top. Horizontal stripe a brilliant blue-green. Lower part of body bright red, belly white.

This living jewel is without a doubt the most gorgeous of all aquarium fishes. The Cardinal Tetra does best in aquaria which are not too bright and have soft, slightly acidic water. The tank should have a dark background and dark gravel. The species is very peaceful and should be kept with fishes of a similar nature. Furthermore, Cardinal Tetras should be kept in groups of six or more, as they like to school and are most appealing when they move together.

This is not an easy fish to breed. Soft, acid (pH 6.0-6.5) water is required with a temperature between 23 and 24°C. It is best to use small aquaria with 8- to 10-liter capacities. Plant the tank with small bunches of *Myriophyllum*. The fish should be put into the tank only after the water has matured. Males are slimmer than the females and have a slightly depressed belly. Weakly adhesive eggs are laid in the plants. After spawning, the pair should be removed and placed back into their original tank. Fry hatch in 25 to 28 hours depending upon the temperature of the water; they should be fed infusoria for the first week or so.

Cheirodon axelrodi, the Cardinal Tetra. Photo by Dr. Herbert R. Axelrod.

Cheirodon axelrodi

F D X 4 9 0 X N N 5

[Dr. Herbert R. Axelrod]

Chilodus punctatus [F][D][X][4][9][1][X][N][N][9]
Chonerhinus naritus [F][D][X][4][9][2][X][N][N][9]

[Kremser]
[J. Elias]

CHILODUS PUNCTATUS Müller & Troschel / *Spotted Headstander*

Range: Northeastern South America between the Amazon and the Orinoco.
Habits: Very peaceful; pays no attention to the other fishes. Rather shy, and should be moved as little as possible.
Water Conditions: Slightly acid to neutral water, very soft. Temperature should range between 24 and 27°C.
Size: About 9 cm.
Food Requirements: Diet should be largely vegetarian; lettuce or spinach leaves are nibbled frequently. Some dried food and live food also.

This peaceful fish forms an interesting addition to any community aquarium. It swims in a normally head-down position and is very fond of nibbling algae from rocks and plants. As additional vegetable nourishment, lettuce and spinach leaves are enjoyed. Females are about 1 cm longer than the males, and the body is considerably heavier. A large aquarium is preferred, with much clear space for swimming. An account of their breeding tells how there was always a lettuce leaf in the aquarium for them to nibble on. During spawning a remarkable change in coloration takes place. The horizontal line disappears and a large, round, dark shoulder-spot which is visible at no other time shows up. Eggs which are non-adhesive are released near the surface and sink unmolested to the bottom. After 4 days they hatch.

CHONERHINUS NARITUS (Richardson) / *Bronze Puffer*

Range: Southeast Asia, primarily Burma, the Malay Peninsula and Thailand.
Habits: A fin-nipper and not to be trusted, even with fishes much larger than itself.
Water Conditions: Softness and acidity factors not critical as long as extremes are avoided, but the addition of non-iodized salt at the rate of about one teaspoonful for every 8 liters of tank capacity will help the fish. This is a warmth-loving species, and the temperature should not be allowed to fall below 21°C for more than a day at a time.
Size: Up to 30 cm in nature.
Food Requirements: Live foods, especially tubificid worms, are best, but meaty prepared foods are accepted.

Chonerhinus naritus differs from the fishes of the more popular puffer genus *Tetraodon* most obviously in its markings (or lack of markings, actually), because although all of the *Tetraodon* species that are seen with any degree of regularity in the aquarium trade are highly patterned species with stripes, bars, vermiculations and spots over their bodies, *Chonerhinus naritus* is of an over-all single color. Other physical differences are much less immediately obvious. One thing that *Chonerhinus naritus* shares with other puffers is that nice set of powerful teeth that all use to good effect in crushing snails and nipping fins. All of the puffers have the dentition to inflict wounds.

CHROMIDOTILAPIA GUENTHERI (Sauvage) / *Günther's Mouthbrooder*

Range: West Africa, Sierra Leone to Cameroon.
Habits: Aggressive, especially to others of its own species.
Water Conditions: Hard, alkaline water preferred and best for spawning. Temperature 24 to 27°C.
Size: 15 cm; smaller specimens most usually offered for sale.
Food Requirements: Accepts all meaty live, frozen and freeze-dried foods.

This species is one of the best mouthbrooders for study, in that the parent fish take great pains in protecting their young. After the spawning pair has established a territory within the tank, male and female join in scooping out a depression in the gravel bottom. After the eggs have been laid and fertilized, the male picks them up in his mouth and carries them mouthbrooder-fashion during the incubation period and until they are able to fend for themselves. During this time, the female is very zealous in helping the male drive off intruders into their territory, and she helps shepherd the free-swimming fry on the occasions that they leave the male's mouth. In this species the female is slightly more colorful than the male, exhibiting a reddish area around the belly that is completely missing in the male.

CICHLA OCELLARIS (Bloch & Schneider) / *Peacock Cichlid, Lukanani*

Range: Widely distributed throughout tropical South America, except in the La Plata System.
Habits: A predatory fish which cannot be kept with smaller species; it will even attack others of its own size.
Water Conditions: A large, well-aerated aquarium is an absolute necessity. Temperature about 25°C.
Size: To 75 cm.
Food Requirements: Will eat only living things like large earthworms, smaller fish, dragonfly and other large larvae, tadpoles, etc.

This fish is widespread throughout South America and is considered to be one of the most important game fishes on the continent. The Peacock Cichlid is one of the largest members of the family Cichlidae, and because it grows so large only the juveniles are suitable for an aquarium. Temperatures should not fall below 20°C, and the aquarium should be well aerated. This fish is a predator and should not be trusted with any other fish. It will attack fishes that are its own size and will eat anything that it can swallow.

In nature *Cichla ocellaris* spawns in shallow water. As spawning time approaches, mature males develop a hump behind the head and their coloration intensifies. Holes are dug in the mud and several nests are formed. The female lays over eight thousand eggs. After the eggs hatch, both parents guard the young fry for about three weeks; the male then chases the female away so that he can guard the young on his own. This fish can be recommended only for extremely large aquaria, pools or ponds.

Chromidotilapia guentheri F R X 4 9 3 X N N D   [R. Zukal]
Cichla ocellaris F C X 4 9 4 X N N B   [Harald Schultz]

494

Cichlasoma centrarchus ⓕⓕⓍ④⑨⑨Ⓧ Ⓝ Ⓝ Ⓒ [Dr. R.J. Goldstein]

Cichlasoma coryphaenoides ⓕⒺⓍ⑤⓪⓪ⓍⓃⓃⒹ [Aaron Norman]

CICHLASOMA CENTRARCHUS (Gill and Bransford) / *Flier Cichlid*

Range: Costa Rica and Nicaragua.
Habits: Territorial but gets along well with other fishes of the same size if given plenty of room.
Water Conditions: Not critical as long as conditions are not extreme. Temperature 24 to 27°C.
Size: 20 to 22 cm in the aquarium; larger in nature.
Food Requirements: Not a fussy eater. Will take a variety of frozen and prepared dry foods.

Cichlasoma centrarchus, introduced into the aquarium hobby in 1967 by Dr. William Bussing, follows the typical breeding pattern adhered to by the majority of the New World cichlids: that is, it is an open-substrate-spawner. The spawning site seems to be chosen by the male, but once the pair has spawned the female becomes the dominant fish. They are not particularly choosy about where they spawn and are as likely to lay their eggs on the aquarium glass or the slate bottom as on a rock. The eggs hatch in a few days, and the fry are free-swimming within a week. At this time they appear to graze on the algae-covered plants or rocks. Whether they are eating the algae or the minute animals that dwell among the algal fibers is not known. At this stage the fry begin the glancing behavior commonly seen in some other New World cichlids: they seem to be eating tiny chunks of their parent's body slime. The parents and fry should be separated at this time.

CICHLASOMA CORYPHAENOIDES (Heckel) / *Chocolate Cichlid*

Range: Widely distributed in the Amazon region, but not common.
Habits: Not peaceful; even when kept with their own kind, the bigger ones are very apt to pick on the smaller.
Water Conditions: Not critical, but temperature requirements are a bit high. 26°C is best, and never let the water go below 21°C.
Size: Males up to 25 cm; female slightly smaller.
Food Requirements: Greedy eaters, preferring large chunks. Earthworms, pieces of beef heart or canned dog food are best.

One of the harder-to-keep large cichlids, this one is seldom imported. They are big, ferocious and a bit touchy where temperature is concerned. The hobbyist who likes their coloration, which is admittedly attractive, soon tires of their greed and inability to get along with any tankmate which can't lick them, of which there are many. Because they are not ready sellers, most breeders have preferred not to try propagating them, even if they had the proper amount of space required. Add to this the fact that the fish does not occur in great numbers in any part of the Amazon where collecting is done, and you have the reason why we seldom see the fish.

CICHLASOMA CYANOGUTTATUM (Baird & Girard) / *Texas Cichlid*

Range: Southern Texas and northern Mexico.
Habits: All the bad cichlid habits: digs a great deal and uproots plants; usually quarrelsome if kept with other fishes.
Water Conditions: Not critical; not sensitive to temperature drops. Best breeding temperature about 24°C.
Size: In native waters up to 30 cm. In captivity seldom exceeds 15 cm.
Food Requirements: Larger specimens require chunks of food, such as cut-up earthworms or pieces of beef heart or other lean meat.

Most of the larger cichlids have very little in the way of good qualities, and this one is no exception. One unusual thing which can be said of it is that it is the only cichlid which is native to United States waters. It is the northernmost American cichlid, found as far up as the Rio Grande and some of its tributaries in southern Texas. Those who intend to keep *C. cyanoguttatum* should provide them with a Texas-size aquarium, 150 liters or better. Once they have made themselves at home here, a pair may some day begin digging holes all over the place. Once the surroundings are bare enough for their satisfaction, they usually select a flat stone and begin to clean it carefully and meticulously. Then the female, after acting coy for awhile, will allow herself to be coaxed to the stone and will deposit 500 eggs or more on it, closely followed by the male who sprays them with his sperm. The fry hatch in 5 to 7 days.

CICHLASOMA FACETUM (Jenyns) / *Chanchito*

Range: Southern Brazil (Rio Grande do Sul, Rio Parana and tributaries).
Habits: Likely to be quarrelsome and uproot plants. Should not be kept with smaller fishes.
Water Conditions: Not critical. Temperature should be between 24 and 27°C.
Size: In their habitat, up to 30 cm; in the aquarium, 20 cm.
Food Requirements: Greedy eaters; larger specimens may be fed canned dog or cat foods in addition to insects, garden worms, water beetles, tadpoles and pieces of fish or lean beef. Will only eat dried foods if very hungry.

The reputation which many cichlids have gotten, whether it be for being quarrelsome or for digging plants and raising the devil in general, may be traced back to the behavior of the Chanchito. Whatever their bad habits may be, they are usually good parents. They lay their eggs on a flat stone, flower-pot or one of the glass sides of the aquarium and then both parents take meticulous care of their spawn, mouthing them often to make sure that no dirt settles on them. In 3 to 4 days the young hatch and are immediately transferred to holes which the parents have been digging previously. The yolk-sacs are absorbed in about another week, and the youngsters then begin to swim out of the holes, to be herded back by the watchful parents.

501

Cichlasoma cyanoguttatum ⟨F⟩⟨E⟩⟨X⟩⟨5⟩⟨0⟩⟨1⟩⟨X⟩⟨N⟩⟨N⟩⟨D⟩   [H. J. Richter]
Cichlasoma facetum ⟨F⟩⟨E⟩⟨X⟩⟨5⟩⟨0⟩⟨2⟩⟨X⟩⟨N⟩⟨N⟩⟨D⟩   [Gerhard Marcuse]

Cichlasoma festivum 〔F〕〔H〕〔X〕〔5〕〔0〕〔3〕〔X〕〔N〕〔N〕〔A〕 [R. Zukal]
Cichlasoma friedrichsthali 〔F〕〔E〕〔X〕〔5〕〔0〕〔4〕〔X〕〔N〕〔N〕〔D〕 [Al Engasser]

CICHLASOMA FESTIVUM (Heckel) / *Flag Cichlid*

Range: Widely spread all over the central Amazon region.
Habits: Fairly peaceful for a cichlid; small specimens make good community tank fish, but when they grow larger they should have their own tank.
Water Conditions: Conditions are not as important as the fact that the water should be clean and have an exceptionally high oxygen content. For this reason they should be given plenty of room.
Size: Up to 15 cm.
Food Requirements: Varied diet of living foods; will eat dried foods unwillingly.

No danger of confusion here with any of the other cichlid species. The line which runs upward diagonally from the mouth to the tip of the dorsal fin identifies it without question. Differentiating between the sexes is another story; males are a bit larger, with longer fins, but a not fully developed male and a fully developed one could easily be mistaken for a pair, and the only way to be really sure is by comparing the genital papillae, or breeding tubes, when they are ready to spawn. The female's tube is much thicker than the male's. This fish is found in a very large area in the central Amazon region, and fish collectors often find them a nuisance when netting other species.

CICHLASOMA FRIEDRICHSTHALI (Heckel) / *Friedrichsthal's Cichlid*

Range: Atlantic coast of southern Mexico (approximately from Rio Coatzacoalas east) to Costa Rica.
Habits: Aggressive, even with very large cichlids. Not so aggressive with members of its own species, however.
Water Conditions: Not critical. This species can withstand temperature extremes of near 10°C to almost 35°C for short periods of time.
Size: Up to about 20 cm.
Food Requirements: Will eat most aquarium foods. Live foods preferred.

Friedrichsthal's Cichlid is very aggressive and cannot safely be housed even with cichlids larger than itself. If other cichlids are to be placed in the same tank, be sure they are well able to take care of themselves. At breeding time *C. friedrichsthali* will make short work of any tankmates.

Spawning has been accomplished and the behavior is quite typical in many respects. There are the usual fin-spreading displays and jaw-locking behavior as well as the scouring of a flowerpot or rock surface in preparation for egg deposition. The male will usually dig a pit or two some distance from the selected spawning site in preparation for the moving of the fry. The female will deposit some 700 golden-orange eggs on the flowerpot or slate where they are continuously fanned by one parent while the other stands guard. After about 4 days the eggs hatch and the wrigglers are moved by both parents to one of the previously dug pits, where they are still guarded vigorously.

CICHLASOMA KRAUSSI (Steindachner) / *Sharpheaded Cichlid*

Range: Northern Colombia and northwestern Venezuela from the Rio Atrato to around Maracaibo.
Habits: Very aggressive; has been compared in temperament to *Hemichromis fasciatus*.
Water Conditions: Not critical.
Size: To about 26 cm total length.
Food Requirements: Will eat almost any aquarium fare including small fishes, beef heart, brine shrimp, etc. Heavy feeders.

If you have several individuals of *Cichlasoma kraussi* in a tank (and it had better be a large tank)—and if you are lucky—they might establish a pecking order in which each fish knows its place and aggression is minimal.

Spawning is fairly typical. The pair will cooperate in cleaning a flat rock, piece of slate or flowerpot that has been put into the tank for that purpose. The immediate area will also be cleaned up, which means the removal of any plants or other fishes in the vicinity. A number of pits are dug in the gravel as well. Courtship consists of displaying in front of the female and shimmying or trembling when parallel to her. Immediately before egg deposition the male will tap or nudge the female repeatedly in the area of her vent. When the female is ready she will lay a string of eggs on the flat surface and the male will follow along to fertilize them. This continues until all the eggs are laid and fertilized. Be prepared for a large spawn, as there are reports of more than 1,000 eggs being deposited at one time, covering a large surface area.

CICHLASOMA LABIATUM (Günther) / *Red Devil*

Range: Nicaragua and Costa Rica.
Habits: Very vicious; should be kept by themselves.
Water Conditions: About neutral and fairly soft. Temperature 24 to 26°C.
Size: To about 38 cm.
Food Requirements: Carnivorous; will eat small living fish and can be trained to accept strips of fish fillets. Young specimens will take dry foods.

Think your Oscars are big? These fellows when fully grown will put an Oscar to shame. There is a great deal of variability in the structure and coloration of this species: some are bright red; others are white or yellow; some have black-tipped fins and tail and black lips; and some have thick rubbery lips. All are scrappy and should have a large tank to themselves. There is a bit of a problem when it comes to providing food for them; they seem to like to eat living fish, and while in many places it is not too difficult to get them live bait fish, they can probably be "trained" to eat clams, mussels or food shrimp, or pieces of fish fillet. In their home waters, they can be caught on hook and line, using the same tactics as for bass.

Cichlasoma kraussi ⌧⌧⌧⌧⌧⌧⌧⌧⌧   [Dr. A. Fernandez-Yepez]
Cichlasoma labiatum ⌧⌧⌧⌧⌧⌧⌧⌧⌧   [M.F. Roberts]

Cichlasoma kraussi Ⓕ Ⓐ Ⓧ ⑤ ⓪ ⑤ Ⓧ Ⓝ Ⓝ Ⓑ   [Dr. A. Fernandez-Yepez]
Cichlasoma labiatum Ⓕ Ⓔ Ⓧ ⑤ ⓪ ⑥ Ⓧ Ⓡ Ⓝ Ⓓ   [M.F. Roberts]

1. *Cichlasoma managuense* ⬚F⬚G⬚X⬚5⬚0⬚7⬚X⬚N⬚N⬚7   [Dr. R.J. Goldstein]
2. *Cichlasoma managuense* ⬚F⬚E⬚X⬚5⬚0⬚8⬚X⬚N⬚N⬚D   [Dr. R.J. Goldstein]

CICHLASOMA MANAGUENSE (Günther) / *Managuense*

Range: Nicaragua.
Habits: A quarrelsome species that will kill smaller (and sometimes larger) fishes if given the chance.
Water Conditions: Not critical; fish does well in waters ranging from moderately soft and acid through hard and alkaline.
Size: Up to 35 cm.
Food Requirements: Eats all meaty foods.
Color Variations: Pattern very variable in the placement of the vermiculations and blotchings according to the mood of the fish.

Cichlasoma managuense is a specialty fish for fanciers of big cichlids, although small individuals are often purchased by hobbyists unsuspecting of what their new tank inhabitants will turn into . . . and usually they turn into killers. Most *C. managuense* specimens will want to rule the roost, and they'll take on anything in their way on the road to that objective. It's not odd that a fish that is territorial by nature will be aggressive, especially where it is kept in cramped quarters with other fishes that cannot help but intrude on its territory, but this species carries things a little too far, since the territory it stakes out for itself usually seems to include the entire tank. Its belligerence, however, is tempered by its intelligence, and grown *C. managuense* exhibit well developed individual personalities, showing distinctive likes and dislikes of a type to endear them to some hobbyists. The species is hardy and prolific, the only real demand they make upon their owners being that they require a large tank in order to put on size. Some hobbyists consider them attractive, but in general they are considered to be too big and too mean at full size to be fit aquarium subjects for anyone not willing and able to give them very large tanks; they, and this includes even very young *C. managuense,* are certainly not suitable candidates for the normal community aquarium tank.

1. *Cichlasoma managuense*, juvenile (p507).
2. *Cichlasoma managuense*, adult (p507).

Cichlasoma managuense. Photo by P.V. Loiselle.

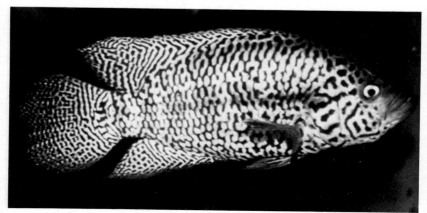

CICHLASOMA MEEKI (Brind) / *Firemouth*

Range: Northern Yucatan.
Habits: Peaceful for a cichlid; will get along with most fishes which do not harass it.
Water Conditions: Not critical; requires large tank with some open space and rocks for shelter.
Size: 12.5 cm; females about 10 cm.
Food Requirements: Predominantly living foods, such as daphnia, tubifex worms, grown brine shrimp, etc.

One of the most beautiful and popular cichlids. Pairs usually get along fairly well together, but when spawning the male may forget his manners if the female is not ready for him and may kill her if she is not removed until her eggs are developed. At this time the male shows his colors at their best. There is a bright red area which extends over his belly and his chin, even to his mouth. The female's colors are much more subdued, and her fins are shorter. They are usually good parents, and the young are easily raised. This species was first introduced in 1937, at which time its beauty created quite a commotion among aquarists in this country and in Europe. This fish is recommended only if the hobbyist has a large aquarium which presents a good number of hiding places. There have been a number of reports where this fish has spawned in a community aquarium and raised its young without injuring any other fishes kept with it.

1. *Cichlasoma meeki* (p510).
2. *Cichlasoma meeki*, mated pair after spawning (p510).
3. *Cichlasoma meeki*, with extended branchiostegal membranes, protecting spawn (p511).

Cichlasoma meeki, the Firemouth Cichlid. Photo by L.E. Perkins.

1. *Cichlasoma meeki* ⬛F⬛E⬛X⬛5⬛0⬛9⬛X⬛N⬛N⬛B
2. *Cichlasoma meeki* ⬛F⬛Q⬛X⬛5⬛1⬛0⬛X⬛N⬛N⬛B
3. *Cichlasoma meeki* → ⬛F⬛E⬛X⬛5⬛1⬛1⬛X⬛N⬛N⬛B

Cichlasoma meeki fry (above) grow very quickly (photo by G. Marcuse). Below is a pair of *Cichlasoma meeki* guarding their fry (photo by R. Zukal).

CICHLASOMA NIGROFASCIATUM (Günther) / *Convict Cichlid*

Range: Guatemala, El Salvador, Costa Rica and Panama.
Habits: A typical cichlid not to be trusted with smaller fishes.
Water Conditions: Not particular about water. Moderately hard water suits it fine, with temperatures between 20 and 27°C.
Size: To 15 cm; breeds at 8 cm.
Food Requirements: Eats everything but does exceptionally well on frozen brine shrimp and frozen beef heart. The young thrive on microworms from their free-swimming stage on.

This is a typical cichlid which exhibits extremes of color variation between the 15 cm adults and the young which may have as many as ten dark vertical bands covering the body. As the fish gets older the stripes disappear until some specimens raised in the author's tanks have lost almost all of their stripes. These fish are very simple to breed if they are given the barest of essentials. Set up a 60- to 80-liter aquarium. The bottom should be sand to a depth of about 5 cm. The pair will select a spawning site on a rock or inverted flowerpot and spawn as soon as they have been prepared for the reproductive act with copious feedings of frozen brine shrimp, beef heart and tubifex worms. They exercise extreme parental care of the spawn and will probably dig holes in the sand after the young are free-swimming in which to herd the young. The fry do very well on microworms until they are old enough for larger forms of live foods.

If their aquarium has plants in it, the plants will usually be ruthlessly uprooted and chewed to bits before the breeders feel secure enough to breed.

1. *Cichlasoma nigrofasciatum* (p514).
2. *Cichlasoma nigrofasciatum*, above spawn (p 515).

Cichlasoma nigrofasciatum, the Convict Cichlid. Photo by R. Zukal.

1. *Cichlasoma nigrofasciatum*
F E X 5 1 4 X N N C
[H.J. Richter]

2. *Cichlasoma nigrofasciatum* ⬚F⬚ ⬚F⬚ ⬚X⬚ ⬚5⬚ ⬚1⬚ ⬚5⬚ ⬚X⬚ ⬚N⬚ ⬚N⬚ ⬚C⬚　　　　[H. J. Richter]
Cichlasoma octofasciatum ⬚F⬚ ⬚Q⬚ ⬚X⬚ ⬚5⬚ ⬚1⬚ ⬚6⬚ ⬚X⬚ ⬚N⬚ ⬚N⬚ ⬚D⬚

Cichlasoma octofasciatum conducting a mating ritual. Photo by R. Zukal.

CICHLASOMA OCTOFASCIATUM (Regan) / *Jack Dempsey*

Range: Veracruz, Mexico to Honduras.

Habits: Very aggressive and loves to dig and uproot plants. Should be kept only with large fishes which can take care of themselves.

Water Conditions: Not critical; temperature should average about 25°C, slightly higher when it is desired to spawn them.

Size: 20 cm for males; females slightly smaller.

Food Requirements: Has a healthy appetite; chopped-up earthworms are a delicacy, as is chopped beef heart small enough to be swallowed easily.

Color Variations: Mature males are deep brown to black, with a black round spot at the center of the body and another at the tail base.

Were it not for their beauty we would seldom see these fish. Besides the background colors mentioned above, the males are peppered with light blue spots all over the body and fins. Females show only a few of these spots and have shorter fins. Another point of beauty on the male is the bright red edges on the dorsal and anal fins. A pronounced roughneck, it is almost sure to harass smaller fishes put in with it, so make sure if it is going into a community tank that its tankmates are of a comparable size. For all its other bad habits, the Jack Dempsey is a very gentle parent and breeding a pair is not usually fraught with a great deal of difficulty. Both parents take excellent care of eggs and fry, and the youngsters are quite pretty when they are about 2.5 cm long. At this time the large spot on the sides is very prominent and ringed with blue or greenish yellow. It is possible with a healthy, vigorous pair to raise as many as 1000 youngsters in a single season.

CICHLASOMA SALVINI (Günther) / *Salvin's Cichlid, Yellow-Belly*

Range: Central America, from Guatemala and Honduras into southern Mexico.
Habits: Can be very rough against other fishes and its own species, but in appropriately large tanks provided with rocks and caves it may be entirely peaceful.
Water Conditions: Not critical; the species is especially tolerant of cool water.
Size: To about 15 cm.
Food Requirements: Takes all meaty foods.

Cichlasoma salvini is a very good example of the type of transition in coloration that can be made in a fish according to the influence of its urge to spawn. Generally a drab, washed-out lemony yellow or gray, both sexes of *C. salvini* become an intensely attractive deep yellow at spawning time and after, when the eggs and fry are being cared for. Spawning colors of the female, which usually is smaller than a male of the same age, are even more intense than those of the male. Eggs and fry will be cared for very well, incidentally, because members of this species are excellent parents.

The eggs are laid on a firm base, usually a rock that forms part of a cave or shelter in which the fish will spawn, although they don't always spawn in a cave, sometimes laying the eggs on a rock surface in open water. The eggs hatch within three days at a temperature of around 26°C, and the fry are zealously guarded and herded. In some cases both parents care for the fry, but sometimes the female alone will undertake all parental supervision; in no case in which both parents are left with the eggs and fry will it be the male alone who cares for the babies.

CICHLASOMA SEVERUM (Heckel) / *Severum*

Range: Northern South America to the Amazon River, except in the Magdalena River.
Habits: Typical of the large cichlids, it will become quarrelsome when breeding time rolls around. Requires a large aquarium and will uproot plants and dig many holes in the gravel.
Water Conditions: Not critical; clean, slightly alkaline water seems to be best.
Size: Up to 20 cm.
Food Requirements: Small specimens may be fed with all the various live foods; when they become large chopped garden worms should be given on occasion.

Like *Astronotus ocellatus,* young specimens of this fish do not greatly resemble their parents and often create a problem when they grow up. Young fish are usually quite peaceful and their owner gets the mistaken impression that this attitude will continue. As they get bigger, they will "pair off" in the usual cichlid fashion and proceed to prepare a site for spawning. Every other fish which dares to come near is driven away fiercely, and bloody fights may ensue. If given their own tank, spawning proceeds normally as a rule, and eggs and fry are seldom eaten. There is also an albino variety of this fish available today, with a light golden body and pink eyes.

Cichlasoma salvini F E X 5 1 7 X N N B
Cichlasoma severum F E X 5 1 8 X N N C

[Dr. Herbert R. Axelrod]
[Aaron Norman]

Cichlasoma spilurum ⬚F⬚E⬚X⬚5⬚1⬚9⬚X⬚N⬚N⬚C ⬚ [R. Zukal]
Cichlasoma temporale ⬚F⬚E⬚X⬚5⬚2⬚0⬚X⬚N⬚N⬚C ⬚ [H. Hansen, Aquarium Berlin]

CICHLASOMA SPILURUM (Günther) / *Blue-Eyed Cichlid*

Range: Central America.
Habits: Relatively peaceful for a large cichlid.
Water Conditions: Not critical.
Size: Up to 18 cm; females smaller.
Food Requirements: Needs the addition of vegetable material such as spinach to its diet.

Central America has been exploited by tropical fish collectors to a much smaller extent than has the Amazon region. Increased interest in the last few years in this region has resulted in the introduction of several new species of tropicals, notably in the cichlid group. *Cichlasoma spilurum* is one of the species which seems to have found a secure place in the hobby.

This is not an especially difficult species to breed, breeding in the familiar cichlid manner. Pairs are inclined to be somewhat secretive about spawning, but a sure sign is the change in the coloration of the female. The head and breast become dusky and the gold band on the side becomes more brilliant. The ventral fins become coal black. It was thought for a time that *C. spilurum* and *C. nigrofasciatum* were color variations of the same fish. Both species are known to occur in the same bodies of water, which is taken as evidence that the color patterns of the living fishes play an important part in preventing hybridizing in nature. These species, however, have been successfully crossed under aquarium conditions, producing hybrids which resembled *C. spilurum* more than *C. nigrofasciatum*. The hybrids were more pugnacious than either parent.

CICHLASOMA TEMPORALE (Günther) / *F Cichlid*

Range: Central Amazon.
Habits: A typical cichlid with earth-moving habits when spawning. They tear up plants when planning to spawn. They will eat fishes small enough to gulp down in one swallow. Best kept with large plastic plants.
Water Conditions: A very hardy fish. Tolerates water from 6.0 to 8.4 pH. Temperature from 21 to 29°C. Hard or soft water is agreeable.
Size: To 20 cm.
Food Requirements: They eat most fish foods.

They are easily recognized by the two vertical spots and the long lateral line marking which, when viewed with the fish's head down, looks like an "F"; this has given this cichlid its common name.

Spawning is quite simple, merely a matter of putting a male and female in the same aquarium with plenty of space and good feedings of freeze-dried foods. The young are free-swimming in about 4 to 5 days depending upon the temperature. Remove the parents after spawning.

CLARIAS ANGOLENSIS Steindachner / *Brown Clarias*

Range: Widespread through western and central Africa.
Habits: A voracious catfish not to be trusted with smaller fishes.
Water Conditions: Needs warm water, 24 to 30°C, but is not otherwise demanding as to water characteristics.
Size: Up to 36 cm.
Food Requirements: Takes all meaty foods; live tubifex worms are preferred by small individuals of the species.

CLARIAS BATRACHUS Linnaeus / *Pla Duk Dam, Albino Clarias*

Range: India, Sri Lanka, Burma, Malaysia, East Indies, Philippines, Indo-China and Thailand.
Habits: An amazing fish which jumps out of aquaria and walks for long distances without dying.
Water Conditions: Hardy and tolerant to any water which is not too salty or too cold. Can tolerate temperatures from 10 to 32°C.
Size: Grows to at least 46 cm in nature.
Food Requirements: Eats anything usually offered to aquarium fishes.

The catfishes of the genus *Clarias* are an extremely interesting group of fishes, for they have a huge accessory breathing organ in the branchial cavity which enables them to utilize atmospheric oxygen in the same way that higher animals do. As a result, their gills have atrophied to the point where they are practically useless and it has been demonstrated that if they are maintained in an aquarium with a floating glass cover, where they are unable to gather atmospheric air to breathe, they die of suffocation.

COBITIS TAENIA Linnaeus / *Weatherfish, Spined Loach*

Range: Extremely wide, covering parts of both Europe and Asia.
Habits: Peaceful and inclined toward shyness.
Water Conditions: Water conditions for this species are not of special importance, as long as extremes of pH and DH are avoided. Can take temperatures lower than 16°C, but a range in the low 20's (°C) is best.
Size: Up to 10 cm.
Food Requirements: Takes all foods, but particularly likes living foods which congregate near the bottom, such as worms.

The range of this fish is so wide that many authorities, no doubt working at least in part on the theory that no single animal should be allowed to cover so much territory, have broken the species up into at least seven subspecies according to geographical origin. No matter where it comes from, this little loach is a peaceful addition to the community tank, where it is most often kept as a scavenger under the mistaken notion that the fish lives by choice on left-over food particles. This same fate overtakes many of the hapless catfish within the genus *Corydoras;* looked upon as garbage disposal units, the fish, whether loach or catfish, gradually wastes away.

Clarias angolensis ⟦F⟧⟦D⟧⟦X⟧⟦5⟧⟦2⟧⟦1⟧⟦X⟧⟦N⟧⟦N⟧⟦D⟧ [R. Zukal]
Clarias batrachus ⟦F⟧⟦H⟧⟦M⟧⟦5⟧⟦2⟧⟦2⟧⟦X⟧⟦A⟧⟦N⟧⟦D⟧ [P.Tsang]

Cobitus taenia ⟦F⟧⟦D⟧⟦B⟧⟦5⟧⟦2⟧⟦2⟧⟦X⟧⟦N⟧⟦N⟧⟦7⟧ [G. Marcuse]

Cochliodon plecostomoides FDX523XNNC

Coelurichthys microlepis FQX524XNN5

COCHLIODON PLECOSTOMOIDES Eigenmann
Spoon-Toothed Sucker Catfish

Range: Villavicencio, Valencia Basin, Colombia.
Habits: Non-aggressive algae eater, safe even with smaller fishes (but not babies). Large specimens may uproot all but sturdy plants.
Water Conditions: Wide range acceptable. Temperature 18 to 28°C.
Size: To 20 cm.
Food Requirements: Omnivorous; almost any food accepted. Beef heart, brine shrimp, pellet foods and cooked oatmeal eagerly accepted. Algae or substitute vegetation required occasionally.

Except for its teeth this catfish is very similar to *Hypostomus* (formerly *Plecostomus).* Concerning coloration and pattern, this handsomely spotted loricariid catfish with its beautiful sail-like dorsal fin is certainly among the most handsome of sucker catfishes. Like other members of its family, its dorsal surface is covered with bony armor plates for protection. Designed for bottom living and grazing over stumps, stones and other surfaces for algae and other organic matter, *Cochliodon* and other loricariids have long coiled intestines for digestion of such material. The intestine is also utilized in a form of accessory breathing in which air is "swallowed" and forced into the intestine, where oxygen is extracted and carbon dioxide exchanged.

COELURICHTHYS MICROLEPIS (Steindachner) / *Croaking Tetra*

Range: Southeastern Brazil, Rio Grande do Sul.
Habits: Peaceful and active; does not disturb plants.
Water Conditions: Should be kept in a roomy aquarium at a temperature slightly lower than most tropical species, 21 to 24°C.
Size: Males about 5.5 cm; females about 4.5 cm.
Food Requirements: Not a fussy eater; besides live foods, will also eat dried foods.

As the name implies, this fish has the power to make tiny croaking noises. These noises are made by getting a gulp of air at the surface of the water, then swimming below and releasing it. This is likened to the chirp of an insect by some. Something which has not yet been fully explained goes on when this fish breeds. There is an active driving beforehand, but then the female leaves the male and lays the eggs without any further contact with the male. The usual explanation for this is that some sort of internal fertilization takes place, and this has been backed by some authorities who have cut open females and removed eggs and a sac which was found to contain sperm. They were able to fertilize the eggs with this sperm, but one thing still remains to be fully explained: how did the sperm-sac get there? A similar problem exists with a few other fishes, such as *Corynopoma riisei* and *Pseudocorynopoma doriae.*

COELURICHTHYS TENUIS Nichols / *Tenuis Tetra*

Range: Southern Brazil, Paraguay and northeastern Argentina.
Habits: Peaceful and very active; prefers to swim in schools. Does not harm plants.
Water Conditions: Soft acid water which is clean and well aerated. Temperature about 24°C.
   Tank should be in a sunny location. Prefers tannic acid stained water (brown water).
Size: 5 cm.
Food Requirements: Should be generously fed with live foods.

Coelurichthys tenuis looks more like a member of the genus *Danio* than one of the characins. They are always alert and forever on the move, traveling in schools whenever a number of them are put into the same aquarium. They love sunlight and are especially happy and active when the sun shines into their tank. In their native habitat they inhabit small, fast-flowing, cool streams where the water is rich in oxygen, and for this reason they should have adequate aeration in their tank. Males of this fish have an odd characteristic: the horizontal stripe extends into the lower rays of the tail. Where the dark rays occur the tail is not evenly notched, but the dark rays come out and give an almost square appearance to the lower caudal lobe. This characteristic is only slight in the females, which gives a sure method for choosing pairs. They have been spawned on a few occasions, but reports do not tell much beyond the fact that they spawned in a similar manner to the other small characins, that the eggs hatched in one day and that the fry were very hard to raise. Many imported specimens which are seemingly healthy seem to waste away for some mysterious reason in the aquarium.

COLISA CHUNA (Hamilton-Buchanan) / *Honey Gourami*

Range: India.
Habits: Peaceful and shy.
Water Conditions: Soft, slightly acid water desirable. Temperature 24 to 28°C.
Size: 6 cm.
Food Requirements: Will accept some dry foods, but prefers small living foods, especially crustaceans.

Although the Honey Gourami is a pleasing fish of warm but not startling coloration, it is no rival to its relative *Colisa lalia,* the male of which is truly a beautiful fish. *Colisa chuna* is a bubblenest builder which spawns like the Dwarf Gourami, but *chuna* uses less vegetable matter in the construction of its nest. Also, the male Honey Gourami is inclined to be more tolerant of the hesitancy of the female to spawn, whereas the male *Colisa lalia* will damage the female if she is not provided with enough refuge. Like the Dwarf Gourami, *Colisa chuna* does best at a temperature between 24 and 28°C.

Coelurichthys tenuis ⬚F⬚D⬚X⬚5⬚2⬚5⬚X⬚N⬚N⬚5 [Harald Schultz]
Colisa chuna ⬚F⬚E⬚X⬚5⬚2⬚6⬚X⬚N⬚N⬚5 [H. J. Richter]

Colisa fasciata ⬚F⬚E⬚X⬚5⬚2⬚7⬚X⬚N⬚N⬚B   [H. Hansen, Aquarium Berlin]
Colisa labiosa ⬚F⬚E⬚X⬚5⬚2⬚8⬚X⬚N⬚N⬚A   [Dr. Herbert R. Axelrod]

COLISA FASCIATA (Bloch & Schneider) / *Giant Gourami*

Range: India: Coromandel Coast, Northwest and North Provinces, Assam.
Habits: Peaceful; a good community fish.
Water Conditions: Not critical; they like warm water. Temperature 25 to 26°C.
Size: Males about 12 cm; females a little smaller.
Food Requirements: They eat anything and have tremendous appetites.

This attractive fish looks somewhat like a larger edition of the popular Dwarf Gourami. Because it is considerably larger, some people tend to shy away from it, fearing that it might be aggressive. This is not so; it is even a bit shy and tends to be scary if placed in a tank where it cannot hide when real or imaginary danger threatens it. Breeding is very easily accomplished, and a well-mated pair may easily make a nuisance of themselves by breeding too often. Like the other *Colisa* species, they prefer to anchor their bubblenest to a floating plant, and a few should be provided. When they are ready to spawn, the water should be reduced to only 8 to 10 cm deep. After a number of false tries, the pair will eventually produce as many as 800 eggs which hatch in about 24 hours. The fry become free-swimming in two more days, at which time the male may be removed; the female should be removed when she is finished laying eggs. The fry should be fed liberally with fine dried food, and it is an advantage to add aeration at this time. Sorting the fry after they begin growing will prevent cannibalism.

COLISA LABIOSA (Day) / *Thick-Lipped Gourami*

Range: India and Burma.
Habits: Peaceful and rather shy; a good fish for the community aquarium.
Water Conditions: Requires warmth, otherwise not critical as to water conditions if extremes are avoided. Temperature about 25°C.
Size: 10 cm; usually somewhat smaller.
Food Requirements: Live foods preferred, but in the absence of these, prepared foods are acceptable.

The Thick-Lipped Gourami, while not as popular or quite as colorful as the Dwarf Gourami, is also worth of a place in the community aquarium. Like the other members of the genus *Colisa,* this fish is a bit on the shy side and should have an aquarium which is rich in plant life and permits the fish to duck out of sight if it feels circumstances warrant it. *C. labiosa* is one of the easiest of the gouramis to breed. The males seem to get a kick out of making bubblenests and are less likely to get rough when a female is not ready for spawning. Care must be taken not to combine this or for that matter any other thread-finned fish with a greedy species such as some of the barbs, or in a very short time the long, thin ventral fins will be reduced to stumps. In time the fins grow back, but the new fin is often a bit crooked at the point where growth began.

COLISA LALIA (Hamilton-Buchanan) / *Dwarf Gourami*

Range: India, Bengal and Assam.
Habits: Very peaceful; likely to be shy and retiring if kept with fishes which annoy it.
Water Conditions: Water should be neutral to slightly acid; enjoys a tank which gets a good
   amount of sunlight. Temperature 24 to 27°C.
Size: Largest males never exceed 6 cm; females 5 cm.
Food Requirements: Not a fussy eater. Dried foods accepted, but should be alternated with
   live foods.

The Dwarf Gourami is one of the beloved hardy perennials of the aquarium
fish world. Even in its native India it is extensively kept in aquaria, which is
an unusual thing because with aquarium fishes there is usually no respect for
a native fish. At least this seems to be the case in the United States, where
there are some native fishes which are valued in other countries as aquarium
specimens but scarcely ever seen here. The Dwarf Gourami is unusual among
the bubblenest builders in that it includes bits of plants, twigs and other
debris in its nest. The result is a firm bundle which holds together for a long
time after the fry are hatched. The eggs are tiny, and if not provided with fine
infusoria at first the fry are likely to starve. Once past the critical stage,
however, when they are large enough to handle newly hatched brine shrimp,
they prove hardy and growth is rapid.

COLOMESUS PSITTACUS (Schneider) / *South American Puffer*

Range: Venezuela, Guianas, the upper Amazon, Rio Branco and Rio Araguaia.
Habits: Generally peaceful but may occasionally nip a fin or two.
Water Conditions: Neutral to slightly alkaline hard water. Temperature 24 to 26°C. Tank
   should be well planted.
Size: To 15 cm; usually smaller.
Food Requirements: Especially fond of snails or will take the larger-sized live foods. Prob-
   ably could be trained to take strips of raw fish.

Most of the puffers we keep in the aquarium are from the East Indies and
there are also a few from Africa and Thailand. The saltwater species are, of
course, native to the warm and temperate waters of most of the world. But for
one to come from South America, and far upstream in the Amazon at that, is
highly unusual. They have been seen very occasionally among the dealers.
You will find that this puffer is not quite as nasty as some of the others and
that you can keep them in a community aquarium if you do not put them with
such juicy morsels as smaller fishes.

Colisa lalia ⬚F⬚E⬚X⬚5⬚2⬚9⬚X⬚N⬚N⬚6
Colomesus psittacus ⬚F⬚D⬚X⬚5⬚3⬚0⬚X⬚N⬚N⬚6

[H. J. Richter]
[Harald Schultz]

Colossoma oculus F C X 5 3 1 X N N 7   [Dr. Herbert R. Axelrod]
Copeina guttata F Q X 5 3 2 X N N 9   [Dr. Herbert R. Axelrod]

COLOSSOMA OCULUS (Cope) / *Red-Finned Pacu*

Range: Branches of the Amazon.
Habits: Not to be trusted with small fishes.
Water Conditions: Soft, slightly acid water is indicated but is probably of no great importance. Temperature 21 to 27°C.
Size: Up to 20 cm.
Food Requirements: Very reluctant to accept dry foods, but will take live and frozen foods.

All of the *Colossomas* are big, ungainly fishes with few attributes that would suit them to the home aquarium. First of all, they are big and must consequently be maintained in big tanks; also, they are closely related to piranhas and share, at least to a small degree, the nasty temperaments of their more notorious cousins. Of course, these very qualities are what makes the piranha species attractive to some hobbyists, and it sometimes happens that a *Colossoma* will be billed in a dealer's display tank as a "man-eating fish" to attract attention.

COPEINA GUTTATA (Steindachner) / *Red-Spotted Copeina*

Range: Central Amazon region.
Habits: Peaceful; good community tank fish if not kept with others much smaller than themselves.
Water Conditions: Not critical; a wide range of temperatures is tolerated, with optimum temperatures around 24°C.
Size: Wild specimens attain a size of about 10 cm; in captivity 15 cm.
Food Requirements: Heavy eaters which will take prepared foods, but they should also be given live foods whenever possible.

It is highly unusual for a fish which is kept in captivity to grow as large as it would in its natural waters. But every rule has its exceptions, and with this fish it is a rare one indeed: *Copeina guttata* becomes larger in captivity than it does in the wild. There may be several reasons for this, but in all probability the answer is in the food supply. In their natural waters *Copeina guttata* occur in large schools and there is a very good chance that they might not get enough food to satisfy their robust appetites. The same has been observed with trout and other fishes which occur in habitats where there was a food shortage. The fish matured but remained much smaller. *Copeina guttata* has another claim to being unusual. It is a true characin but does not spawn in a manner which is usual for characins; their behavior is more like that found among the cichlids. The male scoops out a depression in the gravel in an open spot, and a large number of eggs are deposited into this depression. Here they are guarded and fanned by the male. Fry hatch after 30 to 50 hours and are easily raised. *Copeinas* are jumpers, so be sure to keep their tank covered at all times.

COPELLA ARNOLDI (Regan) / *Splash Tetra, Jumping Characin*

Range: Amazon River, in the region of Rio Para.
Habits: Very peaceful, but should always be kept in a covered aquarium because of its jumping habits.
Water Conditions: Neutral to slightly acid. Temperature between 24 and 26°C.
Size: 8 cm; females about 6 cm.
Food Requirements: Live foods preferred, but will take dry food when hungry.

We have seen many odd ways of reproduction in aquarium fishes, but this species probably has the oddest. In nature, a pair will seek out an overhanging leaf and together leap out of the water and cling to this leaf long enough to paste several eggs there. They then drop back, to repeat the process again and again until there are more than 100 eggs in a closely packed mass on the underside of the leaf. The eggs do not hatch until 3 days later, during which time the male remains under the leaf and every 15 minutes or so splashes water on them with his tail to keep them from drying out. The reason for this behavior is not definite, but a study of the ecology of this fish would probably disclose that there are some egg-eating predators, maybe snails, present in these waters which would wipe out any unprotected eggs in the water but could not catch the tiny fry once they began swimming. In the aquarium, these fish will breed if the tank is half full of water and a piece of slate is leaned against the inside edge so that half is out of water. Once the fry hatch and fall into the water, the parents should be removed.

1. *Copella arnoldi* (p534).
2. *Copella arnoldi*, jumping from the water toward a leaf (p534).
3. *Copella arnoldi*, spawning on a leaf above the water (p534).

Copella arnoldi jump out of water to spawn on a leaf. Photo by R. Zukal.

1. *Copella arnoldi* [F][E][X][5][3][3][X][N][N][8]   [H. Hansen, Aquarium Berlin]
2. *Copella arnoldi*   [F][Q][E][5][3][4][X][N][N][8]   3. *Copella arnoldi*

[R. Zukal]

[R. Zukal]

Copella eigenmanni ⬚F⬚Q⬚X⬚5⬚3⬚5⬚X⬚N⬚N⬚6 [Harald Schultz]
Copella nattereri ⬚F⬚R⬚X⬚5⬚3⬚6⬚X⬚N⬚N⬚6 [Dr. Herbert R. Axelrod]

COPELLA EIGENMANNI (Regan) / *Eigenmann's Copella*

Range: Guyana to Para, Brazil.
Habits: Peaceful; prefers to swim in the upper reaches of the tank. A skillful jumper; tank must be kept covered.
Water Conditions: Soft, slightly acid water. Temperature about 25°C.
Size: To 6 cm.
Food Requirements: They accept dry food but prefer live foods which remain near the top.

The *Copella* group is a bit of a paradox. *Copella arnoldi* has the unusual, almost freakish, method of spawning where the pair jumps out of the water and fastens their eggs to the underside of an overhanging leaf or rock, then splashing water up against the eggs until they hatch. *Copella callolepis* usually spawns on a submerged leaf. If large submerged leaves are not present, *Copella eigenmanni* will spawn in depressions in the sand. The male will often clean the spawning area for many hours before coaxing the female to lay eggs. The male then fans the eggs with his fins, and if they are laid on a leaf, most will eventually fall to the bottom of the aquarium. After 24 hours the small fry hatch out and move to the water's surface. They can only be fed on very fine foods such as infusoria. The adults should be separated from the fry. These fish can jump through the smallest openings and their tank should be covered.

COPELLA NATTERERI (Steindachner) / *Spotted Copella*

Range: Amazon Basin.
Habits: Peaceful; a good community fish. Should be kept in a covered tank.
Water Conditions: Soft, slightly acid water. Temperature 22 to 28°C.
Size: Up to 8 cm.
Food Requirements: Not too particular, but not all dry foods are accepted.

There is a simple beauty to this fish. Not flashy in color, *Copella nattereri* is possessed of a subdued warm coloring that is highlighted by occasional bright spots of red and lavender. The most striking of these spots lies immediately between the gill covers and the pectoral fins; under correct lighting, this spot shows up like a brilliant jewel. Also, the fish has a gliding swimming motion which lends additional grace to its appearance. All in all, *Copella nattereri* gives the impression of refined elegance, especially if it is kept with fishes more stubby in body form, for then the streamlined charm of the Spotted Copella is most pronounced. Distinguishing the sexes is easy with mature specimens, because the male's dorsal fin is very definitely longer and more tapered; also, he is more elongated in shape. Although *Copella nattereri* closely resembles *Copella arnoldi*, its breeding pattern is quite different. Instead of jumping from the water to lay its eggs, the Spotted Copella deposits its eggs on submerged plants, usually broad-leaved plants such as broad-leaf Amazon sword plants. At a temperature of 25°C the eggs hatch in about a day, and the fry require small foods.

COPELLA VILMAE Géry / *Rainbow Copella*

Range: Brazilian Amazon.
Habits: A very typical member of the *Copeina-Copella* group. Keep in covered tank as this species may jump.
Water Conditions: Prefers warm, slightly acid, soft water. Temperature 24 to 28°C.
Size: To about 6 cm.
Food Requirements: Eats any small particle food, especially dried pelletized foods. Also requires some live foods or frozen brine shrimp in order that the male will keep his beautiful colors.

Copella vilmae is a small fish which spends most of its time in the upper layers of the water. The fins of the female are not very large, but the males have elongated dorsal fins, and the upper lobe of the caudal fin is longer than the lower lobe. This species is delicate and should be given a large aquarium which is sparsely planted with broad-leaved plants. The tank should also be given plenty of sunlight. Soft, slightly acidic water is preferred, which can be obtained by filtering through peat moss. Small live foods are best and will help the male to keep his colors. This fish is a very good jumper and the tank should be completely covered.

Copella, Pyrrhulina and *Copeina* are closely related genera with very similar breeding habits (with the exception of *Copella arnoldi*). These fish prefer to spawn on broad-leaved, submerged plants. The male prepares the spawning site by cleaning the nesting area for up to several hours, and then he coaxes the female toward the spot. He does this by swimming around the female and occasionally nudging her with his mouth. The male cares for the spawn, which hatches in about 24 hours. The fry are very small and should be fed infusoria. They move to the surface of the water soon after they are hatched. The adults should be removed from the breeding tank.

CORYDORAS ACUTUS Cope / *Blacktop Catfish*

Range: Upper Amazon.
Habits: Peaceful.
Water Conditions: Soft, slightly acid water desirable. Temperature 23 to 26°C.
Size: 6 cm.
Food Requirements: Accepts all foods.

Although this little catfish is rarely seen, it makes a good aquarium subject, as it is peaceful and hardy. Specimens of this fish are usually found among importations of more popular *Corydoras* species. In dealers' tanks they are almost always mixed in with other *Corydoras*, as there have been no direct attempts at importing this fish as a separate species, for it is little known and has no following among the aquarium public in general. For the casual tropical fish store browser, *Corydoras acutus* has no special charm, and when purchased it is usually the last, or one of the last, specimen to be chosen from the general "scavenger" tank.

Copella vilmae FAX537XNN6

[Harald Schultz]

Corydoras acutus FDX538XNN5

[Dr. S. Weitzman]

1. *Corydoras aeneus* F Q T 5 3 9 X N N 7
2. *Corydoras aeneus* var. F H M 5 3 9 X A N 6   [R. Zukal]

Corydoras agassizi F D X 5 4 0 X N N 6   [Dr. Herbert R. Axelrod]

CORYDORAS AENEUS Gill / *Aeneus Catfish*

Range: Widely distributed over South America from Trinidad to the La Plata.
Habits: Very peaceful; constantly going over the bottom for scraps of leftover food. Useful in keeping the tank clean.
Water Conditions: Neutral to slightly alkaline; water should have no salt added to it. These fish come from absolutely fresh water. Temperature 22 to 26°C.
Size: 7 cm; usually a bit smaller.
Food Requirements: All dried foods are accepted, but to keep them in really good shape an occasional feeding of tubifex worms should be given.

This is probably the most well-known among the popular armored catfishes, and its popularity is well deserved. They are comical fellows, their alert eyes always looking around while grubbing around the bottom in search of food. Probably their eyes are not as useful in finding food as their barbels, which are their accessory taste organs and permit them to find food where many other fishes cannot, even in the dark. This fish has little to fear from any enemies; it has sharply spiked anal and dorsal fins which would make a larger fish feel as though it were biting into a pincushion. His armor plates, which he wears on his body in place of scales, give a hard, bony surface to a smaller fish which would feel inclined to nibble on him. With such protection, who needs teeth? The natives have an odd way of catching these fish. They choose a small pond where the ripples tell them that there are catfish there surfacing for air. Then they build a dam where the water enters and they let the pond run dry. This leaves the catfish flopping about in the mud.

1. *Corydoras aeneus*, normal variety (p539).
2. *Corydoras aeneus*, albino (p539).

CORYDORAS AGASSIZI Steindachner / *Agassiz's Catfish*

Range: West Brazil; Amazon region, Nauta, Ambyacu River, Maranon, Rio Jurua.
Habits: Peaceful; useful in that it feeds off the bottom and gets much food left by other fishes.
Water Conditions: Neutral to slightly alkaline; water should have no salt content. Temperature 22 to 26°C.
Size: 6 cm.
Food Requirements: Will do a good clean-up job, but if really good fish are desired, should get frequent live food feedings.

This attractive little catfish has a shorter, thicker body than most of the other species, almost like *Brochis splendens*. Although it has been known to science as far back as 1912, aquarists did not see them until a single specimen was brought into Germany in 1936. This is one species which cannot be sexed by color alone, as indeed very few of them can. We cannot go by fin shapes either, although usually the dorsal fin of the males is more pointed. The best way to arrive at a fairly accurate conclusion is to look at them from above. The females are a little bigger and their body shape is heavier.

CORYDORAS ARCUATUS Elwin / *Skunk Catfish, Tabatinga Catfish*

Range: Amazon region, above the city of Tefé.
Habits: Peaceful; being a bottom-feeder makes it especially valuable for finding and eating left-over food.
Water Conditions: Neutral to slightly alkaline water; it is important to leave out any salt. Temperature about 25°C.
Size: About 4.5 cm.
Food Requirements: Besides food left by other fishes, an occasional feeding of live food should be given.

Probably the most important reason why the common *Corydoras* species are so seldom bred is because most hobbyists consider them as strictly scavengers and will put one into each of their tanks to eat any food left by the other fishes in that tank. If two are used, no attention is paid to whether they are a pair or not. We would doubtless hear of many spawnings if pairs were given their own tanks and were well fed with living foods. Sexing is not the near impossibility it once was considered. Looking at a group of mature fish from above, it will be seen that some of them are wider in their body than the others; these are the females. These catfish do not eat their eggs; all that is required is that there are no other fish in the tank to eat eggs or fry. In Germany this species is known as "Stromlinien-Panzerwels" or "Streamlined Armored Catfish." Many thousands of them have been imported since 1938, when they were first introduced to the aquarium hobby. It would be interesting to see a batch of youngsters; probably the stripe down the back does not appear right away but develops later.

CORYDORAS BARBATUS (Quoy and Gaimard) / *Banded Corydoras*

Range: Brazil (Southeast).
Habits: Peaceful.
Water Conditions: Soft, slightly acid water desirable. Temperature 22 to 28°C.
Size: Up to 13 cm.
Food Requirements: Takes all foods.
Color Variations: Light brown body covered by large black markings. Belly color pink.

While *Corydoras barbatus*, because of its size, is not considered to be one of the better catfishes for the community tank, the fish is occasionally brought into the country and put on the market. Usually only young specimens are sold, and many purchasers are amazed to find that their catfish, which they originally supposed would grow no larger than the popular *C. aeneus*, is soon outgrowing its tank. For hobbyists with big tanks this is no problem, but for the hobbyist who buys a couple of *Corydoras* just to fit into the general framework of a small community tank, *Corydoras barbatus* is best left alone.

1. *Corydoras barbatus*, normal variety (p542).
2. *Corydoras barbatus*, extended pattern (p542).

Corydoras arcuatus ⬚F⬚ ⬚D⬚ ⬚X⬚ ⬚5⬚ ⬚4⬚ ⬚1⬚ ⬚X⬚ ⬚N⬚ ⬚N⬚ ⬚5⬚   [S. Frank]

1. *Corydoras barbatus* ⬚F⬚ ⬚D⬚ ⬚M⬚ ⬚5⬚ ⬚4⬚ ⬚2⬚ ⬚X⬚ ⬚N⬚ ⬚N⬚ ⬚8⬚   [Dr. Herbert R. Axelrod]
2. *Corydoras barbatus* ⬚F⬚ ⬚A⬚ ⬚B⬚ ⬚5⬚ ⬚4⬚ ⬚2⬚ ⬚X⬚ ⬚N⬚ ⬚N⬚ ⬚8⬚   [Dr. B. Frank]

Corydoras caudimaculatus ⎡F⎤⎡D⎤⎡X⎤⎡5⎤⎡4⎤⎡3⎤⎡X⎤⎡N⎤⎡N⎤⎡5⎤   [Dr. Herbert R. Axelrod]

Corydoras elegans ⎡F⎤⎡R⎤⎡X⎤⎡5⎤⎡4⎤⎡4⎤⎡X⎤⎡N⎤⎡N⎤⎡5⎤   [Dr. Herbert R. Axelrod]

CORYDORAS CAUDIMACULATUS Rössel / *Tail-Spot Corydoras*

Range: Rio Guaporé, Brazil.
Habits: Peaceful; will not disturb fishes or plants.
Water Conditions: Slightly alkaline water is best. Avoid sharp edges on rocks or gravel, as the mouth is easily damaged. Temperature 22 to 27°C.
Size: About 5 cm.
Food Requirements: All food which falls to the bottom is eaten, but there should be some live as well as prepared food.

The short body might almost lead one into believing that this is a species of *Brochis,* but the profile of the head is rounded like the other members of *Corydoras.* The German breeders have been very successful in breeding this fish, and there are no deviations from the usual *Corydoras* breeding procedure. One unusual thing about this species is that even the adipose fin carries a number of dots.

As a general rule, *Corydoras* species are not easy to breed. The sexes can be distinguished most easily when the fish are ripe. The females are larger and fuller, with larger bellies. The dorsal fin is often pointed in the male while rounded in the female. One ripe female should be mated with two or three males. This fish has a typical *Corydoras* spawning ritual, where the males nudge and push against the female. After a period of time the female begins to swim about the tank with the males in hot pursuit. Several potential spawning sites are cleaned during this process and actual spawning can take place in several locations.

CORYDORAS ELEGANS Steindachner / *Elegant Corydoras*

Range: Amazon Basin (Upper).
Habits: Peaceful.
Water Conditions: Slightly acid to slightly alkaline medium-soft water. Temperature 23 to 28°C.
Size: 5 cm.
Food Requirements: Accepts all foods, but is particularly fond of small worms.

The "Elegant" in this fish's popular name is derived from its specific scientific name, not from any special coloring or markings that would entitle it to such a fancy name. It is certainly a lot plainer than many of the other *Corydoras* species, some of which have been extracted from the "scavenger" category and are now being kept for their good looks alone. However, it is a good community catfish, and its desirability is enhanced by the fact that it is small, seldom reaching over 5 cm in length. Breeding has not been observed, although attempts have been made to spawn this fish. The fish pictured are still fairly young; as they mature, they will develop heavier bodies with more of a dorsal "hump." The irregular outline of the dorsal fin of one of the fish is a result of damage suffered during transportation; it is not to be relied on as a sexual characteristic.

544

CORYDORAS GRISEUS Holly / *Gray Catfish*

Range: Brazilian Amazon region, in small tributary streams.
Habits: Peaceful. Will not bother other fishes, even very small ones.
Water Conditions: Slightly alkaline water is best, with no salt content. Temperature about 25°C.
Size: About 5 cm.
Food Requirements: Although dried foods are picked up eagerly from the bottom, live foods should also be fed regularly.

It is possible that this rare little catfish has often been passed up by collectors who considered them a little plain for the average hobbyists' tastes. However, their greatest charm lies in their simplicity of color. It seems that there are never enough aquarists who are interested in the *Corydoras* species to propagate them in quantity. Catching these fish seems like simplicity itself: schools numbering in the hundreds can be seen browsing over a flat sandy bottom. A long seine is spread out and held in place, and then the fish are driven into this with another seine which is pulled along the bottom. A goodly amount of them are seen swimming ahead of the seine, and a large haul is anticipated. Then when the stationary net is approached and the fish see that they are about to be trapped, suddenly they seem to vanish into thin air (or should it be thin water?). They quickly bury themselves in the sand and let the net pass over them, coming up again and swimming away when the danger has passed.

CORYDORAS JULII Steindachner / *Leopard Catfish*

Range: Small tributaries of the lower Amazon.
Habits: Very peaceful and active. Constantly poking on the bottom for bits of food which were overlooked by the others.
Water Conditions: Not critical; best water is slightly alkaline and not very hard.
Size: To 6 cm.
Food Requirements: All sorts of foods are taken, but enough should be fed so that the catfish will get his share.

One of the most popular and attractive members of the *Corydoras* family is *Corydoras julii*. Fortunately the supply is usually good. It is a strange thing about the *Corydoras* catfishes: practically all of the fish we see for sale have been caught wild in South America and imported into this country. The *Corydoras* species are not as difficult to spawn as many others which our hatcheries produce, but nobody wants to spawn *Corydoras*. Like the Neon Tetra, it is cheaper to import them than it would be to raise them. If we were ever cut off commercially from South America (Heaven forbid!) our breeders would soon bend their efforts to producing *Corydoras,* and as a result the collectors would lose a good-sized chunk of business when things were straightened out again.

545

Corydoras griseus F D X 5 4 5 X N N 5
Corydoras julii F D X 5 4 6 X N N 6

[Dr. Herbert R. Axelrod]
[Dr. B. Frank]

Corydoras metae [F][D][X][5][4][7][X][N][N][6] [Dr. Herbert R. Axelrod]
Corydoras microps [F][D][X][5][4][8][X][N][N][6] [Dr. Herbert R. Axelrod]

CORYDORAS METAE Eigenmann / *Masked Corydoras, Bandit Catfish*

Range: Rio Meta, Colombia.
Habits: Peaceful and active.
Water Conditions: Medium soft water; pH slightly acid to slightly alkaline. Temperature 23 to 29°C.
Size: 6 cm.
Food Requirements: Accepts all foods, particularly tubifex worms.

This pretty catfish looks a lot like *C. arcuatus* and *C. myersi,* and the three are often confused by hobbyists. Unfortunately, while *C. metae* must be given the nod over the other two in good looks, it is seen less frequently and is therefore less often available to the hobbyist who would like to own some relatively pretty catfish. *Corydoras metae* will take part in a mass spawning activity in which the males and females gather round a central location and begin the ritual of laying, fertilizing and finally depositing the eggs. As with *Corydoras paleatus,* the females are more aggressive than the males in initiating the reproductive maneuvers; at the end of the courting actions the male lies passively on its side and allows the female to make contact between her mouth and the male's genital pore. Then the female swims to the place to deposit the eggs, usually a spot on the glass sides of the aquarium, cleans the spot with her mouth and in so doing deposits some of the sperm which she has taken from the male. With *C. metae* the eggs are deposited singly, and they soon become tough and tightly bound to the surface on which they're laid. The fry, which hatch in about five days, are large.

CORYDORAS MICROPS Eigenmann and Kennedy /*Light-Spot Catfish*

Range: Rio Sao Francisco, Sao Paulo, Paraguay, Rio de La Plata.
Habits: Peaceful.
Water Conditions: Neutral water, medium soft. Temperature 20 to 24°C.
Size: 6 cm.
Food Requirements: Takes all foods.

One of the more distinctively marked *Corydoras, C. microps* is no longer available in good quantity today, although it was at one time imported for a short while. Perhaps the reason that it was seen for so short a time is due to the fact that this catfish, coming as it does from a spot far removed from the equatorial regions where other South American species originate, is not suited to a really "tropical" tank with temperatures in the high 20's (°C). Under such conditions *Corydoras microps* is uncomfortable and becomes subject to diseases which would not plague it if it were kept in cooler water. *Corydoras microps* has never been bred in the home aquarium, but there is good reason to believe that it spawns in the same manner as its cousins within the genus *Corydoras.*

548

CORYDORAS MYERSI Miranda-Ribeiro / *Myers' Catfish*

Range: Small tributaries of the Amazon above the mouth of the Rio Negro.
Habits: Very peaceful and active; harmless to all but the smallest fry.
Water Conditions: Neutral to slightly alkaline. Temperature about 25°C.
Size: To 6 cm, usually a little smaller.
Food Requirements: All sorts of food are taken, but enough should be fed if other fishes are present to give the catfish their fair share.

Corydoras myersi is frequently sold in this country as *Corydoras rabauti*, but *C. rabauti* is a much smaller species from a different habitat. Probably aquarium hobbyists have never seen the real *C. rabauti* as yet. *C. myersi* is one of the few *Corydoras* species which the author has been privileged to observe in the act of spawning. There is a great deal of hustle and bustle, which ends with one of the males lying on his side on the bottom. The female swims up to him and nuzzles him in the region of the vent, at the same time releasing two or three eggs into a pocket formed by her ventral fins. She then swims up to a spot on the glass which was previously cleaned off and rubs her mouth against this spot. Then she pushes her belly against the same spot and the sticky eggs are pasted against the glass. A very interesting color change comes over the young: until they are about 1 cm long they are real beauties. The front half of the body, including the head, is green and the after half is red! Unfortunately these colors are not permanent and a remarkable thing happens: the green becomes darker and forms the stripe, while the red fades and covers the rest of the body.

CORYDORAS NATTERERI Steindachner / *Blue Catfish*

Range: Brazil, Rio de Janeiro to Sao Paulo.
Habits: Peaceful.
Water Conditions: Neutral, medium soft water. Temperature 22 to 28°C.
Size: Up to 8 cm.
Food Requirements: Accepts all regular foods.

Corydoras can very definitely be attractive, and their attractiveness is usually achieved through markings, such as stripes and spots, rather than through general body color. Although *Corydoras nattereri* does possess a stripe, this is not its distinctive feature, because stripes are not rare on the catfish, but color is. Unfortunately, the color of this fish is not always at its brightest, and it takes a while for this catfish to show up at its best. Rarely will *Corydoras nattereri* live up to its potential in the tanks of dealers, who have neither the time nor the space to give the fish the conditions it needs. In the tanks of a hobbyist who is willing to provide this little catfish with more than the bare essentials, however, it soon rewards its owner by assuming the coloration that sets it apart from all *Corydoras* species. Unfortunately, *Corydoras nattereri* is no longer in good supply.

Corydoras myersi F R X 5 4 9 X N N 6   [Dr. Herbert R. Axelrod]
Corydoras nattereri F D X 5 5 0 X N N 6   [Dr. Herbert R. Axelrod]

Corydoras paleatus ⟦F⟧⟦R⟧⟦X⟧⟦5⟧⟦5⟧⟦1⟧⟦X⟧⟦N⟧⟦N⟧⟦8⟧   [H. J. Richter]
Corydoras punctatus ⟦F⟧⟦D⟧⟦X⟧⟦5⟧⟦5⟧⟦2⟧⟦X⟧⟦N⟧⟦N⟧⟦5⟧   [Dr. Herbert R. Axelrod]

CORYDORAS PALEATUS Jenyns / *Peppered Corydoras*

Range: Southern Brazil and parts of northern Argentina.
Habits: Peaceful.
Water Conditions: Neutral, medium soft water. Temperature 21 to 27°C.
Size: Up to 8 cm.
Food Requirements: Accepts all regular aquarium foods; especially likes worms.
Color Variations: Original type was a dark gray fish with mottled patches of black on the body and spots on fins. An albino variety now exists.

Corydoras paleatus is a comparatively dark species with many dark blotches, irregularly joined, on its sides. This original variety was one of the first of the *Corydoras* species to become popular in this country, but it has fallen by the wayside and is no longer as popular as it once was. However, the fish has maintained at least a small degree of its past popularity in Germany, where the albino form was developed. One of the first *Corydoras* species to be bred (and one of the easiest), *C. paleatus* follows the pattern whereby the male, after an attentive courtship of the female, lies on his back or side and allows the female to lie across him, her mouth in contact with his underside. She then swims away from him and attaches her eggs, which have been expelled during the "contact" position, to a spot which she has cleaned with her mouth. This spot may be a leaf, a rock or a part of the aquarium glass. The first eggs are usually deposited singly, but as the process is repeated more eggs are deposited at each trip.

CORYDORAS PUNCTATUS (Bloch) / *Spotted Catfish*

Range: Guianas to the Amazon.
Habits: Peaceful; useful for picking up food missed by others.
Water Conditions: Neutral to slightly alkaline water. Temperature 23 to 24°C.
Size: To 5.5 cm.
Food Requirements: Willingly eats any kind of foods, but should get live or frozen foods several times a week.

Although this is a fairly common species of *Corydoras* to be found in the hobbyist aquarium, not a great deal is known about its behavior. The sexes are not hard to distinguish when the female is gravid; the female is larger when the fish is fully mature and sexually ripe females have a fuller belly. As a general rule this fish is not a picky eater and will accept most kinds of prepared aquarium foods.

Although breeding *C. punctatus* has been accomplished in the aquarium, it is not a common occurrence. Soft, dark bottom soil should be provided. Clumps of plants and rocks should be placed in the tank to provide hiding areas. Spawning is sometimes stimulated by a temperature change through the addition of fresh water. Several males should be placed with one ripe female.

CORYDORAS PYGMAEUS Knaack / *Dwarf Corydoras, Pygmy Corydoras*

Range: Amazon Basin, Mato Grosso, Paraguay.
Habits: Very peaceful and inoffensive.
Water Conditions: pH and hardness values not of great importance, as long as extremes are
   avoided. Temperature 21 to 29°C.
Size: 4 cm.
Food Requirements: Accepts all regular foods.

Here is a little catfish which represents a departure from normal *Corydoras*
body shape and behavior. First of all, it is a good bit smaller and more streamlined than other *Corydoras,* the difference in body shape being so marked as to
lead to this fish's being placed by some authorities into a separate genus,
Microdoras. Whatever its scientific standing, the Dwarf Corydoras is an interesting addition to a community tank. Contrary to the actions of its
relatives, *Corydoras pygmaeus* swims mainly in the middle reaches of the
water; it spends little time on the bottom, or at least much less than the other
Corydoras. Generally considered as one of the easiest catfishes to spawn and
raise, the Dwarf Corydoras goes through the rather frenzied mating procedure of the other catfishes, but the fish is much more likely to choose plants
for the site of egg deposition; the fry are large for so small a fish.

CORYDORAS RETICULATUS Fraser-Brunner / *Network Catfish*

Range: Amazon Basin.
Habits: Peaceful.
Water Conditions: Neutral to slightly alkaline, medium soft to slightly hard water.
   Temperature 22 to 28°C.
Size: About 5 cm.
Food Requirements: Takes all common aquarium foods, but not so fond of worms as other
   Corydoras.

Although this catfish is very rarely seen, it would make a nice addition to a
collection of *Corydoras,* for it is an attractive fish. The vermiform markings
covering the body and head give a striking appearance to the fish; luckily,
these markings are not subject to appearance or disappearance depending on
the mood or physical condition of the fish. The markings are always there in
fairly distinct form, although it is possible that they can become less clear
when the fish is kept under extremely poor conditions. *Corydoras reticulatus*
does, however, have one prominent marking which is not present at all times,
although, again, this is not subject to mood or to physical condition. Rather, it
is dependent on age; the spot is present in the dorsal fin of young specimens
but absent in the dorsal fin of older fish. Older fish, instead of having the spot,
have a pattern of small dark dashes similar to the markings in the tail, but less
dense.

Corydoras pygmaeus ⬚F⬚D⬚X⬚5⬚5⬚3⬚X⬚N⬚N⬚4 [Dr. Herbert R. Axelrod]
Corydoras reticulatus ⬚F⬚D⬚X⬚5⬚5⬚4⬚X⬚N⬚N⬚5 [Dr. Herbert R. Axelrod]

Corydoras schwartzi ⬚F⬚D⬚X⬚5⬚5⬚5⬚5⬚X⬚N⬚N⬚5   [Dr. Herbert R. Axelrod]

Corydoras simulatus ⬚F⬚D⬚X⬚5⬚5⬚6⬚X⬚N⬚N⬚6   [Dr. Herbert R. Axelrod]

CORYDORAS SCHWARTZI Rössel / *Schwartz's Corydoras*

Range: Brazil, near the mouth of the Purus River.
Habits: Peaceful in any kind of company.
Water Conditions: Not critical as long as the water is clean. Temperature 22 to 26°C.
Size: About 5 cm.
Food Requirements: Will scavenge uneaten food, but should be given their own tank if they are to be fed properly. Live or freeze-dried tubifex worms are ideal and should be alternated with good prepared foods.

Identifying the *Corydoras* species is becoming a constantly more difficult, almost impossible task. At the present time there are over 80 species known to the scientific world, with many more, no doubt, to be added. An interesting thing which is common to most *Corydoras* species which are kept in the hobbyist aquarium is how difficult they are to catch in the wild. When frightened, they quickly and expertly cover themselves with the bottom silt, allowing the seine that was meant to trap them to pass harmlessly over their heads. *Corydoras schwartzi* comes from an area around the mouth of the Rio Purus, which empties into the Amazon a little ways upriver from Manaus.

CORYDORAS SIMULATUS Weitzman & Nijssen / *Copy Catfish*

Range: Colombia's Rio Meta river system.
Habits: Peaceful and active.
Water Conditions: Medium soft water; pH slightly acid to slightly alkaline. Temperature to 29°C.
Size: 6 cm.
Food Requirements: Accepts all foods, particularly tubifex worms.

This little catfish looks very much like *Corydoras metae* and for many years was thought to be just that. Its name is derived from the Latin word *simulare*, meaning to imitate. This is due to the similarity in color pattern between this fish and *C. metae.*

C. simulatus spawns in mass. This activity takes place in a central location around which the males and females gather. Here they begin a ritual that includes egg laying, fertilizing and final depositing of the fertilized eggs. The females are more active than the males at initiating the reproductive behavior. When the courting is complete, the male lays passively on its side and allows the female to make contact between her mouth and the male's genital pore. After this action, the female leaves the male to find a suitable surface on which to lay her eggs. She first cleans the site with her mouth and simultaneously deposits the sperm from the male. Eggs are deposited one at a time and become tightly bound with the surface on which they are laid. The fry are large and hatch in four to five days.

CORYDORAS TREITLII Steindachner / *Long-Nose Corydoras*

Range: Eastern Brazil.
Habits: Peaceful.
Water Conditions: Neutral water desirable, but pH may vary slightly above or below this value; soft water not necessary, but advisable. Temperature 22 to 28°C.
Size: Up to 8 cm.
Food Requirements: Takes all regular aquarium foods.

Although this fish has been known to ichthyologists since 1906, when it was classified by Steindachner, it has never appeared in quantity on the American market, or at least not under its correct name. However, it was seen in Germany in the early 1930's, but it did not attract much attention there, even though German hobbyists worked with it for a while in an effort to breed it. It defied these efforts and soon dropped out of circulation, but not before it had stirred up a little controversy regarding its correct taxonomic stature. This was mainly because of the peculiarly shaped head which was different from the head shape of *Corydoras* species known to hobbyists at that time, being much more elongated. Because of a similarity in coloring, it was also supposed for a short time to be a variety of *Corydoras elegans*, but this point was later resolved.

CORYDORAS UNDULATUS Regan / *Wavy Catfish*

Range: Eastern South America, La Plata region.
Habits: Does not grub into the bottom like most other species; peaceful.
Water Conditions: Temperature 23 to 25°C. Tank should be clean, with no sediment on the bottom.
Size: Females 5 cm; males slightly smaller.
Food Requirements: This fish is not a scavenger, so it should be given generous quantities of live foods.

There are many species of *Corydoras*, and it seems that there are always more coming in. Because of the mistaken idea by many hobbyists that they are strictly scavengers which will live happily on the leavings of other fishes, they are too often kept one to a tank where they lead a miserable half-starved existence. The *Corydoras* have vigorous appetites, and in order to get them to breed they should be fed generously with living foods. Under these conditions they can be gotten to breed quite frequently. *Corydoras undulatus* has not been introduced in any numbers until quite recently, although it was first imported into Germany in 1909. So far there have been no accounts of their having been bred in captivity, but there is no doubt that their breeding procedure is no different from that of other members of the genus. Males are easily distinguished from the females: they are considerably smaller and much more slender. This species is very active and once they have become accustomed to a tank will live for a long time.

Corydoras treitlii ⬚Ⓕ⬚Ⓓ⬚Ⓧ⬚⑤⬚⑤⬚⑤⬚⑦⬚Ⓧ⬚Ⓝ⬚Ⓝ⬚⑦ [Dr. Herbert R. Axelrod]
Corydoras undulatus ⬚Ⓕ⬚Ⓓ⬚Ⓧ⬚⑤⬚⑤⬚⑧⬚Ⓧ⬚Ⓝ⬚Ⓝ⬚⑦ [Dr. Herbert R. Axelrod]

[Burkhard Kahl]

Corydoras julii
F D T 5 5 9 X N N 6

Corydoras aeneus
F D M 5 5 9 X N N 7

Corydoras hastatus
F D B 5 5 9 X N N 4

Corydoras melanistius melanistius
F D T 5 6 0 X N N 5

Corydoras schultzei
F D M 5 6 0 X N N 5

Corydoras pygmaeus
F D B 5 6 0 X N N 4

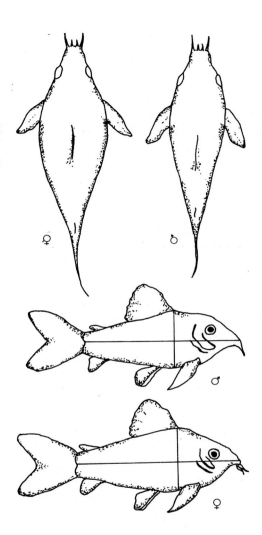

Schematic diagrams showing the sex differences between the male and female *Corydoras.* The female has a thicker body than the male, and a side view shows the female deeper in body than the male.

The following four black and white pages and four color pages are of *Corydoras* species which are identified but not further discussed. These fishes are not very popular. They do, however, appear from time to time and are included herein for identification purposes. Drawings are by Ingeborg Weirich.

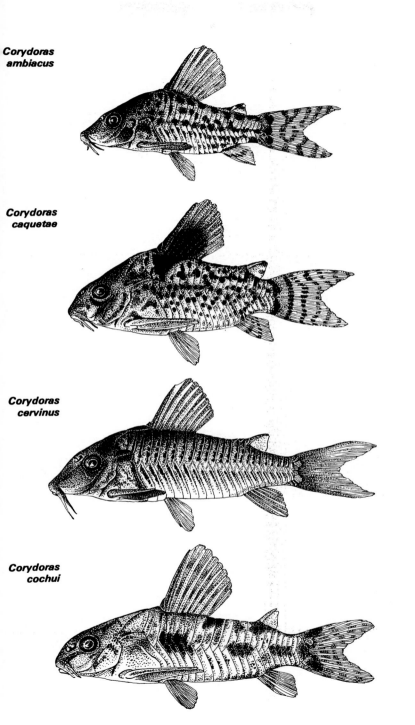

*Corydoras
ambiacus*

*Corydoras
caquetae*

*Corydoras
cervinus*

*Corydoras
cochui*

Corydoras armatus [F][D][X][5][6][1][X][N][N][5]   [Dr. Herbert R. Axelrod]
Corydoras axelrodi [F][D][X][5][6][2][X][N][N][5]   [Dr. Herbert R. Axelrod]

Corydoras bondi [F][D][X][5][6][3][X][N][N][5]
Corydoras deckeri [F][D][X][5][6][4][X][N][N][5]

[Dr. Herbert R. Axelrod]
[Dr. Herbert R. Axelrod]

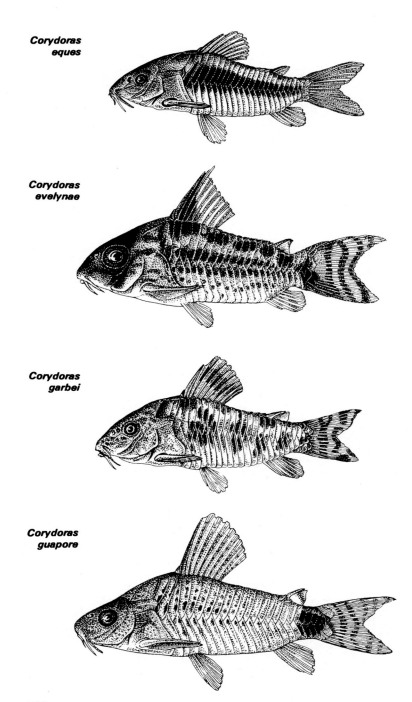

*Corydoras
eques*

*Corydoras
evelynae*

*Corydoras
garbei*

*Corydoras
guapore*

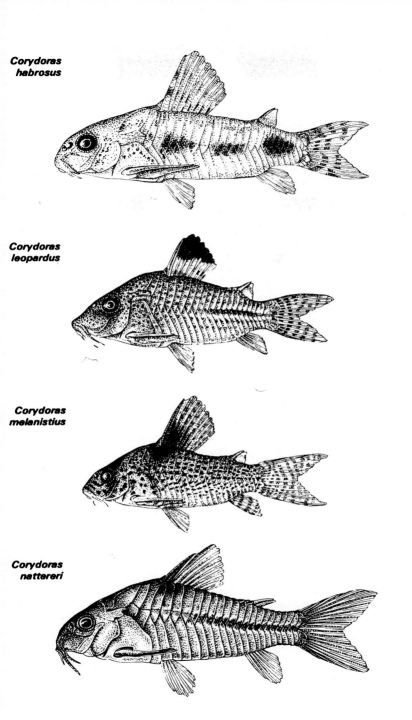

Corydoras
habrosus

Corydoras
leopardus

Corydoras
melanistius

Corydoras
nattereri

Corydoras haraldschultzi ⬛Ⓕ Ⓓ ⓧ ⑤ ⑥ ⑤ ⓧ Ⓝ Ⓝ ⑥   [Dr. Herbert R. Axelrod]

Corydoras melini Ⓕ Ⓓ ⓧ ⑤ ⑥ ⑥ ⓧ Ⓝ Ⓝ ⑤   [Dr. Herbert R. Axelrod]

Corydoras osteocarus ⑤ ⑤ ⑤ ⑤ ⑤ ⑤ ⑤ ⑤ ⑤ ⑤   [Dr. Herbert R. Axelrod]

Corydoras sterbai ⑤ ⑤ ⑤ ⑤ ⑤ ⑤ ⑤ ⑤ ⑤ ⑤   [Dr. Herbert R. Axelrod]

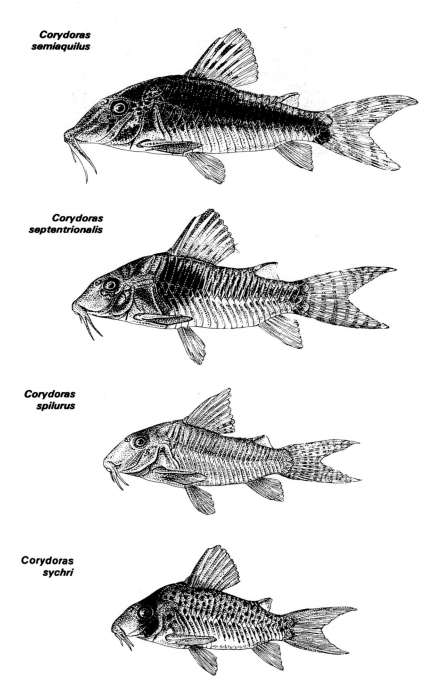

*Corydoras
semiaquilus*

*Corydoras
septentrionalis*

*Corydoras
spilurus*

*Corydoras
sychri*

568

CORYNOPOMA RIISEI Gill / *Swordtailed Characin*

Range: Trinidad, Colombia and Venezuela.
Habits: Peaceful and hardy; a good community fish.
Water Conditions: Not critical. Temperature between 22 to 28°C. A sunny, well-planted tank and clear water show it at its best.
Size: Males 6 cm; females 5 cm.
Food Requirements: Will take prepared foods. Best foods are daphnia, tubifex worms and especially white worms, of which they are very fond.

What first strikes the eye is the magnificent finnage of the males and also a peculiar paddle-like extension of the gill plates, which reaches more than halfway down the sides of the males. What the exact function of these extensions is has been argued back and forth for many years. They are kept folded back except during courtship, when the male swims toward the female with these paddles extended at right angles. Strangely enough, there seems to be some sort of internal fertilization, because females which have been separated from their mates for some time have surprised their owners by laying eggs which hatched!

COTTUS BAIRDI Girard / *Mottled Sculpin*

Range: North America from about the Tennessee River system of Alabama and Georgia to Labrador, west to Lake Manitoba in Canada. A second area of distribution includes parts of Washington, Oregon, Idaho, Montana and adjacent regions of southwestern Canada.
Habits: Because of the temperature needs, the Mottled Sculpin should be given a tank by itself.
Water Conditions: Best to use water from the stream it was collected in. Needs clean, clear water with a temperature of 5 to 18°C.
Size: Reaches a length of over 13 cm.
Food Requirements: Prefers live foods such as stonefly nymphs, chironomids, aquatic crustaceans, etc.

For best results the Mottled Sculpin needs clear, cool, unpolluted water with a high oxygen content. This is reflected in the clear mountain streams and riffle areas of narrow woodland creeks that it inhabits.

Spawning has been accomplished in an aquarium. An 80-liter tank was used with the bottom covered with about 5 cm of well-washed river sand and gravel. The water was filtered water from the area where the fish were captured. Strong aeration and filtration were provided, with the temperature about 15 to 17°C (spawning in nature was seen when the water temperature was as low as 10°C). A wide flat stone set at an angle can provide the fish with shelter (normally they hide under rocks). The male should be placed in the aquarium first and then the female shortly after. The male will court the female, sometimes resorting to a nip or two to hurry things along, until she decides to follow him to his chosen nest site (which is usually under the flat rock). The eggs are deposited on the roof of the cave and fertilized there, after which the female leaves or is driven off.

Corynopoma riisei F Q X 5 6 9 X N N 6   [R. Zukal]

Cottus bairdi F A X 5 7 0 X N N B   [D. H. Lewis]

Craterocephalus stercusmuscarum [Dr. Herbert R. Axelrod]

F D X 5 7 1 X N N 8

1. *Crenicara filamentosa* ♂ F E M 5 7 2 X N N 8   [H. J. Richter]
2. *Crenicara filamentosa* ♀ F F B 5 7 2 X N N 8   [H. J. Richter]

CRATEROCEPHALUS STERCUSMUSCARUM Günther
Fly-Specked Hardyhead

Range: East coastal drainage system of Queensland, Australia.
Habits: Fairly peaceful; a good jumper and fast swimmer.
Water Conditions: Soft, slightly acid water. Temperature 24 to 27°C.
Size: To 13 cm.
Food Requirements: Not a choosy eater. Will take prepared as well as live or frozen foods.

This fish is seldom seen in this part of the world because it is rarely imported. With the exception of rainbowfishes, atherinids are seldom kept in the aquarium hobby. These fish typically produce large eggs that have many long filaments. These filaments are adhesive and cause the eggs to become attached to the surrounding vegetation in the water.

CRENICARA FILAMENTOSA Ladiges / *Checkerboard Lyretail*

Range: Rio Negro area of the Amazon Basin.
Habits: Peaceful with other species, but somewhat combative among themselves.
Water Conditions: Not critical.
Size: Up to about 8 cm for males; slightly smaller for females.
Food Requirements: Does best on live foods, especially small crustaceans, but will accept most prepared foods.

Crenicara filamentosa is a demure dwarf cichlid species that often goes unappreciated because it is not seen at its best. Often it is imported almost by accident and finds its way into shipments of tetras and other South American staple sellers, eventually to end up as part of a tankful of "mixed dwarf cichlids" in a dealer's showroom. When it is in good coloration, however, the fish is easily appreciated because of its elegant good looks, and at its absolute best (which is when it's spawning) it is breathtaking. At spawning time the male and female *C. filamentosa* trade their basic color and pattern for much more eye-catching dress. The change is especially dramatic in the male, because his entire body becomes very dark brown, almost black, highlighted by beautiful green and blue iridescence.

The species spawns on broad leaves or flat rocks, and the eggs are guarded very jealously by the female, who will actively attack intruders, including the male. Usually there is no male-female confrontation, because the male makes no attempt to get involved with the eggs and stays well clear of the female. *Crenicara filamentosa* shows to its best advantage when maintained only in the company of its own species, but it will live well with other dwarf cichlids if the fishes are accommodated in a tank large enough to allow the establishment of territories without fighting. It is not a very scary species and will remain within view unless housed in tanks that contain bigger and more aggressive fishes.

1. *Crenicara filamentosa,* male (p571).
2. *Crenicara filamentosa,* female above eggs on a leaf (p571).

CRENICARA MACULATA (Steindachner) / *Checkerboard Cichlid*

Range: Central Amazon region.
Habits: Fairly peaceful, but should have their own tank.
Water Conditions: Soft, neutral to slightly acid water. Temperature about 25°C.
Size: Males 10 cm; females to 5 cm.
Food Requirements: Varied live foods.
Color Variations: Body yellowish with two rows of alternate square spots on the sides. Male's ventral fins have blue and orange streaks.

Many hobbyists who have seen the Checkerboard Cichlid were not unduly impressed at first. This is because the fish is seldom seen under the best conditions. Put a lot of half-grown fish in a bare tank and they hardly ever rate a second look. But put a fully grown pair which is ready to spawn into a well-planted tank which is to their liking and you have a male which will outshine most of the cichlid family. The Checkerboard Cichlid is a fish which, it seems, nobody can produce in quantity. A pair will produce a beautiful spawning and the next time under identical conditions everything will go wrong. Possibly with this fish the time of sexual ripeness varies between spawnings, and a pair which achieves this state once may not come due again at the same time. Keeping several pairs and observing them closely would probably do the trick, but good pairs are quite expensive and not easily come by. This is a member of the cichlid family which is just about too big to be considered a dwarf cichlid and still too small to be called a regular-sized one. Although it has been known to science since 1875, aquarium hobbyists did not see it until 1938.

CRENICARA PUNCTULATA (Günther) / *Hercules Cichlid*

Range: Upper Amazon and Peru.
Habits: Very sensitive for a cichlid; prefers hiding in dark corners.
Water Conditions: Prefers warm, soft, slightly acid water.
Size: To 10 cm.
Food Requirements: Prefers small earthworms, bits of beef and frozen brine shrimp. Eats coarse grained dry foods, especially pelletized foods.
Color Variations: During spawning the males become very colorful.

Cichlids are, as a general rule, among the most popular fishes to keep in one's aquarium. But when they want to spawn, they will tear up all the plants and attack fishes that come near their nest. This species acts more like an African cichlid than a South American cichlid. It hides on the bottom and prefers dark corners to an open stone. Every time we saw a pair spawn it ate its eggs, so not much information about their spawning is available. At any rate, fishes of the genus *Crenicara* spawn very readily, so it shouldn't be anticipated that there will be any trouble with this species.

Crenicara maculata F D X 5 7 3 X N N 5
Crenicara punctulata F A X 5 7 4 X N N 8

[K. Paysan]
[Braz Walker]

Crenicichla dorsocellata F C X 5 7 5 X N N 7   [Harald Schultz]

Crenicichla geayi F D X 5 7 6 X N N B   [Dr. Herbert R. Axelrod]

CRENICICHLA DORSOCELLATA Haseman / *Eye-Spot Pike Cichlid*

Range: Amazon River and its tributaries near Santarem and Manaus.
Habits: Slightly more peaceful than the other *Crenicichla* species, but cannot be trusted with other fishes. Should be provided with a number of hiding places as retreats for any which are attacked.
Water Conditions: Not critical. Temperature 24 to 26°C.
Size: Up to 20 cm in their native waters.
Food Requirements: Generous feedings of live foods are necessary. They take dried foods only when very hungry.

Many beautiful fishes are shunned by hobbyists because of their vicious, predatory habits. This is often the case with the *Crenicichla* species. Without a doubt they are handsome fishes, but to keep them in company with other fishes would be placing the lives or at least the fins of their tankmates in jeopardy. There is a *Crenicichla* species, *Crenicichla alta,* which is known as "sunfish" in Guyana. This fish has a gorgeous array of colors, but it is the most hated predator of all the fishes in that country. Fish farms which store fishes for shipment abroad will sometimes get a tiny "sunfish" into one of their pools and not have any inkling that it is there until the ragged fins and dead bodies of the other fishes are noticed. The culprit must then be netted out and removed before the pool can yield any more saleable fishes again. *Crenicichla dorsocellata,* although it is a fairly nasty customer, is not quite so ferocious as its cousins.

CRENICICHLA GEAYI Pellegrin / *Half-Banded Pike Cichlid*

Range: Central Amazon region.
Habits: Predatory and vicious. Can only be trusted with fishes with similar habits in large aquaria.
Water Conditions: Not critical. Temperature 23 to 25°C.
Size: To 20 cm; imported specimens usually much smaller.
Food Requirements: Large living foods, preferably live smaller fishes.

The Half-Banded Pike Cichlid is another of the "rough customers" among the cichlid group. This one does not even have the distinction of having any gay colors to ornament it, but it is a good illustration of how a fish's color and markings can be an asset to its habits when it is on the lookout for a meal, which is almost constantly during the daylight hours. Picture this fish almost motionless in a clump of aquatic plants. The resemblance to a slime-covered twig with shadows of plant leaves on it would be close enough to deceive any smaller fish and lull it into a very false sense of security. When the prey gets close enough a rush of that torpedo-shaped body, followed by a gulp of that big mouth, reduces the small fish population by one and the Pike Cichlid is already thinking about how good the next victim will taste. As is the case with most predators, at spawning time they usually become the best of parents.

CRENICICHLA LEPIDOTA Heckel / *Pike Cichlid*

Range: From the Amazon south to northern Argentina.
Habits: A predator which cannot be trusted with other fishes, especially those of a size it can swallow. Tank should be well-planted and afford a number of hiding places.
Water Conditions: Not critical. Temperature 23 to 25°C.
Size: To 20 cm.
Food Requirements: Large living foods, preferably smaller fishes.

The *Crenicichla* species have very little to recommend them. True, they are not unattractive to the eye, but in mixed company they are real terrors. They select a spot among the plants where they are likely to be unobserved, and when a smaller fish swims by they dart out, pike-like, and swallow it. In order to keep them in the best of shape, their owners should have a constant supply of larger-sized live foods like larvae and water-beetle larvae, or best of all some "expendable" smaller fishes like Guppies which are either deformed or do not make the grade as fancy stock with the Guppy breeders. As is usually the case with "nasty" cichlids, a well-mated pair almost always proves to be good parents. Spawning takes place in a depression in the gravel, and a great number of small white eggs result. When the fry hatch the male takes charge of the brood, but the female need not be removed. She soon realizes that she must keep her distance, and does so. While guarding eggs and fry, they should be fed heavily to lessen the temptation to eat their own eggs and fry.

1. *Crenicichla lepidota* (p578).
2. *Crenicichla strigata* (p578).
3. *Crenicichla wallacei* (p578).

Crenicichla lepidota will swallow any fish small enough to stuff in its mouth. Photo by H. Schultz.

Crenicichla lepidota ⬚F⬚ ⬚C⬚ ⬚X⬚ ⬚5⬚ ⬚7⬚ ⬚7⬚ ⬚X⬚ ⬚N⬚ ⬚N⬚ ⬚B⬚   [Harald Schultz]

Crenicichla strigata ⬚F⬚ ⬚D⬚ ⬚M⬚ ⬚5⬚ ⬚7⬚ ⬚8⬚ ⬚X⬚ ⬚N⬚ ⬚N⬚ ⬚C⬚   [Aaron Norman]
Crenicichla wallacei ⬚F⬚ ⬚C⬚ ⬚B⬚ ⬚5⬚ ⬚7⬚ ⬚8⬚ ⬚X⬚ ⬚N⬚ ⬚N⬚ ⬚8⬚   [Harald Schultz]

1. *Crenuchus spilurus* 〔F〕〔A〕〔T〕〔5〕〔7〕〔9〕〔X〕〔N〕〔N〕〔6〕   [Dr. Herbert R. Axelrod]
2. *Crenuchus spilurus* 〔F〕〔B〕〔M〕〔5〕〔7〕〔9〕〔X〕〔N〕〔N〕〔6〕   [Dr. Karl Knaack]

Ctenobrycon spilurus 〔F〕〔D〕〔X〕〔5〕〔8〕〔0〕〔X〕〔N〕〔N〕〔7〕   [Dr. Herbert R. Axelrod]

CRENUCHUS SPILURUS Günther / *Sailfin Tetra*

Range: Guyana and central Amazon region.
Habits: Probably a predator; do not keep them with any smaller fishes.
Water Conditions: Soft, definitely acid water is required. Temperature 24 to 26°C, never lower.
Size: To 6 cm.
Food Requirements: All sorts of live foods, preferably the larger ones like cut-up earthworms and young livebearers.

We hear some conflicting things about this very beautiful tetra. One authority says they are peaceful, but the concensus seems to be that they are predatory and may not be trusted in mixed company. Judging by the size of the mouth, we are inclined to side with the latter school of thought. There are also two camps on the question of spawning habits. All authorities agree that the fry have never been raised, but some say that they spawn characin-fashion among plant leaves while others have them laying their eggs on rocks and large-leaved plants. According to one source, the eggs are bright red and are guarded cichlid-fashion by the male.

1. *Crenuchus spilurus,* male (p579).
2. *Crenuchus spilurus* (p579).

CTENOBRYCON SPILURUS (Cuvier & Valenciennes) / *Silver Tetra*

Range: Northern South America from Surinam to Venezuela.
Habits: Peaceful with fishes of its own size or larger, but likely to pick on smaller ones.
Water Conditions: They prefer clean water, and their tank should be large. Temperature may range from 20 to 25°C.
Size: About 8 cm.
Food Requirements: Greedy eaters, they may extend their appetites to some of the plants. Will also take all kinds of dried foods.

Many people buy this fish at a stage where they are half-grown because of their lively habits and pretty silvery coloring. After they have had them for some months, they find that the fish has grown to a size much larger then they have bargained for. In a large aquarium and with no smaller fish to pick on, the Silver Tetra will live for a long time and always be out in front where they can be readily seen at all times. Breeding them does not present much difficulty; given enough room and a partial change of water, driving is apt to be vigorous and some plants uprooted. A large female may produce as many as 2000 eggs. Mating is accomplished by the pair swimming with tilted bodies in tight circles. As with most of the tetra family, the parents must be removed as soon as they have finished spawning or they will find most of the eggs and eat them. Fry emerge after 50 to 70 hours and become free-swimming after the third or fourth day. Once they have put on a little growth they are easily raised, and what to do with them all may become a problem.

CTENOLUCIUS HUJETA (Valenciennes) / *Blunt-Nosed Gar, Hujeta*

Range: Tropical South America.
Habits: Aggressive; eats small fishes and flying insects. A jumper, so keep the tank covered. A nocturnal fish.
Water Conditions: Not sensitive to changes in water conditions. Does well in water from 21 to 29°C with a pH from 6.0 to 7.6. Prefers soft water, but doesn't suffer too much in hard water.
Size: Up to 25 cm.
Food Requirements: Loves floating insects or live baby Guppies.

The author (HRA) collected this specimen in the northern Rio Branco. The specimen was 20 cm long. It was collected at night with a dip net as the fish was swimming on the surface of the water. The snout is very interesting and there is an external flap of skin projecting from the lower jaw. The upper jaw folds over the lower jaw giving this harmful-looking fish a disadvantage of having an inferior mouth. Its teeth are relatively small and it either swallows its prey whole or jumps for small flying insects.

CTENOPOMA ACUTIROSTRE Pellegrin / *Leopard Ctenopoma*

Range: Middle and lower Congo River tributaries.
Habits: Predatory; should never be kept with fish they can swallow. Peaceful with larger fishes; inclined to be shy in small tanks.
Water Conditions: Not critical. Temperature 25 to 28°C.
Size: To 15 cm; usually much smaller in captivity.
Food Requirements: Any food with a high meat or fish content; very fond of smaller live fish, pieces of earthworm, etc. Frozen brine shrimp is excellent.

The Leopard Ctenopoma is one of the most handsome members of the genus and is a model citizen among a mixed group, as long as its tankmates are of a size where they cannot be swallowed. This size must be figured generously, because the Leopard Ctenopoma has a large mouth. This fish is also a predator which hunts and consumes smaller fishes in its native waters, where it is a very hardy and durable fish which inhabits bodies of water that frequently become quite foul in the dry season. In the aquarium they like their food in large chunks, just small enough that they can be swallowed.

Although some of the other *Ctenopoma* species have been spawned, we have no records of this feat having been accomplished with this one. The *Ctenopoma* species may well be described as the "gouramis" of Africa. Labyrinth fishes are very scarce in this part of the world. This species has been known to science for quite a time; Pellegrin named them in 1899, and they were first made available to hobbyists in 1952.

Ctenolucius hujeta F D X 5 8 1 X N N D   [Dr. Herbert R. Axelrod]
Ctenopoma acutirostre F D X 5 8 2 X N N B   [H. J. Richter]

1. *Ctenopoma ansorgei* 🄵🄰🆇🄵🄼🄵🅇🄼🄼🄵 [Dr. R.J. Goldstein]
2. *Ctenopoma ansorgei* 🄵🅀🆇🄵🄼🅀🅇🄼🄼🄵 [H. J. Richter]

CTENOPOMA ANSORGEI (Boulenger) / *Ornate Ctenopoma*

Range: Tropical West Africa.
Habits: Peaceful when given plenty of space and kept with fishes of the same size or larger.
Water Conditions: Not critical, but the water must be kept warm, 25 to 29°C.
Size: To 7 cm.
Food Requirements: Large live foods, preferably small living fish. Cut-up earthworms or pieces of beef heart are also taken greedily.
Color Variations: Body brownish, with 6 or 7 bluish to greenish bars on the sides, extending into the dorsal and anal fins.

Africa has few labyrinth fishes to offer, and members of the genus *Ctenopoma* are almost the only ones. Most of them make good aquarium citizens, but they must be kept with fishes of their own size or larger. They usually will not harm a fish they cannot swallow, but they can handle a sizeable mouthful, having a large mouth. *Ctenopoma ansorgei* is easily the most attractive member of the family with its alternating reddish and bluish bars which not only cross the body but also extend into the dorsal and anal fins. The *Ctenopoma* species are quite hardy and might even be classified as "tough," but *C. ansorgei* is a bit of an exception in that it is somewhat sensitive to lowered temperatures. This species has been spawned in captivity. The male, distinguished by its brighter colors, is said to build a firm bubblenest. The young are easy to raise. This fish is a greedy eater and very fond of the larger live foods, especially small fishes. Their tank should be a roomy, well-planted one. It is interesting to watch a *Ctenopoma* stalk its prey. It glides rather than swims, its large eyes never losing sight of its prey. An unbelievably quick lunge, and the little fish is gone!

1. *Ctenopoma ansorgei* (p583).
2. *Ctenopoma ansorgei* pair in the aquarium (p583).

Ctenopoma ansorgei in a spawning embrace. Photo by H.J. Richter.

CTENOPOMA CONGICUM (Boulenger) / *Congo Ctenopoma*

Range: Lower Congo River.
Habits: Fairly peaceful with larger fishes. Likes a large, well-planted tank.
Water Conditions: Not critical, but temperature should be kept high, about 25°C.
Size: To 8 cm.
Food Requirements: Large live foods, small living fishes preferred. They can be trained to accept pieces of fish, shrimp, etc.

This is one of the less attractive members of the family; it has only an indistinct mottled pattern on the sides. The only distinct mark is a bright "eye-spot" at the base of the tail. It has been proven with some of the marine butterflyfishes that this "eye" at the other end of the body serves to confuse an enemy or a prospective meal. Whether this is also true with this species has never been observed, but it has been found that these eye-spots usually serve such a purpose. For instance, there is a moth with a large eye-spot on each under-wing which uses these spots to frighten away birds by imitating the eyes of an owl. *Ctenopoma congicum* is said to be quite easy to spawn, although the feat is seldom attempted because of the small demand for this fish. The male chooses a dark corner of the tank, often a spot under a floating leaf. Here he builds a bubblenest. When this is completed he concentrates on getting the female to cooperate by getting under the nest. He wraps his body around her like a *Betta* and everything proceeds accordingly. Eggs hatch in 24 to 30 hours and the fry become free-swimming in 2 to 3 days.

CTENOPOMA KINGSLEYI (Günther) / *Kingsley's Ctenopoma*

Range: Widely scattered from Senegal to the Congo region.
Habits: Very predatory and nasty; should not be kept with other fishes.
Water Conditions: Not critical, but temperature should be high, about 25°C.
Size: To 20 cm.
Food Requirements: Will eat just about everything, but prefers living fish.

Ctenopoma kingsleyi is the largest known species of the ctenopomas. It is also the least desirable species to keep. It gets big, up to 20 cm, and quite nasty. This species could be easily confused with *C. congicum*. There is also an eye-spot of sorts on the caudal base but no pattern on the sides. This unusual group of fishes occurs in places where the water sometimes partly dries out. They are able to cover considerable distances over land and through wet grass, thanks to their air-breathing ability. When the pool in which they are living dries out, they hop out and flop along until they locate another pool. They do not have the panicky terror which most fish have when out of water and seldom get stranded; they usually manage to find a pool before they dry out. Because of their lack of colors, large size and predatory habits this fish is seldom exported from Africa, and we scarcely ever see them.

Ctenopoma congicum F D X 5 8 5 X N N 8   [J. Elias]
Ctenopoma kingsleyi F D X 5 8 6 X N N B   [H. J. Richter]

Ctenopoma oxyrhynchus ⬚F⬚ ⬚C⬚ ⬚X⬚ ⬚5⬚ ⬚8⬚ ⬚7⬚ ⬚X⬚ ⬚N⬚ ⬚N⬚ ⬚5⬚   [Dr. Herbert R. Axelrod]
Cubanichthys cubensis ⬚F⬚ ⬚R⬚ ⬚X⬚ ⬚5⬚ ⬚8⬚ ⬚8⬚ ⬚X⬚ ⬚N⬚ ⬚N⬚ ⬚4⬚   [S. Frank]

CTENOPOMA OXYRHYNCHUS (Boulenger) / *Mottled Ctenopoma*

Range: Tributaries of the lower Congo River.
Habits: Peaceful with fishes of the same size or larger.
Water Conditions: Not critical, but temperatures should be kept high, 26 to 29°C.
Size: To 10 cm.
Food Requirements: Larger live foods preferred, especially living fishes.

Ctenopoma oxyrhynchus is one of the beauties of the group. Its marbled sides and varying shades and the fact that it does not grow as big as most of its cousins makes it the most desirable member of a not very desirable genus. According to Ladiges, the younger specimens have a coloration very similar to the South American Leaf Fish and stalk their prey in the same manner. As they grow older the permanent markings appear. The females are distinguished by their more rounded fins. This species does not build a bubblenest like the others, nor is one needed. The eggs have an oil content which makes them lighter than water and causes them to float at the surface. During this time the tank should be tightly covered. Like the other *Ctenopoma* species, this one also requires warm water. Breeding temperatures should be 28 to 29°C. An uncovered tank where the fish are kept at high temperatures and are gulping atmospheric air at room temperatures would obviously lead to trouble unless the room is heated to tank temperatures. Eggs hatch in 24 to 32 hours and the fry become free-swimming in 2 to 3 days. Having a large mouth, they are easily fed and grow rapidly.

CUBANICHTHYS CUBENSIS (Eigenmann) / *Cuban Minnow*

Range: Western Cuba.
Habits: Will do well in an uncrowded and well-planted aquarium; although it sometimes occurs in brackish waters, an addition of salt is unnecessary.
Water Conditions: Should be kept in a sunny location. Temperature 24 to 26°C.
Size: About 4 cm; usually smaller.
Food Requirements: This species will seldom eat dried foods unless very hungry. All sorts of living foods are taken.

The scientific name of this attractive little fish means "Cuban fish from Cuba." This fish shares a breeding habit with a few of the other cyprinodonts. Instead of a few single eggs being expelled at a time and hung on plants, the female expels the eggs in a bunch, and they hang like a tiny bunch of grapes on a string from her vent. This string is quite durable, and she may swim around with it for hours before it is torn off, leaving the eggs hanging on a plant leaf or anything she might brush against. The fry hatch after 10 to 12 days and are very small at first. The water should be kept warm, about 25°C, and for the first week infusoria should be fed. Once they have grown to where they can take brine shrimp, the rest is fairly easy.

CULAEA INCONSTANS (Kirtland) / *Brook Stickleback, Five-Spined Stickleback*

Range: Northeastern and north-central United States into southern Canada.
Habits: A mildly aggressive fish except during the breeding season, when the males become extremely pugnacious.
Water Conditions: Neutral to slightly alkaline, moderately hard water. Temperature 5 to 18°C.
Size: 8 cm.
Food Requirements: Strictly carnivorous, preferring live foods, but will adapt to bits of fresh meat.

The Brook Stickleback normally inhabits cool waters, but it can be kept in the low twenties (°C) if its aquarium is well aerated. (Fish that have evolved in cool water have functionally adapted to the higher oxygen content of that water.) In addition, it will readily breed at this temperature.

The male stakes out a territory and begins to build a bullet-shaped nest constructed of bits of dead plant leaves, threads of algae and particles of fine sand. This material is cemented together into a hollow tubular shape with a material that is secreted by the male's kidneys. The male then lures a ripe female into the nest. As part of their highly ritualized spawning behavior the male gently nudges the posterior end of the female that remains just outside the nest. This seems to be the releaser that causes the female to expel her eggs. The female then breaks through the opposite end of the nest as the male swims into the nest behind her to fertilize the eggs. Before the male takes up his guard duties, several other females may be lured into the nest to spawn. Finally, the male chases all the females away and positions himself just outside the nest as he continually fans fresh water through the nest by using his pectoral fins or tail. Occasionally he will swim into the nest to "inspect" the eggs and remove the dead ones. The eggs will hatch in about a week at 21°C, and the fry become free-swimming in a few days.

CURIMATA MICROCEPHALA Eigenmann & Eigenmann / *Curimata*

Range: Northern Brazil.
Habits: Peaceful; may be a plant nipper.
Water Conditions: Soft, slightly acid water. Temperature 23 to 26°C.
Size: About 8 cm.
Food Requirements: Eats all kinds of foods.

Members of this species are disregarded or discarded by collectors, who net them frequently but have no use for this fish. Many hobbyists consider *C. microcephala* colorless and uninteresting. Hobbyists who want colorful specimens or those which have interesting habits to make them desirable usually pass this fish by.

589

Culaea inconstans [F][D][X][5][8][9][X][N][N][7]
Curimata microcephala [F][D][X][5][9][0][X][N][N][8]

[Aaron Norman]
[Harald Schultz]

Cyclocheilichthys apogon ꜰ ʀ X 5 9 1 X ɴ ɴ C   [Dr. Herbert R. Axelrod]
Cynolebias adloffi ꜰ ʀ X 5 9 2 X ɴ ɴ 5   [Harald Schultz]

CYCLOCHEILICHTHYS APOGON (Valenciennes) / *Skin-Head Barb*

Range: Java, Borneo, Sumatra and other islands of the East Indies to Malaysia, Burma and Thailand.
Habits: Peaceful; does well in a community aquarium with fishes its own size.
Water Conditions: Not critical. Temperature 21 to 24°C.
Size: To about 25 cm, but not reaching quite that size in aquaria.
Food Requirements: Will take most aquarium foods that are "wet" (brine shrimp, beef heart, etc.) or live. Not particularly fond of dried foods.

Cyclocheilichthys apogon, when kept alone, is a peaceful, quiet fish moving sedately around the aquarium in contrast to the other barbs that seem always to be on the move. When more active fishes are added to the aquarium the *C. apogon* increases its activity also, perhaps caught up in the motion of the others or just to get its share of the food. It has been said that it becomes very quiet in confined quarters, perhaps as a result of the reduced oxygen supply.

The tank can be set up in a variety of ways, but this fish prefers plenty of vegetation where it can find shady places to "hang out" for a while. The plants will not be disturbed.

CYNOLEBIAS ADLOFFI Ahl / *Banded Pearl Fish*

Range: Southeastern Brazil.
Habits: Should be kept by themselves. Males become scrappy.
Water Conditions: Tank should have a layer of about an inch of peat moss on the bottom. Temperature 22 to 25°C.
Size: Males to 5 cm; females a little smaller.
Food Requirements: Live foods of all kinds which are small enough for easy swallowing.

There is no problem distinguishing between males and females in the Banded Pearl Fish, or for that matter any other *Cynolebias* species. The female has almost no color, and the male often seems to have enough for both. Besides, note carefully the great difference in the dorsal and anal fins of the two sexes; one would swear that they were different species! Although they are extremely interesting fishes and beautiful as well, we do not see them offered very frequently for sale. Dealers are reluctant to stock them. Their short life span necessitates making a quick sale, and customers who expect to have their fish for a long time often complain bitterly when their fish dies a perfectly natural death after two or three months. If one can get a few half-grown specimens, it is an amazing thing to see how quickly they grow and blossom into full adulthood. Spawning them is an easy matter. A layer of peat moss on the bottom and a healthy pair is all that is needed. After the female has become considerably thinner the peat moss is netted out and stored in a slightly moist state for three to five months. Eggs hatch in a few hours after the peat moss is put back in the water.

CYNOLEBIAS ALEXANDRI Castello and Lopez / *Entre Rios Pearl Fish*

Range: State of Entre Rios, Argentina.
Habits: Pugnacious with members of its own species; generally peaceful with other fishes.
Water Conditions: Not critical.
Size: To about 5 cm.
Food Requirements: Accepts most meaty foods.

This attractive annual fish is relatively new to science, having been described in 1974; the description appeared in the September, 1974 issue of *Tropical Fish Hobbyist* magazine, with Drs. Hugo Patricio Castello and Rogelio Bartolome Lopez as the authors. Like the other known *Cynolebias* species, it is an annual fish that lays its eggs at the bottom of ponds that dry out during the South American summer; when the ponds again fill up, the fry are liberated and take up their short lives, repeating the spawning process before they die when the ponds dry up again. Under aquarium conditions, *C. alexandri* spawns in a peat substrate, with both parents actually submerging themselves in the peat while the eggs are individually expelled and fertilized. The peat is collected at intervals of one or two weeks and stored for three to four months. The peat should then be placed into a small tank and gently crumbled while tank water is added to the tank. If the eggs were fertile to begin with and nothing has happened to destroy them during the storage period, the fry will begin to hatch within a few hours.

1. *Cynolebias alexandri,* male (p594).
2. *Cynolebias alexandri,* male in an aquarium above a spawning medium (p594).
3. *Cynolebias alexandri,* female (p594).

This is the paratype male of *Cynolebias alexandri;* it was collected by J.O. Fernandez-Santo and J. Castelli at Gualeguachu, Argentina. Photo by Dr. Hugo P. Castello.

1. *Cynolebias alexandri* ♂ F E T 5 9 4 X N N 5 [Dr. B. J. Turner]

2. *Cynolebias alexandri* ♂ F E M 5 9 4 X N N 5 [H. J. Richter]
3. *Cynolebias alexandri* ♀ F F B 5 9 4 X N N 5 [H. J. Richter]

Cynolebias melanotaenia F E X 5 9 9 X N N 5   [H. J. Richter]
Cynolebias nigripinnis F E X 6 0 0 X N N 4   [H. J. Richter]

CYNOLEBIAS MELANOTAENIA (Regan) / *Fighting Gaucho*

Range: Southeastern Brazil.

Habits: Do not put two males in the same tank or they will fight until one or both are badly mutilated or dead.

Water Conditions: Occurs in ditches and water holes, some of which dry out in the hot season; can adapt to almost any water.

Size: Males about 5 cm; females slightly smaller.

Food Requirements: Should be given live food of all kinds. Dried foods are accepted, but not willingly.

Like all *Cynolebias* species, the fighting gaucho is a fish which is short-lived and therefore not often found in the tanks of dealers, who prefer fishes which they can keep over a period of time if they cannot sell them quickly. These fish occur in a variety of conditions, which leads one to wonder just exactly what their breeding habits are. One authority says that they lay their eggs in the mud like the other *Cynolebias* species and that the eggs undergo a drying-out process. Then there is another authority who says that they spawn like the *Aphyosemion, Aplocheilus* and *Rivulus* species, laying their eggs in bushy plants near the surface. We consider the first authority correct.

CYNOLEBIAS NIGRIPINNIS Regan / *Black-Finned Pearl Fish*

Range: Parana River region in Argentina, above Rosario.

Habits: Peaceful toward other fishes, but does best when kept with only their own kind.

Water Conditions: Soft, slightly acid water. Temperature 22 to 25°C.

Size: To 4 cm; females smaller.

Food Requirements: Small live foods are best. Frozen foods are accepted, but only as a second choice.

"Like stars in a summer night" is the very appropriate way one writer describes the color pattern of this beautiful fish. The entire body and fins are a velvety black, sprinkled with small light green to light blue dots. The contrast between the colors becomes very much greater while the fish are spawning, at which time the males may be classed among the most beautiful aquarium fishes. As with the other *Cynolebias* species, the females are so different that it is difficult to recognize them as belonging to the same species as their gorgeous mates. The fins as well as the body are much smaller. She does not share the black color at all; her body color is a light tan to brown, mottled and spotted with a slightly darker color. Males are eager breeders, and they are constantly seeking out the females and trying to coax them to the bottom, which should have a layer of peat moss. They assume a side-by-side position, then almost stand on their heads and push into the peat moss to deposit their eggs. The peat moss is then removed and stored in a slightly damp condition for three or four months. Water is then added and the young hatch in short order.

CYNOLEBIAS WHITEI Myers / *White's Pearl Fish*

Range: Savannah ponds of the Mato Grosso region, Brazil.
Habits: Peaceful toward other fishes, but best if kept to themselves.
Water Conditions: Soft, slightly acid water. Temperature 22 to 24°C.
Size: To 8 cm; females slightly smaller.
Food Requirements: Live or frozen foods. Dried foods accepted only when very hungry.

The fish was named by Dr. George S. Myers for General Thomas D. White, who discovered it in southeastern Brazil, in the Mato Grosso region. Like the other annual fishes, it occurs in ponds that disappear in the dry months, to fill up again when the rainy season gets under way. Naturally such a fish has a very short life span and most dealers shy away from them, but a fish with so much beauty generally finds takers in short order, and if the fish is still fairly young when he gets it, it will not be old when he sells it. The usual method of spawning is the same as for the other *Cynolebias* species, with peat moss as the spawning medium, but it has been found by breeders who have spawned this fish that it will also accept fine-grained sand for the purpose. This is much easier to work with than peat moss; the sand is placed in a shallow dish on the bottom and removed when there are eggs. Procedure from here is the same as for the other species of the genus.

CYNOLEBIAS WOLTERSTORFFI Ahl / *Wolterstorff's Pearl Fish*

Range: Southeastern Brazil.
Habits: Aggressive and pugnacious. Not adaptable for community tanks. Should be given their own well planted tank.
Water Conditions: Neutral to slightly acid. Temperature 24 to 26°C.
Size: Males to 10 cm; females slightly smaller.
Food Requirements: Frequent feedings with live or freeze-dried foods.

Cynolebias wolterstorffi occurs in temporary water holes in southeastern Brazil. It is found in places where it would never be suspected that fish life could be supported, places where the water disappears completely in the hot dry season. The eggs survive for months in the mud where they were buried by the parents, and when the rains begin to fill up the holes again, the eggs hatch and become ravenous fry. Tiny animalcules and, later, insect larvae are gobbled up at a great rate, and in an amazingly short time the former fry are capable of producing and fertilizing eggs. Their maturation process is a race against death, for the water dries up once more and leaves them stranded soon after they lay their eggs. Obviously, such a short-lived vertebrate animal would make an intriguing subject for a student of geriatrics, the study of the ravages of age. Here we have a vertebrate which is hatched, grows to maturity and dies within a period of six to eight months!

Cynolebias whitei ⬚F⬚E⬚X⬚6⬚0⬚1⬚X⬚N⬚N⬚8 [H. J. Richter]
Cynolebias wolterstorffi ⬚F⬚A⬚X⬚6⬚0⬚2⬚X⬚N⬚N⬚8 [Harald Schultz]

1. *Cynotilapia afra* F A X 6 0 3 X N N 8   [G. Meola - African Fish Imports]
2. *Cynotilapia afra* var. F A X 6 0 4 X N N 8 [Dr. Herbert R. Axelrod]

CYNOTILAPIA AFRA (Günther) / *Dogtooth Cichlid, Dwarf Zebra*

Range: Likoma Island, Lake Malawi, Africa.
Habits: A quarrelsome fish. Best kept to themselves in large tanks.
Water Conditions: Requires hard alkaline water at temperatures of 24 to 26°C.
Size: About 8 cm.
Food Requirements: An omnivorous fish requiring some vegetable matter in its diet. Adapts well to dry prepared foods.

Cynotilapia afra derives the first part of its generic name, Cyno, from its dog-like teeth. Although this fish closely resembles *Pseudotropheus zebra*, with which it is sympatric, it can be distinguished, on close examination, by its unicuspid teeth, whereas *P. zebra* has bicuspid teeth in the front row and tricuspid teeth in the inner rows. *C. afra* is somewhat smaller than *P. zebra*. It is also known as the Dwarf Zebra.

C. afra breeds in a manner similar to most of the other Malawian mbuna, being a maternal mouthbrooder. It does, however, produce a smaller clutch size than most other mbunas. There are some behavioral differences between this fish and most of the other mbuna which suggest that *C. afra* may be either evolving in a different direction or may be evolving toward the "typical" mbuna. For instance, the fish tends to form schools of up to 100 in number, and it has been observed feeding on plankton. It has a fairly long jaw gape which equips it for feeding on larger planktonic organisms and small fish.

1. *Cynotilapia afra,* normal variety (p603).
2. *Cynotilapia afra,* color variety (p603).

A rocky outcrop in Lake Malawi around which thousands of cichlids live. Photo by Dr. Herbert R. Axelrod.

Cyphotilapia frontosa individuals photographed in relatively deep water among the rock-strewn bottom of Lake Tanganyika. Photo by P. Brichard.

CYPHOTILAPIA FRONTOSA (Boulenger) / *The Frontosa*

Range: Lake Tanganyika, Africa.
Habits: Peaceful, especially in consideration of its size.
Water Conditions: Hard, alkaline water preferred; temperature 24 to 28°C.
Size: To about 30 cm.
Food Requirements: Accepts most standard aquarium foods.

Although it is not scarce in the wild, being one of the most widely distributed species in Lake Tanganyika, it is a deep-water fish, not a dweller of the shorelines, and therefore is difficult and consequently expensive to collect. Additionally, the desirability of the fish as an aquarium species greatly increases the demand for it, and the combination of scarcity and high demand has kept the price high. In mid-1975, for example, adults were being offered for as much as $250 apiece. Domestic breeding, however, has resulted in a greater availability of this and many other lake cichlids, so prices have now dropped considerably. Good looks are not the fish's only good point; it is also a peaceful species, that, despite its size, doesn't go looking for trouble. The fact that *C. frontosa* is not an aggressive species does not mean that it is not territorial. The fish does establish territories and will guard them, but it is less zealous in their defense than some other African cichlid species. *Cyphotilapia frontosa* is a mouthbrooder; the female, which normally is not too roughly treated during the pre-spawning period, holds the large eggs for 2½ to 4 weeks. The most important factor in determining the length of incubation time is the temperature; at the lower range of spawning temperature, 26°C, incubation takes longer. For a fish of its size, the number of eggs produced at each spawning is small. When released, the fry are large even for mouthbrooder fry, and they are not difficult to feed. Sexing of mature fish can be done fairly reliably according to the size of the hump on the head, which is much larger on males than on females.

1. *Cyphotilapia frontosa*, mature male with large hump above the eye (p606).
2. *Cyphotilapia frontosa*, female without hump (p606).

605

1. *Cyphotilapia frontosa* ♂ | F | A | X | 6 | 0 | 5 | X | N | N | D | [Dr. Herbert R. Axelrod]
2. *Cyphotilapia frontosa* ♀ | F | G | X | 6 | 0 | 6 | X | N | N | A | [H. J. Richter]

Cyprinodon macularius ⬚F⬚A⬚X⬚6⬚0⬚7⬚X⬚N⬚N⬚7
Cyprinodon nevadensis ⬚F⬚R⬚X⬚6⬚0⬚8⬚X⬚N⬚N⬚6

[H. J. Richter]
[G. Wolfsheimer]

CYPRINODON MACULARIUS Baird & Girard / *Desert Pupfish*

Range: Salton Sea, Colorado delta, and Rio Sonoyata, southwestern United States.
Habits: Usually peaceful, but best kept by themselves because of their water requirements and spawning type.
Water Conditions: Hard, alkaline water with temperatures from 24 to 32°C. Some salt may be added to the water.
Size: Up to to about 6 to 8 cm.
Food Requirements: Prefers live foods like tubifex and brine shrimp but can be coaxed onto frozen, flake or other types of foods.

The Desert Pupfish needs very little to keep it well and happy. A moderate-sized tank with some bushy plants placed in 2 to 5 cm of gravel will suffice. The water should be hard and alkaline (some aquarists recommend that a teaspoon of salt per gallon be added).

Spawning can be left to occur naturally by placing several pairs or trios (more females than males) in an aquarium, feeding them well and waiting for developments. It can be speeded up a little by separating males and females and conditioning them with a heavy diet of live foods.

The male will display before the female, circling around her and in general trying to entice her into a suitable spawning site. This will be a clump of fine-leaved or bushy plants or, if continuous egg retrieval is desired, nylon spawning mops. These mops can be placed in the tank (there are reports of success with both high-placed and low-placed mops) and checked periodically for the eggs deposited on them. These fish often will eat their eggs if they are left in the tank too long. The eggs hatch in about ten days and the fry are able to handle newly hatched brine shrimp right away.

CYPRINODON NEVADENSIS Eigenmann & Eigenmann
Amargosa Pupfish

Range: Nevada.
Habits: Usually peaceful, but best kept by themselves because of their high temperature requirements.
Water Conditions: Water should be somewhat alkaline and warm, about 29°C.
Size: Up to 6 cm.
Food Requirements: Live foods preferred, but they can probably be trained to accept frozen foods.

Commonly called the Amargosa Pupfish or Desert Minnow, *Cyprinodon nevadensis* inhabits a number of isolated marshes and springs along the Amargosa River drainage system in Nevada. This species was most likely widespread during the period when, many years ago, this entire area was covered with water. Since that time, however, the fish has become isolated in many small bodies of water. Because of this isolation, six different subspecies of this fish have evolved. Due to man's constant tampering with the fragile Nevada ecosystem, however, at least two of these subspecies are thought to be extinct.

CYPRINUS CARPIO Linnaeus / *Carp*

Range: Originally from the temperate waters of Asia, now widespread.
Habits: Young specimens are peaceful, but constantly stir up the bottom in search of food.
Water Conditions: Will adapt to any water; best is slightly alkaline. Temperature 5 to 24°C.
Size: In natural waters they sometimes exceed a meter in length.
Food Requirements: Will eat anything edible.
Color Variations: Entire body and fins olive green to reddish, with some dark brown markings on sides.

Cyprinus carpio has been introduced into many ponds and streams in temperate waters, where it adapts quickly, often living a good many years and, if food is sufficient, growing to a large size. Sport fishermen consider the Carp a troublesome nuisance and they do not like to catch them. An old sport has been adapted by archers with a view to reducing the numbers of Carp: fish-shooting. Most small to medium-sized fish are shot with a bow and arrow, and larger ones are speared. The Carp is much more respected in Europe and the Asiatic countries. Only young specimens can be kept in the home aquarium. These are useful in that they keep the bottom free of all leftover food; the trouble is that they stir things up very vigorously.

1. *Cyprinus carpio*, Koi, school in a pond (p610).
2. Aka Bekko, the Red Tortoiseshell Koi (p610).
3. Tancho Sanshoku, the Redheaded Tricolor Koi (p611).

Cyprinus carpio exists in several forms. The mirror carp has large reflective scales. Photo by Kocar Miloslav.

1. *Cyprinus carpio* F H X 6 0 9 X V N D [Dr. Herbert R. Axelrod]
2. *Cyprinus carpio* F H X 6 1 0 X V N D [Kodansha Ltd.]

3. *Cyprinus carpio* F H X 6 1 1 X V N D
[Kodansha Ltd.]

CYPRINUS CARPIO Linnaeus var. / *Koi, Japanese Colored Carp*

Habits: Peaceful with all but the smallest fish.
Water Conditions: Slightly alkaline water is best. Temperature from 5 to 24°C.
Size: To about 50 cm.
Food Requirements: Omnivorous; should get and will eat a variety of foods, live, frozen or dried.
Color Variations: Wide range of color varieties from almost all black to pure white.

Koi are highly developed forms of the common Carp in a similar way that fancy-tail Guppies are highly developed forms of the common Guppy. The Koi is particularly well suited to keep in a garden pool, where its touch of brilliant colors would add a great deal of decorative effect. The Koi was produced by Japanese breeders. The results came in a great variety of color variations, and selective breeding did the rest. At the present time there are at least 19 recognized varieties, with the possibility of many more to come. Finnage is still very close to that of the original Carp species, but remember how long it took to produce some of the present-day Goldfish strains! The patient Japanese, who are not appalled at setting a goal which may be achieved by their grandchildren, are the logical ones to depend on for such a task, and we may yet some day see the Koi with long, flowing finnage such as is sported by our Goldfish. The Nishiki-Koi is already very popular among the Hawaiian hobbyists, and many have shown up here on the mainland.

KOI VARIETIES

Although the greatest degree of enthusiasm for Koi in the United States is centered in Hawaii and California, these extremely variable and interesting fish have fans all over the country.

Because of their size, Koi are basically pool fish and do best in an outdoor environment. They are able to withstand a wide temperature range and are undemanding as to water composition, provided that their water is richly supplied with oxygen. In an outdoor pool, suitable filtration and aeration can easily be provided through the use of the pool filters designed specifically for use with garden ponds. Feeding Koi presents no great problems, as they are heavy eaters and accept a wide variety of foods. Worms, shrimp, insects and insect larvae form the major portion of the Koi diet, but vegetable materials in the form of chopped terrestrial and aquatic plants must be included as regular portions. Although Koi are heavy eaters, they will not eat food that is left to stagnate in their pool, so all uneaten food should be removed immediately. After they become accustomed to their surroundings Koi are quite willing to accept food right from their owner's fingers.

Koi breed substantially the same as goldfish, scattering their eggs into the fine leaves or root systems of plants (water lettuce and water hyacinths are ideal) after a vigorous chase by the males of the females. Normally, more than one male per female is used. Sex differences among mature Koi are easily distinguishable; viewed from directly above, females will be seen to be much stockier from behind the head to just behind the dorsal fin.

1. Kohaku, the Red-and-White Koi (p614).
2. Ki Bekko, the Yellow Tortoiseshell Koi (p614).
3. Showa Sanshoku, the Showa Tricolor Koi (p615).
4. Koshi No Hisoku, the Green Carp (p618).
5. Kin Matsuba, the Golden Pine Needle Koi (p619).

Koi pools have become very popular in many parts of the world.

1. *Cyprinus carpio* F H X 6 1 3 X V N D [Kodansha Ltd.]
2. *Cyprinus carpio* F H X 6 1 4 X V N D [Kodansha Ltd.]

3. *Cyprinus carpio* F H X 6 1 5 X V N D

[Kodansha Ltd.]

Cyprinus carpio grows to about one meter. Large specimens are usually kept in pools. Smaller ones like the fish above can be kept in aquaria (photo by G. Senfft). The underslung mouth can be seen in the lower photo.

Cyprinus carpio is a bottom-feeder. The barbels act as chemosensors in detecting a food source. Their mouths are adapted to bottom-feeding. Upper photo by G. Marcuse and lower photo by L.E. Perkins.

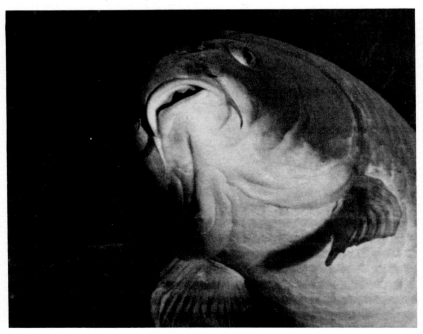

617

4. *Cyprinus carpio*
FHX618XDM
[Kodansha Ltd.]

5. *Cyprinus carpio*
F H X 6 1 9 X D M D
[Kodansha Ltd.]

Danio aequipinnatus will spawn among and above bushy plants, as can be seen above. The Giant Danio lays adhesive eggs in a manner similar to the barb species. Photos by R. Zukal.

DANIO AEQUIPINNATUS (McClelland) / *Giant Danio*

Range: Quite common on the west coast of India and Sri Lanka.
Habits: Peaceful in the community aquarium; will not bother anything it cannot swallow.
Water Conditions: Prefers clean, sunny water; pH and hardness not important. Temperature 24 to 26°C.
Size: Wild specimens are said to attain 15 cm; in the aquarium they seldom exceed 10 cm.
Food Requirements: Will consume dried as well as live foods; like any active fish, it should be generously fed.

This is one of the old favorites among aquarium hobbyists. It has good reason to be popular: it is peaceful, active, easy to breed and colorful. It is at home in any aquarium, as long as it is not too small for its size and active habits. Unless it is abused pretty badly, it is seldom attacked by disease. Unlike the *Brachydanio* species, the Giant Danio lays adhesive eggs in the manner of the barb species. A thicket of bushy plants is placed at one end of a large aquarium (about 80 liters or more) If possible, the aquarium should stand in a sunny spot. The water should always be fresh and clear, and the bottom may be covered with glass marbles or pebbles, because the fish sometimes will spawn in the open areas and the eggs could be eaten. Driving is very active, and hundreds of eggs often result. When finished, the parent fish should be removed. Fry hatch in one to two days, but some will take a little longer. For the next three to five days, until the yolk-sac is absorbed, the youngsters will be seen hanging from the glass sides and plants. Then when they begin swimming, food must be provided.

DANIO DEVARIO (Hamilton-Buchanan) / *Bengal Danio*

Range: Northwest India, Orissa, Bengal and Assam.
Habits: Peaceful, very active; should not be combined with nervous, slower-moving fishes.
Water Conditions: Not critical; water should be near neutral, clean and not too hard.
Size: To 10 cm.
Food Requirements: A hearty eater; will take dried as well as live or frozen foods.

Danio devario is a slightly smaller fish than *Danio aequipinnatus,* the well-known Giant Danio. It would probably be every bit as popular, but its colors are not nearly as brilliant. Like the Giant Danio it is a very active species and could easily cause a tankmate with more sluggish habits to become very nervous. It is always a good policy when mixing fishes in a so-called "community aquarium" to pay attention not only to whether the fishes will hurt each other or not but also to choose fishes with almost equal dispositions. There is no place, for instance, for a nervous, timid fish in the same tank as such ever-active fellows as the danios. It would not be able to stand the constant hustle and bustle and would not get anywhere near its share of the food.

Danio aequipinnatus ⌊F⌋⌊Q⌋⌊X⌋⌊6⌋⌊2⌋⌊1⌋⌊X⌋⌊N⌋⌊N⌋⌊A⌋   [R. Zukal]

Danio devario ⌊F⌋⌊Q⌋⌊X⌋⌊6⌋⌊2⌋⌊2⌋⌊X⌋⌊N⌋⌊N⌋⌊8⌋   [H. J. Richter]

Datnioides microlepis ⬚F⬚ ⬚D⬚ ⬚X⬚ ⬚6⬚ ⬚2⬚ ⬚3⬚ ⬚X⬚ ⬚N⬚ ⬚N⬚ ⬚D⬚ [P. Tsang]

Datnioides quadrifasciatus ⬚F⬚ ⬚C⬚ ⬚X⬚ ⬚6⬚ ⬚2⬚ ⬚4⬚ ⬚X⬚ ⬚N⬚ ⬚N⬚ ⬚B⬚

[Dr. Herbert R. Axelrod]

DATNIOIDES MICROLEPIS Bleeker / *Siamese Tiger Fish*

Range: Thailand, Sumatra and Borneo.
Habits: Peaceful; will not harm any fish it cannot swallow.
Water Conditions: Neutral to slightly acid. Temperature 23 to 26°C.
Size: To 38 cm in its natural waters; much smaller in the aquarium.
Food Requirements: Larger live foods or chunks of shrimp or raw lean beef.
Color Variations: Body yellow to cream or pinkish, with black vertical bars.

Datnioides microlepis is a handsome fish, the black and yellow bands of the body forming a pleasant contrast to the green of a well-planted tank. It is a large fish with a big mouth, and although peaceful enough toward other fishes of an equal size, it cannot be combined with tankmates which could be swallowed. In its native Thailand it is said to attain a length of 38 cm, but in the aquarium it could not be expected to attain half that size. We have had reports that when a *D. microlepis* is displeased with its surroundings it not only sulks but loses its yellow coloring and becomes almost entirely black. Feeding is not much of a problem. Smith, in his book *The Freshwater Fishes of Siam, or Thailand,* mentions keeping them in an aquarium where they thrived on shrimp and raw meat. They have not yet been bred in captivity, and it still remains to be seen if they attain maturity at the smaller sizes attained in the aquarium. In Thailand this fish is highly respected as food, so highly that the fishermen keep them for themselves and market the rest of the catch.

DATNIOIDES QUADRIFASCIATUS (Sevastianov)
Many-Barred Tiger Fish

Range: Thailand, India, Burma and the Indo-Australian Archipelago.
Habits: Peaceful; will not molest other fishes, but will swallow those which are small enough to be eaten.
Water Conditions: Neutral to slightly acid. Temperature 23 to 26°C.
Size: To 38 cm in their natural waters.
Food Requirements: Larger live foods, chunks of shrimp or raw fish.
Color Variations: Yellowish to coppery in color with 8 to 10 dark brown bars, some of which unite as the fish grows older.

Our picture shows a young specimen of *Datnioides quadrifasciatus,* the Many-Barred Tiger Fish. When it has grown a little more the fish will look more like our picture of *Datnioides microlepis.* One of the ways of telling them apart is that *D. microlepis* has much smaller scales, 105 in the lateral line, while *D. quadrifasciatus* has only 70. One must not take the name *quadrifasciatus* too literally ("four bars"). We turn again to H.M. Smith as our authority with the statement that there may be as many as 8 to 10 vertical bars, some of which remain distinct at all ages.

DERMOGENYS PUSILLUS van Hasselt / *Malayan Halfbeak*

Range: Malaysia, Sumatra, Borneo and Thailand.
Habits: Should be kept by themselves; if more than one male is put into a tank, they will fight continually.
Water Conditions: Water should have an addition of one quarter teaspoon of salt to every liter of water. Temperature 23 to 26°C.
Size: Males to 5 cm; females to 6.5 cm.
Food Requirements: Living foods like daphnia or mosquito larvae.

Every once in a while an East Indian shipment contains a number of halfbeaks, which should be enough to ensure a constant supply of these interesting livebearers. This is not so; the fact is, this livebearer is a very difficult fish to breed and even to keep. They occur in brackish as well as fresh water, and the addition of some salt to their water is beneficial. Probably there is some item of food in their native waters which we cannot or do not give them, and as a result they are short-lived in the aquarium. Males often indulge in battles which result in injury to the beak, the result of which is death. Females will give birth once or twice to a dozen or so young, and then most subsequent young are premature or are born dead for some other reason. Another possibility which comes to mind is that there might be some tiny trace element which is native to their home waters but which is absent in the aquarium. Perhaps some day we will have the answer or someone will take extra pains with them and produce a healthy strain which will be hardy and fertile. Even if it does happen, the bellicose nature of the males will always be a drawback to their popularity.

DIANEMA LONGIBARBIS Cope / *Porthole Catfish*

Range: Peru (Rio Ambyiacu) and Brazil (Amazon system).
Habits: Peaceful.
Water Conditions: Not critical.
Size: Attains a length of about 10 to 12 cm.
Food Requirements: Live foods preferred although it can be trained to accept prepared foods.

Dianema longibarbis is very similar to *D. urostriata* and, in fact, if the tails were covered it would be very difficult to tell them apart. However, with the tail fins present there is no problem. In *D. urostriata* the caudal fin is banded horizontally with black, while in *D. longibarbis* it is plain.

The Porthole Catfish has also been misidentified as a species of *Hoplosternum, H. thoracatum,* but catfish experts quickly set everybody straight as to its proper name. Its common name apparently originated from the generally straight line of spots along the side of the fish, although as can be seen by the accompanying photo there are more spots present and they are not always aligned in a regular row.

Dermogenys pusillus ⬚F⬚D⬚X⬚6⬚2⬚5⬚X⬚N⬚N⬚5   [K. Quitschau]

Dianema longibarbis ⬚F⬚D⬚X⬚6⬚2⬚6⬚X⬚N⬚N⬚9   [Dr. Herbert R. Axelrod]

Distichodus noboli ⬚F⬚C⬚X⬚6⬚3⬚1⬚X⬚N⬚N⬚7   [H. J. Richter]

Distichodus sexfasciatus ⬚F⬚D⬚X⬚6⬚3⬚2⬚X⬚N⬚N⬚D

DISTICHODUS NOBOLI Boulenger / *Nobol Distichodus*

Range: Lower Congo River System.
Habits: Peaceful; a good community tank fish, but requires a large aquarium. Nibbles plants.
Water Conditions: Soft, slightly acid water. Temperature 24 to 27°C.
Size: To 10 cm.
Food Requirements: Large amounts of live or frozen foods, with an addition of vegetable matter like lettuce or spinach leaves. Will occasionally accept flake food.

The genus *Distichodus,* which is endemic (exclusively native) to Africa, includes riverine fishes which live in the lower levels of the water. *D. noboli* is a peaceful species which because of its very active nature needs a large aquarium in which to live. Because this fish has a great appetite for shoots and fine leaves, heavy aquarium planting is not recommended. Sex distinctions are not obvious.

DISTICHODUS SEXFASCIATUS Boulenger / *Six-Barred Distichodus*

Range: Lower Congo region.
Habits: Peaceful toward other fishes, but will nibble plants.
Water Conditions: Neutral to slightly acid. Temperature 24 to 27°C.
Size: To 25 cm.
Food Requirements: Large amounts of live or frozen foods, supplemented with green foods like lettuce or spinach leaves.
Color Variations: Body pinkish to white with six dark bands. Fins are brilliant deep red.

The Six-Barred Distichodus is a large, handsome fish which is better adapted to a large tank in a public aquarium than to the comparatively cramped quarters a hobbyist can offer. It is fairly well distributed throughout the Congo basin but does not occur in the upper reaches. There is a similar species which grows bigger and has almost identical coloring and markings, *Distichodus lusosso.* The most outstanding difference between the two is that *D. lusosso* has a head that is ridiculously small and pointed for the big, wide body while that of *D. sexfasciatus* is shorter and in better proportion. As with the other *Distichodus* species, this one should also get a generous proportion of green foods in its diet and will supplement these with any plants it may find. Some hobbyists who wish to have a planted tank and also keep a plant-eater like this one set up a background of plants and then insert a glass pane in the back. This robs the tank of some of its area but is a good way to keep the fish and plants separated. If the fish are fed a good amount of green foods, they will not feel frustrated if they cannot get at the growing plants.

DORMITATOR MACULATUS (Bloch) / *Spotted Sleeper*

Range: Atlantic coastal waters from the Carolinas to Brazil.
Habits: Inactive and predatory; should not be kept with small fishes.
Water Conditions: Water should have a salt content, about a quarter teaspoonful per liter. Temperature 21 to 24°C.
Size: To 25 cm.
Food Requirements: Eats anything and everything; bits of raw fish are especially relished.

The Spotted Sleeper is not strictly a tropical species, although its range extends down into Brazil. The northernmost extreme of its habitat is the Carolinas. This is one of the highly adaptable fishes which is found in salt water as well as brackish and fresh waters. In the aquarium it displays a constantly vigorous appetite which belies its sluggish nature. It is an omnivorous eater, and smaller fishes of a size to be swallowed are considered special tidbits. This species has been spawned in captivity. They spawn very much like many of the cichlid family. Both fish clean off a rock, and a large number of eggs are deposited by the female and fertilized by the male. The tiny fry hatch in a day at 24°C, and when the fry begin to swim it is best to remove the parents. Infusoria should be fed at first, followed by newly hatched brine shrimp and later by larger foods. Not a very satisfactory aquarium fish, the Spotted Sleeper is as inactive as its name indicates and spends most of its time in hiding.

EIGENMANNIA VIRESCENS (Valenciennes) / *Green Knife Fish*

Range: Widely distributed all over northern South America.
Habits: Mostly nocturnal; very greedy eaters which are best kept by themselves.
Water Conditions: Water should be well aged and clean. Temperature 24 to 27°C. This fish is very sensitive to fresh water.
Size: To 45 cm.
Food Requirements: Almost any food is taken greedily; preferred of course are the larger live foods, but they also eat chunks of beef heart and oatmeal.

The knife fishes are a very interesting group because of their unusual shape and manner of swimming. Most of them are nocturnal by nature and are happiest when in a well-shaded tank. Their swimming motions are most interesting, and it is difficult to understand how a fish which is equipped with only pectoral fins and an anal fin can swim so rapidly and maneuver so well. Propulsion is accomplished by a rippling motion of the anal fin. If the fish is swimming forward and wishes to reverse direction, it simply reverses the rippling motion and swims backward just as easily. The Green Knife Fish grows to a large size, about 45 cm, which puts it in a class where it is adaptable only for large show aquaria when fully grown.

Dormitator maculatus ⬚F⬚ ⬚D⬚ ⬚X⬚ ⬚6⬚ ⬚3⬚ ⬚3⬚ ⬚X⬚ ⬚N⬚ ⬚N⬚ ⬚C⬚   [Harald Schultz]

Eigenmannia virescens ⬚F⬚ ⬚D⬚ ⬚X⬚ ⬚6⬚ ⬚3⬚ ⬚4⬚ ⬚X⬚ ⬚N⬚ ⬚N⬚ ⬚E⬚   [Dr. Herbert R. Axelrod]

Eirmotus octozona ⒡⒭Ⓧ⑥③⑤Ⓧ ⓃⓃ⑥   [Dr. Herbert R. Axelrod]

Elassoma evergladei ⒡⒭Ⓧ⑥③⑥Ⓧ ⓃⓃ②   [R. Zukal]

EIRMOTUS OCTOZONA Schultz / *False Barb*

Range: Bung Borapet, Thailand.
Habits: Peaceful and inoffensive toward other fishes and plants.
Water Conditions: Soft, slightly acid water is best. Temperature 23 to 27°C.
Size: To about 6 cm.
Food Requirements: Not choosy; will eat dried as well as live or frozen foods readily.

This handsome little fish was sent to our office way back in 1957, and we were quite sure that it was a barb species of some kind. However, after a careful search through our literature, we could not find a description that exactly fitted the fish. The big surprise came when Dr. Leonard P. Schultz, then Curator of Fishes at the National Museum in Washington, D.C., made a complete taxonomic examination of the specimens we sent him and informed Dr. Axelrod that this was not only a new species, but it was also a new genus. It differed from the known genera which we call the "barb" group by having several lines of sensory papillae on the head and lacking a complete lateral line. Because it looked and acted like a barb but it was not a barb, we gave it the popular name "False Barb."

ELASSOMA EVERGLADEI Jordan / *Everglades Pygmy Sunfish*

Range: Florida and Georgia.
Habits: Very timid with other fishes; should be kept by themselves in a small aquarium.
Water Conditions: Slightly alkaline water. Room temperatures, about 18 to 20°C, are perfect.
Size: About 3 cm; females a little smaller.
Food Requirements: Small live foods are best, like sifted *Daphnia,* newly hatched brine shrimp, etc.

Why is it that the aquarium hobbyist places such a high value on fishes which come from another part of the world and ignores the beautiful and interesting species which he can find in his own country? Our native American fishes, by and large, are not the most colorful and practical aquarium fishes in the world, but there are some which certainly deserve a little more attention. The Everglades Pygmy Sunfish is one of these. Coming from the Everglades in Florida, they can withstand a variety of temperatures. Because of their tiny size, a pair can be kept quite comfortably in a 4- or 8-liter aquarium. Eggs are usually placed on a plant leaf and hatch in two to three days. Spawnings vary from 30 to 60 eggs. Parents guard the eggs and young, which are easily fed in their first days on dust-fine foods. This fish has at times an odd manner of propelling itself along the bottom: the long ventral fins are alternately swished back and forth along the bottom, giving the fish the appearance of "walking." The Pygmy Sunfish can be highly recommended for an outdoor pool during the warm months.

ELECTROPHORUS ELECTRICUS (Linnaeus) / *Electric Eel*

Range: Middle and lower Amazon basin.
Habits: Because of this species's electric properties it is not suitable as a community tank fish. More than one specimen can sometimes be kept in a tank, but this is risky.
Water Conditions: Soft, slightly acid water is optimal, but not important.
Size: Up to 1.8 meters; aquarium specimens much smaller.
Food Requirements: Live fishes are preferred; small specimens will take worms and may be taught to accept liver and similar foods.
Color Variations: Young specimens olive-brown with yellowish markings. Adults olive-brown with orange throat. Eyes emerald green.

The Electric Eel is a novelty rarely offered to the aquarist. Among the most popularly known fishes, it is one of the least satisfactory from the point of view of most aquarists. In nearly all cases it demands an aquarium of its own as well as special handling to avoid shock. Although there are several species of fish which possess electric organs, *E. electricus* has developed them to the greatest extent, with approximately four-fifths of the length of the body being occupied by these elements. The eel does not discharge when at rest, but as it starts to move it emits impulses at the rate of about 50 per second at a strength of up to 1 ampere. The impulses apparently perform the dual functions of navigating device and defensive-offensive mechanism. It is said that the eel stuns its prey before eating it. Electric Eels kept in the same aquarium frequently fight by assuming a head-to-tail position and engaging in tail-slapping, biting and discharging electricity. It is necessary when handling the Electric Eel to wear rubber gloves to prevent being shocked. The heavy gloves used domestically for dish washing are much to be preferred to the thin types used by surgeons. The aquarium provided for the Electric Eel must have enough rocks so that the fish may conceal itself from time to time. This fish has never been bred in captivity, possibly because it does not reach sufficient size in the home aquarium.

ENNEACANTHUS CHAETODON (Baird) / *Blackbanded Sunfish*

Range: New Jersey south to northern Florida, coastal.
Habits: Usually peaceful, but should not be trusted with smaller fishes. Also shy and gets nervous when with very active fishes.
Water Conditions: Water should be kept alkaline and a part of it frequently changed. Temperature around 21°C.
Size: 8 cm.
Food Requirements: Live foods only; it might be possible to induce them to eat frozen foods, but they will seldom take dried foods.
Color Variations: Body silvery to light yellow, with a number of dark bars running vertically. First ventral rays are orange.

Electrophorus electricus F D X 6 3 7 X N N D   [K. Paysan]

1. *Enneacanthus chaetodon* F Q X 6 3 8 X N N 8   [H. J. Richter]

2. *Enneacanthus chaetodon* F H X 6 3 9 X N N 8   [H. J. Richter]
Enneacanthus gloriosus F D X 6 4 0 X N N 6   [Dr. Herbert R. Axelrod]

Here is a fish which our readers in most of the states along the Atlantic Seaboard can catch for themselves, game laws permitting. The Blackbanded Sunfish is found in ponds and cypress swamps along the Atlantic Coast from New Jersey down to northern Florida. The best time to hunt them is the early summer, when the young ones have left the nest and are found along the shore in shallow water. These youngsters are best able to make the change to aquarium life, and there are fewer losses. There may be a great temptation to catch some adult specimens, but if you do this be prepared to lose some of your catch, as they do not acclimate themselves as easily to the aquarium. When transporting them do not crowd the containers; remember, a few live healthy fish are better than a lot of dead ones! This fish is a great favorite with European hobbyists. The males build a nest by digging out a depression in the gravel. The females are then lured to this nest and a great many eggs are expelled. These eggs are sticky and adhere to the gravel. Females are driven away and should be removed. Males guard the eggs and later the young but should be removed when the young leave the nest.

1. *Enneacanthus chaetodon,* mating pair in an aquarium (p638).
2. *Enneacanthus chaetodon* (p639).

ENNEACANTHUS GLORIOSUS (Holbrook)
Diamond Sunfish, Bluespotted Sunfish

Range: Eastern coastal United States from New York to Florida.
Habits: Peaceful when kept with fishes of its size.
Water Conditions: Slightly alkaline water which is kept unheated at room temperature.
Size: To 8 cm.
Food Requirements: Variety of live or frozen foods. Dried foods are accepted unwillingly.

Enneacanthus gloriosus is doubtless one of the most beautiful of our American sunfishes, as well as one of the most peaceful. Occurring as it does in the eastern coastal states of the United States, it should be rated as a cold-water species and should not be kept in a heated aquarium unless there is danger of the water freezing. They may be kept in company with other cold-water species. One way the coldwater species differ from our tropical aquarium fishes is that spawning usually takes place at a very definite time of the year and egg ripeness cannot be induced at any other time by heavy feeding, higher temperatures, adding fresh water or all the other tricks we use with the tropical species. With this particular species there are usually two periods of ripeness, one in the spring and the other in late summer. As is often the case, we must turn to the European authorities for information on how to spawn an American fish in the aquarium. Spawning takes place among fine-leaved plants. At this time the male may treat the female with excessive roughness. The female should be taken out when finished. Fry hatch in three days and are very easy to raise.

ENNEACANTHUS OBESUS (Girard) / *Banded Sunfish*

Range: Eastern United States from Massachusetts to northern Florida, coastal.
Habits: Because of the cooler temperatures enjoyed by this species it should probably have a tank all to itself.
Water Conditions: Not critical. Should have partial periodic changes. Temperatures for breeding a cool 20°C.
Size: About 8 cm.
Food Requirements: Feed a wide variety of live foods such as daphnia, cyclops, chironomid larvae, brine shrimp, etc. and perhaps some frozen or freeze-dried prepared foods.

For those who wish a change from "tropicals," some of our local sunfishes are ideal. They require cooler temperatures and will actually breed at temperatures of 18 to 20°C. To imitate their natural cycle as closely as possible they should be kept at cooler temperatures during the winter and brought up to 20°C in the spring (around May). The tank should be as large as possible and well planted with *Myriophyllum, Nitella* or *Cabomba*.

Spawning is not difficult. As the temperature is raised, the male's colors will intensify if he's in good condition and ready to spawn. He will select a spawning site among the plants (if not enough plants are available he will use a shallow pit in the sand). The male will wait at his chosen spawning site for the female and at her approach will swim toward her in his most vivid coloration and with fins spread. He will prod her with his snout and lead her to the preferred site. There with some quivering the spawning process occurs. As the eggs are laid the male will create a strong current with his fins and sweep the eggs into the plants, where they become stuck. This continues off and on for about two to three hours, after which the female is chased (it is best at this point to remove her from the tank).

EPALZEORHYNCHUS KALOPTERUS (Bleeker) / *Flying Fox*

Range: Sumatra and Borneo.
Habits: Peaceful, even toward the smallest fishes.
Water Conditions: Not critical. An active fish; therefore aquarium should be of a good size. Sunny location best as it provides algae.
Size: Said to attain 14 cm, but specimens in captivity do not usually exceed 10 cm.
Food Requirements: Omnivorous; should have some vegetable substances in its diet, such as is provided by algae.

Most of our so-called "scavenger" fishes are only tolerated because of their useful habits. They keep a tank bottom clear of uneaten food, and many of them also clear the rocks and plants as well as the glass sides of an aquarium of algae. Here we have a fish which does all these things and is beautiful and active as well.

Enneacanthus obesus F D X 6 4 1 X N N 8   [Aaron Norman]

Epalzeorhynchus kalopterus F D X 6 4 2 X N N 6   [Dr. Herbert R. Axelrod]

1. *Epiplatys chevalieri* ⬚F⬚E⬚X⬚6⬚4⬚7⬚X⬚N⬚N⬚6   [Col. J. J. Scheel]

2. *Epiplatys chevalieri* ⬚F⬚Q⬚X⬚6⬚4⬚8⬚X⬚N⬚N⬚6   [H. J. Richter]

EPIPLATYS CHEVALIERI (Pellegrin) / *Chevalier's Panchax*

Range: Zaire.
Habits: Relatively peaceful; should be treated like other species of panchax.
Water Conditions: Slightly acid (pH 6.0-6.5) water with DH of about 7-10. Temperature of at least 24°C.
Size: Attains a length of about 6.5 cm.
Food Requirements: Live food of all kinds preferred; can be coaxed onto prepared foods.

This small species of panchax has often been confused with *Epiplatys macrostigma* and *E. chaperi sheljuzhkoi,* at least in the literature.

Chevalier's Panchax is relatively peaceful and can be kept with other suitable fishes in a community tank. It does not reach a large size, 6.5 cm being maximum, 6 cm being more usual. The tank need not be too large, and the water should have a pH of about 6.0-6.5 and a hardness of about 7-10 DH. The temperature should be above 24°C all the time. Since this is a strictly freshwater fish, salt should not be added to the aquarium.

The sides of the fish glow with intense greens and golds. During the spawning season, however, the female's iridescent green glow disappears and in both sexes the lower two rows of red spots are overshadowed with a broad blue-black band. To further distinguish the sexes, the males have a spike or pointed lower edge of the caudal fin, and their dorsal and anal fins appear more pointed.

During the actual spawning the eggs are deposited among the roots of floating plants or the leaves of plants like *Myriophyllum.* These eggs are usually larger (about 1.1-1.3 mm) and less numerous than those of most other species of *Epiplatys.* Chevalier's Panchax is not particularly an egg-eater, so it is safe to leave the eggs in with the parents (providing they are properly fed). However, if you are desirous of rearing all the young it is always a good idea to separate parents from eggs to prevent any accidents from happening. The young are also safe from their parents. The eggs hatch in about two weeks at a temperature of 26°C or about 19 days at 24°C. The young grow slowly and are only ready for reproduction after about six months. They are fully grown with full color after about nine months.

1. *E. chevalieri* (p647) is very similar in appearance to *E. macrostigma.*
2. *Epiplatys chevalieri* pair in an aquarium (p647).

EPIPLATYS DAGETI Poll / *Red-Chinned Panchax*

Range: Southwestern Liberia to southeastern Ghana.
Habits: Energetic and active; aggressive toward fishes its own size and smaller.
Water Conditions: Slightly acid, soft water is preferred. Temperature 24 to 26°C.
Size: To 5.5 cm.
Food Requirements: For this species live foods are best, but it will accept freeze-dried feedings.

This lovely fish has as subspecies *Epiplatys dageti dageti* and *Epiplatys dageti monroviae*. It first became known to hobbyists in a shipment of aquarium fishes from West Africa in 1908. J.P. Arnold inspected this shipment, and it is said that all of the individual *E. dageti monroviae* kept by aquarists up until 1963 probably originated from the original pair that J.P. Arnold selected from that early imported stock. These pretty fish, regardless of their complicated historical origins and troublesome taxonomic considerations, require relatively uncomplicated aquarium maintenance procedures. Floating plants will serve them well, since they remain at the surface of the aquarium water most of the time. In their natural habitat they live in still, murky water, such as pools. Consequently, if their aquarium waters are kept in constant movement, this condition is likely to be very uncomfortable for them. Spawning this species is not too difficult, since they are typical of the *Epiplatys* genus.

EPIPLATYS FASCIOLATUS (Günther) / *Striped Panchax*

Range: Sierra Leone, Liberia to Nigeria.
Habits: Not safe with smaller fishes; should be kept in a covered tank to prevent them from jumping.
Water Conditions: About neutral and not very hard (10 to 15 DH) with a quarter teaspoon of salt added for every liter.
Size: To 8 cm.
Food Requirements: Prefers the larger sizes of live foods, but can be trained to take frozen foods.

Epiplatys fasciolatus are easily spawned as a rule, laying their eggs in the plants near the upper reaches of the aquarium. The eggs in the female ripen only a few at a time, and for this reason spawning is extended over a prolonged period. As a result the young hatch a few at a time as well. With such assorted sizes growing up together it would naturally follow that once the biggest of the lot got big enough to swallow the smallest it would do so, and for this reason the hobbyist who wants to raise the most fish possible has to have a number of well-planted tanks ready rather than just one and must periodically grade his youngsters as to size. *Epiplatys* eggs are somewhat light-sensitive, and the incubating eggs will fungus readily if they are not shaded.

Epiplatys dageti F E X 6 4 9 X N N 6

[Col. J. J. Scheel]

Epiplatys fasciolatus F E X 6 5 0 X N N 7

[H. J. Richter]

Epiplatys grahami F A X 6 5 1 X N N 6   [Col. J. J. Scheel]

Epiplatys longiventralis F E X 6 5 2 X N N 6   [Col. J.J. Scheel]

651

EPIPLATYS GRAHAMI (Boulenger) / *Graham's Panchax*

Range: Southern Nigeria.
Habits: Lively and peaceful with others of about its own size.
Water Conditions: Soft, slighly acid water is best. Temperature 24 to 26°C.
Size: To 5.5 cm; females slightly smaller.
Food Requirements: Live foods in variety; dried foods only in an emergency.

This species can easily be confused with some others which are very similar in appearance, *E. macrostigma* and *E. chaperi sheljuzhkoi*. The only distinguishing mark is a bright red band on the lower jaw. Although it is an active fish, it is not as productive as most of the other *Epiplatys* species. It should be kept in a well-planted and not too brightly lighted aquarium, to approximate the conditions in the weedy, well-shaded jungle streams where they are found. As they are skillful jumpers, their aquarium should be kept covered at all times. You will find that if a pair or more are kept in their own tank, a few youngsters will be found every once in a while swimming at the surface; they can be lifted out with a spoon to a tank of their own where they are not in constant danger of being swallowed. Of course, if more young are desired the eggs must be hunted out and hatched in a tank of their own. Hatching time is 10 to 14 days, and the young are able to swim and eat at once. Raising them is no problem, as they have sharp eyes and are skilled at hunting their food. They should be sorted frequently to prevent cannibalism.

EPIPLATYS LONGIVENTRALIS (Boulenger) / *Banded Panchax*

Range: Tropical West Africa, principally southern Nigeria.
Habits: Peaceful toward any fish it cannot swallow.
Water Conditions: Soft, slightly acid water. Temperature 24 to 27°C.
Size: To 5.5 cm.
Food Requirements: Live foods preferred; dried foods only when nothing else is available.

E. longiventralis is definitely not a fish which could be combined with smaller specimens in a community aquarium. Those which it could swallow would be stalked and engulfed, and the others which would be a little too large for these attentions would be bullied. It is also a mistake to keep two large males together. Even if there are enough females to keep them both busy, there would be a constant struggle for supremacy. A healthy pair will spawn readily, hanging their eggs in fine-leaved plants near the surface. The so-called "spawning mops" of nylon yarn are also accepted in lieu of plants. Eggs hatch in 12 to 14 days and during the incubation period should not be exposed to bright light. While they are growing, fry should be sorted frequently to keep the same sizes together; otherwise there will be many losses among the smaller ones from being eaten by the larger ones.

EPIPLATYS MACROSTIGMA (Boulenger) / *Spotted Panchax*

Range: Congo tributaries toward the mouth, Africa.
Habits: Peaceful toward any fish it cannot swallow.
Water Conditions: Slightly acid, soft water. Temperature 24 to 26°C.
Size: To 6 cm.
Food Requirements: Living foods; accepts prepared or frozen foods only when very hungry.

This attractive little fish is likely to be very shy in an aquarium which is sparsely planted, and for this reason it should be kept in a tank which is not too strongly lighted and is well planted. Like the other *Epiplatys* species, it is a fairly ready spawner and keeping two or three females to one male not only reduces the wear and tear on the female but also results in more eggs. These hatch in just about two weeks' time and have a fairly hard shell, making them easy to handle. If the owner desires, he can mail them by air for quite a distance, as long as they are placed in water again before they hatch. The best way to pack them is in a small box which is then put in a larger one with paper towels for insulation against shocks.

EPIPLATYS SEXFASCIATUS (Gill) / *Six-Banded Panchax*

Range: West coast of Africa from southern Liberia to the mouth of the Congo River.
Habits: Fairly peaceful with fish of their own size.
Water Conditions: A well-established, well-planted tank which is not too small is preferred. Water should be soft and slightly acid. Temperature 24 to 26°C.
Size: Large specimens attain a length of 10 cm; average is smaller.
Food Requirements: Any kind of living food is preferred; frozen or dried foods are usually passed up.

This attractive little fish is not quite as brightly colored as the others in the "panchax" group and is therefore not seen as often in dealers' tanks. In a community aquarium they are inclined toward shyness and often keep themselves hidden. Two things they seem to like are a light which comes down on them from above and some broad-leaved plants. The males take up a position under the leaves, and when a female or another male swims by, they scoot out with flashing colors. It is advisable once they are established in an aquarium which is to their liking to move them as little as possible. This is of course good advice with any fish, but some adapt to varying conditions more easily than others, and the Six-Banded Panchax is not one of these. When spawning this fish it is best to use a ratio of two or even three females to one male. If only one female is used and the male still wants to spawn after she is depleted of her eggs, she is likely to be beaten up pretty badly. Eggs are deposited singly on plants near the surface and may be removed to small containers where they will hatch in 10 to 14 days. Fry are easily raised.

Epiplatys macrostigma F E X 6 5 3 X N N 6
Epiplatys sexfasciatus F E X 6 5 4 X N N A

[H. J. Richter]
[Col. J. J. Scheel]

1. *Eretmodus cyanostictus* 🄵🄰🄭6️⃣5️⃣5️⃣🄭🄽🄽8️⃣   [A. Roth]
2. *Eretmodus cyanostictus* 🄵🄳🄭6️⃣5️⃣6️⃣🄭🄽🄽7️⃣

ERETMODUS CYANOSTICTUS Boulenger / *Striped Goby Cichlid*

Range: Lake Tanganyika, Africa.
Habits: Generally inoffensive with other species, although combative among themselves.
Water Conditions: Hard, alkaline water preferred. Temperature 23 to 26°C.
Size: Up to 8 cm.
Food Requirements: Accepts all standard aquarium foods; the size of the fish's mouth should be considered in selecting foods.

Eretmodus cyanostictus is an odd-looking fish that has a sedate charm appreciated by hobbyists who are more interested in the behavior of their fishes than in their color and shape. Unprepossessing in appearance and ungraceful in movement, the fish still offers its keepers much in satisfaction. It is small and can be maintained in small tanks, it is generally peaceful and not given to chasing and nipping other fishes, and its habits are interesting to observe. The species is a bottom-dweller that moves from place to place in the tank by a "hopping" motion rather than a more normal swimming motion. This similarity to the fishes of the family Gobiidae is one of the main reasons for use of the name goby cichids as a general common name for *Eretmodus* and some other bottom-dwelling cichlids *(Spathodus, Tanganicodus)* of Lake Tanganyika. When maintained without other species, *Eretmodus cyanostictus* will be less of a bottom-hugger and will make regular visits to other levels in the tank, especially upon introduction of food, but when kept with rough species in a deep tank it will usually stay almost entirely at the bottom. Because of this, the hobbyist keeping *Eretmodus* in company with larger, more aggressive species should make sure that *Eretmodus* gets its share of the food. This is a mouthbrooding species; the female broods the eggs for between five and six weeks and is much more temperamental in her handling of the eggs than many other mouthbrooding females. A slight upset during the brooding period often causes her to eat or expel the eggs, which usually number no more than 25 regardless of the size of the female. The sexes are very hard to distinguish, as there are no reliable indicators of sex. The slight hump-headed appearance of mature males is often a characteristic of females as well, and coloration can not be used at all to differentiate the sexes.

1. *Eretmodus cyanostictus* spends most of its time on or near the bottom of the aquarium (p655).
2. *Eretmodus cyanostictus* (p655) use their pectoral fins for balance and support when resting on the aquarium gravel.

ERIMYZON SUCETTA (Lacépède) / *Lake Chubsucker*

Range: Eastern North America to midwest, from southern New York to Florida, west to Texas, and north to Minnesota, Michigan and Wisconsin.
Habits: A specialty fish that should be kept in cool water aquaria.
Water Conditions: Variable except that temperatures higher than 21°C usually cause problems.
Size: Reaches a length of about 25 cm.
Food Requirements: Will usually take daphnia, brine shrimp, chironomids, copepods.

For those aquarists who have the time and inclination to collect native fishes for their aquaria, the Lake Chubsucker should be quite familiar. The young chubsuckers differ greatly from the adult in color, having a broad black band from caudal base to eye and then downward to tip of snout. In the adult this band disappears or breaks up into blotches, sometimes forming vertical bars.

The aquarium can be set up to match as closely as possible the natural habitat with plants from the collecting site and perhaps a few stones (well worn) as well. The water should be clean. Rain water mixed with tap water has been recommended. Filtered natural water is also used. The temperature of the stream or pond should be taken and the aquarium water adjusted to that. Normally the temperature should not be greater than about 21°C. As the Lake Chubsucker is a bottom-feeder, usually searching for its natural foods such as copepods, cladocerans and chironomid larvae, the tank needs good filtration as the fish stirs up the bottom quite regularly. The tank should also be covered to prevent the fish from jumping out.

In nature these fish spawn in early spring (although they can spawn as late as early July). The male cleans an area amid the gravel for egg deposition (although in some cases the eggs are simply scattered). The female lays up to 20,000 eggs over a two-week period. In about six to seven days they hatch out if the temperature is in the upper range, about 22°C or more.

ERYTHRINUS ERYTHRINUS (Schneider) / *Short-Finned Trahira*

Range: Northern and central South America.
Habits: A predatory fish with pike-like habits; it will lie motionless and wait for prey to pass by before striking. The species becomes more active at night.
Water Conditions: Soft to medium hard water; neutral water (pH 7). Temperature 24 to 25°C.
Size: Up to 20 cm.
Food Requirements: Live food recommended.

This fish requires a large aquarium with dense vegetation and dim lighting. As this fish is predatory, it can only coexist with other large fishes if it is to be kept in a community aquarium. Males have an elongated dorsal fin which is drawn to a point. The females have shorter dorsal fins which are rounded. *Erythrinus erythrinus* has not yet been bred in captivity.

Erimyzon sucetta [F][D][X][6][5][7][X][N][N][B]
Erythrinus erythrinus [F][D][X][6][5][8][X][N][N][B]

[Dr. Warren E. Burgess]
[Aaron Norman]

Esomus danrica 〔F〕〔R〕〔X〕〔6〕〔5〕〔9〕〔X〕〔N〕〔N〕〔5〕 [G. Wolfsheimer]

Esomus malayensis 〔F〕〔R〕〔X〕〔6〕〔6〕〔0〕〔X〕〔N〕〔N〕〔7〕 [G.J.M. Timmerman]

ESOMUS DANRICA (Hamilton-Buchanan) / *Flying Barb*

Range: Singapore and parts of India; numerous in ditches of rice paddies.
Habits: Peaceful; spends most of its time at or near the surface.
Water Conditions: Not critical, as long as the water is clean.
Size: Said to attain 13 cm in native waters; in the aquarium about 6 cm.
Food Requirements: Should have food that floats or stays near the top, such as daphnia (which will gather under a light) or mosquito larvae (which come up for air).

A covered tank is a necessity with these fish; their large pectoral fins have enough drive to send them on a good-sized leap out of the water, and they will soon learn to restrain themselves if they bang their heads a few times on the cover-glass. The *Esomus* species have a distinguishing characteristic: a pair of long "whiskers" flows from the corners of the upper lip underneath the body. These barbels are almost half the entire length of the body. This is another fish which is likely to "go begging" because many hobbyists pass it by due to a lack of bright colors. However, there is a vast difference between the bare tanks in a dealer's establishment and a well-planted, well-lighted tank; once established in one of these, our fish takes on a different appearance. A small school of Flying Barbs is attractive in a tank where most of the other fishes are found in the middle and lower reaches, and they provide some action in the upper reaches. Males are smaller and slimmer than the females. They are very prolific spawners, usually in floating plants in the corners.

ESOMUS MALAYENSIS Ahl / *Malayan Flying Barb*

Range: Malaysian Peninsula and adjacent Southeast Asia.
Habits: Peaceful and very active, preferring to swim in schools near the surface.
Water Conditions: Not critical, but the water should be clean and well aerated. Temperature 22 to 24°C.
Size: To 8 cm.
Food Requirements: Good eaters; accept dried as well as live or frozen foods.

The Malayan Flying Barb is distinguished from the others by having an indistinct horizontal stripe and at the base of the tail a black spot approximately the diameter of the iris of the eye. Around this is a ring of gold. Nature provides many fishes with "eye-spots" on the body, and it is easily understood how a larger fish looking for a meal and swimming into a school of these fish could be greatly confused by seeing so many real and false eyes staring at him and shift his area of operations elsewhere. An eye-spot is also a protection to a fish swimming by itself. A predatory fish on the lookout for a meal might mistake the spot for the real eye and snap at a point behind it where the body should be, to his disappointment. The Malayan Flying Barb should be provided with a tank which affords a good deal of swimming space, and the tank must be kept covered to prevent the fish from jumping out.

ETROPLUS MACULATUS (Bloch) / *Orange Chromide*

Range: India and Sri Lanka.
Habits: Fairly peaceful with fishes of its own size, but cannot be trusted completely.
Water Conditions: Water should be fresh and clean, with about a quarter teaspoon of salt added to each liter.
Size: About 8 cm.
Food Requirements: Should be provided with living or frozen foods; dried food taken only when very hungry.

Asia provides us with a great many of our finest tropical fishes of many kinds, but it is extremely stingy with the aquarist when it comes to cichlid species, most of which come from South America and Africa. Here is one exception which has become very popular in the half-century it has been known to the aquarist. Colors are a happy combination of yellow and black, which always gives a good contrast against the green of the plants. A healthy pair in a well-planted aquarium is particularly beautiful when an additional contrast of black gravel is provided. In form these fish greatly resemble the sunfishes of North America, and their breeding habits are very similar. Sometimes a rock or wide plant leaf is selected, but this fish prefers to find an open space and dig an excavation there until it reaches the aquarium bottom, which it will then clean meticulously. The female usually provides little help, leaving this job to the male. Eggs are attached to this surface and then carefully tended by both parents. Young hatch in four to six days, and about a week later they begin to swim. Newly hatched brine shrimp may then be fed.

ETROPLUS SURATENSIS (Bloch) / *Banded Chromide*

Range: India and Sri Lanka; in the mouths of streams and bays.
Habits: Somewhat quarrelsome; should be trusted only with fishes of its own size or bigger.
Water Conditions: Requires a generous addition of salt to the water, a tablespoonful for every 4 liters, or 10% sea water added.
Size: Wild specimens may measure up to 40 cm, but we seldom see them more than 8 cm in length.
Food Requirements: Should be generously fed with a variety of live foods or frozen full-grown brine shrimp.

This fish is better known to the natives of India as an article of food than as a candidate for the average aquarium. They are usually found in the brackish river mouths and sometimes ascend the rivers into fresh water, like the scats which come from the same area. They seem to prefer these brackish waters to marine environments and are seldom found in salt water. Occasionally some small specimens come in with shipments as a rarity, but their "chip-on-the-shoulder" attitude with their tankmates, along with their inability to do well in fresh water, will always keep them from becoming favorites among aquarium hobbyists.

Etroplus maculatus F E X 6 6 1 X N N 7 [R. Zukal]
Etroplus suratensis F D X 6 6 2 X N N 8 [Dr. Herbert R. Axelrod]

Eutropiellus debauwi 🄵🄳🆇6️⃣6️⃣3️⃣🆇🄽🄽8️⃣
Exodon paradoxus 🄵🄴🆇6️⃣6️⃣4️⃣🆇🄽🄽🄰

[Dr. Herbert R. Axelrod]
[H. J. Richter]

EUTROPIELLUS DEBAUWI (Boulenger) / *Three-Striped Glass Catfish*

Range: Stanley Pool region of the Congo River.
Habits: Very active and peaceful; should be kept in groups rather than singly.
Water Conditions: Soft, slightly acid water is preferable. Temperature 24 to 26°C.
Size: Maximum a little over 7.5 cm.
Food Requirements: Live foods such as daphnia, tubifex worms and white worms.

If you are looking for a catfish which does not look or act like one, this little beauty is for you. The fish in our picture has attained maturity; young specimens do not show their lateral stripes this plainly. A group of about a half-dozen of these makes for a picture of ceaseless nervous activity, and the fish looks as if it would sink to the bottom if it did not struggle constantly to stay afloat. This is definitely a school-fish, and single specimens are generally short-lived. The dorsal fin is small and as is characteristic of the group it appears far in front, near the head. The pectoral and dorsal fins are each provided with a sturdy, sharp first spine. These are held stiffly out and a netted fish is sometimes difficult to disentangle. The barbels are very short, but there are three pairs. Although scientific literature on this fish goes back as far as 1901, hobbyists did not make their acquaintance until 1954.

EXODON PARADOXUS Müller & Troschel / *Bucktoothed Tetra*

Range: Guyana and Brazil.
Habits: Small specimens are mostly peaceful toward other fishes; bigger ones are likely to fight among themselves.
Water Conditions: Should have a large, sunny tank with plenty of vegetation. Rather high temperatures are required, not under 25°C.
Size: Attains a size of about 15 cm, but specimens in the aquarium seldom exceed 10 cm.
Food Requirements: Should get mostly live foods, but will also take frozen foods and pieces of fish, shrimp, etc.

This is a prolific fish in its native waters; wherever it occurs, there are huge schools of them. The natives have an amusing use for them: when they have any dirty dishes to clean, they merely set them in the river and let the "Miguelinhos," as they are called locally, pick them clean. The always-hungry hordes soon find the easy pickings and nibble every bit of food off of the dishes. The native women have a warm affection for this little fish and come to look upon them almost as pets. South American aquarists tell us that a number of these little beauties can be raised together and never cause any trouble. The sad truth is that if a number of grown specimens are put in the same tank, they soon injure each other in many cases. However, there have been a few accounts of them spawning in the aquarium. According to these accounts, they spawned in the usual tetra fashion; that is to say, they scattered eggs in bushy plants. The eggs hatched and the fry were of good size and easy to raise.

FUNDULUS CHRYSOTUS (Günther) / *Golden Ear, Golden Topminnow*

Range: Eastern United States from South Carolina to Texas.
Habits: Peaceful if kept with fishes of its own size.
Water Conditions: Although it sometimes comes from brackish water, it greatly prefers fresh water. Temperature 23 to 26°C.
Size: To 8 cm.
Food Requirements: Has an excellent appetite and will eat dried as well as live or frozen foods.
Color Variations: Sides greenish with rows of red dots. Females have less color and fewer dots. Bright golden spot on each gill-cover.

As with most of our American fishes which are suitable for the aquarium, the Golden Ear finds little respect in its own country. In this case its unpopularity is largely undeserved. It is not uncomfortable at temperatures which we reserve for our tropical species and it is a willing spawner. Even when it is kept in a community tank it is not unusual to find a few youngsters from time to time which have escaped the depredations of the bigger fishes. At spawning time it is not advisable to keep too many males together or there may be fights. It is also a good idea (in the interest of the females) to use two or three females for each male when spawning this fish, because the males are hard drivers. Eggs are laid in bushy plants at the rate of a few each day. They hatch in eight to fifteen days, and if they are not removed daily the parents will eat every egg they find.

FUNDULUS CINGULATUS Cuvier & Valenciennes / *Banded Topminnow*

Range: South Carolina, Georgia, Florida; found in standing water near the coastline.
Habits: Peaceful when kept with fishes its own size.
Water Conditions: It is advisable to add one teaspoon of salt to every 20 liters of aquarium water. Temperature 23 to 25°C.
Size: To 7 cm.
Food Requirements: Will eat most aquarium fish foods, including dried flake food, freeze-dried food and live food.

Fundulus cingulatus should be given an aquarium with plenty of swimming space. The tank should be well planted (although not to the extent that it impedes the fish's swimming) and put in a location where it can get plenty of sunshine. This species is usually peaceful with other species, although the males may sometimes fight among themselves. Sexing is easy as the males are more brightly colored than the females and also have a more robust body and longer fins.

Fundulus cingulatus is not a difficult species to breed. The fish lay their eggs on the plants during a spawning period which lasts several days. After spawning, the parents should be removed from the breeding tanks before they have a chance to eat their eggs. The young will hatch in one to two weeks and should be fed at once. The fry grow slowly.

Fundulus chrysotus ⒻⓇⓍ⑥⑥⑤ⓍⓃⓃ⑧

[Dr. Herbert R. Axelrod]

Fundulus cingulatus ⒻⓇⓍ⑥⑥⑥ⓍⓃⓃ⑦

[Dr. Herbert R. Axelrod]

Fundulus heteroclitus Ⓕ Ⓡ Ⓧ ⑥ ⑥ ⑦ Ⓧ Ⓝ Ⓝ Ⓐ   [Dr. Herbert R. Axelrod]

Fundulus notatus Ⓕ Ⓡ Ⓧ ⑥ ⑥ ⑧ Ⓧ Ⓝ Ⓝ ⑧   [G. Wolfsheimer]

FUNDULUS HETEROCLITUS (Linnaeus) / *Zebra Killie, Mummichog*

Range: Atlantic Coast from Canada to Florida.
Habits: Fairly peaceful, but may pick on smaller fishes.
Water Conditions: Water should be alkaline and hard (about 20 DH), with some salt added, at least a teaspoonful to every 4 liters; will take full salt water. Should be kept at room temperature.
Size: To 20 cm.
Food Requirements: All kinds of live foods, also dried foods which have a vegetable content, such as the so-called "Molly food."

The Zebra Killie is probably the most common small fish along the Atlantic Coast, ranging from Canada down to Florida. It prefers the brackish waters of the bays and river mouths but is occasionally found in fresh water. During the summer months most of the establishments that sell live bait along the New Jersey coast have a supply of live "killies" at all times. In the aquarium they are peaceful if not very colorful citizens which thrive very well once they have become established. Tanks are best left unheated. Males are vigorous drivers. The eggs are laid in plant thickets near the bottom. Incubation period is six to twelve days.

FUNDULUS NOTATUS (Rafinesque) / *Blackstripe Killifish*

Range: Texas, Louisiana and Mississippi north to Wisconsin.
Habits: Fairly peaceful unless kept with fishes it can swallow.
Water Conditions: Should be kept in unheated aquaria at room temperatures.
Size: About 8 cm; fish from the northern part of the range are smaller.
Food Requirements: Should get live foods only; they take dried foods only when very hungry.

Many of the *Fundulus* species have a very odd characteristic which is shared by the *Epiplatys* species of Africa: there is a shiny spot on top of the head. The purpose of this spot has been the source of much conjecture among scientists, and most of them agree that these spots reflecting up from a school of fish swimming near the surface would look like a swarm of insects and would attract real insects to a spot just above the water's surface, where the hungry fish could snap at them. *Fundulus notatus* is distinguished by a black stripe which is indistinct in young specimens, becoming distinctly defined with age. The stripe is especially distinct with mature males. It must be remembered when keeping this and other *Fundulus* species that they are native to much cooler waters than the tropical species and should be kept in an unheated aquarium at room temperatures. Eggs are laid in bushy plants and hatch in about ten to fourteen days.

668

FUNDULUS NOTTI (Agassiz) / *Star-Head Topminnow, Masked Minnow*

Range: South Carolina to Iowa and Texas.
Habits: Best kept only with their own kind, as they are likely to attack other species kept with them.
Water Conditions: A good-sized tank should be provided, with thick vegetation and good aeration. Should be kept at room temperature.
Size: 6 cm.
Food Requirements: Live foods are preferred; dried foods taken only as a last resort.

Living habits are similar in their natural waters: large schools swim mostly just below the surface of the water, in contradiction to their name *Fundulus,* which means "bottom." Most males of the *Fundulus* species are vigorous drivers at breeding time, and it is best to provide each one with several females in order to prevent them from getting hurt. Eggs are deposited on bushy plants and are usually left alone by the parents. It is best to leave the parents in the breeding tank for a week to ten days, as there are only a few eggs deposited each day. Hatching takes place in twelve to fourteen days. The young are free-swimming at once.

GAMBUSIA AFFINIS (Baird & Girard) / *Mosquito Fish*

Range: Southern United States from eastern Texas to Virginia; widely introduced.
Habits: Aggressive and pugnacious; not for the community aquarium.
Water Conditions: Will tolerate a wide variety of water conditions, with temperatures ranging from almost freezing to about 29°C.
Size: Males to 3 cm; females to 5.5 cm.
Food Requirements: Wide variety of foods is eaten greedily, especially live foods.

Although it is not a desirable aquarium fish, *Gambusia affinis* is without a doubt the most useful member of the fish world which we will ever see. It has been introduced into many bodies of water all over the warm parts of the world, there to thrive and multiply and, most important of all, to satisfy its greedy appetite with the hordes of mosquitoes which would otherwise go unchecked to plague the human population and cause many outbreaks of disease. *Gambusia affinis* is a livebearing fish which is particularly well adapted for the job. It can make itself at home in fairly dirty waters and is as much at ease in tropic temperatures as it is in the sometimes near-freezing waters of its native climes. Its appetite is enormous; a healthy fish can consume its own weight in mosquito larvae every day. It is prolific and the young grow very rapidly. But put this fish in an aquarium and we quickly become aware of its true nature. It is very aggressive toward its tankmates, frequently tearing their fins to shreds. It is strange that one of man's most useful fishes should be given a generic name derived from the Spanish slang word *gambusino,* which means "worthless."

Fundulus notti ⬛F⬛R⬛X⬛6⬛6⬛9⬛X⬛N⬛N⬛6 [G. Wolfsheimer]
Gambusia affinis ⬛F⬛R⬛X⬛6⬛7⬛0⬛X⬛N⬛N⬛2 [R. Zukal]

1. *Garmanella pulchra* ⬚F⬚E⬚X⬚6⬚7⬚1⬚X⬚N⬚N⬚3   [H. J. Richter]

2. *Garmanella pulchra*   3. *Garmanella pulchra*

⬚F⬚Q⬚E⬚6⬚7⬚2⬚X⬚N⬚N⬚3   ⬚F⬚Q⬚D⬚6⬚7⬚2⬚X⬚N⬚N⬚3

GARMANELLA PULCHRA Hubbs / *Yucatan Pupfish*

Range: Yucatan, Mexico.
Habits: Relatively peaceful with species of the same size, but males are aggressive toward females of their species.
Water Conditions: Accepts a wide range of water conditions; slightly brackish is best.
Size: To about 3.5 cm.
Food Requirements: Accepts all standard aquarium foods and will also eat loose algae; this species is a heavy feeder.

Garmanella pulchra is a very attractive killifish species that is new to the aquarium hobby. It is hardy and non-demanding as to the conditions it requires and is a reliable and prolific breeder, which means that it can easily be made available in good quantity if it finds favor with hobbyists in general as well as with killie specialists.

Males are easily differentiated from females by coloration and the length of the dorsal fin, which is much larger in the males; the females do not have red in the dorsal and anal fins and are much drabber than the males, although they are more distinctive than many other cyprinodont females. The best way to spawn this species is to use an artificial spawning mop anchored near the bottom of the tank. The males will drive the females very actively and sometime injure them, so it is best to keep an eye on the tank to make sure that a female doesn't get mauled too severely; in any event, the tank should contain a place for her to hide and escape the immediate attentions of the male. The mop should be removed after a week's exposure in the tank. If left in the spawning tank much longer than that, the fry will hatch and be eaten by the parents. The fry don't resorb their yolk-sacs entirely until about a week after they've hatched, but once the yolk-sac is absorbed they must be fed heavily.

Garmanella pulchra and its spawning behavior have been studied in depth by the German aquarist H.J. Richter. In an article in the February 1975 issue of *T.F.H. Magazine*, he described the spawning behavior of the fish as follows: "The mating ceremony is opened by the male's swimming around the female. Circling around is followed by aggressive driving, with the male attempting to get near the female from all sides. To start with the female tries to escape, but once it is ready to spawn it allows the male to swim alongside it. The latter now lays its dorsal fin over the back of the female, and a slight trembling can be observed in both animals as the single egg is expelled and fertilized. Abruptly the fish draw apart. The glass-clear egg with a diameter of about 1 mm disappears in the spawning wool. The whole process is repeated fairly frequently."

1. *Garmanella pulchra* male in breeding colors (p671).
2. A pair of *G. pulchra* above the vegetation preparing to spawn (p671).
3. *G. pulchra* pushing their sides together during spawning (p671).

GARRA TAENIATA Smith / *Siamese Stone-Lapping Fish*

Range: Thailand.
Habits: Peaceful toward even the smallest fishes.
Water Conditions: Slightly alkaline water with a good amount of sunlight. Tank should be well-planted and afforded some hiding places. Temperature 20 to 25°C.
Size: To 15 cm; becomes mature at half that size.
Food Requirements: Accepts all foods, but should be allowed to browse occasionally in an aquarium which has a growth of algae.
Color Variations: Back reddish brown, belly silvery; deep black horizontal line from gill-covers to caudal base. All fins reddish.

It used to be a problem what to do to get rid of algae in the aquarium, but now with the many algae-eating fishes which have become available the situation reverses itself. Some of these fishes, which include *Epalzeorhynchus, Gyrinocheilus* and others, do their clean-up jobs so well that the hobbyist often wonders if they are getting *enough* algae. *Garra taeniata* is well known to the natives of Thailand, who call it *pla lia hin,* or "stone-lapping fish." Its actions may well be described as stone-lapping, and the probability is that it comes from briskly flowing streams where it would have to use its mouth not only for removing algae from rocks or other firmly anchored objects but also to hang on when the current would make it a hard job to use its fins for swimming against it. Like *Epalzeorhynchus kalopterus* this is a very handsome fish and it is hoped that in the near future there will either be more importations or that some breeder with a "wet thumb" will supply them in quantity. Keep this fish in a covered aquarium, as it is a skillful jumper which can find its way through small openings such as those allowed for heaters, etc.

GASTEROPELECUS MACULATUS Steindachner / *Spotted Hatchetfish*

Range: Panama and western Colombia.
Habits: Peaceful surface fishes which may be combined with other non-aggressive fishes in the community aquarium.
Water Conditions: Clean, fairly soft water. Temperature 24 to 26°C. Tank should be well planted, but the water surface should be mostly clear.
Size: To 9 cm; mostly smaller.
Food Requirements: Difficult to feed; should get live food which remains at or near the surface.
Color Variations: Sides bluish silvery with rows of vertical dark spots. Females have a deeper body with less distinct colors.

There are quite a few kinds of hatchetfishes known to science, and they are all very similar in many ways: they are surface fishes, they all have a keeled

1. *Gasteropelecus maculatus* (p674) has wing-like pectoral fins.
2. *G. maculatus* (p675) can be kept alone, as seen here, or with other non-aggressive fishes in a community aquarium.

Garra taeniata F D X 6 7 3 X N N B   [Dr. Herbert R. Axelrod]
1. *Gasteropelecus maculatus* F D X 6 7 4 X N N 8   [Aaron Norman]

Gasteropelecus sternicla [F][D][X][6][7][5][X][N][N][6]
2. *Gasteropelecus maculatus* [F][D][X][6][7][6][X][N][N][8]

belly and long, wing-like pectoral fins with which they can skim along the surface with considerable speed, and in the aquarium they often prove a little difficult to keep and very difficult to spawn. Probably the main reason for this is that the aquarist is hard-put to duplicate exactly the living conditions of this very attractive fish. Their main article of diet, as can be seen by the shape of the mouth, is insect life which swims at the surface or flies just above it. Mosquitoes are a perfect example of this sort of life. Their larval and pupal stages are spent in the water, where they must make frequent trips to the surface for air. The adult winged form flies close to the water when laying eggs. However, feeding mosquito larvae in the home aquarium has its attendant difficulties, and some hobbyists have used wingless fruit flies (*Drosophila*) with success, but there are still no records of the Spotted Hatchetfish being spawned in captivity.

GASTEROPELECUS STERNICLA (Linnaeus) / *Silver Hatchetfish*

Range: Peruvian Amazon, Guianas and the Orinoco Basin in Venezuela.
Habits: A top-feeder which spends most of its time waiting quietly for a passing insect.
Water Conditions: Prefers warm, soft water with a pH of about 6.4. Temperature 24 to 26°C.
Size: About 6 cm maximum.
Food Requirements: Floating foods, wingless *Drosophila* flies and floating bits of frozen brine shrimp.

The Silver Hatchetfish is typical of the fishes in the family Gasteropelecidae in that it has a very compressed body and head. This species inhabits the upper reaches of the water and waits patiently for passing insects. It is a very good jumper and has the ability to emerge from the water and glide for distances of 3 m or more in the air. The power for this "flight" comes from the rapid movement of the fish's pectoral fins. The powerful musculature for the pectoral fins can be seen as an extension in the breast region in which there is a corresponding shoulder-girdle enlargement. Because of this fish's propensity for jumping, the Silver Hatchetfish should be kept in a long, well-covered aquarium. The water should be from 24 to 26°C, soft and slightly acidic (pH of about 6.4). Live foods are most appreciated, including small crustaceans, midge larvae, fruit flies and small cockroaches. The Silver Hatchetfish is peaceful and well suited as a member of a community aquarium.

Although this is not an impossible fish to spawn, little is known about its breeding habits. Sex distinctions are not obvious except when a female is especially gravid.

GASTEROSTEUS ACULEATUS Linnaeus / *Three-Spined Stickleback*

Range: Most of Europe, both coasts of North America, northern Africa and northern Asia.

Habits: Inclined to be pugnacious toward other fishes, and therefore should have their own tank.

Water Conditions: Water should be slightly alkaline with a salt content of about a quarter teaspoonful of salt per liter. Temperature 16 to 18°C.

Size: Up to 10 cm.

Food Requirements: Living foods only, such as daphnia, tubifex worms and white worms.

The Three-Spined Stickleback is one of the most widely distributed freshwater fishes in the temperate zone. Not only does it occur in completely fresh water, but it is also especially numerous in brackish water bays and estuaries. It is an interesting fish for a cold water aquarium, especially in the early and middle spring months. At this time the males put on their brilliant colors and go into their interesting courting activities. They become distinctly unfriendly toward other males who intrude into their territories, and they drive the females very actively. The correct ratio during breeding is two or three females to every male. A number of rooted grasslike plants like *Vallisneria* are a help to the male, who anchors his nest among the leaves. This nest is built in the shape of a ball with a hole through the middle. As a building material bits of plants, etc., are used. These are held together by a sticky secretion from the male's kidneys. After she has laid her eggs the female is driven out of the nest and frequently one or two more add their eggs as well. The eggs hatch in 10 to 14 days, and the fry are carefully guarded.

1. *Gasterosteus aculeatus* fry seeking shelter in its father's mouth (p678).
2. *G. aculeatus* mating pair (p679) in an aquarium.
3. *G. aculeatus* building a nest (p679).

This *Gasterosteus aculeatus* has its third dorsal spine lowered close to the body and inconspicuous. Photo by G. Senfft.

1. *Gasterosteus aculeatus* ⬛F ⬛G ⬛X ⬛6 ⬛7 ⬛8 ⬛X ⬛N ⬛N ⬛O

2. *Gasterosteus aculeatus* F R X 6 7 9 X N N A [S. Frank]

3. *Gasterosteus aculeatus* F A X 6 8 0 X N N A

Gasterosteus aculeatus breeds in rooted grass-like plants. A number of these plants, like *Vallisneria,* are a help to the male, who anchors his nest among the leaves. Photos by G. Senfft.

GENYOCHROMIS MENTO Trewavas / *Malawian Scale-Eater*

Range: Lake Malawi, Africa.
Habits: Aggressive, dangerous to other fishes; a scale- and fin-eater.
Water Conditions: Neutral to hard alkaline water preferred, but not strictly necessary. Temperature 22 to 26°C.
Size: To 18 cm.
Food Requirements: Accepts all standard aquarium foods, but will also eat scales and fins of other fishes kept with them.

Some of the fishes of Lake Malawi in Africa exhibit strange feeding patterns. *Genyochromis mento,* however, is as far as is known the only mbuna (rock-dwelling cichlids of Lake Malawi) to eat scales; it also eats fins. If the oddness of its feeding habits were all that *Genyochromis mento* had to recommend it, it probably would soon be forgotten, but it happens to be an attractive fish and therefore has found some acceptance among hobbyists. This fish has the habit of lurking among hiding places at the bottom of the aquarium and making sudden attacks upward. Both male and female *G. mento* regularly attack other fishes' scales and fins; it is not necessary, though, to provide *G. mento* with long-suffering tankmates in order to maintain the species in good health, because they will accept and do well on more normal aquarium fare. This mouthbrooding species has not been spawned with the degree of regularity attained with other mbunas.

A pair of *Genyochromis mento* between the two pieces of wood. Photo by A. Ivanoff.

Genyochromis mento ⬚F⬚⬚D⬚⬚X⬚⬚6⬚⬚8⬚⬚1⬚⬚X⬚⬚P⬚⬚N⬚⬚C⬚ [Arkadi Ivanoff]

1. *Geophagus balzanii* ♂ ⬚F⬚⬚E⬚⬚X⬚⬚6⬚⬚8⬚⬚2⬚⬚X⬚⬚N⬚⬚N⬚⬚D⬚ [H. J. Richter]

2. *Geophagus balzanii* ♀ F F X 6 8 3 X N N D [H. J. Richter]
3. *Geophagus balzanii* ♀ F F X 6 8 4 X N N D [H. J. Richter]

GEOPHAGUS BALZANII Perugia / *Paraguay Mouthbrooder*

Range: Paraguay (Rio Parana).
Habits: Peaceful; timid.
Water Conditions: This species is tolerant of a wide range of water conditions varying from very soft to medium-hard, pH 6.5 to 7.5 and water temperatures of 20 to 27°C.
Size: To about 18 cm for males; females slightly smaller.
Food Requirements: Takes all standard aquarium fare, both living and prepared; pieces should not be too small.

Here is a South American fish import that has much to recommend it for keeping by both non-specialized hobbyists and dedicated cichlid fans. Although it is a comparatively large species by aquarium fish standards, it is completely peaceful. As a matter of fact, it is a little too peaceful, for it is a timid fish that will allow itself to be bullied. It is a vigorous digger much like its better known cousin *Geophagus jurupari* and will spend time picking up mouthfuls of gravel and then expelling the gravel through the gill openings. It disturbs plants in the tank very rarely. In a tank containing a lot of gravel that could have a tendency to become fouled by becoming a repository for organic matter, *Geophagus balzanii* will serve as an active cleaner of the tank—provided, of course, that the tank is equipped with suitable filtration for removing the debris stirred up by the fish.

Like *G. jurupari, G. balzanii* also is a mouthbrooder. The female broods the eggs for a week to ten days after picking them up in her mouth, and when she releases them they are easily large enough to accept newly hatched brine shrimp.

1. *Geophagus balzanii* male (p682) in an aquarium.
2. *G. balzanii* female (p683) releasing her brood from her mouth.
3. *G. balzanii* female (p683) collecting her fry in her mouth as they seek shelter.

Geophagus balzanii female in a breeding aquarium. Photo by H. J. Richter.

GEOPHAGUS BRASILIENSIS (Quoy & Gaimard)
Brazilian High-Hat, Pearl Cichlid

Range: Eastern coastal regions of South America from Bahia to the La Plata.

Habits: Fairly peaceful for a cichlid. Larger specimens should be kept only with their own kind or with other cichlids their own size.

Water Conditions: Not critical. Temperature should be about 26°C. A pair should have a wellplanted tank of about 80 liters.

Size: In their native waters, about 30 cm; about half that in captivity.

Food Requirements: Live foods preferably; can be accustomed to pieces of fish or shrimp, etc.

This is a popular food fish in the parts of Brazil where it occurs. As the fish matures, a peppering of mother-of-pearl spots becomes more and more prominent. A large black spot on the sides is very variable in intensity. Until the fish become large, the only sure way to tell sex is by comparing the breeding tubes when the fish are ready for spawning. That of the male is slender and pointed, and the female's is blunt. Older males develop a fatty accumulation which gives them a considerable lump atop their foreheads. A preferred spawning site is a cleft between two rocks, which could be replaced by an empty flowerpot standing upright. Eggs and young are seldom eaten. The young, which hatch in four or five days, are carefully tended by the parents, who keep moving them from place to place in holes dug for them. When the fry have begun to swim, it is best to separate them from their parents who might at any time forget their affection for their babies and eat them.

1. *Geophagus brasiliensis* (p686) in an aquarium.
2. *G. brasiliensis* (p686) digging a nest.

Geophagus brasiliensis, the Pearl Cichlid. Photo by L. E. Perkins.

1. *Geophagus brasiliensis* ⬚F⬚A⬚X⬚6⬚8⬚5⬚X⬚N⬚N⬚C   [H. J. Richter]
2. *Geophagus brasiliensis* ⬚F⬚A⬚X⬚6⬚8⬚6⬚X⬚N⬚N⬚C   [H. J. Richter]

Geophagus hondae  [H. J. Richter]
Geophagus jurupari FAX6888XNND [H. Hansen, Aquarium Berlin]

GEOPHAGUS HONDAE Regan / *Redhump Geophagus*

Range: Northern Colombia from the Rio Magdalena and Rio Cauca. One specimen was collected in the Rio Sinu.
Habits: Peaceful, although the male might get rough with the female at times.
Water Conditions: Not critical. Temperatures should be in the mid 20's (°C).
Size: From about 10 to 12 cm; spawns at 6 cm.
Food Requirements: Not fussy; will eat whatever aquarium-type food is available.

The most interesting character of this species, at least physically, is the hump that is developed on the head in the adult male. This hump is normally a reddish brown color but brightens considerably during spawning (thus the name Redhump).

Spawning is not difficult to achieve with the Redhump Geophagus. The aquarium (40 liters or bigger is best) should have gravel, some flat rocks (maybe even the usual flowerpots), and can be planted to provide shelter to one of the partners should the spawning become too combative. The pair can be conditioned with proper feedings in the spawning tank. The lightening of the colors and the dancing displays coupled with the extensions of the breeding tubes are the immediate precursors of egg laying. The site selected, a flat rock or the flowerpot, will have been previously cleaned by both members of the pair. After a few passes over the site actual egg laying commences. The eggs are immediately picked up by the female, and she starts nudging the male in the area of the vent (much like some of the Malawi cichlids). About four to six eggs are deposited at a time until the entire batch of up to 40 is laid. The male, upon completion of spawning, will drive the female away and can be removed from the aquarium to allow the female to incubate the eggs in her mouth.

GEOPHAGUS JURUPARI Heckel / *Eartheater, Demon Fish*

Range: Northern South America.
Habits: Generally peaceful; fond of digging in the sand and searching for edible bits, but seldom uproots plants if they are well rooted. Mouthbrooder.
Water Conditions: Temperature should be kept high, about 26°C. Water should be neutral to slightly acid.
Size: Up to 23 cm in the wild state; not over 15 cm in captivity.
Food Requirements: Will eat dried foods, but should be given an occasional feeding with live foods; white worms and tubifex preferred.

The large, flat, pointed head of this cichlid, with its big eyes, is what usually attracts the hobbyist to this fish. It is constantly digging for food particles in the bottom. Their real claim to being something unusual is their manner of breeding. They will lay their eggs in typical cichlid fashion, then guard and fan them for a day or so. The eggs are then picked up by the male or female or both and incubated in the mouth. After they hatch, the babies will seek refuge in the parents' mouths.

GEOPHAGUS SURINAMENSIS (Bloch) / *Surinam Geophagus*

Range: Amazon Basin and the Guianas.
Habits: Slightly aggressive; typical diggers and earthmovers.
Water Conditions: Not critical; a pH of 7.0 or slightly on the acid side, and hardness 15 to 30. Temperature in the mid 20's (°C).
Size: To 24 cm.
Food Requirements: Will accept almost any aquarium food including brine shrimp (frozen or live), beef heart, flake food, etc. (but prefers to take them from the bottom).

The Surinam Geophagus has become one of the more popular species of *Geophagus* recently, and information on its habits and breeding behavior has become available. The tank size should be adequate, at least 80 liters or more, and supplied with a layer of bottom gravel. The decorations should be selected with the habits of these fish in mind; they are earthmovers and, at least at breeding time, plant destroyers. Therefore a few rocks would be best although plants can be used if you are so inclined and are willing to see them torn apart by the Surinams. The temperature should be within the normal limits of tropical fishes, with spawning temperatures a few degrees higher. A pH of somewhere around neutral is recommended, although it has been reported that its native waters are on the acid side. Perhaps if you are having trouble spawning this fish you might try dropping the pH down to between 6.2 and 6.5 to see if it will help. The hardness is apparently not important; anywhere from 15 to 30 seems to be acceptable and perhaps the tolerance may even go further.

GEPHYROCHARAX CAUCANUS Eigenmann / *Arrowhead Tetra*

Range: Rio Cauca, Colombia.
Habits: In constant motion; active to the point of always having to do something, including bothering its tankmates.
Water Conditions: Temperature should range between 24 to 26°C. They prefer water that is somewhat soft and a pH that is slightly on the acid side.
Size: Up to 6 cm.
Food Requirements: Live foods best, but will accept freeze-dried feedings; dry foods will be accepted if very hungry.

In 1965, when Dr. Axelrod and his special T.F.H. Colombian expedition collected some of these fishes, the aquarium world was able to receive more information and a more critical review of this species. Jacques Gery's critical redescription of these same fishes was highly praised by the scientific world. This fish species is best kept in a tank which has plenty of elbow room, since they are in constant motion. Also, keeping groups of them, besides being more attractive to the eye, is very practical, since there is less of a tendency for them to quarrel among themselves.

Geophagus surinamensis F A X 6 8 9 X N N D [H. J. Richter]
Gephyrocharax caucanus F R X 6 9 0 X N N 6 [Dr. Herbert R. Axelrod]

Girardinus metallicus ⬚Ⓕ ⬚Ⓡ ⬚Ⓧ ⬚⑥ ⬚⑨ ⬚① ⬚Ⓧ ⬚Ⓝ ⬚Ⓝ ⬚⑤   [K. Quitschau]

Glandulocauda inequalis ⬚Ⓕ ⬚Ⓓ ⬚Ⓧ ⬚⑥ ⬚⑨ ⬚② ⬚Ⓧ ⬚Ⓝ ⬚Ⓝ ⬚⑥   [Dr. Herbert R. Axelrod]

GIRARDINUS METALLICUS Poey / *The Girardinus*

Range: Cuba.
Habits: A livebearing fish which greedily gobbles its young if they are not protected with a heavy planting of fine-leaved plants.
Water Conditions: Does best in hard water with a slightly alkaline pH of 7.4.
Size: Females reach 7.5 cm; males about 5 cm.
Food Requirements: They eat everything, but they should have some frozen brine shrimp or live foods in their diets from time to time.

A very heavily planted aquarium with hard water is necessary to have these fish at their best. The German aquarists feed them mosquito larvae, probably their natural food, and enjoy much success with them, but only the very serious aquarist would consider having them at all, as they are as colorless as any fish can be.

The males have an unusual double-pointed gonopodium which is very long proportionately compared to most livebearers. Females are much larger, sometimes being twice as large as the males. The female will drop about 20 to 30 fry per month on a very predictable schedule if conditions are uniform. Unfortunately neither this little fish nor the very similar Yellow Belly *(Girardinus falcatus)* are commonly imported any longer.

GLANDULOCAUDA INEQUALIS Eigenmann / *Croaking Tetra*

Range: Southeastern Brazil, Rio Grande do Sul.
Habits: Peaceful and active; does not disturb plants.
Water Conditions: Should be kept in a roomy aquarium at a temperature slightly lower than most tropical species, 21 to 24°C.
Size: Males about 6 cm; females about 5 cm.
Food Requirements: Not a fussy eater; besides live foods, will also eat dried foods.
Color Variations: Body brownish above, silvery white below. Front and upper edge of eye bright red. Dorsal and anal edged yellow, with black below.

The croaking tetras are an interesting group of characoids that were last reviewed by Gery in 1966. The group includes *Glandulocauda melanogenys, G. melanopleura, G. terofali* and possibly *G. inequalis,* this last species being of uncertain generic status. As *G. inequalis* is so rarely seen, it does no harm to temporarily leave it in the genus *Glandulocauda.* As a group, the croaking tetras are very rare and, from a biological point of view, not very well known.

This species, like the other tetras in its group, has the power to make tiny croaking noises. The fish ingest a gulp of air at the surface of the water. When they release it below the surface, a croaking noise is also emitted.

Not a great deal is known about the breeding habits of this species. Courtship involves active driving and terminates in the laying of eggs.

Glandulocauda inequalis (arrow) together in an aquarium with *Coelurichthys microlepis* (p691).

GLOSSOLEPIS INCISUS Weber / *New Guinea Rainbowfish*

Range: New Guinea.
Habits: Peaceful, a schooling fish that requires a large aquarium.
Water Conditions: Slightly alkaline water with a hardness of 18 to 25 DH. Temperature between 24 and 26°C.
Size: Up to 15 cm.
Food Requirements: Accepts flake foods but prefers such live foods as daphnia, mosquito larvae and cyclops; also accepts lean beef.

Dr. Gerald R. Allen, world authority on rainbowfishes, has recently demoted *Glossolepis* to the subgeneric level and placed it within the genus *Melanotaenia*. Since it is already known in the trade as *"Glossolepis"* and further revisions are said to be forthcoming, we have chosen to leave the species in *Glossolepis* until a conclusive review of the taxon is completed.

The New Guinea Rainbowfish has obvious sexual color differences. The males are much more brightly colored than the females. The male's entire body, including its fins, is a deep salmon-red color. The females have a basic olive coloration with a golden iridescence to the scales. The fins are transparent light yellow.

Glossolepis incisus is a schooling fish which is constantly on the move. It should be given a relatively large tank with a good deal of swimming area. The species shows off its best coloration when kept with several of its own kind, as opposed to keeping the fish with other unrelated species.

Like most of the melanotaeniids kept in the aquarium hobby, the New Guinea Rainbowfish is not difficult to spawn. It spawns in a manner similar to the African killifishes. Several males should be kept for every female. Courtship involves a good deal of chasing. When the male finally catches the female, the two come together over bushy vegetation where the eggs are laid and then fertilized. It should be noted that this species should be given Java moss on which to spawn. The Java moss should be removed (and replaced) from the breeding tank about once a week and transferred into an incubator aquarium with a temperature of about 27°C. The eggs are very adhesive and should be clear. The eggs will hatch about two weeks after they are laid, depending upon the temperature of the water. The fry should be fed immediately. They will head for the surface for food and can be given newly hatched brine shrimp. Because the New Guinea Rainbowfish mates several times a day over a period of time, the eggs in the incubator tank will hatch at different times. The resulting fry from several spawnings will be of different sizes and, for obvious reasons, it is necessary to separate the larger fry from the smaller fry and the eggs.

1. *Glossolepis incisus* male above female (p694).
2. *G. incisus* male is bright orange-red and the female is silver-brown (p694).

1. *Glossolepis incisus* ⊞ⓇⓍ⑥⑨③ⓍⓃⓃⒸ   [H. J. Richter]
2. *Glossolepis incisus* ⊞ⒶⓍ⑥⑨④ⓍⓃⓃⒸ   [B. Mayers]

Gymnocorymbus thayeri F D X 6 9 9 X N N 5   [Dr. Herbert R. Axelrod]

Gymnotus carapo F D X 7 0 0 X N N E   [Dr. Herbert R. Axelrod]

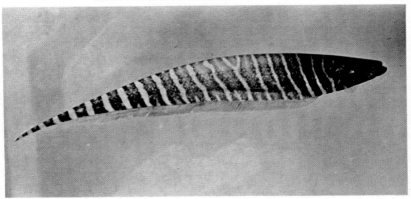

GYMNOCORYMBUS THAYERI Eigenmann / *Straight-Finned Black Tetra*

Range: Upper Amazon, Bolivia and Colombia in warmer waters.

Habits: A fast swimming fish which should be well fed at all times if kept in a community aquarium.

Water Conditions: Prefers warmer, softer and more acid waters than its much blacker cousin, *G. ternetzi*. Temperature 24 to 26°C.

Size: Not larger than 5 cm.

Food Requirements: Prefers copious feedings of live foods, but does equally well if fed frozen brine shrimp and a varied diet of prepared foods. Some live food should be offered weekly.

Undoubtedly many of the black tetras swimming around in aquariums now under the name of *Gymnocorymbus ternetzi* are *G. thayeri*. This fish is much smaller than its cousin, reaching 5 cm maximum in nature. The photo shows a fish collected from the Rio Guapofe. This is really an intermediate area for *G. thayeri* and may represent a new subspecies. *Ternetzi is* relatively deep-bodied, the depth going 1.6 into body length while *thayeri* has a length which is twice its depth; thus, this is the real test. Of course, the fish becomes more rounded as it grows older and only fully grown fishes can pass this "test." this "test."

Spawning of this species is very simple and is merely a matter of separating the sexes and finding enough live foods to bring them into the peak of condition. Any live foods can do it, though daphnia and tubifex worms seem to be best.

GYMNOTUS CARAPO Linnaeus / *Banded Knife Fish*

Range: Guatemala south to the La Plata.

Habits: Mostly nocturnal; a predatory species best kept by itself.

Water Conditions: Not critical. Temperature 24 to 26°C.

Size: Is said to attain 58 cm; imported specimens seldom over 15 cm.

Food Requirements: Pieces of beef heart, fish or shrimp; prefers small fish above all.

The knife fishes are extremely interesting oddities in the aquarium. There is no dorsal fin or caudal fin; where a fish would normally have a tail, the body simply comes to a point. There are pectoral fins, but they contribute little to the fish's locomotion and simply serve to steer it. It propels itself by means of a rippling motion of the long anal fin. This rippling motion can be reversed instantaneously and the fish can swim backward with the same ease as forward. *Gymnotus carapo* is not adapted for keeping in a community aquarium. Its favorite food is smaller fishes, on which it generally feeds while the tank is in almost complete darkness. These fish do not congregate in schools when in their natural waters; the author saw them caught in Guyana, and at no time were there more than three or four among a netful of other fishes.

GYRINOCHEILUS AYMONIERI (Tirant) / *Chinese Algae-Eater*

Range: Widely distributed throughout Thailand.
Habits: Small specimens usually peaceful.
Water Conditions: Clean, well-aerated, slightly alkaline water. To promote algal growth, a generous amount of sunlight should enter the tank.
Size: Seldom exceeds 13 cm in the aquarium.
Food Requirements: Vegetarian; grazes on algae much of the time. Will also take dried foods or a piece of crushed lettuce or spinach leaf.

Whoever got the wild notion of calling this fish the "Chinese Algae-Eater" was far off base. Thailand, its home, is a long way from China. *Gyrinocheilus aymonieri*, although it has been known to science since 1883, was not imported alive until 1955. In its native waters it attains a length of about 25 cm, but in the aquarium a length of more than half that is unusual. Like many of our sucker catfishes, *Gyrinocheilus aymonieri* has an underslung mouth which forms a sucking disc. With this it is able to anchor itself to a rock or some other stationary object in swiftly moving water. There is an unusual thing in connection with this: in addition to the slit behind the gills where the water is exhaled there is another slit which admits fresh water for breathing. The observed respiratory rate is 230 to 240 per minute. This interesting fish has strictly vegetarian habits and will do an excellent job of cleaning up algae in a surprisingly short time. If no algae are available, a crushed lettuce or spinach leaf will do nicely. So far nothing is known of their reproductive habits.

1. *Gyrinocheilus aymonieri* sucking slime and algae off of the rocks (p702).
2. *G. aymonieri* resting on the bottom of an aquarium (p702).

Gyrinocheilus aymonieri with its sucker up against the aquarium glass. Photo by R. Zukal.

1. *Gyrinocheilus aymonieri* ⬚F⬚ ⬚D⬚ ⬚X⬚ ⬚7⬚ ⬚0⬚ ⬚1⬚ ⬚X⬚ ⬚N⬚ ⬚N⬚ ⬚B⬚   [H. J. Richter]

2. *Gyrinocheilus aymonieri* ⬚F⬚ ⬚D⬚ ⬚X⬚ ⬚7⬚ ⬚0⬚ ⬚2⬚ ⬚X⬚ ⬚N⬚ ⬚N⬚ ⬚B⬚   [K. Paysan]

Halophryne trispinosus F D X 7 0 3 X N N D [Aaron Norman]
Haplochromis annectens F A X 7 0 4 X N N D [Dr. Herbert R. Axelrod]

HALOPHRYNE TRISPINOSUS (Günther) / *Toadfish, Freshwater Lionfish*

Range: India to Thailand, Java, Borneo, Sumatra, Malaysia.
Habits: A voracious species that is not safe to keep with any small fishes.
Water Conditions: Not critical; can do well in semi-brackish water.
Size: Over 30 cm in the wild; usually seen much smaller in the aquarium trade.
Food Requirements: Prefers whole fish as food; most individuals will take either live or frozen fish. Smaller individuals will accept smaller non-fish foods.

This odd fish is often sold under the trade name of "Freshwater Lionfish" because of its superficial resemblance to the poisonous lionfishes of the marine family Scorpaenidae. Whether a fish is poisonous or not (this fish is not) is of course a very important consideration, so *all* fishes that look like the subject portrayed here should be viewed with suspicion, and hobbyists should be very careful in relying on sketchy identifications before purchasing any fish which could be poisonous. *Halophryne trispinosus* is a drab species that shows almost no bright coloration at all. They are relatively very inactive except at feeding time, when the introduction of live food can stimulate them to a frenzy of swift motion to capture their prey. The species dislikes bright light and usually seeks caves and other hiding places in which to lurk, making only occasional forays around the tank. Larger fish of the species will bully smaller individuals and keep them from food, although even smaller individuals are greedy eaters. *Halophryne trispinosus* has been spawned under aquarium conditions, but fry have not been successfully reared. Large yellowish eggs were laid in a cave and guarded by the female.

HAPLOCHROMIS ANNECTENS (Regan) / *Annectens*

Range: Lake Malawi, Africa.
Habits: Relatively aggressive (especially during spawning time), but can be kept with other Malawi cichlids that are not timid or easily dominated.
Water Conditions: Hard, alkaline water. Temperature 24 to 28°C.
Size: To about 20 cm.
Food Requirements: Takes all of the usual aquarium foods.

Haplochromis annectens spawns like most of the Malawi mouthbrooders. The male will set up a territory of sorts and start shifting the bottom gravel around until the whole tank is upset and he is eventually satisfied. The female is enticed to the spot where spawning occurs, the female winding up with a mouthful of pale beige eggs some 2½ mm in length. When the bulging gular area of the female is noticed, wait a day or two and then move her to more secluded quarters. Be sure again that the tank is large enough; an 80- or 100-liter aquarium should suffice. The incubation period is again similar to the mbuna, being about three weeks in duration. A trio (one male and two females) is recommended, although a larger group is okay—but keep an eye on them in case a dominant male starts to bully the other males out of the tank.

HAPLOCHROMIS BURTONI (Günther) / *Burton's Mouthbrooder*

Range: Widespread in Africa south of the Sahara.
Habits: Usually too aggressive to be kept with smaller fishes; should have a tank of their own.
Water Conditions: Neutral to slightly acid. Temperature 24 to 26°C.
Size: About 10 cm; females slightly smaller.
Food Requirements: A greedy eater; some vegetable substances should be given.

Haplochromis burtoni is a very aggressive fish which is best kept on its own or with other large fishes which can hold their own. The species is relatively hardy and easy to breed. As with most *Haplochromis* species, *H. burtoni* is a maternal mouthbrooder. The spawning rituals include chasing and whirling movements. The pair end up above shallow pits or rock ledges. Fifty to a hundred eggs are laid and then immediately picked up by the female. They develop in ten days to two weeks. The eggs are fertilized when the female nibbles at the anal fin of the male soon after she picks up her eggs. The male's anal fin has several yellow-orange spots on it. A German scientist, Dr. Wolfgang Wickler, has made a very interesting observation about the function of these spots. The female turns around and picks up the eggs almost as soon as she lays them. When she has a mouthful of eggs the male spreads his orange-spotted anal fin on the bottom in front of her. The spots resemble more eggs and she pecks busily at his fin, trying to pick up the spots. As she does this he releases his sperm, which mixes thoroughly with the eggs in her mouth.

1. *Haplochromis burtoni* male in spawning colors (p706).
2. *H. burtoni* mating pair in an aquarium (p706). The female has an extended buccal cavity full of eggs and is about to collect some sperm from the male's vent.

Haplochromis burtoni with fry. Photo by A. van den Nieuwenhuizen.

1. *Haplochromis burtoni* ♂ F A X 7 0 5 X N N A [A. van den Nieuwenhuizen]
2. *Haplochromis burtoni* F Q X 7 0 6 X N N A

Haplochromis callipterus ⬚F⬚A⬚X⬚7⬚0⬚7⬚X⬚N⬚N⬚9 [Dr. Herbert R. Axelrod]

Haplochromis compressiceps [K. Lucas, Steinhart Aquarium]
⬚F⬚A⬚X⬚7⬚0⬚8⬚X⬚N⬚N⬚D

HAPLOCHROMIS CALLIPTERUS (Günther)
Callipterus

Range: Lake Malawi, south to southern Mozambique.
Habits: Very quarrelsome.
Water Conditions: Hard and alkaline. Temperature 24 to 26°C.
Size: About 10 cm.
Food Requirements: Live or frozen foods, with an addition of foods with a vegetable origin.

Until recently we did not yet have any really reliable breeding information on *Haplochromis callipterus,* but being a *Haplochromis* species, we thought that it might be well to start with the assumption that they will breed like others of the genus *Haplochromis.* This was found to be true, as *H. callipterus* proved to be a maternal mouthbrooder. A close eye should be kept on the females; separate them when there is a mouthful of eggs in evidence. Like the others of this Malawi group, their habitat provides a great deal of algae which is eaten in addition to their normal diet, and if we can provide some hair algae for nibbling purposes, all the better. We still have much to learn about this very attractive species, and its natural bellicose manner may be a stumbling block to keeping it at first. Like so many other formerly aggressive species, a few years of captivity may work wonders toward taming these fish down.

HAPLOCHROMIS COMPRESSICEPS (Boulenger) / *Malawian Eye-Biter*

Range: Lake Malawi, Africa.
Habits: A predator that will eat any small fishes which it can completely engulf.
Water Conditions: Similar to most Malawi fishes, the water for this species should be hard and alkaline with a pH of 7.6 or more. Temperature should be about 22 to 28°C.
Size: Reaches a maximum length of about 25 cm.
Food Requirements: Eats small fishes in nature but will take many of the standard foods for other cichlids.

Haplochromis compressiceps is a predator and is quite successful at its trade. Its compressed head and body, its coloration and its behavior all combine to allow it to approach a victim undetected. The flattened body with dark stripes makes this fish hard to see among the *Vallisneria* beds in which it hunts. It suspends itself in the water at an oblique angle (like a headstander) and moves among the grass with movements of its pectoral and soft portions of its dorsal and anal fins until it comes close enough to make a sudden dash at its prey. Its reputation as an eye-biter has been largely unsubstantiated. Being a predator, it is possible that this fish may dislodge the eye of its prey while in the course of trying to entrap it.

The Malawian Eye-Biter is a maternal mouthbrooder and spawns in a manner similar to other species of Lake Malawi *Haplochromis.* The eggs and fry are tended for about three weeks, after which they are released and are on their own. Fry can take newly hatched brine shrimp or fine flake food.

708

HAPLOCHROMIS EUCHILUS Trewavas / *Euchilus, Big-Lips*

Range: Lake Malawi, Africa.
Habits: Fairly peaceful for a Malawi cichlid; somewhat less aggressive and territory-minded than other Malawi cichlids.
Water Conditions: Prefers hard, alkaline water. Temperature 24 to 26°C.
Size: To 33 cm.
Food Requirements: Much prefers live foods but will accept frozen foods and freeze-dried foods, also good flake foods.
Color Variations: Color and pattern vary greatly according to the age of the fish. Adult specimens show a lot more blue on both body and fins and have other highlights not present in younger fish.

Many of the African cichlids, especially the mouthbrooding species, are very variable in appearance. Some vary mostly according to mood, some according to geographical race, some according to age, some according to other factors. With *Haplochromis euchilus,* the differences are attributable mostly to age: the fish looks much better as an adult than it does as a juvenile.

For a mouthbrooder, *H. euchilus* is not a very easy fish to get to spawn. If not conditioned properly and put into the best possible health, it will refuse to propagate. Luckily, it is not an overly temperamental species as to water and food requirements and therefore doesn't need to have too many concessions made to it in order to be kept in good health. One area of importance is temperature: the species does not like cool water and is very intolerant of abrupt changes in temperature, even more so than most other species. *H. euchilus* is a mouthbrooding species in which the female cares for the eggs and fry. Upon release by their mother, the fry are able to take newly hatched brine shrimp immediately. The fry grow comparatively quickly, but only if they receive regular and substantial changes in their tank water. Tank-raised *H. euchilus* are much less likely to disturb plants than wild fish are.

Haplochromis euchilus, commonly called Euchilus or Big-Lips, is a usually peaceful Malawian cichlid that is less territorial (except when breeding) than most other Rift Lake cichlids of its size. Growing up to 33 cm in the wild, this fish lives in the rocky littoral zone (shallow enough to allow photosynthetic flora to exist) of the lake.

Here *Haplochromis euchilus* grazes on the heavy algae carpeting the rocks, feeding largely upon the insects that in turn live off the algae. Juvenile specimens lack the large lips of the adults. Adults are of a blue-silver color and have two dark bands running along their flanks and back. Sexing live specimens is usually difficult.

In the aquarium, this species will accept freeze-dried and frozen foods, although it usually prefers and thrives on live foods. It is often difficult to get this fish to accept flake foods.

1. A juvenile *Haplochromis euchilus* whose lips are not yet fully developed (p710).
2. An adult *H. euchilus* in a photo tank (p710).

1. *Haplochromis euchilus* [H. Hansen, Aquarium Berlin]
F B X 7 0 9 X N N B

2. *Haplochromis euchilus* F A X 7 1 0 X N N D [Dr. Herbert R. Axelrod]

Haplochromis horei F A X 7 1 1 X N N B [Glen S. Axelrod]

Haplochromis labrosus F A X 7 1 2 X N N B [Dr. Herbert R. Axelrod]

HAPLOCHROMIS HOREI (Günther) / *Spothead Haplochromis*

Range: Found only in Lake Tanganyika.
Habits: Aggressive and generally predatory on smaller fishes.
Water Conditions: Hard and alkaline. Temperature 23 to 28°C.
Size: Attains a length of over 18 cm.
Food Requirements: Will accept almost any type aquarium food, including small fishes.

These are definitely shore fish. They keep very close to the coastline and even penetrate up the estuaries of some of the rivers that empty into the lake. *H. horei* does not venture into deep water and is more likely to be found at depths of less than one meter. In its natural habitat it will feed on higher plants and fishes; Poll found stomachs filled with clupeids (most likely *Limnothrissa*). In an aquarium, however, it accepts almost any type of suitable food, live or prepared. Since it is a predator, make sure you choose the tankmates with care.

The tank should be set up in typical African lake cichlid format with plenty of rockwork and hard, alkaline water. The bottom should be covered with a few centimeters of gravel.

HAPLOCHROMIS LABROSUS Trewavas / *Labrosus*

Range: Lake Malawi, Africa.
Habits: Typical of most Malawi cichlids; aggressive (especially with members of its own kind) but does well in a community situation with other Malawi cichlids.
Water Conditions: Hard, alkaline water. Temperature near 26°C.
Size: To about 13 cm.
Food Requirements: Easy to feed; will take most of the common live or prepared foods generally available for cichlids.

Mature Labrosus have large, fleshy lips from which their name is derived. Although the young *H. labrosus* are similar in appearance, as they grow the males become more recognizable. As they mature and become dominant and finally ready to breed, their bodies take on a more golden color between the vertical dark bars. More golden color is seen on the gill covers and as a streak along the edges of the unpaired fins. Light barring appears between the eyes and small orange spots develop in the anal fin. The female is more plain-colored (usually brownish to reddish brown) and lacks the spots in the anal fin.

Spawning occurs in typical fashion, with the male sporting his best colors, displaying in front of the female and trying to entice her into his territory. As the female fills with eggs she is more likely to succumb to his "charms" and follow him, whereupon spawning commences. The female picks up the eggs in her mouth and incubates them. It is best to remove her from the community tank and let her brood the eggs in peace. It has been reported that she might spit the eggs out if moved immediately.

HAPLOCHROMIS LINNI Burgess and Axelrod
Elephant-Nose Polystigma; Linn's Haplochromis

Range: Lake Malawi, Africa.
Habits: Not too aggressive; well suited to a community tank of the larger African lake cichlids.
Water Conditions: Prefers hard, alkaline water. Temperature between 23 and 28°C.
Size: Reaches a length of at least 35 cm.
Food Requirements: Will eat a wide variety of larger sized aquarium foods as well as small fishes.

In almost all respects the Elephant-Nose Polystigma resembles the other members of the blotched-spotted group (*Haplochromis polystigma, H. livingstoni,* etc.), requiring a relatively large tank, plenty of rocks and artificial plants with perhaps a small open sandy space. Two things have been reported as different for this fish. It is less aggressive than the others and fits very well into a community tank. Secondly, it is more sensitive to dissolved waste buildup and the water quality has to be more carefully monitored.

Spawning follows the pattern of the blotched-spotted group of species. The female will carry up to 200 or more eggs for about three weeks. When the fry are released they are about 10-15 mm in length and resemble the female closely.

Haplochromis linni (upper specimen) is compared with *H. polystigma* lower specimen) to show the similarity in color pattern (p714, upper photo).

HAPLOCHROMIS LIVINGSTONI (Günther) / *Livingstoni*

Range: Lake Malawi, Africa.
Habits: Aggressive.
Water Conditions: Hard, alkaline water. Temperature 23 to 28°C (breeding occurs at upper end of range).
Size: Over 30 cm, but usually does not attain this extreme size in aquaria.
Food Requirements: Will take a variety of foods including small fishes.

Haplochromis livingstoni is very similar to and often confused with its close relative, *H. polystigma.* Both have the typical large blotches, but *polystigma* has, in addition, many small spots over the body and fins that are lacking in *H. livingstoni.*

Spawning can be accomplished in a community tank (the male will keep all other fishes at bay during the spawning), and best results are obtained by using one male and two or more females. Spawning itself follows the normal circling pattern with the female at times mouthing the male's vent, possibly ensuring fertilization of the eggs. Up to 200 eggs are laid and brooded by the female for about three weeks. When released, the fry look very much like the female. They can be fed with newly hatched brine shrimp, crushed flake food or other suitably small and nutritious fare.

Haplochromis linni 　F D X 7 1 3 X N N D 　　　　[Dr. Herbert R. Axelrod]

Haplochromis livingstoni 　F D X 7 1 4 X N N D 　　　[M.K. Oliver]

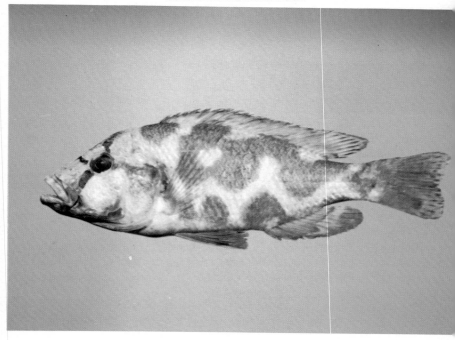

1. *Haplochromis moori* F A X 7 1 5 X N N D   [G. Marcuse]
2. *Haplochromis moori* F F X 7 1 6 X N N D   [G. Schubert]

HAPLOCHROMIS MOORI (Boulenger) / *Blue Lumphead, Blue Moori*

Range: Lake Malawi, Africa.

Habits: Peaceful for a comparatively large cichlid, but not completely inoffensive; the degree of aggressiveness is very variable from individual to individual.

Water Conditions: Prefers hard, alkaline water. Best temperature around 24°C.

Size: Up to 23 cm.

Food Requirements: Takes all normal aquarium foods, especially live and frozen.

Color Variations: Both sexes have an over-all blue color, but individuals vary greatly in the amount of black markings on the fins and back according to their geographical origin.

This is a distinctive fish: in addition to the blue color which is present in all representatives of the species, even if it does vary in intensity, *Haplochromis moori* also has a pronounced hump on the head. The two characters, possession of a hump and over-all blue coloration, don't exist in combination in any other aquarium fish known at present. Other African cichlids *(Steatocranus casuarius, Cyphotilapia frontosa)* have the hump and a number of other African cichlids are of an over-all blue color, but no other African cichlid couples blue color and frontal hump. The size of the hump, like the blue color, is variable from one individual of *H. moori* to another. On some it is very large and on others it is relatively reduced; both males and females show the hump, and although some females have larger protrusions than certain males, males on the average possess larger humps.

Haplochromis moori is a mouthbrooding species in which the female alone incubates the eggs; the length of time the female holds the eggs in her mouth is variable according to temperature and the age and condition of the fish, but in most cases incubation lasts three to four weeks. The fry at the time of release by their mother are able to take newly hatched brine shrimp right away.

This species is much less dependent on the provision of rock jungles in its tank to make it feel comfortable than some of the other Malawi cichlids are, and it is less strictly territorial. *H. moori* is relatively scarce in both the aquarium trade and nature, and good specimens command a high price. *Cyrtocara moori* is the name under which this species was originally described (by Boulenger in 1902), and this name is still sometimes used in reference to it in aquarium literature.

1. *Haplochromis moori*, the Blue Lumphead, with a well-developed bump on his head. This fish is a male (p715).
2. *H. moori* fry entering the buccal cavity of the female parent for protection (p715).

HAPLOCHROMIS POLYSTIGMA Regan / *Polystigma, Polly*

Range: Lake Malawi.
Habits: Aggressive; highly territorial.
Water Conditions: Hard, alkaline water preferred but not strictly required. Temperature 23 to 27°C.
Size: Over 26 cm; usually seen much smaller.
Food Requirements: Accepts all meaty foods.

This large, aggressive Malawian cichlid is a greedy eater and fast grower; it is, in fact, one of the fastest-growing of all African cichlids. Because of its size and potential for being a bullying killer when maintained in close quarters with other fishes, it should be housed in a large tank that is generously provided with hiding places. *Haplochromis polystigma* is similar in color pattern to a number of other Lake Malawi cichlids (*Haplochromis linni, Haplochromis rostratus, Haplochromis pardalis, Haplochromis livingstonï, Haplochromis fuscotaeniatus* among them) but is more commonly seen than any of these species. *H. polystigma* is a mouthbrooding species in which the female broods the young. At a temperature of around 27°C the young can be released from her mouth within ten days; at lower temperatures the hatching/release process takes longer. The female is fiercely protective of the young for a short time after their initial release but generally loses interest in them (and they in her) in about five days. *H. polystigma* is among the most prolific of Lake Malawi mouthbrooders, spawns often numbering over 100. When kept in a tank bottomed with gravel, both male and female will do much moving of the gravel; even immature individuals will engage in some gravel rearrangements. This species is like some of the other large cichlid species in its appreciation by hobbyists.

Haplochromis polystigma has an interesting behavior pattern with regard to its spawning and feeding. During spawning the aggressive male takes on a light coloration and will herd the female away from the other males. In the aquarium, the dominant male will force all of the other males into a confined area of the aquarium, usually into an upper corner. The dominant male will exhibit a light coloration and the cowering males will be very dark. If the submissive males are not removed from the aquarium, there is a good chance that they might be killed.

During the feeding the color patterns are very different from that of breeding. The hunting fish are dark brown and have a similar appearance to cowering males. The fish is known to lie on the bottom of the aquarium, feigning unobtrusiveness with its dark coloration. When the prey comes within range, however, the predator strikes out, engulfing the unsuspecting fish.

1. *Haplochromis polystigma* in an aquarium (p718).
2. *H. polystigma* female releasing fry in an aquarium (p718).

1. *Haplochromis polystigma* ⬚F⬚H⬚X⬚7⬚1⬚7⬚X⬚N⬚N⬚C

2. *Haplochromis polystigma* ⬚F⬚F⬚X⬚7⬚1⬚8⬚X⬚N⬚N⬚C

Haplochromis rostratus [F] [C] [X] [7] [1] [9] [X] [N] [N] [8] [Dr. Herbert R. Axelrod]

Hasemania nana [F] [Q] [X] [7] [2] [0] [X] [N] [N] [5] [Dr. Herbert R. Axelrod]

HAPLOCHROMIS ROSTRATUS (Boulenger) / *Rostratus*

Range: Lake Malawi, Africa.
Habits: Aggressive. Does fairly well with other Malawi cichlids of comparable size. Needs a large aquarium.
Water Conditions: Hard, alkaline, very clean water. Temperature 22 to 28°C.
Size: To about 33 cm.
Food Requirements: Takes all normal aquarium foods.

Haplochromis rostratus is a species endemic to Lake Malawi. It grows rather large, to 33 cm (with the females not quite so big) and, in contrast to the mbuna and other rock-inhabiting species, occurs mostly over the sandy areas of the lake. It is basically a silvery colored fish adorned with neat rows of black spots along the upper sides and back. Some yellow tints can be seen in the fins. In open water over the sand the background color is almost invisible and the fish appears as a series of black spots (the eye would appear as the first spot in the mid-lateral series). It has been reported that when they are threatened they dive into the sand much like the marine wrasses of the family Labridae. When the danger passes, of course, the fish appear out in the open again and continue their feeding or whatever they were doing when interrupted.

Sexing *Haplochromis rostratus* is easy with adult fish, because the males take on a bluish color with maturity. The dominant male is darker than the subordinate males and becomes very dark, almost black, with a blue-black head. The females and juveniles retain the spotted pattern. They spawn over the sand, usually (but not always) in a depression. The female and male can be seen going in circles over the selected spawning site with the female laying her eggs and the male following after. The female will pick up the eggs on the next go-round and apparently mouth the area of the male's vent. This continues until she has deposited all her eggs. The male tolerates the female in the same tank while she is incubating the eggs and early fry, but it is best to separate her for the safety of the fry or in case the male gets ideas about spawning again. In three to four weeks the fry are let out of her mouth and she can begin her recovery from the long fast (although females have been observed sneaking in a bite or two during the incubation period). The number of fry varies, depending on the size of the female and the condition of the breeders, but it may be as many as 100 or more.

HASEMANIA NANA (Reinhardt) / *Silver-Tipped Tetra*

Range: Rio S. Francisco basin, southeastern Brazil.
Habits: Very peaceful; should be kept in a school of not less than six.
Water Conditions: Slightly acid and soft water. Temperature 24 to 26°C.
Size: To 5 cm.
Food Requirements: Prepared foods accepted, but live or frozen foods are preferred.

This is not a very popular fish, although several specimens have found their way into the aquarium trade.

HELOGENES MARMORATUS Günther / *Marbled Helogenes*

Range: Guyana and lower Amazon region.
Habits: Peaceful and nocturnal.
Water Conditions: Not critical, but water should be clean and uncontaminated at all times. Temperature 23 to 26°C.
Size: To 10 cm.
Food Requirements: Eats all sorts of foods, but should have an occasional meal of live foods.

This attractive fish has a great disadvantage: its nocturnal habits make it a fish that is practically impossible to find in a heavily planted aquarium during the daylight hours. It has a very wide anal fin that extends from just behind the anus almost to the caudal base, and the adipose fin is very small. It eats almost any type of food, live as well as prepared. It is useful to keep in an aquarium where other fishes leave some food behind.

HELOSTOMA TEMMINCKI Cuvier and Valenciennes / *Kissing Gourami*

Range: Thailand, Indonesia, Sumatra, Borneo, Java, Malay Peninsula and Cambodia.
Habits: Prefer a large aquarium. Plants are not necessary though they do enjoy "chomping" on them to remove whatever has fallen onto them or grown over them. They are easily overcrowded and unless they are given plenty of room their growth is stunted, they develop a "hollow belly" and they die.
Water Conditions: The water conditions are not critical, but they do much better in slightly hard water with a pH of 7.0. Temperature 26°C.
Size: Up to 30 cm.
Food Requirements: A greedy eater which never tires of looking for food. Their major diet should consist of frozen brine shrimp and woms now and then. They seem to get along very well on salmon eggs (the dried prepared form available as a fish food) and shredded shrimp, though this usually fouls the water.

The Kissing Gourami is a relatively peaceful fish which is also very timid. These fish have broad lips which are widely extended. They press these lips against the aquarium rocks, glass, plants and also the sides of other fish so that they may injest the slime that covers them. These fish also have the habit of touching one another and temporarily locking lips. Some researchers postulate that this behavior pattern is a form of threat display. This mouth action is also responsible for the fish's popular name, Kissing Gourami.

Helostoma temmincki is a rapidly growing fish which requires a rather large aquarium. The species is omnivorous and needs both plant and animal matter in its diet in order to thrive. The fish does not do well in cold water and the aquarium temperature should not drop below 24°C. This fish is not easy to breed and it is difficult to distinguish the sexes.

1. *Helostoma temmincki* trio in an aquarium (p722).
2. *H. temmincki* "kissing" as their extended lips meet (p722).

Helogenes marmoratus ⬚F⬚D⬚X⬚7⬚2⬚1⬚X⬚N⬚N⬚A   [Dr. Herbert R. Axelrod]

1. *Helostoma temmincki* ⬚F⬚H⬚M⬚7⬚2⬚2⬚X⬚N⬚N⬚A
2. *Helostoma temmincki* ⬚F⬚H⬚B⬚7⬚2⬚2⬚X⬚N⬚N⬚A

Hemiancistrus niceforoi 🄵🄳🆇🔢7️⃣2️⃣3️⃣🆇🄽 🄽🄴   [Harald Schultz]

Hemiancistrus vittatus 🄵🄳🆇7️⃣2️⃣4️⃣🆇🄽 🄽🄴   [Dr. Herbert R. Axelrod]

HEMIANCISTRUS NICEFOROI Fowler / *Clown Sucker Catfish*

Range: Upper Amazon and Colombia.

Habits: A typical sucker catfish of the "plecostomus" type. It likes to loaf about the bottom or attach itself to the glass front on the aquarium.

Water Conditions: Not sensitive to water conditions as long as the water is warm (over 24°C) and not too hard or alkaline. Tolerates a pH of 6.0 to 7.0 and water less than 15 DH.

Size: Up to 26 cm.

Food Requirements: As a scavenger, it doesn't require too much in the way of live foods, but it does like plenty of frozen brine shrimp and pelleted dry foods.

What a beautiful fish this is! When Fowler first described it in 1943 in the *Proceedings* of the Academy of Natural Sciences in Philadelphia, from a specimen collected in the city of Florencia on the Rio Orteguasa, Colombia, he couldn't believe that such a fish existed. How often had he heard tales of a "Brick Red Plecostomus"? But this was a scientific report by a famous ichthyologist. Then, nearly 20 year later, a TFH expedition found the fish again and photographed it for the files and records of TFH.

HEMIANCISTRUS VITTATUS (Steindachner) / *Striped Sucker Catfish*

Range: The Amazon and the Rio Paraguay.

Habits: A typical bottom-feeder which spends most of its time loafing about the bottom of the aquarium, chomping on plant leaves trying to get every bit of the algal growth from them. Shy and spends much time hiding.

Water Conditions: Prefers water a bit on the cool side, around 21°C.

Size: Up to 23 cm.

Food Requirements: Does very well on frozen brine shrimp and pellet foods; should be offered some tubifex worms now and then.

In 1882 Steindachner described this fish as *Chaetostomus vittatus* in a Viennese scientific journal. He listed the exact location of the type as coming from the Amazon, with other specimens coming from the Tajapuru, Rio Xingu to Porto do Moz and the Rio Madiera. Throughout its history since that time it has had various names. Eigenmann and Eigenmann in 1889 called it *Hemiancistrus vittatus;* Regan, in 1904, put it into the genus *Ancistrus;* Ribeiro and Gosline, individually, called it *Peckoltia vittata.* The authors feel that this designation, *Hemiancistrus vittatus,* is as correct as possible.

It is one of the more attractive catfishes, but there doesn't seem to be enough of them in any one place to warrant an all-out collecting trip for them. They will probably continually come into this country a few at a time, but as soon as helicopters are available in quantity to help fish collecting, this is one of those fish which will most benefit.

HEMICHROMIS BIMACULATUS Gill / *Jewel Cichlid*

Range: West and central Africa.
Habits: Besides being very pugnacious, it has the nasty habit of digging up plants.
Water Conditions: Not critical. Temperature should be quite high, about 27°C.
Size: To about 15 cm; usually smaller.
Food Requirements: Live foods preferred; frozen foods accepted.

It is strange that such a nasty, pugnacious cichlid species as the Jewel Cichlid is one of the most docile and devoted of parents. If it were not for their own mean disposition, this beauty would certainly be one of the most popular of the cichlid group. The body colors of both sexes undergo quite a change when the time for breeding comes. The sides, which normally are a yellowish green, take on an intense red hue sprinkled with gleaming blue dots, which no doubt gives rise to the popular name. Once they begin spawning their owner may soon be faced with a problem: what to do with all the young Jewel Cichlids which everybody seems to admire but nobody wants. Once a pair has mated, there is seldom any trouble with them afterwards, but selecting a well-mated pair sometimes presents a problem. If you get a male that is ready to spawn and a female that is not, very often the result is a dead or mangled female. Always make sure that when a pair is introduced into a tank there is plenty of refuge such as rocks and plant thickets. A flowerpot placed in a dark corner will usually be the preferred site for spawning, which takes place in the usual cichlid manner.

1. *Hemichromis bimaculatus* spawning pair among their newly hatched brood (p726).
2. *H. bimaculatus* female depositing eggs on a rock with the male nearby (in the background) (p726).

Hemichromis bimaculatus fanning its eggs soon after spawning. Photo by R. Zukal.

Hemichromis bimaculatus var. ⬚F⬚Q⬚X⬚7⬚2⬚5⬚X⬚R⬚N⬚B⬚   [H. J. Richter]
Hemichromis bimaculatus ⬚F⬚Q⬚X⬚7⬚2⬚6⬚X⬚N⬚N⬚B⬚

Hemichromis fasciatus F A X 7 2 7 X N N D [K. Paysan]

Hemigrammocypris lini F R X 7 2 8 X N N 4 [Dr. S. Weitzman]

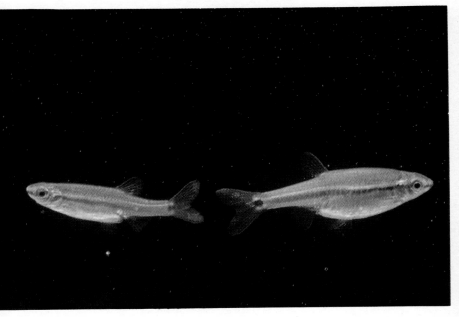

HEMICHROMIS FASCIATUS Peters / *Five-Spotted Hemichromis*

Range: West Africa, widely distributed from Senegal to the Congo.
Habits: Very quarrelsome toward other fishes; should be kept by themselves.
Water Conditions: Occurs in both fresh and brackish waters. In the aquarium they adapt to any water condition.
Size: Fully grown, about 30 cm.
Food Requirements: Will consume any unwanted fish or will settle for chunks of fish or beef heart.

Some hobbyists like nasty fishes and choose a fish like this with the full knowledge of what they are getting; others buy a fish without realizing how big it will get and buy them more or less blindly. A fish like this will prove a disappointment to those people, and they soon realize that the bigger they get, the nastier. Many breeders keep a few of these fish as a sort of "garbage can with fins" which will eat any and every unwanted fish. The five large spots on the side often turn into bands, and when they decide to spawn, a startling transformation in color takes place: the entire body becomes suffused with blood-red, the bands become deep black and the dorsal fin develops stripes of red, yellow and white. Sexes are difficult to distinguish; males have slightly more pointed dorsal and anal fins.

HEMIGRAMMOCYPRIS LINI Weitzman & Chan / *Garnet Minnow*

Range: Southeastern China.
Habits: Peaceful and fast-swimming; always active.
Water Conditions: Not a truly tropical species, so can take much cooler water than most; tolerates a wide range of pH and hardness values.
Size: Up to 5 cm.
Food Requirements: Accepts all standard aquarium foods.

Since the early 1950's there has been some controversy as to the exact taxonomic status of a fish imported in 1951, a pretty little Asiatic cyprinid that in the opinion of many looks a good deal like the very popular White Cloud, *Tanichthys albonubes*. Originally identified as an *Aphyocypris* species, it was later specifically placed as *Aphyocypris pooni*. For years a mild argument ensued among hobbyists as to whether *A. pooni* was really a distinct species or whether it was simply a variant of *Tanichthys albonubes* or perhaps the result of a hybridization between *T. albonubes* and a related species. It wasn't until 1966 that the controversy was resolved definitely, by Dr. Stanley Weitzman of the U.S. National Museum and Lai Lee Chan of the Fisheries Research Station in Hong Kong. Weitzman and Chan's findings, published in the June, 1966 issue of *Copeia*, showed that there were two distinct races of White Clouds and that (1) the fish in question was not a White Cloud of either race, (2) *Aphyocypris pooni* is an invalid name, and (3) the fish in question is correctly known as *Hemigrammocypris lini*.

HEMIGRAMMOPETERSIUS CAUDALIS (Boulenger)
Yellow-Tailed African Characin

Range: Congo River and its tributaries.
Habits: Peaceful unless kept with smaller fishes which it could devour.
Water Conditions: Water should be soft, slightly acid and well aerated. Aquarium should be kept covered to prevent jumping. Temperature 25°C.
Size: About 8 cm.
Food Requirements: Will take dried foods, but a preponderance of live foods should be given.

Here we have another beautiful example of the kind of characin which can be found in the region of the Congo River. Like one of its relatives, *Phenacogrammus interruptus*, the males are very easy to distinguish from the females. One distinction is that the dorsal fin is considerably larger in the males and bright yellow, edged in white and tipped with black. Mature specimens have a frayed edge on this fin. The tail fin also has a distinct characteristic: the middle rays are black and form a point of their own. Females have only a slight tinge of yellow in the fins. There is no existing account that this fish has ever bred in captivity; being an active swimmer, there is a possibility that the comparatively tiny confines of even a large aquarium hinder it to such an extent that it will not try. However, a ripe, mature pair is very likely to attempt spawning even when circumstances do not permit them to do the same things which they do in their native waters. The aquarist who wants to be the first to spawn an unusual species must begin by carefully conditioning his fish with frequent feedings of the best foods available to him and then making close observations.

HEMIGRAMMUS BELLOTTII (Steindachner) / *Dash-Dot Tetra*

Range: Upper Amazon tributaries.
Habits: Peaceful and active; prefer to swim in a group of their own kind.
Water Conditions: Soft, acid water preferred. Temperature 24 to 27°C.
Size: To 2.5 cm.
Food Requirements: Because of their size, small foods of all kinds are recommended.

What a wealth of characin species there is to be found in the Upper Amazon region! And the only reason we see them so seldom is because they share their home waters with the Neon Tetra, which outshines anything in that part of the river for beauty of colors. An unusual situation was created because Neons were at first so difficult to spawn: they were collected in their native waters in such numbers that now when spawning is not so difficult it does not pay the professional breeder to breed and raise them; it is cheaper to *import* them. We can get some idea of what other characins there are in these waters by the ones which are included accidentally with these shipments, and *Hemigrammus bellottii* is one of these.

Hemigrammopetersius caudalis 	F A X 7 2 9 X N N 8
Hemigrammus bellottii 	F R X 7 3 0 X N N 1 	[Dr. Herbert R. Axelrod]

Hemigrammus caudovittatus ⬛F ⬛D ⬛X ⬛7 ⬛3 ⬛1 ⬛X ⬛N ⬛N ⬛A   [Dr. Herbert R. Axelrod]

Hemigrammus coeruleus ⬛F ⬛D ⬛X ⬛7 ⬛3 ⬛2 ⬛X ⬛N ⬛N ⬛6   [Dr. Herbert R. Axelrod]

HEMIGRAMMUS CAUDOVITTATUS Ahl / *Buenos Aires Tetra*

Range: Region around Buenos Aires.
Habits: Fairly peaceful with fishes about its size; should not be kept with thread-finned fishes, whose fins it nips.
Water Conditions: Neutral to slightly acid. Can withstand temperatures around 21°C for a time; should be kept about 25° normally.
Size: About 10 cm.
Food Requirements: Seems to like dried foods as well as live foods; has a good appetite and should be fed generously.

This is one of the most easily kept of the tetra family. Being a rather large species, one of the requirements is a tank which will give them a generous amount of swimming room. Another requirement is a generous amount of food. Lacking this, they are likely to take a few mouthfuls out of the plants. Another habit which is not exactly to their credit is their habit of attacking an Angelfish or gourami and trimming its fins down to stubs. This is not viciousness on their part, just hunger. When properly and generously fed, they will not resort to these antics. Coming as they do from semi-tropical Buenos Aires, aquarium temperatures need not be very high. They will be quite comfortable in the low 20's (°C) and around 25°C they will usually exhibit a willingness to spawn. A bunch of bushy plants should be placed at one end of the tank and about one-fourth of the water drained off and replaced with fresh water. The pair is best separated for a day or two and well fed. When placed in the breeding tank they will soon begin to drive and scatter a large number of eggs all over.

HEMIGRAMMUS COERULEUS Durbin / *Coerulean Tetra*

Range: Manacapuru, Brazil.
Habits: Peaceful when kept with fishes of its own size.
Water Conditions: Neutral to slightly acid. Temperature 23 to 26°C.
Size: To about 7.5 cm.
Food Requirements: Will accept prepared foods, but should also get live and frozen foods.

This species was always thought to be deep red. In the interests of finding this fish and providing fish hobbyists with another beautiful species, perhaps one which could be bred more easily than the Neon or Cardinal Tetras, Dr. Axelrod decided early in 1964 to search for them once more. After much trouble, the proper stream was found by Drs. Axelrod and Terofal with the expert help of Harald Schultz, who was another member of the expedition. They netted tirelessly but could find no characins like the Coerulean Tetra. Finally they put poison in the water and began to put the fishes collected in this manner in formalin. Then came the big surprise: some of the characins in the formalin began to turn *red!* Taxonomic examination confirmed that this indeed was the described species, which only turned red after death.

HEMIGRAMMUS ERYTHROZONUS (Durbin) / *Glowlight Tetra*

Range: The Guianas and adjacent regions of the Amazon.
Habits: One of the most peaceful of all tetras.
Water Conditions: Should have a clean aquarium at all times, with slightly acid, soft water. Temperature 23 to 26°C.
Food Requirements: Will eat dry food, but this should often be augmented with live and frozen foods.
Color Variations: Body greenish and very transparent, with a brilliant, glowing red or purple line running from the upper edge of the eye to the caudal base.

The early and middle 1930's brought fish hobbyists two of the most beautiful aquarium fishes. One was the Neon Tetra and the other was the Glowlight Tetra. To show off the Glowlight Tetra to its best advantage, some pains must be taken to provide it with its proper setting. The bottom should be covered with black gravel and nicely planted. A moderate light should come from above. All that needs to be done then is to place our little jewels in their setting and wait a few hours for them to get used to their surroundings. A dozen or more swimming about in a school will make the most hardened fish fancier sit up and take notice.

HEMIGRAMMUS HYANUARY (Durbin) / *January Tetra*

Range: Amazon tributaries near Leticia, Colombia.
Habits: Very peaceful; prefers to be in a school with others of its own kind.
Water Conditions: Not critical; best is water which is neutral to slightly acid in character. Temperature 23 to 26°C.
Size: About 4 cm.
Food Requirements: Live or frozen foods are of course preferred, but dried foods are also accepted eagerly.

The January Tetra is a fish which is not regularly imported into this country, and most of the specimens we get to see have come inadvertently mixed in with shipments of such fishes as Neon Tetras or Cardinal Tetras. These are often collected when very small, and weeding out all the unwanted specimens from a shipment of less than half-grown fish is almost an impossibility. Overlooking its lack of colors, the January Tetra is an attractive fellow with peaceful habits who will never harm your other fishes or plants. Their small claim to color lies in a horizontal golden stripe and a good-sized squarish black spot in the lower half of the middle caudal rays. Males have a black adipose fins. The fact that they are hardy is fairly obvious to anyone who has ever kept them. Probably the reader is wondering why this fish is called the January Tetra. The original specimens were collected in a place called Lake January by the great ichthyologist Eigenmann in 1918.

Hemigrammus erythrozonus ⬚F⬚A⬚X⬚7⬚3⬚3⬚X⬚N⬚N⬚5 [K. Paysan]
Hemigrammus hyanuary ⬚F⬚Q⬚X⬚7⬚3⬚4⬚X⬚N⬚N⬚4 [J. Elias]

Hemigrammus marginatus F D X 7 3 5 X N N 5
Hemigrammus ocellifer F D X 7 3 6 X N N 4

[Dr. Herbert R. Axelrod]
[S. Frank]

HEMIGRAMMUS MARGINATUS Ellis / *Bassam Tetra*

Range: Venezuela to Argentina.
Habits: Peaceful.
Water Conditions: Fairly soft and slightly acid. Temperature 24 to 26°C.
Size: To 7 cm.
Food Requirements: Live or frozen foods preferred; will also accept prepared foods.

Although it has long been known to German aquarists, the Bassam Tetra is seldom seen in this country. It is a very attractive fish, too. Instead of the plain silvery body that so many of the tetra species have, this one has a violet iridescence like that seen in the *Rasbora* species. This is varied by the deep pink forward tail section followed in the lobes by a black area. The fish was named by Ellis in 1911 and probably comes from waters that are somewhat outside of the usual range of professional collectors, so we seldom get to see it. Spawning, we are told, is in the standard tetra manner, the fish laying eggs in bunches of bushy plants and then eating all they can find until they are taken out. In their home waters they probably spawn in schools, but in the comparatively narrow confines of an aquarium, using more than a pair results in two fish spawning and the rest following and gobbling up the eggs.

HEMIGRAMMUS OCELLIFER (Steindachner) / *Head and Tail Light*

Range: Widely distributed throughout the Amazon region, especially in the southern part.
Habits: Mostly peaceful, if kept with fishes their own size.
Water Conditions: Not critical, but warm temperatures are preferred. Temperature 25 to 26°C.
Size: About 4 cm.
Food Requirements: Will get along very well on dry foods.

This popular tetra has become a favorite among hobbyists since the first ones were introduced into the United States in the early 1930's. It has much in its favor: it is peaceful, does not get too large, will not chew plants and will gratefully accept almost anything in the way of food which is offered. Add to these qualities the fact that it is attractive and easily bred, and there is no mystery as to the reason for its popularity. This fish should not be kept singly or in pairs. A small school of at least six in a roomy aquarium which is lighted from above will show up best; here we are able to see the gleaming spots of gold in the upper half of the eye and at the base of the tail flashing as the fish move about in the open portions of the aquarium. Males are distinguished by their longer, more slender bodies and also a thin streak which runs horizontally across the anal fin. A breeding tank of about 30 liters should be provided, with a layer of glass marbles on the bottom.

HEMIGRAMMUS PULCHER Ladiges / *Garnet Tetra*

Range: Peruvian Amazon, Loreto region.
Habits: Peaceful; will not bother plants or other fishes.
Water Conditions: Prefers a roomy, well-planted tank. Most important requirement is warmth, 26 to 27°C.
Size: About 5 cm.
Food Requirements: Will not refuse dried foods, but should be given frequent changes to live or frozen foods.
Color Variations: Greenish body with a small shoulder spot and indistinct horizontal line. Upper half of caudal base deep red, with black area below.

Because it resembled *Rasbora heteromorpha* in body form and had a large black spot in the after end of the body, this fish was known for a time as the "poor man's rasbora." As so often happens with some names, the situation has become reversed and the rasbora has dropped considerably in price since the days when the Garnet Tetra first made its appearance in 1938, and at the present time there are not very many Garnet Tetras on hand. Therefore one will usually find that the Garnet Tetra commands a higher price. Notwithstanding, it is a very attractive little fish and a small group of them will make a beautiful appearance in any tank. One of the few things which can be said against them is that they are slightly sensitive to disease if their aquarium is allowed to drop in temperature. Given a good thermostatic heater which will keep the water at a constant 26 to 27°C, they will put on their most glowing colors. Males and females are equally beautiful, and the females are distinguished by their stockier build and slightly deeper bellies. Not a ready spawner, but patience and good feeding will sometimes be rewarded.

Hemigrammus pulcher, the Garnet Tetra. Photo by Dr. Herbert R. Axelrod.

Hemigrammus pulcher F Q X 7 3 8 X N N 5
[H. J. Richter]

Hemigrammus rhodostomus [F][D][X][7][3][9][X][N][N][5] [K. Paysan]

Hemigrammus rodwayi [F][R][X][7][4][0][X][N][N][5] [Dr. Herbert R. Axelrod]

HEMIGRAMMUS RHODOSTOMUS Ahl / *Rummy-Nose Tetra*

Range: Lower Amazon region, around Aripiranga and Para.
Habits: Peaceful; is most at home with lively fishes of about its own size.
Water Conditions: Best kept in a well planted, well established, well heated tank. Temperature about 26°C.
Size: 4 to 5 cm.
Food Requirements: Will get along fairly well on dried food, but should get an occasional meal of live or frozen food.

To be a good aquarium citizen, a fish should be small, peaceful, nicely colored and not shy. Our friend here is all of these things. When kept in an aquarium which is well established and well planted, a small school of these fish flit around always active and alert, their noses glowing. Take the same group of fish and place them in a bare tank where the temperature is about 24°C or lower and the water is not to their liking, and immediately the fish become almost unrecognizable. The nose fades to the palest of pinks, and the black markings on the tail are so indistinct that they can scarcely be seen. This fish has been the despair of many dealers. When they display them in a community aquarium, everybody wants them, and when they fish them out of their stock tanks, the customers quickly decide that they don't want them after all. Often no amount of explaining will convince the customer that once they have spent a few days in an aquarium at home they will be every bit as pretty as the ones in the dealer's aquarium. This fish is one of the more difficult ones to breed, and once this is accomplished the tiny young are very difficult to raise.

HEMIGRAMMUS RODWAYI Durbin / *Gold Tetra*

Range: Guianas and the Upper Amazon.
Habits: Peaceful; prefers to be kept in a school.
Water Conditions: Not critical, but water should be somewhere near neutral.
Size: About 5 cm.
Food Requirements: Live foods preferred, but frozen and prepared foods are also readily accepted.

The Gold Tetra is a fish which looks as if it were sprayed with gold paint all over the body. A large, well planted tank with a school of these very attractive fish constantly and playfully on the move needs little else to recommend it. When the author visited Guyana, he was told that this fish was very common in the drainage ditches around the sugar fields and rice paddies just outside of Georgetown. There is a peculiar thing about this little beauty: they do not lose their color in captivity and they breed readily, but the offspring do not have the golden color! In their native waters, they are always golden.

HEMIGRAMMUS SCHMARDAE (Steindachner) / *Schmard Tetra*

Range: Upper Rio Negro River, Brazil.
Habits: Very peaceful.
Water Conditions: Soft, acid water preferred, but not essential. Temperature 24 to 27°C.
Size: Up to 5 cm.
Food Requirements: Dried as well as live foods.

The Schmard Tetra is a very peaceful and undemanding fish. The species requires an aquarium of 30 liters or larger with some unvegetated areas for free swimming. Thick clumps of plants near the sides of the aquarium are appreciated and are required for spawning. The tank should have a dark background to help show off the fish. The water should be mature and slightly on the acid side of neutral. The correct aquarium set-up will heighten the chances of spawning. The tank should be placed in such a location that it will receive morning sunshine. Females can be distinguished from the males by their heavier bodies when gravid. Spawning is a stormy affair with the males and females diving into the plants and pressing their sides together. The eggs are laid and fertilized in the open water and then fall into the dense clumps of plants. The parents should be separated from the eggs after the spawning process concludes or they will most likely eat them.

HEMIGRAMMUS ULREYI (Boulenger) / *Tetra ulreyi*

Range: The upper reaches of the Paraguay, where it enters Brazil.
Habits: Peaceful; will not harm plants or other fish.
Water Conditions: Most important thing is temperature, which should be kept from 25 to 27°C.
Size: Males about 5 cm; females about 4.5 cm.
Food Requirements: Will eat dried foods, but should be varied with live or frozen foods.

For many years this fish has gone unrecognized and another one has masqueraded under its name. Finally, the distinction has been made and the other fish which has gone under the name of *"Hemigrammus ulreyi"* for many years has been classified as *Hyphessobrycon heterorhabdus*. Because it was considerably less attractive, *Hemigrammus ulreyi* was not collected. At first the bigger, fatter, less colorful females were not thought to be the same species and were thrown back, with the result that breeders tore their hair out looking for infinitesimal differences and selecting what they thought were pairs and getting no results because they were actually working with two males! The males are considerably smaller and more slender. Another way of sexing them is by a look at the silvery sac which contains the organs, easily discernible by placing a light behind them. The female's sac is blunt and the male's is pointed. Most of the tetra species can be sexed in this manner, and it is much more reliable than going by outward appearances. According to even the latest works, this species has not yet been bred.

Hemigrammus schmardae ⬚F⬚D⬚X⬚7⬚4⬚1⬚X⬚N⬚N⬚5   [Dr. Herbert R. Axelrod]

Hemigrammus ulreyi ⬚F⬚Q⬚X⬚7⬚4⬚2⬚X⬚N⬚N⬚4   [Harald Schultz]

Hemigrammus unilineatus ⬚F ⬚Q ⬚X ⬚7 ⬚4 ⬚3 ⬚X ⬚N ⬚N ⬚5   [Dr. Herbert R. Axelrod]

Hemigrammus vorderwinkleri ⬚F ⬚Q ⬚X ⬚7 ⬚4 ⬚4 ⬚X ⬚N ⬚N ⬚4   [S. Frank]

HEMIGRAMMUS UNILINEATUS (Gill) / *Featherfin Tetra*

Range: Trinidad and northern South America from Venezuela to Brazil.
Habits: Peaceful; a heavy eater which should have plenty of swimming room.
Water Conditions: Should have a sunny aquarium with fairly high temperatures, 26 to 27°C.
Size: Attains a length of 5 cm; most specimens smaller.
Food Requirements: Like all active fish, a heavy eater. If possible, should be fed several times daily. Will take dried foods, but live foods should also be fed.
Color Variations: Body silvery with a gold horizontal stripe. First rays of the dorsal and anal fins white, with a black streak behind. Brazilian variety has red fins.

This is not one of our most colorful of the tetras, but the fish enjoys a great popularity nevertheless, because of its ceaseless activity. Besides always being on the go, it is always out where it can be easily seen. One of our old favorites, this fish has been known to aquarium hobbyists since 1910, when it was first imported from Para in Brazil. Since then shipments have also been made from Venezuela and Trinidad, proof of the fish's wide range. Like most of the tetras, it is best to keep a small school of them. A sunny aquarium with clear water and a temperature of about 25°C will have them chasing around all day. Given a tank to themselves a pair, or better yet two males and one female, will soon begin driving about madly and depositing eggs all over the bushy plants. When the female begins to hide from the males and egg hunts are begun, the parents should be immediately removed or there will soon be very few eggs left. A successful spawning may number as many as 500 eggs which hatch in about 60 hours. After two to four days the fry become free-swimming, at which time they may be fed very fine dried food or infusoria. Growth is very rapid under good conditions. Brazilian males have an anal hook.

HEMIGRAMMUS VORDERWINKLERI Gery / *Vorderwinkler's Tetra*

Range: Upper Rio Negro River, Brazil.
Habits: Very peaceful.
Water Conditions: Soft, acid water preferred. Temperature 24 to 27°C.
Size: About 4 cm.
Food Requirements: Dried foods accepted as well as living or frozen kinds.
Color Variations: Silvery bluish, dorsal fin orange, upper part of eye as well as the base of the caudal lobes red.

H. vorderwinkleri is durable, peaceful and not a bit fussy about eating any kind of food provided for them. As the specimens which were sent to Dr. Gery had to be preserved beforehand, there was no time to attempt spawning them. The *Hemigrammus* species, however, are fairly easy spawners and no particular problems would be anticipated.

744

HEMIODOPSIS GOELDII (Steindachner) / *Goeldi's Hemiodus*

Range: Guianas and the Rio Xingu, Brazil.
Habits: Peaceful and highly active; likely to jump out if the tank is not covered.
Water Conditions: Neutral to slightly alkaline. Temperature 24 to 27°C.
Size: To about 15 cm.
Food Requirements: Prepared foods accepted, but likes to nibble on plants occasionally. Lettuce or spinach leaf should be provided for this reason.

This species is frequently confused with *Hemiodopsis gracilis* and has the same short line running from an oval-shaped black spot on the side and widening until it becomes quite prominent in the lower caudal lobe. There is a great deal of similarity, it is true, but they do differ. Dr. Gery describes the differences on page 72 of the November, 1964 issue of *Tropical Fish Hobbyist.* Unless the few imported specimens breed prolifically, and it is not likely that they do, it is doubtful that we will ever see many of them in the aquaria of hobbyists. However, nothing is impossible. Then again, a collector may stumble on a large number of these in an out-of-the-way stream and get them on the market. Like *Hemiodopsis gracilis,* this is a very active fish and should not be put in with quieter fishes that dislike being disturbed. They are also very fond of jumping, and their tank should be kept covered.

HEMIODOPSIS GRACILIS (Günther) / *Slender Hemiodus*

Range: Guyana and the middle Amazon River region.
Habits: Peaceful toward other fishes. An active swimmer and skillful jumper.
Water Conditions: Soft and slightly acid. Temperature about 24°C.
Size: To about 15 cm; imported specimens about half this size.
Food Requirements: Greedy eaters which should get green vegetable foods in addition to prepared and freeze-dried foods.

Usually the *Hemiodopsis* species commonly seen in this country is *H. gracilis.* What distinguishes it is the red streak on the bottom edge of the lower tail lobe. This fish is a very agile swimmer, and a tank left even partly uncovered is an invitation for it to jump out, which it does surprisingly well. Give these fish a tank in which they will have enough room to swim about without too much restriction. For some strange reason there have been no reports of their ever spawning in captivity. Why? Perhaps, being such active swimmers, they require briskly flowing water in which to lay their eggs. Or they might spawn in deep water where they come from, deeper than we could give them in an aquarium. The hemiodus group is composed of very greedy eaters and should get some vegetable foods.

1. *Hemiodopsis gracilis* in an aquarium (p746).
2. This *Hemiodopsis* sp. is unidentified but considered a member of the *H. gracilis* group (p746).

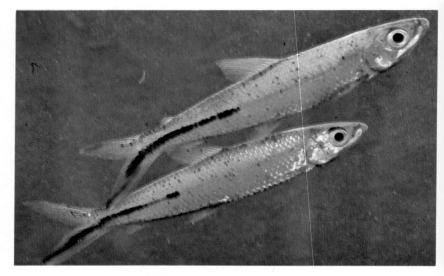

Hemiodopsis goeldii [F][D][X][7][4][5][X][N][N][B]

1. *Hemiodopsis gracilis* [F][D][M][7][4][6][X][N][N][A]
2. *Hemiodopsis* sp. [F][D][B][7][4][6][X][N][N][8]

Hemiodopsis quadrimaculatus F D X 7 4 7 X N N B
Hemiodopsis sterni F D X 7 4 8 X N N A   [Harald Schultz]

HEMIODOPSIS QUADRIMACULATUS (Pellegrin) /*Barred Hemiodus*

Range: Upper Amazon and Guianas.
Habits: Peaceful and active; prefers to be kept in groups. A jumper; tank must be kept covered.
Water Conditions: Neutral to slightly alkaline, with good planting and a sunny location.
Size: To almost 13 cm.
Food Requirements: Should be given a good percentage of vegetable foods in addition to the usual live or frozen foods.
Color Variations: Body brownish with a violet shimmer. Three black bands cross the body; caudal peduncle black. Caudal lobes have black edges.

The genus *Hemiodopsis* is represented by many species which are found in the Amazon Basin and northern South America. This species, like most others in the genus, is a peaceful but active fish. It is a good jumper and will find its way out of your aquarium if given a small opening through which to jump. Its tank should be well aerated to accommodate its high metabolism.

HEMIODOPSIS STERNI Gery / *Stern's Hemiodus*

Range: Upper Juruena River, Brazil.
Habits: Peaceful but should be kept with other very active fish.
Water Conditions: Neutral to slightly alkaline. Temperature 23 to 26°C.
Size: To about 10 cm.
Food Requirements: Dried foods accepted, but live or frozen foods needed occasionally. Vegetable substitutes like lettuce leaves are recommended.
Color Variations: Body yellowish tan with three large spots on the sides and a spot on the lower part of the caudal base which ends in a black streak on the tail lobe.

This species is a member of the so-called *"quadrimaculatus* group," which includes in addition *Hemiodopsis quadrimaculatus* and *H. huraulti*. It would take a trained ichthyologist to tell these species apart by eye. This species was found further south than the other three, in the upper Juruena region of Brazil. This species, according to the specimens examined, is smaller than *H. huraulti* and *H. quadrimaculatus*. One thing noticeable in this picture distinguishes this species: the bar at the caudal base does not extend all the way up, but is merely a black spot in the lower half and meets a black streak in the lower caudal lobe. Although there are no complete reports on their behavior as yet, a safe bet is that they are as active as the rest of the group and should not be kept with lazy species which would be made nervous by their constant activity. Another safe bet is that they will accept a partly vegetable diet.

HEPSETUS ODOE (Bloch) / *African Pike*

Range: Widely distributed all over tropical Africa.
Habits: Vicious, greedy and predatory; can only be kept with their own kind or larger fishes.
Water Conditions: Not critical, but soft, slightly acid water is best. Temperature 24 to 27°C.
Size: To 30 cm.
Food Requirements: Living smaller fishes only; possibly they may be trained to eat strips of raw fish.
Color Variations: Body olive green, belly golden. Young specimens have dark spotted fins.

All over the world Mother Nature has some fishes which serve to keep the waters from being overpopulated. These are the predators, the fishes which feed ravenously on smaller living fishes. They have large mouths and appetites to match. The eyes are large and keen, and everything which moves and is small enough to be swallowed is sought out by them. The teeth are designed for holding the struggling prey; they turn inward and a fish impaled on them and managing to get off will only find himself nearer the hungry, greedy throat. The temperate waters of the world have similar counterparts to this fish, namely the pikes, pickerels and muskellunge. *Hepsetus odoe* has been known to science since 1794 and is very rarely imported. It would be no problem for a collector to find them; they occur all over tropical Africa. Although they might make interesting showpieces for public aquariums, only young ones would be of a size small enough for the average hobbyist's tanks, and very few hobbyists would find them interesting enough for theirs.

Mtapa Creek in Kenya illustrates the *H. odoe* habitat. Photo by Dr. W. Klausewitz.

Hepsetus odoe ⬚F⬚⬚D⬚⬚X⬚⬚7⬚⬚4⬚⬚9⬚⬚X⬚⬚N⬚⬚N⬚⬚D⬚   [H. Hansen, Aquarium Berlin]

1. *Herotilapia multispinosa* ⬚F⬚⬚E⬚⬚X⬚⬚7⬚⬚5⬚⬚0⬚⬚X⬚⬚N⬚⬚N⬚⬚A⬚   [H. J. Richter]

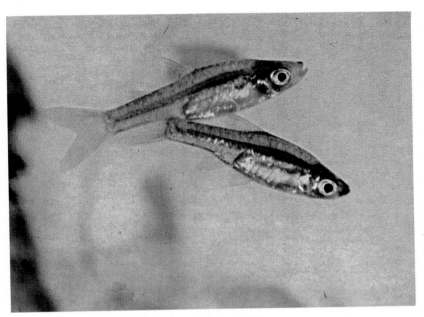

Horadandia atukorali 🇫 🇩 🇽 7 5 9 🇽 🇳 🇳 2
Hyphessobrycon agulha 🇫 🇷 🇽 7 6 0 🇽 🇳 🇳 5

[Dr. Herbert R. Axelrod]
[Harald Schultz]

HORADANDIA ATUKORALI Deraniyagala / *Midget Minnow, Green Carplet*

Range: Sri Lanka.
Habits: Peaceful and active; timid in the presence of larger fishes.
Water Conditions: Can take both soft, acid water and hard, alkaline water, as long as extremes are avoided. Temperature 22 to 28°C.
Size: 3 cm.
Food Requirements: Accepts all foods that are small enough to be swallowed.

A little fish whose size would lead one to the belief that the species is delicate, *Horadandia atukorali* is really pretty tough and is able to live under conditions that would soon kill off other species. Originally thought to be a *Rasbora* species, this hardy cyprinid was first brought into the United States by Captain Henri Carpender, a sea captain who was able to purchase or trade for new fishes during his many voyages around the world. The Midget Minnow spawns by laying adhesive eggs in plant thickets; the eggs, as is to be expected from the size of the parents, are very small. The newly hatched fry are also very small, and they therefore require feedings of infusoria, as they are unable to swallow brine shrimp nauplii during the first days of their life. *Horadandia atukorali* eggs have a fairly short incubation period (about a day and a half to two days); perhaps it is fair that the fish should be able to begin its free-swimming life comparatively quickly, because it doesn't get a chance to enjoy life very long. They are considered past their prime at an age of one year.

HYPHESSOBRYCON AGULHA Fowler / *Red-Tailed Flag Tetra*

Range: Upper Amazon region.
Habits: Peaceful; likes to swim in schools.
Water Conditions: Soft, slightly acid water. Temperature 24 to 26°C.
Size: About 5 cm.
Food Requirements: Will accept dried foods, but live or frozen foods should be given frequently.

Like *Hemigrammus bellottii*, young specimens of *Hyphessobrycon agulha* are frequently mixed in with Neon Tetras when shipments come in. Here we have a fish which, when it grows to its full size, is a very attractive proposition and an asset to any aquarium. It greatly resembles *Hyphessobrycon heterorhabdus*, the popular Flag Tetra. There is even an added touch of color: the tail of the male is bright red. Here again we have a fish which will come in only once in a while, and then by accident. The collectors who catch and ship Neon Tetras make a comfortable living on this fish alone, and a visit to the compounds where they store their fish usually shows as many Neons as all other species combined. As long as there is a ready market for Neons, they have no need to ship anything else. They reason that as long as they've got a good thing, they won't bother to try developing other good things until what they have ceases to pay off.

HYPHESSOBRYCON BENTOSI Durbin / *Rosy Tetra*

Range: Amazon Basin and Guianas.
Habits: Peaceful; should be kept in groups of at least six.
Water Conditions: Soft, slightly acid water is best. Temperature 24 to 27°C.
Size: To 5 cm.
Food Requirements: Prepared foods accepted, but live and frozen foods preferred.

The Rosy Tetra is the largest member of the so-called *"callistus* group." A handsome fish such as this deserves a few extra pains to bring out its best colors. To do
this, rule number one is to give it a dark background. If your tank has its back to a
wall and gets its light from the front, that is good. If the front light is sunlight,
that is even better. As for the background, paint the back glass with dark green
paint, either the ordinary type or the crackle finish paint sold for this purpose by
most petshops. When this is done, cut down the glare still further by using black
gravel instead of the natural color. Planting of course should be concentrated in
the back and on the sides, with an open area in front center. This done, and of
course the other fixtures attached, the stage is set for the star attraction, a group of
Rosy Tetras.

HYPHESSOBRYCON BIFASCIATUS Ellis / *Yellow Tetra*

Range: Southeastern Brazil, near the coast.
Habits: Very peaceful; will not attack other fishes or plants.
Water Conditions: Neutral to slightly acid. Temperature 22 to 24°C.
Size: Up to 5 cm.
Food Requirements: All foods gratefully eaten, prepared as well as live or frozen.

This looks like a larger, yellow version of the Flame Tetra. We do not often see
it because there is little collecting done in the regions to which they are native,
and besides no collector will ever get rich collecting this species. They are not particularly colorful and the demand for them would be very light. They are extremely hardy in the aquarium and stand up very well even when slightly abused.
Young specimens of the Yellow Tetra are considerably prettier than the fully
grown ones. Their fins when half-grown are an attractive red and make a nice
contrast to the yellow color of the body as well as the two black streaks. As the fish
grows older the red leaves the fins completely and the yellow color as well as the
black streaks become washed out. This is an easy species to breed. Spawning
takes place among the bushy plants, and the parents must be removed as soon as
the spawning is completed. Eggs hatch the day after they are laid, after which the
tiny young can be seen hanging from the glass sides and the plants. Once the
yolk-sac is absorbed and they begin to swim, feeding may be begun with very fine
foods, to be followed in a few days with newly hatched brine shrimp.

Hyphessobrycon bentosi  F Q X 7 6 1 X N N 5   [Dr. Herbert R. Axelrod]
Hyphessobrycon bifasciatus F Q X 7 6 2 X N N 5   [Dr. Herbert R. Axelrod]

Hyphessobrycon callistus ⬚F ⬚Q ⬚X ⬚7 ⬚6 ⬚3 ⬚X ⬚N ⬚N ⬚4   [S. Frank]

Hyphessobrycon erythrostigma ⬚F ⬚Q ⬚X ⬚7 ⬚6 ⬚4 ⬚X ⬚N ⬚N ⬚6

HYPHESSOBRYCON CALLISTUS (Boulenger) / *Callistus Tetra*

Range: Rio Paraguay.

Habits: Peaceful and active; should have a well-planted tank and be kept in a school of not less than six individuals.

Water Conditions: Fish will show their best colors if the water is slightly acid and very soft. Temperature best around 24°C.

Size: About 4 cm.

Food Requirements: Prepared foods accepted, but to keep them in the best of condition they should get live or frozen foods frequently.

Hyphessobrycon callistus is probably one of the most misnamed of all aquarium fishes. This is one of the cases where for years a fish is known by a certain accepted name, in this case *Hyphessobrycon serpae,* as with this one. Then later on, after taxonomic investigation, the apple-cart is upset by the announcement that this is not *H. serpae,* but *H. callistus.*

The Callistus Tetra is a peaceful and active fish that requires an aquarium 30 liters or larger. The tank should have a dark background and soft, slightly acid water. This species does best when it is in the company of its own kind and, although it makes a good community aquarium fish, should be kept in groups with a minimum of six individuals. The Callistus Tetra spawns in a similar manner to the Flame Tetra, *H. flammeus.*

HYPHESSOBRYCON ERYTHROSTIGMA (Fowler)
Bleeding Heart Tetra, Tetra Perez

Range: Upper Amazon.

Habits: Peaceful if kept with fishes of its own size.

Water Conditions: Slightly acid, soft water. Temperature 23 to 26°C.

Size: To 8 cm.

Food Requirements: Live or frozen foods preferred; prepared foods taken if hungry.

For some months after its introduction this very attractive fish was known to the hobby only as "Tetra Perez." At that time a large number of immature fish were found by a collector and shipped from Colombia. It is amusing to see how some of our present-day authorities took these immature specimens and jumped to conclusions. Professor Sterba in his book *Süsswasserfische aus Aller Welt* gives their maximum size as 3.5 cm and illustrates his account of the fish with a sketch of obviously half-grown specimens, which purports to show them in their natural size. To everyone's surprise, these little fellows which arrived in 1956 grew and grew until they became larger by far than the Rosy Tetra. Most of the color is concentrated in the bright pink of the dorsal fin with its large black area in the middle, and in the startling blood-red spot just above the belly region. This is not a fish for the small aquarium; it is an active species which requires a good deal of "elbow room" and should get it. Given this, a well-conditioned pair will spawn readily and in a manner similar to that of the other *Hyphessobrycon* species.

HYPHESSOBRYCON FLAMMEUS Myers / *Flame Tetra, Red Tetra, Tetra from Rio*

Range: Region near Rio de Janeiro.
Habits: Peaceful; best kept with other small fishes and in a school of at least six.
Water Conditions: Not critical; water is best if slightly acid and soft, but this is not absolutely essential. Temperature of 24 to 26°C.
Size: To 4 cm.
Food Requirements: Prepared foods accepted, but live or frozen foods are preferred.

The aquarium hobbyist who wishes to try his hand at spawning one of this group is strongly recommended to try the Flame Tetra. Not only is the task an easy one which is usually successful, but the rewards enjoyed later on are well worth the effort. A good sized, well-planted aquarium which contains a good number of healthy, colorful youngsters is a sight at which even a hardboiled old-timer will gaze repeatedly. There is nothing shy and retiring about a Flame Tetra; they enjoy being out in the open and disporting themselves, looking for all the world like a flock of tiny red-winged butterflies. Sexing is not much of a problem: besides being less full-bodied and having brighter colors, the males have a slightly wider black margin on the anal fin, which has a straighter edge than that of the females. Spawning occurs among fine-leaved plants, and their owner is sometimes amazed at the amount of eggs which can be released by such a small female. Hatching occurs in two to three days, and once the fry begin to swim they must be fed with very fine-grained prepared foods or infusoria. Growth proceeds rapidly; with good attention, the fry are raised to maturity in about six months.

HYPHESSOBRYCON GRIEMI Hoedeman / *Griem's Tetra*

Range: Brazil, in the vicinity of Goyaz.
Habits: Perfectly peaceful; like the other small members of the family, they also prefer to be kept in groups of at least six.
Water Conditions: Soft, slightly acid water is best but not necessarily essential. Temperature 24 to 26°C.
Size: About 4 cm.
Food Requirements: Prepared foods are accepted, but live or frozen foods are preferable.

This fish was collected in 1956 and named by Hoedeman in 1957. In size and shape it resembles *Hyphessobrycon flammeus,* and the same two streaks appear on the sides. The picture only hints at the slightly greenish color of the sides, which become lighter around the second streak of black. The deep pink of the caudal and anal fins is only slightly indicated in most available specimens, but with good care and feeding it becomes increasingly evident. This color is also often lost when the fish is frightened by being placed in a too-bare aquarium or in an aquarium where it is being constantly pursued by larger fishes.

Hyphessobrycon flammeus ☐F☐ ☐H☐ ☐X☐ ☐7☐☐6☐☐5☐ ☐X☐ ☐N☐ ☐N☐ ☐4☐ [R. Zukal]
Hyphessobrycon griemi ☐F☐ ☐Q☐ ☐X☐ ☐7☐☐6☐☐6☐ ☐X☐ ☐N☐ ☐N☐ ☐4☐ [S. Frank]

Hyphessobrycon herbertaxelrodi [F][Q][X][7][6][7][X][N][N][3]   [S. Frank]
Hyphessobrycon heterorhabdus [F][Q][X][7][6][8][X][N][N][5]   [S. Frank]

HYPHESSOBRYCON HERBERTAXELRODI Gery / *Black Neon Tetra*

Range: Rio Taquary, Brazil.
Habits: Peaceful toward other fishes; prefers to be kept in a group of at least six.
Water Conditions: Soft, slightly acid water preferred but not essential. Temperature 25°C.
Size: About 3 cm.
Food Requirements: Hearty eaters; prepared foods as well as live or frozen foods are eaten with equal gusto.

The so-called "Black Neon" has caused quite a furor in German aquatic circles. In the author's opinion this is indeed a handsome fish, but not handsome enough to cause such excitement. Like the Neon Tetra, the contrasts are very striking, even if in this case the colors are only black and white. In a well-planted aquarium, a number of them swimming around makes a pleasing sight with the broad, velvet-black area on the lower half of the sides and the startling, enamel-white stripe above it. When the light comes from above, this white stripe takes on a gleaming light blue color which we cannot see in the picture. Another color which is only faintly indicated is the red in the upper half of the eye. Discovery of this species can be attributed to the sharp eyes of Mr. Karl-Heinz Stegeman, who spotted them in a shipment of fishes coming from the Rio Taquary in the State of Mato Grosso, Brazil. This was in the early part of 1960, and the taxonomic description by Dr. J. Gery was published in the May, 1961 issue of *Tropical Fish Hobbyist.*

HYPHESSOBRYCON HETERORHABDUS (Ulrey)
Flag Tetra, False Ulreyi

Range: Lower and middle Amazon region.
Habits: Peaceful and very active.
Water Conditions: A little sensitive if not given soft, slightly acid water. Temperature should be kept around 25°C.
Size: About 5 cm.
Food Requirements: Will take dried food readily, but should also get frequent feedings of live or frozen foods.

This very attractive tetra masqueraded under a false name for many years. When it was first introduced into Germany in 1910, it was mistaken for *Hemigrammus ulreyi*. Call it what you may, it is a pretty little fish and an asset to any aquarium. Trouble is, we seldom get to see any numbers of tank-raised specimens, and we are still dependent upon imported specimens for our aquaria. They usually take very well to captivity, and the females seem to fill up with eggs, but the usual result is either nothing at all or only a few youngsters.

HYPHESSOBRYCON METAE Eigenmann & Henn / *Purple Tetra*

Range: Rio Meta, Colombia.
Habits: Peaceful, but tends to be shy; should not be kept with large or aggressive fishes.
Water Conditions: Soft, slightly acid water is best, especially for breeding purposes. Temperature 24 to 28°C.
Size: To 5 cm.
Food Requirements: Although live foods are preferred, frozen foods will be accepted without trouble; will often accept flake foods as well.

Almost all *Hyphessobrycon* species, like the *Hemigrammus* species, are very peaceful and may be kept together in a community aquarium. They are most at home and most attractive when kept in schools of a moderate size. For breeding purposes, bunches of fine-leaved plants such as *Myriophyllum* or *Amblystegium* should be placed in the aquarium. If these are unavailable, artificial spawning material should be used. The water should be soft and on the acid side of neutral. Water may be made acid by filtering it through peat moss or by adding tannic acid. Only females which appear gravid should be used. The spawning ritual may appear violent, with the fish pressing up against each other and diving into the plants. Parents should be removed from the breeding aquarium soon after spawning, as they are known to be egg-eaters. To further protect the eggs, the plants should be densely bunched and glass beads or marbles should be placed on the floor of the breeding aquarium.

HYPHESSOBRYCON PERUVIANUS Ladiges / *Loreto Tetra*

Range: Peruvian Amazon.
Habits: Peaceful and a bit shy; should not be kept with large or aggressive fishes.
Water Conditions: Soft, slightly acid water is best but is not absolutely essential. Temperature 24 to 28°C.
Size: 5 cm; most specimens smaller.
Food Requirements: Live foods preferred, but frozen or prepared foods are accepted without any trouble.
Color Variations: Back light brown to olive, with a deep black stripe below; dorsal fin reddish, and caudal fin deep red.

The Loreto Tetra is similar in shape to the Neon Tetra. Males of this species are slimmer than the females and their swimbladders are completely visible when the fish is seen against a light. The more robust females have only a partially visible swimbladder. The Loreto Tetra is a hardy and undemanding fish. Under optimum conditions these fish will develop a brilliant purple coloration.

Hyphessobrycon metae F E X 7 6 9 X N N 5   [S. Frank]
Hyphessobrycon peruvianus F D X 7 7 0 X N N 5

[Dr. Herbert R. Axelrod]

770

Hyphessobrycon pulchripinnis [F] [Q] [X] [7] [7] [1] [X] [N] [N] [5]   [S. Frank]
Hyphessobrycon scholzei [F] [D] [X] [7] [7] [2] [X] [N] [N] [5]   [K. Paysan]

HYPHESSOBRYCON PULCHRIPINNIS Ahl / *Lemon Tetra*

Range: Brazil, in the vicinity of Pará.
Habits: Peaceful; happier in a group of at least six.
Water Conditions: Soft, acid water is desirable but not essential. Temperature 24 to 27°C.
Size: To 5 cm.
Food Requirements: Live foods preferred, but frozen and prepared foods are accepted.

The males of this species are more colorful than the females. The females have a fuller, deeper body and a narrower black edge on the anal fin, if indeed any edge exists at all. As can be readily seen, this is not a highly colorful fish, but the small streaks of brightest lemon yellow in the fins and the bright red upper part of the eye make it an excellent "contrast fish," especially when combined with other tetras which have a good deal of red in them. Spawning these little beauties is not always simple. Females frequently have a bit of trouble expelling eggs, and it may sometimes be necessary to combine a male with several females before a successful spawning is achieved. Eggs are laid in fine-leaved plants in the usual *Hyphessobrycon* manner. Once the fry have hatched they sometimes prove to be a bit "touchy" at first, and the mortality rate is likely to be high. Once through these trying stages, however, they are fairly easy to raise.

HYPHESSOBRYCON SCHOLZEI Ahl / *Black-Lined Tetra*

Range: Vicinity of Pará, Brazil.
Habits: Peaceful; will not harm other fishes or plants.
Water Conditions: Soft and slightly acid water is preferable but not essential. Temperature 23 to 26°C.
Size: To 5 cm.
Food Requirements: Prepared foods accepted readily, but they should be supplemented with frozen and live foods.

The Black-Lined Tetra is not one of the flashy species which take the aquarium world by storm, but it has a quiet charm which has kept it in the tanks of aquarium hobbyists with a fair amount of consistency ever since its introduction in 1936. The reason most probably is that it has just about all the desirable traits except color. And if one sees this fish in the proper light, there is some color which is quite evident. When in a position where sunlight bounces off its scales, these show an opalescent gleam and the black stripe has a bluish, almost luminous glow at its upper edge. Besides, all the unpaired fins have a slight pink tinge when the fish is in good condition. All these things are lost when they are put in a tank where there are not enough plants and the lighting is not proper, and the Black-Lined Tetra becomes just a silvery fish with a black stripe. This is one of the easiest members of the genus to breed. They spawn like many other *Hyphessobrycon* species, hanging their eggs among fine-leaved plants.

HYPHESSOBRYCON SERPAE HARALDSCHULTZI Travassos
Harald Schultz's Tetra

Range: Ilha do Bananal, Goiaz, Brazil.
Habits: Peaceful; should be kept with a number of their own kind.
Water Conditions: Soft, slightly acid water. Temperature 24 to 26°C.
Size: Just under 2.5 cm.
Food Requirements: Will take prepared foods, but live or frozen foods are better.
Color Variations: Body color rosy pink, the belly white; fins reddish except dorsal, which has a black spot in a white area; small black shoulder spot.

Here we have another example of what happens all too frequently with so many of our aquarium fishes. When Harald Schultz found this little fish in the Ilha do Bananal in Goiaz, Brazil, he made a rough sketch of it in its life colors and sent it along to us. This sketch showed the color of the body and all fins, with the exception of the dorsal, to be a brilliant red. When a shipment of the living fish came and we got them into an aquarium, we wondered if they could possibly be the same ones. These had only a slight rosy flush, somewhat less than that of the Rosy Tetra. This we attributed to the rigors of their long journey, but their colors never brightened again. Nevertheless, even with its paler-than-original colors the fish is very attractive and peaceful as well. The taxonomic description by Dr. Haraldo Travassos appeared in the February, 1960, issue of *Tropical Fish Hobbyist,* and he here mentions that this species is closely related to *H. callistus* but distinguished from that species by the black spot in the dorsal fin and also by differences in dentition. Coloration and dentition differences also distinguish it from other members of the group.

Hyphessobrycon serpae haraldschultzi. Photo by Harald Schultz.

Hyphessobrycon serpae haraldschultzi 🄵🇶🆇🄷🄷🄷🆇🄽🄽🄸

1. *Hyphessobrycon serpae serpae* 🄵🄷🆇🄷🄷🄷🆇🄽🄽🄸 [H. J. Richter]

2. *Hyphessobrycon serpae serpae*
[H. J. Richter]

F Q X 7 7 5 X N N 2

HYPHESSOBRYCON SERPAE SERPAE Durbin / *Serpae Tetra*

Range: Amazon River (Madeira and Guaporé regions) and upper Paraguay.
Habits: Mostly peaceful, but will sometimes take a dislike to a fish and nip fins.
Water Conditions: Soft, slightly acid water. Temperature should not drop below 24°C at any time.
Size: Up to 4 cm; usually smaller.
Food Requirements: Does very well on dried foods, but of course should get occasional feedings with live or frozen foods.

It is a pity that we cannot give this beautiful tetra an absolutely clean record for behavior. With other fishes of the same approximate size it is usually a model citizen, but put it with something smaller, like a Neon Tetra, and it will often pursue them unmercifully. The Serpae Tetra is a very durable fish and once accustomed to its surroundings will usually live a long time. It is easily spawned, and the fish are not difficult by the usual methods. It is seldom imported, but many other species are incorrectly sold under the name *H. serpae.*

If breeding is intended for this fish, thick bunches of fine-leaved plants such as *Myriophyllum* or an artificial spawning foliage should be provided. Bottom soil is not required. The water should be soft and slightly acid. It can be helpful to filter the water through peat moss. Lighting in a proper fashion also helps to stimulate spawning. These fish seem to enjoy morning sunlight.

1. *Hyphessobrycon serpae serpae* in an aquarium enjoying the morning sunlight (p774).
2. *H. serpae serpae* pair (p775).

Hyphessobrycon serpae, the Serpae Tetra. Photo by R. Zukal.

HYPHESSOBRYCON SIMULANS Gery / *False Neon*

Range: Rio Negro, Brazil.
Habits: Peaceful; likes to travel in schools.
Water Conditions: Water should be acid and very soft. Temperature 24 to 26°C.
Size: About 2.5 cm.
Food Requirements: Small living foods preferred; probably would accept prepared or frozen foods readily.
Color Variations: Bright blue iridescent streak from opercle to caudal base, with an area of red above the anal fin.

It is an odd thing that the Neon Tetra and later on the Cardinal Tetra were both originally classified as belonging to the genus *Hyphessobrycon,* where neither one remained. The Neon Tetra was known as *Hyphessobrycon innesi* for many years before it was reclassified as *Paracheirodon innesi.* The Germans tried calling the Cardinal Tetra *Hyphessobrycon cardinalis,* but it is now *Cheirodon axelrodi.* A third "neon" came along and Dr. Jacques Gery assured us that it is a genuine *Hyphessobrycon.* He named it *Hyphessobrycon simulans* in the April, 1963, issue of *Tropical Fish Hobbyist.* Perhaps this one will not suffer the same fate as its predecessors and will retain its original name. The fish arrived in Switzerland as part of a shipment from the Aquario Rio Negro in Brazil and might have been sold unnoticed if it were not for the eagle eye of Chris R. Schmidt, Jr., a young scientist who spotted "something different" among the Cardinal Tetras. The Rio Negro and its tributary streams are far from being completely studied, and probably there are many more new and beautiful species to be found there for the fish hobbyist.

HYPHESSOBRYCON STEGEMANNI Gery / *Savannah Tetra*

Range: The savannahs of northeastern Brazil, between the lower Rio Tocantins and the Rio Capim.
Habits: Peaceful; likes to travel in schools.
Water Conditions: Soft, slightly acid water. Temperature should not drop lower than 24°C.
Size: To 5 cm.
Food Requirements: Does very well on dried foods, but should also get occasional feedings with live or frozen foods.

This fish comes from clear, swiftly-moving river waters which have a relatively stable temperature of 24°C. The pH of the water varies with the time of year. During the summer dry season, the pH of the river water varies from 5.2 to 5.8. During the heavy downpours of the rainy season, however, the pH will move toward the alkaline side of neutral. This is due to the salts in the surrounding savannah lands which are washed into the rivers. The process is reversed when the floods come and the decaying vegetation that results sends the pH back into the acid range.

Hyphessobrycon simulans F D X 7 7 7 X N N 1   [H. J. Richter]
Hyphessobrycon stegemanni F Q X 7 7 8 X N N 4   [Dr. E. Schmidt]

Hyphessobrycon takasei Ⓕ Ⓐ Ⓧ ⑦ ⑦ ⑨ Ⓧ Ⓝ Ⓝ ③   [Harald Schultz]
Hyphessobrycon vilmae Ⓕ Ⓡ Ⓧ ⑦ ⑧ ⓪ Ⓧ Ⓝ Ⓝ ④   [Harald Schultz]

HYPHESSOBRYCON TAKASEI Gery / *Coffee Bean Tetra*

Range: Amapa Territory in northern Brazil.
Habits: Very peaceful; will not harm plants or other fishes.
Water Conditions: Soft, acid water is optimal. Temperature 24 to 26°C.
Size: About 3 cm.
Food Requirements: Prefers live foods, but will accept frozen, freeze-dried or dried foods as well.

The Coffee Bean Tetra is another member of a large and confusing group of tetras referred to as the *"callistus*-group" which includes such aquarium favorites as *Hyphessobrycon callistus* and *H. serpae*. The Coffee Bean Tetra is separable from all other tetras to date by the very large humeral or shoulder spot which is unique not only because of its size but also because of its coffee bean shape. This species was first collected in the Serra do Navio above Macapa in Amapa Territory, Brazil in December of 1961. It was subsequently imported into Germany in 1962 and sold under the incorrect name *"Megalamphodus takasei."* This species is best given extremely soft water of a pH between 6.8 and 6.5. A temperature range between 24 and 26°C seems to suit it.

HYPHESSOBRYCON VILMAE Gery / *Vilma's Tetra*

Range: Northern and central Brazil.
Habits: A lively nature yet not aggressive, but can be a fin-nipper.
Water Conditions: Somewhat on the acid size; a small fluctuation of DH will be tolerated. Temperature 24°C.
Size: To 4 cm.
Food Requirements: Will accept freeze-dried foods and also dry foods; live foods are naturally relished.

This tetra was discovered by Harald Schultz in the savannahs and primeval forest bordering the upper Rio Arinos in Brazil. This charming little species inhabits those small creeks and burity palm swamps which are not far from the village of Diamantino. Mr. Schultz decided to have this new species named in honor of his wife, Vilma. The enthusiasm that the great explorer Harald Schultz felt for this new member of the genus *Hyphessobrycon* was shown in his own personal written description of this species: "Colors are even more brilliant than on the accompanying slide; the upper band, which goes through eyes, is old gold, with a thin blood-red line below it; the lower band, beginning at the opercle and ending at the tips of middle caudal rays, is deep black; the fins and to a certain degree the body are bluish." This gorgeous fish is not readily available, but maybe one day, if there is a demand, *Hyphessobrycon vilmae* might become as popular as some of the other well-known aquarium tetras; some say that this species is even more appealing to the eye than *Hyphessobrycon stegemanni,* another species which Mr. Schultz also discovered.

HYPHESSOBRYCON SP.

Range: Lower Amazon region.
Habits: Peaceful; prefers to be kept in a school of fishes its own size or, better yet, its own
 species.
Water Conditions: Soft, slightly acid water preferred. Temperature 24 to 26°C.
Size: About 4 cm.
Food Requirements: Prepared foods readily accepted, but live or frozen foods preferred.

Hyphessobrycon species are, in general, hardy, peaceful fish that come in a
variety of shades and colors. This species, like many others in the genus,
prefers to school with its own kind but will sometimes be seen schooling with
other species in the genus. Because of the popularity of the *Hyphessobrycon*
tetras, many of the species in this genus can be found in the aquarium hobby.
They are closely related and very often difficult to identify to the species level
even by the most noted scientists working with this group of fish. When a
shipment of *Hyphessobrycon* species arrive in this country, there are often a
number of questionable, unidentifiable or unidentified species included in the
shipment.

HYPOPOMUS ARTEDI (Kaup) / *Spotted Knife Fish*

Range: Brazil and the Guianas.
Habits: Peaceful toward other fishes which are not small enough to be swallowed; likely to be
 belligerent toward their own kind.
Water Conditions: Not critical, but the fish is sensitive to fresh water. The tank should be
 well planted and offer a number of places to hide. Temperature about 24°C.
Size: To 43 cm.
Food Requirements: Prefers large live foods or chopped lean beef.
Color Variations: Yellowish to brownish with darker spots.

Tell a non-hobbyist that there is a fish which has no dorsal fin, no tail fin and
no ventral fins, and also has its anus just below its head, and he will doubt
your sanity! Then tell him that this fish swims by rippling its anal fin and can
swim as easily backward as forward by reversing this rippling motion, and
your friend will begin to make excuses to get away as quickly as possible
before you get violent. So you better have one of these fish around to show him
before you tell him these things. There are knife fishes fairly well distributed
in tropical Asia, Africa and South America. They are seldom caught in large
numbers, and putting together two males often results in a pitched battle in
which the defeated fish is likely to be killed if it is not rescued. In spite of this
seeming bloodthirstiness, *Hypopomus artedi* is rather shy in its behavior
toward other fishes, provided of course that they are not small enough to
become an item on its menu. This shyness unfortunately manifests itself by
the fish's almost constant hiding among the plants and rocks.

Hyphessobrycon sp. 　Ⓕ Ⓓ Ⓧ ⑦ ⑧ ① Ⓧ Ⓝ Ⓝ ④　[Dr. Herbert R. Axelrod]
Hypopomus artedi 　Ⓕ Ⓓ Ⓧ ⑦ ⑧ ② Ⓧ Ⓝ Ⓝ ⑨　[Dr. Herbert R. Axelrod]

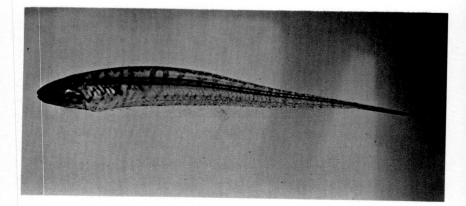

1. *Hypostomus plecostomus*   F D X 7 8 3 X N N D
2. *Hypostomus plecostomus*   F D X 7 8 4 X N N D

HYPOSTOMUS PLECOSTOMUS (Linnaeus) / *Sucker Catfish, Plecostomus*

Range: Most of South America.

Habits: Peaceful toward other unrelated fishes, but sometimes very scrappy among themselves.

Water Conditions: Slightly hard, alkaline water preferred. Temperature 24 to 27°C.

Size: To 60 cm in natural waters; most captive specimens get no bigger than 30 cm.

Food Requirements: Live worms or frozen foods are eaten greedily, also cut-up pieces of earthworms.

Not all of our aquarium fishes are beautiful; a few are so ugly that their unbelievable ugliness makes them interesting, and the Plecostomus is one of these. The eyes, for example, do not look like anything that any living creature could see through but rather like a pair of lumps. There seems to be no transparency to them. The mouth is a round, underslung affair with which the fish can attach itself to a flat surface and rasp off the algae, of which it is very fond. This makes it a very useful citizen in a tank which is plagued by algal growths. The Plecostomus is a fish which is most active at night and during the day generally remains hidden by the hour in the shade of some rock. Do not let this preference for a shady spot argue you into putting this fish into a tank where there is little sunlight, because our friend will always find a spot to its liking during the daylight hours and at night come out and graze on the algae prone to proliferate in a tank which is sunny and has fairly alkaline water. Perhaps it has been bred, but if so the feat is a rare one.

1. *Hypostomus plecostomus* resting on a rock in an aquarium (p783).
2. *H. plecostomus* head close-up. Note the interesting eye (p783).

Hypostomus plecostomus in its albino form. Photo by Dr. Herbert R. Axelrod.

HYPSELEOTRIS GUENTHERI (Bleeker) / *Chameleon Sleeper*

Range: Sumatra to New Guinea, the Solomons and east to Fiji and Samoa.
Habits: Peaceful; all foods readily accepted.
Conditions: Slightly alkaline, fairly hard water preferred; brackish water is tolerated. Temperature 23 to 26°C.
Size: About 6 cm.
Food Requirements: Will eat anything, but may also include plants in its menu; should get live foods occasionally.
Color Variations: Usually a muddy brown with a darker horizontal stripe. The male's fins have a blue edge, the dorsal fin with blue dots.

This seldom-imported fish has a wide range in the western Pacific islands. It is a regular chameleon in the way it can undergo color changes with startling speed. Its usual color is a rather muddy brown with a darker horizontal stripe, but in no time at all it can assume darker colors. Along with the darker colors the fish frequently develops a pair of startling light blue eyes. Most of the goby group are not good swimmers. Some have very inadequate swimbladders and merely hop about on the bottom from one place to another. Not so with this one; it swims normally and prefers the middle reaches of the aquarium. They are very hardy, and the author has kept some for a number of years without any special attention. Males can be distinguished by a blue edge on the fins and a number of large blue dots in the dorsal fin. The female's fins are transparent and the blue edge is missing.

HYPSELEOTRIS KLUNZINGERI (Ogilby) / *Australian Pink Sleeper*

Range: The coastal waters of Australia.
Habits: A fin-nipper which should only be kept with fishes its own size.
Water Conditions: Prefers slightly alkaline, hard water; brackish water is tolerated.
Size: It is rarely found to exceed 10 cm.
Food Requirements: Prefers live foods, but takes pelleted foods and frozen foods readily.
Color Variation: Some specimens have red, brown and blue edges on their fins.

When kept in a school of about a dozen fish in an 80-liter aquarium with hard water, the fish become very active and colorful, but they seem to be extremely short-lived. The longest that one has stayed alive (on record) is less than a year; perhaps this is due to the manhandling the fish gets before it is shipped.

Aquarists in Australia receive the fish very well and claim it to be an excellent community fish, but our experience here is that the fish is nasty and nips the fins of larger fishes while swallowing fishes up to half its own size! It is not recommended for the community aquarium regardless of what our friends from "down under" say.

Hypseleotris guentheri ⬚F ⬚R ⬚X ⬚7 ⬚8 ⬚5 ⬚X ⬚N ⬚N ⬚6   [Dr. Herbert R. Axelrod]

Hypseleotris klunzingeri ⬚F ⬚R ⬚X ⬚7 ⬚8 ⬚6 ⬚X ⬚N ⬚N ⬚9   [G. Wolfsheimer]

1. *Ictalurus punctatus* var. [F][H][T][7][8][7][X][A][N][4]   [M. F. Roberts]
2. *Ictalurus punctatus* [F][H][M][7][8][7][X][N][N][9]   [Aaron Norman]

Iguanodectes spilurus [F][D][X][7][8][8][X][N][N][9]   [Dr. Herbert R. Axelrod]

ICTALURUS PUNCTATUS (Rafinesque) / *Channel Catfish*

Range: U.S.A., Great Lakes to Florida and Texas.
Habits: Small ones are excellent scavengers and peaceful.
Water Conditions: Not critical as long as the water is clean and not too warm. Temperature about 18°C.
Size: Only babies are recommended for the aquarium; reaches 90 cm in length.
Food Requirements: Tubifex worms and frozen brine shrimp are eaten with gusto by juveniles, but adults have large mouths and large appetites.

If you should ever get one of these, don't expect to raise it to full size. Literature on this species tells us that it is one of the larger catfishes, attaining a weight of 12 kg or more! Kept in an aquarium, however, small specimens take a long time to grow to a size where they must be given to a public aquarium. We kept an 8 cm specimen for several months in the TFH main office, where it was very well-behaved and did its cleaning-up duties very efficiently. It is very interesting to note the local names for this catfish and its close relative the Blue Catfish: catfish of the lakes, great fork-tailed cat, Mississippi cat, Florida cat, mathameg, flannel-mouth cat or ugly fish. Albino specimens are rather rare in nature because any fish with a white color becomes a target for predators and seldom attains any size. Because of an albino's rather poor eyesight, it also has another point against it by not seeing an attacker and not being able to get away in time. Therefore, it is a real advantage to an albino fish to be raised in an aquarium, where it is protected from predatory fishes.

1. *Ictalurus punctatus* albino (p787).
2. *I. punctatus* with a normal coloration (p787).

IGUANODECTES SPILURUS (Günther) / *Slender Tetra*

Range: Middle and lower Amazon region and the Guianas.
Habits: Peaceful and active; very likely to jump.
Water Conditions: Not critical, but best suited to soft, slightly acid water. Temperature from 24 to 28°C.
Size: To 9 cm.
Food Requirements: Live foods preferred, but others accepted.

Once in a while a few specimens of this fish find their way into "mixed" shipments; most dealers have a hard time making an identification, in case their customers should ask. Note the long, gracefully streamlined body, which proclaims the fish as an active swimmer. No long, flowing, decorative fins here! Fish like this are also capable of prodigious leaps, and their aquarium should be covered at all times. The black upper caudal lobe and colorless lower one give one the feeling that the fish has suffered an injury or that something is wrong, but this is the normal coloration.

INDOSTOMUS PARADOXUS Prashad & Mukerji / *Paradox Fish*

Range: Lake Indawgyi, northern Burma.
Habits: Peaceful; given to resting on the bottom for long periods or drifting through the water slowly.
Water Conditions: Soft water; pH about 6.8. Temperature 20 to 24°C.
Size: About 2.5 cm.
Food Requirements: Live baby brine shrimp preferred, but it may be trained to accept substitutes.

Ichthyologists have accused the Paradox Fish of being related to the trumpetfishes (Aulostomidae), ghost pipefishes (Solenostomidae) and the tubenoses (Aulorhynchidae). For the aquarist, *I. paradoxus* is a fascinating species that seldom exceeds 2.5 cm in length and is ideally suited to a 20-liter aquarium. Because of its coloration, it blends in very easily with its background and may be difficult to locate at times. Although a sedentary species, the Paradox Fish is completely capable of lightning-like bursts of speed which may carry it completely out of the water. The aquarium should be covered. Temperatures between 20 and 21°C are tolerated, although around 24°C seems best. There are no reports of spawning.

INPAICHTHYS KERRI Gery & Junk / *Blue Emperor*

Range: Upper Rio Aripuana, Mata Grosso, Brazil.
Habits: Similar to the Emperor Tetra, but perhaps more timid.
Water Conditions: Water should be soft to medium hard with a pH around neutral. Temperature about 26 to 28°C.
Size: Reaches a length of at least 5 cm.
Food Requirements: Will accept frozen or dried foods but prefers live foods.

Inpaichthys kerri is one of the most recently described tetras, and its beauty will probably make it one of the more sought-after of the emperor-like tetras.

Spawning is similar to that of the Emperor Tetra. Males can be distinguished from the females as follows: the female is tan with a broad dark stripe from snout tip to base of caudal fin, and the adipose fin is dark red to orange; the male is similarly colored on the body, but when excited or in advantageous lighting it shines bright blue with violet overtones, and the adipose fin is a bright blue. After one or two days the pair introduced to a spawning tank will quiet down some and usually start spawning. The tank itself can be as small as 20 liters, should not be very bright and should be planted to a moderate extent with some fine-leaved plants. The male will display vigorously in front of the female before spawning and will try and entice the female into the fine-leaved plants by swimming into them and back to the female, trying to press his body against hers. When the female follows him they swim through the plants, where the female will stop over a chosen spot and the male will press his body against hers again in typical tetra fashion.

Indostomus paradoxus F D X 7 8 9 X N N 1

[J. Mehrtens]

Inpaichthys kerri F E X 7 9 0 X N N 5

[W. Junk]

Iodotropheus sprengerae 　F E X 7 9 1 X N N A　　　[S. Frank]

1. *Iriatherina werneri* ♂　F E M 7 9 2 X N N 4　　[Dr. W. Foersch]
2. *Iriatherina werneri* ♀　F F B 7 9 2 X N N 4　　[Dr. W. Foersch]

IODOTROPHEUS SPRENGERAE Oliver & Loiselle / *Rusty Cichlid*

Range: Lake Malawi, Africa.

Habits: Pugnacious toward its own species and territorial, but much less destructive than some of the larger mbuna.

Water Conditions: Hard, alkaline water is best; a teaspoonful of non-iodized salt added per 4 liters of aquarium water may be beneficial.

Size: About 9 cm for females; 10 cm for males.

Food Requirements: Will take all standard aquarium foods, but the basic diet should consist of meaty items like live tubifex worms and frozen brine shrimp.

Iodotropheus sprengerae is a mouthbrooding species. The female parent incubates the eggs in her mouth for about three weeks before releasing the fry, and she will continue to care for the fry until they no longer need her. The female should be placed in a tank by herself as soon as it is certain that spawning has been completed and no more eggs will be laid and picked up after fertilization by the male, and she should be allowed to remain with the released fry until they no longer need her—which will be evident from the fact that she no longer pays them any attention. The mother should not be returned to the presence of the male, whether he is by himself or in a community tank, until after she has been given a chance to rest and fatten up after her brooding activities.

IRIATHERINA WERNERI Meinken / *Featherfin Rainbow*

Range: West Irian (on island of New Guinea).

Habits: Peaceful and active.

Water Conditions: pH and hardness are not critical, as long as extremes are avoided. Temperature 24 to 27°C.

Size: To about 4 cm.

Food Requirements: Accepts most standard aquarium foods, but only in small sizes.

Iriatherina werneri is a non-spectacular but interesting species of rainbow fish (family Atherinidae). Although it is not highly colorful, its small size and peaceful nature, coupled with the graceful good looks of the males in their long-finned elegance, make it a desirable fish. So far as is now known, this species is restricted in distribution to only western portions of the Republic of West Irian on New Guinea. The water in which the original specimens were collected was turgid, slow-moving and weed-choked, but they probably exist in clearer and more swiftly flowing waters as well. When presented with specimens, Dr. Meinken determined that the fish is sufficiently different taxonomically from other East Asian atherinid fishes to be placed into a new genus. Discovered in 1973, the fish has not yet been imported or bred in numbers sufficient to give it a real foothold in the hobby.

1. *Iriatherina werneri* male (p791).
2. *I. werneri* female (p791).

792

JORDANELLA FLORIDAE Goode & Bean / *American Flagfish*

Range: Florida, especially in the southern portion.
Habits: Males are apt to be very quarrelsome, especially at spawning time; it is best to give pairs their own aquarium.
Water Conditions: Prefers a sunny aquarium with slightly alkaline water. Temperature should be around 21°C, slightly higher for spawning.
Size: About 5 cm.
Food Requirements: Will eat dried as well as live foods, but should get a good deal of vegetable matter in its diet.

A fish, like a prophet, is often without honor in its own country. The European hobbyists value this cyprinodont highly, but in American aquaria it is quite rare. This also holds true for a great number of other beautiful native American fishes. Of course, temperatures which we give to our tropical species are a bit too high for these beauties, but even a small aquarium at room temperature suits them fine. Its breeding habits are unusual for a cyprinodont. Eggs are often hung among surface plants in the usual cyprinodont manner, but sometimes we also find them near the bottom or on the bottom, guarded by the male. It is not usually necessary to remove the female; she is rarely molested. Spawning may last over a period of a week. The male takes care of the young cichlid-fashion after they hatch. Incubation lasts five to six days.

JULIDOCHROMIS DICKFELDI Staeck / *Dickfeldi*

Range: Lake Tanganyika, Africa.
Habits: Territorial in nature and aggressive toward members of its own species.
Water Conditions: Hard, alkaline water. Temperature 24 to 27°C.
Size: Reaches a length of almost 10 cm.
Food Requirements: Not critical, so can be coaxed onto most of the standard aquarium foods.

Julidochromis dickfeldi is territorial and will not tolerate members of its own species being too close. If the aquarium provided is too small, the territory guarded will encompass the entire tank and any additional individuals will be forcibly ejected or killed.

In the center of a territory there is usually a cave or some place of refuge. It is within this cave that spawning usually takes place. If a compatible pair is obtained, this can be accomplished by having a large tank which will house safely several Dickfeldis or by introducing a ripe female or two into the male's tank and watching over them to see that no harm comes to them. The cave and the area immediately surrounding it are cleaned and cleared by the female or both partners. The female is nudged by the male in the area of the vent and displays before her until she starts the egg laying on the roof of the cave. The male follows in the same upside down posture and fertilizes the eggs. Both parents tend eggs and young.

Jordanella floridae F E X 7 9 3 X N N 5

Julidochromis dickfeldi F A X 7 9 4 X N N 9

[H. J. Richter]

[P. Brichard]

Julidochromis marlieri ⬚F⬚⬚E⬚⬚X⬚⬚7⬚⬚9⬚⬚5⬚⬚X⬚⬚N⬚⬚N⬚⬚A⬚   [Wardley Products Co.]
Julidochromis ornatus ⬚F⬚⬚Q⬚⬚X⬚⬚7⬚⬚9⬚⬚6⬚⬚X⬚⬚N⬚⬚N⬚⬚8⬚   [H. J. Richter]

JULIDOCHROMIS MARLIERI Poll / *Marlier's Julie*

Range: Lake Tanganyika, Africa.
Habits: Adult males are apt to become very scrappy unless given a large aquarium.
Water Conditions: Hard, alkaline water. Temperature 24 to 27°C.
Size: About 10 cm.
Food Requirements: Living foods are preferred, but will take frozen foods if they are not available.

Julidochromis marlieri is a fairly aggressive cichlid from Lake Tanganyika. Although this species is probably the most scrappy of the *Julidochromis* species, it is also thought by many to be the most attractive. Because it is very territorial, this fish requires a large aquarium if it is to contain more than one male cichlid. *J. marlieri* is a substrate-spawner which lays its eggs in rocky caves. There will be one to two hundred fry in a typical spawn, and they are fairly large when they become free-swimming. It is not necessary to separate the parents from the fry, as they get along very well. The fry are large enough at birth to eat newly hatched brine shrimp or finely crushed flake food.

JULIDOCHROMIS ORNATUS (Boulenger) / *Julie*

Range: Lake Tanganyika, Africa.
Habits: Because of their special water requirements, they should be kept by themselves. If more than one male is kept, each should have his own spot.
Water Conditions: Very hard and alkaline water made by treating it with sodium bicarbonate and calcium. Temperature 24 to 27°C.
Size: About 7.5 cm.
Food Requirements: Very finicky eaters which seem to prefer tubifex worms and glassworms.
Color Variations: Lemon-yellow with three dark brown horizontal stripes in the upper half of the body and a large dark spot at the caudal base.

Julidochromis ornatus, commonly called Julie or Ornatus, is a relatively peaceful cichlid from Lake Tanganyika. Nevertheless, this species is territorial, and males must be given enough room so that they do not fight each other. *J. ornatus* is a golden yellow fish with three chocolate-brown stripes in the upper half of its body. It reaches about 7½ cm in length.

This species is omnivorous, eating both algae and insects. In the aquarium, however, *J. ornatus* is a very picky eater. This species seems to prefer live food such as tubifex worms and glassworms.

Little research has been done on this fish's breeding habits. It is a substrate-spawner that lays many eggs in comparison to the small number of large eggs laid by many mouthbrooders in the Rift Lakes.

JULIDOCHROMIS REGANI Poll / *Convict Julidochromis*

Range: Lake Tanganyika, Africa.

Habits: Territorial, but not overly aggressive; seldom bother unrelated species that don't intrude into their territories.

Water Conditions: Hard, alkaline water preferred. Some aquarists add a quarter teaspoon of salt per liter to aquaria housing all *Julidochromis* species and all other fishes from Lake Tanganyika; although most such saline additions do the fish no harm, they are not strictly necessary. Temperature 24 to 27°C.

Size: About 10 cm.

Food Requirements: Will take all standard meaty foods; young fish do well on foods incorporating vegetable matter, especially algae.

Of all the many African cichlids that have come into the aquarium hobby, the species of *Julidochromis* are among the most sought after. Like *J. ornatus* and *J. marlieri*, *J. regani* lays its eggs in dark recesses in or around the cave-like rocky structures in which it prefers to spend most of its time. Spawns are not large, but the parents usually leave the fry alone. Since *Julidochromis* fry are fairly large when they become free-swimming, they are easy to feed on brine shrimp nauplii and suitable substitutes and therefore are fairly easy to raise. Juveniles get along well with their parents if they are maintained in the same tank, but they often fight among themselves.

1. *Julidochromis regani* in its normal form (p798).
2. *J. regani*, the yellow variety (p798).

JULIDOCHROMIS TRANSCRIPTUS Matthes / *Masked Julidochromis*

Range: Lake Tanganyika, Africa.

Habits: Territorial in nature; aggressive with fishes that do not respect its territorial boundaries.

Water Conditions: Hard, alkaline water preferred. Temperature 24 to 27°C.

Size: About 10 cm is average adult size.

Food Requirements: Not finicky; will take standard aquarium fare. Foods that include a high proportion of vegetable materials should be offered occasionally.

Julidochromis transcriptus is odd in that the black stripe running through and obscuring the lower portion of its eye gives the fish a rather sinister look which seems not to fit at all with the delicate and attractive edge-band pattern of the dorsal and caudal fins. This eye stripe, of course, has given rise to the common name of Masked Julidochromis. Despite its appearance, however, *J. transcriptus* is no more of a bad actor than its cousins within the genus. Like them, it is an attractive, interesting fish that feels most at home weaving and darting its way among rocky labyrinths erected in its tank to simulate the conditions of the rocky crannies in which it lives in Lake Tanganyika. Provision of rocky shelters or a close substitute is absolutely necessary to the well-being of *J. transcriptus* and the other *Julidochromis* species.

1. *Julidochromis regani* FAT797XNNA   [T. Brichard]
2. *Julidochromis regani* var. FDM797XNN9   [Glen S. Axelrod]

Julidochromis transcriptus FDX798XNN8   [B. Kahl]

Kryptopterus bicirrhis ⬚F⬚D⬚X⬚7⬚9⬚9⬚X⬚N⬚N⬚A [Wardley Products Co.]
Kryptopterus macrocephalus ⬚F⬚D⬚X⬚8⬚0⬚0⬚X⬚N⬚N⬚B

KRYPTOPTERUS BICIRRHIS (Cuvier & Valenciennes) / *Glass Catfish*

Range: Thailand to Indonesia.
Habits: Peaceful; should not be kept singly, and should also not be kept with very active fishes.
Water Conditions: Water should be slightly alkaline and have a hardness which does not surpass 10 DH. Temperature about 24°C.
Size: To 10 cm.
Food Requirements: Should be given living foods such as tubifex worms, white worms, daphnia, etc.

As with most of the transparent catfishes, the body organs are enclosed in a silvery sac which shows how compressed and far in front these organs are in some fishes. As they are nocturnal in their habits, they need a darkened aquarium. They are also happier when kept in a group and should not be combined with other fishes which are highly active. Their tanks should be well planted, and they seem to enjoy getting under a broad leaf and remaining there with their fins undulating. They are not a bottom-grubbing species, and food which reaches the bottom is seldom retrieved by them. Note how the two long barbels or "whiskers" stand straight out rather than point downward, as do those in the bottom-feeding catfishes.

KRYPTOPTERUS MACROCEPHALUS (Bleeker)
Poor Man's Glass Catfish

Range: East Indies.
Habits: Harmless and very peaceful; should be kept in groups.
Water Conditions: Soft, neutral to slightly alkaline water best; slightly acid water is tolerated. Temperature about 24°C.
Size: To 11 cm.
Food Requirements: Prefers small living foods, but will take freeze-dried, dried and frozen foods, provided the pieces are not large.

K. macrocephalus has been referred to as the Poor Man's Glass Catfish primarily because its chief claim to prominence, its "transparency," is less pronounced than that of its more popular look-alike, the true Glass Catfish, *K. bicirrhis*. In many cases *K. macrocephalus* is accepted only as a second choice in the absence of *K. bicirrhis*. Like its relative, it is a completely inoffensive member of the community aquarium, living at peace with every other fish, even those much smaller than itself. Rather timid, it should be maintained in a well-planted aquarium that provides refuge and alternating light and dark areas. Neither of the Glass Catfishes is exceptionally hardy, but they are not overly delicate, either. This is a mid-water species that is not an active swimmer and is not able to compete for food against swifter species. The more-or-less continuous tail-down hovering position of the fish is normal and is not an indication of sickness.

LABEO BICOLOR Smith / *Red-Tailed Shark*

Range: Thailand.
Habits: Apt to be a bit scrappy among themselves, but peaceful toward other fishes.
Water Conditions: Slightly alkaline water and a hardness of about 10 DH. Temperature 24 to 26°C.
Size: To 12 cm.
Food Requirements: All kinds of live foods, besides some vegetable matter like lettuce or spinach leaves.
Color Variations: Deep brown to black body color ending in a red caudal base and tail.

The person who first referred to this group of fishes as "sharks" certainly had a healthy imagination. True, the *Labeo* species have a rather high dorsal fin, but its shape does not even faintly resemble the sickle-shaped dorsal fin of the real sharks which are seen so frequently in marine waters. There is no other resemblance either between the shy, mild-mannered Red-Tailed Shark and its vicious, ever-hungry namesake. The only time the Red-Tailed Shark gives any inkling of a "chip on its shoulder" is when one male intrudes into another's territory. With most fishes which stake out a claim this is the signal for a fierce battle, and there is a great deal of bustle and bluster with the Red-Tailed Sharks as well. The only thing is that, lacking the dental equipment and sharp fin rays, the Red-Tailed Shark is at a real disadvantage and his ferocity is mostly bluff. Lately there have been shipments of many small specimens, and it is suspected that the Thai breeders propagate them in their pools. Females are recognizable by their heavier bodies and we have seen accounts which stated that they had been bred, but no details were given.

LABEO ERYTHRURUS Fowler / *Rainbow Shark*

Range: Thailand, Mekong River.
Habits: Peaceful toward other fishes; tend to fight among themselves if not given enough tank room.
Water Conditions: Water 10 DH and slightly alkaline. Temperature 24 to 27°C.
Size: To 12 cm.
Food Requirements: Does best with live or frozen foods and will sometimes accept flake foods; vegetable matter should be included in the diet.

The Rainbow Shark is very much like its close relative the Red-Tailed Shark. Their aquarium should not be given much light and should be provided with an ample amount of hiding places. Although *Labeo erythrurus* is generally peaceful toward other species, it tends to be belligerent with its own kind. *Labeo erythrurus* is generally slimmer than *L. bicolor*.

Vegetable matter should be included in its diet in addition to the usual flake and frozen foods. If the Rainbow Shark does not get enough greens, it will tend to pick at the aquarium plants.

Labeo bicolor F D X 8 0 1 X N N B
Labeo erythrurus F D X 8 0 2 X N N A

[Braz Walker]

Labeo forskali [F][D][X][8][0][3][X][N][N][D]
Labeo variegatus [F][D][X][8][0][4][X][N][N][C]

[R. Zukal]
[Braz Walker]

LABEO FORSKALI Rüppell / *Plain Shark*

Range: Northeastern Africa.
Habits: Peaceful with other species; quarrelsome with members of its own species.
Water Conditions: Not critical, provided extremes are avoided. Temperature 22 to 26°C.
Size: To about 50 cm in nature; usually seen much smaller.
Food Requirements: Takes all standard aquarium foods; should have vegetable matter included in diet.

Not much on brilliance of color, *Labeo forskali* is nonetheless a pleasing species for those who appreciate large fishes. It looks very much like the popular conception of a big minnow, but it differs considerably from some of its smaller cyprinid cousins in being highly aggressive under conditions that bring out the beast in it . . . those conditions being that it is placed in a situation under which it has to share tank space with its own species. *Labeo forskali* has not been bred in the aquarium and little is known of sex differentiations, so it is not known whether combativeness between individual *L. forskali* is related to the sex of the fish; males are probably more aggressive than females, especially toward other males. In common with a number of other *Labeo* species, *L. forskali* also has a peculiarly shaped mouth as an adaptation for grazing algae, and it should be provided with suitable vegetative fare. It is not, however, an active eater of plants. The species should be housed in a large tank in keeping with its growth potential; the tank should be kept well covered, because it is a good jumper.

LABEO VARIEGATUS Pellegrin / *Harlequin Shark*

Range: Upper Congo.
Habits: Aggressive; should not be kept with fishes that cannot take care of themselves.
Water Conditions: Water quality is not critical, but avoid extremes. Temperatures may vary from 21 to 27°C.
Size: To over 30 cm in nature; usually much smaller in the aquarium.
Food Requirements: Will take almost any live, frozen or dried food used for aquarium fishes; a heavy feeder.

For those aquarists who want a variety of "sharks" and want to get away from the usual blacks and red fins, *Labeo variegatus* is the answer. It is a hardy, quite attractive fish that will be around for a long time. The juveniles are yellowish, mottled with various shades of black and brown, with perhaps some red thrown in for good measure.

Caring for the Harlequin Shark is easy. All it needs is a large, well-planted aquarium with plenty of aeration. Water conditions are not a problem, and a wide temperature range is tolerated (the suggested temperatures are from about 21 to 27°C).

LABEOTROPHEUS FUELLEBORNI Ahl / *Fuelleborn's Cichlid*

Range: Lake Malawi, Africa.
Habits: One of the most peaceful of the Malawi cichlids, but should be kept with large fishes.
Water Conditions: Should be fairly hard and alkaline. Temperature 24 to 27°C.
Size: Over 12 cm.
Food Requirements: Largely vegetarian, but animal foods are taken; will accept large dried foods with gusto.
Color Variations: Very similar to *Pseudotropheus zebra*, with dark bars on a blue background and the posterior portions of anal and dorsal with large orange spots—many color varieties.

Most fishes of the genera *Pseudotropheus* and *Labeotropheus* are to some degree adapted to scrape algae from rocks. The genus *Labeotropheus*, however, is extremely well adapted for this type of feeding. The mouth is underslung, allowing the fish to more easily contact submerged objects with its lips. One of the results of this adaptation is a hooked "nose" which gives the fish a rather unintelligent look. The teeth are also adapted to feeding on the algae by the fact that they have broad, spatulate tips which are slightly bent inward. These adaptations allow Fuelleborn's Cichlid to scrape even the most tenacious algae from rocks. This fish has several color forms surprisingly like *Pseudotropheus zebra*, but it is comparatively slimmer. Females of the genera *Pseudotropheus* and *Labeotropheus* often exhibit two different color patterns. One is more or less similar to the male of the respective species and the other is a white, black and orange mottled pattern similar to that found in Shubunkin Goldfish. Like *Pseudotropheus zebra*, male *Labeotropheus fuelleborni* have spots on the anal and dorsal fins. These are called "egg spots" and are found in many, but not all, mouthbrooding cichlids.

This species is one of the most peaceful cichlids from Lake Malawi. There are several color varieties (morphs) of this species, the most common variety being blue with 9 to 12 vertical bars on its sides. As far as is known, all forms of this species have identical behavior and food requirements.

As was previously mentioned, this fish is an herbivore with very specialized dentition for grazing algae off the substrate. The majority of aquarium foods, including meat (beef heart, etc.), will be accepted, however. Nevertheless, it is important that this fish be fed a good amount of vegetable foods and plant matter.

Labeotropheus fuelleborni is a maternal mouthbrooder with an incubation period of three to four weeks. Broods range in size from 25 to 75 offspring, and the fry are fairly large upon release. Adults grow to over 13 cm, with the males being slightly larger and more colorful than the females.

1. *Labeotropheus fuelleborni* normal male (p806).
2. *L. fuelleborni* mottled female (p806).
3. *L. fuelleborni* marmalade cat male (p807).
4. *L. fuelleborni* red-top marmalade cat male (p807).

1. *Labeotropheus fuelleborni*
2. *Labeotropheus fuelleborni* var.

F E X 8 0 5 X N N B
F F X 8 0 6 X P N B

3. *Labeotropheus fuelleborni* var.   F A X 8 0 7 X P N B

4. *Labeotropheus fuelleborni* var.   F E X 8 0 8 X M N B

Labeotropheus fuelleborni newly released fry (above) are seen against a scale in mm. The female *L. fuelleborni* (below) mouths the male's vent during spawning and receives sperm to fertilize the eggs in her mouth. Photos by Dr. D. Terver, Nancy Aquarium.

LABEOTROPHEUS TREWAVASAE Fryer / *Red-Top Trewavasae*

Range: Lake Malawi, Africa.
Habits: Should be kept in large aquaria with ample hiding places to prevent bullying.
Water Conditions: Should be fairly hard and alkaline. Temperature 24 to 27°C.
Size: About 10 cm.
Food Requirements: Largely vegetarian, but will accept animal foods.
Color Variations: Males blue with about 12 darker bars, dorsal red; females gray or tan, mottled black and orange—many color varieties.

The Red-Top Trewavasae is one of the most colorful cichlids to ever be offered to aquarists. Color, however, is largely confined to the male. His gleaming indigo tones are sharply contrasted with the brilliant dorsal which is colored brownish red to scarlet-red except for the posterior tip, which is striated with black markings. The posterior edges of the dorsal and the anal are marked with large orange spots. A white mask stripe runs over the forehead, connecting the eyes. The female is uniformly mottled black, yellow and, sometimes, blue. There are, however, many different color forms. The species is a mouthbrooder. The female broods the offspring, and when they are molested they may return to the protection of her mouth. This may occur as late as three or four weeks after hatching. The young are all colored like their mother. Although the Red-Top is highly adapted for scraping algae from rocks, it accepts all foods readily. If algae cannot be supplied, cooked spinach can be substituted. Like most of the Malawi cichlids, the Red-Top is aggressive. Males bully females and weaker males without end, and if peace is desired a large aquarium with many hiding places is necessary. After spawning, the male should be removed to prevent him from worrying the female while she is brooding.

If you start with a big tank and decide to add new cichlids at a later date, it is a good idea to completely rearrange the rocks first. Mature males placed into a new tank will challenge each other until they have divided up all the available territory. The most dominant male will command what he considers to be the most preferable area and the other males will divide up what is left. If a new male is added to the aquarium, he will be abused by the others wherever he may swim. This problem can be rectified by rearranging the rocks within the aquarium and confusing all of the fishes.

Generally speaking, African Rift Lake cichlids are very hardy and will withstand a wide range of conditions. Nevertheless, conditions simulating those of the Rift Valley Lakes are necessary if you desire to spawn your fish, want them to live long and want them to exhibit optimum coloration.

1. *Labeotropheus trewavasae* red-top male (p810).
2. *L. trewavasae* normal male in front of a normal female (p810).
3. *L. trewavasae* orange sparsely mottled female (p811).
4. *L. trewavasae* orange-blotched female (p811).

1. *Labeotropheus trewavasae* var. FEX809XNNA
2. *Labeotropheus trewavasae* FRX810XMNA [Dr. Herbert R. Axelrod]

Ladigesia roloffi ⬚F ⬚R ⬚X ⬚8 ⬚1 ⬚5 ⬚X ⬚N ⬚N ⬚4   [E. Roloff]

Lamprichthys tanganicanus   ⬚F ⬚D ⬚X ⬚8 ⬚1 ⬚6 ⬚X ⬚N ⬚N ⬚B

[Dr. Herbert R. Axelrod]

LADIGESIA ROLOFFI Gery / *Jelly Bean Tetra*

Range: Sierra Leone, West Africa.
Habits: Initially very shy; it will attempt to jump out of tank, so a covered tank is a definite necessity; reasonably hardy and peaceful.
Water Conditions: Temperature should be from 24 to 26°C, and the pH should be on the acid side, 6.7.
Size: To 4 cm.
Food Requirements: Will accept dry foods after a certain amount of training; freeze-dried foods are accepted willingly and live foods are never refused.

"Ladigesia" is derived from the name of the well-known Dr. Ladiges of Hamburg, Germany; *"roloffi"* is based on the name of the internationally recognized aquarist from Karlsruhe, Mr. E. Roloff, who collected the specimens used for identification. In the wild this new species is very difficult to catch because it is an amazingly fast swimmer, so the hobbyist will have to rely heavily upon aquarium-raised stock as his source of supply. Even though the tank-raised specimens are not as intensely colored as the individuals captured in Africa, they are nevertheless still a shining example of subtle beauty. The sexes in this fish follow a familiar pattern in aquarium fishes whereby the male is much more colorful and larger in size. Spawning, if attempted by the aquarist, should be patterned after the naturally existing conditions of the Jelly Bean Tetra's home in Africa: slowly running forest brook water, temperature 26°C, hardness 5.1 (German scale) and no aquatic plants except for ferns growing on protruding rocks.

LAMPRICHTHYS TANGANICANUS (Boulenger)
Tanganyika Pearl Killie

Range: Lake Tanganyika, Africa.
Habits: Peaceful and quite shy; should be kept in a well-planted, covered tank.
Water Conditions: Slightly alkaline. Temperature about 24°C.
Size: Males about 15 cm; females slightly smaller.
Food Requirements: Living foods such as daphnia, tubifex worms and adult brine shrimp.

Lake Tanganyika is a place where the ichthyologist has long had a field day with many species which were known from no other place. There is also much to interest the aquarist, among them some gorgeous specimens like this fish. Seeing a pair swimming around with the sun shining on them is a sight guaranteed to make any aquarist gasp. The rows of tiny dots gleam brightly with an incandescent blue. The picture gives a good idea, but the fish must be seen in the proper light to be appreciated. They are peaceful, even timid. Other fishes kept with them which are large enough not to be swallowed are left alone. Being an active fish, a large tank is preferable and should be covered to prevent their loss by jumping.

LAMPROLOGUS BRICHARDI Poll / *Lyretail Lamprologus*

Range: Lake Tanganyika, Africa.
Habits: Scrappy among themselves, but usually not pugnacious toward other species.
Water Conditions: Medium-hard to hard water preferred. Temperature 24 to 27°C.
Size: Up to about 9 cm.
Food Requirements: Live foods, especially live brine shrimp, are best, but frozen and flake foods accepted; sometimes refuses to eat granulated dry foods. Diet should include vegetable substances.

This comparatively common Tanganyika import has much to recommend it, its main point of attraction being its graceful configuration and its subdued yet very pleasing coloration. Its overall appearance provides an odd combination of power and refinement, and one of the nicest things about the species is that its good looks and gracefulness actually remain on display within the tank, because the fish is much less shy than some of the other Tanganyika cichlids on the market. A part of its tank should be given the same rocky, rubble-strewn setup as would apply to a tank of *Julidochromis*, for example, but the *Lamprologus* will not hide all day among the rocks. The species' willingness to put itself on display, however, does not extend to breeding time, for when *Lamprologus brichardi* spawns it becomes a recluse; the eggs are deposited within the caves and crannies formed by the rock piles in the tank, and in most cases their owner doesn't even know the fish has spawned until he sees baby *Lamprologus*. This species was once called *Lamprologus savoryi elongatus*, but this was changed because there was another species that had the same name for a longer time.

LAMPROLOGUS COMPRESSICEPS Boulenger / *Compressiceps*

Range: Lake Tanganyika, Africa.
Habits: Peaceful toward other fishes, but cannot be trusted with those it could swallow.
Water Conditions: Alkaline water, about pH 8.0. Temperature 24 to 27°C.
Size: 10 to 11 cm.
Food Requirements: Medium-sized living foods, such as grown brine shrimp, small fishes or cut-up earthworms.

This fish is as fragile as it is graceful. It is very susceptible to disease and is also a very picky eater. It does best on living foods such as tubifex worms, large fully grown brine shrimp and small fishes. In the lake it feeds on small fishes and copepods.

Not a great deal is known about the breeding habits of this species. It is a substrate spawner that spawns among the rocks in the littoral region of the lake. It prefers privacy; mating takes place in narrow and enclosed caves. It is extremely difficult to spawn in the aquarium unless the conditions are ideal.

Lamprologus brichardi ⬚F⬚ ⬚G⬚ ⬚X⬚ ⬚8⬚ ⬚1⬚ ⬚7⬚ ⬚X⬚ ⬚N⬚ ⬚N⬚ ⬚6⬚   [H. J. Richter]
Lamprologus compressiceps ⬚F⬚ ⬚D⬚ ⬚X⬚ ⬚8⬚ ⬚1⬚ ⬚8⬚ ⬚X⬚ ⬚N⬚ ⬚N⬚ ⬚B⬚   [Wardley Products Co.]

LAMPROLOGUS LELEUPI Poll / *Lemon Cichlid*

Range: Lake Tanganyika, Africa.
Habits: Inoffensive; can be kept with other fishes which can tolerate their water conditions.
Water Conditions: Alkaline water, about pH 8.0. The tank should be well planted and other hiding places provided as well. Temperature 24 to 27°C.
Size: To 10 cm.
Food Requirements: Prefers living foods on the small side, such as daphnia.

The males are distinguished by a larger head and more robust body. Pairs should be selected and given tanks of their own, which besides plants contain flowerpots from which the bottoms were knocked out. The pairs will spawn cichlid-fashion in the flowerpots, and the eggs will hatch in three days. The parents should then be left with the eggs, and the females will assume all of the parental responsibility. Of the approximately 150 eggs which each pair lay, most hatch. The fry are raised without difficulty.

LAMPROLOGUS TRETOCEPHALUS Boulenger / *Five-Bar Cichlid*

Range: Lake Tanganyika, Africa.
Habits: Territorial; provide plenty of caves and hiding places, as each individual male will set up a territory and defend it.
Water Conditions: Moderately hard water with a pH of around 7.6-8.0. Temperature in the middle 20's (°C).
Size: To about 14 cm.
Food Requirements: Not critical; will eat most live and prepared aquarium foods.

Their tank should be large and set up with rockwork typical of that used for other lake cichlids. About six small individuals can be used as a starting point (large mated pairs are very expensive) with the hopes that at least one or more natural pairs will form. *Lamprologus tretocephalus* is a territorial species, and you will find that each individual has selected a particular area (often a cave) in which it will remain much of the time and will defend.

When the *L. tretocephalus* reaches sexual maturity a pair may form; pair formation usually is followed by some digging by the female. At this time the female is somewhat darker, the white areas between the dark bars turning gray. This may be a behavioral ploy to allow the female to enter the male's territory without being chased. Breeding tubes are evident at the approach of egg-laying, and a flat rock, slate or flowerpot is cleaned for that purpose. The eggs are laid and fertilized and the female then takes up the chore of fanning them while the male returns to his territory and does not take part. The eggs are small, about 1.5 mm long, and white. Hatching takes some three to four days, whereupon the female moves them to the "security" of one of the pits she has prepared. In about another four days the fry have become free-swimming.

Lamprologus leleupi F E X 8 2 1 X N N A   [H. J. Richter]
Lamprologus tretocephalus F D X 8 2 2 X N N A   [D. Scheuermann]

Laubuca dadiburjori ⬛F⬛R⬛X⬛8⬛2⬛3⬛X⬛N⬛N⬛3
Laubuca laubuca ⬛F⬛R⬛X⬛8⬛2⬛4⬛X⬛N⬛N⬛6

[Dr. Herbert R. Axelrod]
[Dr. Herbert R. Axelrod]

LAUBUCA DADIBURJORI Menon / *Dadio*

Range: Vicinity of Bombay, India.
Habits: Active fish which if possible should be kept in a small group; a jumper, so keep their tank covered.
Water Conditions: Soft to medium-hard water. Temperature 22 to 25°C.
Size: 3 cm.
Food Requirements: Accepts dried foods as enthusiastically as live or frozen foods.

The Dadio is never likely to win any prizes for its coloration alone, but it has everything else to recommend it. It is active, gregarious and will accept anything in the food line which comes its way. It is not particularly sensitive to water conditions and seems to breed readily. The specific name honors its discoverer, Shri Sam J. Dadyburjor of Bombay, India. In June, 1960, we received a few specimens and sent them to Herr E. Roloff in Karlsruhe, Germany. He gave them a long tank of their own, such as is used for spawning the *Danio* species. In one corner he placed a nylon "mop," which is merely a tassel of nylon yarn attached to a cork to make it float. The tank was otherwise bare and the fish had no choice but to spawn in the nylon threads. Herr Roloff thinks, however, that they normally attach their eggs to the underside of a broad plant leaf. There were less than 100 eggs laid, and the parents were removed immediately afterward. Hatching began on the next day, but the fry did not begin to swim until the sixth day.

LAUBUCA LAUBUCA (Hamilton-Buchanan) / *Indian Hatchetfish*

Range: India, Burma, Sumatra and Malaysia.
Habits: Peaceful fish which prefers the upper reaches of the aquarium; active swimmers and skilled jumpers, so keep their aquarium covered.
Water Conditions: Neutral to slightly acid, soft water for spawning; otherwise water conditions are unimportant. Temperature 24 to 27°C.
Size: Up to 6 cm.
Food Requirements: Will eat any food; being top-feeders, they prefer a food which does not sink rapidly.

Here we have a fish which is quite attractively colored, easily fed, not difficult to spawn and easy to keep; still, hobbyists never seem to get excited about it. This is a paradox which exists with some species. Sometimes, suddenly, a fish "catches on," and people who have known and avoided a particular species for years suddenly fall all over each other to get them. The spawning act of *Laubuca laubuca* is interesting. An aquarium with a large water surface is best. There need be no precautions against the eating of eggs by the parents; if well-fed they show little inclination to do so. Males are distinguished by their thinner bodies and brighter colors, and little attention is paid to the females until about dusk. After an active pursuit the male embraces the female from the left with his fins, and a large number of eggs result. They hatch in about 24 hours at a temperature of 26°C.

824

LEIOCASSIS BRASHNIKOWI Berg / *Russian Catfish*

Range: Russia, in central reaches of Amur River.
Habits: An active species, more crepuscular than nocturnal; peaceful, but not to be trusted with fishes small enough to be swallowed whole.
Water Conditions: Acidity/alkalinity factors are not critical, but the species will not tolerate prolonged maintenance under temperature conditions prevailing in tropical aquaria. Temperature 10 to 18°C.
Size: Up to almost 12 cm.
Food Requirements: Takes all live foods and most meaty prepared and frozen foods.

L. brashnikowi has two advantages over the bullheads when considering coldwater catfishes: it is smaller than any of them, growing to a maximum of about 12 cm, and it is less of a strictly nocturnal fish, which makes it much more visible in the tank, since it does not have the same tendency toward secretiveness as the bullheads.

This species has not been bred under aquarium conditions, but it is known to deposit its large eggs among tangles of roots. Sex distinctions are unknown.

LEIOCASSIS SIAMENSIS Regan / *Barred Siamese Catfish*

Range: Thailand.
Habits: Peaceful toward fishes it cannot swallow; mostly nocturnal in its habits.
Water Conditions: Soft, slightly acid water which has been aged for at least a week. Temperature 22 to 25°C.
Size: To 16 cm.
Food Requirements: All sorts of live or frozen foods.

This is a comparatively rare species of catfish which was first offered to hobbyists in 1953. Today we do not see them offered for sale very frequently, but fish shows seldom fail to attract quite a number of entries. This is a clear indication that the fish has a long life span. There is a considerable variation in the body colors. Most specimens have an attractive light pattern on a coffee-brown background color, but others are a bluish black or grayish blue. These are probably local color variations, because the colors change very little with the moods of the fish. Being a nocturnal species, hiding places will be sought out and used during the bright daylight hours. They prefer the larger sizes of living foods, and a special delicacy is a medium-sized earthworm cut up into several pieces. There are no visible sex differences, and thus far there have been no accounts of their reproductive habits. A characteristic of this group is the large adipose fin, which is also seen in the *Synodontis* species from Africa. The large mouth indicates that it could swallow smaller fish in the same aquarium, so do not keep your fancy Guppies or Neon Tetras in its company or they might disappear.

Leiocassis brashnikowi Ⓕ Ⓒ Ⓧ Ⓐ Ⓐ Ⓐ Ⓧ Ⓝ Ⓝ Ⓐ   [V. Elek]

Leiocassis siamensis Ⓕ Ⓓ Ⓧ Ⓐ Ⓐ Ⓐ Ⓧ Ⓝ Ⓝ Ⓑ   [Aaron Norman]

Lepidarchus adonis 🄵🅁🅇⑧②⑦🅇🅽🅽④　　　　　　　　[E. Roloff]

Lepisosteus osseus 🄵🄲🅇⑧②⑧🅇🅽🅽⑦　　　　　　　　[Braz Walker]

LEPIDARCHUS ADONIS Roberts / *Adonis*

Range: Restricted range in southern Ghana.
Habits: Peaceful; prefers subdued light.
Water Conditions: Soft, clean, acid water is best for this species but not critical. Temperature 24 to 26°C.
Size: 4 cm for both males and females.
Food Requirements: Small live foods preferred, aquatic crustaceans being the preferred first food; also accepts finely granulated or shredded dry foods.

Lepidarchus adonis offers no great problems in its propagation, except that it lays only a small number of eggs at each spawning. Some pairs maintained by E. Roloff of Karlsruhe, Germany, spawned readily enough in small aquaria containing water at a pH of 6.0 and a hardness of about 2 DH. The temperature of the water in the spawning tanks was 25°C. The eggs, which had been deposited in spawning mops, hatched in about 36 hours when maintained at the spawning temperature, but the fry didn't become free-swimming until a week passed. They are large enough to take brine shrimp nauplii immediately upon becoming free-swimming, and they grow quickly. One big drawback in the production of this species by commercial breeders is the small number of eggs produced at each spawning. An average of only 25 eggs or so per spawning does not make for wholesale production, but it is hoped that individuals that become adapted to aquarium life will be more prolific. This almost scaleless species prefers to keep out of bright light, so their aquarium should provide shady areas.

LEPISOSTEUS OSSEUS (Linnaeus) / *Longnose Gar*

Range: North America; Gulf states, Mississippi Basin northward to Great Lakes, eastern seaboard.
Habits: Highly predatory and not to be trusted with fishes small enough to swallow; rather slow-moving most times, but capable of great bursts of speed.
Water Conditions: Not at all critical; often found surviving where other fishes have succumbed. Tolerates a wide temperature range, so suitable for the coldwater or tropical aquarium.
Size: To 2 meters in nature, much less in aquaria; size can be reasonably controlled, although very large aquaria are eventually required.
Food Requirements: Live fishes preferred; acclimated fish can often be converted to strips of beef heart or other substitutes.

The gars of the family Lepisosteidae, of which the Longnose Gar is the most widespread and common, once flourished in Europe but are now extinct except in North America. Here they have prospered since the Eocene, still retaining certain features long since abandoned by the other modern fishes. One such feature is the hard, bony, diamond-shaped scales they possess. Locked each to the other by a peg-and-socket arrangement, they form excellent armor. Gars are capable of breathing air. The air is "swallowed" at the surface into the gas bladder, which serves as a respiratory organ.

LEPOMIS GIBBOSUS (Linnaeus) / *Sunfish, Pumpkinseed*

Range: Maine to Florida west to the Mississippi.
Habits: Should be kept by themselves or with others of the same genus.
Water Conditions: Tank should be roomy and the water clean. Room temperatures suffice without any additional heat.
Size: Seldom larger than 15 cm.
Food Requirements: Hearty eaters which require frequent feeding with large live foods such as chopped earthworms or frozen foods like beef heart.

Lepomis gibbosus is easily acclimated to a clean, good-sized aquarium tank and is quite colorful besides. The best ones to get for aquarium keeping are caught in the early summer months and are 3 to 5 cm long. At this size they accept captivity well if they are uncrowded and are not likely to be as belligerent toward each other as larger ones would be. As is the case with so many of our native fishes, they are quite popular in Europe as coldwater aquarium fishes, and much space is devoted in foreign literature to their spawning habits. The male fans out a depression in an open space and then lures the female into it. Eggs are laid here and guarded by the male, who drives away the female after she has finished. Eggs hatch in two to three days, and the fry are easily raised.

LEPOMIS MEGALOTIS (Rafinesque) / *Longeared Sunfish*

Range: Eastern United States, Canada to Mexican border.
Habits: Best kept by themselves.
Water Conditions: Not critical, but water should be clean and well aerated.
Size: Wild specimens 20 cm; in the aquarium seldom over 13 cm.
Food Requirements: Hearty eaters whose live food diet can be supplemented with chopped beef heart, liver, etc.

The Longeared Sunfish occurs in the same habitats as the other common sunfishes. Its chief mark of distinction is an elongated extension of the black tab at the point of the opercle or gill-plate. In colorful males this "ear" is edged blue, sometimes yellow or red. They are often regarded as "panfish" and are accepted as food by fishermen when the larger ones they are seeking prove scarce or elusive. Their flesh makes excellent eating, but they are very bony. In the aquarium it will be found that medium-sized specimens which have recently reached maturity are the most brightly colored and that these colors tend to "wash out" as the fish grow larger. It will be found that the Longeared Sunfish prefers a little more sunlight than the others, and their tank should be in a position where it gets a few hours of direct sunlight daily. During the winter months these fish should get a "rest period" of lowered temperatures, about 4 to 7°C. This is essential to their well-being, and if they do not get this period the number and quality of the eggs laid the following spring may easily be a disappointment.

Lepomis gibbosus Ⓕ Ⓓ Ⓧ ⑧ ② ⑨ Ⓧ Ⓝ Ⓝ ⑧   [Dr. Herbert R. Axelrod]
Lepomis megalotis Ⓕ Ⓓ Ⓧ ⑧ ③ ⓪ Ⓧ Ⓝ Ⓝ Ⓓ   [Braz Walker]

Leporinus agassizi  [Harald Schultz]

Leporinus arcus [Dr. Herbert R. Axelrod]

LEPORINUS AGASSIZI Steindachner / *Half-Striped Leporinus*

Range: Central Amazon region.
Habits: Fairly peaceful and fond of nibbling algae from glass or plants.
Water Conditions: Neutral to slightly acid. Temperature 23 to 26°C.
Size: About 9 cm in the aquarium; likely to grow much bigger.
Food Requirements: Will take prepared foods, but live and frozen foods are preferred; fond of nibbling a lettuce leaf.

This species is very hardy and peaceful. The Half-Striped Leporinus appreciates a large aquarium that is not too densely planted. The aquarium should have a gravel bottom. Frequent water changes are suggested, but one must be careful not to let the temperature drop below 21°C. Although this fish is not particular about its food, it should be given a fair amount of vegetable matter. If *L. agassizi* does not get a sufficient amount of greens, it will tend to nibble at the aquarium plants. Specimens up to 9 cm are usually noted in the aquarium, but it is known that this fish will grow to a larger size if given enough room. Most *Leporinus* species are collected when they are very small to reduce the cost of shipping each fish.

LEPORINUS ARCUS Eigenmann / *Lipstick Leporinus*

Range: Venezuela, the Guianas and parts of Brazil.
Habits: Peaceful; likely to jump out of an uncovered tank.
Water Conditions: Neutral to slightly acid. Temperature 23 to 26°C.
Size: Reaches 40 cm, but only 5-10 cm when imported.
Food Requirements: Live and frozen foods preferred; should have an occasional lettuce leaf to nibble on.

Scientific works mention the similarity between this *Leporinus* species and another one, *L. striatus.* Our color pictures show a few differences. There may, however, be more differences as the fish fully mature or show their breeding colors. Note that the light body stripes have a yellowish tinge, while those of *L. striatus* are purple. Perhaps some day someone with a very large tank will raise this beauty to a size where the female's eggs and the male's sperm ripen. I wonder what a tankful of baby *Leporinus* would look like! Most of the *Leporinus* species are very skillful jumpers and for this reason are very difficult to capture in a seine. This also means that their tank must be kept covered or on some morning an unpleasant surprise will await their owner; they will be found on the floor.

LEPORINUS FASCIATUS (Bloch) / *Banded Leporinus*

Range: Widely distributed in South America from the Guianas to the La Plata.
Habits: Active and peaceful toward other fishes, but inclined to be destructive to plants; keep their tank covered because they jump.
Water Conditions: Neutral to slightly alkaline water. Being active, they require a good-sized tank. Temperature 23 to 26°C.
Size: In their home waters to 33 cm; in captivity, seldom over 15 cm.
Food Requirements: Omnivorous, with a preference for vegetable matter; crushed lettuce leaves or spinach leaves should be frequently provided.

The Banded Leporinus is doubtless the most popular and brightly colored fish of this group. The alternating black and light yellow bands stand out very effectively against a green plant background. Young specimens have only a few black bands, and as the fish grows older these bands split and form two separate ones. In their native waters they swim in a head-down position and constantly graze on the algae which cover the plant surfaces. In the aquarium they will do the same, and when all the algae have been cleared away they will switch their attentions to the soft shoots and plant leaves. A good substitute is to give them a frequent supply of crushed lettuce leaves, but of course there is always the danger that they will pass up the lettuce and re-direct their attentions to the aquatic plants again. Another ruse, which many aquarists will frown upon, is to use plastic plants. They resemble the real article and provide shelter for the fish, but once they get a few trial nips they are left strictly alone.

LEPORINUS FRIDERICI (Bloch) / *Friderici*

Range: The Guianas to the Amazon River.
Habits: Peaceful toward other fishes; a jumper, so the tank must be kept covered.
Water Conditions: Neutral to slightly alkaline. Temperature 24 to 27°C.
Size: In nature, up to 41 cm; in captivity, seldom over 15 cm.
Food Requirements: Live or frozen foods, with frequent feedings of vegetable substances such as crushed lettuce leaves or chopped spinach.

Most of the *Leporinus* species are prized for food in their native countries, and collectors who net them must make it very plain to their native workers that they may keep only fish above a certain size and that the smaller ones go into the cans. This is a difficult fish to catch in their native waters, and many of them go sailing high over the top of the net in magnificent leaps when they feel confined. The native boys who handle the nets must duck with lightning-like reflexes when a fish comes flying at them or they could easily get a black eye. This jumping ability is shown to a lesser degree in the confines of an aquarium, and a cover must be kept on at all times. Kept in large public aquaria, the fish can attain a size up to 41 cm, as it does when wild. Usually they are sold at a size of 8 to 10 cm and do not grow larger than about twice this size, even in a large home aquarium.

Leporinus fasciatus F D X 8 3 3 X N N 6 [Dr. Herbert R. Axelrod]
Leporinus friderici F D X 8 3 4 X N N 8 [Dr. Herbert R. Axelrod]

Leporinus melanopleura FDX835XNN9 [Dr. Herbert R. Axelrod]
Leporinus pellegrini FDX836XNN8 [Dr. Herbert R. Axelrod]

LEPORINUS MELANOPLEURA Günther / *Spot-Tailed Leporinus*

Range: Eastern Brazil, between the Amazon River and Rio de Janeiro.
Habits: Peaceful toward other fishes; a jumper which must be protected by keeping its tank covered.
Water Conditions: Neutral to slightly alkaline. Temperature 24 to 27°C.
Size: To 20 cm; usually sold at 8 to 10 cm.
Food Requirements: All live foods and frozen foods; prepared foods are also accepted, and an addition of vegetable matter is very beneficial.

Leporinus melanopleura is distinguished by having a body which is not quite as elongate as that of the other *Leporinus* species. Another distinguishing trait is a number of tiny brown dots on the caudal base. Whether or not it is a sexual characteristic is questionable, but some specimens have a dark edge on the dorsal and caudal fins. These are presumed by some to be the males and the plainer colored ones the females. This species does not attain the size of most of the other *Leporinus* species, but with a maximum size of 20 cm it is by no means a small fish. The first ones to be sold to hobbyists reached the market as early as 1926, but to date there have been no accounts of any spawnings. One of the theories as to why some aquarium fishes have eluded all efforts to spawn them is that the larger species which have been stunted for some time in an aquarium (which does not allow them full development) never attain sexual maturity.

LEPORINUS PELLEGRINI Steindachner / *Pellegrin's Leporinus*

Range: Upper and lower Amazon, Peru, Espirito Santo, Rio de Janeiro, Sao Paulo, Rio Paraguay, Guianas.
Habits: Peaceful and active; should have a covered tank, as it is likely to jump.
Water Conditions: Neutral to slightly acid; water should be well aged. Temperature about 24°C.
Size: 7 to 10 cm in the aquarium.
Food Requirements: A good eater; will eat dried foods as well as all kinds of live foods.

Tank-raised specimens of *Leporinus pellegrini* should be much easier to spawn than their wild ancestors, having been in aquaria all of their lives and accustomed to the comparatively cramped quarters allotted to them. It was at one time considered impossible to spawn the Angelfish in the aquarium, but after the first ones were successfully raised it became easier with each successive generation, and now some beginners raise them. Pellegrin's Leporinus is said to spawn very much like the barbs, scattering eggs all over the aquarium and then eating them if not taken out. This should be one fish which would be easy to raise, judging by the appetite the grown ones have. Like the other *Leporinus* species, a little green food should be given.

LEPORINUS STRIATUS Kner / *Striped Leporinus*

Range: Amazon River south to the Parana in Uruguay.
Habits: Peaceful and very active; tank should be kept well covered. Temperature 23 to 26°C.
Water Conditions: Neutral to slightly alkaline.
Size: About 30 cm in nature; in captivity about half that.
Food Requirements: Omnivorous; likes to nibble on plants, so should be given an occasional lettuce or spinach leaf.

This is a relatively hardy species that should be given a large aquarium with both planted and open swimming areas. Although this species is not a particularly picky eater, it should be given a good amount of vegetable matter in its diet. The Striped Leporinus is both peaceful and active. *Leporinus* species are all confined to South America, where they inhabit gravel-bottomed, slow-moving streams. Juveniles are more strikingly colored than adults. This species, like the rest of the genus, tends to be a head-stander. Sexual distinctions are not known. To the best of our knowledge, this fish has not yet been bred in captivity.

1. *Leporinus striatus,* the Striped Leporinus (p838).
2. An unidentified *Leporinus* species (p838).

LEPTOLUCANIA OMMATA (Jordan) / *Swamp Killie, Pygmy Killifish*

Range: Southern Georgia to Florida, in swamps.
Habits: Peaceful, but should not be kept with larger fishes.
Water Conditions: Neutral to slightly acid water; tank should be well planted. Temperature 21 to 24°C.
Size: To about 4 cm.
Food Requirements: Small living foods are preferred, but dried foods are accepted.

The body shape of this little minnow bears a great resemblance to a related genus of cyprinodonts native to parts of Africa, the *Aplocheilichthys* species. The Swamp Killie is not a particularly beautifully colored fish, but it makes up for this by being peaceful and hardy. Females are slightly larger than their mates and are easily distinguished by the fact that they have one more spot, an extra spot just above the anal fin. The males have an ocellated spot at the caudal base; this spot is not as distinct in the females. With good feeding and a constant temperature of 24°C, a pair will soon spawn among fine-leaved plants. The eggs are very small and hatch in about ten days. At first they should be fed infusoria. Once they have graduated to larger live foods such as baby brine shrimp, growth is very rapid. It is interesting to speculate as to why an "eye-spot" occurs in some fishes. Probably the reason is that a predatory fish which sees the eye-spot going by in dim waters would be fooled into thinking that this was the real eye and snap at where the body should be, getting a mouthful of water instead of a mouthful of fish.

1. *Leporinus striatus* ⬚F⬚D⬚T⬚8⬚3⬚7⬚X⬚N⬚N⬚9 [Dr. Herbert R. Axelrod]
2. *Leporinus* sp. ⬚F⬚D⬚M⬚8⬚3⬚7⬚X⬚N⬚N⬚A [Aaron Norman]

Leptolucania ommata ⬚F⬚D⬚X⬚8⬚3⬚8⬚X⬚N⬚N⬚4 [G. Wolfsheimer]

1. *Limnochromis auritus* F D X 8 3 9 X N N C [Dr. Herbert R. Axelrod]

2. *Limnochromis auritus* F D X 8 4 0 X N N C [Dr. Herbert R. Axelrod]

LIMNOCHROMIS AURITUS (Boulenger) / *Auritus*

Range: Lake Tanganyika, Africa.

Habits: Relatively shy and retiring; this fish will not display well unless it feels completely at home in its tank.

Water Conditions: Hard, alkaline water is best, but softer and more acidic waters are accepted, especially by tank-raised fish. Best temperature range, 24 to 28°C.

Size: About 12 cm.

Food Requirements: Live foods are especially relished, but all standard prepared foods are taken; avoid a steady diet of tubifex if feeding live foods.

Limnochromis auritus is different in a number of ways from many of the other African Rift Lake cichlids that have been introduced into the aquarium hobby. It is, for one thing, a more live-and-let-live fish, and it doesn't go in for the Murder Incorporated act that has become a standard part of the repertoire of a number of bad-tempered Rift Lake imports. That is not to say that *Limnochromis auritus* is absolutely the most peaceful aquarium species you can find—it's just that it's relatively peaceful as African cichlids go. Occasional squabbling will be seen between it and other species and between the sexes of *Limnochromis* individuals, but in the main it's well behaved. The good point is unfortunately offset to some extent by the species' shyness; it has a tendency to keep itself out of view until it feels completely established in a tank, and if maintained in an aquarium that is subject to much turmoil—regardless of whether the turmoil is generated from inside the tank by the actions of other fishes or from outside the tank by the activities of the hobbyist and his family—it might never get around to showing well. Very bright lighting definitely should be avoided, partly because it has a tendency to increase the timidity of the species and partly because it does nothing to enhance the looks of the fish, whose metallic spangles show best in a subdued lighting.

This species, however, differs most greatly from the other popular African cichlid species in its post-spawning behavior and in the number of eggs and fry produced. It is a mouthbrooder, but instead of producing a very limited number of comparatively very large eggs it produces instead many small eggs, enough to provide upward of 400 fry from a single spawning. Occasionally enough eggs are produced that even a large female can't cram them all into her mouth, and the male in such cases usually will then accommodate the leftover eggs in his. He is less dedicated to the welfare of the young than the female would be and is much more inclined to eat the eggs he picks up than she would be, but the fact that he picks up any at all is worthy of note—as is the act that if left with the female during the brooding period he won't kill her and might even take turns with her in mouthing and shepherding the brood.

1. *Limnochromis auritus* in an aquarium (p839).
2. *L. auritus* in a photo tank (p839).

LORICARIA FILAMENTOSA Steindachner / *Whiptail*

Range: Central eastern South America.
Habits: Peaceful with other fishes; males are aggressive among themselves.
Water Conditions: Softness and acidity factors are of no great importance provided that extremes are avoided. The best temperature range is 23 to 25°C.
Size: Up to 25 cm; usually seen much smaller.
Food Requirements: Will eat all normal aquarium foods; an active algae-eating species.

A number of different sucker-mouth fishes are popular in the aquarium hobby, including South American loricariid catfishes like *Loricaria, Hypostomus* and *Ancistrus, Gyrinocheilus, Gastromyzon* and *Pseudogastromyzon.* Just about any fish whose mouth is adapted to let it obtain a suction-based grip is generally seized upon for use in the hobby as an algae-eater and is often used expressly for that purpose in hobbyist's tanks. *Loricaria filamentosa* is one such species, and the fish will indeed do a creditable job of removing soft algae from the glass panes of an aquarium and even to a lesser extent from the leaves of plants, including artificial plants, but it would be a mistake to feed the fish nothing besides algae; it needs and should have other foods.

Loricaria filamentosa is not a difficult species to keep, and it is fairly easy to spawn as well, even under community conditions. One thing that a prospective spawning pair of Whiptails should have is a tubular cave. This cave can be either natural (such as a hollowed out bamboo cane) or artificial (such as a cut-down length of PVC drain or plumbing pipe); regardless of material, the tube should be opaque. *Loricaria* will on occasion spawn without having been provided with a tube shelter, but providing the pipe greatly increases chances for success. The inside, and often also the outside, of the pipe is thoroughly cleaned, and spawning takes place inside the pipe, where the eggs are placed. The male parent takes good care of the eggs, which hatch in about eight days at a temperature of 26°C. The fry are able to swim as soon as they hatch, and they should be fed very small live foods. They are fast growers and will reach a size of about 6 cm within three months if properly fed; they will themselves be capable of breeding when they are about eight months old. Sexing adult *Loricaria filamentosa* is not difficult: the male has tuft-like growths on the side of his head and the female doesn't.

Loricaria filamentosa was recently placed in a new genus, *Dasyloricaria,* by Isbrücker and Nijssen.

1. *Loricaria filamentosa* resting on the floor of an aquarium (p842).
2. *L. filamentosa* with   eggs on a leaf (p842).

1. *Loricaria filamentosa* [F] [B] [X] [8] [4] [1] [X] [N] [N] [D] [R. Zukal]
2. *Loricaria filamentosa* [F] [A] [X] [8] [4] [2] [X] [N] [N] [D] [H. J. Richter]

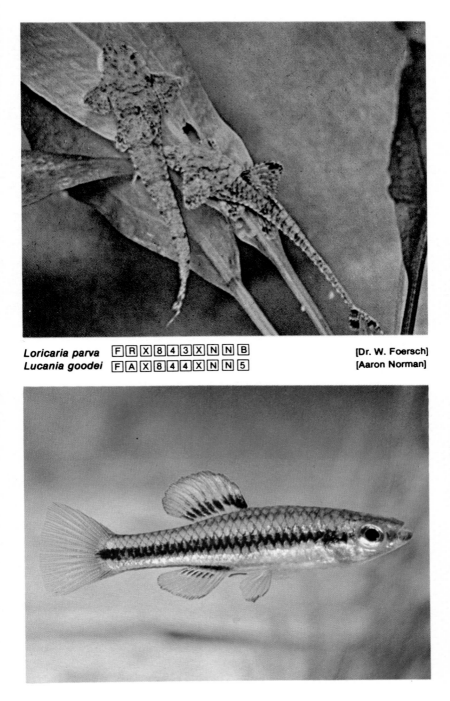

Loricaria parva [F][R][X][8][4][3][X][N][N][B]
Lucania goodei [F][A][X][8][4][4][X][N][N][5]

[Dr. W. Foersch]
[Aaron Norman]

LORICARIA PARVA Boulenger / *Whiptailed Catfish*

Range: Paraguay and the La Plata region.
Habits: Occurs in fast-flowing streams and therefore requires well-aerated water; peaceful toward other fishes.
Water Conditions: Temperatures should be kept in the lower 20's (°C).
Size: Up to 11 cm.
Food Requirements: Food should be small; tubifex worms are taken greedily, but most important is some vegetable matter, like lettuce leaves.

The Whiptailed Catfish is very likely to be overlooked in the average aquarium. Its colors blend with most gravel bottoms, and the fish spends a great deal of time motionless on the bottom with fins folded. Its form is interesting, reminding one of some of the armor-plated fossil fishes seen pictured now and then. Up to a short time ago, it was considered impossible to breed this fish, but the job has since proved to be far from impossible. Thanks to the skill of some German breeders, we know that they require a large quantity of vegetable matter in their diet to get them into condition. After that comes the hard job: raising the young. They breed in dark places like the inside of flowerpots or tubes about 4 cm in diameter. The male guards the eggs until they hatch.

The species was recently placed in the genus *Rineloricaria* by Isbrücker.

LUCANIA GOODEI Jordan / *Bluefin Killifish*

Range: Southern Florida.
Habits: An active species which will sometimes pursue other fishes, but seldom attacks.
Water Conditions: Should be kept in roomy aquaria, well planted and cool (15°C).
Size: 5 cm.
Food Requirements: Small live foods only; dried foods are accepted only if the fish are starving.

This is a common little fish in Florida, but in spite of this we seldom see it offered by dealers. Probably the reason they do not like to handle them is that many people who buy them try to crowd them into a tank with tropical species, a thing which this fish does not like at all. They should not be crowded, and they cannot stand the 24 to 27°C temperatures we give to most of our tropical species. Given a roomy tank which is well planted and temperatures which range from 15 to 18°C, the males will put on a nice display and spawnings will be observed among the fine-leaved plants. Only three to five eggs will be expelled by one female per day, but this is kept up for about five weeks. The eggs hatch in about 14 days at 18°C. Higher temperatures result in many infertile eggs. When they hatch, they can be brought to the surface by placing a light over the darkened tank. They are then lifted out with a spoon and transferred to a rearing tank with similar water. After a week of infusoria feedings they are able to take newly hatched brine shrimp.

844

LUCIOCEPHALUS PULCHER (Gray) / *Pike-Head*

Range: Malaysia, Sumatra and Borneo.
Habits: Predatory fish which should never be kept with smaller ones.
Water Conditions: Soft, slightly acid water. Temperature 26 to 29°C.
Size: To 18 cm.
Food Requirements: Small living fishes are preferred over anything else.

It is a pity that we only see this fish once in a while and then very shortly. It does not take very kindly to captivity, and even skilled aquarists often despair after losing a few in spite of their expert attentions. A study of their home conditions may be of some help in determining what is needed. They prefer to lie in the more placid waters of flowing streams, always on the lookout for any morsel they can swallow. This tells us that among other things Pike-Heads require a good deal of oxygen and that their tank should be well aerated and filtered. The Pike-Head is a predator which feeds on all sorts of smaller creatures such as small fishes and the larger aquatic insects and their larvae. Their method of catching food is very interesting: the mouth opens very quickly to a funnel shape, causing the water to flow into it and take the greatly surprised prey with it. Their appetites should never be underestimated, and the owner often wonders where all those Guppies go.

LUCIOSOMA SETIGERUM (Valenciennes) / *Long-Finned Apollo Shark*

Range: Borneo, Sumatra and Thailand.
Habits: Aggressive with its own kind and with other active fishes that frequent the surface.
Water Conditions: Not critical, but extremes should be avoided.
Size: To about 25 cm.
Food Requirements: Not particular; will take a high quality flake food and other items that sink slowly, and *Drosophila* and small mealworms are excellent.

The Long-Finned Apollo Shark gets to be quite large (about 25 cm) for an aquarium fish and is very active in the upper layers of water. It therefore needs plenty of open space (*i.e.,* a very large tank) to be shown off to its best advantage. With proper lighting the scales of its back reflect iridescent blues and greens, and the longitudinal dark line and dark streaks in the caudal fin add to the streamlined appearance of this fish.

The Long-Finned Apollo Shark is aggressive toward members of its own kind and will also attack other active surface fishes. If more than one are kept in an aquarium, be sure to provide some hiding places (plants will do nicely) for the losers of any battles. Fortunately, the Long-Finned Apollo Shark usually ignores the more sluggish bottom fishes, but do not trust it with fishes too much smaller than itself.

1. *Luciocephalus setigerum* juvenile in an aquarium (p846).
2. *L. setigerum* pair (p846).

Luciocephalus pulcher F D X 8 4 5 X N N C

[K. Paysan]

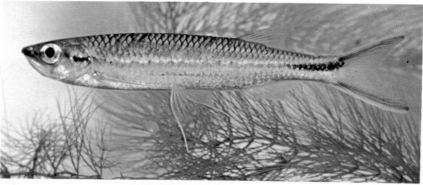

1. *Luciosoma setigerum* F D M 8 4 6 X N N A
2. *Luciosoma setigerum* F D B 8 4 6 X N N D

[Braz Walker]

Macrognathus siamensis F D X 8 4 7 X N N D
Macropodus cupanus cupanus F E X 8 4 8 X N N 8

[H. J. Richter]

847

MACROGNATHUS SIAMENSIS (Günther) / *Spot-Finned Spiny Eel*

Range: Thailand.

Habits: Fairly peaceful with fishes its own size or not too much smaller, but it has been known to attack tiny species and half-grown individuals of large species.

Water Conditions: Soft, slightly acid water is best. Temperature 24 to 29°C.

Size: Up to 25 cm.

Food Requirements: Usually reluctant to accept dry foods, although will sometimes pick these up from the bottom; tubifex worms are eagerly accepted.

Spiny eels in general appeal to hobbyists because of their interesting habits and odd shape, although it is true that some of them are also considered attractive because their various bars and spots form pleasing patterns. The fish are definitely eel-like in shape, but they are not considered to be true eels, even though authoritative ichthyologists of the last century classified them as such. The most interesting habit of spiny eels (both *Macrognathus* and *Mastacembelus* species are known by the popular name) is their ability to dig into and remain buried in the aquarium gravel, where they sometimes remain for long periods of time with just the head sticking out, or even completely buried. Another characteristic, but one of more annoyance and less pleasure for their owner, is their propensity to escape from whatever tank they are kept in. This is accomplished more by a "climbing" maneuver than by jumping.

MACROPODUS CUPANUS CUPANUS (Cuvier)
Spike-Tail Paradise Fish

Range: Southern India and Sri Lanka.

Habits: Generally peaceful.

Water Conditions: Water should be fairly soft and acidic. 23 to 26°C is the best temperature range; slightly higher for breeding.

Size: To about 8 cm.

Food Requirements: Accepts all standard aquarium foods.

This fish is a bubblenester, but the nest is not constructed initially at the surface of the water; instead, the male usually chooses the underside of a broad leaf that has outer margins that curl down, providing a cupped hollow, and he places the bubbles into the hollow. After the parents embrace under the nest and the female expels the eggs; the male retrieves the sinking eggs and places them into the nest. The female often attempts to help with the egg-retrieval chore, but after spawning is over the male becomes much more of a bully than he has been previously, and at this point it is best to remove the female. The male tends the eggs carefully, and many times he moves the nest from the spawning area to the water surface. If the water is maintained at the spawning temperature of about 27°C, the fry will hatch within 40 hours. The fry begin to swim freely in another three days, and the male should be removed before they have reached the free-swimming stage.

MACROPODUS CUPANUS DAYI (Köhler) / *Day's Paradise Fish*

Range: Southeast Asia.
Habits: Peaceful and easy to keep.
Water Conditions: Not critical as long as clean and warm. Temperature 24 to 28°C.
Size: Up to 8 cm.
Food Requirements: Not at all choosy; will thrive on most foods (prepared, frozen, etc.).

The body of Day's Paradise Fish is a reddish brown with two darker stripes, but the most striking characteristic is a bright blue edge on the caudal and anal fins plus the tips of the ventrals. The fin rays in the caudal fin of some specimens of this species are divided in the center. This sometimes happens but is not normal. The tail should come to a point, like that of a male *Apistogramma agassizi*. The fins of the female are less developed and have less color. The best colors are shown when higher temperatures are provided. Spawning begins with the construction of a bubblenest by the male. A lively chase follows, the eggs falling to the bottom, where they are retrieved by both parents and spit into the bubblenest, which is often quite small. At 28°C the eggs hatch in about a day. The fry are guarded by the male.

MACROPODUS OPERCULARIS (Linnaeus) / *Paradise Fish*

Range: China and Formosa.
Habits: Very quarrelsome, even toward their own kind.
Water Conditions: Very adaptable to any water conditions. An unheated aquarium suffices, and for breeding 21 to 24°C is high enough.
Size: About 8 cm.
Food Requirements: A greedy eater which should be fed often and generously; all kinds of foods are accepted.

The Paradise Fish is the granddaddy of all tropical aquarium fishes. Actually, it can only be called a semi-tropical species, and they have been known to survive freezing temperatures when kept in outdoor pools. A pair of Paradise Fish in top condition is a breathtaking sight, and it is a pity that such a gorgeous creature should have so much against it as a community fish. They cannot be kept in a community tank with other fishes, especially smaller ones. In any case the temperatures which would be comfortable for most tropicals would be too high for the Paradise Fish. Anyone who has despaired of ever being able to breed any aquarium fishes could get a pair of these and be almost sure of success. The males build bubblenests very frequently, and a female which is not yet ready for egg-laying should be kept away until she is or the nasty-tempered male may mutilate or even kill her. A great number of eggs which float are laid, gathered by the male and placed in the nest. The male's ferocity becomes most apparent when spawning is over and he guards the nest, so the female should be removed. Young hatch in 30 to 50 hours and are very easy to raise.

Macropodus cupanus dayi ⬚F⬚E⬚X⬚8⬚4⬚9⬚X⬚N⬚N⬚8 [H. J. Richter]
Macropodus opercularis ⬚F⬚E⬚X⬚8⬚5⬚0⬚X⬚N⬚N⬚8 [H. J. Richter]

Malapterurus electricus [F][D][X][8][5][1][X][N][N][D]   [Dr. Herbert R. Axelrod]
Malpulutta kretseri [F][A][X][8][5][2][X][N][N][4]   [H. J. Richter]

MALAPTERURUS ELECTRICUS (Gmelin) / *Electric Catfish*

Range: Tropical Africa, except for some lake and river systems.
Habits: Decidedly predatory, so not safe with other species.
Water Conditions: Neutral water in the medium-soft range is best. Temperature 23 to 28°C.
Size: Over 60 cm in nature, but rarely seen at this size when offered for sale.
Food Requirements: Wants small live fishes which are usually swallowed whole; will also eat plants.

Usually kept for its attraction as a novelty, the Electric Catfish is a real show specimen, for it is both interesting and, in a subdued way, attractive. The most interesting point about *Malapterurus* is, of course, the fish's capacity for discharging an electric current. This current is much weaker than that generated by the South American Electric Eel, *Electrophorus electricus,* but much stronger than that of the African elephant-noses of the family Mormyridae. Much speculation has gone into the problem of discovering the exact use to which the Electric Catfish puts its odd talent, with some authorities claiming that the catfish uses its electricity as a weapon of offense by which *Malapterurus* stuns its prey, and others claiming that it is used chiefly as a type of sonar, for the Electric Catfish has very small and poorly developed eyes. Perhaps the former conclusion is closer to the truth, because *Malapterurus* is a very clumsy swimmer and definitely needs help in catching its victims.

MALPULUTTA KRETSERI Deraniyagala / *Malpulutta*

Range: Sri Lanka.
Habits: Peaceful; should be kept only with small species.
Water Conditions: Soft, slightly acid water is optional. Temperature 24 to 27°C.
Size: About 4 cm.
Food Requirements: Mosquito larvae eagerly taken; can be trained to take frozen and freeze-dried foods.

The anabantoid family Belontiidae offers relatively few novelties to the aquarist in the sense that most genera of the family have at one time or another been made available to the aquarist and have been established as regularly breeding species. Malpulutta is an exception to this, being correctly classed as a rarity. This species is apparently not common even in the wild, where it is found in streams in the company of such species as *Anabas testudineus, Rasbora daniconius, Aplocheilus dayi, Ompok bimaculatus, Puntius chola, P. vittatus* and *Macropodus cupanus.* Males build a nest containing a few bubbles between floating plants. The embrace is typical of the family, and the amber eggs are lighter than water. The fry hatch in two days at 27°C and become free-swimming in three more. The entire mating procedure is gentle, and the adults can be left with the fry if necessary.

852

MASTACEMBELUS ARMATUS (Lacépède) / *White-Spotted Spiny Eel*

Range: India, Sri Lanka, Thailand and Sumatra.
Habits: Mostly nocturnal; should have places where it can hide.
Water Conditions: Not important as long as the water is clean. Temperature 24 to 27°C.
Size: To 76 cm in native waters.
Food Requirements: Living or frozen foods, especially worms.

This is the largest of the spiny eels, and throughout its wide range it is highly valued as a food fish. Its sharp spines and slippery body make it a difficult fish to handle, and because of its size only very young specimens can be considered for the home aquarium. Fish as long as 76 cm have been recorded, and it is obvious that a fish even half that size is much too big for the average aquarium. The family Mastacembelidae has a fairly wide distribution which covers the southern half of Africa and most of the East Indies, but there are none in South America or Australia. *Mastacembelus armatus* is probably the most handsome of the spiny eels while young, a fact that the accompanying picture graphically bears out. Like many of the eel-like fishes, the spiny eels are nocturnal in their habits. Have no fear that tubifex worms will get into your bottom gravel and foul the water while they are there! The spiny eels are excellent diggers and will do a thorough job of getting every one out. Some even sleep under the gravel! Known to science since 1798, this species was first introduced to aquarium hobbyists around 1922. The unpaired fins are all connected in this species.

MASTACEMBELUS ERYTHROTAENIA Bleeker / *Spotted Fire Eel*

Range: Java, Borneo and Sumatra.
Habits: Mostly nocturnal and a bit shy at first; hiding places should be provided.
Water Conditions: Not important as long as the water is clean. Temperature 24 to 26°C.
Size: To 46 cm.
Food Requirements: Very fond of worms and other live foods such as daphnia and brine shrimp.

A real oddity which sometimes reaches our shores is the Spotted Fire Eel. Its unusual body shape, color pattern and hooked, trunklike snout make it a stand-out in any collection. Like so many species that can undulate the dorsal as well as the anal fin, it can swim backward as well as forward and is a mighty tricky proposition to get into a net. It is largely nocturnal in its habits and unfortunately does not come out often, except when it is hungry and smells food. It is most at ease when a number of hiding places such as rocks or plant thickets are provided. Often, too, it burrows into the gravel with only its eyes and snout protruding.

Mastacembelus armatus 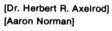 [Dr. Herbert R. Axelrod]
Mastacembelus erythrotaenia [Aaron Norman]

Mastacembelus zebrinus F D X 8 5 5 X N N D [Dr. Herbert R. Axelrod]

Megalamphodus axelrodi F Q X 8 5 6 X N N 3 [Dr. Herbert R. Axelrod]

MASTACEMBELUS ZEBRINUS Blyth / *Zebra Spiny Eel*

Range: Burma.
Habits: A generally peaceful fish, but not above eating baby fishes.
Water Conditions: Not critical if extremes are avoided. Temperature 22 to 26°C.
Size: Up to 46 cm in the wild; usually seen at no more than 13 cm.
Food Requirements: Small moving live foods are preferred, but prepared foods are readily accepted, provided pieces are not too large.

The Zebra Spiny Eel is less colorful than some of the other spiny eels from Africa and Asia that have found their way into aquarists' tanks, but it is attractive nonetheless and shares with its relatives within the family Mastacembelidae the odd appearance and interesting habits that have made these fishes popular over the years. The habit that has apparently given the spiny eels the most claim to attention by hobbyists is their ability and willingness to dive into the gravel and remain there either completely submerged or with just the head sticking out. *Macrognathus* also behaves in a similar manner.

The Zebra Spiny Eel should be maintained in a dimly lighted, well-planted tank that offers it many hiding places. Aquarists keeping the species will note that fish maintained under these conditions will show much less of a tendency to enter the gravel. Since constant movement through aquarium gravel, which is much harder and sharper than the silty bottoms underlying the fish's native waters, can be harmful to the species in the long run, providing proper hiding places will make the Zebra Spiny Eel much more comfortable. *M. zebrinus* definitely suffers if kept in a tank that is too brightly illuminated.

MEGALAMPHODUS AXELRODI (Travassos)
Calypso Tetra, Red Pristella

Range: Trinidad.
Habits: Peaceful; likes to swim in schools.
Water Conditions: Soft, slightly acid water. Temperature 24 to 27°C.
Size: About 3 cm.
Food Requirements: Takes all foods eagerly, including dried flakes, but should have an occasional meal of live or frozen food.

Anyone who has had experience with other *Megalamphodus* species finds it very difficult to recognize this as one of them. Probably the only reason it had missed being "found" in all the biological surveys of the fishes of Trinidad is its close resemblance to *Pristella maxillaris*. When one of the authors found these fish in a small pool at the edge of the Piarco Airport, the collecting party gasped at the sight of a hundred "drops of blood" in the net. No fish as red as this one had ever before been found in Trinidad, which has more fish collectors per square mile than any other country in the world!

MEGALAMPHODUS MEGALOPTERUS Eigenmann
Black Phantom Tetra

Range: Brazil.
Habits: Peaceful and active.
Water Conditions: Soft, acid water is best, especially for breeding. Temperature 23 to 26°C.
Size: 4 cm.
Food Requirements: Accepts live, frozen and dried foods.

The Black Phantom Tetra is a very pretty fish whose colors can best be described as a combination of the markings of the Black Tetra and the Serpae Tetra. Additionally, it is a small fish and, unlike some of its tetra relatives, a peaceful one. The Black Phantom Tetra can be sexed easily when mature, so there is no problem picking pairs for breeding purposes. The male has a much larger dorsal fin, although this difference is not as noticeable as with some of the other easily sexed characins, like *Hyphessobrycon erythrostigma*, the Bleeding Heart Tetra. But just to make sure that there is no confusion, the fish makes it a little easier for prospective breeders by adding another sure sign of sex, this one holding good even before the fish have reached maturity: the ventral and adipose fins are blood red on the females and black on the males. *Megalamphodus megalopterus* spawns in thick bundles of plants (nylon spawning mops may also be used), and for a small fish it is quite prolific, sometimes scattering up to 400 eggs at one spawning. The eggs hatch in a little over a day at a temperature of 25°C, but they are quite susceptible to fungus, especially if put into a tank with too much light.

1. *Megalamphodus megalopterus* female (p858).
2. *M. megalopterus* pair in an aquarium (p858).

Megalamphodus megalopterus male. Photo by van Raam.

1. *Megalamphodus megalopterus* ♀ [F][F][X][8][5][7][X][N][N][4] [H. J. Richte
2. *Megalamphodus megalopterus* [F][Q][X][8][5][8][X][N][N][4] [H. J. Richte

Megalamphodus sweglesi

m. J. Richard

MEGALAMPHODUS SWEGLESI Géry / *Swegles' Tetra*

Range: Amazon region near Leticia, Colombia.

Habits: Peaceful; like the other tetras, they prefer to be in schools.

Water Conditions: Soft, slightly acid water is preferred. Temperature 24 to 26°C.

Size: About 4 cm.

Food Requirements: Easily fed; prefers live foods, but frozen and prepared foods also accepted.

Color Variations: Body reddish brown with a large lateral spot of black. Male's dorsal fin is high and pointed, the female's smaller and round.

Megalamphodus sweglesi is a very beautiful fish species which was named by Dr. J. Géry in the May, 1961, issue of *Tropical Fish Hobbyist* magazine. The specific name honors Mr. Kyle Swegles of Chicago, who found them near Leticia, in Colombia, in 1960. The fish closely resembles species of the genus *Hyphessobrycon*, and it is not evident that this is a member of a different group altogether until a painstaking taxonomic examination is made by an ichthyologist. The region from which the fish comes is an interesting one. Leticia lies at a point on the Amazon where several other rivers meet it, and the small feeder streams are especially rich in fish life. The exotic birds and plant life where the jungle comes to the water's edge put the viewer in another world, one which changes at every turn of the stream. It is here that the Peruvian Amazon begins and we enter into the region from which comes the Neon Tetra.

Megalamphodus sweglesi. Photo by Dr. Herbert R. Axelrod.

MELANOCHROMIS AURATUS (Boulenger)
Auratus, Malawi Golden Cichlid

Range: Lake Malawi, Africa.
Habits: This fish should be kept in large aquaria with large fishes; males are particularly aggressive.
Water Conditions: Should be fairly hard and alkaline. Temperature 24 to 27°C.
Size: About 20 cm; aquarium-bred specimens usually smaller.
Food Requirements: Accepts all standard aquarium foods.

Melanochromis auratus, commonly called Auratus or the Malawi Golden Cichlid, is a very territorial, aggressive fish from Lake Malawi. This species is born with a bright golden yellow color. Juveniles have two black stripes on the upper portions of their sides and another black stripe through the dorsal fin. As the fish gets older, bright blue streaks line the black stripes. At maturity the males change color and become almost the inverse of the female and juvenile coloration. The males are black with golden stripes.

This species is a maternal mouthbrooder with an incubation period of three to four weeks. The size of its brood ranges from 12 to 40, depending upon the conditions of the aquarium and the age of the fish. Fish carrying their first broods usually have few fry. It should be noted that this species is very aggressive when mating. Males always seem to be looking for a mate and will disrupt fish three times their size to prevent them from spawning in their territory. This species was formerly called *Pseudotropheus auratus.*

1. *Melanochromis auratus* female (p862).
2. *M. auratus* pair with the male below (p862).

Melanochromis auratus discharging orally incubated young. Photo by A. F. Orsini.

1. *Melanochromis auratus* [F][B][X][8][6][1][X][N][N][A]   [Dr. Herbert R. Axelrod]
2. *Melanochromis auratus* [F][Q][X][8][6][2][X][N][N][A]

1. *Melanochromis johanni* ♂ F A T 8 6 3 N N B [U. Werner]
2. *Melanochromis johanni* ♀ F B M 8 6 3 N N B [Dr. Herbert R. Axelrod]

3. *Melanochromis johanni* ♂ F A X 8 6 4 N N B [Dr. Herbert R. Axelrod]

MELANOCHROMIS JOHANNI (Eccles) / *Johanni*

Range: Lake Malawi, Africa.

Habits: Quarrelsome and aggressive; males are active bulliers of other males and active killers of uncooperative females.

Water Conditions: Hard, alkaline water preferred but not strictly necessary. Aquarium-raised individuals are especially tolerant of water quality variations from the ideal. Temperature 24 to 27°C.

Size: Up to 12 cm.

Food Requirements: Accepts all standard aquarium foods.

Color Variations: There are two major color variations among adult males of this species: a striped type in which the basic dark body color is overlaid with two blue stripes along the flanks and a type in which the dark body color is interrupted by a pattern of blue blotches. In both types the blue color is carried into the dorsal fins, and the dorsal is edged in blue in both types. Females and young fish are an overall golden to orange color.

Melanochromis johanni is very close in temperament and (at least in the males) in looks to *Melanochromis auratus* (formerly known as *Pseudotropheus auratus*), probably the longest-established African Rift Lake cichlid in the tanks of aquarium hobbyists. Like *M. auratus,* it is a quarrelsome species in which each male tries to dominate all of the others in its tank and directs its belligerence at other species as well. Unless these fish are maintained in a community rich in hiding places formed from rocks and shale or some inert man-made substance and rich also in the type of perpetual motion that prevents attackers from zeroing in on a single victim, the weakest are going to get killed. If they don't get killed outright from direct attack they'll die a lingering death from being prevented from getting to food and being made the object of continual strength-sapping bites.

This fish is a reliable spawner. It is very easy to differentiate the sexes, as adult males are dark-bodied with blue stripes or spots, whereas females are light-bodied, ranging from yellowish to orange in overall coloration. Young *M. johanni* of both sexes have the coloration of the females, but the fish that turn dark are males. Unfortunately, the hobbyist can't always be certain that a large fish that shows female coloration definitely is a female, for adult males that have been cowed by being kept in the presence of more dominant males often revert to their immature coloration. Like the other fishes in the *Melanochromis* complex, *M. johanni* is a mouthbrooder in which the female broods the eggs. There are comparatively few eggs laid, but the eggs are large and so are the fry; the fry are therefore easy to feed and to raise. Females that have finished brooding a group of young should be given a period of rest and recuperation.

1. *Melanochromis johanni* male (p863).
2. *M. johanni* female (p863).
3. *M. johanni* male (p863).

MELANOCHROMIS VERMIVORUS Trewavas / *Purple Mbuna*

Range: Lake Malawi, Africa.
Habits: Quarrelsome; smaller fish of the species tend to be greatly bullied by larger individuals.
Water Conditions: Hard, alkaline water is best. Temperature should be maintained at 23 to 27°C.
Size: Up to about 11 cm.
Food Requirements: Takes all standard aquarium foods; should have vegetable matter added to the diet.
Color Variations: Extremely variable according to age, mood, condition of the fish and its status within its own community.

Melanochromis vermivorus is typical of many of the Lake Malawi mbuna cichlids in many regards: it is aggressive, it is a mouthbrooder, it is very variable in coloration and pattern and it is attractive and interesting. The best conditions to offer this species consist of a tank set up with hard, alkaline water and lavishly furnished with rockwork in which the fish can indulge their tendency to dart in and out among the rocky shelters thus created. The tank need not be very large if only a few *M. vermivorus* are to be housed in it, but the supply of rocky refuges should be ample and should be well distributed throughout the tank. The same conditions apply if the fish is to be maintained among a community of other mbuna cichlids, as is often the case. This species is aggressive and can give a good account of itself in battles with fishes of other species, even fishes a good deal larger than itself; it is especially aggressive among members of its own kind, and the less self-assertive fish in a group of *M. vermivorus* will usually be hounded by bullying from the more successfully assertive individuals in the group. In many cases the weaker fish will be literally hounded to death by being prevented from eating and resting and by being continually picked at.

Melanochromis vermivorus is a mouthbrooding species; a female brooding eggs should be removed to the relative security of a small tank by herself in which she can release and tend her fry, and she should not be returned to the community from which she came until she has been allowed to regain her pre-brooding condition. If she is returned too soon, she is in great danger of attack and in her weakened condition probably would not be able to defend herself successfully.

Good aeration and filtration are particularly important while the female is brooding. The eggs are extremely susceptible to fungus, and the developing eggs, with their high metabolism, need a good supply of oxygen. Partial water changes of not more than 25% are recommended weekly for tanks lacking a good biological filter.

1. *Melanochromis vermivorus* female in an aquarium (p866).
2. *M. vermivorus* male changing from female pattern. (p866).
3. *M. vermivorus* male (p866).

1. *Melanochromis vermivorus* [F][B][T][8][6][5][X][N][N][B] [G. Marcuse]
2. *Melanochromis vermivorus* [F][A][M][8][6][5][X][N][N][B]

[H. Hansen, Aquarium Berlin]

3. *Melanochromis vermivorus* [F][A][X][8][6][6][X][N][N][B] [Dr. Warren E. Burgess]

1. *Melanotaenia maccullochi* [F][R][T][8][6][7][X][N][N][7] [H. J. Richter]
2. *Melanotaenia maccullochi* [F][A][M][8][6][7][X][N][N][7] [H. J. Richter]

Melanotaenia nigrans [F][A][X][8][6][8][X][N][N][8] [Dr. G. R. Allen]

MELANOTAENIA MACCULLOCHI (Ogilby) / *Dwarf Australian Rainbow*

Range: Northeastern Australia in the region of Cairns.
Habits: Peaceful; prefers being kept in small groups.
Water Conditions: Slightly alkaline water to which a little salt (about a quarter teaspoon per liter) has been added is best. Temperature 23 to 26°C.
Size: Up to 7 cm.
Food Requirements: Not a choosy eater; prepared foods accepted as readily as live or frozen foods.

The Dwarf Australian Rainbow comes very close to being an ideal aquarium fish. It is generally peaceful, hardy and easily fed. It spawns quite readily and seldom eats its eggs except when very hungry. It does not uproot plants, nor does it nibble on them. Add to these traits a set of very attractive colors and you obviously have a fish which is fairly hard to improve upon. The male has something special to offer in the way of colors which we have never seen photographed: when pursuing a female during spawning time the colors not only become intensified, but a wide lemon-yellow stripe appears on the sides, to disappear as quickly as it came. Eggs are laid in bushy plants; young hatch in seven to ten days and are very easily raised.

1. *Melanotaenia maccullochi* pair in an aquarium (p867).
2. *M. maccullochi* male (p867).

MELANOTAENIA NIGRANS (Richardson) / *Dark Australian Rainbow*

Range: Northeastern Australia as far south as Sydney.
Habits: Peaceful and very hardy; prefers to be kept in small groups.
Water Conditions: Neutral to slightly alkaline water to which a small amount of salt has been added. Temperature 19 to 24°C.
Size: To 10 cm.
Food Requirements: Easily fed; accepts prepared foods as readily as live or frozen foods.

This is the original Australian rainbow which has been known to the hobby since about 1927. By old standards it was quite large for the average tank, but the use of larger tanks has become more commonplace since those days, as well as better accessory equipment for aeration, filtration, etc. Breeding rainbows is not at all difficult. A well-conditioned pair is placed into a tank of at least 60 liters capacity which has been planted with *Myriophyllum, Cabomba* or some other fine-leaved plant. It is not necessary to watch the fish and remove them the minute they have finished spawning. They seldom touch their eggs. When a good amount of eggs can be seen hanging by little strings from the plants and the fish have lost interest in each other, the parents can be removed. The incubation period is seven to ten days. The fry are hardy.

MELANOTAENIA SPLENDIDA (Peters)
Pink-Tailed Australian Rainbow

Range: Queensland, Australia.
Habits: Peaceful; a good community fish.
Water Conditions: Soft, slightly acid water preferred. Temperature 24 to 26°C.
Size: To 12 cm.
Food Requirements: Not a choosy eater; will take prepared as well as live or frozen foods.

The Pink-Tailed Australian Rainbow is a very peaceful fish which makes a good community aquarium member. It should be kept in a spacious, moderately planted aquarium with a temperature between 24 and 26°C. Fine-leaved plants should be provided for spawning purposes, and the aquarium should be put in a position where it can receive the morning sunshine. Breeding this species is not difficult, and spawnings will often occur on several consecutive mornings among the fine-leaved plants. The eggs attach to the plants with fine filamentous tentacles. The eggs hatch in eight to ten days depending upon the temperature, which should be about 25°C. The parents may be left in the breeding tank until the young hatch. It should be noted that the parents place the eggs in an area of the aquarium that is sheltered from the light.

METYNNIS HYPSAUCHEN (Müller & Troschel) / *Plain Metynnis*

Range: Amazon region; widely distributed.
Habits: Peaceful; fond of swimming in schools.
Water Conditions: Must be kept in a large aquarium. Water should be 10 to 15 DH and slightly acid; pH 6.8. Temperature 24 to 26°C.
Size: Up to 15 cm.
Food Requirements: Will take and should get live or frozen foods, but the most important item is vegetable nourishment, such as lettuce leaves, etc.

Decorating with the artificial plants one sees sold nowadays could cause a great deal of frustration to a fish which sees something which looks good to eat but isn't, but the fact is that a fish depends more on its sense of smell when it comes to locating its food than on its sight, which with many fishes is far from good. One must remember, too, that water is not by a long shot as transparent as air, and a fish with poor eyesight is not as badly off as one which has been deprived of its senses of smell and taste. To get back to the subject, *Metynnis hypsauchen* has been spawned on occasion. A pair will swim through a plant thicket and cuddle against each other tetra-fashion, releasing as many as 2000 eggs. These hatch in 70 hours at about 26°C, and the fry do not begin to swim freely until about a week later. They are easily raised on brine shrimp and finely chopped spinach.

Melanotaenia splendida F A X 8 6 9 X N N B

Metynnis hypsauchen F D X 8 7 0 X N N C

[K. Paysan]

Metynnis maculatus ⬜F⬜D⬜X⬜8⬜7⬜1⬜X⬜N⬜N⬜8 [H. J. Franke]
Micralestes acutidens ⬜F⬜D⬜X⬜8⬜7⬜2⬜X⬜N⬜N⬜5 [Dr. Herbert R. Axelrod]

METYNNIS MACULATUS (Kner) / *Spotted Metynnis*

Range: Guianas down to the Rio Paraguay.
Habits: Peaceful toward other fishes of comparable size; are happiest when kept in groups.
Water Conditions: Soft, slightly alkaline water is best. The tank should be roomy and afford some shelter. Temperature 22 to 24°C.
Size: To 18 cm; usually collected and sold at about 5 cm.
Food Requirements: Special attention must be given to their vegetable diet requirements by giving them lettuce and spinach leaves plus live foods.

The *Metynnis* species are related to the vicious piranhas which are known and feared throughout most of tropical South America. Although there is a superficial similarity in body form, to an ichthyologist there is an immense difference in skull structure and in the digestive organs. The piranhas are of course strictly carnivores, while the *Metynnis* species are almost as strictly vegetarians. Thus the hobbyist who keeps them in a community aquarium and feeds them as he does his other fishes is making the mistake of depriving them of their most important diet ingredient, vegetable substances. If their tank is planted, the *Metynnis* will make up for this lack by chewing up the plants until they are all gone. This places a considerable strain on the ingenuity of the hobbyist: how to achieve an attractive background for his fish without using plants. This can be done surprisingly well by using rocks, driftwood and decorative roots. Males of this species are distinguished by the shape of the anal fin, which is considerably indented, while that of the female is straight or slightly rounded.

MICRALESTES ACUTIDENS (Peters) / *Sharp-Toothed Tetra*

Range: Nigeria to Angola and the Zambezi basin.
Habits: Peaceful and active fish which require adequate swimming room.
Water Conditions: Soft, slightly acid water which is clean and well aerated is best. Prefers warmth, about 26°C, but a drop to 23°C or so is tolerated.
Size: 6 cm maximum.
Food Requirements: Not critical; may be maintained on dried foods with only occasional feedings of live foods.

What the Sharp-Toothed Tetra lacks in bright colors it makes up for in good activity and good behavior; it minds its own business and bustles around without bothering the others. Don't let the name "Sharp-Toothed" scare you. These teeth do no damage to other fishes or plants. Because the collectors have so many highly colored and therefore better-selling species to offer, we do not often get to see these lesser-colored fish, and to the best of our knowledge they have not yet been spawned in captivity. Again we have the possibility that the breeders have not tried very hard to propagate a fish which might be a "hard seller."

872

MICROGLANIS POECILUS Eigenmann / *Dwarf Marbled Catfish*

Range: Brazil, Surinam, Guyana and Venezuela.
Habits: Peaceful and nocturnal; the tank in which they are kept should have a number of retreats where the fish can hide when the light is bright.
Water Conditions: Soft, slightly alkaline water is best. Temperature 24 to 26°C.
Size: To 7 cm.
Food Requirements: Live foods are preferred, especially worms; frozen foods are second choice, then dry foods.

The catfishes are a tremendous group. They include fishes which are downright ugly, some which are not quite as ugly but are kept for strictly utilitarian reasons and others which are quite pretty. Some have no objection to a brightly lighted tank, but others will come out into the light only when there is food available and they are hungry enough to subjugate their fear and hatred of the light to come out of hiding and quickly gobble up as much food as they can get into their mouths and then rush back again. *Microglanis poecilus* belongs to a minority group by being very pretty to look at and never getting to a size where the owner wonders whether to purchase a larger tank or cook it for dinner.

MISGURNUS ANGUILLICAUDATUS (Cantor) / *Weatherfish*

Range: Japan and northern China.
Habits: Peaceful with other species.
Water Conditions: Water conditions are not too important, as long as extremes are avoided. Temperature 21 to 26°C.
Size: Up to 20 cm.
Food Requirements: Takes all regular aquarium foods, but living worms are preferred.

Like the other cobitid fishes, most *Misgurnus* species are often thought to be eels because of their elongated cylindrical shape. The name "Weatherfish" is derived from the fact that the fish are known to be sensitive to changes in barometric pressure, and their changes in motion during periods in which the barometric pressure changes sharply have given the fish the reputation for being able to forecast the weather accurately. Changes in activity accompanying a drop in pressure, signifying a storm, are especially noteworthy. In the home aquarium the fish are interesting for their habit of diving headfirst under the gravel, sometimes keeping the whole body completely out of sight, other times keeping the head or part of the head above the level of the sand. This makes it difficult to tell at a glance exactly how many *Misgurnus* are in a tank (if the tank contains a bottom in which the fish can hide), and it is always a surprise for a viewer to find four or five healthy, active fish in a tank which to all intents and purposes contained nothing just a few minutes before.

Microglanis poecilus ⬚F⬚D⬚X⬚8⬚7⬚3⬚X⬚N⬚N⬚7   [H. J. Richter]
Misgurnus anguillicaudatus ⬚F⬚D⬚X⬚8⬚7⬚4⬚X⬚N⬚N⬚C   [Dr. Herbert R. Axelrod]

Moenkhausia sanctaefilomenae F D X 8 7 9 X N N 7 [Dr. Herbert Axelrod]
Mogurnda mogurnda F D X 8 8 0 X N N A [H. Hansen, Aquarium Berlin]

MOENKHAUSIA SANCTAEFILOMENAE (Steindachner)
Yellow-Banded Moenkhausia

Range: Paraguay Basin.

Habits: Peaceful toward other fishes and very active.

Water Conditions: Not critical, but slightly acid, soft water is preferred. Temperature 24 to 26°C.

Size: To 7 cm.

Food Requirements: Omnivorous, with a good appetite; if fed with a good amount of vegetable substances, it will not nibble plants to any great extent.

This very attractive *Moenkhausia* species was introduced to aquarium hobbyists around 1956 and scored quite a hit. It does not get as large as *M. oligolepis* and is not as hard on the plant life in the aquarium. The yellow band on the caudal base ahead of the black region makes distinction between the two species simple. Sex distinction among young and half-grown fish is not easy, but with maturity the females become rounder in the belly. Spawning is quite simple: a pair, where the male is active and the female has become heavy with eggs, is placed in an aquarium which is clean and has several plant thickets. The water should be fairly soft, about 5 German DH, and is best left to filter through peat moss for several days. The temperature should be brought to 27°C, when the male will soon be observed chasing the female. Eggs are laid among plant thickets. The pair should be removed as soon as they lose interest in each other and begin searching for eggs. Hatching takes a day or two, depending on temperature and other conditions.

MOGURNDA MOGURNDA (Richardson) / *Purple-Striped Gudgeon*

Range: Eastern and northern coastal Australia.

Habits: Should be kept with its own kind or larger fishes which can take care of themselves, or it may bully its tankmates.

Water Conditions: Alkaline water with a slight addition of salt is best. Temperature 22 to 26°C.

Size: 10 cm.

Food Requirements: Should get a preponderance of live or frozen foods.

Many a nipped fin can be traced to this species. Old-time aquarists often counsel: "Beware of a fish with a large mouth." This does not necessarily mean that all large-mouthed fishes are nasty. The all-time "nasty prize" goes to the African *Phago* species, which will pursue and pick at a fish until its fins are gone and then proceed to pick at its scales and skin until it is dead. And they have small mouths! To return to the Purple-Striped Gudgeon, they spawn quite willingly on rocks and the glass sides of the aquarium. The male takes charge of the eggs and keeps fanning them thoroughly for about a week, at which time they begin to hatch. It is best to remove him at this time and leave the fry to fend for themselves.

MONOCIRRHUS POLYACANTHUS Heckel / *Leaf Fish*

Range: Tropical South America; Amazon, Rio Negro, Guianas.
Habits: Occurs in sluggish streams, where it feeds on smaller fishes and aquatic insects; peaceful in the aquarium toward anything it cannot swallow.
Water Conditions: Soft, slightly acid water. Temperature about 26°C.
Size: Up to 10 cm.
Food Requirements: Small ones may be fed with the usual live foods; larger ones must get living smaller fishes.

Unless he knows what to look for, a collector would probably pass by dozens of these before he realized that they were fish, so perfect is their camouflage. Not only does their color make them look like a dead leaf in the water, but they also have the faculty for swimming like one. They can turn on their sides and drift along almost imperceptibly by paddling their almost transparent pectoral fins. Not only does this throw their enemies off guard, but it also permits them to get close to their unsuspecting prey. They work their head toward a selected morsel and then suddenly open a surprisingly large mouth. The prey is sucked in along with inrushing water, and the Leaf Fish has had his meal. In the aquarium these conditions must be duplicated, as the Leaf Fish will consider it beneath its dignity to forage for food and prefers to stalk it. A supply of small expendable fishes must therefore always be on hand. Some hobbyists who are possessed of infinite patience and have a great deal of time at their disposal find that it is sometimes possible to tame Leaf Fish and get them to swallow a strip of cut fish by dangling it in front of them. They breed easily and lay sticky eggs under a leaf.

1. *M. polyacanthus* compared to a leaf (p883).
2. *Monocirrhus polyacanthus,* commonly called the Leaf Fish, living up to its name as it hangs onto the vegetation at the bottom of an aquarium (p882).

A pair of *Monocirrhus polyacanthus* . Photo by G. Senfft.

Morulius chrysophekadion ⬚F⬚D⬚X⬚8⬚8⬚7⬚X⬚N⬚ ⬚N⬚ ⬚D⬚   [K. Paysan]
Myleus rubripinnis ⬚F⬚A⬚X⬚8⬚8⬚8⬚X⬚N⬚ ⬚N⬚ ⬚D⬚   [H. Azuma]

MORULIUS CHRYSOPHEKADION (Bleeker) / *Black Shark*

Range: Thailand.
Habits: Peaceful toward other fishes, but likely to be scrappy among themselves.
Water Conditions: Water should be slightly alkaline, about 10 DH. Temperature 24 to 27°C.
Size: To 60 cm.
Food Requirements: Will take practically any food, but exceptionally fond of algae and other vegetable matter.

Be sure you have a large tank if you intend keeping Black Sharks! In nature they attain a length of about 60 cm, and although they do not get to be this big in captivity, specimens 30 cm long are not unusual. Needless to say, the ones offered for sale are only 8 to 10 cm long. This is a fish with an excellent appetite; it spends most of its waking hours in search of food. Vegetable matter is preferred, and they can always be counted on to do an excellent job of cleaning up an algae-infested aquarium. Lacking this, a leaf of lettuce or spinach is also appreciated. Probably because ordinary-sized aquaria inhibit their growth, chances are that very few Black Sharks attain sexual maturity, and both males and females look so much alike that they would have to be dissected to distinguish them.

MYLEUS RUBRIPINNIS (Müller & Troschel) / *Redhook Metynnis*

Range: Guyana and Surinam to Brazil.
Habits: Peaceful and shy if kept by itself, but less so if kept in small groups; cannot be safely kept with vegetation because of their plant-eating tendencies.
Water Conditions: Clean, soft and highly oxygenated water is necessary. Temperature (at least for breeding) should be about 25 to 27°C.
Size: Matures at about 9 to 12 cm; maximum size not known.
Food Requirements: Takes a variety of foods, but their diet must contain vegetable matter.

Redhook Metynnis should be kept in a large tank. A single Redhook is usually very shy, and it is therefore recommended that several be kept together as a small "school." Several fish of this size require lots of space, so a tank of 200 liters or more should do nicely. Plants are out of the question—Redhook Metynnis are plant-eaters.

Actual spawning consists of the male coming close to the female, almost appearing to wrap his anal fin around her. The eggs are scattered over the bottom during a period of about three to six hours. After that time there may be as many as 300 to 500 pale yellowish eggs some 1.8-2.2 mm in diameter covering the floor of the tank. At this time the eggs should be removed as there is evidently no parental care whatsoever.

In 50 to 60 hours the eggs hatch; in another week the fry are already able to accept newly hatched brine shrimp. The fast-growing youngsters reach a length of about 20-25 mm in about one month.

MYLOSSOMA DURIVENTRE (Cuvier) / *Hard-Bellied Characin*

Range: Southern Amazon region, Paraguay, Paraná, La Plata.
Habits: Peaceful toward other fishes, but larger specimens are likely to damage plants.
Water Conditions: Soft, slightly acid water in a well-planted tank. Temperature 24 to 28°C.
Size: To 23 cm in their natural waters; imported specimens much smaller.
Food Requirements: All kinds of live and frozen foods, supplemented with some vegetable substances like chopped spinach, etc.

For many years this species was imported and sold as *Mylossoma aureum,* but it was found that these fish were merely young specimens of *Mylossoma duriventre* and the real *Mylossoma aureum* had not yet been imported. What probably contributed to the confusion was that, as is the case with many other fishes, there are several color changes as they grow up. Thus a dealer can easily be fooled into believing he has two different species when actually he merely has two sizes of the same species. *Mylossoma duriventre* gets to be 23 cm long in its native waters, but it is rarely that we ever see them even approach this size in captivity. Like the *Metynnis* species, the larger ones (8 cm and up) are likely to destroy plants, about the only thing that can be said against them. There are no recognizable sexual differences given in the reference works; probably if they ever show up we would see them only in grown specimens.

NANDUS NANDUS (Hamilton-Buchanan) / *Nandus*

Range: India, Burma and Thailand.
Habits: A voracious species which will eat any fish up to three-fourths of its own size.
Water Conditions: Soft, acid water is optional. Temperature 22 to 26°C.
Size: Up to 20 cm.
Food Requirements: Live fishes; some can be trained to take worms and beef.

Not only is the Nandus the type species for its genus, which also includes *Nandus nebulosus,* but it is also the type for the small family Nandidae. The nandids are without exception predatory species which greatly prefer living fishes as food. Some species will starve before they will eat anything else. There is a great similarity among members of the family in spite of the fact that they come from three different continents (Asia, South America, Africa). One of the most characteristic things about the family is the startling transparency of the posterior sections of the dorsal and anal fins and of the caudal fin. This doubtless has survival value to a fish which stalks its prey. These sections of the anal and dorsal and the caudal are used extensively for locomotion, and their colorlessness makes them difficult to see even when in motion. The Nandus is best kept in a dimly lighted aquarium with plenty of plants and rockwork. This will help to overcome the fish's great shyness. It is difficult to select tankmates which are neither so small that they will be eaten nor so large that they might take advantage of the Nandus' retiring nature.

Mylossoma duriventre  F C X 8 8 9 X N N 6   [Dr. Herbert R. Axelrod]
Nandus nandus F D X 8 9 0 X N N D

Nannacara anomala ⎡F⎤⎡Q⎤⎡X⎤⎡8⎤⎡9⎤⎡1⎤⎡X⎤⎡N⎤⎡N⎤⎡5⎤   [B. Kahl]
Nannaethiops unitaeniatus ⎡F⎤⎡D⎤⎡X⎤⎡8⎤⎡9⎤⎡2⎤⎡X⎤⎡N⎤⎡N⎤⎡6⎤   [K. Paysan]

NANNACARA ANOMALA Regan / *Golden Dwarf Cichlid*

Range: Northern South America.
Habits: Peaceful and shy except when guarding young.
Water Conditions: Neutral to slightly alkaline. Temperature 23 to 26°C.
Size: Males to 8 cm; females to 5 cm.
Food Requirements: Prefers live foods but can be trained to take ground beef heart.

Nannacara anomala is the perfect answer for the hobbyist who wants to observe the family life of cichlids and does not have the large tank which would be required to spawn one of the larger kinds. A 20-liter tank is ample for the purpose, and it does not take long to get a pair ready. A week's feeding with a variety of live foods is generally all that is needed to get a healthy female almost bursting with eggs and an equally healthy male to put on his brightest colors. A flowerpot laid on its side is often a preferred spot, but the male may pick out a rock or clean off the glass in a corner of the tank. Fifty or seventy-five eggs is an average spawning, and it may happen that the pair will share the duties of caring for the eggs and young. It may also happen, and usually does, that the little female will begin to harass her bigger mate and force him into hiding. If the male is left in, he may be badly injured or even killed, so he should be taken out. Eggs hatch in two to three days and the youngsters become free-swimming in five more days. Feeding then may be begun with newly hatched brine shrimp, and growth is very rapid.

NANNAETHIOPS UNITAENIATUS Günther / *One-Lined African Tetra*

Range: Equatorial Africa.
Habits: Peaceful; a good community fish which does not bother plants.
Water Conditions: Soft and slightly acid. Requires some warmth, about 24 to 26°C.
Size: Males 5 to 6 cm; females slightly larger.
Food Requirements: Live food preferred, but will take dry foods otherwise.

When this fish became known as "The" African tetra, there were not very many tetra species available from the Dark Continent. Nowadays this popular name would cause confusion because there are many. In fact, this fish is seldom seen at the present time, where once it was in fairly good supply. A hardy species, it may live for years once it has become accustomed to its surroundings. This is also one of the easier tetra species to spawn, and it may prove to be quite prolific. Females may be distinguished by the deeper body and larger size, while the males have a more pronounced horizontal stripe and a wider dark marking in the first dorsal rays. Eggs are scattered all over the plants and bottom. They hatch in 40 to 50 hours, and the tiny young begin to swim in about five days. An infusoria culture is a necessity for the first few days, but once they have survived this stage and are able to handle newly hatched brine shrimp the battle is won and the fish grow well from then òn.

NANNOPERCA VITTATA (Castelnau) / *Australian Pygmy Perch*

Range: Western Australia.
Habits: Peaceful; will not harm other fishes or plants.
Water Conditions: Water should be clean and have an addition of a quarter teaspoon of salt to each liter of water. Temperature 16 to 24°C.
Size: To 8 cm.
Food Requirements: Live or frozen foods; they can be taught to take dried foods, but do not like them.

Many Australian freshwater fishes, like the native fishes of our own temperate climate, tend to be colorful only when the spawning season arrives, which is the case with *Nannoperca vittata*. Most of the year they are just a muddy brown with the horizontal stripes barely distinguishable. In Australia the breeding season occurs between the months of July and January, at which time the fish takes on brilliantly intense colors. There is a black area on the back which gives way to an orange stripe from the forehead to the caudal base, and below this an orange area which covers the entire belly region. Eggs are laid in plants near the bottom, eight to ten being laid each day until a total of about 60 is attained. They hatch in 62 to 74 hours. According to the reports, the fry are hardy and grow slowly.

NANNOSTOMUS ARIPIRANGENSIS Meinken / *Aripiranga Pencilfish*

Range: Region around Aripiranga, lower Amazon River.
Habits: Completely peaceful toward other fishes and plants.
Water Conditions: Soft, slightly acid water which has been aged for at least a week. Temperature 23 to 27°C.
Size: About 5 cm.
Food Requirements: Because of the small mouth, small live foods are best; will also accept frozen and dried foods.

The Aripiranga Pencilfish is so closely related to *Nannostomus beckfordi* that it is possible to produce hybrids by crossing the two species. These hybrids are not usually sterile, and as a result many of the present-day *N. aripirangensis* have been crossed at some time in a previous generation; unless we are sure that our fish are a direct importation from the Aripiranga region we cannot be sure that we have the real thing. Some unusual experiments have been made in animal behavior by hybridizing two closely related fish species of which each has a different method of spawning. The result was a hybrid which was utterly confused when spawning was attempted, giving the animal behaviorists ample opportunity to make exhaustive observations and put out reams of scientific papers. Not so with our *N. aripirangensis-N. beckfordi* hybrids: both species have exactly similar spawning habits. The result is a healthy, more robust fish which seems to excel its forebears in color as well: the body has a great deal more red color such as is found in the male.

Nannoperca vittata ꇫꇫꇫꇫꇫꇫꇫꇫꇫꇫ   [Dr. Herbert R. Axelrod]

Nannostomus aripirangensis ꇫꇫꇫꇫꇫꇫꇫꇫꇫꇫꇫ [Dr. Herbert R. Axelrod]

1. *Nannostomus beckfordi* ♀   F F X 8 9 5 X N N 5   [H. J. Richter]
2. *Nannostomus beckfordi* ♂   F E X 8 9 6 X N N 5   [H. J. Richter]

NANNOSTOMUS BECKFORDI Günther / *Beckford's Pencilfish*

Range: Guianas, Paraná, Rio Negro, middle and lower Amazon.
Habits: Peaceful toward other fishes and plants; should be kept in a group of their own kind or other related species.
Water Conditions: Prefers soft, slightly acid water but is not intolerant to other types. Temperature 24 to 27°C.
Size: To 5 cm.
Food Requirements: Prefers the smaller living foods, but can be accustomed to taking frozen or dried foods when the others are not available.

Beckford's Pencilfish is fairly well distributed through most of the small streams of Guyana, along with most of the other pencilfish species. This species is fairly easy to breed, but the young in the first stages are difficult to feed because of their tiny mouths. For this reason most of the pencilfishes sold are still imported. In their native waters there are large schools to be found in the backwater streams, and collecting them is a very simple matter. As with most wild-caught fishes, the colors are unbelievably brilliant and lovely, and it is hard to believe that the comparatively pale fish one brings home and puts into the aquarium are the same ones. Rarely do the original colors ever return to their former beauty, but a pair which is spawning in the sunlight comes pretty close. Most of the pencilfishes have an odd characteristic. At night, the body markings change greatly. This species loses its horizontal stripe and replaces it with three large spots; if one lights up a dark tank and then tries to identify some pencilfishes, it is strongly advisable to wait awhile before doing so until their real colors come back.

1. *Nannostomus beckfordi* female (p895).
2. *N. beckfordi* male (p895).

Nannostomus beckfordi. Photo by Dr. Herbert R. Axelrod.

NANNOSTOMUS BIFASCIATUS Hoedeman / *Two-Striped Pencilfish*

Range: Guyana, Surinam, French Guiana.
Habits: Peaceful toward other fishes and plants.
Water Conditions: Soft, slightly acid water. Temperature 24 to 27°C.
Size: About 5 cm.
Food Requirements: Small live foods are preferred, but frozen and dried foods are also accepted.
Color Variations: Body brown with two dark stripes, one from the top of the eye to the upper caudal base and another from the snout to the lower caudal base.

One of the lesser-known pencilfishes is *Nannostomus bifasciatus,* the Two-Striped Pencilfish. The reason for this is that there are not as many fishes being collected where they come from as there are in the other regions where pencilfishes occur. Under certain ecological conditions streams simply swarm with every imaginable kind of pencilfish, and yet few people are able to breed them in quantity. In Guyana thousands of pencilfishes are collected in the small, almost dried-out streams which meander across the savannahs in the Rupununi District. Many of the streams are shaded by palms, and the water is slightly brown from decaying vegetation. There must be multitudes of tiny infusoria in these waters when the eggs hatch, and it would be very interesting and helpful to science in general and the hobby in particular to know just what these organisms are and the exact chemical composition of the water in which they thrive. It would help greatly in breeding the fishes which have tiny fry.

NANNOSTOMUS EQUES Steindachner / *Brown-Tailed Pencilfish*

Range: Guyana and Orinoco to lower Amazon.
Habits: Peaceful; swims with the head tilted upward, and prefers to swim in schools.
Water Conditions: Soft, neutral to slightly acid water. Temperature 24 to 27°C.
Size: To 5 cm.
Food Requirements: Most foods are taken from or near the surface; mosquito larvae are particularly relished by mature fish.

Pencilfishes are generally popular aquarium fishes due to their peaceful nature, small size and attractive coloration. In particular this is true for the Brown-Tailed Pencilfish. This species naturally inhabits slow-flowing, heavily vegetated, mildly acidic waters. This fish feeds on insects in the upper water layers or on the water's surface, but it will take most aquarium foods while in captivity. Males of this species are much slimmer than the females and are also more colorful. This fish prefers to breed on *Ludwigia* or *Hygrophila* leaves and is not difficult to spawn in an aquarium. The water should be aged, soft and acidic; the aquarium should be well planted; the water temperature should be on the warm side of its suggested range.

Nannostomus bifasciatus ⬚F⬚R⬚X⬚8⬚9⬚7⬚X⬚N⬚N⬚5 [Dr. Herbert R. Axelrod]
Nannostomus eques ⬚F⬚R⬚X⬚8⬚9⬚8⬚X⬚N⬚N⬚5 [H. J. Richter]

Nannostomus espei FQX8999XNN5   [H. J. Richter]
Nannostomus marginatus FQX9000XNN3   [H. J. Richter]

NANNOSTOMUS ESPEI (Meinken) / *Barred Pencilfish*

Range: Guyana.
Habits: Peaceful and active; a skilled jumper whose tank should be covered.
Water Conditions: Soft water, neutral to slightly acid. Temperature 24 to 27°C.
Size: To 5 cm.
Food Requirements: Not choosy as to foods, but very partial to live daphnia.

This is the most distinctively marked of all the pencilfishes. The five black bars in the lower half of the body make it unmistakable even from 6 meters away. The fish was found in Guyana by our good friend Louis Chung in 1956, and large numbers of them found their way to American and European dealers. The author (HRA) helped collect many species of pencilfishes in the Rupununi District savannahs with Mr. Chung, but this was not one of them. Of course this is no help in pinpointing their habitat, but at least we know two things: they *do* come from Guyana and they do *not* come from the savannah waters in the southwestern part of that fascinating country. They are active and like to swim in small groups. Both sexes show a similarity of finnage, but the deeper body and more irregular markings of the female make it easily recognizable. They are said to spawn in bushy plants like most of the other pencilfishes.

NANNOSTOMUS MARGINATUS Eigenmann / *Dwarf Pencilfish*

Range: Guyana to Colombia and the lower Amazon.
Habits: Very peaceful; an excellent community fish.
Water Conditions: Neutral to slightly acid; requires heat, about 26°C.
Size: Maximum about 3 cm.
Food Requirements: Prefers small live foods, but will take dry food if necessary.

The pencilfishes are very popular, and this is probably the most popular member of the group. Its small size makes it a candidate for a community tank containing only small, peaceful fishes. Many people make the error of mixing fishes of all sizes, as long as they do not harm each other. This is a mistake, because in many cases a fish like, for instance, this one, is constantly frightened by larger fishes swimming near it, and as a result it spends much of its time hiding. Sexes are not easy to distinguish, except for the female's slightly heavier body and a little more red in the dorsal and anal fins of the male. Breeding them is made difficult because of the fact that the parent fish are very quick to eat their own eggs. These eggs have very little adhesive power and most of them fall to the bottom. A bed of glass rods which lets the eggs through and holds back the parents is used with success here. The young are very small when they hatch, which makes them difficult to feed.

NANNOSTOMUS TRIFASCIATUS Steindachner
Three-Lined Pencilfish

Range: Upper Amazon region.
Habits: Peaceful toward other fishes and plants; should not be kept with active fishes.
Water Conditions: Soft, slightly acid water which has been run through peat moss. Temperature 24 to 27°C.
Size: To 6 cm.
Food Requirements: Small live foods are best, with frozen or dried foods given only when living foods are not available.
Color Variations: Three black stripes at side of the body, with red markings on anal, ventral, dorsal and caudal fins.

Most hobbyists who keep pencilfishes consider *Nannostomus trifasciatus* the beauty of the group and are usually unanimous in expressing the opinion that this species is the most difficult to spawn. Strangely enough, in its habitat in Guyana this was the most common species everywhere we (HRA and the T.F.H. expedition) fished. The usual catch was about as many *Nannostomus trifasciatus* as all the rest of the *Nannostomus* species put together. Our best catch was made in a little stream which meandered across a savannah in the vicinity of Lethem, near the Brazilian border. The banks were lined with palm trees and there was grass growing knee-deep right up to the water. The bottom was only slightly muddy, and the water was stained brownish by decaying vegetable matter. The stream was no more than hip-deep in most places, but the variety of characins caught there was no less than amazing. We even caught some piranhas in this little stream, which was seldom more than 30 m wide, scarcely enough to call it a creek. *Nannostomus trifasciatus* is one of the larger pencilfishes, attaining a length of 6 cm. It is happiest in a sunny tank with a number of its own kind.

NANNOSTOMUS UNIFASCIATUS Steindachner / *One-Lined Pencilfish*

Range: Middle and lower Amazon tributaries, Rio Negro, Guyana, Orinoco.
Habits: Peaceful and somewhat timid; prefer to be kept in a small group.
Water Conditions: Soft, slightly acid water. Temperature 23 to 26°C.
Size: To 6 cm.
Food Requirements: Live and prepared foods of small size, preferably food which will remain at or near the surface.

The One-Lined Pencilfish has been known to science since being named by Steindachner in 1876, yet we see them so seldom that many works do not even list them. This species is an attractive aquarium fish which is easy to keep and not difficult to breed. Males have an anal fin that is rounded from below and brilliantly colored, while the females have an anal fin that is straight. This species should be kept in a well-planted aquarium with soft, warm, well-aged, acidic water.

Nannostomus trifasciatus FRX901XNN4 [Harald Schultz]
Nannostomus unifasciatus FRX902XNN6 [Dr. Herbert R. Axelrod]

Nanochromis dimidiatus ⌐F⌐A⌐X⌐9⌐0⌐3⌐X⌐N⌐N⌐6   [H. J. Richter]
Nanochromis splendens ⌐F⌐R⌐X⌐9⌐0⌐4⌐X⌐N⌐N⌐8   [H. J. Richter]

NANOCHROMIS DIMIDIATUS (Boulenger) / *Dimidiatus*

Range: Congo basin.
Habits: Usually very peaceful in the community aquarium.
Water Conditions: Soft, slightly acid water. Temperature 24 to 26°C.
Size: Males 9 cm; females 6 cm.
Food Requirements: All sorts of live foods, preferably those which sink to the bottom; frozen foods also accepted.
Color Variations: Body dusky with a purplish sheen; horizontal dark line may be present; back part of dorsal fin and top of caudal fin bright red.

The genera *Nanochromis* and *Pelvicachromis* are very closely related, and a quick glance at *Nanochromis dimidiatus* might give rise to the suspicion that it is a *Pelvicachromis* species, the two being almost exactly alike in body form. This species will breed readily if given the proper conditions and a tank of its own. *Dimidiatus* prefers to spawn on the sloping face of a flowerpot. After spawning, the female cares for the eggs and later the brood. The eggs hatch in about three days and the fry are free-swimming in an additional three to four days.

NANOCHROMIS SPLENDENS (Boulenger) / *Congo Dwarf Cichlid*

Range: Congo basin.
Habits: Apt to be a bit quarrelsome at times; best kept by themselves.
Water Conditions: Soft, slightly acid water is best. Temperature 24 to 26°C.
Size: Up to 8 cm for males; females about 2 cm smaller.
Food Requirements: Live foods of all kinds; at times when none is available, frozen foods may be provided temporarily.
Color Variations: Sides of body blue, belly bright green; dorsal fin is orange with a black tip and white edge; upper half of tail striped.

There are many fishes from Africa which could be properly referred to as dwarf cichlids, and the *Nanochromis* species are among these. As with so many cichlids, peace is never assured when more than one male is kept to a tank, unless the tank is a large one which provides territories for all the males. For the first few hours after being placed in an aquarium, each male will search busily for a sheltered spot where he can spend his time and keep a constant lookout for intruders. When an invasion occurs, an otherwise peaceful male will become a raging tyrant until the other fish beats a retreat. For this reason provision for a number of places where an attacked fish can hide is highly important where any dwarf cichlids are concerned, especially *Nanochromis splendens*. Females are a docile lot and submit meekly to the advances of the males when they are ready to spawn. When the male has finished his duties of fertilizing the eggs, the erstwhile meek little female turns into a tigress and gives the male a severe drubbing every time he gets anywhere near the eggs. For his safety he should be removed at this time and put into another tank while the female guards the eggs and fry.

NEETROPLUS NEMATOPUS Günther / *Little Lake Cichlid*

Range: Nicaragua (the Great Lakes) and Costa Rica.
Habits: Generally peaceful except when spawning; a territorial species.
Water Conditions: Prefers hard alkaline water to which some salt has been added. Temperature not critical, but should have sufficient aeration.
Size: Reaches a standard length of just over 9 cm.
Food Requirements: Will take any normal aquarium foods.

Neetroplus nematopus is expected to be a very popular aquarium cichlid by virtue of its interesting habits and engaging personality. It is relatively hardy (although it needs adequate aeration), easily fed (will take any of the normal aquarium foods) and easily bred. Unfortunately its dependence on adequate oxygen makes it difficult to ship so that its availability will be limited until better shipping methods or domestic breeding can supply the demand.

Neetroplus is territorial by nature and will set up its defended area around rockwork or flowerpots set up in the tank. Usually within this territory is a flat rock, somewhat sheltered, that can serve as a breeding site. The female that is ready to spawn will enter this territory and become one of its prime defenders. The site preparation goes on for a couple more days until the actual spawning. About 50 to 250 or more reddish or wine-colored adhesive eggs are laid in a protected spot in the territory (often the roof of a cave) that can be readily defended. The small (under 2 mm) oval eggs hatch in about one to one and a half days at 26 to 29°C. In another four to five days the fry are free-swimming. Both eggs and fry are aggressively defended by both parents. In the early part of the free-swimming stage the female takes over most of the chores, but as the school of fry becomes more difficult to manage the male replaces her as headmaster.

NEMATOBRYCON LACORTEI Weitzman & Fink / *Rainbow Tetra*

Range: San Juan basin, Colombia.
Habits: Peaceful; inclined to be a bit shy.
Water Conditions: Soft, slightly acid water is best. Temperature 24 to 27°C.
Size: To 5 cm.
Food Requirements: Live foods are best, but the fish can be trained to accept frozen and dried foods.

There are two *Nematobrycon* species: *N. palmeri* and *N. lacortei*. *N. lacortei* was known for a time as *N. amphiloxus*. Weitzman and Fink found that the type specimens of *N. amphiloxus* were in fact a variety of *N. palmeri*. They renamed the specimens on the market, which were formerly known as *N. amphiloxus*, *N. lacortei*.

N. lacortei and *N. palmeri* are geographically isolated in nature but will hybridize in the aquarium. They spawn like most tetras, laying their eggs in bushy plants.

Neetroplus nematopus   ⬚F⬚A⬚X⬚9⬚0⬚5⬚X⬚N⬚N⬚8   [H. Ross Brock]

Nematobrycon lacortei   ⬚F⬚R⬚X⬚9⬚0⬚6⬚X⬚N⬚N⬚5   [Dr. Herbert R. Axelrod]

Nematobrycon palmeri ⬚Ⓕ Ⓡ Ⓧ ⑨ ⓪ ⑦ Ⓧ Ⓝ Ⓝ ⑤　　[Dr. Herbert R. Axelrod]
Neolebias ansorgi ⬚Ⓕ Ⓐ Ⓧ ⑨ ⓪ ⑧ Ⓧ Ⓝ Ⓝ ④　　[H. J. Richter]

NEMATOBRYCON PALMERI Eigenmann / *Emperor Tetra*

Range: San Juan basin and Atrato Rivers, Colombia.
Habits: Peaceful and a bit shy; inclined to remain singly or in pairs rather than forming a school.
Water Conditions: Clean, soft, slightly acid water is best. Temperature 23 to 25°C.
Size: To 5 cm.
Food Requirements: Excellent appetite; will accept dried or frozen foods, but of course live foods are preferred.

The Emperor Tetra comes from a very inaccessible region in Colombia, the San Juan basin on the Pacific slope. Fortunately, breeders both in Europe and in the United States found that this fish was far from difficult to breed, and a permanent supply seems to be assured. They spawn like most tetras, laying their eggs in bushy plants. Some breeders prefer to use spawning mops or bundles of fine nylon filaments, both of which are readily accepted and more practical to use than the usual bundles of *Myriophyllum* or other bushy plants.

The breeding aquarium should contain soft, slightly acidic water with a warm temperature on the high end of the recommended range. Live foods are suggested prior to breeding as this will help get the fish into the best condition. The fry are hardy, and it is not difficult to raise the youngsters to maturity. The fry will take newly hatched brine shrimp.

NEOLEBIAS ANSORGI Boulenger / *Ansorge's Neolebias*

Range: Cameroon to lower Congo basin.
Habits: Peaceful and very shy in a community tank; should be kept by themselves.
Water Conditions: Sensitive to hard, alkaline water; water must be well-aged and should never undergo great changes. Temperature 24 to 28°C.
Size: To 4 cm.
Food Requirements: Small live foods only.

Anyone who sees the picture of this fish and then sees it for the first time in a dealer's bare tank is apt to be highly disappointed and accuse the photographer of taking liberties with the colors. The truth of the matter is that here we have a fish which pales very quickly when things around him are not to his entire satisfaction. Even when in color, there are two distinct color varieties, one golden in body and the other green. Both have a large amount of green in the wide horizontal stripe, but in one the rest of the body is greenish to violet, while in the other those portions are golden. One would never suspect that this is one of the tetra family from its body shape. It has the short, heavy body that one generally associates with the barbs, an illusion which is heightened by the fact that there is no adipose fin. The unique square dorsal fin looks like nothing one would find on a tetra, either. The fish is sensitive to water changes and hard water. They breed readily, but the fry are difficult to raise. Eggs are laid in plant thickets and hatch in 20 to 24 hours. The tiny fry have small mouths and must at first be given very fine infusoria.

NEOLEBIAS TREWAVASAE Poll & Gosse / *Trewavas's Neolebias*

Range: Nile to lower Congo River.
Habits: Peaceful and very shy in a community tank; should be kept by themselves.
Water Conditions: Sensitive to hard, alkaline water; water must be well aged and the aquarium should never undergo large percentage water changes. Temperature 22 to 28°C.
Size: To 5 cm.
Food Requirements: Small live foods only, of a size comparable to newly hatched brine shrimp.

Neolebias trewavasae is a micropredator which lives on small animals found on the river bottom or among the plants. In general, *Neolebias* species keep to the bottom water layers in the aquarium. This species prefers a well-planted aquarium with soft, acidic, well-aged water. During breeding time, the temperature should be raised to 30°C. This species breeds among the plants, depositing batches of a dozen eggs at a time. Three hundred or more eggs can be laid. The fry hatch in about one day, depending upon the temperature of the water.

NEOLEBIAS TRILINEATUS Boulenger / *Three-Lined Neolebias*

Range: Congo basin.
Habits: Peaceful and shy.
Water Conditions: Not very critical, but the best is slightly acid and soft water. Temperature 23 to 26°C.
Size: To 4 cm.
Food Requirements: Live and frozen foods greatly preferred, but when not available dry foods can be given for a time.
Color Variations: Back brown, sides silvery with three dark horizontal stripes; fins are reddish.

The African continent is notoriously stingy toward the aquarium hobbyist when it comes to producing tetras. Most of the characins from Africa have some drawback: they become too big for the average home aquarium, they gobble up the plants, they cannot get along with other fishes, they cannot be induced to spawn, etc., etc. The *Neolebias* species are a notable exception. *Neolebias trilineatus* is a small peaceful fish which usually will not bother plants and can easily be gotten to spawn. *N. trilineatus* should be placed in a fairly large aquarium which gets a good amount of sunlight and is not very heavily planted. Best temperatures range from 23 to 26°C. The reason for the fairly large aquarium is that sometimes spawns are surprisingly large. Eggs are scattered among plants and sometimes all over the bottom. At 25°C the fry hatch in 26 to 32 hours, and in five days they become free-swimming. This is a fish which seldom shows its best colors unless conditions are ideal. The lower half of the body should show a pink flush. Males are distinguished by their reddish fins and slightly higher dorsal fins.

Neolebias trewavasae ⬚F⬚A⬚X⬚9⬚0⬚9⬚X⬚N⬚N⬚5   [Dr. Herbert R. Axelrod]
Neolebias trilineatus ⬚F⬚R⬚X⬚9⬚1⬚0⬚X⬚N⬚N⬚4   [Dr. Herbert R. Axelrod]

Noemacheilus fasciatus ☐F☐ ☐R☐ ☐X☐ ☐9☐ ☐1☐ ☐1☐ ☐X☐ ☐N☐ ☐N☐ ☐9☐   [Dr. Herbert R. Axelrod]

Noemacheilus notostigma ☐F☐ ☐D☐ ☐X☐ ☐9☐ ☐1☐ ☐2☐ ☐X☐ ☐N☐ ☐N☐ ☐8☐   [K. Paysan]

911

NOEMACHEILUS FASCIATUS (Cuvier & Valenciennes)
Barred Loach

Range: Sumatra, Java, Borneo.
Habits: Best given a tank of their own; chooses and defends its own territories.
Water Conditions: Soft, slightly acid water. Temperature 24 to 26°C.
Size: To 9 cm.
Food Requirements: Likes worms and other live foods, but not a fussy eater.

Although it has an elongated body and markings like our old friend *Acanthophthalmus kuhli*, the Kuhli Loach, plus a set of barbels, the similarity between the two fishes ends right there. *Noemacheilus fasciatus* does not have the snaky, eel-like motions of the Kuhli Loach and has a more useful-looking and nicer-shaped set of fins. It carries itself more like a fish than like a large worm or small snake. The natives to the countries where the loaches come from are fond of eating small fishes and have an interesting method of catching them. They divert a small stream by damming it and leading it away from its original bed. When the water has run off, they turn over rocks and dig into the gravel bed, capturing a great many loaches of all sorts in the process. We have also heard of the South American collectors doing the same thing when collecting the *Corydoras* catfishes. *Noemacheilus fasciatus* should have a number of hiding places in their tank. Each fish carefully selects and takes possession of one of these nooks and defends it fiercely.

NOEMACHEILUS NOTOSTIGMA Bleeker / *Fighting Loach*

Range: Sri Lanka.
Habits: Best kept by themselves in pairs or several pairs in a large tank with a number of hiding places.
Water Conditions: Not critical, but the water should be clean. Temperature 24 to 27°C.
Size: To 8 cm.
Food Requirements: Any kind of food accepted, but there should be live foods given at times.

The loach family is for the most part a peaceful one. There are a few members, notably the Clown Loach, which will take over a special spot and defend it from intruders, but such action is mostly bluff and seldom results in serious injuries. Our Fighting Loach goes one step further and not only defends its own territory but sometimes goes out looking for trouble. Females, which with most species are the docile ones, are just as pugnacious as the males where the Fighting Loach is concerned. Here is one loach where the males are easy to distinguish: in the male the upper lobe of the tail is considerably longer, looking like a rooster's. Both sexes attain a length of 8 cm. Fighting consists mostly of maneuvers in which one fish attempts to grasp the other's pectoral fin. Although they have no teeth in their jaws, they can manage to tear away pieces of the fin membrane.

NOMORHAMPHUS CELEBENSIS Weber & de Beaufort
Celebes Halfbeak

Range: Celebes, Indonesia.
Habits: Generally peaceful but will eat fishes small enough to swallow; should probably be kept by themselves.
Water Conditions: On the hard side with a pH of 7.0 or higher; regular water changes are recommended. Temperature should be around 23 to 28°C.
Size: May reach 10 cm.
Food Requirements: Must have live foods such as Guppies or brine shrimp.

For the aquarist with a taste for the unusual but who still wants some color in his tank, *Nomorhamphus celebensis* is a natural choice. It is a member of the family Exocoetidae, which now includes the halfbeaks or hemiramphids along with the marine flyingfishes and the aquarium favorite *Dermogenys.*

The sexes are easily distinguished by the color pattern and the size of the protuberance on the end of the lower jaw. Males are much more colorful, with bright red and black fins and a large blue-black protuberance on the lower jaw. The female has traces of red and black in her fins but much less than in the male's, and the lower jaw protuberance is very small.

The Celebes Halfbeak is relatively peaceful and easy to keep except for one problem. It requires live food. Small Guppies and live adult brine shrimp will usually be sufficient for its needs.

Because it is a livebearer, *Nomorhamphus celebensis* should be kept in a well-planted tank. Tankmates should be selected with care as they most likely would make short work of any newly born halfbeaks that they could capture. The Celebes Halfbeak young may be born head first or tail first and are able to swim immediately, so with a little bit of luck they can make it to the shelter of the plants. The same bushy plants used in other livebearer tanks can be used with the Celebes Halfbeak. The tank itself need not be very large, a 20- to 40-liter capacity should be sufficient. Most of the time the halfbeaks will be in the upper layers of the tank, so plan accordingly.

Despite the superficial resemblance to another livebearing halfbeak genus, *Dermogenys,* reproduction is somewhat different. In *Dermogenys* the eggs are fertilized and develop in the ovary until just before birth. In *Nomorhamphus* the eggs are fertilized in the ovary but only partially develop there. The still undeveloped young are released into a uterus where the egg capsules are resorbed. The developing young absorb a nutrient (secreted by the uterus walls) through their body surfaces at first but later only through the mouth opening. Six to eight young may develop in each uterus at one time (never more than sixteen total) and after they are born are replaced by more eggs which were developing in the ovary during this time.

1. *Nomorhamphus celebensis* mating pair in an aquarium (p914).
2. *N. celebensis* have beard-like protuberances extending from their lower jaw (p914).

1. *Nomorhamphus celebensis* ⌐F⌐R⌐X⌐9⌐1⌐3⌐X⌐N⌐N⌐9 [H. J. Richter]
2. *Nomorhamphus celebensis* ⌐F⌐R⌐X⌐9⌐1⌐4⌐X⌐N⌐N⌐9 [H. J. Richter]

1. *Nothobranchius melanospilus* 	F R X 9 1 9 X N N 5 	[Dr. Karl Knaack]
2. *Nothobranchius melanospilus* 	F Q X 9 2 0 X N N 5 	[Dr. W. Foersch]

Nothobranchius melanospilus spawning among bottom vegetation and peat moss. Photos by Karl Knaack.

NOTHOBRANCHIUS MELANOSPILUS (Pfeffer) / *Beira Notho*

Range: Vicinity of Beira, Mozambique.
Habits: Should be kept in their own tank.
Water Conditions: Soft, slightly acid water with a layer of peat moss on the bottom.
Size: Males to 5 cm; females slightly smaller.
Food Requirements: Live foods only, and there should be an almost constant supply.

Nothobranchius melanospilus was found near Beira in Mozambique by E. Roloff. The specific name is a bit puzzling, because *melanospilus* means "black-spotted." One would expect to see a fish with black spots all over, but the spots are only on the head and gill-covers of the male. The female is a very drab proposition by comparison. A hobbyist who keeps several species of *Nothobranchius* has to be very careful to keep the females either in labeled tanks or with their own males, because there is so little difference that things could be hopelessly confused and the result could be either sterile eggs or a lot of unidentifiable hybrids. This species is almost always ready to spawn if kept in good condition, almost too ready. If there is only one female available, a male will soon have her quite battered and she should be given a few days of rest. Like the other *Nothobranchius* species, eggs are buried in a layer of peat moss on the bottom where they may be removed, peat moss and all, when there is a let-up in the spawning. This is kept in a slightly moist stage for three to four months and the eggs hatch when they are put in water again.

1. *Nothobranchius melanospilus* in an aquarium (p919).
2. *N. melanospilus* mating pair (p919).

NOTHOBRANCHIUS PALMQUISTI Lönnberg
Palmquist's Notho

Range: East Africa.
Habits: Somewhat pugnacious; should be kept in their own tank.
Water Conditions: Water should be soft and slightly acid. Temperature 24 to 27°C.
Size: To 6 cm.
Food Requirements: Live foods only.

This species is often a fighter and should be given its own tank. The males are about 25% larger than the females and also much more colorful. This fish should be given an aquarium with a dark background and subdued light. Although it is tempting to add more males to the aquarium than females (due to lack of coloration in the females), it is not advisable as the fish will tend to kill each other.

Palmquist's Notho spawns in a fashion similar to that of other members of its genus. Its eggs have a four-month incubation period when stored in peat moss. Hatched fry should be given infusoria or prepared liquid fry food upon hatching. Egg hatching can be hastened by warm water of about 27°C.

1. *Nothobranchius palmquisti* mating pair (p922).
2. *N. palmquisti* male with his dorsal fin over the female (p922).

Nothobranchius palmquisti pair in a spawning aquarium. Photo by H. J. Richter.

1. *Nothobranchius palmquisti* ⬚F⬚ ⬚Q⬚ ⬚X⬚ ⬚9⬚⬚2⬚⬚1⬚ ⬚X⬚ ⬚N⬚ ⬚N⬚ ⬚6⬚   [H. J. Richter]
2. *Nothobranchius palmquisti* ⬚F⬚ ⬚Q⬚ ⬚X⬚ ⬚9⬚⬚2⬚⬚2⬚ ⬚X⬚ ⬚N⬚ ⬚N⬚ ⬚6⬚   [H. J. Richter]

1. *Nothobranchius rachovi* ♂ [F][E][X][9][2][3][X][N][N][5] [H. J. Richter]
2. *Nothobranchius rachovi* [F][Q][X][9][2][4][X][N][N][5] [H. J. Richter]

NOTHOBRANCHIUS RACHOVI (Ahl) / *Rachow's Notho*

Range: East Africa, in the vicinity of Beira.
Habits: Quarrelsome toward other fishes; should be given their own tank.
Water Conditions: Water should be soft and slightly acid. Temperature 24 to 27°C.
Size: To 5 cm.
Food Requirements: Living foods only.

Any hobbyist who sees a beautiful male *Nothobranchius rachovi* in his full colors will never deny that this is one of the most beautiful freshwater fishes in the whole world. Like the other *Nothobranchius* species, they have a few traits which keep them from being perfect. For one thing, they insist on live foods and will seldom eat anything which is not moving. Males will frequently stage seemingly vicious battles which usually turn out to be harmless, but when kept with other fishes they are likely to become nasty. A jewel such as this deserves its own setting, and it is best to give them a tank with only their own kind. Like the other *Nothobranchius* species, their life span is comparatively short and once they have attained maturity spawnings are frequent and feedings must be generous.

1. *Nothobranchius rachovi* male in spawning colors (p923).
2. *N. rachovi* mating pair (p923).

Nothobranchius rachovi, Rachow's Notho. Photo by R. Zukal.

NOTOPTERUS CHITALA (Hamilton-Buchanan) / *Clown Knife Fish*

Range: Malaysia, southeastern India, Thailand and islands of Borneo and Sumatra.
Habits: Mostly nocturnal, and peaceful at small sizes but distinctly predatory at larger sizes; will usually not bother other fishes about equal to them in size, but will quarrel with members of their own species.
Water Conditions: Soft, acidic water preferred; temperature should be maintained at 24 to 27°C.
Size: In nature, to about 90 cm at the maximum; never seen this large under aquarium conditions.
Food Requirements: Live foods, worms especially, are readily accepted, as are most frozen foods; dry foods are not always accepted by fish over 10 cm long.

This is a big fish. Hobbyists may never see them at their full attained-in-nature size, but they're big enough even at the reduced sizes at which they're generally offered. It is also a nocturnal fish and does not appreciate being forced to exist in a tank in which it cannot escape from bright lighting, so it should be provided with large shaded areas.

N. chitala attaches masses of eggs to upright structures such as large plants. The male devotedly guards the eggs, which hatch within six days at a temperature of about 32°C according to Dr. Hugh M. Smith. This abnormally high temperature might not be too much out of line when you consider the tropical areas the fish inhabit and the fact that the waters in which they live are usually slow-moving or stagnant, allowing the temperature to build up.

NOTROPIS HYPSELOPTERUS (Günther) / *Sailfin Shiner*

Range: South Carolina, Georgia, Florida and Alabama.
Habits: A peaceful, active fish which will not molest its tankmates.
Water Conditions: Clean, soft, slightly acid water and a good-sized, well-planted tank are preferred.
Size: 8 cm.
Food Requirements: Will take dried as well as live or frozen foods.

Notropis hypselopterus is one of our most beautiful native fishes; it occurs in good numbers in Georgia's Okefenokee Swamp region. In spite of its obvious good looks, the usual antipathy toward any fish which does not come from some far-away place exists, and dealers will seldom stock them. The author once saw a tankful of beautiful specimens in a dealer's store, all males. When asked if there were any females available, the dealer said that the collectors had thrown away all of the females and kept only the more brightly colored males, thinking that the females were something else. It is an active but peaceful fish which is usually swimming where it can be seen. For their complete well-being, they should get a period of two to three months each year in an unheated aquarium at room temperatures. At the end of this period their temperature can again be increased gradually.

Notopterus chitala FDX925XNND   [Dr. Herbert R. Axelrod]
Notropis hypselopterus FAX926XNN8   [H. Hansen, Aquarium Berlin]

Notropis lutrensis ⬚F⬚A⬚X⬚9⬚2⬚7⬚X⬚N⬚N⬚8   [Aaron Norman]
Ompok bimaculatus ⬚F⬚D⬚X⬚9⬚2⬚8⬚X⬚N⬚N⬚A   [Dr. Herbert R. Axelrod]

NOTROPIS LUTRENSIS (Baird & Girard)
Red Horse Minnow, "Asian Fire Barb"

Range: Illinois and South Dakota south to Louisiana and Texas.
Habits: Peaceful; will not molest its tankmates at any time.
Water Conditions: Water must be clean and well aerated, and fish should never be crowded. Temperature may go as high as 26°C, but nearer 21°C is better.
Size: 8 cm.
Food Requirements: Prepared foods as well as live foods are eaten, but there should be a preponderance of live or frozen foods.

These fish prefer flowing streams and in order to make them feel at home, their tank should be well aerated and briskly filtered. Mr. Jeff W. Moore has an interesting article about it in the July, 1959, issue of *Tropical Fish Hobbyist*. He tells how a trio kept in a community aquarium which also contained tropical species spawned for him right in the center of the tank. The male fanned away the fine gravel in a small area and then spawned for more than an hour, first with one female and then with the other. Since there were other fishes in the tank the eggs were eaten. Since the fish is plentiful in the Dallas, Texas area, no further attempts were made to isolate and spawn them again. Unfortunately the bright colors of the male only appear for a few months each year.

OMPOK BIMACULATUS (Bloch) / *One-Spot Glass Catfish*

Range: Sri Lanka, Indo-China, Thailand, Burma, Java and Sumatra.
Habits: Only small specimens are adaptable to aquaria, and they should not be kept singly; single fish are short-lived.
Water Conditions: Very adaptable to practically any clean water. Temperature 23 to 28°C.
Size: To 46 cm in native waters; about half that in the aquarium.
Food Requirements: Live or frozen foods preferred.

Ompok bimaculatus is found throughout a rather wide range which includes most of the Indian-Southeast Asia area. It is a very popular fish wherever it occurs, not as an aquarium fish but as an item on the menu. Being fairly common, it is easy to get under ordinary circumstances. The natives often have pools which they stock with these fish, feeding them all sorts of table refuse and eventually reaping a rich harvest. The generic name *Ompok* was originally given to this fish by Lacépède in 1803, and he did a very questionable job on it which caused much confusion later. In his drawing he left out the tiny dorsal fin, and he also failed to mention it in his description. More than 30 years later Valenciennes dug out Lacépède's specimen and discovered that the little fin, which consists of four or five rays, was there all the time. Small specimens are frequently sent to our shores, but they soon outgrow their quarters. In the open, the fish may get to be 46 cm long, but in captivity a fish half that size is quite unusual. Unlike many catfishes, this one is active and does not mind the daylight.

ORYZIAS JAVANICUS (Bleeker) / *Javanese Rice Fish*

Range: Java and Malaysia.
Habits: Peaceful toward other fishes and will not harm plants.
Water Conditions: Water should be neutral to slightly alkaline, with a little salt added. Keep at 26 to 29°C.
Size: Males to 3 cm; females to 4 cm.
Food Requirements: Live foods greatly preferred; other foods are not picked up once they fall to the bottom.

The Javanese Rice Fish is not the most colorful of aquarium fishes, but it is an interesting one nevertheless. The glassily transparent body plainly shows the skeletal structure of the fish, and with the light shining on it from behind the viewer, the large anal fin shows a beautiful blue edge. Most interesting, however, is their manner of spawning. The male drives the female actively until they come to a quivering halt among the plants. Here the eggs are expelled and fertilized. Nothing unusual so far, but here is where the oddity comes in: instead of staying among the plants, the eggs hang in a bunch attached by a tough string to the female's vent and are sometimes carried about in this manner for hours. Finally the string snags against something solid, usually a plant leaf or twig, and the eggs come to rest. Hatching takes place in 10 to 12 days, and until they begin to grow the tiny youngsters must be provided with infusoria.

ORYZIAS LATIPES (Schlegel) / *Medaka*

Range: Japan and nearby islands.
Habits: Active and peaceful, although a male will occasionally rough up a female; a very good community fish.
Water Conditions: Slightly soft, acid water desirable.
Size: Females about 5 cm; males slightly smaller.
Food Requirements: Takes all foods.

The three primary requisites of a good aquarium fish are that the fish be hardy, easy to feed and interesting. The Medaka possesses all three characteristics to a remarkable degree. It is very definitely one of the toughest of all aquarium fishes, outranking even the Guppy and White Cloud in its ability to withstand adverse conditions, particularly where water temperature is concerned. It is easy to feed, accepting dry food day in and day out without declining, although of course it will not be at its best under such a feeding schedule. The Medaka is interesting in both its attractiveness and breeding habits, too. Certainly not a flashy fish, it is still quietly pretty, with its golden body (the old wild strain is no longer seen) set off by iridescent blue-green flecks and the beautiful, large, almost luminescent eyes. The breeding habits of the fish offer a remarkable opportunity to view the life cycle from egg to free-swimming fry, for the eggs can be observed in bunches on the female, and they can later be observed attached to plants.

Oryzias javanicus ⑤ⓇⓍ⑨②⑨ⓍⓃⓃ③　　　　[Dr. Herbert R. Axelrod]
Oryzias latipes ⑤ⒶⓍ⑨③⓪ⓍⓃⓃ⑤　　　　[Dr. Herbert R. Axelrod]

Osphronemus goramy ꞏFꞏCꞏXꞏ9ꞏ3ꞏ1ꞏXꞏNꞏNꞏ9ꞏ   [Wardley Products Co.]
Osteochilus hasselti ꞏFꞏDꞏXꞏ9ꞏ3ꞏ2ꞏXꞏNꞏNꞏAꞏ   [G. Wolfsheimer]

OSPHRONEMUS GORAMY Lacépède / *Giant Gourami*

Range: Great Sunda Islands; introduced in other places as a food fish.
Habits: Peaceful; because of their size they should be kept only with large fishes.
Water Conditions: Not critical as long as the water is clean. Temperature 23 to 28°C.
Size: Up to 60 cm in natural waters; about half that in the aquarium.
Food Requirements: Should get large amounts of shrimp, clams, mussels, etc., to which is also added vegetable matter such as boiled oatmeal.

The Giant Gourami is usually sold in sizes of 5 to 8 cm, at which size they are attractively banded and nicely shaped. The surprise comes when they grow and grow and grow. If allowed plenty of room and full scope is given to its huge appetite, the result is a large, heavy-bodied fish with thick, rubbery lips and a stupid expression. In their native range they are highly regarded as food fish, and the natives consider them quite a delicacy. According to existing literature on the subject, they build a bubblenest and the male stands guard over the eggs and young. Sexes can be distinguished in mature specimens by a roundness in the dorsal and anal fins of the females. In males these fins are pointed. Mature fish 30 cm or more in length are said to be excellent show objects for large public aquariums. Their food should contain a good amount of vegetable matter, such as boiled oatmeal and the like. According to Rachow, old specimens become completely black in color. This fish has been known to science since 1802 and has been known to the aquarium hobby for a long time as well, having first made its appearance somewhere around the year 1895.

OSTEOCHILUS HASSELTI (Cuvier & Valenciennes) / *Hard-Lipped Barb*

Range: Thailand to Java, Borneo and Sumatra.
Habits: Peaceful if kept with fishes of its own size.
Water Conditions: Neutral to slightly acid water; tank should be well planted and of a good size. Temperature 24 to 27°C.
Size: Grows to a little over 30 cm in length in nature; about half that in the aquarium.
Food Requirements: Live foods with an addition of vegetable substances.

Osteochilus hasselti is a well-known food fish in Thailand as well as Java, Borneo and Sumatra. It is a large, handsome, well-formed fish which unusually enough has two pairs of barbels on the upper lip and none on the lower. The mouth is well adapted for algae-nibbling and tearing at other soft plants. The upper and lower lips are lined with papillae, and there is a bony structure behind the lower lip. In central and southeastern Thailand it is called *pla soi khao* because of a fancied resemblance to a dove which is called *nok khao*. The fish gets large in its home waters, having been reported at a little over 30 cm, but this is rarely the case. Most mature specimens are 15 to 20 cm in length. The large dorsal fin is reddish, the pectoral fins are white to greenish and the caudal, anal and ventral fins are red.

OSTEOCHILUS VITTATUS (Cuvier & Valenciennes)
Black-Banded Osteochilus

Range: Thailand, Java, Borneo, Sumatra and the Malay States.
Habits: Peaceful if kept with fishes of its own size.
Water Conditions: Neutral to slightly acid water; tank should be well planted and of a good size. Temperature 24 to 27°C.
Size: To 23 cm in their natural waters; about half that in the aquarium.
Food Requirements: Live foods with added algae or lettuce leaves.

In spite of the fact that it is as abundant in its home waters as *Osteochilus hasselti* and of a smaller, more practical size for the aquarium hobbyist, *Osteochilus vittatus* is seen even less among imported Thailand fishes than its better-known cousin. It is distinguished very easily by its broad black band which extends from the eye through the fork of the tail. In some highly colored specimens the area above this stripe is purplish to purplish black, making the lateral stripe difficult to distinguish. The body of *Osteochilus vittatus* is also distinguished by being more slender, and the dorsal fin is not the magnificent sail-like structure it is with *Osteochilus hasselti.* Seen from underneath, the mouth shows a horseshoe-shaped upper lip which is rough.

OSTEOGLOSSUM BICIRRHOSUM Vandelli / *Arowana*

Range: Guianas and most parts of the Amazon.
Habits: Only small ones may be kept together; big ones are best kept alone.
Water Conditions: Should be moved as little as possible. Temperature 24 to 26°C.
Size: To about 60 cm, but usually much smaller.
Food Requirements: Greatly prefers fishes which can be swallowed whole, but can be trained to take pieces of raw fish, shrimp, etc., from the fingers.

The Arowana gives its viewer a look into an ancient prehistoric world, the Jurassic Age. The Arowana is one of the few remaining living examples of this group. They make very interesting aquarium fishes, but only the largest aquarium will hold a full-grown specimen. Their swimming movements are very lithe and fluid, reminding one of those of a snake. The scales are very large and opalescent, reflecting many colors when the light hits them. The large "landing barge" mouth betrays the predatory nature and healthy appetite. Anyone who decides to keep one of these beauties should have a number of expendable small fishes on hand at all times for food. We have heard of their being trained to accept strips of raw fish from the fingers, which solves the feeding problem when there are no live fishes on hand. Once an Arowana adapts itself to a tank and is given the proper attention, it will usually live to a ripe old age and make an interesting conversation piece. They become very tame and we have had reports that they frequently come up to their owners to be "petted."

Osteochilus vittatus ⬚F⬚⬚D⬚⬚X⬚⬚9⬚⬚3⬚⬚3⬚⬚X⬚⬚N⬚⬚N⬚⬚8⬚   [Dr. Herbert R. Axelrod]
Osteoglossum bicirrhosum ⬚F⬚⬚C⬚⬚X⬚⬚9⬚⬚3⬚⬚4⬚⬚X⬚⬚N⬚⬚N⬚⬚D⬚   [Aaron Norman]

Osteoglossum ferreirai ⬚F⬚C⬚X⬚9⬚3⬚5⬚X⬚N⬚N⬚A [Dr. Herbert R. Axelrod]

Otocinclus affinis ⬚F⬚D⬚X⬚9⬚3⬚6⬚X⬚N⬚N⬚5 [Harald Schultz]

OSTEOGLOSSUM FERREIRAI Kanazawa / *Black Arowana*

Range: Rio Branco tributary of the Rio Negro in Brazil.

Habits: Large specimens won't hesitate to swallow anything they can cram into their very spacious mouths, but neither adults nor young specimens are quarrelsome with fishes not regarded as food; rather unpredictable in temperament, frequently showing disturbance when there is no visible cause for alarm.

Water Conditions: Soft, slightly acid water desirable. Temperature 25 to 28°C.

Size: Wild adult specimens run up to about 40 cm; juveniles of about 8 cm most often seen.

Food Requirements: Variable from individual to individual; some will take prepared aquarium foods, while others refuse all except small live fishes.

In nature, the Black Arowana is usually found in heavily vegetated areas that are shallow and often stagnant. Aquarium water should be soft and slightly acidic. Although this fish will often accept prepared aquarium foods, live foods should be included in their diet. Young Black Arowanas are usually the only specimens available for the average aquarist. Dealers are able to sell the young fish at a much lower price than the adults. Many of the juveniles, however, are offered for sale at such a young age that their yolk-sacs are still attached. These young fish demand greater care than the adults and are much less adaptable to aquarium life.

OTOCINCLUS AFFINIS Steindachner / *Midget Sucker Catfish*

Range: Southeastern Brazil.

Habits: Peaceful.

Water Conditions: Soft, slightly acid water is best, with dense plant growth and good light. Temperature 21 to 29°C.

Size: 5 cm.

Food Requirements: Main staple is algae which are scraped off leaves, rocks and glass sides of the aquarium, but will accept other foods.

This is a good algae-eater for the small tank, or even for the large tank, if enough of them are used. *Otocinclus affinis* busies itself by going around the aquarium using its sucker-like mouth to rasp algae off wherever it may have formed in the aquarium. The fish is particularly useful, because of its size, in removing algae from places which are beneath the notice of large sucker species, like the plecostomus catfishes. But there is a strange thing about this little catfish: there seems to be no middle ground in its adaptability to a given set of tank conditions. The Midget Sucker Catfish will do either very well or very poorly, with no in-between state. Unfortunately, it often works out that the fish does poorly rather than well. This is in many cases directly attributable to a lack of sufficient algal growths (or a lack of the right kind of algae) in the tank to support the fish. Where not enough algae or only the wrong kinds of algae are available, *Otocinclus affinis* will linger for a while but eventually die off. Although the species is bred only infrequently, the feat is not impossible if the species is given good care. Eggs are placed *Corydoras*-fashion against the glass sides of the tank; the small eggs hatch in two days.

OTOCINCLUS ARNOLDI Regan / *Arnold's Sucker Catfish*

Range: La Plata Region.
Habits: Peaceful and will not harm other fishes or plants; cleans algae from plants and rocks.
Water Conditions: Slightly alkaline water and a sunny tank are best. Temperature 23 to 26°C.
Size: To 5.5 cm.
Food Requirements: Tubifex worms are eagerly eaten; the grazing on algae that they do takes care of their vegetable requirements.

Arnold's Sucker Catfish is one of the most useful of all aquarium fishes. The large sucker catfishes often outgrow their quarters and can stir up quite a mess when they are rooting in the bottom. Many species also stake out territories and defend them, getting pretty nasty when doing so. This is not the case with the little *Otocinclus*, which minds its business of grazing on patches of algae and is never a source of annoyance to other fishes. Its small size permits it to get into a lot of nooks and crannies which are not available to its larger cousins and dig out morsels in the form of uneaten food, etc. With the *Otocinclus* we need never worry about shallow-rooted plants being dug out, either. Their only interest lies in what is to be found on the surface of the bottom, and the closest they will come to rooting is when a tubifex worm is found and dragged out. Spawning is very similar to that of the *Corydoras* species. Eggs are fastened to rocks, plant stems and leaves, glass sides or any available solid surface. After two or three days they hatch and begin their never-ending search for food, which may be offered in the form of very fine dried foods.

OTOCINCLUS VITTATUS Regan / *Striped Sucker Catfish*

Range: Rio Paraguay system.
Habits: Peaceful.
Water Conditions: Soft, slightly acid water. Temperature 21 to 28°C.
Size: About 5 cm.
Food Requirements: Prefers algae above all other foods, but some meaty items are taken.

Otocinclus vittatus, like its relatives *O. affinis* and *O. arnoldi*, is considered by aquarists as a miniature version of the larger sucker catfishes. It does an efficient job of eradicating algae, but the fish, being small, has a limited capacity and cannot be relied on to tackle too big a job. One *Otocinclus* in a small tank will suffice, but in a larger tank the hobbyist must be prepared to use more *Otocinclus* or replace them with larger sucker catfishes. This, of course, is based on the assumption that the hobbyist is keeping the little sucker cats primarily for their value as algae-eaters, although some hobbyists prefer to keep them for their interesting habits alone, taking care of the job of algae eradication through their own efforts.

Otocinclus arnoldi $\boxed{F}\boxed{D}\boxed{X}\boxed{9}\boxed{3}\boxed{7}\boxed{X}\boxed{N}\boxed{N}\boxed{5}$ [G. Wolfsheimer]

Otocinclus vittatus $\boxed{F}\boxed{D}\boxed{X}\boxed{9}\boxed{3}\boxed{8}\boxed{X}\boxed{N}\boxed{N}\boxed{5}$ [Harald Schultz]

Oxyeleotris lineolatus F R X 9 3 9 X N N 9
Oxygaster anomalura F D X 9 4 0 X N N 7

[G. Wolfsheimer]
[Dr. Herbert R. Axelrod]

OXYELEOTRIS LINEOLATUS (Steindachner) / *Lined Sleeper*

Range: Queensland, Australia and New Guinea.
Habits: Will eat anything that will fit into its mouth; a predator not suitable for the community aquarium.
Water Conditions: Hard, alkaline water. Temperature about 21°C.
Size: Over 48 cm when fully mature; smaller in aquaria.
Food Requirements: Live or frozen foods.

Oxyeleotris lineolatus is a predator that can grow to over 2.5 kg in weight. They are better known as table fish than they are as aquarium fish. In the wild this fish is seldom seen in the winter. In the summer, however, it can be found close to the surface of the water and is easily caught in a landing net. As a sports fish this species provides little sport as it is very sluggish and will not readily accept bait. It is a fish well worth eating, having white, firm flesh and a pleasant flavor. The Lined Sleeper has been reported to have spawned under aquarium conditions. The male is larger than the female and has longer fins and brighter colors. The male selects the nesting site, pursues the female and later aerates the eggs. The eggs are adhesive and will attach to plants, gravel or rocks.

OXYGASTER ANOMALURA van Hasselt / *Knife Barb*

Range: Thailand, Java, Borneo, Sumatra and Malaysia.
Habits: Peaceful and active; a jumper.
Water Conditions: Soft, slightly acid water is best. Temperature 21 to 30°C.
Size: Up to 13 cm.
Food Requirements: Will accept live, dry and frozen foods; despite its size, this fish prefers small foods.

The Knife Barb, so named for its keeled or "sharp" belly, is a harmless cyprinid which is best suited to larger tanks because it gets big and because it does best in a tank in which it has plenty of room to swim freely. Rarely imported, *Oxygaster anomalura* is not in great demand; it is neither a pretty fish nor is it especially interesting, so no one seems to miss it, although it was offered some years ago on the aquarium market. All of the *Oxygaster* species are restless, nervous fishes. They swim back and forth from one side of the aquarium to the other almost continually, like the *Danio, Brachydanio* and some *Puntius* species. However, *Oxygaster anomalura* keeps more to the upper reaches of the water than to lower and middle reaches; its mouth is definitely adapted to feeding at the surface. The Knife Barb has not been bred in this country, but a spawning report on *Oxygaster atpar* states that the mating pair go through vigorous circular motions before the eggs are laid. The eggs are small and non-adhesive, and they hatch in about a day at a temperature of 26°C. The fry remain near the surface, where they can easily be fed on dust-fine dry foods.

OXYGASTER OXYGASTROIDES (Bleeker) / *Glass Barb*

Range: Thailand and the Greater Sunda Islands.
Habits: Harmless to other fishes and plants; likes to swim in schools.
Water Conditions: Soft, slightly acid water. Temperature 24 to 27°C.
Size: To 20 cm in native waters; in the aquarium about 13 cm.
Food Requirements: Prefers live foods which remain near the surface, like mosquito larvae; can be accustomed to dry foods.

The Glass Barb loses most of its claim to the popular name as it becomes bigger. In their natural water this species attains 20 cm in length, but in the aquarium a fish half that size is considered large. Small fish have a very glassy transparency, much of which is lost later. The dark spots in the caudal lobe also tend to disappear in time and the fish become very plain, greenish silvery with a dark stripe running from behind the gill-plate to the caudal base and another much narrower stripe from behind the belly to the bottom of the caudal base. The upturned mouth indicates that it gets most of its food at or near the surface. Another thing to remember is the size of the pectoral fins. This is the mark of the jumper, a fish which can easily "take off" from the surface and land on your living room rug. Never keep them in an uncovered aquarium.

PACHYPANCHAX HOMALONOTUS (Dumeril) / *Green Panchax*

Range: Madagascar.
Habits: Peaceful with fishes too large to be swallowed.
Water Conditions: Not critical; salt can be added. Temperature 22 to 26°C.
Size: Up to 10 cm; usually smaller.
Food Requirements: Live, frozen or freeze-dried foods accepted.

Although the Green Panchax is much less common than its relative *Pachypanchax playfairi*, in the opinion of many aquarists it is both more beautiful and more ideally suited to the aquarium. The first record of this species being kept in the aquarium appeared in 1951, but it was not generally made available until 1953. Although the upturned mouth would seem to indicate a species given to surface-dwelling, the Green Panchax is in fact at home at all levels of the aquarium. Spawning usually occurs in the morning in fine-leaved plants. The adults will eat the eggs if they find them. The male is a strong driver, and for this reason it is desirable to use a fairly large aquarium or several females. Two or three eggs are generally deposited at a time. Occasionally a female may extrude several eggs at one time which remain attached to her vent until they are brushed off on plants. Unfertilized eggs turn white within half an hour. Hatching takes from 14 to 16 days at 24°C. Fry are large enough to accept newly hatched brine shrimp upon becoming free-swimming. This is a species best kept in groups of three or more. Individuals which have been separated will fight when reunited.

Oxygaster oxygastroides ⒻⓇⓍ⑨④①ⓍⓃⓃ⑨ [Dr. Herbert R. Axelrod]

Pachypanchax homalonotus Ⓕ④Ⓧ⑨④②ⓍⓃⓃ④ [G. Wolfsheimer]

Pachypanchax playfairi ⬚F⬚⬚A⬚⬚X⬚⬚9⬚⬚4⬚⬚3⬚⬚X⬚⬚N⬚⬚N⬚⬚8⬚ [H. Hansen, Aquarium Berlin]
Panaque nigrolineatus ⬚F⬚⬚D⬚⬚X⬚⬚9⬚⬚4⬚⬚4⬚⬚X⬚⬚N⬚⬚N⬚⬚D⬚ [Dr. Herbert R. Axelrod]

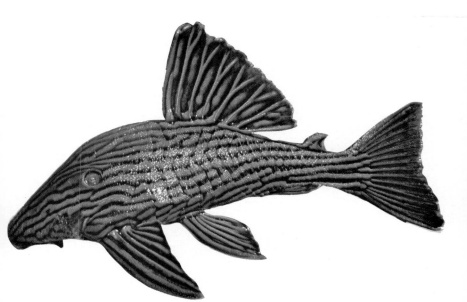

PACHYPANCHAX PLAYFAIRI (Günther) / *Playfair's Panchax*

Range: East Africa, Seychelles and Madagascar.
Habits: Apt to be a bit "bossy" with smaller fishes; should be kept in a sunny, well-planted aquarium.
Water Conditions: Neutral to slightly alkaline water. Temperature 23 to 26°C.
Size: About 8 cm.
Food Requirements: Live foods of all kinds, but will take dried foods if hungry.

Here is a fish you can recommend unhesitatingly to anyone who wants to begin with an "easy" egglaying species. Playfair's Panchax will withstand just about any abuse you can hand out and merrily keep on spawning. This is a species which will lay a small number of eggs daily over a period of time. Males are active drivers, and many breeders keep several extra females so that the male can divide his attentions. Eggs are hung in bushy plant leaves near the surface, where they can be seen hanging by fine threads. The shells are hard enough that they can be picked out carefully with the fingers and placed in a separate tank for hatching. This takes place in 10 to 14 days, and the youngsters can swallow newly hatched brine shrimp at once. Growth is rapid, and the young must be sorted frequently because of the disparity in size between the younger and the older ones. Once they have reached a size where they can no longer swallow each other, all is well. *Pachypanchax playfairi* has an unusual trait which is worth mentioning: the scales, especially along the back, stand out instead of lying close to the body. This is natural and must not be diagnosed as a disease symptom.

PANAQUE NIGROLINEATUS (Peters) / *Panaque*

Range: North-central South America.
Habits: Peaceful with other species but aggressive among themselves.
Water Conditions: Not critical. Temperature 21 to 27°C.
Size: Usually seen at 15 or 18 cm; much larger in nature.
Food Requirements: Accepts most aquarium fare but should be provided with vegetable substances as well.

This species has one big drawback: it gets very large, and only the smallest of available individuals are suitable to housing in tanks of 40 liters or less. It is a daytime hider that dislikes bright light and does most of its feeding at night; individuals that have become accustomed to community tank life over a long time, however, lose some of their shyness and develop a greater tendency to come out into the light. In any event, the species should be provided with a suitable resting place within the tank, because besides being averse to bright light it also is territorial and wants a place to call its own. *Panaque nigrolineatus* has not yet spawned under aquarium conditions; no doubt the species requires a very large tank to house the prospective spawners, which would be very large at maturity.

PANGASIUS SUTCHI Fowler / *Siamese Shark*

Range: Malay Peninsula.
Habits: Relatively peaceful, but will eat fishes small enough to swallow.
Water Conditions: Not critical, but soft acid water preferred. Temperature 22 to 27°C.
Size: 18 cm, but usually smaller.
Food Requirements: Prefers live or frozen foods.

The Siamese Shark is a member of the catfish family Schilbeidae, which has contributed relatively few species to the aquarium. Other species of this family which have found their way to the aquarium are *Irvineia voltae* and *Eutropiellus debauwi*. The latter species bears a great resemblance to *P. sutchi*. *E. debauwi* has much wider white stripes than *P. sutchi*. Like many members of the family Schilbeidae, the Siamese Shark does not possess the characteristic bottom-haunting habits we tend to associate with many other catfishes. Like the Glass Catfish, the Siamese Shark schools in mid-water. Unlike the Glass Catfish, the Siamese Shark is constantly on the move. Schools of this species frequently work themselves into the corners of the aquarium, where they make ceaseless circles up and down the glass. *P. sutchi* has a tendency toward hysteria. When frightened they dash madly around the aquarium, colliding with the sides, rocks, plants and other fishes. These flights are generally terminated by the fish sinking to the bottom where they lie on their sides or backs until they recover. Normally this species is an extremely graceful swimmer which comes to the top periodically for air. *Pangasius sutchi* is a schooling fish which is extremely uncomfortable without company.

PANTODON BUCHHOLZI Peters / *Butterfly Fish*

Range: Tropical West Africa.
Habits: Harmless to other fishes, but better kept by themselves to prevent damage to their filamentous ventral fin extensions.
Water Conditions: Soft, slightly acid water is preferable. The tank should not be too heavily planted; it must have a large surface and be covered. Temperature 23 to 27°C.
Size: To 10 cm.
Food Requirements: Prefers live insects but it can be trained to take bits of shrimp.

Pantodon buchholzi is the only species in the genus, and the genus *Pantodon* is the only one in the family Pantodontidae. Its appearance is also unique. The upturned mouth tells us that it is a surface feeder, and the size of the mouth is an indication that not only mosquitoes and flies but also larger beetles and the like can be handled with ease. The large pectoral fins, which when outspread resemble a butterfly's wings, can be used for gliding over short distances in much the same manner as the oceanic flyingfishes. The Butterfly Fish inhabits weedy, slow-flowing pools where it lies almost motionless near the surface and waits for its prey to pass by.

945

Pangasius sutchi ⬚F⬚D⬚X⬚9⬚4⬚5⬚X⬚N⬚N⬚A   [Dr. Herbert R. Axelrod]

Pantodon buchholzi ⬚F⬚D⬚X⬚9⬚4⬚6⬚X⬚N⬚N⬚A   [H. J. Richter]

1. *Paracheirodon innesi*   F H X 9 4 7 X N N 4
2. *Paracheirodon innesi*   F Q X 9 4 8 X N N 4

[H. J. Richter]

PARACHEIRODON INNESI (Myers) / *Neon Tetra*

Range: Upper course of the Rio Solimoes (= Amazon) and Rio Purus.
Habits: Very peaceful; should be kept only with small fishes or in a tank of their own.
Water Conditions: Soft, clear, slightly acid water is preferred and brings out their best colors. Best temperature about 24°C.
Size: Maximum 4 cm; most specimens seen are about 2.5 cm or less.
Food Requirements: Medium or finely ground dried foods, with occasional feedings of small live foods.

The Neon Tetra is undoubtedly one of the most popular among the egglaying freshwater fishes in aquaria today. Probably its only drawback is its small size, which would make it a meal for larger fishes if put into an aquarium with them. Like the other small tetra species, their brilliance is made even more effective if they are kept in a school of a dozen or more. For contrast, their aquarium should be given a dark bottom. Black gravel is best. The Neon Tetra has an interesting history. It was discovered by natives who showed it to A. Rabaut while he was on a collecting expedition searching for butterflies. Realizing the importance of what he had, he brought back some with him to France. The first ones to reach America were shipped from Germany on the ill-fated dirigible "Hindenburg," which was to crash a short time later. Breeding this beautiful fish is not an impossibility, but many attempts result in failure. The most important ingredient is soft, acid water and a compatible pair. The eggs are very sensitive to light.

1. *Paracheirodon innesi* in an aquarium (p947).
2. *P. innesi* mating pair in an embrace (p947).

Paracheirodon innesi, the Neon Tetra. Photo by J. Elias.

PARAILIA LONGIFILIS Boulenger / *Mottled Glass Catfish*

Range: Zaire, in the region of the Stanley Pool.
Habits: Very peaceful.
Water Conditions: Not critical, as long as extremes are avoided. Temperature 21 to 27°C.
Size: About 10 cm.
Food Requirements: Will accept all usual aquarium foods, although some individuals take a long time to get accustomed to accepting prepared foods.

This is a species of catfish that makes an occasional appearance in shipments of Glass Catfishes from Africa, and although it has much less of the transparency that has given the Asiatic *Kryptopterus* and allied species their common "Glass Catfish" name, they are usually sold under that name. In general body shape and general deportment they resemble *Kryptopterus* greatly, but they are not even in the same family. *Parailia longifilis* is in the family Schilbeidae, whereas *Kryptopterus* species are in the family Siluridae. *Parailia* is a mild-mannered fish, seldom looking for trouble when kept in a mixed community, yet it is not above swallowing its tankmates if they are small enough to be ingested and fall into the catfish's path during its nighttime prowling of the tank.

PARAPOCRYPTES SERPERASTER (Richardson) / *Slim Mudskipper*

Range: Southeast Asia from India to China, most numerous in Malayan Archipelago.
Habits: Aggressive.
Water Conditions: Warm, brackish water required. Temperature 24 to 27°C.
Size: To about 25 cm.
Food Requirements: Will accept only rich, meaty foods, in most cases only living foods; tubifex worms, earthworms and small live fishes are accepted, and will gladly take soft-bodied insects.

The Slim Mudskipper is not in the same genus *(Periophthalmus)* as the mudskippers best known to aquarium hobbyists. But the similarity in looks, temperament and odd habits is striking enough to make this fish's common name quite appropriate. *Parapocryptes* is more directly tied to a watery existence than is *Periophthalmus,* because whereas the latter often leaves the water and emerges onto completely dry land, sometimes even climbing up into mangrove branches, *Parapocryptes* never ventures onto completely dry terrain but strays from the water only as far as mud flats.

This is not an easy fish to keep. In the first place, it demands live food, and even when it is provided with an adequately rich and varied diet it is susceptible to fungal infections of the fins. *Parapocryptes* also is a sluggish fish, remaining mostly in one place and showing liveliness only when offered food or when frightened. The species also is disturbed when maintained in tanks that are brightly lighted, even though it is not a strictly nocturnal species.

Parailia longifilis ⌈F⌉⌈D⌉⌈X⌉⌈9⌉⌈4⌉⌈9⌉⌈X⌉⌈N⌉⌈N⌉⌈A⌉

Parapocryptes serperaster ⌈F⌉⌈D⌉⌈X⌉⌈9⌉⌈5⌉⌈0⌉⌈X⌉⌈N⌉⌈N⌉⌈D⌉

[K. Paysan]

[R. Zukal]

Parauchenipterus galeatus F D X 9 5 1 X N N C [Harald Schultz]

Parauchenoglanis guttatus F D X 9 5 2 X N N B [Braz Walker]

PARAUCHENIPTERUS GALEATUS (Linnaeus) / *Starry Cat*

Range: Northern and eastern South America.
Habits: Generally peaceful, but larger specimens will eat smaller fishes if given the chance.
Water Conditions: Slightly acid, soft water. Temperature 23 to 26°C.
Size: To 18 cm.
Food Requirements: Will accept most aquarium fish foods, but prefers tubifex worms or frozen foods.

The Starry Cat requires a medium to large tank. Although it will accept most prepared aquarium foods, live foods such as tubifex worms should be fed from time to time. *P. galeatus* should only be kept with fishes its own size or larger as it will eat smaller fishes.

PARAUCHENOGLANIS GUTTATUS (Lönnberg)
African Flathead Catfish

Range: Cameroon; Congo basin.
Habits: Nocturnal, and shy and retiring, so should be provided with rocks, caves, etc.; predatory, so do not keep with fishes that might be swallowed.
Water Conditions: Not critical; tolerates most local water types quite well, but, as with other fishes, extremes of pH or hardness should be avoided. A temperature range of 21 to 27°C.
Size: Up to 30 cm.
Food Requirements: Prefers earthworms and other live foods but also relishes ground beef heart, chopped fish and other meat- or fish-based foods; some individuals will accept cooked oatmeal (rolled oats).

Parauchenoglanis guttatus is an attractive member of the catfish family Bagridae. It is found mostly in the Cameroon region and is very similar in appearance and closely related to *P. macrostoma*, the African Spotted Catfish, which comes from Gabon. They can be distinguished most easily by the length of the barbels or whiskers, the outer mandibular pair in *P. guttatus* reaching to the edge, base or middle of the pectoral fins, whereas in *P. macrostoma* these same barbels extend to the end of the pectoral fins. There are also color differences, *P. macrostoma* with transverse series of spots forming about five distinct bars and the fins less spotted than in *P. guttatus*.

The African Flathead Catfish is a typical nocturnal predator which spends the daylight hours in retirement under rocks, in caves or otherwise obscured. With care and patience it can be taught to come out for food while the lights are on (not too brightly please) or before dark. Newly acquired fish, however, require feeding at night. It may even be necessary to place food almost directly in their mouths – which can be difficult if there are tankmates that will snap up the morsels of food right from under their noses. The type of food presents no problem as the African Flathead Catfish will eat a wide variety of food. It will consume rather large quantities of ground beef heart, chopped or scraped fish (fresh or frozen), earthworms or lean meat.

PARAUCHENOGLANIS MACROSTOMA (Pellegrin)
African Spotted Catfish

Range: Tropical West Africa (Gabon).
Habits: Peaceful; usually remains hidden in daylight and comes out at night.
Water Conditions: Soft, neutral to slightly acid water. Temperature 24 to 27°C.
Size: To 25 cm in natural waters; much smaller in the aquarium.
Food Requirements: All sorts of live or frozen foods.

The African Spotted Catfish when fully grown is recorded to attain a size of 25 cm, and at this size it would be adaptable only to very large aquaria. This species is very attractive, but when placed in a large well-planted aquarium even a diligent search often fails to find them. Add to this the fact that they confine most of their activity to the night hours, and it is easily understood why they haven't exactly caused a furor in aquarium circles. Like so many of the other African catfishes, this species has not been spawned in captivity. Probably there have never been enough of them on hand to make any real attempts in this direction, but it is a fairly safe bet that even if a few shipments came in the story would still be the same.

PARODON PONGOENSE (Allen) / *Pongo Pongo*

Range: Peruvian Amazon, Ecuador and Colombia.
Habits: Peaceful; prefer to school.
Water Conditions: Soft acid water is preferred. Temperature from 23 to 30°C.
Size: About 5 cm.
Food Requirements: Prefers live foods but can readily take frozen brine shrimp and prepared dry foods.

One day while visiting a petshop my (HRA) attention was called to this fish because of its unbelievable swimming habits. The fish never stopped swimming at a very rapid rate in a rather tight circle in schools. There were about twelve fish in the school, and they swam very quickly in a circle about 10 cm in diameter, making a complete circle about twice every three seconds. They always swam about 5 cm off the gravel in the aquarium, which was about 30 cm deep. Their activity was anything but relaxing and reminded one immediately that this was probably an unnatural behavior, because the fish were imprisoned in such a small area. I took the fish to my own aquarium and within a few minutes they had schooled again and started the same "ratrace" even though I placed them in a 200-liter aquarium! This behavior didn't seem to disturb the other fishes, though; they all stayed away from the circling group. The only time they broke schooling was when food was introduced into the aquarium. They swam very fast while feeding, but this is a usual characid characteristic.

Parauchenoglanis macrostoma F D X 9 5 3 X N N 8   [Aaron Norman]
Parodon pongoense F R X 9 5 4 X N N 5   [Dr. Herbert R. Axelrod]

2. *Pelvicachromis pulcher* F E X 9 5 9 X N N 6
3. *Pelvicachromis pulcher* F E X 9 6 0 X N N 6

[Dr. Herbert R. Axelrod]

PELVICACHROMIS PULCHER (Boulenger) / *Kribensis*

Range: Tropical West Africa, especially the Niger Delta.
Habits: Peaceful; does some digging, but mostly under rocks, and plants are seldom uprooted.
Water Conditions: Not critical. Temperature 23 to 25°C.
Size: Males up to 8 cm; females to 6 cm.
Food Requirements: Live and frozen foods.

The Kribensis (so-called because it was long known as *Pelmatochromis kribensis)* was an immediate hit when it was first introduced in the early 1950's. One look at the pictures of this georgeous fish is enough to make it obvious why. It is not large enough to really put it in a class with the big cichlids, and at the same time it is rather large to be called a dwarf cichlid. Its behavior in mixed company is very mild, but for its most appealing feature, just look at the colors! It is best when first attempting to spawn a pair to keep them in separate tanks until the female becomes heavy with eggs. The ideal spawning site is a flowerpot with a notch knocked out of the rim and set upside down on the bottom. There will be a great deal of activity, the male carrying out huge mouthfuls of gravel from inside the flowerpot, when suddenly one day both will disappear, to come out very rarely. Then a very comical situation develops. The little female will forcibly eject the male every time he tries to go in. Put him in another tank or he may get hurt. The female takes complete charge of the eggs and young but should be removed when the youngsters become free-swimming.

The male is more slender, bigger, and has a broader forehead than the female. On the edge of his dorsal fin there is a silvery, gold-tinted stripe which ends in the point. In the upper part of the tail fin there are one to five round dark spots which are edged in light yellow. The fins are violet in color. The female has a large wine-red patch on each side of her body.

1. *Pelvicachromis pulcher* mating pair in an aquarium (p958).
2. *P. pulcher* showing dark body stripe (p959).
3. *P. pulcher* lacking mating colors (p959).

Pelvicachromis pulcher at the spawning site. Photo by R. Zukal.

PELVICACHROMIS TAENIATUS (Boulenger) / *Striped Kribensis*

Range: Lower Niger River, West Africa.
Habits: Generally peaceful, even timid except when breeding.
Water Conditions: Soft, slightly acid water is best; the tank should be well planted and provide hiding places. Temperature 24 to 26°C.
Size: Male 8 cm; female slightly smaller.
Food Requirements: Live foods are preferred, but finely chopped beef heart is also accepted and even relished.

Pelvicachromis taeniatus is only slightly different from its much better-known cousin, *Pelvicachromis pulcher*. Both come from West Africa, and the few specimens which are imported now and then are frequently sold as *Pelvicachromis pulcher*. Both are beautiful and highly desirable species, and their habits are identical. When the female becomes heavy with eggs and the male begins to search for a spawning site, it has been found that the best one is a flowerpot with a notch about one inch in diameter cut or broken out of the edge. This is partially filled with gravel, set upright in a dark corner and covered with a piece of slate. The male will soon be swimming in through the notch and returning with mouthfuls of gravel. Then one day it will be noticed that the female has taken possession and will not let him enter. A careful lifting of the slate will reveal that she is guarding eggs. In about ten days the young are free-swimming.

1. *Pelvicachromis taeniatus* male in breeding colors (p962).
2. *P. taeniatus* breeding pair with brood (p962).

Pelvicachromis taeniatus. Photo by G. Marcuse.

1. *Pelvicachromis taeniatus* ♂ F E X 9 6 1 X N N 8   [H. J. Richter]
2. *Pelvicachromis taeniatus* F Q X 9 6 2 X N N 8   [H. J. Richter]

1. *Periophthalmus barbarus* F D X 9 6 3 X N N B [H. Hansen, Aquarium Berlin]
2. *Periophthalmus barbarus* F D X 9 6 4 X N N D [H. Hansen, Aquarium Berlin]

PERIOPHTHALMUS BARBARUS (Linnaeus) / *Mudskipper*

Range: East Africa to Australia.
Habits: Cannot be combined with any other group of fishes; shy at first, but later can be tamed effectively.
Water Conditions: Water must have salt, ½ teaspoon to the liter, added; there should be an area where the fish can climb out. Temperature 24 to 27°C.
Size: To 15 cm.
Food Requirements: Worms and other living insects.

The Mudskipper looks as though it were a fish which began developing into a frog and changed its mind when the metamorphosis was half completed. Its head with the eyes set into lumps on top certainly has a frog-like appearance. The powerful pectoral fins are set in muscular elongations which resemble short forelegs and permit the fish to move over land with amazing nimbleness. They are in fact clumsy swimmers and can move more swiftly over land than they can swim in the water. Their habitat is usually a stretch of muddy tide-flats which become uncovered when the tide moves out. There is almost always a tangle of mangrove roots, and the Mudskippers are very adept at climbing onto these to get a wider range of vision. In the aquarium Mudskippers are not the easiest fish in the world to keep. Their tank should be shallow and have a large surface. Their water, what there is of it, should have about a half teaspoon of salt added to it per liter. The sand should be sloped to come out of the water, and a few flat rocks may be placed at the water's edge. It is important that the air be warm and moist, so the tank must be kept tightly covered.

1. *Periophthalmus barbarus* sitting on a rock out of the water (p963).
2. *P. barbarus* in an aquarium (p963).

PERIOPHTHALMUS PAPILIO Bloch & Schneider
Butterfly Mudskipper

Range: Western Africa from Senegal to the Congo.
Habits: Cannot be maintained with any other class of fishes; they soon overcome their initial shyness.
Water Conditions: Water must have a salt content, about a ½ teaspoon to the liter; areas must be provided for the fish to climb out onto a dry perch.
Size: Attains a size of 16 cm.
Food Requirements: Living insects or small earthworms; tubifex worms are also welcome; can be trained to take other foods.

The expression "helpless as a fish out of water" does not apply to the mudskippers. They actually seem to prefer the land to the water and are awkward swimmers. Students of ecology can see in these fishes a remarkable adaptation of a creature to a highly individual biotope. Mudskippers inhabit muddy tidal flats where very little water is left at low tide. The air is usually swarming with mosquitoes and other flying insects and the frog-like eyes of this fish give it an immense visual range. Observe the pectoral fins, which have evolved into limbs with which the fish can crawl very effectively. The tail can be bent forward to act like a spring and kick the fish wherever he aims his body with those pectoral fins (or "limbs," if you like). Mudskippers make interesting pets and are not exceptionally difficult to keep if their requirements are understood. They become tame once they are accustomed to their surroundings and even take tidbits from the fingers. Coming from coastal water as they do, they require some salt in their water, about a half teaspoon per liter. Their tank should be kept covered at all times to keep in the heat and prevent drafts.

PETITELLA GEORGIAE Géry and Boutiere / *False Rummy-Nose*

Range: Upper Amazon basin.
Habits: Peaceful; best kept in schools.
Water Conditions: Soft, acidic water is preferred but is not crucial. Best temperature is 23 to 25°C.
Size: To 8 cm.
Food Requirements: Accepts all standard aquarium foods and especially relishes live freshwater crustaceans like daphnia.

Petitella georgiae, first described in 1964, happens to be involved in one of the most persistent cases of look-alike mixups that the aquarium hobby has known. The similarity to *Hemigrammus rhodostomus* in external distinguishing marks is indeed remarkable, and it is difficult for even a trained eye to distinguish between the two fishes. The problem was resolved only because the famous ichthyologist Dr. Jacques Géry was unable to satisfy himself as to why there should be a disagreement in anatomical features between samples of *Hemigrammus rhodostomus* collected on the upper Amazon around Iquitos, Peru by himself and specimens coming from the lower Amazon (which is the origin of the specimens described by Ernst Ahl as the basis for naming *Hemigrammus rhodostomus*, the original Rummy-Nose Tetra, in 1924). Géry tracked the differences down and determined that they were sufficient in themselves to place the False Rummy-Nose Tetra as an entirely different species and even to place it in a different genus. The structure of the teeth is especially different in the two fishes, and tooth structure is a very important morphological character in the taxonomic placement of the tetras. In an excellently detailed study that appeared in *Tropical Fish Hobbyist* in the April, 1972 issue ("An Astonishing Similarity: *Hemigrammus rhodostomus* and *Petitella georgiae*"), Dr. Géry presented three major possible explanations for the similarity in looks of the two species.

Petitella georgiae and *Hemigrammus rhodostomus* are similar in all respects as regards their care in the aquarium, except that *Petitella georgiae* can tolerate slightly lower temperatures.

Periophthalmus papilio F D X 9 6 5 X N N B   [G. Marcuse]
Petitella georgiae F Q X 9 6 6 X N N 8   [S. Frank]

1. *Petrotilapia tridentiger* F D X 9 6 7 X N N E [Dr. Herbert R. Axelrod]
2. *Petrotilapia tridentiger* F A X 9 6 8 X N N A [Dr. Warren E. Burgess]

PETROTILAPIA TRIDENTIGER Trewavas / *Blue Petrotilapia*

Range: Lake Malawi, Africa.
Habits: Quarrelsome toward other fishes and therefore should be kept by themselves.
Water Conditions: Hard, alkaline water; the addition of salt is indicated, one-quarter tablespoon per liter. Temperature 24 to 27°C.
Size: Males 10 cm; females a little smaller.
Food Requirements: Live or freeze-dried foods; add some foods of vegetable origin.

Petrotilapia tridentiger is one of the attractive species which originate in Lake Malawi, Africa and are imported for aquarists all over the world. *Petrotilapia* is said to be a mouthbrooder. Males have large yellow spots on the anal fin. These spots have an interesting application: when the female has finished picking up the eggs she has laid, the male spreads out his anal fin before her. She sees the spots and tries to pick them up, thinking she has missed some eggs. Instead she gets a mouthful of sperm, which fertilizes the eggs she has already put in her mouth. Lake Malawi, like Lake Tanganyika, has water that is very hard. Many aquarists have found it advantageous to use ordinary non-iodized table salt to make their water so that the fish thrive in it. A quarter tablespoon per liter should do it. Trouble is, if the salt concentration becomes very heavy you may have to make do without plants—but then, few aquarists keep live plants in lake cichlid tanks anyway.

1. *Petrotilapia tridentiger* has a mouth equipped with many rows of tricuspid teeth (p967).
2. *P. tridentiger* in a photo tank (p967).

Petrotilapia tridentiger guarding its territory.

PHAGO MACULATUS Ahl / *African Pike Characin*

Range: West Africa, in the Niger River.
Habits: A decidedly nasty fish which will kill for the sheer pleasure of killing.
Water Conditions: Neutral, medium-soft water best. Temperature 23 to 24°C.
Size: Up to 20 cm, but usually seen much smaller.
Food Requirements: Wants plenty of meaty foods, preferably live fishes, although it will also accept dead ones.

This mean fish is seldom available because of the irregularity of West African fish shipments, but you can bet that *Phago* is not missed except by a few hobbyists who are willing to put up with its vicious nature for the sake of owning an oddity. In effect, the African Pike Characin is the piscatorial counterpart of the weasel, for *Phago*, like the weasel, kills more than it needs to satisfy its hunger. It almost seems that the fish takes pleasure in killing, and *Phago* even goes the weasel one better by torturing its victims before dispatching them. Most imported specimens are small youngsters. Some authorities place this fish in a family distinct from the family Characidae, in the family Citharinidae.

PHALLICHTHYS AMATES (Miller) / *Merry Widow*

Range: Atlantic coastal regions from Guatemala to northern Panama.
Habits: Peaceful toward other fishes, but very fond of eating its own young.
Water Conditions: Slightly alkaline water is best. Temperature 22 to 24°C.
Size: Males 3 cm; females 7 cm.
Food Requirements: Should have some algae on which to nibble, as well as prepared, frozen and live foods.

The Merry Widow was a very popular livebearer several decades ago, but since then there have been many other more colorful fishes to attract the attention of the hobbyist, and it is rarely seen except in the collections of those who specialize in keeping the lesser-known livebearing fishes. An usual feature of the male of this species is an exceptionally long gonopodium. Males have six to twelve fine vertical bands on their sides and yellowish fins. In the female, the vertical bands are absent and the fish has an overall paler coloration. Although this species is relatively easy to breed, live foods should be fed as a conditioner. Plant food should also be included in their diet. The brood number in a large female is about 45. The young are fully developed at birth and independent of their parents. Growth is very rapid. This is a peaceful species well-suited to a community aquarium. Nevertheless, the parents are known to vigorously pursue the fry.

Phago maculatus F D X 9 6 9 X N N A   [K. Paysan]
Phallichthys amates F R X 9 7 0 X N N 7   [G.J.M. Timmerman]

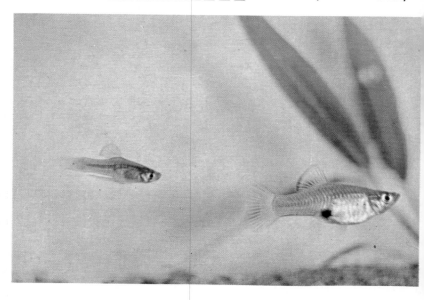

Phalloceros caudomaculatus ⬛F⬛R⬛X⬛9⬛7⬛1⬛X⬛N⬛N⬛6 [R. Zukal]
Phenacogaster pectinatus ⬛F⬛D⬛X⬛9⬛7⬛2⬛X⬛N⬛N⬛5 [Dr. Herbert R. Axelrod]

PHALLOCEROS CAUDOMACULATUS (Hensel) / *Caudo*

Range: From Rio de Janeiro to Paraguay and Uruguay.
Habits: Peaceful at all times; not greatly inclined to eat their young if well fed.
Water Conditions: Slightly alkaline water that is well filtered and clean; the tank should stand in a sunny location. Temperature 23 to 26°C.
Size: Males up to 3 cm; females to 6 cm.
Food Requirements: Small sizes of live and prepared foods, supplemented with algae which is nibbled from plants and glass sides.
Color Variations: Yellowish to golden with black irregular markings.

This is the little fish with the big name. The original "Caudo" is a nondescript little fish which has never found any favor, but this one with the yellowish background and black peppered markings is at least popular enough to be seen occasionally. There is also a golden variety with black markings, but this is uncommon. In this species we have a real disparity in size between the sexes, the female being about twice the size of the male. His 3-cm size makes him an unlikely candidate for the community aquarium unless his companions are all small fishes like himself who would not swallow or bully him. Females are not very productive, and it must be expected that a percentage of the young will revert to the original coloring. The fry are a little delicate at first, but once they begin growing the battle is over. The author (HRA) has always considered the Caudo as a nice little fish which deserves a more respected place in the livebearing group, but in these days of fancy Guppies and a multitude of brilliantly colored breeds of other livebearers, this not unattractive little fellow has fallen into a more or less "ugly duckling" role which it does not deserve.

PHENACOGASTER PECTINATUS (Cope) / *Pectinatus*

Range: Middle and upper Amazon basin.
Habits: Generally peaceful at all times.
Water Conditions: Soft, slightly acid water. Temperature 22 to 27°C.
Size: About 5 cm.
Food Requirements: This species is omnivorous and should be given a mixed diet of plant and animal matter; it will accept prepared flake food but prefers small live or frozen foods.

This species is a lively and very peaceful shoaling fish. In nature it feeds upon aquatic plants, drifting insects and, to a certain extent, the water's surface film. *P. pectinatus* will thrive on small foods such as brine shrimp or daphnia. Tufts of fine-leaved plants should be placed in the aquarium if spawning is to be tried. The spawning ritual is often violent, with fish diving at each other around the aquarium and finally into the plants. If there is a successful breeding, remove the parents before they eat their eggs.

PIMELODELLA GRACILIS (Cuvier & Valenciennes) / *Slender Pimelodella*

Range: Northern Amazon region into Venezuela.
Habits: Peaceful with any fish it cannot swallow; nocturnal.
Water Conditions: Not sensitive; best is neutral to slightly alkaline water. Temperature 24 to 27°C.
Size: Usually to about 18 cm, but has been recorded to twice that size.
Food Requirements: A very greedy eater with strictly carnivorous habits; tubifex worms are consumed very eagerly.

The Slender Pimelodella gets rather large in the aquarium but is otherwise a peaceful fish when kept with others that it cannot swallow. It becomes very numerous in its native waters. Scientists who have studied this species in its natural habitat mention running into hordes of a very similar *Pimelodella* species in the Takatu River in Guyana. During the latter part of the dry season when the river is very low, thousands of squirming, whiskery pimelodellas can easily be caught in the collector's seines. Most collectors find this species so numerous that they are thrown back and the collectors concentrate on rarer species. Prolific as they are in their native waters, there is no record of their breeding in the aquarium. They are greedy eaters and feedings must be generous in order to prevent the fish with them from being cheated out of their fair share of the food.

PIMELODUS CLARIAS (Bloch) / *Spotted Pimelodus*

Range: Central America south to central South America.
Habits: Peaceful with fishes too large to swallow; nocturnal.
Water Conditions: Any clean water suits this hardy fish. Temperature 20 to 26°C.
Size: To 30 cm; only young specimens are suitable for the average tank.
Food Requirements: Larger live foods like cut-up earthworms are preferred, but other foods like chunks of lean beef are also relished.

This handsome catfish looks very much like some of the *Synodontis* species from Africa or *Mystus* from Asia. Because of the large size it attains (about 30 cm), it is not highly suitable for the average home aquarium when it reaches maturity. It has a very wide distribution, all the way from Central America down to central South America. Unfortunately it becomes most active at night and prefers to remain hidden in the daytime. As with most nocturnal fishes, they are seen most frequently in a well-planted tank which does not receive a great deal of sunlight. In such a tank they feel secure and make themselves quite at home. This is not an algae-eating fish. Generous feedings of such foods as cut-up earthworms or other animal fodders should be provided. Chopped beef heart or other beef is excellent, but care must be taken that the fish receive enough during the dark hours and at the same time that there is nothing left to foul the tank in the morning.

Pimelodella gracilis F D X 9 7 7 X N N B
Pimelodus clarias F D X 9 7 8 X N N B

[Harald Schultz]
[R. Zukal]

Poecilia caucana ⬚F⬚R⬚X⬚9⬚8⬚3⬚X⬚N⬚N⬚5 [Dr. Herbert R. Axelrod]
1. *Poecilia latipinna* var. ⬚F⬚E⬚X⬚9⬚8⬚4⬚X⬚K⬚N⬚A [H. J. Richter]

POECILIA CAUCANA (Steindachner) / *Cauca Molly*

Range: Southern Panama to eastern Colombia.
Habits: Peaceful.
Water Conditions: Neutral to slightly alkaline. Temperature about 25 to 28°C.
Size: Males about 3 cm; females about 6 cm.
Food Requirements: Will take prepared foods, but should get occasional feedings of live or frozen foods.
Color Variations: Body blue and belly silver; dorsal fin yellow to orange with a black edge; males have about a dozen light vertical bars.

The Cauca is a good-sized river which crosses the north-central part of Colombia and flows into the Caribbean Sea. It is here that we find the Cauca Molly, as well as in many other parts of that section of Colombia and even southern Panama. This is one of the mollies that looks more like a limia species. The sides are deep blue and the belly silvery. Both males and females have a dorsal fin which is canary yellow to orange and is edged with black.

Males are smaller than the females. Note also that the scales are edged with black, giving a reticulated effect. The males have a series of bars on the sides which are only vaguely indicated in the females. Keep this fish warm, about 27°C. Young are born in relatively small batches, 10 to 25 depending on the age and size of the female. Like all mollies, they should be kept in uncrowded tanks which are well aerated. Unlike most of our mollies, the parents are very quick to eat their young unless they are well protected by plant thickets in which to hide. This species was named by Steindachner in 1880 and was first imported in 1906 by German hobbyists.

Mollies are susceptible to two major maladies: ich and shimmies. Ich is the white spot disease which is caused by a parasite imbedding itself in the skin of the fish and forming a case about itself (that's the white spot). If your aquarium becomes infected with this disease, raise the temperature of the water to 29°C and keep it at that level until all the white spots have disappeared from the body and fins of the mollies. At that time add 650 milligrams of quinine (ask your druggist for the water soluble kind) per 20 liters of water. Add this amount every two days until the fish are cured. In the meantime be preparing some aged water to replace 50% of the treated water once the fish have been cured. If the spots persist raise the temperature higher, say to 32°C, and use common table salt (½ teaspoon per liter of water) along with the quinine.

Shimmies is the disease where the mollies stand in one spot and shake and wiggle. This is usually considered to be the symptom of a digestive malady. It means your fish had too much undigestible matter and not enough live daphnia and green stuff. The shimmies can be helped by raising the water temperature to 31°C until the fish stop shimmying and at the same time feeding daphnia or newly hatched brine shrimp.

POECILIA LATIPINNA (Le Sueur) / *Sailfin Molly*

Range: Southeastern coastal United States south to Yucatan.
Habits: Peaceful toward other fishes, but best kept by themselves.
Water Conditions: Slightly alkaline water with a light addition of salt, a quarter teaspoon to the liter. Temperature 25 to 29°C.
Size: Males to 10 cm; females to 13 cm.
Food Requirements: A hearty eater which should be fed frequently with a preponderance of foods which have a vegetable content.

One of the most abused of all aquarium fishes is the Sailfin Molly. Very seldom does one see them kept with a perfect understanding of their requirements and habits, and consequently the specimens one sees are of a very poor quality. In the first place, the fish in its natural waters usually seeks a place where the water is shallow and becomes quite warm during the day. For this reason fish kept in captivity should be kept at higher temperatures than one generally gives to tropical species. Pursuing the topic still further, the warmer water holds less oxygen than the cooler water and in order to give them the oxygen they require, mollies should have a large, uncrowded tank. A study of their internal organs as well as observation of their habits tells us that they are largely vegetarians, and their food should contain a good percentage of vegetable matter. Coming as they do from mostly brackish water, the addition of salt to their aquarium water is important. Females about to have young should not be moved if possible, and breeding traps should not be used. Given a well-planted aquarium of her own, a molly will seldom eat her young.

Since the early 1920's there have been so many molly hybrids developed that shopkeepers have been having a difficult time properly identifying the various mollies for their customers. For many years aquarists often utilized the name *Poecilia (Mollienesia) sphenops* for the black variety of *Poecilia latipinna*. Many dealers, unknowingly of course, attempt to sell exceptional specimens of *Poecilia (M.) latipinna* for *P. velifera*. They say that they are hybrids between *latipinna* and *velifera*. This may have been the case thousands of years ago when the various species may have interbred more freely in nature than they do now, but there seems to be no hybrid vigor when these two relatives are interbred. A truly magnificent example of hybrid vigor is obtained by crossing the Florida *Poecilia latipinna* and a Gulf of Mexico *P. latipinna*. Give these babies enough room and enough food and they will grow huge dorsal fins.

1. *Poecilia latipinna*, black Sailfin Molly male (p983).
2. *P. latipinna*, black Sailfin Molly male (p986).
3. *P. latipinna*, starburst Molly male (p986).
4. *P. latipinna*, black lyretail male (p986).
5. *P. latipinna*, albino Molly male (p987).
6. *P. latipinna*, marble Sailfin Molly male (p987).
7. *P. latipinna*, balloon Molly of the green non-lyretail strain, female (p987).

2. *Poecilia latipinna* var. ⬚F⬚E⬚T⬚9⬚8⬚5⬚X⬚K⬚N⬚A ⬚⬚⬚⬚[Dr. Herbert R. Axelrod]
3. *Poecilia latipinna* var. ⬚F⬚E⬚M⬚9⬚8⬚6⬚X⬚Q⬚N⬚A ⬚⬚⬚[Dr. Herbert R. Axelrod]

4. *Poecilia latipinna* var. ⬚F⬚E⬚B⬚9⬚8⬚6⬚X⬚K⬚L⬚A ⬚⬚⬚[B. Kahl]

5. *Poecilia latipinna* var. [F][E][T][9][8][7][X][A][N][A] [Dr. Herbert R. Axelrod]
6. *Poecilia latipinna* var. [F][E][M][9][8][8][X][V][N][A] [Dr. Herbert R. Axelrod]

7. *Poecilia latipinna* var. [F][F][B][9][8][8][X][N][Z][A] [H. J. Richter]

Poecilia latipinna, the Sailfin Molly, can be found in a variety of colors and with several fin forms. Above is an albino form, photo by Dr. Herbert R. Axelrod. Below is a marble lyretail form, photo by R. Zukal.

POECILIA MELANOGASTER Günther
Black-Bellied Limia; Blue Limia

Range: Jamaica and Haiti.
Habits: Peaceful toward all but newly born young (including its own).
Water Conditions: Neutral to slightly alkaline. Temperature 22 to 25°C, slightly higher for breeding.
Size: Reaches a length of 6.5 cm for females; 4 cm for males.
Food Requirements: Needs a varied diet and frequent changes of food.

Poecilia (Limia) melanogaster is a lively little fish and should be provided with ample swimming spaces among the plants. The male constantly chases the female, so it is best to have more females than males in the tank. The attentions of males have even caused females to hide continuously and actually starve to death at times.

With sufficient plants in the aquarium and the fish well fed, the Blue Limia can be left to breed in the tank. The babies are rather quick and will use the plants as protection until they are large enough to prevent predation by the parents. For more precise breeding the sexes can be separated until young are wanted. Then the female is placed in the breeding tank first to be followed by the male once she has become acclimated. The gestation period is about 28 days, and broods of 10 to 80 may appear depending upon the size and health of the female.

POECILIA MEXICANA (Steindachner) / Mexicana Molly, Shortfin Molly

Range: Atlantic slope from Rio San Juan, Mexico, southward to Colombia and to the Colombian West Indies.
Habits: The behavior of this species is not consistent; individual specimens vary from completely peaceful to nasty.
Water Conditions: Hard, alkaline water is preferred; the tank should have a good amount of vegetation and be well lighted. Temperature 23 to 26°C.
Size: Up to 11 cm; males 1 cm to 2 cm smaller than the females.
Food Requirements: Should be given a diet with a good amount of vegetable matter, and live foods are taken readily; dry prepared foods are also accepted, although not preferred.
Color Variations: There are many color forms; the principal colors are gray or black on the body with orange markings.

Poecilia mexicana has been a taxonomic problem for many years. In the past, it has been put in and out of synonymy with *P. sphenops* several times. There are several color varieties of *P. mexicana* and two subspecies, *P. m. mexicana* and *P. m. limantouri*. In the wild, this species feeds by removing accumulated algae from rock surfaces, eating both the plant matter and also the small insects and crustaceans that live in the algal matt. In the aquarium, this species should be given a good amount of vegetable matter in its diet. This fish is a livebearer and is not difficult to breed in captivity.

Poecilia melanogaster F R X 9 8 9 X N N 7

Poecilia mexicana F R X 9 9 0 X N N A

[R. Zukal]

[Dr. Herbert R. Axelrod]

2. *Poecilia reticulata* var. F E T 9 9 5 X A V 5 [M. Hill]
3. *Poecilia reticulata* var. F E M 9 9 6 X N T 5 [M. Hill]

4. *Poecilia reticulata* var. F E B 9 9 6 X K V 5 [M. Hill]

A newly born batch of Guppies is, of course, of mixed sex, but this cannot be told until the age of about four weeks is attained. Whether the young Guppies are separated from their mother is in part a matter of choice and in part a question of her tendency to eat them. A variety of guppy traps are used, and about the only advice that can be given at this stage is that a large one be used so that the female is not unduly confined, if one be used at all. If the mother is well fed she will not eat her young, but if there is any danger of this occurring then it is most important that the young and the mother be separated.

The young males and females can be separated from one another at about a month and prior to this stage will not have mated, although a more mature male in the same tank is believed to be capable of fertilizing even very young females. This should, therefore, be avoided. The separated male and female fry should then be raised in groups to the age of three or four months to get as much size on them as possible and to prevent too early breeding.

If one is breeding for fancy fish this procedure involves two most important principles. First, early breeding of females tends to slow down their growth and thus reduce not only the size of the mother herself undesirably, but also to reduce the size and batch size of the young she may produce. Big mothers grow big babies. Secondly, even if it is desirable to mate small batches of Guppies together rather than to try and raise them in pairs, it is not desirable to raise all of a batch of fry together because some degree of selection must be exerted. Even further, if a batch of males of variable development is left together with females, the smaller and smaller-finned males are the quickest to mature and are liable to fertilize the females much more frequently than their larger and slower moving counterparts. This again will result in the reverse type of selection to that which is desired. Nevertheless, it is not desirable to try to raise individual pairs. These are hard to feed properly without water pollution and they do not seem to get on so well as when in the presence of several other pairs, which embodies a degree of competition in feeding and mating and also prevents too great a degree of inbreeding.

The following captions refer to different strains of *Poecilia reticulata*, the Guppy:
1. Winners from a Singapore Guppy show (p994).
2. Red-albino deltatail male (p995).
3. Double-swordtail male (p995).
4. Three-quarter black deltatail males (p995).
5. Half-black blue veiltail male (p998).
6. Half-black bi-color deltatail male (p998).
7. Snakeskin deltatail male (p998).
8. Fancy veiltail male (p999).
9. Fancy female (p999).
10. Bi-color deltatail male (p999).
11. Albino-red deltatail male (p1002).
12. Fancy deltatail male (p1002).
13. Red deltatail male (p1002).

Poecilia reticulata, the Guppy, is known for its many forms and color varieties. Above is a common deltatail whose quality is compromised by the fact that its tail is ragged. Below is a king cobra Guppy. Photos by Dr. Herbert R. Axelrod.

5. *Poecilia reticulata* var. ⬚F⬚E⬚T⬚9⬚9⬚7⬚X⬚M⬚V⬚5 [Dr. Herbert R. Axelrod]

6. *Poecilia reticulata* var. ⬚F⬚E⬚M⬚9⬚9⬚8⬚X⬚M⬚V⬚5 [M. Hill]
7. *Poecilia reticulata* var. ⬚F⬚E⬚B⬚9⬚9⬚8⬚X⬚V⬚V⬚5 [A. Noznov]

8. *Poecilia reticulata* var. ⬛F⬛E⬛T⬛9⬛9⬛9⬛X⬛M⬛ ⬛V⬛5   [Dr. Herbert R. Axelrod]

9. *Poecilia reticulata* var. ♀ ⬛F⬛F⬛M⬛0⬛0⬛0⬛X⬛M⬛ ⬛V⬛5   [V. Datzkevich]
10. *Poecilia reticulata* var. ⬛F⬛E⬛B⬛0⬛0⬛0⬛X⬛M⬛ ⬛V⬛5   [H. Kyselov]

A double swordtail king cobra Guppy (male) above is seen chasing a female. Photo by R. Zukal. A different male (below) positions his gonopodium toward the female. Photo by Dr. M. Gordon.

The male Guppy has his gonopodium fully extended toward the female's vent. Photo by Dr. M. Gordon. Below, the fry are seen at birth leaving the female Guppy. Photo by Milan Chvojka.

11. *Poecilia reticulata* var. ⬚F⬚E⬚T⬚0⬚0⬚1⬚X⬚A⬚V⬚5 [H. Kuceneb]

12. *Poecilia reticulata* var. ⬚F⬚E⬚M⬚0⬚0⬚2⬚X⬚B⬚V⬚5 [H. Kuceneb]
13. *Poecilia reticulata* var. ⬚F⬚E⬚B⬚0⬚0⬚2⬚X⬚R⬚V⬚5 [H. Kyselov]

Potamotrygon laticeps F D X 0 1 1 X N N D   [Harald Schultz]
Priapella intermedia F A X 0 1 2 X N N 5   [V. Elek]

POTAMOTRYGON LATICEPS Garman / *Freshwater Stingray*

Range: Amazon basin.
Habits: Spends all of its time on the bottom, sometimes almost covered; small specimens are bottom-feeders and will seldom attack other fishes.
Water Conditions: Slightly alkaline water with fine gravel on the bottom. Temperature 24 to 27°C.
Size: Up to 122 cm.
Food Requirements: Worms, bits of shrimp, clam, etc.

What is the most feared fish in South American waters? Before you jump to the wrong conclusions and say that it is the piranha, let me hasten to tell you that it is the stingray. There are many times more instances of natives being injured painfully by its whipping tail than there are cases of piranha bites. A stingray will lie on the bottom in the sand and change its colors to blend exactly with its surroundings. Here it is the master of any situation. Other fishes cannot (and will not) attack it, and its only danger is that of being trampled upon. This is where its very effective weapon comes into play. The "stinger" does not make much of a wound going in, but it has many barbs on its surface which rip the flesh when it is withdrawn. There is no injection of poison as with a snake, but the slimy coating causes an agonizingly painful swelling and infection.

PRIAPELLA INTERMEDIA Alvarez / *Blue-Eyed Livebearer*

Range: Eastern Mexico north of the Yucatan Peninsula to Vera Cruz.
Habits: Peaceful.
Water Conditions: Hardness and acidity factors are of no great importance as long as extremes are avoided. Temperatures in the mid 20's (°C) are best. This species is especially susceptible to abrupt chills.
Size: Up to 5 cm; usually seen a bit smaller; males and females both reach the same approximate size.
Food Requirements: Not at all choosy as to types of food accepted, taking all standard live, prepared and frozen foods eagerly. The method of feeding, however, is important, as this species has a tendency to ignore all foods that are not available to it at the top levels of the water; once they hit the bottom, the fish lose interest unless they are very hungry.

This species has made some friends, mostly among fanciers who are attracted to it by its colorful eyes and subdued yet pleasing coloration and by the fact that it is a "different" livebearer. One big difference between *Priapella* and more common aquarium livebearers is the size of the broods delivered: *Priapella* is a much less fecund fish, producing an average of only about 12 babies per brood at intervals of five weeks. Another difference is that in female *Priapella* the dark marking near the vent that indicates gravidity is either absent or so faint as to be indistinguishable.

PRIONOBRAMA FILIGERA (Cope) / *Glass Bloodfin*

Range: Tributaries of the Rio Madeira.
Habits: Peaceful, very active fish which prefer to be in groups.
Water Conditions: Soft, slightly acid water is best; the tank should afford a good amount of swimming room. Temperature 23 to 26°C.
Size: To 6 cm.
Food Requirements: Prepared foods accepted, but live foods should be given at least several times a week.
Color Variations: Body transparent with a light blue tint and dark blue shoulder-spot; anal and caudal fins red at the base; anal with a white edge.

It is frequently the misfortune of a fish that it is overshadowed by another better-known species which it resembles. In this case we have a fish which resembles the popular Bloodfin, *Aphyocharax anisitsi*, to which it is closely related. However, the Glass Bloodfin has a more distinctive finnage. The anal fin of the male is sickle-shaped and white on the front edge. This white edge is usually extended to a definite point. Unlike the common Bloodfin, there is not much red in the anal fin, but a definite amount in the tail. The Glass Bloodfin is an active, attractive fish in its own right and, when kept in a group, provides constant motion and activity. They are skilled jumpers, so the tank in which they are kept should be kept covered at all times. They spawn in a helter-skelter fashion, the males pursuing the females like danios and scattering eggs all over the tank, where most of them fall to the bottom. As soon as the driving is finished the breeders should be removed or the eggs will be eaten. Fry hatch in a day at 26°C and grow rapidly.

PRIONOBRAMA PARAGUAYENSIS (Eigenmann) / *Southern Bloodfin*

Range: Paraguay and Uruguay.
Habits: Peaceful, very active fish which prefer to be among their own kind.
Water Conditions: Soft, slightly acid water; the tank should have ample area for the fish to swim freely. Temperature between 23 and 26°C.
Size: To 7 cm.
Food Requirements: Prefers live foods but will also accept frozen foods or good prepared flake foods.

Prionobrama paraguayensis is very similar to the species discussed above, *P. filigera*. *P. filigera* is common in the Amazon basin. It is thought that *P. paraguayensis* may be a form of *P. filigera* from Paraguay and Uruguay. The behavior of this species is very similar to that of the above, being a very active fish and a skilled jumper. For that reason it is important to keep the tank covered at all times.

Prionobrama filigera F A X 0 1 3 X N N 6   [Aaron Norman]

Prionobrama paraguayensis F R X 0 1 4 X N N 6   [Harald Schultz]

Pristella maxillaris ⬚F⬚Q⬚X⬚0⬚1⬚5⬚X⬚N⬚V⬚5   [R. Zukal]

Procatopus nototaenia ⬚F⬚R⬚X⬚0⬚1⬚6⬚X⬚N⬚N⬚3   [H. J. Richter]

PRISTELLA MAXILLARIS (Ulrey) / *Pristella*

Range: Northern South America.
Habits: Peaceful and active; swims in schools.
Water Conditions: Soft, slightly acid water. Temperature 24 to 26°C.
Size: To 5 cm.
Food Requirements: Not at all choosy; live foods should be offered as often as available.
Color Variations: Sides silvery to yellowish; dorsal and anal fins each have a large black spot on a white background; tail reddish to bright red.

This perky little tetra has long been a prime favorite among hobbyists, and for excellent reasons. It is active, always out where it can be seen and harmless toward other fishes and plants; to top it off, it is a real beauty. For many years there has been an albino variety offered by the trade. These are pink-eyed, rather washed-out in appearance and to the author's (HRA) mind do not begin to compare with the original. For instance, I do not consider a red spot on a pink background to be as effective as a black spot on a white background. Still, there are many who deem this a lovely fish and a great improvement over the original. Breeding the Pristella is not a difficult task, but care must be taken to select a good pair. Picking a ripe female is ridiculously easy; the eggs can be seen plainly through her transparent sides with the aid of a light from behind the fish. The body cavity of the male comes to a point. We can only estimate by their interest in the females whether or not they are ready. It may be necessary to try several males before a proper one is found. Eggs hatch in a day; the fry are hardy and easily raised.

PROCATOPUS NOTOTAENIA Boulenger / *Blue Lady Killie*

Range: Southern Cameroun to southwestern Nigeria.
Habits: Non-aggressive; moderately active.
Water Conditions: Soft, slightly acid water optimal. Temperature 19 to 24°C.
Size: Males 3 cm; females slightly smaller.
Food Requirements: Live, frozen or dried foods accepted.

There are two anatomical peculiarities in this fish. First, the male has a spine-like projection behind the gill covers; second, the ventral fins are placed extremely far forward for a killifish. This dwarf species does not require a large aquarium. The temperature should be between 19 and 24°C. This species does not appreciate warmer temperatures. *P. nototaenia* seems more comfortable in a heavily planted aquarium. This species spawns readily in nylon mops placed near the bottom. The eggs hatch in 14 to 21 days at 21°C. Resting eggs are common, but they may be stimulated to hatch by placement in a small container with a small amount of dried food. This creates an oxygen deficiency which will sometimes stimulate hatching. Infusoria is required as a first food. The fry are difficult to raise and are sensitive to water changes.

PROCHILODUS NIGRICANS Agassiz / *Spotted Small-Mouth*

Range: Amazon basin.
Habits: Peaceful and lively, likes to school and is a very good jumper, so cover the aquarium; should be given hiding places.
Water Conditions: Soft, slightly acid water. Temperature 22 to 27°C.
Size: Grows to over 30 cm.
Food Requirements: Primarily an herbivore and should be given a good amount of vegetable matter such as algae, cooked spinach and lettuce. Some animal matter should also be given.

Prochilodus nigricans, the Spotted Small-Mouth, is a very peaceful fish which prefers the company of its own kind. Growing to over 30 cm, it is wise to provide this fish with a rather large aquarium which is well covered.

PROTOPTERUS ANNECTENS Owen / *African Lungfish*

Range: Widespread from central to southeastern Africa, mostly in low-lying swampy areas.
Habits: Strictly a predator; will ignore small fast-moving fishes but will eat anything slow enough to be caught.
Water Conditions: Not critical.
Size: To well over 60 cm.
Food Requirements: Younger specimens will accept most standard aquarium foods.

The order Dipneusti is a very ancient order of primitive fishes that once, according to fossil records, were widely distributed over the major land masses but are now confined to central South America, central Africa and eastern central Australia. There are two families of these fishes: the Lepidosirenidae and the Ceratodontidae. The family Lepidosirenidae contains the living genera *Lepidosiren* (South America) and *Protopterus* (Africa); the family Ceratodontidae contains only one living genus, the Australian *Neoceratodus*. All of these fishes are commonly called lungfishes because of their capacity for extracting oxygen from the atmosphere as well as from water; the organs by which the lungfishes are enabled to do this are about as close to true lungs as any fish possesses, and they are definitely distinct from the types of auxiliary breathing apparatus possessed by anabantoids and certain other fishes. Their possession of these "lungs" (or, in the case of *Neoceratodus,* a "lung") allows the fishes to survive in waters that dry out completely or almost completely in the dry season that occurs annually in their home areas. With the onset of the dry season, *Protopterus annectens* excavates a burrow in the still-moist ground or pond-bed surrounding its home waters and envelopes itself in a cocoon of mucus; the cocoon covers every portion of the fish except its mouth, through which aperture it must breathe while enveloped in the mud. When the rainy season begins, the fish awakens from its state of estivation and begins its slow-moving predatory existence in its ephemerally watery world.

1. *Protopterus annectens* swimming about in an aquarium (p1018).
2. *P. annectens* on the bottom of the aquarium (p1018).

Prochilodus nigricans ⬚F⬚D⬚X⬚0⬚1⬚7⬚X⬚N⬚N⬚D Dr. Herbert R. Axelrod]
1. *Protopterus annectens* ⬚F⬚D⬚M⬚0⬚1⬚8⬚X⬚N⬚N⬚D Dr. Herbert R. Axelrod]

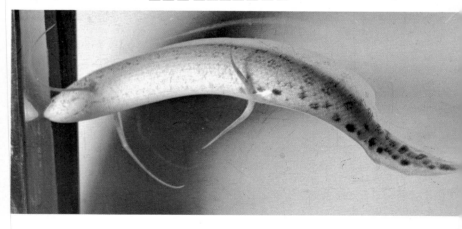

2. *Protopterus annectens* ⬚F⬚D⬚B⬚0⬚1⬚8⬚X⬚N⬚N⬚D [Dr. D. Terver, Nancy Aquarium

Pseudobagrus fulvidraco FDX0019XNND [A. Noznov]
Pseudochalceus kyburzi FDX0020XNN8 [Dr. Herbert R. Axelrod]

PSEUDOBAGRUS FULVIDRACO (Richardson) / *Tawny Dragon Catfish*

Range: China.
Habits: Semi-retiring and generally peaceful with fishes of comparable size except for slow-moving or long-finned fishes; should not be trusted with fishes which might be swallowed.
Water Conditions: Wide tolerance for pH and hardness; extremes best avoided, as with most fishes. Since range extends well into cold water regions, probably withstands temperatures as low as 4°C or less.
Size: 25 cm in nature; probably less than half that in the aquarium.
Food Requirements: Takes live foods such as small earthworms, frozen brine shrimp, beef heart, tablet and pellet foods and probably most foods containing animal protein.

Pseudobagrus fulvidraco is a small to medium size Chinese catfish belonging to the family Bagridae. It is widely distributed in China and is reportedly of considerable commercial importance. It is a handsome fish which has, in addition to the attributes of the other small and medium-sized catfishes belonging to its family, the ability to withstand cold water. Since interest in coldwater fishkeeping is increasing, a beautiful catfish should be a welcome addition of the non-tropical aquarium as well as the tropical. *P. fulvidraco* is suitable for both. Care is not difficult. As with its bagrid relatives such as the Barred Siamese Catfish, *Leiocassis siamensis*, hiding places such as rocks and caves are appreciated. Pieces of well-seasoned and properly conditioned driftwood also make good cover for bagrids and similar catfishes. Requirements are very similar to those for *Pimelodella* species from South America, which belong to another family, Pimelodidae.

PSEUDOCHALCEUS KYBURZI Schultz / *Kyburz Tetra*

Range: Colombia.
Habits: Active and aggressive, even with their own kind.
Water Conditions: Soft, slightly acid water. Temperature 24 to 26°C.
Size: To 8 cm.
Food Requirements: Various live foods including insects.

In 1965, Dr. Herbert R. Axelrod asked Dr. Leonard P. Schultz, then Curator of Fishes at the Smithsonian Institution, Washington, D.C., to identify a characid fish that he had collected in the Rio Calima, Cauca Valley, Colombia, South America. Dr. Schultz determined, after examination and research, that the specimen given to him by Dr. Axelrod represented a new species referable to the genus *Pseudochalceus* Kner. The color of this new fish is quite interesting: its back is yellowish brown, with its mid-side a light purple. Its lower side and belly are grayish white tinged with pink, while its dorsal and adipose fins are a light yellowish hue.

PSEUDOCORYNOPOMA DORIAE Perugia / *Dragonfin Tetra*

Range: Southern Brazil and the La Plata region.
Habits: Will not annoy other fishes or chew plants.
Water Conditions: Soft, slightly acid water. Temperature 21 to 25°C.
Size: To 8 cm.
Food Requirements: Will take any foods, but live foods are of course preferred.

There are never more than a very few Dragonfin Tetras available at any time. It is not the easiest fish in the world to keep and breed, and it does not ship very well. In its native waters it sometimes has to withstand some very cool temperatures, at times as low as 16°C. This of course is not a recommendation to keep it as cool as that, but it is a warning that high temperatures should be avoided. Another thing the fish is sensitive to is drastic changes in water.

PSEUDOCRENILABRUS MULTICOLOR (Hilgendorf)
Dwarf Egyptian Mouthbrooder

Range: All over eastern Africa south to the lower Nile.
Habits: Fairly safe in the community aquarium.
Water Conditions: Not critical. Temperature between 24 and 27°C.
Size: Males to 8 cm; females slightly smaller.
Food Requirements: Live and frozen foods preferred; dry foods are taken.

One of the most unusual and intriguing methods of reproduction is that of the mouthbrooding cichlid species. *Pseudocrenilabrus multicolor* is the smallest of the group and also the most generally available, and it is with this species that the hobbyist usually makes his first acquaintance. The actual egg-laying is frequently missed, and their owner is unaware that there was a spawning until he observes the bulging throat of one of the females. Here is what happens: the male digs a shallow hole, usually in an out-of-the-way corner. This done, he coaxes and almost forces the female to join him in the hole, and eventually 30 to 80 eggs are laid. The female then picks up the eggs in her mouth, which is made more capacious by the presence of a sac in the throat region. Here the eggs remain for ten days until they begin to hatch, constantly provided with circulating water by the breathing motion of the mother and constantly moved around by a sort of chewing motion. When the fry hatch, they are faithfully guarded by the mother; if danger threatens, she opens her big mouth and lets the little ones swim inside, where they are packed in like sardines in a can.

This attractive little fish, usually in good supply and available at very reasonable prices, is a very good species for hobbyists who want to breed and raise cichlids. They lack the size of the mouthbrooding *Tilapia* species and the nasty temperament of some of the mouthbrooding Lake Malawi cichlids.

1021

Pseudocorynopoma doriae ⬚F⬚R⬚X⬚0⬚2⬚1⬚X⬚N⬚N⬚8 [Dr. Herbert R. Axelrod]
Pseudocrenilabrus multicolor ⬚F⬚E⬚X⬚0⬚2⬚2⬚X⬚N⬚N⬚8 [H. J. Richter]

Pseudocrenilabrus philander F E X 0 2 3 X N N 9   [R. Zukal]
Pseudodoras niger F D X 0 2 4 X N N D   [Braz Walker]

PSEUDOCRENILABRUS PHILANDER (Weber)
South African Mouthbrooder

Range: Throughout southern Africa.
Habits: Aggressive; should be kept with species of similar size and temperament.
Water Conditions: Not critical.
Size: 8 to 11 cm.
Food Requirements: All foods accepted eagerly.

The old term "mouthbreeder" should be replaced with the more scientific term "mouthbrooder," since this more accurately describes the breeding habits of these species. *P. philander* is a wide-ranging species and has a number of geographical variations, not only in color but also in size. The most attractive form is from Beira and resembles a large Egyptian Mouthbrooder. The back and belly of the male are iridescent blue. Fins are brilliant red with blue tips. The anal fin is cobalt blue on the anterior portion. The lower lip is blue, and the throat and belly are reddish when the fish is excited. Other forms tend to lack red coloration.

PSEUDODORAS NIGER (Valenciennes) / *Black Doradid*

Range: Guyana through much of Amazon from sea level to 900 meters.
Habits: Very peaceful, even with small fishes; light-shy.
Water Conditions: Not critical. Water should be clean, well filtered and aerated.
Size: To nearly a meter in length and over 7 kg in weight.
Food Requirements: Will take a wide variety of foods but should get some vegetable matter; make sure foods are sinking types as this fish is a bottom-feeder.

The aquarium should be as large as possible. Remember, this catfish grows very large and a larger aquarium will mean less transferring later on. The temperature of the water should be between 21 and 27°C, although a slightly broader range (18 to 29°C) is tolerated. The water should be clean and clear, meaning a good filtration system and plenty of aeration. The pH and hardness do not appear to be critical, although extremes should be avoided and partial water changes made periodically.

The decor of the tank should be such that caves or other sheltered areas are formed. Rocks, driftwood, etc. may be used in their construction, but the main idea is to provide a place where *Pseudodoras niger* can get in out of the light. Particularly light-shy, the Black Doradid will stay in its cave much of the time that the tank is brightly lit. When the lights are dimmed it will start cruising around the tank in search of food. Once at home in a tank the Black Doradid will often dash out into the light for some morsel(s) of food but retreats quickly back to its home.

Food is generally no problem. There may be an initial hesitance in taking the strange new foods, but this is understandable. After all, the natural diet is said to consist mainly of flower buds, petals and seeds.

PSEUDOMUGIL SIGNIFER Kner / *Southern Blue-Eye*

Range: Australian states of Queensland and New South Wales.
Habits: A peaceful, active fish.
Water Conditions: Prefers alkaline, slightly hard water but is adaptable to life in water of different composition. Best temperature range 22 to 26°C.
Size: To about 6 cm for males.
Food Requirements: Accepts all standard aquarium foods except large, chunky prepared foods.

Pseudomugil signifer is a species that is not often seen in aquarium shops and usually is ignored even when it is, for it does not show at its best unless it is given conditions to its liking, and the true elegance of the species doesn't become evident unless the fish are in spawning condition. It is best maintained in a single-species tank; although it will live under community aquarium conditions, it will not be at its best when mixed with a grouping of disparate species. Maintained away from the company of other fishes and under proper conditions, however, it makes an excellent display fish because it is always active and continually flashes through the tank. This is not a difficult species to spawn. Ripe males and females should be maintained in a tank that contains either real or artificial bushy fine-leaved plants; the parents will chase through the tank, entering the plants from time to time to expel and fertilize the eggs, usually one at a time. The eggs will adhere to the spawning medium by a sticky thread and can be harvested individually by removing each egg from the medium or by putting the egg-bearing medium into a separate tank for hatching. The number of eggs deposited of course varies with the number of spawners in the tank and the age and condition of the females; but the spawning process is continual over a period of many weeks, and hundreds of eggs can be garnered from only a single pair. Occasionally the parents will eat the eggs, but most often they do not. At a temperature of about 26°C the eggs take about two weeks to hatch; the fry are ready to take food immediately and should be fed newly hatched brine shrimp.

PSEUDOPIMELODUS TRANSMONTANUS Regan
Peruvian Mottled Catfish

Range: Peruvian Amazon, near Iquitos.
Habits: Peaceful, but should not be trusted with fishes which are small enough for it to swallow.
Water Conditions: Soft, slightly acid water. Temperature 24 to 27°C.
Size: To 13 cm, possibly bigger.
Food Requirements: Will eat almost any kind of food, but should get some live food, especially worms, when available.

It is best to avoid tempting fate too much by remembering that the big mouth is capable of swallowing quite a morsel.

Pseudomugil signifer ⬚F⬚A⬚X⬚0⬚2⬚5⬚X⬚N⬚N⬚6 [H. J. Richter]
Pseudopimelodus transmontanus ⬚F⬚D⬚X⬚0⬚2⬚6⬚X⬚N⬚N⬚C [Aaron Norman]

seudoplatystoma fasciatum ☐F☐D☐X☐0☐2☐7☐X☐N☐N☐D☐ [K. Paysan]

seudotropheus elongatus ☐F☐B☐M☐0☐2☐8☐X☐N☐N☐B☐ [Dr. D. Terver, Nancy Aquarium]

Pseudotropheus elongatus ☐F☐A☐B☐0☐2☐8☐X☐N☐N☐B☐ [Dr. D. Terver, Nancy Aquarium]

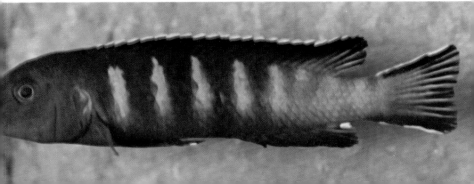

PSEUDOPLATYSTOMA FASCIATUM (Linnaeus)
Tiger Catfish, Shovelmouth

Range: Northern South America.

Habits: A strictly predaceous species that will swallow anything it can catch and engulf; a twilight and nighttime prowler.

Water Conditions: Soft, slightly acid water optimal, but the species can take a fairly wide variation in pH and hardness factors. Temperature 23 to 28°C.

Size: Up to 90 cm, but usually seen much smaller.

Food Requirements: Prefers living small fishes.

Pseudoplatystoma fasciatum is a good-looking, interesting, hardy pimelodid catfish, a very fine species for stocking a large display aquarium, where it is sure to get a lot of attention even from people who ordinarily pay no mind to fish. There are, however, a few problems involved with attempting to maintain the species. First of all, it's big, attaining a size close to 90 cm if given enough food and tank room and usually reaching 30 cm at least even if not given an exceptionally large tank. Secondly, it's sure death on smaller tankmates, which it will happily gobble up during nighttime forays around its tank. In order for a fish to have a chance to live peacefully with a Tiger Catfish, it has to be too big to swallow or too fast to catch; with especially large *Pseudoplatystoma*, a fish has a chance if it's too small to be noticed. Medium-size fishes, especially those that like to stay in a certain area in the tank, will be eaten. Naturally, also, any fish with an appetite like a Tiger Catfish's is bound to present some difficulties in finding enough good food for it.

PSEUDOTROPHEUS ELONGATUS Fryer / *Slender Mbuna*

Range: Lake Malawi, Africa.

Habits: Quarrelsome; should be kept in a well-planted tank by themselves.

Water Conditions: Alkaline and very hard; add one tablespoon of non-iodized table salt for every four liters. Temperature 24 to 27°C.

Size: In the aquarium about 10 cm, but probably larger in nature; females are slightly smaller than males.

Food Requirements: Frozen, freeze-dried or live foods are best.

Pseudotropheus elongatus can easily be distinguished from its mbuna lookalikes by being a little longer and more slender, which is the reason for the name *elongatus*. Both sexes are blue with broad vertical dark bands, but males are much brighter blue with a dark head. This species is not difficult to spawn if adequate conditions are maintained. This fish is a maternal mouthbrooder with an incubation period of two to three weeks. A usual spawning will consist of between 30 and 40 fry.

1. *Pseudotropheus elongatus* female (p1027).
2. *Pseudotropheus elongatus* male in breeding colors (p1027).

PSEUDOTROPHEUS LANISTICOLA Burgess / *Snail-Shell Mbuna*

Range: Lake Malawi, Africa.
Habits: Quarrelsome; many rock caves or holes should be provided if kept with other cichlids.
Water Conditions: Alkaline and very hard. The optimum temperature range is about 24 to 27°C.
Size: Reaches a size of about 9 cm.
Food Requirements: Not fussy; will take almost any food.
Color Variations: Not one of the species known to have color morphs; the pattern and color depicted here is the only one currently known.

Pseudotropheus lanisticola is one of the more interesting of the Lake Malawi cichlids. Although it is currently classified in the genus *Pseudotropheus*, whose members are all mbunas, it does not live among the rocks like the rest of them. It lives instead in the empty shells of a snail, *Lanistes*. Most of the individuals I (WEB) have seen were kept in aquaria supplied with rocks and they seemed to do very well. It might be interesting to place some empty shells in the same aquarium and see if they would take up residence in them. Spawning is similar to that of the other *Pseudotropheus*. The female incubates the eggs in her mouth. She should be removed from the community tank when holding eggs and isolated until the fry are well able to care for themselves. There are generally few eggs, about 20 or so, but the parental care ensures that most of them will have an excellent chance for survival. The sexes are generally similar in appearance and no indication of how to sex them outside the breeding period (aside from examination of the genital papillae) has been recorded. There are bluish individuals and yellowish individuals, the bluish ones typically breeding males.

Most *P. lanisticola* are collected by trawling in relatively shallow water, somewhere between 9 and 15 meters deep. The empty *Lanistes* shells collected in this way are shaken to see if the small fish will fall out. This fish can be caught by chasing it into a shell and then covering the shell's opening with a finger. It is interesting to note that as the fish grow in size they must look for larger and larger shells. Nevertheless, there is enough of an abundance of shells to enable the fish to spend its entire life in a relatively confined area within the lake. This species has recently been very much sought after by Rift Lake cichlid enthusiasts because of its attractive coloration and interesting habits.

1. *Pseudotropheus lanisticola* in a shell that it uses for shelter (p1030).
2. *P. lanisticola* male (p1030).

1. *Pseudotropheus lanisticola* Ⓕ Ⓓ 🅇 🄀 🄁 🄈 🅇 Ⓝ Ⓝ 🄈

[Ken Lucas, Steinhart Aquarium]

2. *Pseudotropheus lanisticola* Ⓕ Ⓐ 🅇 🄀 🄃 🄀 🅇 Ⓝ Ⓝ 🄈

3. *Pseudotropheus tropheops* var. F B X 0 3 5 X P N A [Dr. Herbert R. Axelrod]

4. *Pseudotropheus tropheops* var. F A M 0 3 6 X B N A [K. Paysan]
5. *Pseudotropheus tropheops* var. F D B 0 3 6 X D N A [Dr. Herbert R. Axelrod]

level of competition in the lake which forces the fish to rely on the *aufwuchs* as food. If they were able to get it, they would prefer a more balanced or high protein diet. It has been reported that many of the lake cichlids grow larger in an aquarium than in their natural habitat. This could be due to a better diet than they are able to obtain in the wild.

Spawning is similar to that in most other mbunas. The actual spawning takes place among the rocks, apparently safely away from the other cichlids in the tank, and is not commonly observed. Many aquarists know that spawning has occurred only by the appearance of the female. Once spawning has occurred and she has a batch of eggs in her mouth, the lowered gular area is quite obvious. She is generally removed to more isolated quarters where emergence of the fry occurs some weeks later. The female is usually a good parent and the fry may be left in with her for the early stages of development and while the female regains her strength. It is not advisable to place the female back in the community or spawning tank too soon. In her weakened condition she might not be able to cope with the advances of the males in the tank and might eventually be killed by them. The fry are relatively easy to raise.

When adding mbunas to your tank it is advisable to move the rocks about before their introduction. *P. tropheops* is territorial (like the other mbunas) and will chase any newcomer from any cover or food until it is killed. By moving the rocks the territories are broken up and new ones must be established. Introducing new fishes at this time gives them an equal try at the territories.

Pseudotropheus tropheops varieties:
1. Normal female (p1034).
2. Normal male (p1034).
3. Mottled female (p1035).
4. Blue male (p1035).
5. Gold unknown sex (p1035).

PSEUDOTROPHEUS ZEBRA (Boulenger) / *Zebra, Malawi Blue Cichlid*

Range: Lake Malawi, Africa.
Habits: Very quarrelsome.
Water Conditions: Should be fairly hard and alkaline. Temperature 24 to 26°C.
Size: About 10 cm.
Food Requirements: Omnivorous, and for this reason should get both plant and vegetable foods; does well on a balanced dry food diet.
Color Variations: Body various shades of blue with six to eight bluish black bars and blue fins; anal has some round orange spots and forehead a black bar.

Pseudotropheus zebra, commonly called the Zebra or the Malawi Blue Cichlid, is an mbuna from Lake Malawi and is known to have over a dozen color varieties. Its common name came from its most prevalent color form, which was exported from Lake Malawi in 1964. It has a blue body of varying shades with six to eight vertical bars on its sides (BB morph). As additional collecting work was performed around the lake, many new color varieties were found. These forms include: a solid red morph, called the red zebra; a solid blue morph, called the cobalt blue; a solid green morph, called the green zebra (this morph also is often called a cobalt, as the cobalts can vary in color from blue to greenish blue); an orange-blotched morph called the OB; a mottled form called the marmalade cat; a white morph; a yellow morph; a white form covered with black freckles, called the peppered zebra; a solid orange form called the tangerine form; and an albino form.

This species is usually very pugnacious and territorial. It should be given plenty of room in which to move around and establish its territory. It grows to over 10 cm. Because there are so many forms, it is not always easy to sex unless one is familiar with all or most of the color varieties.

Pseudotropheus zebra is omnivorous and will eat most aquarium foods, including flake food. It is best to give this fish a balanced diet of both animal and vegetable matter.

This species is a maternal mouthbrooder with an incubation period of between three and four weeks. Normal brood sizes are between 30 and 40 fry. Good aeration and filtration are particularly important after the eggs have been laid and collected by the female. The eggs are extremely susceptible to fungus, and the developing eggs, with their high metabolism, need a good supply of oxygen. Partial water changes of not more than 25% are recommended weekly for tanks lacking a good biological filter. Otherwise, regular water changes should be continued for several weeks after the young have been released by the female. Of the total number of fry, over 90% should be properly developed. The deformed fry are not easy to recognize at first, but after a period of time the difference should become apparent. The fry are placed in a secluded area and are closely watched over for several days.

With mouthbrooders, the fry seek refuge in a parent's mouth. Most Rift Lake cichlids are surprisingly gentle with their own fry and seldom need to be

1. *Pseudotropheus zebra* var. ⨻F⨻E⨻T⨻0⨻3⨻7⨻X⨻Q⨻N⨻B

2. *Pseudotropheus zebra* var. ⨻F⨻A⨻M⨻0⨻3⨻8⨻X⨻B⨻N⨻B [Dr. Herbert R. Axelrod]
3. *Pseudotropheus zebra* var. ⨻F⨻H⨻B⨻0⨻3⨻8⨻X⨻R⨻N⨻B [S. Kochetov]

10. *Pseudotropheus zebra* var. ⬚F⬚B⬚T⬚0⬚4⬚3⬚X⬚P⬚N⬚B   [Dr. Herbert R. Axelrod]

11. *Pseudotropheus zebra* var. ⬚F⬚A⬚M⬚0⬚4⬚4⬚X⬚M⬚N⬚B   [Dr. Herbert R. Axelrod]
12. *Pseudotropheus zebra* var. ⬚F⬚A⬚B⬚0⬚4⬚4⬚X⬚P⬚N⬚B   [Aaron Norman]

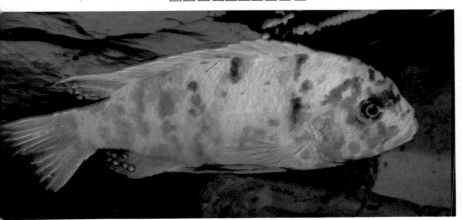

separated from the brood (whereas separation is always essential with many other cichlids). Baby brine shrimp (or other similar fine live foods) should be given to the fry. The fry will remain close to their parents for an additional one to two weeks. During this time the parents will herd the stray fry. The fry grow quickly and should double in size within one month.

With additional collecting around Lake Malawi new varieties of cichlids are constantly being found. *Pseudotropheus zebra* is one species in which the color morphs are becoming better known. Unlike the Angelfish *(Pterophyllum scalare)* varieties, those of *P. zebra* occur naturally in Lake Malawi. They vary from the basic blue with black stripes (BB) to shades of red, white, mottled blue, etc. With the ease of breeding this species it will be interesting to see if some of the crosses in colors will produce entirely new color varieties from those found naturally in the lake.

One of the rarest of the morphs of *P. zebra* is a mottled male generally called the marmalade cat. This morph is similar to the orange-blotched (OB) female which is so common, but it has a bluish tinge to the whitish portions of the pattern. Naturally, being so rare it commands a rather high price at this time and is constantly sought after by aquarists. So far no reports of marmalade cats being found among the progeny of domestically raised fish have been forthcoming.

Pseudotropheus zebra varieties:
 1. Orange male (p1038).
 2. Blue male (p1038).
 3. Red unknown sex (p1038).
 4. Normal male (p1039).
 5. Green unknown sex (p1039).
 6. Tangerine male (p1039).
 7. Peppered female (p1042).
 8. Blotched female (p1042).
 9. Green barred male (p1042).
10. Blotched female (p1043).
11. Red Top male (p1043).
12. Marmalade Cat   (p1043).

PTEROLEBIAS LONGIPINNIS Garman / *Common Longfin*

Range: Northern Argentina northward into southeastern Brazil.
Habits: Peaceful with other species, but males fight among themselves.
Water Conditions: Acidity and hardness factors of the water are not very important, provided the water is clean. Temperature 17 to 22°C; higher temperatures to be avoided.
Size: Males about 8 cm; females 6 cm.
Food Requirements: Does best on live foods; will accept meaty prepared foods but will quickly go off feed if maintained on monotonous diet of dry foods.

Pterolebias longipinnis is a prolific, reliable spawner that can easily be spawned in small aquaria; in fact, small aquaria are better than large ones, as is the case with most annual killies. Male and female completely submerge themselves in the bed of peat moss used as the spawning medium, so the layer of peat moss at the bottom of the tank (or in the spawning pot, if larger breeding quarters are used) should be about 7 cm deep. The damp peat moss containing the eggs should be stored for about seven months; most of the fry will hatch out when the peat moss is covered by 2 cm or so of aged soft water, but some will usually not hatch until the peat moss is drained and subjected to saturation again. The comparatively large fry are able to accept newly hatched brine shrimp right away and grow quickly if given enough food and room. Male *P. longipinnis* are less rough on females than males of some other annual species are, but an occasional male will be rough to the point of killing or badly battering mates.

PTEROLEBIAS PERUENSIS Myers / *Peruvian Longfin*

Range: Upper Amazon region.
Habits: Usually peaceful, but should be kept by themselves.
Water Conditions: Soft, considerably acid water; for spawning, a layer about 2 cm deep of peat moss should be provided on the bottom. Temperature 18 to 23°C.
Size: About 7 cm for males; females about 5 cm.
Food Requirements: Live foods of all kinds.

At the little city of Leticia, Colombia, the author was privileged to travel a short distance up the Amazon River to a point where Peru could be seen across the immense river. Here we went up a small tributary stream to the fish collector's trading post. Most of the smaller, brightly colored fishes in the area were to be found in the storage troughs, and the author recalls being asked for a scientific identification of two species. One was *Colomesus psittacus,* and the other was called "Africano" by the natives. This turned out to be our friend *Pterolebias peruensis.* It would have been highly interesting to see where the Indians were catching these fish, but time did not permit. This is one of the "annual" fishes which lays its eggs in the mud on the bottom of small bodies of water that dry out in the dry season. The fry hatch when the rains begin and the dried-out ponds fill up once more.

Pterolebias longipinnis F R X 0 4 5 X N N 7   [H. J. Richter]
Pterolebias peruensis F R X 0 4 6 X N N 6   [H. Abel]

Pterolebias zonatus ꩜FꩦAꩦXꩦ0ꩦ4ꩦ7ꩦXꩦNꩦNꩦB꩜ [Aaron Norman]
Pterophyllum dumerili ꩜FꩦDꩦXꩦ0ꩦ4ꩦ8ꩦXꩦNꩦNꩦA꩜ [Dr. Herbert R. Axelrod]

PTEROLEBIAS ZONATUS Myers / *Lace-finned Killie, Banded Longfin*

Range: Venezuelan drainage of the Orinoco River.

Habits: Males not overly aggressive, but in close quarters they may nip at each other's fin ray extensions.

Water Conditions: Does well in soft acid water but will readily adapt to neutral or slightly alkaline water. Best maintained between 20 and 24°C.

Size: Males grow to 15 cm in the wild and females reach half that size; aquarium-raised fish are not quite this long.

Food Requirements: Feeds heavily on mosquito larvae and other surface-dwelling insects, but will adapt well to frozen or prepared foods.

Over the years much controversy has ensued over identification of the "sunny" form of this fish found in open pools and the "shady" form which is found in more sheltered habitats. Both forms have been found in very close proximity to each other, but they are not sympatric (found together). Extensive studies of both forms by Dr. Jamie Thomerson have resulted in his finding consistently distinct morphometric and meristic differences between them. The "sunny" form, having more distinct vertical bands, is now being defined as *P. zonatus,* while the "shady" form is now known as *P. hoignei.*

In nature, this is indeed a short-lived fish, since it is most commonly found in the waters of roadside ditches and shallow rain pools which dry up from December through April. In the aquarium, however, as with most other annual killifishes, they can live for considerably longer if they are kept in cooler water, not overfed, and rested from their daily spawning activity for at least one week out of every month.

P. zonatus breeds in the typical fashion of the annual "peat divers," but because of their relatively peaceful nature they can be spawned in drum bowls of four liters or so. The female initiates the spawning activity, and both parents dive down into an 8 to 10 cm layer of peat moss to lay their large (2 mm) adhesive eggs. The eggs must be incubated in this peat moss, which has been dried to the consistency of fresh pipe tobacco, and require a minimum dry period of eight months. Fry are quite capable of taking newly hatched brine shrimp nauplii as their first food.

PTEROPHYLLUM DUMERILI (Castelnau) / *Long-Nosed Angelfish*

Range: Essequibo River to lower Amazon region.

Habits: Peaceful with fishes of its own size.

Water Conditions: Water should be soft and slightly acid. Temperature 24 to 26°C.

Size: To about 10 cm.

Food Requirements: Prefers live or frozen foods, but accepts prepared foods when hungry.

The Long-Nosed Angelfish is not as common or popular as its close relative the Scalare. Because it is a third smaller than the Scalare, the Long-Nosed Angelfish is more suitable for smaller aquaria.

PTEROPHYLLUM SCALARE (Lichtenstein) / *Angelfish, Scalare*

Range: The Amazon basin, the Rupununi and Essequibo Rivers of Guyana, with specimens also found in French Guiana and Surinam.

Water Conditions: Clean, neutral water. Temperature 23°C.

Size: 13 cm in length; 15 cm in depth.

Food Requirements: Freeze-dried or live foods.

Color Variations: This species is found in "ghost" forms without bars, in solid black, in "lace" forms with some black markings and with long fins; these are all mutant forms which have been fixed by inbreeding.

Lichtenstein first described this fish in 1823 as *Zeus scalaris* from Brazil. The name was subsequently changed to *Platax scalaris* in 1831 by Cuvier and Valenciennes and finally to *Pterophyllum scalaris* by Heckel in 1840. Günther changed the *scalaris* to *scalare* in 1862, and so it has been ever since. *P. scalare* is the Angelfish every aquarist is familiar with. Since 1928 when Ahl described *P. eimekei* from the mouth of the Rio Negro in Brazil, there has been considerable confusion as to which species was which. Dr. L. P. Schultz carefully studied specimens of both "species" and found that the counts for the syntype of *P. eimekei* coincide with the median counts of *scalare* and thus concluded that *eimekei* is a synonym of *scalare*. The important lesson to be learned here is that tank-raised fishes sometimes do not have the same meristic characteristics as wild specimens and usually cannot be used in the description of a species.

The Scalare is easy to breed and millions of tank-raised specimens are sold every year all over the world. Many color and finnage varieties have been developed. This species prefers to spawn on broad-leaved water plants. Both parents care for the eggs and fan them with their fins to ensure adequate oxygenation. The fry hatch after 24 to 40 hours at 27 to 31°C. The young are collected by the parents after they hatch and placed in depressions in the bottom gravel for several days until they can swim. A successful brood can have as many as 1000 fry.

NAJA AND WONG GOLDEN ANGELFISH

It was awaited for a long time, and when it finally came it was welcomed with open arms by the aquarium world: the production of the first really golden Angels the hobby had seen. Carl Naja of Milwaukee and Peter Wong of Hong Kong had worked ceaselessly for years to produce something outstanding in the way of a new Angelfish variety, and what they came up with—working quite independently of one another but using the same general technique of ruthless culling and line-breeding—was a fish that had an immediate acceptance among both beginners and experienced fanciers. It had taken Carl Naja about five years from the first appearance of a grayish golden sport in one of the tanks of his large basement breeding establishment until he

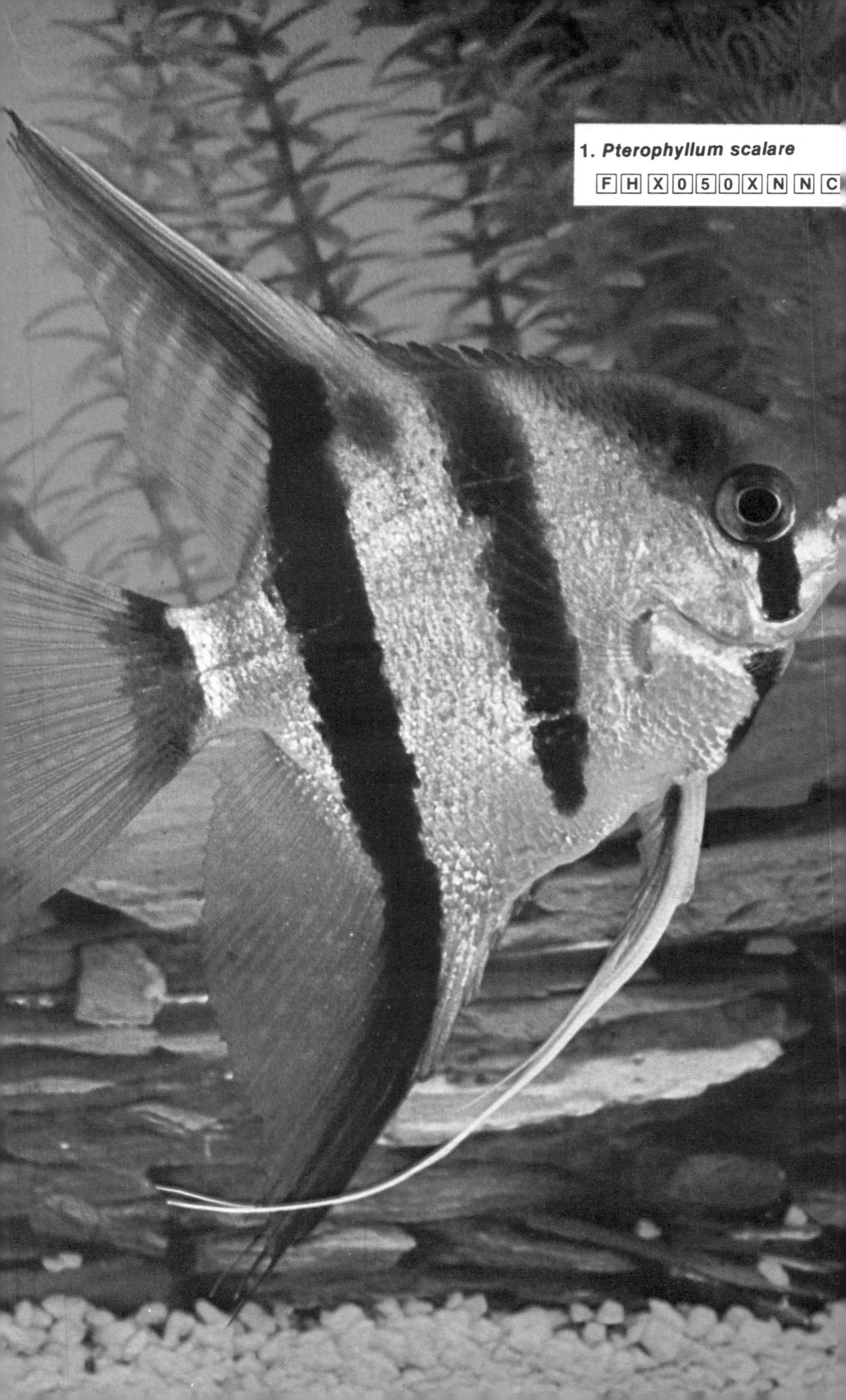

1. *Pterophyllum scalare*

F H X 0 5 0 X N N C

2. *Pterophyllum scalare* var.

F H X 0 5 1 X V N 9

was finally able to feel that his strain was true-breeding enough to be put on the markets, but when they finally arrived they were so well appreciated by hobbyists that mature fish were selling for up to $100 apiece at retail. Babies of the originally marketed strain weren't golden in color immediately upon reaching a recognizable Angelfish shape, some of them taking as long as three months to change from gray to gold and some remaining basically gray throughout their lives, which led to a lot of confusion about whether the Angels were in reality golden at all. But nicely colored pure golden Angels have now become established and their permanence is practically assured.

1. *Pterophyllum scalare* normal type (p1050).
2. *P. scalare* zebra variety (p1051).
3. *P. scalare* marbled variety (p1054).
4. *P. scalare* pair; blushing female and marked gold male spawning on a leaf (p1055).

The Angelfish, *Pterophyllum scalare,* is one of the most popular aquarium fishes. The silver veiltail form, below, is often seen. Photo by Dr. Herbert R. Axelrod.

There are many Angelfish forms and color varieties. In the upper photo, a golden Angelfish (above) and a bleeding heart Angelfish (below) prepare a spawning site. Photo by Dr. Herbert R. Axelrod. The black Angelfish in the lower photo are among the most attractive forms available. Photo by G. Wolfsheimer.

3. *Pterophyllum scalare* var.

F H X 0 5 4 X P N B

[H. J. Richter]

4. *Pterophyllum scalare* var. F Q X 0 5 5 X M N B [H. J. Richter]
Pterygoplichthys bolivianus F D X 0 5 6 X N N C [Dr. Herbert R. Axelrod]

MARBLED ANGELFISH

The Angelfish is a popular fish, and it stands to reason that all attractive new varieties of the basic Angel stock will also be popular. Such is the case with the marbled Angel, a strain that was developed and marketed in quantity by California breeder Charles Ash. (Bud Goddard, a Florida breeder, had produced a marbled Angelfish about five years before Ash produced his, but the Goddard strain was not fixed.)

Among a batch of regular Angelfish youngsters that he was raising, Ash noticed a youngster whose markings differed considerably from those of its brothers and sisters. He separated this fish (it turned out to be a female, and very attractive) and later bred to a regular Angel male; males of the resulting fry, which grew quickly, were subsequently mated to the mother, but a number of spawnings produced only three more marbled young. These three, however, formed the core of a colony that bred true and allowed Mr. Ash to perpetuate his development in quantity. The marbled Angels caught on immediately with aquarium hobbyists, and specimens of the new strain were sold throughout the country.

PTERYGOPLICHTHYS BOLIVIANUS (Pearson)
Bolivian Sucker Catfish

Range: Bolivia, in the Amazon tributaries.
Habits: Seldom bothers other fishes.
Water Conditions: Neutral to slightly alkaline. Temperature 24 to 27°C.
Size: To 15 cm.
Food Requirements: All live and frozen foods eagerly accepted, especially worms; requires algae or a vegetable substitute like lettuce leaves.

The Bolivian Sucker Catfish will surely gladden the hearts of many aquarium hobbyists if it ever becomes generally available. Most of the sucker catfishes are characterized by their extreme ugliness, but it is completely forgotten when this fellow begins waving his banners, in this case a huge sail-like dorsal fin and a deep anal fin, both with large round black dots in neat rows. The tail also carries some rows of black dots, but they are not as round or spaced in as orderly a fashion. Strangely enough, only a few of these dots overflow onto the body, in the belly region. The body is well protected by rows of sharp spines on the sides, and the stiff, sturdy first ray of the pectoral fins is similarly armed, making this fish not only a dangerous one to handle but also a difficult one to remove from the meshes of a net. All of the plecostomus-type catfishes are very difficult to capture in their native waters because they invariably seek out streams where there is a great deal of brushwood in the water where they can hide. Seining is an impossibility, and the fish cannot be driven out into clear spots. They merely dodge from one hiding place to another.

PUNTIUS CONCHONIUS (Hamilton-Buchanan) / *Rosy Barb*

Range: India.

Habits: Very active, continually swimming from one end of the tank to the other; generally well-behaved.

Water Conditions: Water can vary a little way from neutral in either direction; likes a well-planted tank, but must have swimming room. Temperature 22 to 24°C.

Size: Up to almost 15 cm, but usually seen much smaller, about half this size.

Food Requirements: Takes all foods.

The Rosy Barb's popularity has endured the test of time, and it seems destined to be with us always. When in breeding color, the male takes on a gleaming purplish red flush and the black in its fins becomes accentuated. The female, which when not in breeding condition looks like a plain silvery fish, also improves in coloration when in spawning condition, but she never rivals the male in brilliance. They spawn by scattering eggs into bunches of plants like so many of their relatives. Properly conditioned, the species is eager to spawn and requires no special preparations, except that for best results they require big tanks for both spawning and rearing the fry. A very prolific fish, the Rosy Barb is usually in good supply at low prices. Rosy Barbs are very active swimmers and very heavy eaters, often rooting around in the gravel much like Goldfish. They should be kept in long, low tanks, preferably by themselves; kept in a school, the males will swim around each other with fins fully spread and colors at their gleaming best in an effort to outshine their brothers. Although the Rosy Barb is considered a peaceful fish, it occasionally nips slower species.

The longfinned Rosy Barb occurred originally in a mutation of the normal Rosy Barb stock of a fish breeder in Russia; some of the original stock were passed on to skilled hobbyists in eastern Europe and inbred with a stock of Rosy Barbs in which finnage was normal but coloration was exceptionally fine. The resulting youngsters combined the good points of both parental elements, the longfins of the mutation and the excellent color of the regular Rosy Barbs. The new mutation acts in all respects the same way as the normal Rosy Barb and can be treated in the same way, the only exception being that to preserve maximum finnage development on the fish it should not be housed with fin-nippers that would be attracted to the flowing fins. It also is slightly less active than the regular Rosy Barb, since it is somewhat impeded in swimming by the longer fins. Both male and female fish of the longfinned Rosy Barb have the elongated finnage, but in males the fins are longer.

1. *Puntius conchonius*, "Odessa Barb" (p1058).
2. *P. conchonius*, longfinned variety (p1058).
3. *P. conchonius*, normal variety (p1059).

1. *Puntius conchonius* [F][E][X][0][5][7][X][Z][N][9] [H. J. Richter]
2. *Puntius conchonius* [F][H][X][0][5][8][X][N][V][9] [H. J. Richter]

3. *Puntius conchonius* ꊮ F E X 0 5 9 X N N 9   [A. Roth]

Puntius filamentosus F D M 0 6 0 X N N A   [Dr. Herbert R. Axelrod]
Puntius gelius F R B 0 6 0 X N N 4   [G.J.M. Timmerman]

PUNTIUS FILAMENTOSUS (Cuvier and Valenciennes)
Black-Spot Barb

Range: Sri Lanka, India, Burma.
Habits: Peaceful with fishes its own size; a good jumper.
Water Conditions: Slightly acid to neutral; not too hard. Temperature 23 to 26°C.
Size: Up to 13 cm.
Food Requirements: Takes all foods.

This fish deserves the title "longfin barb" almost as much as *Capoeta arulius,* another barb in which the adult males show extended dorsal rays. Colors in these two fishes are also somewhat similar, but *arulius* lacks the prominent dark blotch which shows so strongly on *P. filamentosus.* For breeding, a large tank should be used. The longer the tank, the better the results. Spawning pairs of this species will chase back and forth over the length of the tank a few times before settling down to the actual spawning act; the eggs are laid in bunches of plants, which should cover at least one-fourth of the bottom area of the tank. Once driving by the males has been begun, the fish should not be interrupted, as this often results in a complete cessation of breeding activity for a period of weeks. Eggs hatch in about two days, and the newly emerged fry are soon able to take newly hatched brine shrimp.

PUNTIUS GELIUS (Hamilton-Buchanan) / *Dwarf Barb*

Range: Central India, Bengal and Assam.
Habits: One of the most peaceful of all the barb species; in their native land they occupy quiet waters, usually in small schools near the shore.
Water Conditions: Not critical, but avoid too high temperatures; 22 to 24°C is ample.
Size: Females 4 cm; males 3.5 cm.
Food Requirements: Good eaters, but food should be small.

Its small size and lack of brilliant colors keep this little fellow from being one of the most popular of the barb species, but it has some qualities which should make it deserving of a greater popularity. One is a lack of sensitivity to lower temperatures, and another is that it does not present as many problems when being bred as do most of the other barbs. The spawning act usually takes place in the morning, with the female beginning by chasing and annoying the male until he turns the tables on her and drives her vigorously all over the tank. Unlike most of the other barbs, these do not usually strew their eggs among the bushy plants but prefer to stick them on the underside of broad-leaved plants, which should be provided instead of the usual *Nitella* or *Myriophyllum.* The parents do not indulge in the usual "egg-hunt" after breeding is completed, but leaving them in the breeding tank serves no further purpose. Fry hatch in about 24 hours and may be seen hanging from the plants or glass sides for a time, after which they seem to disappear from sight.

PUNTIUS LINEATUS (Duncker) / *Striped Barb*

Range: Singapore and Malayan Peninsula.
Habits: Peaceful and active; harmless to plants.
Water Conditions: Soft, slightly acid water. Temperature 24 to 27°C.
Size: Up to 10 cm; usually smaller.
Food Requirements: All sorts of food accepted, but occasional meals of live foods are necessary for the best condition.
Color Variations: Body olive-green with four horizontal lines on the sides; dorsal and anal fins show a pink flush at times.

It is a pity that this very attractive barb is seldom available, and then only in limited numbers. It is a perfect aquarium fish with a pretty color pattern and an alert, perky carriage. It is usually out in front where it can be seen and admired, and its not-too-large size makes it practical to keep a number of them in an average-sized aquarium. It does not take bites out of your best plants as some barbs do. The fact that it is one of the most difficult barbs to breed successfully makes it a challenge to the experienced aquarist. The females do not seem to fill up with eggs as they should, and when one of the rare spawnings takes place only a few hatch. Once we get a few generations which have spent their entire lives in the aquarium, the story will be different. A school of half-grown Striped Barbs and another of Tiger Barbs in a large, well-planted aquarium should make a breathtaking exhibit at a fish show, sure to put the exhibitor in the running for a trophy.

PUNTIUS NIGROFASCIATUS (Günther) / *Black Ruby Barb*

Range: Sri Lanka.
Habits: An active swimmer, but inclined to nip fins.
Water Conditions: Soft, slightly acid water. Temperature 24 to 28°C.
Size: 6 cm.
Food Requirements: Accepts all foods, but small living foods are preferred.
Color Variations: Male purplish red with broad black bars and purple-black fins; female lacks male's red color and black fins.

When in color, the male of the Black Ruby Barb is a beautiful fish in which the bright red of the front part of the body is set off against the deep black of the rear portion and the fins. Out of color, it is of no distinction, being a plain grayish yellow banded barb. Sexes are not difficult to distinguish, because the black bars on the male and the black in his fins are always more crisp and distinct than in the female, even when he is not showing his best colors. The Black Ruby Barb spawns in typical *Puntius* fashion, but the fish requires a larger tank than its size would indicate. The fry hatch more quickly if the temperature of the water is kept a degree or two below that used for spawning.

Puntius lineatus F R X 0 6 1 X N N 9   [J. Elias]
Puntius nigrofasciatus F Q X 0 6 2 X N N 6   [H. J. Richter]

Puntius sachsi ⬚F⬚Q⬚X⬚0⬚6⬚3⬚X⬚D⬚N⬚6   [H. J. Richter]
Puntius somphongsi ⬚F⬚D⬚X⬚0⬚6⬚4⬚X⬚N⬚N⬚7   [Dr. Herbert R. Axelrod]

PUNTIUS SACHSI (Ahl) / *Golden Barb*

Range: Malayan Peninsula.
Habits: Peaceful and active.
Water Conditions: Soft, slightly acid water. Temperature 21 to 28°C.
Size: 6 cm.
Food Requirements: Accepts both live and dry foods.

The Golden Barb is a pretty and inoffensive fish which has achieved a good deal of popularity because it is easy to keep, cheap, peaceful and easy to breed. Besides these good points, the fish also offers a very pleasing combination of colors in which the golden yellow of the body is set off nicely by the reddish fins and black markings. The Golden Barb is an easy breeder and a prolific one, although not as prolific as its larger relatives. For spawning, fine-leaved bunch plants or their artificial substitutes, such as nylon mops, are required. The parent fish chase wildly back and forth over the length of the tank until the female is ready to enter the spawning area. Once there, the male and female quiver side by side and the female releases the eggs, which are immediately fertilized by the male. During the first entrances into the plants there may be no eggs expelled, but there are only a few such dry runs before the female is able to produce eggs. The eggs hatch in 24 hours at a temperature of 27°C.

PUNTIUS SOMPHONGSI (Benl & Klausewitz) / *Somphongs' Barb*

Range: Thailand.
Habits: Peaceful and active, but sometimes nips plant leaves.
Water Conditions: Soft, slightly acid water. Temperature 24 to 27°C.
Size: 10 cm.
Food Requirements: Has a good appetite and is not a fussy eater; will accept dried as well as live or frozen foods.

If there is ever to be a good supply of this handsome barb available to hobbyists, it looks as if they will have to be bred somewhere unless a better source of supply is found in Thailand. Somphongs Lek-Aree, who was probably the best-known and most active collector in Thailand, declared that it was the rarest of all rare Thailand fishes and that in all of his collecting expeditions he had found only six. Two died on the return trip and another died in his aquarium. The other three were sent as a Christmas present to Dr. Gerhard Benl in Munich, Germany. He and Dr. Wolfgang Klausewitz promptly named the new barb in the collector's honor. Sometimes these so-called "rarities" are scarce in their home waters not because they are not prolific but because they have a great many natural enemies. Do not take the size given as the absolute maximum.

PUNTIUS STIGMA (Cuvier & Valenciennes) / *Two-Spot Barb*

Range: Common throughout most of India.
Habits: Peaceful and active if kept with large fishes.
Water Conditions: Not critical, but soft, slightly acid water is best. Temperature 20 to 26°C.
Size: To 20 cm.
Food Requirements: Heavy eater which will consume any kind of food.

Chances are that you will never see the Two-Spot Barb, because it is one of those fishes which is common enough in its home country of India but remains unpopular for two reasons: first of all it gets too big; secondly, its size might be overlooked if it had a set of attractive colors, but the only bit of color is a faint streak of red on the side from the head to a black spot at the caudal base. There is another spot at the base of the dorsal fin which is not always evident. As a matter of fact, only the black spot at the caudal base remains at all times and other markings may put in an appearance only when the fish is spawning. The Two-Spot Barb has been known to science since Cuvier & Valenciennes named it in 1843, and hobbyists first saw it in 1927. The fish did not cause any great commotion then, and there have not been many imported since. Spawning is similar to the other barbs but would probably require a large aquarium. Females are distinguished solely by their heavier bodies when the eggs ripen, plus the fact that the red stripe never shows on them.

PUNTIUS STOLICZKAI (Day) / *Stoliczka's Barb*

Range: Eastern Burma, near Rangoon.
Habits: Active and peaceful in the community aquarium.
Water Conditions: Like other barbs, not critical. Temperature 24 to 26°C.
Size: A little over 5 cm.
Food Requirements: Frozen or live foods preferred, but dried foods accepted.

Stoliczka's Barb is often mistaken for *Puntius ticto*. The markings on the body and fins are very similar, but Stoliczka's Barb is slightly higher in the body. It is also distinguishable by the bright golden zone around the dark spot near the caudal base. This and the bright rosy hue of the fins make it a very attractive fish. Their colors are best observed if a number of males are kept together. Some very vigorous but harmless battles take place, but there are seldom any torn fins. Each male tries to make the other retreat, and a great deal of butting and tail-slapping goes on. Although they are fond of searching among the bottom sediment for stray bits of food, they never stir it up or uproot any plants. For spawning, a tank of at least 60 liters should be richly planted, or a great many eggs will be eaten. The eggs do not have any great adhesive power, and a great many fall to the bottom instead of adhering to the plants. Fry hatch in 30 to 36 hours and begin swimming two days later. Finely powdered dry food is fed.

Puntius stigma ⬚F⬚ ⬚D⬚ ⬚X⬚ ⬚0⬚ ⬚6⬚ ⬚5⬚ ⬚X⬚ ⬚N⬚ ⬚N⬚ ⬚9⬚   [Dr. Herbert R. Axelrod]
Puntius stoliczkai ⬚F⬚ ⬚Q⬚ ⬚X⬚ ⬚0⬚ ⬚6⬚ ⬚6⬚ ⬚X⬚ ⬚N⬚ ⬚N⬚ ⬚5⬚   [R. Zukal]

Puntius ticto F E X 0 6 7 X N N 8   [Dr. Herbert R. Axelrod]

Puntius vittatus F R X 0 6 8 X N N 5   [Dr. Herbert R. Axelrod]

PUNTIUS TICTO (Hamilton-Buchanan) / *Tic-Tac-Toe Barb*

Range: Sri Lanka and India.
Habits: Peaceful; inclined to be timid when small and aggressive as it gets older and larger.
Water Conditions: Slightly soft and acid water recommended; not delicate. Temperature 24 to 27°C.
Size: Up to 10 cm.
Food Requirements: Prefers live foods, but accepts dry and frozen foods.

Puntius ticto is considered by some authorities to be identical with Stoliczka's Barb or the two forming subspecies of a single species. Here they shall be considered as two separate species, because hobbyists have long treated them separately and distinguish one from the other by general body outline and color differences. *P. ticto* is a more streamlined fish than *P. stoliczkai*, the male *P. ticto* being especially less deep in body contour. The Tic-Tac-Toe Barb is not continuously available, because importations of this fish are sporadic and because it is not being bred in quantity on a permanent basis by any of the large commercial breeders in this country, in contrast to such established barb favorites as the Tiger Barb and Rosy Barb. The species scatters its adhesive eggs into bundles of plants placed about the spawning tank; like the other barbs, it will eat its own eggs, but in this regard it is not so great an offender as some of the others.

PUNTIUS VITTATUS (Day) / *Banded Barb*

Range: Found mostly in rice paddies throughout India.
Habits: Peaceful and active; prefers to move in schools.
Water Conditions: Not at all critical; will adapt to almost any kind of water. Fairly soft water with a temperature of about 24°C. is best.
Size: 5 to 6 cm.
Food Requirements: Will eat dried as well as live foods; easily kept.

Why this one is called Banded Barb is a bit of a mystery. The only band this barb has runs through the dorsal fin. Although this fish is very abundant in its native waters, its lack of bright colors keeps it among the seldom-seen species. It is, however, one of the most easily kept fishes of the genus. It will accept just about anything in the way of food, and if there is a drop in temperature, these will be among the last to suffer from it. It is easy to distinguish a ripe pair, even if the colors of both sexes are almost alike. The female's body is much deeper, and she is usually somewhat bigger than her mate. *Puntius vittatus* seem to be happier when they are swimming in a school, and in their native waters they are seldom found singly, but usually in large schools. This fish has been compared to *P. conchonius* in ease of keeping. They seldom get sick and make little demands of their owner. They spawn readily, scattering their eggs among plant thickets. Fry hatch in about 36 hours and become free-swimming a day or two later.

1068

PUNTIUS WOEHLERTI (Trewavas) / *Sickle Barb*

Range: Mozambique.
Habits: Peaceful, timid and inclined to hide.
Water Conditions: Soft, slightly acid water. Temperature 22 to 28°C.
Size: 3 cm.
Food Requirements: Prefers small live foods, but will accept dry and frozen foods.

Here's a little barb that you won't see very often, for it is seldom imported. This is unfortunate, because it has some good points that would soon make it popular if it were ever brought into the country and sold in quantity. Apart from its diminutive size, which is enough of an advantage when the fish is compared to some of its close relatives, *Puntius woehlerti* also has another trait working in its favor: with mature specimens, there is no danger of confusing male and female, because there is a very definite physical characteristic which enables the hobbyist to tell the sexes apart. This is unusual in a barb, because with most barbs the aquarist must rely on such changeable evidence as comparative color brilliance, fullness of the body, etc. Although in most cases these are very valuable guides, they are not completely reliable unless the fish are in good enough condition to bring out the differences. Not so with the Sickle Barb! The anal fin of the male of this species is shaped very differently from that of the female. The Sickle Barb breeds in normal barb fashion.

PYRRHULINA BREVIS Steindachner / *Short-Lined Pyrrhulina*

Range: Widespread in South America.
Habits: Very peaceful in the community aquarium.
Water Conditions: Soft, slightly acid water. Temperature 24 to 27°C.
Size: To 6 cm.
Food Requirements: Small live foods preferred, but will take frozen and prepared foods.

The Short-Lined Pyrrhulina, although not as attractive as many of its close relatives, is a very peaceful fish that will not disrupt a well-organized community aquarium. The species has not been seen very often in the aquarium hobby. This is partly due to the confusion concerning this group of fishes; species often appear under the wrong names. *P. brevis* and its close relatives are characterized by a relatively deep body and a very short stripe which extends onto the eye and opercle. There are two subspecies of this fish. *Pyrrhulina brevis brevis* is found in the Rio Negro area; *P. brevis australe* is found farther south from the La Plata-Parana-Paraguay basin to the Rio Guapore basin. Males of the "lugubris" form have the dorsal, anal and ventral fins edged in black. The female has yellowish fins which are not black-edged.

1. *Pyrrhulina* of the *P. brevis* group (p1070).
2. *Pyrrhulina* of the *brevis* group, the form generally called *P. "lugubris"* (p1070).

Puntius woehlerti ⏹F⏹⏹R⏹⏹X⏹⏹0⏹⏹6⏹⏹9⏹⏹X⏹⏹N⏹⏹N⏹⏹3⏹   [E. Roloff]

1. *Pyrrhulina brevis* ♀   ⏹F⏹⏹A⏹⏹M⏹⏹0⏹⏹7⏹⏹0⏹⏹X⏹⏹N⏹⏹N⏹⏹6⏹   [Dr. Herbert R. Axelrod]
2. *Pyrrhulina brevis* ♂   ⏹F⏹⏹A⏹⏹B⏹⏹0⏹⏹7⏹⏹0⏹⏹X⏹⏹N⏹⏹N⏹⏹6⏹   [Dr. Herbert R. Axelrod]

Pyrrhulina spilota ☐F☐ ☐R☐ ☐X☐ ☐0☐ ☐7☐ ☐1☐ ☐X☐ ☐N☐ ☐N☐ ☐6☐ [Dr. Herbert R. Axelrod]

Pyrrhulina vittata ☐F☐ ☐R☐ ☐X☐ ☐0☐ ☐7☐ ☐2☐ ☐X☐ ☐N☐ ☐N☐ ☐7☐ [Dr. Herbert R. Axelrod]

PYRRHULINA SPILOTA Weitzman / *Blotched Pyrrhulina*

Range: South America, specific origin unknown.
Habits: Very peaceful in the community aquarium.
Water Conditions: Soft, slightly acid water. Temperature 24 to 27°C.
Size: 6 cm.
Food Requirements: Small live foods are preferred, but it will also accept frozen and some prepared flake foods.

The attractive dwarf fishes of the genus *Pyrrhulina* are relatively unknown as aquarium fishes compared to many of the other characoids. In general *Pyrrhulina* species are surface fishes with upturned mouths and flat heads. *P. spilota* was described in 1960 by Dr. Stanley H. Weitzman. The specimens that were available to him were imported live from South America by Paramount Aquarium, Inc. for distribution in the aquarium hobby, their exact origin unknown.

Pyrrhulina spilota has a light tan body with four black spots. It has a line from the mouth to behind the operculum. As can be seen when comparing the color photos, *P. spilota* has the same pattern as *P. vittata* but has one more black spot and a significantly more elongate body.

PYRRHULINA VITTATA Regan / *Banded Pyrrhulina*

Range: Amazon in the Santarem region, Rio Tapajoz.
Habits: Very peaceful in the community tank.
Water Conditions: Soft, slightly acid water. Temperature 24 to 27°C.
Size: To 7 cm.
Food Requirements: Small live foods preferred, but will also take frozen and prepared foods.

The Banded Pyrrhulina is an attractive and peaceful little fellow which can always be counted upon to "dress up" a community tank and never upset the equilibrium there. This species is easily distinguished from the others by the short, rather chunky body and the distinct narrow black line which extends from the lower jaw through the eye to a point slightly behind the gill-plates. The three markings on the side could be described as large spots rather than bands, and there is a golden band at the base of the tail. Males are distinguished by a longer dorsal fin and a blue glint in the dorsal and caudal fins. This species is said to be a ready spawner, but sometimes a bit of patience and a number of fish are required for results. A pair will choose a broad submerged leaf and clean it thoroughly, then lay eggs on the clean surface. The male guards and fans them, and the fry hatch in 24 to 28 hours. Once they are swimming there is no point in keeping the parents with them any longer. The youngsters should get infusoria for at least a week, after which fine dried foods and then newly hatched brine shrimp are fed.

QUINTANA ATRIZONA Hubbs / *Black-Barred Livebearer*

Range: Cuba.
Habits: Because of their size, they should be kept only with small fishes; otherwise they may tend to be shy.
Water Conditions: Not critical. Prefers a sunny tank which is well heated, 24 to 26°C.
Size: Males about 2 cm; females about 3 cm.
Food Requirements: Not choosy, but the food particles should be small in size.

Although not very brightly colored, these little livebearers are very interesting. The gonopodium of mature males is very long and reaches almost to the caudal base when folded back. At the tip is a distinct hook, similar to the one found on *Gambusia* species. This fish was first introduced in 1932. These first ones were said to have come from the vicinity of Havana, Cuba and also from Baracoa, in the eastern end of the island. Now there seems to be some doubt as to whether they come from Cuba at all. Time will tell, but it seems strange that we still cannot be sure of the habitat of a fish which has been known since 1932. As with most livebearers, there is no question which are the males. Broods are quite small even with fully grown fish, and more than thirty young is unusual. The fry are tiny and must be carefully fed with very fine foods at first, almost like the fry of egglayers. With proper feeding, however, they grow rapidly and in three to four months are ready to have young of their own. These fish do a little picking on algae from the plants but never extend their appetites to the plants themselves.

RASBORA AGILIS Ahl / *Black-Striped Rasbora*

Range: Sumatra.
Habits: Peaceful, active swimmers; will mix with other active species in a community aquarium.
Water Conditions: Water should be clean, very soft and with a pH of about 6.6. Temperature 24 to 28°C.
Size: About 8 cm.
Food Requirements: Will take dried foods, but live or frozen foods preferred.

Females have deeper bodies. For spawning, a tank of not less than 40 liters should be provided with several bunches of bushy plants. Spawning is sometimes extended over several days, and the usual practice is to leave the breeders in until the first fry are seen. The youngsters grow slowly in the first few days and should be given infusoria as well as finely powdered dry food. After two to three weeks the rate of growth increases, and in a half-year the youngsters attain a size of 4 cm and more. This species is one of the earlier-known rasboras, having been first imported into Germany in 1913.

Quintana atrizona ⬚F⬚R⬚X⬚0⬚7⬚3⬚X⬚N⬚N⬚1 [G.J.M. Timmerman]
Rasbora agilis ⬚F⬚R⬚X⬚0⬚7⬚4⬚X⬚N⬚N⬚7 [Dr. Herbert R. Axelrod]

Rasbora argyrotaenia ⬚F⬚R⬚X⬚0⬚7⬚5⬚X⬚N⬚N⬚8 [Dr. Herbert R. Axelrod]
Rasbora bankanensis ⬚F⬚R⬚X⬚0⬚7⬚6⬚X⬚N⬚N⬚7 [Dr. Herbert R. Axelrod]

RASBORA ARGYROTAENIA (Bleeker) / *Silver Rasbora*

Range: Japan, China, Thailand, Malacca, Malaysia, Java, Bali and Borneo.
Habits: Peaceful toward other fishes, but likely to be shy if kept alone.
Water Conditions: Soft water, about 5 to 8 DH. Should be kept about 23°C, but drops in temperature down to 18°C are tolerated.
Size: Attains a size of 15 cm in natural waters and about 10 cm in captivity.
Food Requirements: Being an active fish, it requires generous feeding; will accept dried foods, but these should be supplemented with live foods.

Even though it lacks much of the color which we associate with the rasbora species, *Rasbora argyrotaenia* lends a great deal of life to the community aquarium with its ceaseless activity, its gleaming silvery body and the black edging of its tail fork. Sexes can only be determined with certainty when mature. At this time the male retains his slim outline, but the female becomes heavier in the belly. As with any other active fish, a cover should be kept on the aquarium to prevent them from jumping out. It is not surprising that a fish with such a wide distribution should have many local varieties and that there should be a certain amount of confusion as to proper identification. For this reason an ichthyologist who is called upon to identify a fish will give hardly any attention to color but will rather note body characteristics like scale counts, ray counts, head measurements, etc. These vary only slightly if at all, but colors may vary greatly depending on location.

RASBORA BANKANENSIS (Bleeker) / *Banka Rasbora*

Range: Island of Banka and the neighboring region of Sumatra.
Habits: Peaceful; likes to swim in schools.
Water Conditions: Soft and slightly acid. Temperature 24 to 27°C.
Size: To about 8 cm.
Food Requirements: Prepared foods accepted, but live or frozen foods should form at least a part of the diet.

The island of Banka, from which this rasbora comes, is frequently spelled "Bangka" and lies off the northern coast of Sumatra. This little fish looks almost completely colorless, but scientific descriptions tell us that it has a blackish stripe which begins faintly at the opercle and gets a little plainer toward the tail. The anal fin on some specimens is said to have a black tip. Dr. Martin Brittan says there are about 45 known species in the genus *Rasbora*, and H. M. Smith says that rasbora species are among the commonest freshwater species found in Thailand. Even if this species is not one of the gorgeously colored ones, there is a certain perkiness in its behavior, just as there is in most rasbora species, which makes them attractive nevertheless. Like most school fishes, they prefer to keep to the open spaces in the aquarium.

RASBORA BORAPETENSIS Smith / *Redtailed Rasbora*

Range: Thailand (Bung Borapet).
Habits: Peaceful; likes to swim in small schools and does not nibble at plants.
Water Conditions: Soft, acid water. Temperature 24 to 27°C.
Size: To 6 cm.
Food Requirements: Eats anything, but should get live foods occasionally.

It would hardly seem appropriate to call this the "Redtailed" Rasbora on the strength of the small amount of color which this picture shows, but this illustrates one of the great but little-known difficulties of fish photography: the fish often change color intensity and it is difficult to photograph them during their period of optimum coloration. Normally, in good color, the fish has a great deal of red in its tail and is a real beauty. Besides, the fish are easy to keep, eat anything and live for a long time in the aquarium. Getting them to spawn is far from being a difficult task; the author knows a breeder who has produced them by the thousands. Still, dealers hesitate to stock them because every time they do they cannot move them, even when the price is very reasonable. For breeding they should be given a tank of at least 40 liters capacity with some bushy plants. The water should be soft, about 2 or 3 DH, and the pH acid, 6.5 or 6.6. A ripe pair, where the female is heavy with eggs and the male active and in good color, is put into this tank and the water temperature raised to 27°C. Eggs are laid in the plants and hatch in 36 hours.

RASBORA CAUDIMACULATA Volz / *Greater Scissortailed Rasbora*

Range: Malaysia and Sumatra.
Habits: Peaceful and active, but should not be combined with small fishes.
Water Conditions: Soft, slightly acid water. Temperature 24 to 27°C.
Size: To 20 cm.
Food Requirements: Eat just about anything, but should get live foods occasionally.

This handsome rasbora has a great resemblance to its smaller cousin *R. trilineata*, the Scissortail, because of the unusual pattern in the tail. Closer examination also shows that the first impression is not so accurate, because the three stripes which are prominent are missing here and there is only one faint stripe. The fish in this photograph were just shipped and the black spot in the lower caudal lobe had evidently been nipped off. This was no great tragedy, because it quickly grew back. There are as yet few reports of any spawnings, and the probability is that this will require a large tank. In their home waters this fish is said to attain a length of 70 cm. Their aquarium should be firmly covered at all times; the author once lost a good pair because the cover glass was not replaced well enough and both jumped out. It is a pity that we do not see this graceful, beautiful fish more often.

Rasbora borapetensis FRX0077XNN6   [Dr. Herbert R. Axelrod]
Rasbora caudimaculata FRX0078XNNC   [Dr. Herbert R. Axelrod]

Rasbora cephalotaenia [F][R][X][0][7][9][X][N][N][9]   [Dr. Herbert R. Axelrod]

Rasbora daniconius [F][R][X][0][8][0][X][N][N][8]   [Dr. Herbert R. Axelrod]

RASBORA CEPHALOTAENIA (Bleeker) / *Porthole Rasbora*

Range: Malaysia, Sumatra and Borneo.
Habits: Peaceful at all times.
Water Conditions: Prefers soft, slightly acid water. Temperature 24 to 26°C.
Size: To 13 cm in natural waters; captive specimens somewhat smaller.
Food Requirements: Takes all foods, but should get live or frozen foods occasionally.

RASBORA DANICONIUS (Hamilton-Buchanan) / *Golden-Striped Rasbora*

Range: Southeastern Asia from Thailand through Burma and Andaman Islands to western India and Sri Lanka.
Habits: Peaceful and hardy; prefers to be in company with others of its own species.
Water Conditions: Medium hard (about 10 DH), neutral to slightly acid (pH 6-7) water kept at a temperature between 22 and 25°C is best for this species.
Size: Reaches a length of 20 cm in nature, but rarely gets to be more than 8 to 9 cm in captivity.
Food Requirements: Not critical; normal aquarium foods, including dried foods, will be accepted. They should be conditioned on live foods for spawning.

Rasbora daniconius is one of those excellent aquarium fishes that are easy to maintain and easy to breed. They are not only resistant to many of the common diseases, but they can also temporarily withstand temperatures as low as 17°C.

Spawning is not difficult, but as typical for a *Rasbora,* the sexes are difficult to tell apart, at least until the female becomes distended with eggs. For best results the sexes should be separated. This prevents inadvertent spawning in the community tank and loss of eggs to the other members of the community. Conditioning should include ample amounts of live foods such as brine shrimp, daphnia, chironomid larvae, etc. The spawning tank need not be overly large, and it should be provided with fine-leaved plants. The water should be quite clean and there should be a layer of gravel on the bottom. The male may be introduced into the tank first (the previous night is good), with the female added the next morning. The courtship consists of displays and chases by the male as the female hides among the plants until she is ready to spawn. Then they assume a side by side position and the male attempts to curl his body around hers. This site has apparently been selected by the female, and the eggs are shed among the leaves of the plants. The process is repeated, with the female choosing other spawning sites. Once spawning has ceased the adult fish should be removed as they often will eat the eggs.

The eggs hatch in a few days, and estimates of some 200 to 300 fry are common. By the end of a week the fry are free-swimming and ready for food. Infusoria is a good starting food and can be followed in a short time with newly hatched brine shrimp.

RASBORA DORSIOCELLATA Duncker / *Hi-Spot Rasbora*

Range: Southern Malaysia and adjacent Sumatra.
Habits: An active fish, usually forming schools near the surface.
Water Conditions: Prefers soft, neutral to slightly acid water and warm temperatures.
Size: To 6 cm.
Food Requirements: This is an active fish which requires frequent feedings; it does well on dried foods, but live foods help bring out the colors.

This interesting rasbora has one of the most attractive and distinctive color patterns to be found in the genus and has been popular in the aquarium since it was first introduced at the beginning of the century. It was first described and named from aquarium specimens, but unfortunately it is no longer easily obtainable. A school of Hi-Spots swimming near the surface is fascinating in its beauty. When the light is right, the lower halves of the eyes and gill-covers shine a deep emerald green and a golden stripe appears on the hind part of the body. The large black blotch on the dorsal fin stands out even more because of the milky border below the spot. The fins often appear slightly yellowish or greenish.

A prolific breeder, the Hi-Spot Rasbora can be successfully bred by using fine-leaved plants such as *Nitella* or *Myriophyllum* or a spawning mop made of nylon yarn. Many eggs are attached to the plant tufts and hatch in one or two days. The fry can be fed infusoria or other fine foods. Spawning is best at 25 to 27°C and can be initiated by feeding live food. Sexes are hard to distinguish, but if kept in a school the fish will find their own mates.

Juvenile Greater Scissortails *(Rasbora caudimaculata)* might be confused with Hi-Spots because both species have black in the dorsal fin. *Rasbora caudimaculata*, however, has black at the *tip* of the dorsal fin and also has black on the caudal lobes. Hi-Spots have clear caudal lobes and the dorsal fin spot is at the *center* of the fin.

RASBORA DUSONENSIS (Bleeker) / *Yellowtail Rasbora*

Range: Thailand, Malaysia, Sumatra and Borneo.
Habits: Peaceful and active; should have a large tank with a tight cover.
Water Conditions: Soft, somewhat acid water. Temperature 24 to 28°C.
Size: 15 cm.
Food Requirements: Not choosy; will eat dried as well as live foods.

This rasbora, and for that matter most other rasboras, is an active jumper and must be protected from its own exuberance by a tight-fitting cover. *R. dusonensis* is frequently confused with *R. argyrotaenia,* which is much more common in the Asiatic collecting areas. The only difference is that the dark stripe is wider and not as pronounced in *R. dusonensis.* Both are beautiful and well worth the trouble of keeping them, but it is necessary to let them have a roomy aquarium which their active nature requires.

Rasbora dorsiocellata ⬚F⬚D⬚X⬚0⬚8⬚1⬚X⬚N⬚N⬚6 [K. Paysan]
Rasbora dusonensis ⬚F⬚D⬚X⬚0⬚8⬚2⬚X⬚N⬚N⬚A [Dr. Herbert R. Axelrod]

Rasbora einthoveni 🄵🅁🅇🄾🄿🄿🄿🅇🄽🄽🄿 [Dr. Herbert R. Axelrod]

Rasbora elegans 🄵🅁🅇🄾🄿🄿🄿🅇🄽🄽🄿 [Dr. Herbert R. Axelrod]

RASBORA EINTHOVENI (Bleeker)
Brilliant Rasbora, Einthoven's Rasbora

Range: Malacca, Malaysia, Thailand, Sumatra and Borneo.
Habits: In its native waters it travels in schools; an active swimmer, so it should be given adequate quarters with a good amount of swimming space.
Water Conditions: Not critical, but prefers soft, acid water and temperatures between 24 to 26°C; for spawning, about 27°C is best.
Size: Up to 8 cm.
Food Requirements: Being an active fish, they should be fed frequently; dried foods are accepted but should be supplemented with frozen foods.

This is a very attractive little fish, and a number of them swimming actively with the sun reflecting from their shiny scales and turning their dark stripe to deep green is a pleasant sight. This species is often confused with some of the other similar species such as *R. taeniata*, *R. daniconius* and *R. cephalotaenia*, all three of which it resembles very closely. Sexes are difficult to distinguish; the only difference is the heavier body of the females. One might have what is thought to be a pair and find that it is a ripe and an unripe female. The species is easily spawned; the non-adhesive eggs fall to the bottom, which should be covered with pebbles to prevent the parents from eating them.

RASBORA ELEGANS Volz / *Two-Spot Rasbora, Elegant Rasbora*

Range: Malaysia and the Sunda Islands.
Habits: Peaceful and active; good community tank fish.
Water Conditions: Soft, slightly acid water. Temperature 24 to 28°C.
Size: To 13 cm.
Food Requirements: Easily fed with live, frozen or dry foods.

No chance of confusing the Two-Spot Rasbora with any other species of the genus. Its outstanding characteristic is a rectangular spot on the sides in the middle of its body. The pigmentation in most fishes occurs in the skin, but the skin and flesh of this attractive fish appear to be quite transparent at this point, and the spot is deeper down. The picture shows this to a certain extent: compare the rectangular spot on the sides with the black streak just above the anal fin. Probably the spot is of equal intensity, but being imbedded more deeply we see some of the light violet of the body on it. Males are usually a bit smaller than the females and have deeper colors. A ripe pair will spawn readily in the same manner as the barbs, with a great deal of driving and hide-and-seek among the bushy plants, coming to a frequent quivering halt among the plants and scattering adhesive eggs. Like the barbs, the breeders will eat their eggs if they are not removed as soon as spawning is completed. Hatching takes place on the following day; fry are easily fed with hard-boiled egg yolk squeezed through a cloth until they are able to handle newly hatched brine shrimp later on.

RASBORA HETEROMORPHA Duncker / *Rasbora, Harlequin Fish*

Range: Malaysia, southern Thailand, Sumatra and Java.
Habits: Peaceful and harmless to even the smallest fishes; they are active swimmers which prefer to travel in schools.
Water Conditions: Comes from very soft and acid waters, and this is what they should get. Temperature 24 to 27°C.
Size: 5 cm; usually a little smaller.
Food Requirements: Will accept dried foods, but should get frequent feedings with live and frozen foods besides.

Almost every picture which depicts a group of tropical aquarium fishes will include Angelfish, Discus and our little friend *Rasbora heteromorpha.* The little red fish with the black triangle is almost as well known as the ubiquitous Guppy. Its popularity is well deserved; besides being unquestionably decorative; it is always out in front where it can be seen and admired and is never in the least aggressive toward its tankmates. This fish was long a mystery to German breeders. They knew that there was a good profit in breeding Rasboras, and some of them were able to breed large numbers of them with very little trouble. These were all in a single district, and other breeders found that the very soft water in this district was the reason for success. As soon as they duplicated the chemical properties of this water, their fish began breeding too. Sexes can usually be distinguished by a fine gold line along the upper part of the triangle in the males and the heavier, deeper body of the females. Eggs are usually laid on the underside of a wide plant leaf and afterward ignored by both parents. Fry hatch in 24 to 26 hours and should be given infusoria feedings at first.

RASBORA KALOCHROMA (Bleeker) / *Big-Spot Rasbora*

Range: Malaysia, Sumatra and Borneo.
Habits: Peaceful and a continuous swimmer.
Water Conditions: Warm (24 to 27°C), soft, acid water.
Size: Reaches a total length of 10 cm.
Food Requirements: Takes dry, frozen and live foods equally well.

A remarkable similarity between the Big-Spot Rasbora and the Two-Spot Rasbora is easily seen. Both fish are of similar size, shape and color and both may be found in the same parts of Malaysia and Sumatra. Yet technical differences such as scale counts and number of fin rays prove that the two species are not so closely related to each other as might be thought from superficial observation. In both the Big-Spot and the Two-Spot, the larger blotch is at midside. In *Rasbora kalochroma,* the small spot is behind the head; in *R. elegans,* it is at the base of the caudal fin. This difference is fine for the aquarist trying to identify his fish, but it brings up the problem of how and why fish evolve such similar, yet different, color patterns.

1085

Rasbora heteromorpha ⬚F⬚ ⬚Q⬚ ⬚X⬚ ⬚0⬚ ⬚8⬚ ⬚5⬚ ⬚X⬚ ⬚N⬚ ⬚N⬚ ⬚5⬚

Rasbora kalochroma ⬚F⬚ ⬚R⬚ ⬚X⬚ ⬚0⬚ ⬚8⬚ ⬚6⬚ ⬚X⬚ ⬚N⬚ ⬚N⬚ ⬚A⬚

1. *Rasbora maculata* ♂ ⬚F⬚E⬚T⬚0⬚8⬚7⬚X⬚N⬚N⬚2   [H. J. Richter]
2. *Rasbora maculata* ♀ ⬚F⬚F⬚M⬚0⬚8⬚7⬚X⬚N⬚N⬚2   [H. J. Richter]

Rasbora myersi ⬚F⬚D⬚X⬚0⬚8⬚8⬚X⬚N⬚N⬚C   [Dr. Herbert R. Axelrod]

RASBORA MACULATA Duncker / *Dwarf Rasbora, Spotted Rasbora*

Range: Parts of India, southern Malaysia, Singapore and Sumatra.
Habits: Very peaceful, but because of their tiny size and special water requirements they should have a tank of their own, which need not be big.
Water Conditions: These fish are only at their best in water which is quite acid, pH 6.2 to 6.4, and very soft, about 2 DH. Temperature 24 to 26°C.
Size: 2 cm.
Food Requirements: Larger foods like tubifex or white worms should be chopped before feeding; dried foods accepted in the finer sizes.

Not one in a dozen people who have seen this lovely little fish has seen it in its full glory, and glory it is. It demands special treatment and when it gets it shows its gratitude by displaying an array of colors which rival those of any fish. These colors are difficult to describe; they must be seen to be appreciated. A proper background must be prepared. Their tank should be well planted around the sides and back, with an open space in front. Here is where you will usually see the little beauties. The bottom should be dark; the black gravel which is now available is perfect for the purpose. Sunlight should come into the tank from behind the observer. These fish love sunlight and will strut around in it like butterflies. At certain angles the sides will take on a deep violet shimmer. Females are a little bigger than the males and almost as brightly colored. Spawning takes place in bundles of bushy plants. The pair should be well fed before being put out to spawn, because the females are very fond of eating their own eggs. Fry hatch in 24 to 36 hours and are surprisingly easy to raise on finely ground dried foods.

1. *Rasbora maculata*, male (p1087).
2. *Rasbora maculata*, female (p1087).

RASBORA MYERSI Brittan / *Myers' Rasbora*

Range: Malaysia, Sumatra, Borneo and Thailand.
Habits: Peaceful toward any other fishes which it cannot swallow.
Water Conditions: Soft, neutral to slightly acid water. Temperature 24 to 27°C.
Size: 15 cm.
Food Requirements: Live, frozen or dried foods taken equally well.

One look at this *Rasbora* species should serve to convince anyone as to why it is so seldom seen in the collections of fish hobbyists. It just simply does not have any outstanding colors, unless you could call attention to that slight tinge of black in the tail. Doubtless collectors in Asiatic waters have the same problems as do the South American collectors: a netful of fish is brought up, and 95 out of 100 are of no value for several reasons: they are or get to be too big for the aquarium, they are undesirable because they are vicious toward other fishes or, most of all, they have no colors to make them decorative and desirable in the aquarium.

1088

RASBORA PAUCIPERFORATA Weber & de Beaufort
Red-Line Rasbora

Range: Sumatra.
Habits: Peaceful and well-behaved in mixed company.
Water Conditions: Water should be somewhat acid, pH 6.2, and soft, DH 2 or 3. Temperature 24 to 27°C.
Size: About 6 cm.
Food Requirements: Live foods preferred, but all kinds are accepted.

A well-planted tank with lighting from above and about a dozen Red-Line Rasboras is all that is needed to make a breathtaking display which will attract anyone's attention and admiration. An added touch may be attained by the use of black gravel, which sets off the colors of the fish and plants. Only a few other fishes have a stripe which matches this one in brilliance. One is the Glowlight Tetra. A little experimenting is necessary to get the best lighting for the most effective results. When just right, the fish lights up from tail to snout like a red neon sign. This fish was named by Weber and de Beaufort in 1916, and hobbyists saw their first specimens in 1928. Spawning is similar to the other long-bodied rasboras: bushy plants should be provided and also a generous amount of swimming space. Males drive actively, coming frequently to a stop alongside a female among the plants and scattering eggs all over, many of them falling to the bottom. Fry hatch in 24 to 36 hours.

RASBORA SARAWAKENSIS Brittan / *Sarawak Rasbora*

Range: Northern Borneo.
Habits: Peaceful and active in the community aquarium.
Water Conditions: Soft, acid water preferred but not essential. Temperature 24 to 27°C.
Size: To 8 cm.
Food Requirements: Eats all foods, but should get live or frozen foods occasionally.

We do not very frequently hear of a fish from Sarawak, situated on the northern part of the island of Borneo. There is little chance that this *Rasbora* species will ever set the hobby on its ear. It reminds one of *Rasbora borapetensis* from Thailand, except that the tail is only a pale yellow while that of our Thai friend is red. We had a couple of pairs in our TFH office aquarium for quite a time and found them, like the other rasbora species, to be as peaceful and easily pleased as any fish in the tank. It seems that there are many more possibilities for aquarium fishes on the huge island of Borneo than we have seen thus far, if there were only somebody to get out there and *find* them! Y. W. Ong sent these to the author (HRA). Many of them, of course, would also be native to Thailand, Sumatra, Malaysia and Java. All of these countries have been fairly well gone over by scientists, but at least there should be a few more than one not-so-attractive *Rasbora* species!

Rasbora pauciperforata 	F	D	X	0	8	9	X	N	N	6	[H. J. Richter]
Rasbora sarawakensis 	F	R	X	0	9	0	X	N	N	8	[Dr. Herbert R. Axelrod]

Rasbora somphongsi 🄵🅁🅇🄾🄾🅉🄸🅇🄽🄽🄾
Rasbora steineri 🄵🅁🅇🄾🄾🅈🄾🅇🄽🄽🄾

[Dr. Herbert R. Axelrod]
[G.J.M. Timmerman]

RASBORA SOMPHONGSI Meinken / *Somphongs' Rasbora*

Range: Thailand.
Habits: Peaceful; a good community fish.
Water Conditions: Soft, acid water desirable. Temperature 23 to 28°C.
Size: About 3 cm.
Food Requirements: All types of food accepted, provided that it is small enough to be swallowed.

Just a little bit bigger than *Rasbora maculata*, the Dwarf or Spotted Rasbora, is *Rasbora somphongsi*, a fish ideally suited to the needs of the hobbyist who has small tanks. Peaceful and hardy, Somphongs' Rasbora is a very good community fish with only one drawback: its preference for strictly soft, acid water. This insistence by the fish of being maintained only in water which is difficult for some hobbyists to duplicate has led to a curtailment of its popularity among hobbyists who can obtain only hard, alkaline water, and *Rasbora somphongsi* finds itself in the same boat as *Rasbora maculata:* it is not seen as often as it deserves, while other less attractive and less accommodating fishes are given preference. For spawning, which is accomplished through the laying of eggs in bunches of plants or synthetic plant fibers, soft and acid water is a necessity. The fry are very tiny, as is to be expected from the size of the parents, and they require plenty of infusoria for the first few days of their free-swimming life. *Rasbora somphongsi* is not a brilliantly colored fish, but its quiet beauty can be shown off better if it is kept in a well-planted tank having a dark background and bottom.

RASBORA STEINERI Nichols & Pope / *Chinese Rasbora*

Range: Southern China, Hainan Province.
Habits: Peaceful and well-behaved with other fishes.
Water Conditions: Soft and considerably acid water. Temperature 23 to 26°C.
Size: Up to 8 cm.
Food Requirements: Live foods preferred, but all kinds are accepted.

Most of China is in the Temperate Zone, and there are very few fishes of interest to the fish hobbyist available today from waters which are warm enough to be considered "tropical." *Rasbora steineri*, from Hainan Province, is one of the exceptions. In appearance it resembles the much better-known *R. borapetensis*, the main difference being that *R. borapetensis* has a shade brighter red in the tail toward the base. There is as yet no record of any spawning of *R. steineri*. Probably it spawns like the other long-bodied rasboras, but any guess may be far off base. It is a logical point from which to start when making an attempt to spawn it, however. But we already have rasboras, many of them far surpassing this one in beauty and, what is more important, readily available.

RASBORA SUMATRANA (Bleeker) / *Sumatran Rasbora*

Range: Thailand, Malaysia, Sumatra, Borneo and Southeast Asia.
Habits: Peaceful toward other fishes which are too large to be swallowed.
Water Conditions: Soft, slightly acid water preferred. Temperature 23 to 26°C.
Size: 15 cm in captivity.
Food Requirements: Not choosy as to foods, but should have live or frozen foods frequently.

The Sumatran Rasbora is a species which requires an expert to identify it positively because of the extreme variability of its colors. Here is how Dr. Martin R. Brittan describes them: "May have dark stripe, a stripe posteriorly only, or none at all; if present, stripe may or may not end in a spot at the base of the tail; spot may be present without stripe. Streak above anal may be variable in shape, and is often absent. Tail may or may not have dark margin or dark tip to lobe." Care and spawning for this species are similar to that of *Rasbora somphongsi*.

RASBORA TRILINEATA Steindachner
Three-Lined or Scissortailed Rasbora

Range: Sumatra and Borneo, where it is common.
Habits: Peaceful; active swimmers who should have plenty of swimming space in their aquarium.
Water Conditions: Soft, acid water with a pH value of about 6.5. Temperature 24 to 26°C.
Size: Up to 10 cm.
Food Requirements: Will accept dried foods as well as live foods.

The Scissortailed Rasbora has become one of the most popular members of the group. This is certainly not due to the presence of any brilliant colors, but the fish has other things to recommend it. For one, it is usually out in front where it can be seen. Another is that it is always on the move. It accepts and thrives on practically any food and never becomes belligerent toward its neighbors. It spawns quite easily and the young are not difficult to raise. Although it is at its best in acid water, it will also get along in alkaline water but might possibly make known its objection to it by refusing to spawn. All in all, it is a very hardy and adaptable species. Females are a trifle longer than the males and considerably bigger around. After considerable driving, the male gets the female into some bushy plants, where he wraps his body about hers and 15 to 25 eggs are expelled and fertilized. The eggs have very little adhesive power and many fall to the bottom. The first of the fry hatch after 24 hours. In five days the youngsters begin to swim, at which time they may be fed with very fine dry food, followed in a week or so by newly hatched brine shrimp.

Rasbora sumatrana ⒡ⒹⓍ⓪⑨③ⓍⓃⓃⒶ   [Dr. Herbert R. Axelrod]
Rasbora trilineata ⒡ⓇⓍ⓪⑨④ⓍⓃⓃ⑦   [Dr. Herbert R. Axelrod]

Rasbora urophthalma $\boxed{F}\boxed{R}\boxed{X}\boxed{0}\boxed{9}\boxed{5}\boxed{X}\boxed{N}\boxed{N}\boxed{2}$ [S. Frank]
Rasbora vaterifloris $\boxed{F}\boxed{R}\boxed{X}\boxed{0}\boxed{9}\boxed{6}\boxed{X}\boxed{N}\boxed{N}\boxed{3}$ [Dr. Herbert R. Axelrod]

RASBORA UROPHTHALMA Ahl
Ocellated Dwarf Rasbora; Exclamation-Point Rasbora

Range: Sumatra.
Habits: Peaceful; because of their diminutive size, they should not be kept with large fishes.
Water Conditions: Soft water, no more than 5 DH, with an acidity of pH 6.5. Temperature 23 to 27°C.
Size: 3 cm.
Food Requirements: Smaller live foods preferred, but dried foods also accepted; they are also fond of picking at algae.

This is one of the small rasboras, easily recognized by the horizontal stripe which is at its widest below the beginning of the dorsal fin and then narrows down to a point toward the tail base. Here there is an ocellated round spot of steel blue ringed with gold. This fish, and the other small rasboras for that matter, requires a well-planted aquarium or it may turn out to be very shy. Given proper conditions and sunlight shining in on them, it will be seen that the dark line is edged above with a delicate gold. Like the other rasboras, this species is very gregarious and happy only when kept in a small group of at least six. Then they are active and always about in the open spaces. Spawning may be accomplished in a small aquarium of 12 to 20 liters which should be planted with one or two broad-leaved plants like *Cryptocoryne* species and a bunch of fine-leaved plants like *Myriophyllum*. Temperature should be gradually raised to 27°C. Driving is not at all vigorous.

RASBORA VATERIFLORIS Deraniyagala / *Singhalese Fire Barb*

Range: Sri Lanka.
Habits: Very peaceful, active fish which should be given adequate swimming space.
Water Conditions: Soft, acid water like the other species. Temperature should not sink below 25°C.
Size: Maximum length 3.5 cm.
Food Requirements: Will accept dried foods as well as live or frozen foods.

Like so many other fishes, this one may be rather pale and uninteresting in a dealer's bare tank, and the hobbyist who does not know what beautiful color this species is capable of might easily pass it up as too drab for his tank. Then he might see the same fish in all their glory in a friend's aquarium and rave about their beauty. Females are easily recognizable by their lighter colors and heavier dimensions. Males are active drivers and pursue the females into plant thickets, where a very rapid spawning act takes place. The eggs have little adhesive power, and most of them fall to the bottom. The pair should come out as soon as the eggs have been laid or most of them will be eaten. The water level should then be reduced to 15 cm. The young will hatch in 36 to 40 hours.

RASBORICHTHYS ALTIOR Regan / *Green False Rasbora*

Range: Singapore.
Habits: A peaceful, schooling species.
Water Conditions: Not critical; soft, slightly acid water is preferred. Temperature 15 to 26°C.
Size: 9 cm.
Food Requirements: Standard foods are accepted readily.

The Green False Rasbora is a species which is best kept in schools of six or more. Groups smaller than this tend to not show the schooling behavior and are much less attractive. This species is reported to be resistant to temperatures down to 10°C, but breeding is best accomplished at about 24°C. Breeding can be accomplished in a 40-liter aquarium heavily planted with bunch-plants such as *Cabomba*. A pair or a trio of two males and one female can be used for breeding. The female should be conditioned separately and introduced into the aquarium at least 24 hours before the males. Water in the breeding aquarium should be soft and slightly acid; spawning is apparently stimulated by sunlight. The eggs are adhesive and hatch in about two days at 24°C. Fry should be fed infusoria for about a week and then converted to newly hatched brine shrimp.

RHADINOCENTRUS ORNATUS Regan
Southern Soft-Spined Rainbowfish

Range: Southern Queensland and northern New South Wales, Australia.
Habits: Active mid-water swimmers; peaceful.
Water Conditions: Neutral to slightly alkaline water to which a little bit of salt has been added. Temperature should range from about 22 to 26°C.
Size: Attains a length of about 8 cm.
Food Requirements: Will readily accept most common aquarium foods, but for best conditioning should have some live foods.

Rhadinocentrus ornatus is an active swimmer and usually can be seen in the mid-water areas of the aquarium. They are peaceful fish, however, and can be used as a community species to fill the area around mid-tank. Live food is preferred, but they will accept almost any of the common aquarium foods.

Spawning is not too difficult and can be accomplished in a manner similar to that of the other rainbowfishes. The tank is set up with some fine-leaved plants and the spawners introduced after about a week of conditioning. Once spawning is completed the parents can be removed, although they are said to leave the eggs alone if well fed. The eggs can be seen hanging by small threads from the plants. Hatching occurs in about one week, and the fry are hardy and rather easy to raise. The first food should be infusoria, but baby brine shrimp can be added before too long.

Rasborichthys altior F D X 0 9 7 X N N 9   [Dr. Herbert R. Axelrod]

Rhadinocentrus ornatus F R X 0 9 8 X N N 8   [Dr. Herbert R. Axelrod]

Rhodeus sericeus F R X 0 9 9 X N N 8   [J. Elias]

1. *Rivulus agilae* ♂ F A M 1 0 0 X N N 5   [J. H. Huber]

2. *Rivulus agilae* ♀ F B B 1 0 0 X N N 5   [J. H. Huber]

RHODEUS SERICEUS (Pallas) / *Bitterling*

Range: Middle Europe.

Habits: Peaceful, but not a good community fish, as it is not a tropical species and cannot take normal aquarium temperatures.

Water Conditions: Water composition is not of great importance as long as extremes are avoided. Temperature 14 to 21°C.

Size: Up to 8 cm.

Food Requirements: Accepts most commercial foods; paste foods are especially good.

Very few American hobbyists have had any experience with this fish, but it is popular in Europe, where there is less stress placed on tropical species and more attention is paid to native fishes. Perhaps the Bitterling is more favored in Europe because of its interesting habits; European hobbyists pay more attention to behavioral characteristics than Americans do. In any event, the Bitterling is fascinating in its breeding pattern. Many fishes go to great lengths to protect their young, but the Bitterling really confounds its enemies: the female uses her extremely long ovipositor to place the eggs within living molluscs, where they are safe from all harm. The hatched fry remain in their living refuge until they become free-swimming. The mollusc, usually a mussel, is not to be considered as a victim, because the young *Rhodeus* are not parasites and take nothing from the bivalve. As a matter of fact, the protection afforded by the young fish only serves to even up the score between mollusc and fish, for many young bivalves spend their larval stages attached to the skin of fishes, who thus transport them to new homes.

RIVULUS AGILAE Hoedeman / *Agila Rivulus*

Range: Coastal Guianas.

Habits: Best kept with its own kind or similar fishes.

Water Conditions: Soft, slightly acid water is best. A temperature around 22°C is best, but gradual drops in temperature are tolerated.

Size: To 5.5 cm.

Food Requirements: Living foods preferred; frozen or prepared foods only accepted when very hungry.

This species was described by J. J. Hoedeman in 1954 and was found in a small rocky stream. It is a small fish which reaches adulthood at five to six months of age and usually reproduces at eight months, when it will have reached only a little more than 5 cm in body length. The Agila Rivulus is most closely related to *Rivulus breviceps* from Guyana and Surinam and to *Rivulus geayi* from French Guiana. *Rivulus agilae* does best when kept at temperatures between 18 and 23°C.

1. *Rivulus agilae* male (p1099).
2. *R. agilae* female (p1099).

RIVULUS CYLINDRACEUS Poey / *Cuban Rivulus*

Range: Cuba.
Habits: Fairly peaceful in the community aquarium.
Water Conditions: Soft, slightly acid water preferred. Temperature 24 to 26°C.
Size: Males slightly under 5 cm; females slightly larger.
Food Requirements: Should get live foods only, but will accept dried foods if hungry.

As with the African *Aphyosemion* species, there is little danger of getting the males and females of this attractive fish confused. Even at an early age, females develop the well-known "rivulus spot." This is an ocellated spot in the upper part of the caudal base. It is totally absent in the males. Besides, the males have much more to offer in the way of color. Both have a lateral stripe, but the male's is a deeper brown and more distinct. The male's dorsal fin has a blue edge, as has the upper part of the tail, and his sides have regular rows of red dots. These fish are very easy to spawn, and a small aquarium suffices. Eggs are laid in bushy plants near the surface, a few each day, and take from 12 to 14 days to hatch. There are several ways to separate the eggs and breeders. One is to pick out the eggs every few days. A simpler method is to leave the breeders in with the eggs, which they seldom eat, for about 10 days and then fish out the parents. Still another is to remove the plants with the eggs every 10 days and place them in similar water to hatch. The fry are free-swimming upon hatching.

RIVULUS HARTI (Boulenger) / *Hart's Rivulus; Giant Rivulus*

Range: Trinidad, Venezuela and eastern Colombia.
Habits: Peaceful and likely to remain hidden; will not harm any fish it cannot swallow.
Water Conditions: Not at all critical, but slightly sensitive to lower temperatures. The temperature should never be allowed to drop below 24°C.
Size: 10 cm.
Food Requirements: Should get live food, but will take dry food when very hungry.

Some of the *Rivulus* species, of which this is one, have a strange habit which is not mentioned in most of the books: they will often jump out of the water and cling to the glass sides of the aquarium above the surface or to the cover glass for considerable periods of time. When they feel themselves beginning to become dry, they drop back, sometimes to repeat the procedure soon afterward. What the reason for this behavior might be is something for animal behaviorists to figure out, and the answer, if we ever get it, might be very interesting. Perhaps in their native waters they escape some natural enemies in this manner; then again, maybe they just *like* to do it! In any case, their tank must be kept covered if these jumpers are to remain in it. Sexes are easily distinguished, as with most *Rivulus* species. The males have rows of red dots on the sides which are only faintly indicated in the females.

Rivulus cylindraceus ☐F☐R☐X☐1☐0☐1☐X☐N☐N☐5 [S. Frank]
Rivulus harti ☐F☐R☐X☐1☐0☐2☐X☐N☐N☐7

Rivulus holmiae ꓒꓒꓒꓒꓒꓒꓒꓒꓒꓒ [R. Zukal]
Rivulus punctatus ꓒꓒꓒꓒꓒꓒꓒꓒꓒꓒ [Harald Schultz]

RIVULUS HOLMIAE Eigenmann / *Golden-Tailed Rivulus*

Range: Guyana.
Habits: Adept at jumping through the smallest opening; peaceful, but will eat small fishes.
Water Conditions: Soft, slightly acid water optimal, but not necessary. Temperature 22 to 25°C.
Size: About 10 cm.
Food Requirements: Will accept living, frozen or freeze-dried foods.

This *Rivulus* species is one of the biggest killifishes kept in the aquarium. Its 10 cm size as well as its nature suit it to a large, well-planted aquarium. For such a large fish, it is unusually shy. The temperature should be about 24°C. The members of the genus *Rivulus* are not particularly active fishes. They are given to staying in one posture, usually at an odd angle, for long periods of time. The fish are capable of quick, rather snaky movements when food approaches. Breeding is not particularly difficult. Raising the temperature to about 25°C and placing the pair in a well-planted aquarium is about all the preparation that is necessary if the pair has been well conditioned. Most members of the genus will spawn immediately upon being placed in the breeding aquarium, but this interesting species frequently will not spawn for several hours. After the pair has gotten used to the aquarium, the male will start courting the female. As he becomes more persistent in his courtship, he presses his body against the female's, forcing her against a plant leaf or against the bottom. At this time the eggs are laid either singly or in groups of two. A single female may lay up to 100 eggs in a twenty-four-hour period if she has been well conditoned. The eggs hatch in 10 to 14 days, and the fry gather near the top. The fry are large enough to accept newly hatched brine shrimp at once.

RIVULUS PUNCTATUS (Boulenger) / *Spotted Rivulus*

Range: Paraguay, Bolivia and western Brazil.
Habits: Generally peaceful, but shy with other fishes.
Water Conditions: Soft, slightly acid water. Temperature 24 to 27°C.
Size: To 8 cm.
Food Requirements: All sorts of live foods; dry foods taken only when very hungry.

The Spotted Rivulus is a real rarity which is seldom seen in hobbyist collections today. Another fish, *Rivulus dorni,* has been mistakenly offered as this species by dealers from time to time. The fish pictured here was caught by Harald Schultz in the Mato Grosso region of Brazil. The V-shaped arrangement of dots in the after part of the body is highly reminiscent of the bars in *R. strigatus,* another very attractive member of the genus. All *Rivulus* species are excellent jumpers and can leap surprisingly high out of the water. A covered tank is therefore a necessity if you do not want to find your precious fish on the floor some morning.

RIVULUS UROPHTHALMUS Günther / *Golden Rivulus*

Range: Guianas to the lower Amazon region.
Habits: Prefer to be kept by themselves, but a large tank is not essential; they like to hide in plant thickets and are very active jumpers.
Water Conditions: Soft, slightly acid water is best. A temperature around 24°C is best, but it is not sensitive to gradual drops.
Size: 6 cm.
Food Requirements: Live foods are essential, preferably those which remain near the surface, like mosquito larvae.

The genus *Rivulus* is one which is not generally noted for its brilliance of colors. Most of the species have a coloration which blends in with their native background, making them a drab lot. *Rivulus urophthalmus* is one of the exceptions, even in the green form which we seldom see. The upper two-thirds of the body is covered with horizontal rows of red dots. This species often has a xanthic variation, which is the one which most hobbyists are offered. Here the entire body is a golden yellow instead of green, and the red dots are exceptionally brilliant. Probably these yellow fish occur quite frequently in their native waters, but such a fish would seldom attain full growth. Its color would be equivalent to a death warrant, because such a fish would find it next to impossible to hide from its many enemies. However, in the aquarium the golden ones can be separated from the green ones in a batch of fry and raised to maturity without being attacked by enemies, and the results are beautiful. This fish is easily spawned. A few eggs are laid daily among floating vegetation. These are best picked out and allowed to hatch separately, which they do in 12 days. The fry are easily raised.

ROEBOIDES SP. / *Glass Characin*

Range: Central and South America.
Habits: Although often said to be peaceful, this fish should not be trusted with smaller fishes.
Water Conditions: Neutral water of medium hardness. Temperature 23 to 26°C.
Size: To about 15 cm.
Food Requirements: Prefers live or frozen foods of all kinds, but will sometimes accept prepared flake foods.

Roeboides is a large genus which contains over 20 species and subspecies. Most species of the genus are characterized by a translucent body similar to that found in *Asiphonichthys* and *Phenacogaster,* the body shape of a *Charax* and a flat, pointed head. Glass Characins swim in a slightly inclined head-down position rather than the normal horizontal position. The lower lobe of the caudal fin in many mature specimens is often stronger than the upper lobe due to its swimming pattern. These fish are very active and should be given adequate room to swim and some sunlight. The fish generally spawn among water plants after active courtship rituals.

Rivulus urophthalmus F R X 1 0 5 X N N 6   [Dr. Herbert R. Axelrod]

Roeboides sp. F D X 1 0 6 X N N B   [Harald Schultz]

Sciades marmoratus F D X 1 1 1 X N N 9
Sciades pictus F D X 1 1 2 X N N C

[Braz Walker]
[Harald Schultz]

SCIADES MARMORATUS Gill / *Marbled Catfish*

Range: Marañón River (Amazon system), Peru.
Habits: Somewhat light-shy and retiring, so rock caves and other shelters should be available; peaceful with fishes which it cannot swallow.
Water Conditions: Not critical; adapts easily to most water conditions as long as extremes of pH and hardness are avoided. Temperature 21 to 27°C.
Size: Attains a length of 60 cm or more in aquaria; reaches a larger size in nature.
Food Requirements: Does best on live foods of suitable size, beef heart and other animal-based foods; freeze-dried, frozen and pellet foods are readily taken by young fish; learns to accept oatmeal.

Sciades marmoratus is almost as attractive as its close relative *Sciades pictus*, the Painted Catfish. Immediately striking in young fish of 50-75 mm are the long, motile barbels (the maxillary barbels reach far beyond the caudal fin) ringed alternately with black and white, and the large, almost sail-like dorsal fin. The adipose fin is also quite large.

The young and adult Marbled Catfish are so different in color and pattern that one would hardly suspect them of being the same fish. As the fish grows older it darkens; the dark spots give way to a beautiful wavy marbled pattern. The caudal fin lobes, which are rounded in the young, become much prolonged and pointed (especially the upper lobe) in the adult.

SCIADES PICTUS (Müller & Troschel) / *Painted Catfish*

Range: Amazon basin.
Habits: Retiring and peaceful for its size but should not be kept with fishes it can swallow; caves, driftwood and other types of shelter should be provided.
Water Conditions: Not critical, although extremes of pH and hardness should be avoided.
Size: Reaches a length of 60 cm or more.
Food Requirements: Takes a wide variety of live, freeze-dried or frozen foods; learns to accept cooked oatmeal.

This handsome catfish is one of the most attractive members of the family Pimelodidae and immediately attracts the attention of hobbyists. Even the long, graceful barbels are alternately ringed with black and white. In younger individuals these barbels reach backward beyond the caudal fin; in mature fish they are relatively shorter but still extend beyond the dorsal fin. *Sciades pictus* is typical of the pimelodid catfishes in that it is naked; that is, it has no scales or other bony armor covering its skin.

The Painted Catfish has a voracious appetite and grows rapidly, therefore requiring a very large aquarium for its permanent quarters. For a large predatory catfish, this species seems to be quite peaceful toward fishes too large for it to swallow.

SCLEROPAGES FORMOSUS (Müller & Schlegel)
Barramundi; Asiatic Arowana

Range: Southeastern Thailand, Sumatra, Borneo and Bangka.
Habits: Will eat small fishes; excellent jumper.
Water Conditions: Not critical. A temperature between 22 and 28°C should suffice.
Size: To 90 cm and a weight of over 7 kilograms.
Food Requirements: Surface feeder in nature on insects but will also take small fishes and crustaceans (shrimp, etc.); smaller individuals will take daphnia, brine shrimp, etc.

The Barramundi is an interesting aquarium fish, but like its cousin the Arowana it needs a very large tank when fully grown. Young fish do well in 200-liter tanks but grow rapidly, and soon one must be looking around for 400- or 600-liter tanks to house their pets.

The species of *Scleropages* are mouthbrooders. It has been proved that *Scleropages formosus* is a maternal mouthbrooder, the eggs being taken into the mother's mouth immediately after they are laid. The incubation period is not known specifically for *S. formosus,* but in another species it is estimated to be about 10 to 14 days. The eggs themselves are large, about 10 mm in diameter on the average, and vary in number from 50 to 200.

1. *Scleropages formosus* in a large aquarium (p1114).
2. *S. formosus* subadult (p1114).

SELENOTOCA MULTIFASCIATA (Richardson) / *False Scat; Silver Scat*

Range: New Guinea to New Caledonia; warm Australian coastal waters.
Habits: Peaceful toward other fishes but cannot be trusted with plants.
Water Conditions: Fairly hard, alkaline water with a teaspoon of salt added per four liters of water. Temperature 23 to 26°C.
Size: To 10 cm.
Food Requirements: Live foods, with the addition of vegetable substances like lettuce or spinach leaves; will also eat frozen foods.

Only a highly trained eye can spot the difference between this attractive fish and one of an entirely different genus, *Scatophagus tetracanthus,* the Striped Scat, with which and as which it is frequently shipped. *Selenotoca multifasciata* has a slightly more elongated body and the soft parts of the dorsal and anal fins are smaller than in the Striped Scat. Otherwise they are practically identical, both in appearance and habits. The Silver Scat has a highly variable number of black bars on the sides which give way to vertical rows of spots. As with many fishes which have barred markings, the bars in young specimens probably split now and then to become two. Exactly the same attention should be given the *Selenotoca* species as was specified for the Scat, and they are very likely to be just as hardy and long-lived as their better-known cousins.

1113

1. *Scleropages formosus* ⬚F⬚ ⬚D⬚ ⬚T⬚ ⬚1⬚ ⬚1⬚ ⬚3⬚ ⬚X⬚ ⬚N⬚ ⬚N⬚ ⬚D⬚   [Dr. Herbert R. Axelrod]
2. *Scleropages formosus* var. ⬚F⬚ ⬚D⬚ ⬚M⬚ ⬚1⬚ ⬚1⬚ ⬚3⬚ ⬚X⬚ ⬚N⬚ ⬚N⬚ ⬚D⬚   [K.W. Bertin]

Selenotoca multifasciata ⬚F⬚ ⬚C⬚ ⬚X⬚ ⬚1⬚ ⬚1⬚ ⬚4⬚ ⬚X⬚ ⬚N⬚ ⬚N⬚ ⬚8⬚   [G. Wolfsheimer]

Semaprochilodus taeniurus [F][C][X][1][1][5][X][N][N][B] [Dr. Herbert R. Axelrod]
Semaprochilodus theraponura [F][D][X][1][1][6][X][N][N][D] [Harald Schultz]

SEMAPROCHILODUS TAENIURUS (Valenciennes) / *Silver Prochilodus*

Range: Amazon basin.
Habits: Peaceful, but very likely to nibble at plants; tanks should be kept covered at all times, as the fish jump.
Water Conditions: Soft, slightly alkaline water. These are active swimmers, and they like a roomy tank. Temperature 23 to 26°C.
Size: To 30 cm.
Food Requirements: Mostly vegetable foods should be offered, such as lettuce or spinach.

Not as often imported as *Semaprochilodus theraponura* but even more beautiful is *Semaprochilodus taeniurus*. The body, which in *S. theraponura* is a slightly golden color and without markings, is silvery white and is covered with horizontal rows of black dashes. In the middle from a point below the dorsal fin to the caudal base is a thin black line which looks as if the pigment in a row of dashes flowed together. The same characteristic stripes seen in *S. theraponura* adorn the caudal and anal fins of *S. taeniurus,* but the intervening areas are white. Note also the difference in the dorsal fins: that of *S. taeniurus* is striped black and white like the tail, while in *S. theraponura* it is unmarked and reddish. The outstanding feature of *S. taeniurus,* however, is the brilliant red of the ventral fins, the only splash of bright color in the whole fish. The thick, rough lips proclaim both species as algae-nibblers, and vegetable matter is an important item in their menu. Lacking this, the fish will become listless, sluggish and prone to disease. A large, well-lighted tank is a necessity with this fish, and another is a tight-fitting cover.

SEMAPROCHILODUS THERAPONURA (Fowler)
Flag-Tailed Prochilodus

Range: Guyana and the central Amazon region.
Habits: Peaceful, but its vegetarian habits may lead it to nip plants; a skilled jumper, so tank must be kept covered.
Water Conditions: Soft, slightly alkaline water. Temperature 23 to 26°C.
Size: To 35 cm; imported specimens seldom exceed 13 cm.
Food Requirements: Mostly vegetable food should be offered, such as lettuce leaves, spinach or boiled oatmeal; live foods also accepted.

This is one of the fishes which we seldom see except as babies. Larger ones would be highly expensive to ship, and the market for them would not be active. In their native Guyana they attain a size of 35 cm, at which size the natives catch them for food. Netting them is difficult; they leap nimbly over the net, often even over the collector's head, as soon as they feel the confines of the seine. A young specimen in full color is certainly a thing of beauty with its reddish fins and large striped tail. As the fish gets older the colors fade and finally it is scarcely recognizable as the same species. As is the case with many of these large fishes, no external sex differences have yet been observed.

SERRASALMUS CALMONI (Steindachner) / *Dusky Piranha*

Range: Guianas to the lower Amazon River.
Habits: Cannot be kept with other fishes, even its own kind; fierce and predatory.
Water Conditions: Soft and slightly acid. Temperature 24 to 27°C.
Size: To about 30 cm.
Food Requirements: Smaller living fishes preferred, but adapts to chunks of raw table fish.

The group of fishes known as piranhas or pirayas, the fishes about which so many blood-curdling tales are spun, includes several subgenera of *Serrasalmus*. *Serrasalmus, Taddyella* and *Pygocentrus* are the nasty, razor-toothed ones that can inflict a severe wound if carelessly handled. According to the wild tales, the piranhas travel in huge schools and are always ready to pounce upon anything that resembles food. The natives in most places where these fishes occur have no apprehension whatever when it comes to entering the water, but they would never think of cleaning a chicken at the water's edge and dipping in their bloody hands to wash them. These fish seem to have a powerful instinct to turn upon and destroy anything that has been injured, even one of their own number.

1. *Serrasalmus* cf *calmoni* in an aquarium (p1118).
2. *S. calmoni* on a photo table (p1118).

SERRASALMUS HOLLANDI (Eigenmann) / *Holland's Piranha*

Range: South of Amazon basin.
Habits: Vicious; cannot even be kept with another of its own kind.
Water Conditions: Soft, slightly acid water. Temperature 24 to 27°C.
Size: About 13 cm.
Food Requirements: Smaller living fishes preferred; can be trained to take strips of raw fish.

The solons who enacted the law forbidding the import, sale and possession of any species of the genus *Serrasalmus* passed a bit of legislation which, even if its intentions were good, left the inspectors in a bit of a dilemma as to deciding what was a dangerous fish and what wasn't. There are many fishes which have the almost identical form of a piranha but which are perfectly harmless. An inspector cannot be expected to open up a carton, open a plastic bag and then stick his hand in; if it comes out without the usual complement of fingers the fish should be confiscated. A little of this and there would soon be a drastic shortage of customs inspectors! Consequently there are now just as many piranhas offered for sale as there were before July 1, 1961, when the law was passed. The hobbyist who keeps a fish with dental equipment sharp and strong enough to amputate a finger or at the very least inflict a serious wound should not do so unless he takes some very important precautions: 1) Keep the tank where children cannot get at it; 2) Be very careful when netting the fish; don't ever put your hand close to it!

1. *Serrasalmus calmoni* F D T 1 1 7 X N N D [Harald Schultz]
2. *Serrasalmus calmoni* - F D M 1 1 7 X N N D [Harald Schultz]

Serrasalmus hollandi F D B 1 1 8 X N N C [Harald Schultz]

rrasalmus nattereri $\boxed{F}\boxed{D}\boxed{X}\boxed{1}\boxed{1}\boxed{9}\boxed{X}\boxed{N}\boxed{N}\boxed{C}$
rrasalmus rhombeus $\boxed{F}\boxed{D}\boxed{X}\boxed{1}\boxed{2}\boxed{0}\boxed{X}\boxed{N}\boxed{N}\boxed{D}$

[Dr. Herbert R. Axelrod]

SERRASALMUS NATTERERI (Kner)
Natterer's Piranha; Red-Bellied Piranha

Range: Widely distributed throughout the Amazon and Orinoco basins.
Habits: Vicious; must be kept alone in the average tank.
Water Conditions: Soft, slightly acid water. Temperature 24 to 27°C.
Size: Up to 30 cm in natural waters; shipped specimens usually much smaller.
Food Requirements: Smaller living fishes or strips of raw fish or beef heart.
Color Variations: Back steel gray with many tiny shining scales; large black spot on sides; throat, belly and anal fin bright red.

Authorities now tend to agree that the piranha on this page properly belongs to the genus *Serrasalmus*. Whatever we call him, he is a nasty customer and can use those razor-sharp teeth and powerful jaws with very telling effect. This is the most widely distributed and most commonly found of the piranha group, and it is also probably the most handsome of the lot. There has been a good deal of controversy as to how dangerous the piranha really is. In the author's opinion a piranha is not really dangerous until it feels it is trapped and confined, and then it attacks in self-defense. Most piranha bites are sustained when the fish are being handled. This is not to say that a hungry piranha is never a dangerous proposition. Usually there is a plenitude of small fish life on which they can forage, but if such is not the case and there is a leg or arm in the water, the temptation to take an experimental nip might prove too great to resist. Once blood is drawn others are attracted to the scene and the bloody shambles that follow have been described all too often and vividly. Natterer's Piranha is frequently seen in public aquariums, and small specimens are often kept by hobbyists.

SERRASALMUS RHOMBEUS (Linnaeus)
White Piranha; Spotted Piranha

Range: Amazon river system and northeastern South America.
Habits: Dangerous to most other fishes; perhaps smaller ones can be kept with larger fishes in a community tank.
Water Conditions: Soft, slightly acid water best. Temperature 24 to 27°C.
Size: To about 32 cm.
Food Requirements: Does well on fishes and raw meat.

Piranhas have often been divided into the very dangerous ones and the less dangerous ones. The White Piranha falls into the latter category, but this does not mean that it cannot inflict a bad wound on a person while being handled. This also does not mean it is not dangerous to other fishes—it is. Any fish placed in a tank with this piranha runs the risk of being killed and eaten, even members of its own kind. It is therefore recommended that only one White Piranha be kept and that one in a tank by itself.

1120

SICYOPTERUS SP. / *Mountain Goby*

Range: Sri Lanka.
Habits: Peaceful; clings to glass or rocks with sucker-like pelvic fins.
Water Conditions: Requires cool (21°C), well-aerated, clear water.
Size: Average 15 cm; females larger than males.
Food Requirements: Prefers a lush growth of algae on rocks and aquarium glass; will also
eat prepared foods containing a large amount of vegetable matter.

Cool temperatures are required if the Mountain Goby is to do well in the aquarium. At temperatures above 24°C, it turns pale and begins to act confused and nervous. The water must be kept clean and be well aerated in order to simulate its stream habitat. Be sure to keep the tank covered tightly, as the Mountain Goby is able to climb up the side of the tank by using its pelvic sucker, and it is able to squeeze through cracks less than 1 cm wide!

1. *Sicyopterus* sp. in an aquarium (p1122).
2. The pelvic fins of *Sicyopterus* sp. are modified to form a sucker.

SIMOCHROMIS DIAGRAMMA Günther
Diagramma; Diagonal Bar Simochromis

Range: Endemic to Lake Tanganyika.
Habits: Generally aggressive but suitable for an African lake cichlid community tank; prone to
chasing each other about the tank, but with little damage done.
Water Conditions: Hard and alkaline water desirable. Temperature should be about 26°C
(24 to 29°C).
Size: Reaches a length of about 18 cm or more, but will breed at about 10 cm.
Food Requirements: Will eat almost any type of normal aquarium foods, but will usually do
better if algae and some vegetable matter are available.

Simochromis diagramma is easily recognized by the 10 or 11 diagonal bars crossing the body. The other species of *Simochromis* may have similar bars, but they are always vertical, not diagonal. It is also the largest species of *Simochromis* in the lake.

The Diagramma is typically a rock-dweller and can be found in most rocky areas of the lake. It is more tolerant of murky water than the other species. They can inhabit the surf-churned waters near the shoreline and can often be seen darting in and out of the rock crevices, the males usually chasing the females. This chasing carries over into the aquarium, and one report indicated the male chased the female for hours on end over a period of several weeks. It was recommended that there be plenty of cover for the female and that the tank, if possible, be extra long to allow these high speed chases to occur without significant damage.

The aquarium should be as large as possible and, as just stated, as long as possible. It should be provided with the rock work so often recommended for African cichlid tanks.

1. *Sicyopterus sp.* ⬚F⬚ ⬚D⬚ ⬚C⬚ ⬚1⬚ ⬚2⬚ ⬚1⬚ ⬚X⬚ ⬚N⬚ ⬚N⬚ ⬚B⬚   2. *Sicyopterus* sp.

Simochromis diagramma ⬚F⬚ ⬚D⬚ ⬚X⬚ ⬚1⬚ ⬚2⬚ ⬚2⬚ ⬚X⬚ ⬚N⬚ ⬚N⬚ ⬚C⬚   [Dr. Herbert R. Axelrod]

1. *Steatocranus casuarius* [F][E][T][1][2][7][X][N][N][A] [Dr. Herbert R. Axelrod]
2. *Steatocranus casuarius* [F][E][M][1][2][7][X][N][N][A] [H. J. Richter]

Steatocranus tinanti [F][R][X][1][2][8][X][N][N][8] [Dr. Herbert R. Axelrod]

STEATOCRANUS CASUARIUS Poll / *Lionhead Cichlid*

Range: Stanley Pool, Zaire.
Habits: Fairly peaceful for a cichlid.
Water Conditions: Should have hard, alkaline water. Temperature 24 to 28°C.
Size: About 10 cm.
Food Requirements: Will rarely accept dry foods, although some frozen foods, particularly frozen adult brine shrimp, are taken.

This fish has one characteristic which makes it noteworthy and without which it would have to be considered as just any drab bottom-dwelling African cichlid. The characteristic is this: males of the species develop a large bump on the head. This protuberance gives the fish an odd appearance, and hobbyists viewing *Steatocranus* for the first time are likely to believe that it is the victim of a cancerous growth, but such is not the case, for the bump is a normal physical development and causes the male *Steatocranus* neither pain nor difficulty. Other cichlids develop a cranial protuberance with age, but in no other case is the bump developed to such a prominent degree. The Lionhead Cichlid breeds by laying its adhesive eggs in cave-like structures, and the male stands guard and takes care of them while they are hatching. After the eggs hatch both parents assume responsibility for their offspring. When the young venture from their cave to depressions which are dug in the gravel by the male, the female hovers over them in an attitude of vigilance and attacks anything that may venture near. This species grows quickly.

1. *Steatocranus casuarius* male with a well developed hump on his head (p1127).
2. *S. casuarius* young male in an aquarium (p1127).

STEATOCRANUS TINANTI (Boulenger) / *Slender Lionhead Cichlid*

Range: Central Africa, especially the Congo River area.
Habits: A bottom-dweller that spends most of its time in hiding.
Water Conditions: Prefers water that is warm (27°C) and neutral, the closer to pH 7.0 and a hardness of 3 degrees, the better.
Size: A maximum size of 15 cm is rare.
Food Requirements: Will only eat live foods, though some pelleted dried foods and frozen brine shrimp serve well.

This is an undemanding and very peaceful species when not breeding. It is not an avid digger and will spawn in an inverted flowerpot with a narrow entrance. Both the male and female prepare the spawning site by carrying away gravel from inside the inverted flowerpot. The male guards the eggs and fans them with his fins. Several weeks after hatching, the young are collected by the parents from inside the artificial spawning cave and placed in a prepared depression in the gravel outside the cave.

STEATOGENYS ELEGANS (Steindachner) / *Mottled Knife Fish*

Range: Northeastern South America, Barra do Rio Negro, Guyana, lower Amazon River and northern tributaries of the middle Amazon.
Habits: Nocturnal; rarely seen during the daytime.
Water Conditions: Not critical; neutral, slightly soft water with a temperature between 24° and 29°C is good.
Size: Grows to a length of 18 to 20 cm.
Food Requirements: Readily accepts live brine shrimp as well as other live foods; will also eat prepared foods, chopped fish and shrimp, etc. with a little coaxing.

These fish are relatively hardy and can be kept in fairly small aquaria. It must be remembered that they are nocturnal and the tank should be as dark as possible if you ever want to see them out in the open. If the light is too bright they stick their head into some cave or hole and remain there until it becomes dark again. Rockwork, flowerpots or roots should be added to provide these hiding places. They are quite peaceful and make very good community tank members (taking into consideration their nocturnal habits) except when kept with members of their own species.

One final unusual aspect of *Steatogenys elegans* is the possession of barbel-like organs in the mental region. Resting in deep grooves under the chin that are open anteriorly but covered posteriorly, these barbel-like organs extend to the back of the head, under the base of the pectoral fins and appear again in open grooves in the shoulder region above the pectoral fins. The construction of these organs is similar to that of some of the electric organs.

1. *Steatogenys elegans* in a photo-tank (p1130).
2. A close-up of the head of *S. elegans* (p1130).

STIGMATOGOBIUS SADANUNDIO (Hamilton-Buchanan)
Knight Goby

Range: Indonesia, Burma, India and the Philippines.
Habits: A bottom-dwelling fish which requires live food.
Water Conditions: Originally from brackish water areas, this fish is not at home in soft water conditions. Add salt to the water, at least one tablespoon for 8 liters.
Size: Up to about 9 cm.
Food Requirements: Must have copious feedings of live foods, preferably worms; frozen brine shrimp is eagerly taken once the fish has become accustomed to it.

Knight Gobies are hard to keep in good health without proper feedings of worms, and they require at least 10% of their water to be sea water or a fair substitute thereof. When all is said and done they will probably jump out of the tank and dry out on your living room rug, but people still buy them. Perhaps you can find a reason for this fish being a member of your community tank, where, if you don't feed him, he'll start chewing on fishes about half his own size.

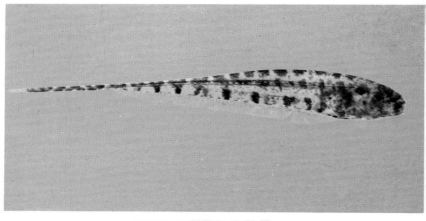

1. *Steatogenys elegans* ⬚F⬚D⬚T⬚1⬚2⬚9⬚X⬚N⬚N⬚C   [Dr. Herbert R. Axelrod]
2. *Steatogenys elegans* ⬚F⬚D⬚M⬚1⬚2⬚9⬚X⬚N⬚N⬚C   [Dr. Herbert R. Axelrod]

Stigmatogobius sadanundio ⬚F⬚A⬚X⬚1⬚3⬚0⬚X⬚N⬚N⬚9

Stoneiella leopardus ⬚F⬚ ⬚D⬚ ⬚X⬚ ⬚1⬚⬚3⬚⬚1⬚ ⬚X⬚ ⬚N⬚ ⬚N⬚ ⬚C⬚   [Dr. Herbert R. Axelrod]

1. *Symphysodon aequifasciata aequifasciata* ⬚F⬚ ⬚H⬚ ⬚X⬚ ⬚1⬚⬚3⬚⬚2⬚ ⬚X⬚ ⬚N⬚ ⬚N⬚ ⬚D⬚

[G. Marcuse]

STONEIELLA LEOPARDUS Fowler / *Orange-Trim Sucker Catfish*

Range: Guyana.
Habits: Peaceful with other species, but sometimes quarrelsome with other plecostomus-type catfishes.
Water Conditions: Soft, slightly acid water should be used if possible, but the fish can take variations from this if not too great. Temperature 22 to 27°C.
Size: Up to 15 cm.
Food Requirements: Will take prepared foods from the bottom, but the biggest part of the diet consists of algae scraped from rocks, leaves and the sides of the aquarium.

This fish, along with some other sucker catfishes, was one of the chief aquarium importations of 1961. The fishes were brought into the country by Paramount Aquarium, and even though the firm had come back from its collecting expedition with quite a few specimens of each species, they soon had to make plans to look for more, because all of these catfishes were eagerly snapped up by dealers throughout the country. *Stoneiella leopardus* was the best looking to come into the country at that time, despite the fact that those years had seen some really attractive new species introduced. One of the main features of the appearance of this fish, besides the touch of color which is such a welcome relief in a type of fish which usually has no color at all, is the magnificent high dorsal fin.

SYMPHYSODON AEQUIFASCIATA AEQUIFASCIATA (Pellegrin)
Green Discus

Range: Brazil (Lago Teffe).
Habits: Peaceful for a cichlid.
Water Conditions: Should have soft, slightly acid water; in extremely hard, alkaline water, this species will waste away. Temperature 24 to 28°C.
Size: 30 cm.
Food Requirements: Dry foods not relished; frozen beef heart willingly accepted, as are live foods, but this fish should not be fed on any one food exclusively, as it needs variety.
Color Variations: Body color a dark brownish green with nine vertical bars which vary in intensity; irregular blue streaks on body.

Discusfishes of any species have always been held in high regard by aquarists because they are beautiful. Also, these fish have an attraction for another reason: discus specimens always sell for a good price, and many hobbyists have attempted to set up prospective pairs in hopes of getting them to spawn, thus providing themselves with a steady source of income. The trouble is that few people have succeeded in spawning the fish and raising some young in great numbers. It is important to leave the parents with the fry, as the babies feed off of the slime on the adults' bodies.

1. *Symphysodon aequifasciata aequifasciata* with its vertical bars partially faded. (p1131).
2. *S. a. aequifasciata* with its vertical bars well defined (p1134).

Symphysodon aequifasciata aequifasciata. Photo by G. Budich.

2. *Symphysodon aequifasciata aequifasciata* ⬚F⬚ ⬚H⬚ ⬚X⬚ ⬚1⬚ ⬚3⬚ ⬚4⬚ ⬚X⬚ ⬚N⬚ ⬚N⬚ ⬚D⬚   [E. Schmidt]

1. *Symphysodon aequifasciata axelrodi*

SYMPHYSODON AEQUIFASCIATA AXELRODI Schultz
Brown Discus

Range: Brazil.

Habits: Peaceful for a cichlid.

Water Conditions: Soft, acid water best. Temperature 24 to 28°C.

Size: About 13 cm.

Food Requirements: Takes all live foods and some frozen foods (beef heart, liver, blood-worms); does not accept any dried food except pelleted brine shrimp.

Color Variations: Body color varies from light to dark brown; nine vertical bars cross body and head; fins yellowish.

The Brown Discus, although less colorful than *Symphysodon aequifasciata aequifasciata* and *Symphysodon aequifasciata haraldi*, is still a pretty fish and one much in demand. Like its relatives, *S. a. axelrodi* feeds its young from a thick coating of slime which forms on the body at spawning time.

1. *Symphysodon aequifasciata axelrodi,* the Brown Discus, in an aquarium (p1135).
2. *S. aequifasciata axelrodi* mating pair (p1138).
3. *S. aequifasciata axelrodi* in a spawning tank (p1138).

Symphysodon aequifasciata axelrodi, commonly called the brown Discus, has a very attractive pattern. Photo by G. Marcuse. The brown Discus fry, like other Discus fry, survive by eating the slime off of their parents' bodies. The brown Discus on the opposite page is surrounded by its fry. Photo by G. Budich.

2. *Symphysodon aequifasciata axelrodi* F Q X 1 3 7 X N N D   [Dr. Terver, Nancy Aq
3. *Symphysodon aequifasciata axelrodi* F Q X 1 3 8 X N N D   [J. Taborsky]

1. *Symphysodon aequifasciata haraldi* ⬚F⬚Q⬚X⬚1⬚3⬚9⬚X⬚N⬚N⬚D [E. Schmidt]
2. *Symphysodon aequifasciata haraldi* ⬚F⬚H⬚X⬚1⬚4⬚0⬚X⬚N⬚N⬚D [E. Schmidt]

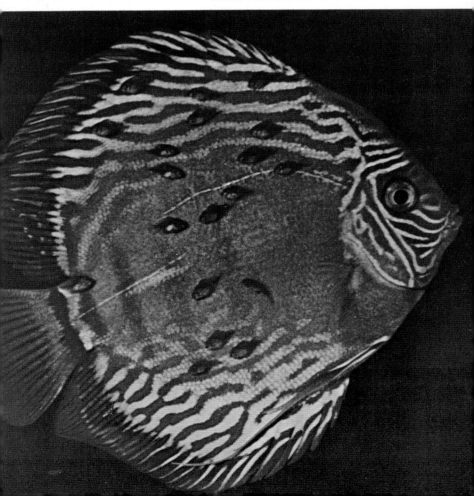

SYMPHYSODON AEQUIFASCIATA HARALDI Schultz
Blue Discus

Range: Rio Negro and its tributaries.
Habits: Very peaceful; requires a large and well-planted aquarium.
Water Conditions: Soft, slightly acid water preferred. Temperature 24 to 29°C.
Size: Up to 20 cm; mature at about half that size.
Food Requirements: White worms, mature brine shrimp and chopped beef heart.

Considered by many to be the most beautiful of the *Symphysodon* group, the Blue Discus possesses the additional advantage of being the hardiest fish in this specialized group. It breeds in the same way as its relatives, and the parents get along very well together. One of the many things that must be done to maintain any discus species in good health is to make many partial changes of water. Two of the world's most successful discus breeders make it an absolutely hard and fast rule to change at least one-third of the water in their discus tanks each week. This is important, as it stimulates the fish to better feeding and consequently better growth, and it is also important in that it builds up the fish's resistance to some of the more troublesome discus diseases.

1. *Symphysodon aequifasciata haraldi* in a spawning tank (p1139).
2. *S. a. haraldi* with fry picking at the slime on its body (p1139).

This adult Discus is a cross between *S. a. haraldi* and *S. discus.* The adult hybrid is tending its eggs. Photo by Dr. Herbert R. Axelrod.

SYMPHYSODON DISCUS (Heckel) / *Red Discus; Pompadour Discus; Heckel's Discus*

Range: Brazil.
Habits: Peaceful for a cichlid.
Water Conditions: Soft, acid water desirable; this species is especially susceptible to abrupt changes in water composition. Temperature 24 to 27°C.
Size: About 15 cm.
Food Requirements: Does best on live foods, but worms should not be fed too often.

When Angelfish were first introduced, hobbyists were quick to dub them "King of the Aquarium Fishes." This was quickly forgotten when the discus first made their appearance around 1932, and the title went to these regal newcomers. Their proud bearing, their wonderful colors and their high price made them seem worthy of the title, and they still are. Although they are not exactly a rarity in their native waters, shipping them was quite a problem in the old days. Small ones were not easily found or caught, and the big ones had to have a shipping can all to themselves. Breeders had difficulty in getting them to spawn, and the fish remained very scarce and high-priced. Nowadays air transport has made their shipping faster, and new methods of packing them have cut down the weight problem.

1. *Symphysodon discus* with mid-body vertical bar outstanding (p1142).
2. *S. discus*, the LoBue albino variety (p1142).
3. *S. discus* with mid-body vertical bar faint (p1143).

Symphysodon discus, the Red Discus. Photo by Mueller-Schmida.

1. *Symphysodon discus* var. ⬚F⬚ ⬚D⬚ ⬚X⬚ ⬚1⬚ ⬚4⬚ ⬚1⬚ ⬚X⬚ ⬚N⬚ ⬚N⬚ ⬚D⬚ [H. Hansen, Aquarium Berlin]
2. *Symphysodon discus* var. ⬚F⬚ ⬚H⬚ ⬚X⬚ ⬚1⬚ ⬚4⬚ ⬚2⬚ ⬚X⬚ ⬚A⬚ ⬚N⬚ ⬚D⬚ [A. Castro]

3. *Symphysodon discus* var. F H X 1 4 3 X N N D

[W. Bechtle]

Symphysodon discus is one of the most prestigious aquarium fish in the hobby. Being almost round, these fish grow to 15 cm in diameter. They have the ability to alter their coloration, varying the intensity of their body and head bars and background. Photos by Goellner.

SYNGNATHUS PULCHELLUS Boulenger / *African Freshwater Pipefish*

Range: Congo region in Africa.
Habits: Peaceful.
Water Conditions: Should be maintained in slightly salty to brackish water. Temperature about 25°C.
Size: 10 cm.
Food Requirements: Usually refuses to eat anything but small living foods, although floating frozen foods may be picked at; aquatic crustaceans and baby livebearers are preferred.

This species is considered to be more desirable than its Asiatic relative, *Syngnathus spicifer*, from the standpoints of ease of maintenance and good looks. It is a more colorful fish and is easier to feed, even though it, like *S. spicifer*, insists on having nothing but living foods. The differential in ease of caring for this species lies in the fact that *S. pulchellus* will accept aquatic crustaceans such as brine shrimp and daphnia more readily than *S. spicifer*, which will accept nothing but newborn livebearers on a regular basis. In other regards the species are much the same, and both share in the peculiar breeding pattern of the family Syngnathidae, whereby the male carries the eggs in a brood pouch until they hatch. *Syngnathus pulchellus* fry are equally as difficult to raise as the fry of *S. spicifer*.

SYNGNATHUS SPICIFER Rüppel / *Indian Freshwater Pipefish*

Range: Sri Lanka and India.
Habits: Peaceful with any fish that cannot be swallowed.
Water Conditions: Should have brackish water, although the salt can vary in concentration from light to heavy; tank should not be too heavily aerated. Temperature 24 to 29°C.
Size: About 13 cm.
Food Requirements: In the home aquarium, this fish will accept only newborn livebearers.

Like its saltwater relatives the seahorses, *Syngnathus spicifer* is covered with rows of bony plates which encase the fish in a suit of armor. The odd trumpet-like mouth is very small at its opening, and the fish has difficulty in eating anything that is not small enough to be ingested whole. This complicates matters for the hobbyist who wants to keep this fish, and it has been found that specimens kept in aquariums will accept nothing but newborn livebearers, which it is quite expert at stalking and catching, despite the lack of speed. However, even some baby livebearers are too big for *Syngnathus* to swallow. In its reproductive methods the pipefish is very odd, for the female lays her eggs in a pouch formed by folds in the abdomen of the male. At a temperature of about 27°C, the eggs hatch in a day and a half to two days. The newly hatched fry are small, and they move through the water in short, jerky motions.

Syngnathus pulchellus | F | D | X | 1 | 4 | 5 | X | N | N | A | [K. Paysan]
Syngnathus spicifer | F | R | X | 1 | 4 | 6 | X | N | N | B | [A. van den Nieuwenhuizen]

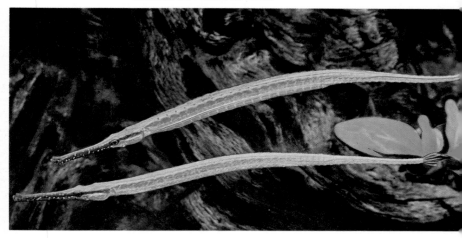

Synodontis angelicus [F][D][X][1][4][7][X][N][N][B]   [Aaron Norman]

Synodontis contractus [F][D][X][1][4][8][X][N][N][8]   [Dr. Herbert R. Axelrod]

SYNODONTIS ANGELICUS *Schilthuis / Angelicus;* *Polka-Dot Upside-Down Catfish*

Range: Tropical West Africa.
Habits: Peaceful with other fishes and will not uproot plants.
Water Conditions: Medium-soft, slightly acid to neutral water; tank should be heavily planted and provided with rock grottoes in which the fish may hide. Temperature 22 to 29°C.
Size: 20 cm.
Food Requirements: Will take prepared and frozen foods; likes algae and worms.

There is a very good reason for the scarcity of this fish on the aquarium market: it is extremely rare in its home waters in the Congo, and fish exporters have a great deal of difficulty in catching them, so the price of the few specimens which are made available remains prohibitively high. It is a nocturnal fish which hides in the mud during the day and comes out to feed only at night, the way many other mochokid (upside-down) catfishes do. But *Synodontis angelicus* seems to have a very distinct choice as to the area in which it will do its feeding; for some reason, the fish is attracted to places inwhich there is a lot of iron. They will congregate around rusty metal submerged in the water, and it almost seems as if they actually graze on the surface of the metal!

SYNODONTIS CONTRACTUS Vinciguerra
David's Upside-Down Catfish

Range: Zaire; localized in and around Stanley Pool near Kinshasha.
Habits: Peaceful and semi-nocturnal; likes to rest in sheltered areas in tank, especially grottoes formed by rocks.
Water Conditions: Soft or medium-soft water slightly on the acid side is best. Temperature shouldn't go below 24°C unless fish is maintained in very large aquarium.
Size: Up to 8 cm.
Food Requirements: Will accept all meat-based aquarium foods, but should have dried or freeze-dried foods that include substantial portions of vegetable materials.

Synodontis contractus, introduced to commercial aquarium channels some 25 years ago as the result of one of Dr. Herbert R. Axelrod's collecting/exploration trips to Africa, has one distinct advantage over *Synodontis nigriventris,* which is still the most common of the upside-down catfishes: it's smaller and can be more comfortably accommodated in smaller tanks. *S. contractus* is also much chunkier in build and a trifle more colorful and attractive, although neither species can lay any claim to being "pretty." Their main attraction is their oddness, which lies primarily in the fact that they normally swim on their backs. There is as yet no substantiated account of the spawning of *S. contractus,* but it is quite probable that the species spawns in a manner very similar to that of *S. nigriventris. S. contractus* eats just about anything and is undemanding concerning water composition, but it should be provided with cave-like structures in order to feel at home.

SYNODONTIS NIGRIVENTRIS David / *Blackbellied Upside-Down Catfish*

Range: Central West Africa, the Congo basin and tributaries.
Habits: Peaceful; prefers to remain hidden in the darker regions of the aquarium and come out for food after dark.
Water Conditions: Soft, slightly acid water with little or no salt content. Temperature should range between 24 and 27°C.
Size: Females up to 8 cm; males a little smaller.
Food Requirements: Enjoys just about all kinds of foods; will come to the surface for dried food and grub in the bottom for worms.

Here we have one of the real oddities of the fish world: a fish which prefers to swim upside-down! Other members of the genus *Synodontis* are seen to do this occasionally, but this fellow does it most of the time. Mother Nature has even seen fit to bow to his whim and has reversed his coloration. Most fish are darker on the back and lighter on the belly. This makes their color blend in with the dark bottom when viewed from above by a bird, and when a larger fish or other enemy looks up at them, the light belly blends in with the glare from the surface. This fish has a lighter back and a dark belly, which would give him the benefits of camouflage when swimming upside-down.

1. *Synodontis nigriventris* resting in non-inverted position (p1150).
2. *S. nigriventris* truly swims upside-down at times (p1150).

SYNODONTIS NIGROMACULATUS Boulenger
Black-Dotted Upside-Down Catfish

Range: Luapula system, Mweru, Bangwelu, Lake Tanganyika, Upper Kasai, Upper Zambezi, Okovango, Cunene and Limpopo.
Habits: Retiring; active around twilight, so needs hiding places such as caves, rocks, etc; peaceful. Swims upside-down less than most *Synodontis*.
Water Conditions: Easily adapted to many conditions; most local water supplies are suitable after dechlorinization. The temperature range is about 18 to 29°C, with 23 to 25°C optimum.
Size: About 30 cm in nature, but only 20 cm in the aquarium.
Food Requirements: Omnivorous; live foods, freeze-dried and fresh or frozen foods.

Synodontis nigromaculatus grows slowly but steadily and may last, with proper care and attention, well over fifteen years in an aquarium. They should be given plenty of room to grow in a dimly lighted aquarium that is provided with dark recesses in which to retire.

Among the interesting or amusing habits of *Synodontis nigromaculatus* are its noise-making and upside-down swimming. The sound is produced in a manner similar to that employed by other catfishes, the rotating of fin spines in the sockets, the sound being carried to and amplified by the swim bladder. The upside-down swimming is less prevalent in this species than in some of the other upside-down catfishes.

1. *Synodontis nigriventris* Ⓕ Ⓒ Ⓣ ① ④ ⑨ Ⓧ Ⓝ Ⓝ ⑥   [Dr. Herbert R. Axelrod]
2. *Synodontis nigriventris* Ⓕ Ⓓ Ⓜ ① ④ ⑨ Ⓧ Ⓝ Ⓝ ⑧   [Dr. D. Terver, Nancy Aquarium]

Synodontis nigromaculatus Ⓕ Ⓓ Ⓧ ① ⑤ ⓪ Ⓧ Ⓝ Ⓝ Ⓒ   [Dr. Herbert R. Axelrod]

Synodontis notatus ⃞F ⃞D ⃞X ⃞1 ⃞5 ⃞1 ⃞X ⃞N ⃞N ⃞D

[K. Paysan]

1. *Tanichthys albonubes* var. ⃞F ⃞H ⃞M ⃞1 ⃞5 ⃞2 ⃞X ⃞N ⃞V ⃞4
2. *Tanichthys albonubes* ⃞F ⃞H ⃞B ⃞1 ⃞5 ⃞2 ⃞X ⃞N ⃞N ⃞4

[H. J. Richter]
[Aaron Norman]

SYNODONTIS NOTATUS Vaillant / *Spotted Synodontis*

Range: Congo basin.
Habits: Reasonably peaceful, crepuscular catfish which does well in large aquaria.
Water Conditions: Not critical. Temperature 20 to 29°C.
Size: 25 cm.
Food Requirements: Omnivorous; prefers beef heart and brine shrimp.

Synodontis notatus, while a member of the "upside-down" catfishes (family Mochokidae) of Africa, does not frequently swim upside-down. Its oddity lies more in its capacity to produce loud growling noises that can be easily heard outside the aquarium. The noise is produced by grinding pectoral and dorsal spines in their sockets; through linkage with the gas bladder by modified vertebrae known as the Weberian apparatus, the vibrations are amplified and broadcast into the water by means of the enlarged surface area of the gas bladder.

TANICHTHYS ALBONUBES Lin
White Cloud Mountain Minnow

Range: Small streams in the vicinity of White Cloud Mountain in Canton, China.
Habits: Peaceful in the community tank; very active and prefers to swim in schools.
Water Conditions: Not critical. Best kept at a relatively low temperature, 18 to 21°C.
Size: 4 cm.
Food Requirements: Will eat dried as well as live foods; when it is desired to spawn them, live foods should be given.

This little fish has the distinction of being one of the easiest aquarium fishes to spawn. A pair placed together in a well-planted aquarium and fed well with live foods, preferably daphnia, will soon produce fry that they show little tendency to eat. When young, the green stripe glows so bright that they are often mistaken for small Neon Tetras. It must be remembered that this is not exactly a tropical species. It comes from comparatively cool mountain streams which are fairly well oxygenated; as a result, they would be very uncomfortable in a warm, crowded community tank. This fish has an interesting history. The first specimens were found by a Chinese scoutmaster named Tan Kam Fei, who gave them to the director of a fisheries experimental station for identification. This man, Lin Shu-Yen, gave them their name, *Tanichthys* (Tan's fish) *albonubes* (White Cloud). This was in 1932, but aquarists did not get to see the fish until about 1938, at which time it became known as "the poor man's Neon Tetra." Since then the status has reversed itself and so many Neon Tetras have come in that the price is lower than that of the White Clouds.

1. *Tanichthys albonubes* is sometimes available as a beautiful long-finned variety (p1151).
2. *T. albonubes* in its normal form (p1151).

1152

TELEOGRAMMA BRICHARDI Poll / *Brichard's Slender Cichlid*

Range: Congo basin.
Habits: Playful, but sometimes quarrelsome with members of its own species.
Water Conditions: Medium-soft, slightly acid water best; tank should have plenty of rocks and caves to make the fish feel at home. Temperature 21 to 27°C.
Size: About 10 cm.
Food Requirements: Live foods much preferred, although some frozen foods are accepted.

Teleogramma species are bottom-dwelling cichlids from the Congo River. These fishes, of which there are three species, generally live under stones and rocks in rapidly moving streams. *T. brichardi* is the most popular of these large-mouthed, elongate fishes. This species is a substrate-spawner where the female is more active than the male. The female, which is also more colorful than the male, develops a red girdle during breeding time. She sets up a territory in a rocky area, courts the male and eventually guards the eggs once they are laid. The eggs are large, few in number and are stuck with an adhesive to the rocks or walls of the nesting site. After spawning, the male is driven off. Hatching occurs in 72 hours.

TELMATHERINA LADIGESI Ahl / *Celebes Rainbow Fish*

Range: Celebes.
Habits: Peaceful; may be combined with other fishes with similar requirements.
Water Conditions: Water should have a slight addition of salt, a teaspoonful per 4 liters; tank should be sunny. Temperature 24 to 27°C.
Size: 8 cm.
Food Requirements: Will take dried foods, but should have frequent supplements of living foods.

This beautiful fish has a reputation which it does not fully deserve. Many who have kept and had trouble with it claim it is delicate, but the only thing which should be criticized is the fact that they did not give it the proper care. There are two things it does require: a little salt in the water (about a teaspoon per 4 liters of water) and a proper amount of heat (25°C suits them fine). Even before they attain their full size and coloration, males may be distinguished by the more pointed body cavity as seen through the transparent sides with a light behind them. When fully grown, of course, there can be no doubt as to which are the males. One look at the gorgeous yellow dorsal and anal fins with the long filaments and black first rays is sufficient. One other thing this beauty is particularly sensitive to is a great deal of moving around. Once they have adapted themselves to the conditions in a tank, they should then be left alone. They are by nature a bit timid, and a tank where they are kept should have a sufficiency of plant life in which they can hide if any real or imagined danger is present. Eggs are laid in bushy plants and hatch in two days.

Teleogramma brichardi ⬛Ⓕ🄰🄾🄰🄸🄰🄾🄸🄸🄰 [P. Brichard]
Telmatherina ladigesi ⬛Ⓕ🄺🄾🄸🄸🄰🄾🄸🄸🄰 [H. J. Richter]

Telmatochromis bifrenatus [F][D][X][1][5][5][X][N][N][B]   [Dr. Herbert R. Axelrod]
Telmatochromis caninus [F][R][X][1][5][6][X][N][N][C]   [H. J. Richter]

TELMATOCHROMIS BIFRENATUS Myers / *Striped Telmat*

Range: Lake Tanganyika, Africa.
Habits: A relatively inactive, non-aggressive, retiring species compared to the vast majority of Rift Lake cichlids; sexes fight among themselves, however, and this species will tend to be more belligerent and territorial during spawning periods.
Water Conditions: Hard, alkaline water; pH between 8.0 and 9.0 is preferred. Temperature between 22 and 26°C.
Size: To 13 cm for males; smaller for females.
Food Requirements: Most aquarium foods are accepted, including live, frozen, freeze-dried and flake foods; vegetable matter should be added to the diet.

Telmatochromis bifrenatus is a Lake Tanganyikan omnivore which is relatively peaceful compared to most Rift Lake cichlids. This species is a substrate-spawner which is not difficult to breed.

TELMATOCHROMIS CANINUS Poll / *Caninus*

Range: Lake Tanganyika, Africa.
Habits: This is a fairly inactive, retiring species that usually causes no great problem because of aggressiveness, but the sexes quarrel among themselves, especially preceding spawning.
Water Conditions: Hard, alkaline water preferred but not strictly necessary. Best temperature range is 23 to 26°C.
Size: To 15 cm for males; smaller for females.
Food Requirements: Most live, frozen and prepared (especially flake) foods accepted; vegetable matter should be added to the diet.

Telmatochromis caninus is one of the Rift Lake cichlids that has neither the pleasing appearance nor interesting behavior that has endeared many other Lake Malawi and Lake Tanganyika cichlids to hobbyists, but it still attracts people. In general it is one of the less aggressive species, probably because it is comparatively sedentary. One almost gets the impression when watching it that it would like to start trouble but doesn't have the energy to go out and look for a fight. The bulging, toothy mouth gives it a more pugnacious appearance than its nature lives up to. For the most part, individual *T. caninus* are content to stay at the bottom of the tank, preferably in some type of shelter provided by their owner in the form of a cave, and leave other fishes alone unless their area is intruded upon. Males of the species, however, are not always content to let their females alone and sometimes actively seek them to punish them. Spawning is almost always preceded by a roughing-up of the female, although sometimes the tables are turned, with the male on the receiving end. This is not a mouthbrooding species. Eggs are laid in cave-like structures; the female does most of the tending to the eggs, with the male usually staying outside the cave. It is best to leave the parents with their fry, as they take good care of them if left undisturbed. The fry are large enough to easily take newly hatched brine shrimp.

TELMATOCHROMIS VITTATUS Boulenger / *Blunt-Headed Telmat*

Range: Lake Tanganyika, Africa.
Habits: Relatively docile for a cichlid.
Water Conditions: Fares best in hard alkaline water but can adapt to less stringent conditions. Temperature 23 to 28°C.
Size: To about 8 cm.
Food Requirements: Takes most standard aquarium foods but especially likes brine shrimp and daphnia.

Sexes in this species look very much alike, and the most reliable guide to sex differentiation is the relative slimness or fullness of the body; the number of iridescent blue speckles on the body and fins is not a reliable sex indicator. *T. vittatus* is a substrate-spawner that enters rocky refuges to deposit its spawn, usually on the roof of the chosen cave. If maintained in good condition, *T. vittatus* readily spawns and the parents take excellent care of the young until they are able to fend for themselves. They even leave the fry alone after their parental obligations have been fulfilled, so it is possible to leave the fry and their parents in the same tank. The fry are free-swimming when they leave the spawning cave but remain at the bottom of the tank for between one and two months.

TETRAODON CUTCUTIA Hamilton-Buchanan / *Malayan Puffer*

Range: Malaysia and parts of India, in fresh and brackish waters.
Habits: Quarrelsome toward other fishes and even among themselves.
Water Conditions: Hard, alkaline water with salt added, one teaspoonful per 4 liters. Temperature 24 to 27°C.
Size: To 15 cm.
Food Requirements: Live foods in the larger sizes or chopped-up pieces of table shrimp; crushed snails are a delicacy.

The puffers are an odd group of fishes which inhabit the fresh, brackish and especially marine waters in many parts of the world. They have the odd capability of being able to inflate themselves with water until their bodies swell up to many times their normal size, and a fish which takes one into its mouth often finds that he cannot swallow it. This one comes mostly from brackish waters, so a small amount of salt is advisable, one teaspoonful per 4 liters. Unfortunately they are very quarrelsome even among themselves and should never be kept with other fishes. They are useful in the aquarium because of their love for snails and will depopulate a snail-ridden tank in short order. Their rabbit-like teeth are useful in crushing the shells and biting the tough flesh. The puffers soon lose their shyness and come begging for food to the surface whenever the tank is approached. Spawning the puffers is not the easiest thing in the world, but it has been done repeatedly. The females are easily distinguished by their larger size and lighter colors.

Telmatochromis vittatus ⬚F⬚D⬚X⬚1⬚5⬚7⬚X⬚N⬚N⬚8   [P. Brichard]
Tetraodon cutcutia ⬚F⬚D⬚X⬚1⬚5⬚8⬚X⬚N⬚N⬚9   [Dr. Herbert R. Axelrod]

Tetraodon miurus ⬚F ⬚D ⬚X ⬚1 ⬚5 ⬚9 ⬚X ⬚N ⬚N ⬚A   [Dr. Herbert R. Axelrod]

1. *Tetraodon palembangensis* ⬚F ⬚D ⬚M ⬚1 ⬚6 ⬚0 ⬚X ⬚N ⬚N ⬚B
2. *Tetraodon palembangensis* ⬚F ⬚D ⬚B ⬚1 ⬚6 ⬚0 ⬚X ⬚N ⬚N ⬚8

TETRAODON MIURUS Boulenger / *Congo Puffer*

Range: Middle and lower Congo River; found in fresh water only.
Habits: A dangerous fish in the community aquarium; should be given a tank by itself or with others of its own kind.
Water Conditions: Soft, slightly acid water. Temperature 24 to 27°C.
Size: To 10 cm.
Food Requirements: Living small fishes, fully grown brine shrimp or pieces of earthworms; they enjoy snails.

The Congo Puffer is a strange little fish. Its body colors are capable of considerable change, and it can match its surroundings quite easily as long as they are some shade of brown, red or gray. Its eyes are set atop the head like those of a frog, and it frequently digs into the bottom to lie completely hidden from its prey, with only the eyes showing. When seen resting on the bottom, the shapeless blob of a body looks like nothing more than a rock lying there. Prey that mistake it for a rock and manage to get too near to its mouth would be in trouble. *Tetraodon miurus* has an unusual feature for a puffer: its mouth, instead of opening straight ahead or slightly downward, points *up*. This must adapt it to a specialized method of feeding. A large specimen cannot be trusted with other fishes in the aquarium, even those it cannot swallow. It seems to enjoy swimming up to a fish and, with a quick snap of its powerful jaws and sharp teeth, chopping it neatly in half.

TETRAODON PALEMBANGENSIS Bleeker / *Figure-Eight Puffer*

Range: Southeastern Asia and Malaysia Peninsula.
Habits: A fin-nipper; tends to be pugnacious.
Water Conditions: Does best in water to which a teaspoon of salt per 4 liters has been added.
Size: Up to 18 cm.
Food Requirements: Prefers larger live foods like fishes or shrimp.

Puffers of all kinds continue to be popular in the aquarium hobby despite the several drawbacks that they present, and the reason lies mostly in the fact that buyers of these odd aquarium fishes buy them usually for their quaintness and what they take to be a nice oddity without realizing that puffers in general can be very bad actors. They look harmless enough, and they usually move at a very slow and deliberate pace, which gives people the idea that they couldn't do any harm even if they wanted to; such is not the case at all, because they often are decidedly pugnacious, and even though they are not the swiftest of swimmers they most times are fast enough or persistent enough to catch up to intended victims.

1. *Tetraodon palembangensis* eating a shrimp in an aquarium (p1159).
2. *T. palembangensis* is an interesting aquarium fish (p1159).

THAYERIA BOEHLKEI Weitzman / *Böhlke's Penguin*

Range: Amazon region of Brazil (especially near Obidos).
Habits: Peaceful, active fish that do well in a small group or school.
Water Conditions: Not critical but do better in neutral to slightly acid water; lights should not be too bright. Temperature 22 to 24°C.
Size: Maximum size is about 8 cm.
Food Requirements: Not critical; will eat most of the usual aquarium foods.

For general keeping, an 80-liter tank with a heavily planted background is ideal for a dozen or so penguins. The water should be clear and, if possible, moving. This can be accomplished through the use of power filters. The pH can vary anywhere from 6.6-7.4, but for breeding purposes a more acid water, down to 6.2-6.4, may be better.

The sexes are very hard to distinguish although at breeding time the female's abdomen is noticeably larger and the male appears slenderer and slightly smaller. For spawning *T. boehlkei* a pair or several females to a male should be placed in the spawning tank. Several females are used because spawning is apt to get a bit rough and a lone female may wind up quite battered after all the chasing. If the spawning fish are ready and they are placed in the spawning tank in the evening, spawning itself should begin at dawn. *Thayeria* generally spawn near the surface, and it should be mentioned here that bright lights are said to cause damage to the eggs and young, so be sure the lights are dim. Male and female will eventually swim side by side with their vents quite close. At this time 30-50 eggs will be ejected into the water by the female as the male fertilizes them.

THAYERIA OBLIQUA Eigenmann / *Short-Striped Penguin*

Range: Middle Amazon region.
Habits: Active swimmers and peaceful; may be kept in the community aquarium.
Water Conditions: Water should be soft and slightly acid. Best temperature 24 to 26°C.
Size: 8 cm.
Food Requirements: Will take dried foods, but these should be alternated frequently with live foods.

Sexes are difficult to distinguish, practically impossible in immature fish. When maturity is reached, the heavier bodies of the egg-laden females identify them easily. Spawning takes place in bushy plants, and the eggs are brown in color. A prolific species, there may be as many as 1,000 eggs laid at a single spawning. It has been found advisable, when spawning is over, to draw off part of the water and replace it with fresh water. Hatching takes place in as little as 12 hours. When they begin to swim, the fry should get very fine foods.

Thayeria boehlkei [F][D][X][1][6][1][X][N][N][8]
Thayeria obliqua [F][R][X][1][6][2][X][N][N][8]

[Dr. Herbert R. Axelrod]

Thoracocharax stellatus ⏽F⏽⏽D⏽⏽X⏽⏽1⏽⏽6⏽⏽3⏽⏽X⏽⏽N⏽⏽N⏽⏽8⏽ [Dr. Herbert R. Axelrod]
Thysia ansorgi ⏽F⏽⏽A⏽⏽X⏽⏽1⏽⏽6⏽⏽4⏽⏽X⏽⏽N⏽⏽N⏽⏽A⏽ [R. Zukal]

THORACOCHARAX STELLATUS (Kner) / *Silver Hatchetfish*

Range: Amazon, Paraguay, Orinoco basin to Venezuela.
Habits: An extremely peaceful surface fish; a good jumper, so its tanks should be covered.
Water Conditions: Soft, slightly acid water a necessity; this fish dies easily if maintained in hard, alkaline water. Temperature 23 to 26°C.
Size: 8 cm.
Food Requirements: Floating foods of all kinds taken, provided they can be swallowed.

This hatchetfish is occasionally offered for sale, but it is rarely identified under its proper name, as it is usually sold just as "a hatchetfish," with no attempt at placing the species. One reason for the lackadaisical attitude shown by both dealers and hobbyists when confronted with the many different hatchetfishes is that these fishes are almost never bred in captivity; since almost no attempt is made to breed them, no one seems to bother to break up shipments of hatchetfishes into species, which would of course be necessary if they were to be bred. None of the hatchetfishes should be considered as a really hardy fish, and they are especially susceptible to some of the more common aquarium diseases, such as ich. Perhaps this is because they are often neglected when kept in a community tank. Unless precautions are taken to see to it that the hatchetfishes are fed in accordance with their specific requirements, that is, that food is made available to them at the top of the water, they will soon decline.

THYSIA ANSORGI (Boulenger) / *Five-Spot African Cichlid*

Range: Liberia to Nigeria, in fresh and brackish waters.
Habits: Peaceful for a cichlid; does some digging, usually around rocks, but plants are seldom uprooted.
Water Conditions: Slightly alkaline, with an addition of about a teaspoonful of salt per 4 liters of water; tank should be well planted. Temperature 24 to 26°C.
Size: Males to about 10 cm; females a little smaller.
Food Requirements: Live foods preferred, but they will also take frozen foods.

The Five-Spot African Cichlid occurs in coastal waters of tropical West Africa, where it is found in brackish as well as fresh waters. With such a fish it is always a good idea to add some salt to the aquarium water, about a teaspoon per 4 liters. This is just enough to make the water a tiny bit brackish but not brackish enough to do any harm to freshwater plants. Females of this species have an unusual marking when sexually mature: they have a gleaming white spot on the sides near the anal opening. They can be distinguished from the males in other ways as well: they are a little smaller in size and the fins are smaller and more rounded. A well-mated pair will usually get along well and spawn regularly, preferring the privacy of an overturned flowerpot with a notch broken out of the rim to allow the pair to get in.

TILAPIA BUTTIKOFERI (Hubrecht) / *Hornet Tilapia*

Range: Central West Africa.
Habits: Peaceful when young, but decidedly aggressive when adult.
Water Conditions: Soft, acid water preferred. Temperature 24 to 28°C.
Size: Up to 26 cm.
Food Requirements: Live foods best although most standard aquarium foods are taken; especially likes live snails.

T. buttikoferi behaved themselves well in a 250-liter tank that also housed some African characins, but when the larger of the two fish reached a length of about 10 cm, the deportment of both fish changed entirely. They became very aggressive and constantly chased the characins and uprooted and destroyed the plants in the tank; they soon started fighting between themselves as well. After repeated unsuccessful attempts to get the fish to breed, Mr. Roloff gave his pair to a scientific institute when the larger of the pair was 26 cm long, but they did not spawn even in the larger tank and generally good conditions provided by the institute. They did well in soft, acid-to-neutral water ranging between 24 and 28°C in temperature, but perhaps they need an unknown stimulus to get them to spawn.

TILAPIA GUINEENSIS (Bleeker) / *Guinea Tilapia*

Range: Coast of the Gulf of Guinea, West Africa.
Habits: Not normally belligerent with other species unless their presence would deprive it of appropriate territory, but very aggressive among members of its own species, especially near spawning time; young fish of about the same size normally will not fight among themselves.
Water Conditions: Not critical as regards composition, but the temperature should remain above 22°C.
Size: To about 30 cm in nature; usually seen much smaller in the aquarium.
Food Requirements: A greedy eater that accepts all standard aquarium foods; should have vegetable matter in its diet.

This African cichlid species is a hardy fish that makes no great demands on its keeper and rewards its owner with constant displays of the type of "personable" behavior that has endeared cichlid species to aquarists for many years. It is a showy, active, non-scary fish that seems to make the best of any situation into which it's introduced. *Tilapia guineensis* is not a truly pugnacious species that seems to be always looking for a fight, but it can take very good care of itself if attacked by other fishes, even much larger fishes. It is a highly territorial fish that will stake out an area in a tank and defend it against all comers almost regardless of size, and at spawning time it of course becomes even more defensive of its territory. *Tilapia guineensis* is a substratum-spawner, not a mouthbrooder, and is a very dedicated and jealous guarder of its eggs and fry. Well-conditioned adults will spawn at a wide range of temperatures, but 24 to 27°C is best.

1165

Tilapia buttikoferi ⬚F⬚⬚D⬚⬚X⬚⬚1⬚⬚6⬚⬚5⬚⬚X⬚⬚N⬚⬚N⬚⬚D⬚ [E. Roloff]
Tilapia guineensis ⬚F⬚⬚A⬚⬚X⬚⬚1⬚⬚6⬚⬚6⬚⬚X⬚⬚N⬚⬚N⬚⬚D⬚ [Dr. D. Terver, Nancy Aquarium]

atocranus jacobfreibergi   F A X 1 7 1 X N N B   [G. Meola - African Fish Imports]
ogaster leeri   F E X 1 7 2 X N N A   [A. Roth]

TREMATOCRANUS JACOBFREIBERGI Johnson / *Jacobfreibergi*

Range: Lake Malawi, Africa.
Habits: Relatively peaceful if kept with other African lake cichlids of its own size; plenty of rocky caves should be provided.
Water Conditions: Hard and alkaline with a pH of 7.6 or higher. Temperature 22 to 28°C.
Size: About 12 cm.
Food Requirements: Not critical; like most Malawi cichlids, they will take a wide variety of fish foods and will do very well on a good flake food and brine shrimp (frozen or live).

Spawning is accomplished in typical fashion with the male displaying before the female with fins spread, swimming in circles around her and shimmying in front of her with his colors greatly intensified. The female cooperates by joining the male to form a quivering circle. The eggs are laid and fertilized and are immediately picked up by the female. The male may pick up some too, but that's the last you will see of those eggs. If the female strays off before spawning is completed, the male will quickly drive her back to the spawning area. After an hour spawning is generally finished and the female is left to wander away. For safety she should be removed to a tank of her own where she can incubate the eggs in peace.

TRICHOGASTER LEERI (Bleeker)
Pearl Gourami, Leeri, Mosaic Gourami

Range: Thailand, Malayan Peninsula, Penang, Sumatra and Borneo.
Habits: Peaceful and inclined to be a bit shy; may be kept in any community aquarium.
Water Conditions: Not critical, but water should be rather warm, about 26°C. A full-grown pair should be kept in a good-sized tank, at least 60 liters.
Size: 10 cm.
Food Requirements: Will eat any kind of dried foods, but should also get live foods occasionally.

This is the king of all the gouramis. Its regal bearing, coupled with the lovely violet sheen of its sides, makes it a very desirable fish to see. The males have longer, more pointed dorsal fins, and at mating time the belly color is a deep orange. The only thing that could possibly be said in their disfavor is that they are apt to be shy and timid. This might result in their not getting the full amount of food that they require if kept with a lot of boisterous, greedy tankmates. Their tank should be roomy and well planted, and if possible it should be in a place which is away from slamming doors and street noises. A healthy pair can easily be induced to spawn in such a tank. The driving which takes place before spawning is not as wild as with the other gouramis; they always seem to maintain themselves with a great deal of dignity. The bubblenest is apt to be large, and the number of eggs may be very high. At this time especially it is important to avoid frightening them. Usually the female may be left with the male while the eggs are being guarded.

TRICHOGASTER MICROLEPIS (Günther) / *Moonbeam Gourami*

Range: Thailand.
Habits: A fairly peaceful fish, but large specimens tend to be bullies, at least with others of their species.
Water Conditions: Soft, slightly acid water best, but this is not of great importance. Temperature 24 to 29°C.
Size: Up to 15 cm.
Food Requirements: Takes prepared, frozen and live foods.

The male builds a large bubblenest which is not very high in form; not much vegetable matter is woven into this nest, and the bubbles are allowed to float rather freely. During spawning, the color of the thread-like ventral fins becomes intensified, changing for a short time from orange to red. For best results in breeding, the water depth in the breeding tank should be low and floating plants should be present to give the fish a feeling of security. The female should also be provided with a thicket of fine-leaved plants into which she may flee if the male shows too much aggressiveness; fortunately for her, the male *T. microlepis* is not a real wife-beater. The fry, which hatch quickly at a temperature of 27°C, are very tiny. As with other anabantoid fry, they are very delicate for the first few weeks of their lives.

TRICHOGASTER PECTORALIS (Regan) / *Snakeskin Gourami*

Range: Southeastern Asia.
Habits: Peaceful and entirely harmless to other fishes, even young ones.
Water Conditions: Soft, slightly acid water. Temperature 24 to 27°C.
Size: To 26 cm in their home waters; mature at 10 cm.
Food Requirements: Not choosy as to food; dry food accepted as well as frozen and live foods.

Even though it grows to a good size, the Snakeskin Gourami cannot be described as anything but peaceful. The colors are very attractive and it is an asset to any group of larger fishes. It is an easy fish to maintain and will accept any food offered. At 8 to 10 cm maturity is attained, and, if allowed to spawn, it will be found that both parent fish will get along harmoniously, which is not the case with many other labyrinth fishes. The male builds a large bubblenest and, if she is of good size, the female will be found to be extraordinarily productive. Another thing in their favor is that the parent fish will never eat their young. They also cannot be coaxed to eat the young of other fishes or even snails. This gives the hobbyist the opportunity of raising a family of Snakeskins without ever having to remove the parents, as long as the tank is large enough to accommodate all of them. The youngsters can be raised easily by feeding progressively larger sizes of dried foods, beginning with the finest sizes and as the fish grow giving them coarser sizes. Naturally an occasional feeding with live foods such as newly hatched brine shrimp is a welcome change in the diet.

Trichogaster microlepis [F][D][X][1][7][3][X][N][N][C]   [R. Zukal]
Trichogaster pectoralis [F][Q][X][1][7][4][X][N][N][B]   [Dr. Herbert R. Axelrod]

1. *Trichogaster trichopterus* var. ☐F☐E☐T☐1☐7☐5☐X☐V☐N☐C☐ [Harald Schultz]

2. *Trichogaster trichopterus* ☐F☐E☐M☐1☐7☐5☐X☐N☐N☐C☐ [H. J. Richter]
3. *Trichogaster trichopterus* var. ☐F☐H☐B☐1☐7☐5☐X☐D☐N☐C☐ [H. J. Richter]

TRICHOGASTER TRICHOPTERUS (Pallas)
Three-Spot Gourami, Blue Gourami

Range: Southeastern Asia and the Indo-Malaysian Archipelago.
Habits: Peaceful in a community tank with fishes which are not too small.
Water Conditions: Not critical, but slightly acid, soft water is best. Temperature 24 to 28°C.
Size: To 15 cm.
Food Requirements: Takes any food, dried as well as live or frozen.

The Blue Gourami, a cultivated color pattern, has become so popular that it has backed the plainer wild Three-Spot Gourami right out of the picture, so much so that only the real "old-timers" still know what a Three-Spot looks like. The Blue Gourami is a very attractive fish and by far the most available color form. A pair can almost always be counted on to spawn in a tank which is to their liking; that is to say, one which has a fair amount of plants, a good-sized surface and enough heat. About 26°C is a good spawning temperature, and one does not need to worry about there being too much depth as one does with the Siamese Fighting Fish. A large bubblenest is built, usually in a corner. Here the male coaxes the female until she gets the idea and lets him wrap his body around hers. Many works insist that the eggs are squeezed from her in this process, but the pressure, if any, is very light. If she is well filled a spawning may be huge, 700 to 800 eggs. Although she is seldom damaged by the male, it is still advisable to remove the female after she has finished with her egg-laying chores. The male takes good care of his babies but should be taken out when they are free-swimming.

As mentioned above, the Three-Spot Gourami is the wild form of this species. In fact, it only has two spots on the body and the third spot is generally considered to be the eye. In addition to the Blue and Three-Spot, a Gold Gourami and a Cosby Gourami have been developed. The Cosby Gourami has irregular vertical bands on its flanks.

The golden color variation of the Cosby strain of the Blue Gourami was developed in East Germany in 1970 and has been seen on the American aquarium market since early 1971. The fish was not deliberately planned for, but was the result of random matings by Blue Gouramis that had been housed outdoors during warm weather. Gold Gouramis are the same as Blue Gouramis in all important respects except color, but no one has succeeded in raising Gold Gouramis equalling the maximum size of some of the Blue Gouramis in the trade.

1. *Trichogaster trichopterus*, the Cosby strain (p1175).
2. *T. trichopterus*, the normal variety (p1175).
3. *T. trichopterus*, the gold strain (p1175).

TRICHOPSIS PUMILUS (Arnold) / *Pygmy Gourami*

Range: Vietnam, Thailand, Malaysia and Sumatra.
Habits: Peaceful, but because it is shy it is best to keep them only with their own kind.
Water Conditions: A large aquarium is not required. 26°C is good; for spawning 29°C.
Size: Males about 3 cm; females slightly smaller.
Food Requirements: Will take prepared as well as the smaller live foods.

Colisa lalia, referred to as the Dwarf Gourami, was generally considered to be the smallest of the labyrinth fishes, and it was until this little beauty moved into the picture, so now we have a fish which we have to call the Pygmy Gourami. A tankful of these with the sun shining on them makes a lovely picture, with their deep blue eyes and purplish spots sprinkled all over the body and fins. Sexes are not always easy to distinguish, but the males usually have a bit of light edging on their dorsal and anal fins, and these fins are a bit larger and come to more of a point. These fish love a warm temperature and are apt to be "touchy" to keep if it is not given to them. Spawning them is very much dependent upon the compatibility of the pair. We have seen the rankest amateurs get spawning after spawning, while some of the so-called "experts" are unable to get them to breed at all. There is a small bubblenest, usually hidden under a floating broad leaf, into which about 50 eggs are laid. They hatch in about 30 hours, and the male takes care of the brood.

TRICHOPSIS SCHALLERI (Ladiges) / *Three-Striped Croaking Gourami*

Range: Thailand.
Habits: Peaceful; emits a faint croaking sound, especially during spawning activity.
Water Conditions: Soft, slightly acid water. Temperature 23 to 25°C.
Size: About 6 cm.
Food Requirements: Live or frozen foods of all kinds; dry foods would probably be accepted.

Most of us have at some time or another become acquainted with the original Croaking Gourami, *Trichopsis vittatus,* which has been kept by aquarium hobbyists for many years. This new species was sent to E. Roloff, the well-known German authority, from Bangkok, Thailand. Herr Roloff was quick to recognize it as a new species. The fish were collected by Dieter Schaller about 220 km northeast of Bangkok, where he found them in ponds and small pools in clear, lightly brown-tinted water with a fairly heavy plant growth. Roloff placed a pair in a small tank which was planted with a single *Cryptocoryne* plant. The male built a small bubblenest under one of the leaves. They embraced in typical labyrinth fish fashion, and after each frequent embrace three to six eggs were produced. The male guarded the eggs, which hatched on the third day. He was a good father and guarded the more than 200 fry very closely. They became free-swimming on the seventh day and were easily raised.

Trichopsis pumilis [F][E][X][1][7][7][X][N][N][3] [H. J. Richter]
Trichopsis schalleri [F][A][X][1][7][8][X][N][N][5] [H. J. Richter]

Trichopsis vittatus <u>F</u> <u>Q</u> <u>X</u> <u>1</u> <u>7</u> <u>9</u> <u>X</u> <u>N</u> <u>N</u> <u>6</u>

Trigonectes strigabundus <u>F</u> <u>R</u> <u>X</u> <u>1</u> <u>8</u> <u>0</u> <u>X</u> <u>N</u> <u>N</u> <u>6</u>

[H. J. Richter]

[Harald Schultz]

TRICHOPSIS VITTATUS (Cuvier & Valenciennes) / *Croaking Gourami*

Range: Vietnam, Thailand, Malaysia, Sumatra, Java and Borneo.
Habits: Peaceful and shy; should be kept by themselves because of their high temperature requirements.
Water Conditions: A well-covered, well-heated aquarium is necessary or this fish may prove to be sensitive. A temperature of 27 to 29°C should be maintained.
Size: Males a little over 6 cm; females slightly smaller.
Food Requirements: Will take dried foods if hungry, but prefers live foods, especially white worms.

The most attractive feature of this otherwise rather plain fish is its beautiful deep-blue eyes. Another unusual thing about it is that it is able to make tiny croaking noises, usually while spawning. One must listen quite attentively to hear them, but they are distinct. The species is by no means a newcomer, having been known to hobbyists in Germany since before the turn of the century. The old-time hobbyists who had to heat their aquaria with gas or alcohol flames had trouble keeping this fish alive, but nowadays when it is a simple matter to boost the temperature with a thermostatically controlled electric heater and hold it in the upper 20's(°C), it is not difficult to keep such fishes. If given a sunny aquarium which is shallow and well covered, pairs will begin to spawn in the spring months. A few broad-leaved plants should be there with the leaves floating, for the preferred spot will be under these leaves. Fry hatch in 24 to 35 hours and are tiny at first.

TRIGONECTES STRIGABUNDUS Myers / *Brazilian False Panchax*

Range: Rio Tocantins, Brazil.
Habits: Peaceful with fishes it cannot swallow.
Water Conditions: Soft, slightly acid water. Temperature 24 to 26°C.
Size: To 6 cm.
Food Requirements: Live foods of all kinds; can be trained to take frozen foods.

At first glance, if one did not know that the fish came from South America, one would be led to believe that this handsome fish is a species of *Aplocheilus* from Asia or Africa. The long, pointed dorsal fin and filamentous rays of the male's ventral fins certainly make it look like a "panchax" of some sort or other, but the fish comes from South America and is closely related to the well-known *Rivulus* species. This fish comes from the Rio Tocantins in Brazil, where it was found by our good friend Harald Schultz. The sexes are unmistakable: note that the female, the upper fish, lacks the black chin sported by the male and has shorter, more rounded fins. When we had several pairs of these fish in our office we were fortunate to have them spawn for us. The female expelled about a dozen eggs which were fertilized by the male and hung from her vent for quite a time by a thread until they were brushed off and hung from a plant.

TRIPORTHEUS ANGULATUS (Spix) / *Narrow Hatchetfish*

Range: Middle and Lower Amazon, Rio Madeira, Rio Negro, Orinoco and the Guianas.
Habits: Active and peaceful with other fishes of its own size.
Water Conditions: Not critical; tank should be in a sunny location and permit ample swimming space. Temperature about 25°C.
Size: Wild specimens attain a size of about 20 cm.
Food Requirements: Not very fond of dried foods, so should be richly fed with living foods such as daphnia or adult brine shrimp.
Color Variations: Body silvery with large scales; faint horizontal line; middle rays of tail are black and elongated beyond the caudal lobes.

This fish has no bright colors but is an active species which will always remain in the open spaces and will not bother the other tankmates. Its long pectoral fins and keeled belly identify it as a jumper, and a tank with these in it should always be kept covered or they are very likely to be found on the floor. This species has long been known to science; it was first identified in 1829 as *Chalcinus angulatus,* but recently it was reclassified as *Triportheus.* There is an interesting peculiarity of structure which this species shares with some of the African characins: the middle rays of the caudal fin are elongated and black in color, waving like a pennant far behind the tips of the caudal lobes. If the fish were not such an active swimmer, this elongation would make an irresistible target for other fishes and would often get nipped off. What the purpose of such an ornament might be could be the basis for much conjecture, and we will not attempt to make any guesses. One thing we do know: if this tip does get nipped off, it will quickly regenerate itself. So far there have been no recorded spawnings and there are no known external sex differences.

Triportheus elongatus, the Elongated Hatchetfish. Photo by Dr. Herbert R. Axelrod.

Triportheus angulatus 🄵🄳🆇①⑧①🆇🄽🄽🄱   [Dr. Herbert R. Axelrod]
1. *Tropheus duboisi* 🄵🆁🆇①⑧②🆇🄽🄽⑨   [Glen S. Axelrod]

2. *Tropheus duboisi* var. ⬚F⬚C⬚T⬚1⬚8⬚3⬚X⬚N⬚N⬚5 [P. Brichard]
3. *Tropheus duboisi* var. ⬚F⬚D⬚M⬚1⬚8⬚3⬚X⬚N⬚N⬚7 [Dr. W. Staeck]

4. *Tropheus duboisi* var. ⬚F⬚D⬚B⬚1⬚8⬚3⬚X⬚N⬚N⬚9 [P. Brichard]

TROPHEUS DUBOISI Marlier / *Duboisi*

Range: Lake Tanganyika, Africa.
Habits: Peaceful for a cichlid.
Water Conditions: Hard, alkaline water preferred. Temperature 24 to 26°C.
Size: About 9 cm.
Food Requirements: Live foods, preferably tubifex and white worms.

Tropheus duboisi is a very popular cichlid from Lake Tanganyika. In its natural environment, it lives among algae-covered rocks in the littoral region of the lake. Several color morphs are known, the most common being the narrow olive-banded, the wide olive-banded, the white-banded and the rainbow. Sexes are difficult to tell apart, although males usually grow larger than the females and are more aggressive in their defense of territory. The juveniles look nothing like the adults in terms of color pattern. Adults have a dark blue coloration with a light vertical band through the center of their bodies. Juveniles do not have the vertical band but rather a series of white dots in vertical rows across their flanks.

Tropheus duboisi is a difficult fish to breed under the best conditions. The species is a maternal mouthbrooder that lays few (6 to 12) comparatively large eggs. These eggs are about 4 mm in diameter. The mother carries the eggs for about four weeks depending upon the temperature of the water.

1. *Tropheus duboisi* pair in an aquarium (p1182).
2. *T. duboisi* juvenile is covered with rows of white spots (p1183).
3. *T. duboisi* losing its white spots and developing its white bar as it matures (p1183).
4. *T. duboisi* yellow-barred variety (p1183).

Tropheus duboisi juveniles. As the fish mature, the white spots on their head and body disappear and are replaced with a body band of varying widths. Photo by Wilhelm Hoppe.

TROPHEUS MOORII Boulenger / *Moorii*

Range: Lake Tanganyika, Africa.
Habits: Inhabits rocky bottoms in Lake Tanganyika and should be provided with some rocks in the aquarium.
Water Conditions: Slightly alkaline. Temperature 24 to 28°C.
Size: Up to 10 cm; sometimes slightly larger.
Food Requirements: Live foods, but will also eat grated beef heart; should have vegetable matter as well.
Color Variations: Many color variations.

To give the reader an idea of the wealth of fishes in Lake Tanganyika, allow us to point out that there are no less than 144 species of cichlids alone in this big, deep lake. This gives the aquarist a whole new world of fishes which are just becoming available.

Tropheus moorii, commonly called Moorii, is a relatively peaceful Tanganyikan cichlid that has become very popular. This fish inhabits the rocks in the littoral region of the lake. Over 30 color varieties of this species have been found around the lake, possibly more color morphs than have been found in any other Rift Lake cichlid. These color varieties include an olive form, yellow-bellied form, brown form, green form, red-striped form, orange-striped form, rainbow form, black form, solid orange form, yellow form, blue-black form, red and yellow form and tangerine form.

This species grows up to 10 cm. It is peaceful with other fishes but can be rough with its own kind if crowded into too small an area or when breeding.

Tropheus moorii, brown variety. Photo by Wilhelm Hoppe.

1185

1. *Tropheus moorii* var. F A T 1 8 6 X Y N A   [Glen S. Axelrod]
2. *Tropheus moorii* var. F D M 1 8 6 X C N A   [Glen S. Axelrod]

3. *Tropheus moorii* var. F D B 1 8 6 X C N A   [Glen S. Axelrod]

4. *Tropheus moorii* var. [F][A][M][1][8][7][X][U][N][A] [Dr. W. Staeck]
5. *Tropheus moorii* var. [F][A][T][1][8][7][X][N][N][A] [Dr. W. Staeck]

6. *Tropheus moorii* var. [F][A][B][1][8][7][X][N][N][A] [P. Brichard]

Sexing is difficult unless one knows the color morphs that one is working with. Males are usually larger than the females and more colorful.

Tropheus moorii is an omnivore that eats both algae and insects from the rocks. It has specialized dentition very similar to that of the *Simochromis* species. This fish will take most aquarium foods without question and should be given vegetable matter as a supplement to its diet.

The initial courtship for African Rift Lake cichlids is seemingly ritualistic and very interesting to watch. The male notices the female when her belly is full and protrudes with ripe eggs. The courtship begins with the male chasing the female around the tank. The female is at first elusive and plays "hard to get." This might go on for hours or days. The female will hide from the male among the rocks until she is also ready to breed. Eventually the male will be able to approach the female. The courtship includes fin movements and body twitchings. The two fish stay close together, with the male usually following the female around the tank. The male will situate himself in a certain area of the tank and defend its "terrain" from intruders. It is important to place the cave nesting areas far enough apart so that the range of territories does not overlap.

After the initial courtship is over and the territorial range has been established, the male will usually prepare a nesting site and can often be seen cleaning the rock surfaces. After the nest is prepared, the male will again chase the female throughout the tank. Finally the female will enter the nest with the male in "hot pursuit." Her body trembles during the egg-laying process.

This species is a maternal mouthbrooder that lays few (6 to 12) comparatively large eggs. These eggs are about 4 mm in diameter. Incubation periods range from four to five weeks. It is important not to disturb this species when brooding, as it is temperamental and will eat or spit out its eggs. This nature, along with its long incubation period and small egg number, helps account for this fish's high price.

When setting up aquaria with the intention of breeding Rift Lake cichlids, at least 40 liters of water should be allowed for each fish. The fish can best be bred in 80-liter tanks accommodating one pair each, or a larger tank may be used to breed several pairs. Ignoring esthetics, is often better for the beginner to place mated pairs in individual tanks. This eliminates the problems of competitive territoriality that the fish will display when they develop the spawning site; it will also eliminate the problem of territorial defense during and after spawning. The breeding tank should not be well planted but must be adequately aerated.

Mouthbrooders often have difficulty brooding while in captivity; many of them either swallow their eggs or spit them out. This is also a problem with young fishes that have spawned for the first time. In order to help solve the problem of destroyed eggs, especially with rare or expensive species, several types of artificial incubation have been developed. A modification of several of these incubation ideas results in what I (GSA) think is an excellent artificial system in which to hatch mouthbrooder cichlid eggs.

To begin with, the fish carrying the eggs must be caught after you are sure that the eggs have been fertilized. This is not always an easy task, especially if there are many rocks in the aquarium. The carrying fish instinctively hides among the rocks and is very defensive. Chase the brooding fish into a flower-pot, and then remove the pot plus the fish from your tank. Quickly grasp the fish in your palm. (Make sure that your hands are wet before you handle any live fish.) Point the head of the fish down and gently rub the buccal cavity (mouth) from below with your thumb. Hold the fish above a net that is touching the surface of the aquarium water but not completely submerged. As you rub the brooding fish under the mouth and it gasps for air, the eggs will spill from its mouth into the net. You can usually look into the mouth to make sure that all of the eggs have been expelled. Return the adult fish to an aquarium where it can recover without being bothered or chased by other fishes. As this process takes a certain developed manual dexterity, I recommend that the uninitiated practice on inexpensive fishes before handling prize specimens.

Submerge half of the net containing the eggs into a small (about 8 liters) aquarium, making sure that all of the eggs are covered by at least 1 cm of water. The chemistry of the water should be the same as that in the Rift Lake cichlid aquarium. The temperature of the water should be 25 to 28°C. This tank should not have an undergravel filter or a particulate filter. No filtration system is needed. Fix the net to the aquarium so as to hold it in the pre-described fashion. Run water through an airlift and bubble it over the eggs in the netting so that the water gently splashes down on the submerged eggs. Also place an airstone on the bottom of the small aquarium, directly under the net containing the eggs. Gently aerate so that the bubbles hit the bottom of the netting. Mouthbrooder eggs must be constantly aerated and rotated, but in a gentle manner. The combination of slow aeration and splashing water will accomplish this.

Tropheus moorii varieties (Moorii):
1. Kigoma yellow-belly (p1186).
2. Brown yellow-fin (p1186).
3. Kigoma brown (p1186).
4. Blue (p1187).
5. Rainbow (p1187).
6. Red-black (p1187).
7. Orange (p1190).
8. Kigoma yellow-barred (p1190).
9. Gold (p1190).

7. *Tropheus moorii* var. F D T 1 8 9 X N N A [Glen S. Axelrod]
8. *Tropheus moorii* var. F D M 1 8 9 X N N A [Dr. Herbert R. Axelrod]

9. *Tropheus moorii* var. F A B 1 8 9 X N N A [P. Brichard]

Xenentodon cancila ⒡Ⓓ☒①⑨⑤☒ⓃⓃⒹ
Xenocara dolichoptera ⒡Ⓓ☒①⑨⑥☒ⓃⓃⒷ

[S. Frank]
[Harald Schultz]

XENENTODON CANCILA (Hamilton-Buchanan) / *Silver Needlefish*

Range: Southeastern Asia.
Habits: Surface-swimmer and will jump out of tank if it is not covered; at times it appears to be motionless, as if hanging in air.
Water Conditions: An addition of some sea-salt would be beneficial. Temperature range from 22 to 26°C.
Size: Up to 30 cm.
Food Requirements: Prefers live foods including all kinds of smaller fishes.

This very odd-looking creature belongs to the family Belonidae, whose geographical range is truly worldwide. If you were to look at some of our North American gars, you couldn't help but notice some of the striking similarities between them and this family of needlefishes. But most members of this group of fishes are inhabitants of ocean waters, with only a few species found in fresh waters. As far as their swimming habits are concerned, they are very fast and can usually be found at the surface of the water. Because of the size *X. cancila* attains and its tremendous food requirements when mature, it is probably only suitable for large public aquaria. Even though the younger specimens are not as choosy about their eating habits, they nevertheless grow quite rapidly, and before you know it you would have to face the great task of providing it with all kinds of live fishes. Another bad characteristic of this species is its ability to jump in such an extraordinary fashion.

XENOCARA DOLICHOPTERA (Kner) / *Bushy-Mouthed Catfish*

Range: Northeastern South America.
Habits: Peaceful; will not harm even the smallest fishes.
Water Conditions: Can take a very wide range of water conditions, as long as abrupt changes are not made.
Size: Up to 13 cm.
Food Requirements: Accepts all foods and is especially fond of algae.

This armored catfish is one of the few that has ever been bred in home aquariums. They spawn in cave-like shelters, which may be duplicated in the home aquarium by rock caves or tubular shelters; of the latter, perhaps bamboo tubes are best, as these have been used on many occasions with good success in the breeding of this bewhiskered species. The male, which sometimes spawns with more than one female at a time, cleans off a space on which to deposit the adhesive eggs. The male guards the eggs and fans them vigorously all during their five- to seven-day incubation period; the fry do not become free-swimming until about four days after they have hatched, but as soon as they are able to swim well they hide themselves within the tank. On chopped tubifex worms and dry food they grow fast, reaching a size of about 4 cm in less than a month and a half.

XENOMYSTUS NIGRI Günther / *African Knife Fish*

Range: Broad east-to-west range in tropical Africa.
Water Conditions: Soft, acid water is best. Temperature range 24 to 28°C.
Habits: A nocturnal prowler; should be provided with good cover within the tank. Young, small fish are peaceful, but older fish are quarrelsome among themselves and definitely predatory upon small tankmates.
Size: Up to 20 cm; usually seen much smaller.
Food Requirements: Accepts all standard aquarium foods, but especially prefers live foods and frozen foods; floating dry foods are usually not accepted.

This rather colorless but highly interesting fish has been popular in the hobby for a long time, popular in the sense that whenever a dealer has them for sale they are usually bought out very quickly, for their novelty appeals to many hobbyists who are looking for something different. Unfortunately, once they get the fish home and into a tank they wonder why it seems to be uncomfortable, always seeking a place to hide. The reason, of course, is that *Xenomystus nigri,* like the other African knife fishes, is primarily a nocturnal species. It is not active when in the light, and it retreats from brightness whenever it has a chance.

XENOTOCA EISENI (Rutter) / *Red-Tailed Goodeid*

Range: Mexico, Rios Tepic and Compostela south into Jalisco at least to Magdalena; Rios Tamazula and Tuxpan in southern Jalisco south to Atenquique.
Habits: Peaceful; does well with others of the same species of all sizes, except possibly for equal sized males which may tend to be scrappy over females.
Water Conditions: Not critical as far as pH is concerned (pH 6-8 presents no problems), but hard water (DH 8-10 is sufficient) is necessary. Temperature 20 to 29°C.
Size: Reaches a length of 8 cm.
Food Requirements: Omnivorous; accepts a wide variety of live or prepared fish foods, and vegetable-based flake food is recommended to balance the diet.

The males go through a complex courting procedure (which may differ in details in different populations in the wild) including a simple stopping in front of the female, assuming a sigmoid body shape with his head toward the female and with the upper part of the body tilted toward her and dorsal and anal fins conspicuously bent toward her, and a very elaborate dance in which he performs figure-eights before the female.

Young females may drop up to a dozen young, but older and more mature females can have broods of 50 to 75 young every six weeks. The embryos are nourished in a uterus through a cord and placental arrangement apparently equivalent to that found in mammals. The young are born with the cord and placenta still attached (but dropped within the first 24 hours), upside-down and tail first. They are relatively large at birth, averaging about 12 mm.

Xenomystus nigri   F D X 1 9 7 X N N D
Xenotoca eiseni   F R X 1 9 8 X N N 8

[H. J. Richter]

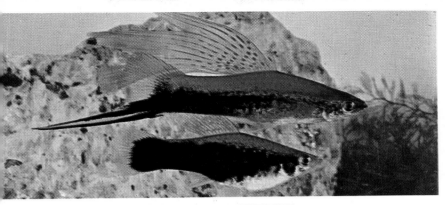

1. *Xiphophorus helleri* var. F Q T 1 9 9 X T S A   [Dr. Herbert R. Axelrod]
2. *Xiphophorus helleri* var. F Q M 1 9 9 X D N A   [Dr. Herbert R. Axelrod]

3. *Xiphophorus helleri* var. F Q B 1 9 9 X S N A   [H. J. Richter]

XIPHOPHORUS HELLERI Heckel / *Swordtail*

Range: Southern Mexico to Guatemala.

Habits: This fish is very variable in temperament; some specimens show very little aggression toward other fishes, while others, especially large males, are out and out bullies.

Water Conditions: Slightly alkaline, medium hard water; an addition of salt is sometimes of benefit, but this is not necessary. Temperature 21 to 27°C.

Size: Wild specimens up to 13 cm; almost always seen much smaller than this.

Food Requirements: Accepts all regular aquarium foods, but there should be variety.

Color Variations: Swordtails come in many different colors, with many different patterns. Red, green, black, albino and other forms are available.

The Swordtail is an extremely popular fish and one of the prettiest. Easy to keep, easy to breed, colorful, fast-growing, always available. . .the list of the fish's good points could stretch on and on. The male Swordtail is a beautiful fish, and his "sword," which is an extension of the caudal fin, is one of the most striking physical characteristics possessed by any aquarium fish. Unfortunately, many Swordtails of today do not have the same majestic tail of the original Swordtail, but they do have color, and this makes up somewhat for their lack of tail development. One of the prime factors which has served to popularize the Swordtail is the fact that the fish is a livebearer and thus can be bred with extreme ease. Even beginners in the aquarium hobby have no great difficulty in sexing and breeding this species, although they do often run into the problem of raising good-size young, something that the beginner is not able to do until he has mastered at least the fundamentals of aquarium management. Large females can give birth to more than 150 young at one time at intervals of about a month, so it is easy to see why this is considered a prolific fish.

Xiphophorus helleri, the Swordtail. A pair of black-spotted forms with the male below.

Xiphophorus helleri can be found in many color forms. Above is a pair of green Swordtails. Photo by Dr. Herbert R. Axelrod. Below is a gold wagtail Swordtail male. Photo by R. Zukal.

4. *Xiphophorus helleri* var.  [Dr. Herbert R. Axelrod]

5. *Xiphophorus helleri* var. F F M 2 0 2 X R L A
6. *Xiphophorus helleri* var. F Q B 2 0 2 X R N A [Dr. Herbert R. Axelrod]

7. *Xiphophorus helleri* var. F E T 2 0 3 X V S A   [K. Quitschau]

8. *Xiphophorus helleri* var. F E M 2 0 3 X R V A   [K. Quitschau]
9. *Xiphophorus helleri* var. F Q B 2 0 3 X Z N A   [A. Roth]

It happens every once in a while that there is a freak among the Swordtails where a male develops two swords instead of one. When this happens to the fish of a professional fish farmer with a hatchery, we can expect to see enough to ensure at least a small distribution to the fish hobbyists. This was the case with Oren Adams of the Adams-Prevatt Fish Farm in Gibsonton, Florida. About 10 years ago he noticed that some of his green wag Swordtails had a sword above, on the upper fin rays of the tail, as well as below. He segregated and inbred these fish, and now a batch averages about half with these unusual "swords." The males of these fish have one other characteristic: an unusually long gonopodium, sometimes as long as 6 cm. From the original green wag specimens, Adams now has red, red wag, brick, and brick wag varieties. Another unusual thing about this Adams strains is that the females as well as the males have the swords, a thing that would never happen in the regular strain. The lyretail characteristic does not affect the strain's fertility in any way.

Because all of the fins of the lyretail Swordtail, a comparatively new sword-tail sport, have been lengthened to a certain extent, giving the original lyretail Swordtail a dorsal fin a little higher than that of a normal Swordtail, hobbyists have confused the lyretail Swordtail with the Hi-Fin lyretail Swordtail. There are two reasons why there is so much difficulty in differentiating the lyretail Swordtail from the Hi-Fin lyretail Swordtail. First of all, both varieties when young exhibit exactly the same characteristics and are impossible to tell apart; it is not until they are about three or four months old that a definite distinction can be made. Secondly, the varieties are alike in more than the appearance of the lyretail and extended dorsal; both also exhibit the greatly extended anal fin that is present on all Swordtails with lyre-shaped tails. Adult male Hi-Fin lyretail Swordtails can be differentiated from the much more common lyretail Swordtails by the length of the dorsal fin (which in the former is much longer and more flowing than in the latter) and by the "splintered" appearance of the anal fin. Adult females of the Hi-Fin strain have a much longer and fuller dorsal fin than plain lyretail Swordtail females.

Xiphophorus helleri varieties (Swordtails):
1. Tuxedo Hi-Fin (p1199).
2. Marigold (p1199).
3. Green (p1199).
4. Tuxedo (p1202).
5. Red lyretail (p1202).
6. Red (p1202).
7. Variegated Hi-Fin (p1203).
8. Red Hi-Fin lyretail (p1203).
9. Green (p1203).

The specimen above is a Swordtail male with both a double caudal fin and double gonopodium. *X. helleri* (below) shows the male, with an extensive dorsal fin and well developed sword, above the female. Photos by R. Zukal.

1. *Xiphophorus maculatus x X. helleri* F E T 2 0 6 X T N 8

2. *Xiphophorus maculatus x X. helleri* F F M 2 0 6 X T Z 8 [G. Entlinger]
3. *Xiphophorus maculatus x X. helleri* F E B 2 0 6 X Q S 8 [Dr. Herbert R. Axe

Xiphophorus variatus var. ⬚F⬚E⬚T⬚2⬚1⬚1⬚X⬚V⬚N⬚6 [Dr. C. D. Zander]

2. *Xiphophorus variatus* var. ⬚F⬚E⬚M⬚2⬚1⬚1⬚X⬚T⬚N⬚6 [A. van den Nieuwenhuizen]
3. *Xiphophorus variatus* var. ⬚F⬚Q⬚B⬚2⬚1⬚1⬚X⬚Y⬚N⬚6 [Dr. Herbert R. Axelrod]

XIPHOPHORUS VARIATUS (Meek) / *Sunset Platy, Platy Variatus*

Range: Mexico.

Habits: Peaceful and active; excellent for the community aquarium.

Water Conditions: About neutral, fairly hard water is best but not essential. Temperature about 24°C.

Size: Females about 6 cm; males a little smaller.

Food Requirements: Will accept any and all foods, whether dry or living.

Color Variations: Very variable, with no two males alike; males have yellow to green body with black spots; dorsal yellow and tail red.

This very attractive livebearer has been bred to so many color varieties and hybridized by crossing with *X. helleri* and *X. maculatus* that at the present time it is just as difficult to find the pure-bred original strain as it is to find a Guppy which has not yet responded to the breeder's touch. This is a very hardy fish, and the females make up for their almost complete lack of color by producing a great number of offspring regularly (some strains have colorful females). The fry are very easily raised but try their owner's patience because the males do not show any color until after they have reached maturity. However, their beautiful colors are usually worth waiting for. Although they were first described by Seth Meek in 1904 as *Platypoecilus variatus,* aquarists did not get to see them until 1932, when they scored an immediate hit and became one of the best-liked livebearing species. Today there are many color varieties, thanks to the variability of coloration and the breeder's art, plus the fact that it crosses readily with the other *Xiphophorus* species. A sunny spot and good plant growth are preferred by the Sunset Platy, and like its close relatives the mollies it likes to pick algae.

The *Xiphophorus variatus* male is smaller than the female, as can be seen in the lower photo. Photo by Dr. Herbert R. Axelrod.

The specimen pictured above is a hybrid between *Xiphophorus helleri* and *X. variatus*. Photo by R. Zukal.

DELTA TOPSAIL VARIATUS

Sooner or later it was bound to happen. The famous Simpson Hi-Fin Swordtails just *had* to be crossed with other *Xiphophorus* species to get that gorgeous fin on other fishes. It fell to the lot of Bill Hearin of the Delta Fish Farm in Miami, Florida, to take these magnificent Swordtails and try his hand at it. The goal he set for himself was to get a variegated Platy and develop that tremendous dorsal fin on this fish. The idea was fine, but as is usual with such ideas, results were not so encouraging at first. Bill, a perfectionist, wanted only the dorsal fin of the Simpson Swordtails without the "sword" which is characteristic of the Swordtail. This took a lot of careful breeding, and a person with less patience and perseverance might have given up when a short sword kept showing up to remind him of the fish's Swordtail ancestry. But now we have them, in not only one strain but three: red, variegated and yellow, all with gorgeous flowing dorsal fins in the males. Females have these dorsals as well but not in the magnificent colors sported by the males. Only a very slight hint of a point remains at the bottom of the tail.

Xiphophorus variatus varieties (Sunset Platies):
1. Normal Sunset (p1211).
2. Tuxedo (p1211).
3. Gold (p1211).
4. Brushtail (p1214).
5. Hearin's Hi-Fin (p1214).
6. Hi-Fin (p1215).
7. Tuxedo lyretail (p1215).

4. *Xiphophorus variatus* var. ⊞ ⊞ ⊠ ② ① ③ ⊠ ⊡ ⊡ ⑥ [G. Entlinger]
5. *Xiphophorus variatus* var. ⊞ ⊞ ⊠ ② ① ④ ⊠ ⊡ ⊡ ⑥ [Dr. Herbert R. Axelrod]

6. *Xiphophorus variatus* var. ⬚F⬚E⬚X⬚2⬚1⬚5⬚X⬚Y⬚S⬚6 [S. Frank]
7. *Xiphophorus variatus* var. ⬚F⬚H⬚X⬚2⬚1⬚6⬚X⬚T⬚V⬚6 [Dr. Herbert R. Axelrod]

Xiphophorus variatus, purple Platy males become quite dark upon maturity. Note the spike tail in the male. The lower photo shows a female above a male. The fish are the result of hybridization between a Swordtail and a Platy. Photo by G. J. Timmerman.

Aerial view of a Florida fish farm.

Raising Tropical Fishes Commercially

Introduction

The breeding of tropical fishes on a commercial basis is being done today all over the world. While Russia does not have a tropical fish industry as we know it, there are at least two tropical fish stores in Leningrad, three in Moscow and perhaps others in the rest of the country. The proprietors of these establishments must, by virtue of the system under which they live, conduct their business after normal working hours, as they perform other duties for the State during the day. The vast majority of the fishes sold in these shops are produced in Russia by hobbyists. In Hungary, also, the State has not yet nationalized pet shops.

Florida, in the United States, is by far the major tropical fish producing area. Other large and important breeding centers are to be found in West Germany, Hong Kong, Singapore, California, England, Holland, Denmark and Belgium.

It is easy to see from the photo above why fish farms require a large supply of fresh water, either from lakes, rivers or wells, which is close at hand.

Tropical fish are today available to anyone at nearly any point. The risk of loss in transport has virtually disappeared. Superior methods of packaging and insulating shipments bring the fishes to their destination in fine and robust health, which is a welcome change from the conditions existing just 20 years ago.

The scope of the tropical fish industry (which a few facts and figures will reveal) immediately indicates that it is far from a small endeavor.

Tropical fishes are one of the largest single air freight items from the state of Florida. In an average week between five and six thousand boxes containing an average of 175 individual fish per unit are shipped. This means that better than one million fishes are produced and sold in Florida each week. Fifty million fishes each year is a conservative total. This does not include Goldfish, and this is *just* from Florida.

In the Tampa area alone there are 27 individuals who do nothing but raise various types of egglaying and livebearing fishes to supply the fish farmers with items they do not or cannot raise in sufficient quantity. These people in the most part derive their entire income from this work. They never ship fish, but they devote all of their energies to supplying the various shippers in their neighborhood. In all instances their production is specialized. This illustrates further the magnitude of the industry. In other parts of the United States this type of supplementary breeding also is being done, although in most instances by advanced hobbyists. The demand for good quality fish has never been satisfied. It apparently never will.

1218

Setting Up The Hatchery

You will learn in the following pages how tropical fishes are bred commercially.

It is absolutely essential before any such venture is started that you have a complete understanding of what is involved. It would be extremely foolhardy for any individual to invest any amount of money in equipment before knowing whether or not he can accomplish satisfactory results. This can be learned by breeding a few species on a small scale and keeping accurate records of your results. Only then can a valid conclusion be reached.

FOOD REQUIREMENTS

In order to raise healthy fishes fast, they must be fed an adequate and varied diet. Most large hatcheries mix their own dry foods and wet mashes, though commercial diets are usually better. Live foods are fed once or twice every day. Fishes are fed a minimum of three times each day. Feeding less often will give poor results, whereas feeding more often will further reduce cannibalism and increase rate of growth.

Dry food is fed first, usually the first thing each morning. The amount of food used depends upon the amount of fishes in the raising container. It should all be eaten in less than five minutes. The food is scattered over the surface of the container. It should *not* be delicately dropped into one corner. When the dry food is in a small area the larger fishes crowd out the smaller ones and they are deprived of an equal share.

Commercially prepared dry foods are sifted into three sizes:

(a) A dry powder for tiny fishes.

(b) A medium-small grind for larger fishes and full-grown fishes such as small tetras, danios, etc.

(c) A large coarse grind for breeding stock and young of fishes that will grow to a large size, such as *Cichlasoma meeki, C. severum, Pterophyllum scalare,* etc.

Fish meal is the basic ingredient of commercial dry foods. Various supplementary foods in dehydrated form such as shrimp meal, crab meal, blood meal, salmon egg meal, pablum, clam meal, beef meal, daphnia and fish roe are added. The important things are variety, balance and high protein.

Live food is fed several hours after the dry food, by which time the dry food should have been consumed. If it is not all eaten the fishes are being overfed.

The very best and safest live food is brine shrimp. The tiny newly hatched nauplii are essential for breeding success. The danger of introducing harmful enemies such as hydra, insect larvae, leeches, etc., is eliminated, since brine shrimp are free of freshwater parasites.

Some species are held in tanks under screened roofs (1 and 2) so that preying birds cannot get to them. A staff member (3 and 4) collects fishes from holding tanks to fill an order.

During the colder times of the year the ponds in Florida are covered with large plastic sheets to help insulate them.

Daphnia is a live food that is cultured by all large fish hatcheries. It can be screened and separated into various sizes for feeding different sized fishes. With a bit of care most of the dangerous pests that are introduced with daphnia can be removed. Newly hatched brine shrimp can be raised to maturity in about 25 days if you have the skill and ability to do it. This can be used instead of daphnia.

Daphnia is usually raised outdoors in large dirt pools without running water. The pool must be allowed to develop a goodly amount of protozoan life before daphnia can be raised. Sheep manure and cottonseed meal are the usual fertilizing agents. As the water clears additional amounts of fertilizer must be added or the culture will disappear.

Cyclops and rotifers are other smaller forms of live food that can be raised in the same manner as daphnia.

Tubifex worms can be raised, but this is difficult and seldom practical. These can be collected in fair quantities in most places and stored for a considerable length of time. It is best to leave their collection to specialists.

Mosquito and midge larvae (wigglers) are superior live foods presenting a dilemma for each user to work out for himself. If overfed you have just raised yourself a batch of mosquitoes!!

Fishes eat fishes, and baby fishes are wonderful foods. Prolific fishes such as the Blue Gourami, Red Paradise, Guppy, etc., are raised for food in many places.

White worms, *Drosophila*, bloodworms, glass worms, *Gammarus*, microworms, fairy shrimp, pond and ramshorn snails, mealworms and earthworms are other forms of live foods that are used. They are available intermittently, and the attendant difficulties in rearing them in quantity make their use at times impractical.

WET MASHES AND COOKED FOODS

All of these can be prepared in quantity and frozen until needed. The following are all excellent fresh-cooked foods that can be fed singly or in combination with each other: chicken, turkey, fish, beef liver, muscle meats, fish roe, minced clam, boiled shrimp, lobster and crab.

Hatcheries all prepare a pastelike cooked mash. There is no best formula, although there are many different formulas. After cooking, the material is rendered pastelike with a blender. The mash is stiffened to the required consistency by the addition of dry food. It should be packaged in individual units each equivalent to a day's supply and frozen.

The basic ingredient of such a mash is quick-cooking oatmeal. To this is added shrimp, liver, spinach and/or egg yolk. Ingredients can be purchased already cooked and simply combined. The strained and chopped baby foods are perfect.

WATER AND WATER TREATMENT

Before you can breed fishes you must be able to keep them alive and healthy. This is a great deal more complicated than most people realize.

You must research your fishes. It is essential that you learn as much as possible about the fishes' natural habitat. This information will give you the knowledge to be able to offer the fishes:

    (a) the correct temperature range,

    (b) the proper water composition,

    (c) its natural foods and

    (d) correct amounts of light.

All of the large successful hatcheries bring water from various locales for mixing and coloring the available natural waters. This is done to enable them to breed a large variety of fishes, which would be impossible if they were limited to one fixed type of water.

Some fish houses have warm water pipes under each tank and these act as both support for the holding aquaria and a source of heat.

Deep-well waters are almost sterile, as the lack of light inhibits bacterial and protozoan growth. Not so with river, pond and swamp waters. Exposed water must be treated before it can be used. Prolonged storage in the dark will help purify the water, but this isn't practical. Boiling the water is one safe method to kill off most of the undesirable life. Another method is to use chlorine water followed in about an hour's time by treatment with sodium thiosulphate (15 mg per liter of water). This will not alter the pH or hardness of the water to any appreciable extent.

Local water departments will supply accurate and correct analysis of your water without charge at any time. In addition, most water departments for a small fee will analyze any water you might bring them. This is very important. There is no excuse for blind groping when the information is easily available.

If your breeding stock is raised in water radically different from the water in which they are to breed, results will be very disappointing. The vast majority of egglayers come from soft waters on the acid side. When these fishes are kept in alkaline water and not bred, the eggs nearest the vent apparently calcify, making it impossible for the fishes to reproduce. Such fishes are not

Each of the tanks in this long row is supplied with air from a central compressor. The building as a whole is heated to a uniform temperature.

necessarily useless as breeding stock, for these calcified eggs can be stripped by hand with a gentle downward pressure. In a matter of weeks the fishes can be bred. This isn't a technique that everyone can manage easily, but it can be done successfully with a bit of practice.

For good results, it is essential that fishes be *reared* and *bred* in the same water. If you are aware of the type of water these fishes will be kept in when offered for sale to the consumer, they can be gradually acclimated to this type of water. Healthy fishes have remarkable tolerance to pH and hardness changes.

There are many types of good water softening apparatuses available today, and unless you are fortunate enough to have soft water from your tap, such an investment is almost a necessity. Water can be permanently demineralized with little difficulty, but I have never found a practical method to permanently acidify water. All of the recommended methods will acidify water, but within 24 hours the pH is back to where it started.

Fishes have a remarkable tolerance to wide temperature ranges. The danger is sharp fluctuations in temperature. An Angelfish will live happily at 15°C and also at 32°C, but only if the change is made gradually. The higher the temperature the higher the metabolism, so fishes require more food, more room and more oxygen at higher temperatures. The body processes slow down as the temperature is lowered. If it is too low, growth will be inhibited. A happy medium is desired. A temperature range between 22° and 25°C will give excellent results. When breeding, the temperature is raised. A practical and simple method of doing this automatically is to store breeding stock in the tanks closest to the floor and place the breeding tanks higher. Since heat rises, the breeding tanks will be 3° to 6°C warmer at all times.

Prevention and Treatment of Disease

Prevention is the key. If you meticulously adhere to certain basic rules you will be rarely troubled with disease. Briefly, these are the most important steps in preventing disease:

1. Nets and hands must be *wet* before a fish is handled.

2. A net is used *one* time in *one* container, and then it is sterilized before being used again. Potassium permanganate solutions and super-saturated copper solutions are used for sterilization purposes in most commercial establishments. Nets must, of course, be thoroughly washed before re-use.

3. Temperature control must be adequate. Nothing causes disease faster than rapid temperature changes. This is just as important up as down. The secret is constant thermostatically controlled heating equipment.

4. All new fishes must be isolated. Three weeks is a minimum safe period to be certain the new stock is healthy before mixing them with other breeding stock.

5. Wild-caught live foods such as cyclops, daphnia, tubificid worms, glass worms, etc., must be watched carefully, particularly if they are to be used with young fishes. Hydra, water tigers, water boatmen, etc., are almost always introduced with live food.

In order to treat a sick fish it is mandatory that you be aware of what malady affects the fish. The use of a microscope is not essential, but it is at times a very useful tool.

A quick synopsis of the accepted commercial treatments is given below.

ICH *(Ichthyophthirius)*. Success is often measured by rapidity in noticing the disease. If it first becomes apparent by the time the fishes are already dead and dying it is difficult to check and cure, but if observed early enough it can be cured without any loss at all. Mercurochrome in a regular commercial solution of 2% is very effective, but this must not be used on fishes being raised for breeding stock or for your current breeders, as you can cause sterili-

ty with this treatment. When using Mercurochrome the proper dosage is two drops to every four liters of water. If your water needs changing, siphon it down and add fresh water before treatment starts. Do not move the fish unless it is absolutely necessary. In addition to the Mercurochrome use one teaspoonful of Epsom salts to every 12 liters of water.

Malachite green in most cases is just as effective as Mercurochrome and will not sterilize your fish. A solution made of five grams of malachite green in a liter of distilled water is used. Put one drop to every four liters of affected water. This solution must be kept refrigerated or it will soon lose its potency.

Methylene blue and quinine, both of which are frequently mentioned as cures, are worthless in comparison with the above.

VELVET. Of all the common ailments velvet is the most difficult to diagnose. It is often confused with ich. The velvet granules are considerably smaller than ich, and unless you have unusually sharp eyes they will appear as a velvety coat on the fish's body.

Acriflavine and copper sulphate are the accepted and most successful treatments. To use copper sulphate obtain some of the chemical commonly known as "bluestone" and dissolve two heaping tablespoons in 500 ml of water. This will not completely dissolve, but it will give you a super-saturated solution to work with. Use care in handling copper, for an overdose will be fatal. Use one drop to every 20 liters of water. If the fish are not improved within 24 hours repeat the dose. This is the absolute maximum that can safely be employed.

Acriflavine can also kill fish and should not be overdosed. This is the same dye that the European chemists refer to as "trypaflavine." Tablets (125 mg) can be purchased. A stock solution is made by dissolving eight tablets in 500 ml of hot distilled water. Twenty-five drops to 10 liters will give excellent results. Store in a dark bottle out of the sun, and the solution will keep its strength for a long time.

Holding rooms have many tanks that are isolated from each other (they do not share the same water supply). This factor helps prevent the spread of disease. Photo by Dr. Herbert R. Axlerod.

NEON TETRA DISEASE. Using commercial formaldehyde, five drops per 10 liters will cure tetras in a matter of hours.

MOUTH FUNGUS, TAIL ROT, INFECTED WOUNDS, BADLY BRUISED FISHES. All are best treated with tetracycline hydrochloride. Unfortunately this is a very expensive drug. A minimum daily dosage is 250 mg to 20 liters, and double this amount is advised.

Two other invaluable medications are methylene blue and Epsom salts. The former is a most effective and safe germicidal agent. The latter stimulates the secretion of body slime on fishes. In reasonable doses neither can harm fishes, and these are best used in combination with the drugs mentioned specifically to treat the various common diseases.

Any observant person will in time be able to recognize trouble even if he is 10 meters from the afflicted aquarium. Sick fishes do not act in their normal manner. Each species is different, but by observation you will unconsciously recognize that something is wrong by the fishes' behavior. You must immediately discover what is wrong and try to correct it.

1228

How to Breed Fishes

BREEDING STOCK. Adult fishes should be avoided and purchased only when no other stock is available. Your potential breeders should be raised in the same water in which they will be spawned. When your fish are of an age to attempt breeding, sexes should be separated. By keeping them isolated in this manner a larger yield will result. However, this can be a dangerous practice unless your breeders are being used on a prearranged schedule. If mature egg-layers are kept by themselves and not bred often enough, many will become eggbound.

SETTING UP. All breeding establishments set up a minimum of 10 tanks of a specific species at a time and more often a setup will consist of 75 to 100 tanks of the item to be bred. Disregarding for the moment the more difficult fishes, an average of eight spawns out of every ten setups is considered fair. The really fine breeders often will have complete success and achieve a fertile spawn in every tank setup. The obvious point, of course, is that fishes which are not properly conditioned and ready to breed should never be utilized.

Most fishes will spawn within 24 hours. Some fishes (Lemon Tetras, Black Ruby Barbs, etc.) will not start spawning until 48 to 72 hours have elapsed. With the exception of fishes that are permanently set up (Scalare, Ramirezi, Kribensis, Bumble Bees, etc.), all breeding attempts will be abandoned after five days without results. Fishes are never fed while set up.

REMOVE BREEDERS. The majority of spawns will occur in the first hours of the new day. There is never a mad rush to remove the parents, for even the worst egg-eaters will not eat their eggs until spawning is completed. This is not a matter of a few minutes, but often many hours. If spawning commences at daybreak the parents should not be removed for at least four hours. A 12 cm net with a 4 mm mesh should be used so that the net itself will hold the parents but will allow all of the eggs to slip through. After the parent fish are captured and before they are completely removed from the spawning tank, the net should be sharply struck on the side of the aquarium to dislodge any eggs that may have adhered.

BREEDING EQUIPMENT AND RACKS. There are no hard and fast rules in so far as constructing racks is concerned. As the tanks must be moved on and off the rack frequently, the ease with which this can be accomplished should be kept in mind. Angle iron cut to shape and bolted together makes the most practical rack. Bolting, not welding, is suggested, because if it becomes necessary to move your installation it can then easily be accomp-

Many fish are collected from each outdoor pond.

lished by removing a few bolts. If possible the breeding rack should be in the center of the room. Utilize the floor by building completely around the perimeter of the room a series of concrete vats. Size is dependent on the number of fishes they are to be used to hold or raise. Breeding stock can be kept in these vats, but it is more practical to use them for rearing young and new breeders. The actual current breeders should be in glass-fronted containers where they can be constantly observed. Large wooden casks are to be had for a fraction of their worth from importers of Spanish olives. These hold about 800 liters and are ideal containers for treating, holding and ageing water. An electric pump to facilitate the moving of water is most important.

The roof of the breeding room should be modified to allow for an ample amount of natural sunlight. The cost of skylights can be repaid quickly by utilizing the light to raise aquatic plants in your concrete vats. There is always a ready market for fine aquatic plants. As a tremendous amount of water must be used, be aware of the need for adequate floor drains. Drains are simple to install during construction but very troublesome when an afterthought.

Breed your fish in ample-sized aquariums. An oversized container will help, but an undersized restrictive container will inhibit breeding efforts. Containers smaller than 32 liters are seldom used. The use of all-glass tanks is wise, though plain galvanized aquariums may be used. A well-made aquarium is a sound investment. A bargain aquarium invariably costs three times what you think you are saving. It will fail you when it is most needed. Before purchasing your aquariums be sure to have a complete written understanding of your guarantees with the seller.

The breeding room should be kept in as close to a sterile condition as possible. Visitors should be discouraged. Cleanliness is essential.

Commercial Breeding Techniques

Zebra Fish *(Brachydanio rerio)* and **Pearl Danio** *(B. albolineatus)*

Since these fishes can be handled in an identical manner we will discuss them together as group-spawners that drop non-adhesive eggs. They are best spawned in a breeding trap. As many as six trios (two females and one male) are placed in the spawning trap, depending upon the size of the trap. The best results are obtained when the breeders are covered with no more than 3 cm of water. Fifteen to twenty setups are worked at the same time. The breeders are left in the breeding traps until the young start the free-swimming stage. This is usually the fourth day after the fish have been set up. The fry should be fed with infusoria often and copiously. After three days the fry are removed to larger vats for raising. If the weather is warm enough, fry can be put outdoors directly into concrete or dirt pools for raising. These fishes can stand an outside temperature as low as 0°C when grown and acclimated, but the babies will succumb if the temperature is below 15°C when they are put outside. The breeders often injure themselves in the confined traps while breeding. It is advisable to medicate them with sodium sulfathiozole and Epsom salts after removal from the breeding trap. Zebra Fish are voracious egg-eaters if given the opportunity.

Giant Danios *(Danio malabaricus)*

Unlike their smaller cousins described above, Giant Danios have adhesive eggs. This makes spawning traps impractical. Giant Danios are egg-eaters, and a thick spawning medium must be utilized. The most common *egg receiver* is Spanish moss, which is placed thickly and completely over the bottom of the spawning tank. A single pair is set up in each aquarium. Breeders are 8 to 10 cm in length, and a medium aquarium should be used (40 to 60 liters). A well-conditioned pair will throw 600 to 1,000 eggs. They grow fast. The secret of raising quantity is to give the young plenty of room.

Three-Spot or Blue Gourami *(Trichogaster trichopterus)*

This is a hardy fish that will withstand temperatures as low as 13°C. The adults are better able to withstand cold than the youngsters. The fish will spawn naturally in a dirt pool, but no production can be achieved this way.

The standard procedure is to set up about 30 pairs at a time, each pair in 32-liter aquaria. Water should be 10 cm deep. They spawn prolifically in water on the hard and alkaline side. A few water hyacinths or similar floating plants should be put in each tank. This helps anchor the bubblenest. The tank should be empty of all foreign matter except for the floating plants. There does not have to be a wild rush to remove parents after spawning, because this fish seldom will eat its young. Two days after the fry are free-swimming the parents can be removed. This fish is extremely prolific, and it is usual to hatch more than 1,000 fry from a spawn. The parents can be bred again within two weeks. If the fry are to be raised indoors the problem will be to feed the young sufficient food and yet keep the container clean. Most Blue Gouramis raised commercially are bred from April through July and, depending on the size of the vats or pools available, taken outside and released when six or eight days old. They are harvested in the fall before extreme cold weather sets in and held inside for sale throughout the winter months. The fish does not command a high price, so it is impractical to attempt to supplement stocks by indoor raising.

Opaline or Cosby Gouramis are handled in a manner identical to the above, but as this is a higher-bred strain of *T. trichopterus,* yields are smaller and the percentage of successful spawns will be lower.

Pearl Gouramis *(Trichogaster leeri)* are handled in a similar manner, with the following exceptions. The fish is extremely soft-bodied and unusually susceptible to fungus. They must be handled with extreme care. Since they will not trap it is dangerous to attempt to raise them in an outside dirt pool. It is more practical to raise them in large concrete vats where they can be safely caught with nets.

Siamese Fighting Fish or Betta *(Betta splendens)*

This is one of the most simple egglayers to breed. The ability to raise a majority of the spawn is the difficult part. The fish breeds simply in a small container. A 4-liter tank is sufficient. Water level should be no more than 8 cm. The female must be given a hiding place, which can be done with clean aquatic plants, pieces of slate or other rocks. The male will, in most instances, kill the female unless precautions are taken. Remove the female immediately upon completion of spawning. The male will then repair the nest and return the young that fall through. It is safe to keep the male with the young for 48 hours after the babies are free-swimming. The young are fed heavily with infusoria and after another 48 hours are moved to a larger rearing tank or vat. At this time various spawns can be combined.

If you are to raise Bettas successfully they must get adequate food often and plentifully. If the male is removed from the spawn prematurely the young will drown. All labyrinth fishes grow unequally. While this is true to some extent with most fishes it is more pronounced in this family. As the Bettas grow, the males, which will be obvious by their longer fins, are removed and placed in individual pint jars. They are raised in isolation or they will tear each other's fins apart. Bettas should be raised on live food only, because it is difficult to

Although Siamese Fighting Fish are one of the most simple egglayers to breed, they are difficult to raise to maturity. The fish will breed in small containers. As the Bettas grow, the males, which will be obvious by their longer fins, are removed and placed in individual pint jars as seen above. They are raised in isolation or they will tear each other's fins apart.

feed dry foods in a confined space without fouling the water and losing the fish. Brine shrimp, tubificid worms and daphnia are the best foods. It should take no more than five months to raise a male Betta to maturity. If it takes longer the fault lies in the diet.

Bettas can survive in terribly foul water by utilizing their labyrinth chambers. However, to raise good males the water must be changed at least one time before sale and more often if possible. A percentage of all jars should be changed each week. If this is done methodically it can be accomplished without undue labor, but if it is allowed to accumulate there will never be sufficient empty jars to move a quantity into clean water at the same time. The technique is simple. The entire jar is poured (including the fish) through an 8 cm net and then the fish is dumped into a shallow pan. When the pan contains 25 to 50 fish they are netted out individually and placed into clean jars. The dirty jars are then cleaned and filled with proper water. They are then ready for next week's changes.

Rainbow Pumilus Gourami *(Trichopsis pumilus)*

This is a most delightful fish with no bad habits and is easily raised. The fully grown Pumilus is barely 4 cm. They should be spawned like *Betta splendens,* the exception being that the male is not aggressive and will not injure the female. The Pumilus nest is considerably smaller than a Betta nest and seldom as large as a nickel. The nest is invariably built in a corner of the tank; as it is small, the plastic frame corners of the tank can obscure it from view, so you must check carefully. Pumilus is a prolific but slow-growing fish.

Angelfish *(Pterophyllum scalare)*

This is certainly one of the very best fish for the small breeder to produce. Spawns are large and the young, if properly fed, can be of saleable size in eight weeks. Most important, there is always a ready market for the fish. Once a compatible pair is obtained they can be expected to produce some 25 spawns per year which should yield some 5,000 to 10,000 saleable fry.

When selecting breeders it makes little sense to attempt to short cut and purchase a so-called "mated pair." Invariably what you will obtain will be a proven pair, but the hitch is that the fish are rapidly approaching the end of their productive life as breeders. The only practical approach is to purchase young, medium-sized fish and grow them to maturity together in a large tank. In this maturing aquarium is usually a piece of slate, but any number of other types of inert material can be used, such as colored rigid plastic tubing or sheeting, rocks, a large Amazon sword plant of the broad leaf variety or a sheet of ground glass or other opaque glass. When the fish have attained sexual maturity they will pair off by themselves. The trick is to be able to single out the pair from the group. This can be done with a bit of practice.

It is perhaps more common with Angelfish than any other cichlid for two females to pair off. This necessitates accurate records of spawns so that if infertile eggs are obtained three consecutive times the pair (?) can be discarded.

The breeding tank, which should be of about 40 liters, will contain an airstone, a piece of slate, suitable water and nothing else.

Success in breeding Angelfish is more dependent on food than any other single factor. Variety is the secret. The very best foods are, in order:

  Baby Guppies (first heavily feed the Guppies with dry food)
  Tubifex worms
  Mosquito larvae
  Water boatmen
  Earthworms (chopped and cleaned)
  Daphnia
  White worms.

The eggs should always be removed from the breeding tank on the slate upon which they were laid. They should be placed in 4-liter aquariums containing water identical to that in the breeding tank. A moderate stream of air from an airstone should be played against the slate, which should be slanted. This is important to prevent an accumulation of detritus on the eggs. The water should be colored with methylene blue to prevent excessive bacterial activity.

When the babies are free-swimming they must be fed infusoria. After they have been fed for four days they can be removed to larger quarters for raising. At this point they are able to take newly hatched brine shrimp. Feed a little at a time until you are sure they are able to take it, and then keep food in front of them constantly. They will grow very fast.

Breeders that consistently throw a percentage of malformed young should be destroyed.

Fancy Angelfish (veiltails, black lace, all-blacks and the various combinations of these) are handled identically. However, you will find much larger percentages of runts in these spawns. These are not necessarily bad or weak fish and generally are the more desirable specimens since they rarely eat their spawn. At 30 days of age all of the smallest fish should be removed and raised separately. They will quickly put on normal growth when they no longer have to compete with their larger brothers and sisters for the available food.

Large Cichlids are probably more popular now than ever before, with greater emphasis on old standbys and newer South American and African species. Old favorites include the following.

Astronotus ocellatus (Oscars) are huge fish, and full-grown fish are seldom seen outside of breeding establishments. They are extremely long lived and very hardy. Breeding pairs as old as 14 years have been known to still produce young in normal quantities.

These fish are extremely difficult to pair and must be allowed to pair themselves. As it takes a minimum of two years to raise a breeder, and the breeders need enormous amounts of space, it isn't a task to be lightly undertaken. In addition, the fish require copious amounts of live food (such as small Goldfish, ghost shrimp, crawfish and bait fish), and this is not always easily available. When the fish are finally old enough to breed they must be paired. Unless watched closely, incompatible fish will kill each other, and then two years of work are ruined.

If you are still interested and haven't given up the idea of breeding Oscars by this time, look at the other side of the story. A proven pair is like a money machine. If properly fed and conditioned they will breed continually. An average of 25 spawns per pair per year is not unusual, and this should yield at least $3,000.00 at 25¢ per baby.

Cichlasoma severum is another large cichlid, although not quite so huge as Oscars. They will produce almost as many as Oscars in number of young, but unlike Oscars, there is a task to sell all that a good pair will produce.

C. festivum, C. meeki, Aequidens pulcher and *C. nigrofasciatum* are all bred and sold in limited quantities. *Geophagus braziliensis* is a common member of the genus that is easily bred. It is a beautiful fish and sells very well. Of course African cichlids of all types are good sellers, and the mouth-brooders are easy to breed.

Symphysodon species are unquestionably the most desirable of all tropical fish from a strictly commercial outlook. The very finest professional and amateur breeders have devoted many years to breeding these fishes but complications such as the fry feeding off the parents' slime make them difficult to raise in quantity.

Dwarf cichlids

Dwarf cichlids are also much more popular than ever before. They do not have any of the objectionable habits of their larger brethren and are very hardy fish. Temperature plays an important part in breeding this group. *Apistogramma ramirezi* will spawn best at 32°C and none will breed easily at less than 26°C. Small tanks are adequate; slate bottoms are best and they should be covered with a centimeter of well-washed gravel. Broken flowerpots make ideal spawning mediums and enough should be put into the breeding tank to give the fish room to hide. Young can be raised with the parents, although most breeders will remove the parents and raise the young in the breeding tanks. Some of the dwarf cichlids from Africa, such as *Julidochromis*, some *Lamprologus, Nanochromis* and *Pelvicachromis* species, are among the prettiest of all tropical fish.

Halfbeaks *(Dermogenys pusillus)*

This unique livebearer is bred with great success as follows. A large shallow aquarium or wooden vat should be employed. An 8 cm square wooden rod is cut to the length of the opposite corner and when floated in the vat will divide the container into two equal triangles. One half is left completely bare and the other half is thickly filled with hornwort. The advantage of hornwort over most other floating plants is that it will resist decay for a long period of time even in dim light. Fifteen female and five male Halfbeaks are placed into the vat for breeding purposes. Live food should be in front of the breeders at all times, for these fish are extremely cannibalistic. The combination of adequate hiding space and ample food ensures success. Breeding occurs at any hour and continually. Babies should be individually captured and removed. Thirty to forty young daily is the average yield. Be alert for the inevitable introduction of dangerous aquatic insect enemies with live food. If these get to be a problem the best and easiest cure is to re-make the entire setup.

White Clouds *(Tanichthys albonubes)*

Although extremely easily bred, this fish is often in short supply. The outstanding advantage this fish possesses is the fact that it will eat neither its eggs nor its young. This is a decided advantage to a breeder who cannot always be with his fish when success demands his presence. There are many ways to breed this fish, but the two methods described below yield the greatest results (the first is often favored).

(a) Two trios are placed in a 30-liter tank that is bare except for a fair-sized clump of Spanish moss. The aquarium should be checked daily until the first young are observed. The breeders are removed 24 hours after and rested for 10 days before being set up again. At this point the young must be given infusoria. They are very small when hatched, so they should be fed on this for at least one week. At that point a bit of brine shrimp is added, but the infusoria must be continued. As eggs are laid over a period of days, new young will hatch days after the first are observed.

(b) Larger quantities of breeders are kept in concrete vats or large wooden vats. The container is heavily stocked with plants and usually is old and mulm-filled to ensure a ready stock of infusoria. White Cloud babies come to the surface and stay there the first few days of their free-swimming life so it is a simple matter to remove them with a small net and rear them separately.

White Clouds do best in hard, alkaline water. The best method to distinguish sex is by body shape; if the females aren't quickly apparent they are not yet ready to breed. Males have longer and more colorful dorsal fins.

Barb species (*Puntius, Capoeta, Barbodes*)

All are bred in an identical manner. The size of the breeders determines the size of the container. While not as fussy as characins in so far as water is concerned, they do best in soft, slightly acid water. This group has a tendency to get eggbound, and care must be taken to see that breeders are bred frequently or left together so that the females may rid themselves of eggs. Spanish moss "skeletons" are the best spawning medium, but any similar sterile material will work. Commercial breeders do not like to use plants, the reason being that plants are carriers of enemies. Synthetic fibers are used with wonderful success.

Tanks should be bare except for the spawning medium. Spawning starts an hour after daylight, and breeders should be removed as soon as they are finished. The newborn young are relatively large and after a few days on infusoria are ready to take brine shrimp. After three days on brine shrimp they should be removed to a larger container for raising. Barbs as a group require a great deal of oxygen and cannot be crowded. They are susceptible to *Oodinium* (particularly *oligolepis* and *nigrofasciatus*). A copper sponge placed in the raising container will eliminate this trouble.

Unless you have a large or varied outlet for sales it is impractical to breed the more exotic varieties. The best commercial barbs in order of importance are *tetrazona, titteya, everetti, nigrofasciatus* and *schuberti.* Two very good though difficult species are *hexazona* and *lineatus.* The largest and most prolific spawners are *everetti, lateristriga, filamentosus* and *arulius.* Two of the most dramatic are the seldom seen African *candens* and *hulstaerti.* These are found in such extremely acid water that it is doubtful they will ever be adjusted to normal water conditions. I wouldn't advise wasting time with them, although the returns would be very high if successful. *Gelius* is a lovely small fish with not much demand. *Oligolepis* is very pretty but grows very, very slowly and only large specimens are in demand. Africans such as *callipterus, holotaenia, usumbarae* and *viviparus* are not pretty enough to be of lasting interest. Not much has been done with *schwanenfeldi* and the specimens available have all been expensive; it is a pretty fish but grows very large. No mention has been made of *conchonius* or *ticto,* because these will breed by themselves in dirt pools and are tremendously prolific. They sell at low prices so it would be of little practical use to breed these where space is limited.

Rasboras

The most popular *Rasbora* is *heteromorpha,* the "Harlequin." Unfortunately, this fish is seldom bred in a practical manner. It is very common in its native Malaysia and large quantities of imported specimens make it available at reasonable prices. This fish can be bred in pairs or in community schools. The best method is three females and two males. The species most commonly and easily bred is *trilineata,* the Scissortail. This is a larger than the average *Rasbora* and very prolific. A good spawning will yield 500 young. The fish supposedly grows to 20 cm in length, but it is rare to see a fish larger than 10 cm and the average breeders are 6 to 8 cm in length. They are a soft-bodied fish and great care must be taken in handling them, as they bruise and fungus very easily. Other varieties of *Rasbora,* such as *maculata, pauciperforata, dorsiocellata* and *borapetensis,* are bred commercially but in very limited numbers. *Trilineata* should be bred in large aquaria for best results. The water should be on the acid side and soft. Spanish moss is an ideal medium. If spawning hasn't been accomplished in 48 hours, chances are that they will not spawn. It is impractical to leave them set up for longer periods. They grow fast and are omnivorous. If fed properly the young will be saleable in 90 days.

Catfishes

Catfishes of suitable aquarium size can be sold with little effort. Even the most bizarre and rare types can be sold easily, as this entire group holds great interest for advanced hobbyists and owners of family community tanks. Tremendous quantities of the more easily obtainable types are imported. The various South American collectors ship in excess of eight million wild-caught specimens each year. The only catfishes that are bred commercially are

Pieces of plastic corrugated roofing material are inserted into the water along the edge of a *Corydoras aeneus* breeding pond to serve as egg depositories for the catfish.

Callichthys, Hoplosternum thoracatum, Corydoras, mostly *aeneus* and *pygmaeus,* and one variety of African glass catfish.

Callichthys and *Hoplosternum* are bred in an identical manner. They require large quarters that should have a minimum of 2000 square cm of surface. Water depth should be 12 cm. Water should be slightly alkaline and medium soft. These fish are bubblenest builders and must have something floating to anchor the nest and eggs. The following egg anchorers have been used successfully: a 40 cm square of polystyrene, an aluminum pie plate, a piece of wood and various floating plants. The parents guard the nest and young and are not interested in eating either eggs or progeny. They spawn prolifically but are not easy to induce to spawn. Breeders are 10 to 18 cm long and the young grow rapidly. The female is invariably larger than the male. The young can immediately take brine shrimp.

Corydoras are bred as follows: It is most important that the breeders be large enough and old enough. The aquarium should be of at least 40 liters capacity. The bottom should be covered with well-washed gravel. A few clean *Cryptocoryne* plants will give the breeders more security. Breeders should be placed in the spawning tank at night and, if in condition, will spawn the following morning. If spawning is not accomplished in 48 hours, change breeders. Eggs will be placed on the plant leaves or sides of the aquarium and will number two to three hundred. While it is true the parents do not show any further interest in the eggs and usually will not eat them, it is best to remove the parents immediately after spawning. After this is done add methylene blue to the tank. Raise the young in the breeding tank. The eggs hatch in five days and the yield is never more than 30 or 40% of the eggs laid.

Why there is such a consistent number of infertile eggs has never been satisfactorily explained. The young are large enough to take brine shrimp and microworms immediately. 7.4 pH and medium soft brown water yield best results.

Characins (tetras)

Breeders *must* be properly grown and conditioned; this is the most important factor in breeding. If correctly handled any common member of this family can be spawned every three weeks. If time and space permit, best results will be realized by keeping the sexes separate. The danger, of course, is in not utilizing your egg-filled females often enough. This will cause an egg-bound vent and makes subsequent breeding attempts difficult and sometimes impossible. The size of the breeding container necessarily depends on the size and number of breeders to be used. Characins, more than any other group, can successfully be bred by utilizing more than one pair at a time. When group spawnings are attempted the usual ratio used is two males for every three females. The danger of eggs being eaten is greatly increased in group spawnings, and constant vigil must be employed to prevent a large loss through negligence. The most widely employed spawning mediums are Spanish moss, knitting yarns and fine-leaved plants such as hornwort or *Cabomba*. Live plants are being used in large commercial establishments less frequently as, despite all precautions, they will carry undesirable organisms into the spawning tanks.

The water used for tetras depends upon the fish although the vast majority prefer a soft, light brown water of 6.4 to 6.8 pH. You must research your chosen fish to best determine the characteristics of the natural conditions where it is found in the wild. The pH figures given above would yield poor results with Rummy-Nose Tetras and Bleeding Heart Tetras, as these fish require *extremely* acid water. The exact opposite type of water (hard and alkaline) is preferred by Bloodfins and Swordtail Characins. This group should be of particular interest to those of us who have limited space.

Two problems plague the Florida fish farmers—unwanted animals and the weather. Fences surround the pond areas to keep out snakes, toads, etc., and an electric wire runs through the middle of the fence to restrain cattle and other grazing animals.

Many tetras can be sold easily and in good volume, and there are many common and uncommon species that can profitably be bred and sold.

Neons, Pencilfish, *Metynnis,* Hatchetfish, *Anostomus, Leporinus* and *Chilodus* are impractical to breed either because of difficulty in propagating or the extremely low prices for imported specimens. All are available in large quantities from foreign exporters of tropical fish.

Killifishes

Killifishes are a group which can only be described in broad language, as the variety of reproductive habits they employ would easily make a full length book. The group is tremendously fertile, but few species are given to large spawnings. The most commercial killies are:

Flag Fish *(Jordanella floridae),*
Fire Killies *(Nothobranchius* species),
Medaka *(Oryzias latipes),*
Panchax Lineatus *(Aplocheilus lineatus),*
Lyretails *(Aphyosemion* species) and
Panchax Chaperi *(Epiplatys chaperi).*

This is a most interesting family of fishes and will give a devotee much delight in accomplishment. The suspense attendant to a six-month delay in hatching *Nothobranchius rachovi* makes any of Hollywood's suspense dramas tame by comparison.

There apparently is a very steady demand for all varieties of "panchax." This group would be a worthwhile specialty for any small breeder.

Catching pond fishes is not an easy job. Prior to filling the pond, a hole is dug in its center. A wire screen barrel is then inserted into the hole. Later on, to catch the fishes, the pump hose is inserted into the barrel and the water is pumped out leaving the pond at a very low level. The screen barrel prevents the fishes from being sucked into the pump. From the remaining shallow water, the fishes are netted out.

Raising Livebearers in Outside Pools

The dirt pool method of propagating tropical fishes is of comparatively recent origin. Albert Greenberg of Tampa and the late H. Woolf, who dug their first dirt pools by hand in the early 1930's, started an industry that today supplies the majority of all tropical fishes sold. Their choice of location (in the vicinity of Tampa, Florida) has proven to be excellent. Today this area supports some 30 different fish farms. The water table is extremely high and even in the driest years fresh water remains within 1.5 m of the surface. For the most part the temperature seldom falls to a chilling point. Vast underground water reserves are available, and by utilizing the pressure from deep wells (200 to 400 m) a flow of warm water (23°C constant the year round) can be fed into each pool. This not only warms the water in the winter and cools it in the summer, but it also helps control the ever-present dangers of fouling, stagnation and drought.

The sizes of individual dirt pools vary. The preference of the individual operator is the governing factor, but generally speaking a pool of 25 to 30 m in length, 5 m wide and 2 m deep (at the deepest end) is most commonly used. The water level will remain constant, as an 8 cm overflow drain is provided for each pool. This carries the excess water off into drainage ditches.

A dirt pool such as the one described above can be dug in two and a half hours. A half-yard bucket dragline is used. The dirt removed is banked around the perimeter of the pool to give additional protection against flood and erosion. One end is always dug deeper than the other. This enables the water to collect at the deepest end when a pool must be pumped dry, thus facilitating cleaning and poisoning.

As a general rule varieties are not mixed in the same pool. The reason for this is not necessarily because the fish will or can interbreed, but rather that the eventual culling operation makes it far too time-consuming to be practical.

The most important single factor for a successful operation is the quality of the original stocking. Quality of a livebearer is determined by two equally important factors: *(a)* color and body development, and *(b)* purity of strain. These desirable traits are accomplished by careful selective breeding. This is a constant and most important part of the fish farmer's work. New strains are always in the process of development. For many years the wide variety of livebearer strains has made a virtual riot of rich colors available to everyone at most reasonable prices.

It is a constant source of pleasure and wonder to realize that from the original dull greens and grays available from the wild platy selective breeding has produced over 20 standard varieties. To further illustrate this tremendous variety, simply check any offering sheet from a Florida fish farmer and you will see that they all work with five basic species. These are Guppies, mollies, swordtails, platies and Platy Variatus. One recent list indicated that from these five original species 67 different color varieties are offered.

The life span of the average pool is approximately one and a half years. At the end of that period the dirt pool must be completely reset. This means that the pool must be pumped dry. This is done with a portable 10 cm water pump run by a gasoline motor. As soon as the pool is dry the treatment starts. Hydrated lime is carefully thrown on the now exposed sides and bottom, one hundred and fifty pounds being the minimum amount used. This will sweeten the soil and also kill any remaining fish. The pool is then allowed to refill itself. This will usually take 48 hours. Another three or four days are allowed to pass, and then the pool is fertilized with cottonseed meal, sheep manure, etc. This will start the food cycle (bacteria ⟶ protozoa ⟶ crustaceans ⟶ fish). A few days after the application of the fertilizer live daphnia is added. At the end of three weeks the pool is ready to receive fish, and if all has been properly done the pool will be teeming with microscopic life. This

Mud ponds are still very much in use. Here a worker sprays down the mud after the pond was emptied.

will give the new stock a fast start. It will take a minimum of eight to twelve months before this pool is ready for harvest. During this time the pool must be kept clean of weeds; this is best done with arsenic compounds which must be carefully applied. Frogs, snakes, birds, water insects, crawfish, drought, flood, excessive heat, excessive cold, water fouling and the introduction of wild fish by birds are just some of the problems that beset the fish farmer. It is not a business for faint hearts or weak backs.

Fishes are removed from the pools by trapping. The bait used is a fishmeal paste. Two types of traps are employed. The most popular trap is a large wire basket trap which is set in the afternoon and allowed to fill with fishes until needed the next day. As these are made of 6 mm hardware cloth and cannot be overcrowded, there is no danger of the fishes suffocating. Smaller plastic or glass "barrel traps" are used during the day. These must be carefully supervised. If too many fishes are trapped too quickly they will suffocate. Work starts at the crack of dawn, as the most productive trapping can be done in the first two hours of daylight.

Portable gasoline driven water pumps are used in the field to move water from one pond (or well) to another pond.

Two methods of grading are currently being employed. The older and more efficient method from a cost point of view is to have the fish graded on the spot in the field. There is no advantage to this other than speed and the subsequent savings in labor cost. The disadvantages are many. The people grading are not supervised and they always have the pressure of time on them, as they have other traps working which must be watched closely. As a result they must at times work faster than is possible to do a good job. In addition, the grading is done outdoors and it is inevitable that at times of extreme heat or cold the water used for the grading purposes will become overheated or severely chilled. The other system, which is employed by all of the most progressive firms, is an indoor grading operation. The fish are removed from the pools and then immediately taken to a grading room. The fish are then carefully and accurately graded for size and color. Off-color fish are removed and destroyed so that when the fish are returned to the pool the strain will be strengthened by the removal of any poor quality fish.

Orders are assembled 48 hours before shipment. The fishes are held in various chemical solutions which will condition them for the rough trip they must make to their ultimate destination. The very best drugs for livebearers are germicidal dyes such as acriflavine and methylene blue. These apparently prevent disease by sterilizing wounds and sores. Tetracycline, Terramycin or sodium sulfathiozole is used in combination with one of these dyes to heal the wounds. Epsom salts stimulate the secretion of the fish's body slime, which further protects it from disease. When the fishes are ready for shipment they are in top condition.

Livebearing fishes are also produced in the Miami, Florida, area in concrete pools of large size. As the cost of construction of these pools is so much greater than a comparably sized dirt pool, all of the Miami farmers have small pools and the quantity of fishes produced is much lower. In recent years the Miami operations have more and more specialized in imported wild fishes and the raising of egglayers. A very great percentage of the livebearers sold from Miami are actually produced in the Tampa area and sent to Miami for conditioning, sizing and eventual sale.

The Importance of Fast Air Transport

In recent years, the price of fishes, especially the rarer species, has come down considerably. Hobbyists, of course, are reluctant to look a gift horse in the mouth. They have given little thought to the reasons behind the lower prices; they are much more likely to have pocketed their savings and been grateful for the price reduction. But whether they've thought about it or not, there are some basic economic factors involved in their windfall. Increasing popularity of the hobby is one big reason. As more people make a demand for fishes, dealers are able to rely more and more on a large volume of small-markup sales instead of a few high-markup sales. Individual unit prices therefore decline, to the benefit of hobbyists.

But there are other factors, too, one of the biggest being the availability of fast air freight to large commercial breeders and importers. Air freight is an asset to hatcheries because it is a time saver. When shipping tropicals, anything that saves time saves lives; the longer a fish is in transit, the greater are the chances that it will arrive dead or dying. Mortality of transported fishes is a very real expense. Whether this cost be absorbed by wholesaler or retailer matters little to the hobbyist; what does matter is that the cost of fishes killed or debilitated on the way to his favorite fish store is ultimately passed on, at least in part, to him. What hurts the dealer hurts the hobbyist; con-

This holding building is one of several such facilities located at intervals between the mud ponds.

versely, anything that helps the dealer also helps the hobbyist. Fast air freight applied to the tropical fish field has helped a lot, and not only in the area of price. Without air freight it would be next to impossible to bring in some of the weird beauties that are on the market today. Some of the most colorful fishes, especially marine fishes, would be completely unobtainable.

But although air transport has had a healthy effect on the hobby, there are still problems. Airlines are still hampered by the weather, more so than other transportation media. Also, the advantages of speed of transport must be paid for; air rates are high. Luckily, progressive shippers have been able to develop methods for safely shipping many fishes in just a little water, thus cutting down on freight costs and allowing the advantages gained by rapid delivery to be passed along to the hobbyist.

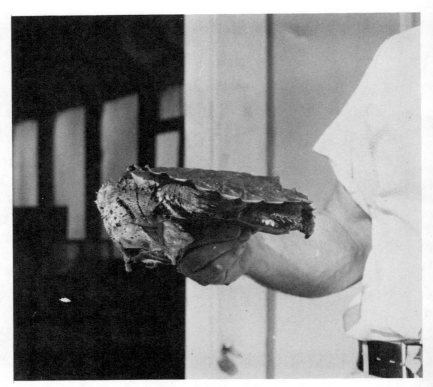
Turtles and other animals are forever taking up residence in the fish ponds.

One method used to reduce the weight of shipments is to pump pure oxygen into a large plastic shipping bag filled with water to only about one-seventh of its capacity. The fishes have less room to swim, but they can be packed closely because the water constantly absorbs fresh oxygen. This process can be made doubly effective by putting tranquilizers into the water. In this way the fishes are less active and give off less carbon dioxide, the real killer when fishes are crowded.

Even these new methods, however, cannot eliminate the painstaking work done by the commercial people to provide hobbyists with a large selection of healthy tropicals. The fishes still have to be bred and raised to good size, collected, sorted, acclimated and packed. So far there have been few shortcuts in these systems. The most efficient transportation in the world can neither help a breeder to raise nice Sailfin Mollies nor give him a hand in sorting and checking his stock so that only the healthiest, most vigorous fishes are shipped. These things are still done mostly by hand. There's a lot of work involved, but it's worth it.

COMPREHENSIVE INDEX

The following is a comprehensive index covering the four basic sections (Aquarium Management, Plants, Tropical Fish, and Commercial Breeding) of *EXOTIC TROPICAL FISHES,* EXPANDED EDITION. Like the text of this book, this index reflects the latest changes in scientific nomenclature. This index will be expanded periodically to take into account additional supplement books added to the basic text.

Use of the index:
A straight-forward page reference system is used in this index. All valid scientific names of fishes, plants or other organisms are indicated by *bold italic type* while all junior synonyms (invalid scientific names) are indicated by *non-bold italic type.* Page numbers in **bold type** refer to full-color plates.

This index uses a cross referencing system for fish and plant scientific nomenclature. Each species is listed under its full scientific name (genus name followed by specific name), under its specific name (species, genus) and under its common name(s). If the species was recently known under a name which is now a junior synonym, the junior synonym is listed under its generic name and also under its specific name; both of these listings   refer   the reader to the organism's present valid scientific name.

About *Exotic Tropical Fishes* Supplement Books

Looseleaf binding is a very useful feature in a book designed to meet the needs of people involved in a dynamic pastime like the tropical fish hobby. New fishes are being introduced to the market all the time, so to help readers keep up to date on new developments we issue Supplement Books to *Exotic Tropical Fishes* at regular intervals, and the looseleaf binding makes it very easy to include the supplement pages right in the basic volume.

Some readers, however, prefer non-looseleaf bindings. Therefore we have produced the Expanded Edition of *Exotic Tropical Fishes* in both looseleaf and non-looseleaf form, and buyers can take their choice. Since the form in which we produce the Supplement Books makes it possible to use the pages *regardless of which type of binding a reader has,* owners of the non-looseleaf version don't lose the valuable grow-along-with-the-hobby feature that the Supplement Books provide.

Free Supplements Available with *Tropical Fish Hobbyist Magazine*

Subscribers to *Tropical Fish Hobbyist* Magazine receive their supplement pages automatically and at no extra charge, because each monthly issue of the magazine contains looseleaf-holed supplement pages that can be removed from the magazine and easily inserted into *Exotic Tropical Fishes.* Subscribers therefore receive their supplement pages at no extra cost—they save both money and effort and never have to worry that they'll miss any supplements. If you're not already a subscriber to *Tropical Fish Hobbyist,* the world's most exciting and informative aquarium magazine, please use the handy subscription form provided to start your subscription right now.

Non-subscribers don't receive their supplements free or automatically, but they can keep their books up to date at all times by buying the Supplement Books. The Supplement Books are issued on a regular basis and are available at pet shops everywhere.

INDEX

1053, **1054, 1055,** 1056

Angelfish; commercial breeding, 1234, 1235

Angelicus, **1147,** 1148

Angelicus Pimelodus, **979,** 980

angelicus, Synodontis, **1147,** 1148

angolensis, Clarias, 521, **522**

anguillicaudatus, Misgurnus, 873, **874**

Anguillula, 71, 73

angulatus, Triportheus, 1181, **1182**

anisitsi, Aphyocharax, 301, **302**

Annectens, **703,** 704

annectens, Haplochromis, **703,** 704

annectens, Protopterus, 1017, **1018**

annulatus, Epiplatys, **643,** 644

anomala, Nannacara, **891,** 892

anomalura, Oxygaster, **939,** 940

anomalus, Nannostomus, see *Nannostomus beckfordi*

Anoptichthys jordani, see *Astyanax fasciatus mexicanus*

Anostomus anostomus, 293, **294**

anostomus, Anostomus, 293, **294**

Anostomus taeniata, see
  Anostomus taeniatus

Anostomus taeniatus, **295,** 296

Anostomus trimaculatus, **295,** 296

ansorgei, Ctenopoma, **583,** 584

ansorgei, Neolebias, **907,** 908

ansorgei, Phractura, **975,** 976

Ansorge's Neolebias, **907,** 908

ansorgi, Pelmatochromis, see
  Thysia ansorgi

ansorgii, Thysia, **1163,** 1164

Antibiotics, 79, 82, 86

antipyretica, Fontinalis, 140

antipyretica var. *gracilis, Fontinalis,* 140

Anubias afzelii, 181, **195**

Anubias lanceolata, 181

Anubias nana, 179, 181, **194**

Anubias species, 148, 178, 180

Apareiodon pongoensis, see *Parodon pongoense*

Apeltes quadracus, 297, **298**

Aphanius dispar, 297, **298**

Aphanius iberus, **299,** 300

Aphanius mento, **299,** 300

Aphredoderus sayanus, 301, **302**

Aphyocharax anisitsi, 301, **302**

Aphyocharax axelrodi, see *Megalamphodus axelrodi*

Aphyocharax dentatus, **303,** 304

Aphyocharax erythrurus, **303,** 304

Aphyocharax rubripinnis, see
  A. anisitsi

Aphyosemion ahli, 305, **306**

Aphyosemion arnoldi, 305, **306**

Aphyosemion australe, 120, 121, **307** 308

Aphyosemion australe australe, see
  A. australe

Aphyosemion bertholdi, **307,** 308

Aphyosemion bivittatum, 309, **310**

Aphyosemion bivittatum hollyi, see
  A. bivittatum

Aphyosemion bualanum, 311, 312

Aphyosemion calliurum, 313, **314**

Aphyosemion calliurum ahli, see *A. ahli*

Aphyosemion calliurum calliurum, see
  A. calliurum

Aphyosemion chaytori, 313, **314**

Aphyosemion christyi, 315, 316

Aphyosemion cinnamomeum, 315, 316

Aphyosemion coeruleum, see
  A. sjoestedti

Aphyosemion cognatum, 317, **318**

Aphyosemion filamentosum, 317, **318**

Aphyosemion gardneri, **319,** 320

Aphyosemion geryi, 321, **322**

Aphyosemion guineense, **323,** 324

Aphyosemion labarrei, **323,** 324

Aphyosemion liberiense, 325, **326**

Aphyosemion occidentalis, 325, **326**

Aphyosemion petersi, **327,** 328

Aphyosemion seymouri, **327,** 328

Aphyosemion sjoestedti, 329, **330**

Aphyosemion striatum, 329, **330**

1261

Free Supplements Available With *Tropical Fish Hobbyist* Magazine

Subscribers to *Tropical Fish Hobbyist* magazine receive their supplement pages to *Exotic Tropical Fishes* automatically as they're issued. Refer to pages at the end of this book for handy subscription form.

Cyprinodonts, breeding, 120, 121
Cyprinus carpio, 609, **610, 611,** 612, 613, **614, 615,** 616, 617, **618, 619**

D

dadiburjori, Laubuca, **823,** 824
Dadio, **823,** 824
dageti, Epiplatys, 649, **650**
dageti monroviae, Epiplatys, 649
daguae, Astyanax, 365, **366**
daniconius, Rasbora, **1079,** 1080
Danio aequipinnatus, 620, 621, **622**
Danio devario, 621, **622**
Danio malabaricus, see *D. aequipinnatus*
Danio malabaricus, commercial breeding, 1231
danrica, Esomus, **659,** 660
Daphnia, 63, 64
Daphnia, commercial use, 1222
Dark Australian Rainbow, **867,** 868
Dash-Dot Tetra, 729, **730**
Datnioides microlepis, **623,** 624
Datnioides quadrifasciatus, **623,** 624
daubenyana, Nymphaea, 241
David's Upside-Down Catfish, **1147,** 1148
dayi, Aplocheilus, 353, **354**
Day's Panchax, 353, **354**
Day's Paradise Fish, 849, **850**
debauwi, Eutropiellus, **663,** 664
deckeri, Corydoras, **563**
deissneri, Parosphromenus, **955,** 956
demersum, Ceratophyllum, 163, 170, 176, 236
Demon Fish, **687,** 688
densa, Egeria, 163
densa, Elodea, 161, 162, 173, 213, **216,** 217
dentatus, Aphyocharax, **303,** 304
Dermogenys pusillus, 625, **626**
Dermogenys pusillus, commercial breeding, 1236
desertorum, Aponogeton, 187, 188
Desert Pupfish, **607,** 608
devario, Danio, 621, **622**

Devil's lilac, 152, 154
Diagonal Bar Simochromis, 1121, **1122**
Diagramma, 1121, **1122**
diagramma, Simochromis, 1121, **1122**
Diamond Killifish, **271,** 272
Diamond Sunfish, **639,** 640
Diamond Tetra, 877, **878**
Dianema longibarbis, 625, **626**
Dianema urostriata, **627,** 628
Diaptomus, 65
Dichotomous, 253
dichroura, Moenkhausia, **875,** 876
Dickfeldi, 793, **794**
dickfeldi, Julidochromis, 793, **794**
difformis, Hygrophila, 133, 165, **230,** 245
Dimidiatus, **903,** 904
dimidiatus, Nanochromis, **903,** 904
Dioecious, 253
discorhynchus, Hippopotamyrus, 753, **754**
Discus, 1132
discus, Symphysodon, 1140, 1141, **1142, 1143,** 1144
Disease prevention, 1226
dispar, Aphanius, 297, **298**
distachyus, Aponogeton, 145, 187, 188
Distichodus affinis, **627,** 628,
Distichodus fasciolatus, 629, **630**
Distichodus lusosso, 629, **630**
Distichodus noboli, **631,** 632
Distichodus sexfasciatus, **631,** 632
djambi, Cryptocoryne, see *Cryptocoryne johorensis*
Dogfish, 285, **286**
Dogtooth Cichlid, **603,** 604
Dog-with-two-tails, 187, 188
dolichoptera, Xenocara, **1195,** 1196
dolichopterus, Austrofundulus, **371,** 372
Dolphin Cichlid, **275,** 276
doriae, Brachygobius, 429, **430**

maruloides, Ophiocephalus, see *Channa maruloides*
Mashes, wet commercial use, 1223
Masked Corydoras, **547,** 548
Masked Julidochromis, 797, **798**
Masked Minnow, 669, **670**
Mastacembelus armatus, 853, **854**
Mastacembelus erythrotaenia, 853, **854**
Mastacembelus zebrinus, **855,** 856
maxillaris, Pristella, **1015,** 1016
Mealworms, commercial use , 1223
Medaka, 929, **930**
Medaka, commercial breeding, 1241
Medications, 76
meeki, Cichlasoma, 117-119, 509, **510, 511,** 512
Megalamphodus axelrodi, **855,** 856
Megalamphodus megalopterus, 857, **858**
Megalamphodus sweglesi, **859,** 860
megalopterus, Megalamphodus, 857, **858**
megalotis, Lepomis, 829, **830**
melanampyx, Capoeta, **447,** 448
melanistius, Corydoras, **559,** 565
Melanochromis auratus, 861, **862**
Melanochromis johanni, **863,** 864
Melanochromis vermivorus, 865, **866**
melanogaster, Poecilia, 989, **990**
melanopleura, Leporinus, **835,** 836
melanopleura, Sarotherodon, 236
melanopterus, Balantiocheilos, 377, **378**
melanopterus, Channa, 482
melanopterus, Ophiocephalus, see *Channa melanopterus*
melanosoma, Channa, 482
melanosoma, Ophiocephalus, see *Channa melanosoma*
melanospilus, Nothobranchius, **919,** 920
melanotaenia, Cynolebias, **599,** 600

melanotaenia, Cynopoecilus, see *Cynolebias melanotaenia*
Melanotaenia maccullochi, **867,** 868
Melanotaenia nigrans, **867,** 868
Melanotaenia splendida, 869, **870**
melanozonus, Micropoecilia, see *Poecilia parae*
melanurus, Bryconops, 437, **438**
melini, Corydoras, **566**
mento, Aphanius, **299,** 300
mento, Catoprion, **467,** 468
mento, Genyochromis, 681, **682**
Mercurochrome, 1226, 1227
Merry Widow, 969, **970**
Mesogonistius chaetodon, see *Enneacanthus chaetodon*
metae, Corydoras, **547,** 548
metae, Hyphessobrycon, 769, **770**
metallicus, Girardinus, **691,** 692
Methylene blue, 80, 1227, 1228, 1246
Metynnis hypsauchen, 869, **870**
Metynnis maculatus, **871,** 872
Metynnis schreitmuelleri, see *M. hypsauchen*
Mexican Swordtail, 1209, **1210**
Mexican Tetra, **367,** 368
mexicana, Azolla, 138
Mexicana Molly, 989, **990**
mexicana, Poecilia, 989, **990**
mexicanus, Astyanax, see *Astyanax fasciatus mexicanus*
Micralestes acutidens, **871,** 872
Micranthemum orbiculatum, see *Hemianthus orbiculatum*
Microbrycon fredcochui, see *Boehlkea fredcochui*
microdon, Najas, 237
microcephalus, Abramites, see *Abramites hypselonotus*
microcephala, Curimata, 589, **590**
microfolia, Sagittaria, 143
Microglanis poecilus, 873, **874**
microlepis, Acestrorhynchus, 267, 268
microlepis, Coelurichthys, **523,** 524
microlepis, Datnioides, **623,** 624

1280

microlepis, Trichogaster, 1173,
1174
micropeltes, Channa, 477, **478, 479,**
480, 482
micropeltes, Ophiocephalus, see Channa
micropeltes
microphylla, Rorippa, 245
Micropoecilia melanozonus, see Poecilia
parae
microps, Corydoras, **547,** 548
microstoma, Pseudotropheus, 1033,
1034
Microworms, 71, 73
Microworms, commercial use, 1223
Midget Minnow, **759,** 760
Midget Sucker Catfish, **935,** 936
Mimagoniates inequalis, see Glandulocauda inequalis
Mineral blocks, 19
Minerals, fishes' requirements of, 60
Minerals, relative compositions in various waters, 19
minimum, Nuphar, see N. pumilum
minor, Elodea, 158
minor, Najas, **235**
minor, Utricularia, 151
Misgurnus anguillicaudatus, 873,
874
miurus, Tetraodon, **1159,** 1160
modesta, Botia, 421, **422**
Moenkhausia dichroura, **875,** 876
Moenkhausia oligolepis, **875,** 876
Moenkhausia pittieri, 877, **878**
Moenkhausia sanctaefilomenae, **879,**
880
Mogurnda mogurnda, **879,** 880
mogurnda, Mogurnda, **879,** 880
Mollienesia caucana, see Poecilia
caucana
Mollienesia latipinna, see Poecilia latipinna
Mollienesia sphenops, see Poecilia
sphenops
Mollienesia velifera, see Poecilia
velifera
monniera, Bacopa, 189

Mono, **883, 884**
Monocirrhus polyacanthus, 881,
882, 883
Monodactylus argenteus, **883,** 884
Monodactylus sebae, 885, **886**
montezumae, Xiphophorus, 1209,
1210
Moonbeam Gourami, 1173, **1174**
Moorii, 1185, **1186, 1187,** 1188, 1189
1190
moorii, Haplochromis, **715,** 716
moorii, Tropheus, 1185, **1186, 1187,**
1188, 1189, **1190**
Mormyrops engystoma, 885, **886**
morsus-ranae, Hydrocharis, 154,
155, 166, 176
Morulius chrysophekadion, **887,** 888
Mosaic Gourami, **1171,** 1172
Mosquito Fish, 669, **670,** 753, **754**
mossambica, Tilapia, see Sarotherodon
mossambicus
mossambicus, Sarotherodon, **1107,**
1108
motleyi, Barclaya, 144
Mottled Ctenopoma, **587,** 588
Mottled Glass Catfish, 949, **950**
Mottled Knife Fish, 1129, **1130**
Mottled Sculpin, 569, **570**
Mountain Goby, 1121, **1122**
Mourning Tetra, **755,** 756
Mousetail Knife Fish, 1193, **1194**
Mozambique Mouthbrooder, **1107,**
1108
mucronata, Marsilea, 141
Mudfish, 285, **286**
Mudskipper, **963,** 964
mullerti, Ludwigia, 232
Mulm, 10
Mulm (removal), 24, 25
multicolor, Haplochromis, see Pseudocrenilabrus multicolor
multicolor, Pseudocrenilabrus,
1021, **1022**
multifasciata, Selenotoca, 1113, **1114**
multifasciatus, Leporinus, see Leporinus
fasciatus

Scatophagus argus, 1109, **1110**
schalleri, Ctenops, see *Trichopsis*
  schalleri
schalleri, Trichopsis, 1177, **1178**
Schilbe marmoratus, 1109, **1110**
Schmard Tetra, 741, **742**
schmardae, Hemigrammus, 741,
  742
schoelleri, Aplocheilichthys, 351,
  352
scholzei, Hyphessobrycon, 771, 772
schomburgki, Polycentrus, 1009,
  1010
Schomburgk's Leaf Fish, 1009, **1010**
schreitmuelleri, Metynnis, see *Metynnis*
  hypsauchen
schultzei, Corydoras, 559
schultzei, Myloplus, see *Myleus*
  rubripinnis
schwanenfeldi, Barbodes, 389, **390**
schwartzi, Corydoras, 555, 556
Schwartz's Corydoras, **555,** 556
Sciades marmoratus, **1111,** 1112
Sciades pictus, **1111,** 1112
Scissortailed Rasbora, 1093, **1094**
Scleropages formosus, 1113, **1114**
Scott, 162
Scud, 65, 67
sebae, Monodactylus, 885, **886**
Selenotoca multifasciata, 1113,**1114**
Semaprochilodus taeniurus, **1115,**
  1116
Semaprochilodus theraponura,
  1115, 1116
semiaquilus, Corydoras, 568
**semicinctus, Acanthophthalmus,
  263,** 264
semifasciolatus, Capoeta, 451,
  452
septentrionalis, Corydoras, 568
sericeus, Rhodeus, 1099, 1100
**serpae haraldschultzi, Hyphesso-
  brycon,** 773, **774**
**serpae serpae, Hyphessobrycon,
  774, 775,** 776
Serpae Tetra, **774, 775,** 776

serperaster, Parapocryptes, 949, **950**
Serrasalmo hollandi, see
  Serrasalmus hollandi
Serrasalmo nattereri, see
  Serrasalmus nattereri
Serrasalmus calmoni, 1117, **1118**
Serrasalmus hollandi, 1117, **1118**
Serrasalmus nattereri, 1119, 1120
Serrasalmus rhombeus, 1119, 1120
Sessile, 253
sessiliflora, Limnophila, 133, 165
setacea, Isolepis, 157
setigerum, Luciosoma, 845, **846**
Seven-Spotted Archer Fish, 1169, **1170**
Severum, 517, **518**
severum, Cichlasoma, 517, **518**
Sex differences, 95
sexfasciatus, Distichodus, 631, 632
sexfasciatus, Epiplatys, 653, **654**
Sexual reproduction, plant, 130
seymouri, Aphyosemion, 327, 328
Seymour's Killifish, **327, 328**
Shark-Tailed Distichodus, 629, **630**
Sharpheaded Cichlid, 505, **506**
Sharp-Toothed Tetra, **871,** 872
shelfordi, Acanthophthalmus, 263,
  264
Shelford's Loach, **263,** 264
sheljuzhkoi, Epiplatys, see
  Epiplatys chaperi sheljuzhkoi
Sheljuzhko's Panchax, 645, **646**
Shell grit, 49
Shimmies, 31, 90
Shipment of fishes, 1246-1248
Short-Bodied Catfish, **431,** 432
Shortfin Molly, 989, **990**
Short-Finned Trahira, 657, **658**
Short-Lined Pyrrhulina, 1069, **1070**
Short-Striped Penquin, 1161, **1162**
Shovelmouth, **1027,** 1028
Shovelnose Catfish, **1123,** 1124
Shrimp, brine, 66-69
Shrimp, brine (commercial use), 1219
Shrimp, fairy (commercial use), 1223
siamensis, Cryptocoryne, 148, **203**
siamensis, Epalzeorhynchus, **643,**644

About *Exotic Tropical Fishes* Supplement Books

Looseleaf binding is a very useful feature in a book designed to meet the needs of people involved in a dynamic pastime like the tropical fish hobby. New fishes are being introduced to the market all the time, so to help readers keep up to date on new developments we issue Supplement Books to *Exotic Tropical Fishes* at regular intervals, and the looseleaf binding makes it very easy to include the supplement pages right in the basic volume.

Some readers, however, prefer non-looseleaf bindings. Therefore we have produced the Expanded Edition of *Exotic Tropical Fishes* in both looseleaf and non-looseleaf form, and buyers can take their choice. Since the form in which we produce the Supplement Books makes it possible to use the pages *regardless of which type of binding a reader has,* owners of the non-looseleaf version don't lose the valuable grow-along-with-the-hobby feature that the Supplement Books provide.

Free Supplements Available with *Tropical Fish Hobbyist Magazine*

Subscribers to *Tropical Fish Hobbyist* Magazine receive their supplement pages automatically and at no extra charge, because each monthly issue of the magazine contains looseleaf-holed supplement pages that can be removed from the magazine and easily inserted into *Exotic Tropical Fishes.* Subscribers therefore receive their supplement pages at no extra cost—they save both money and effort and never have to worry that they'll miss any supplements. If you're not already a subscriber to *Tropical Fish Hobbyist,* the world's most exciting and informative aquarium magazine, please use the handy subscription form provided to start your subscription right now.

Non-subscribers don't receive their supplements free or automatically, but they can keep their books up to date at all times by buying the Supplement Books. The Supplement Books are issued on a regular basis and are available at pet shops everywhere.

Individual supplement pages in each Supplement Book (and in the magazine, of course) are hole-punched and perforated for easy removal. Additionally, they are keyed by page number, making it easy for readers to put them into their proper places in the basic volume after they are removed from the Supplement Books or from the magazine. Owners of the non-looseleaf version of the basic volume can keep their supplements in a looseleaf (T.F.H. stocks a separate binder for just such usage) or can leave them within the sturdy covers of the Supplement Books.

Since twenty-five Supplement Books were issued to the Original Edition, the Supplement Books to the Expanded Edition begin with Supplement Book #26. Owners of this, the Expanded Edition, do not need any of the first 25 Supplement Books, as every fish covered in these Supplement Books has been covered in the basic volume of the Expanded Edition. Owners of the Expanded Edition can make their books completely up to date by beginning their Supplement Book series with Book #26—and of course owners of the Original Edition can keep their books up to date simply by continuing their sets of Supplement Books, because Supplement Books #26 and all succeeding Supplement Books can be used as supplements to both the Original Edition and the Expanded Edition.

IMPORTANT NOTICE

In 1980 an expanded edition of *EXOTIC TROPICAL FISHES* was published in both a looseleaf form and in the usual hardcover form. This 1980 edition contains all the supplements issued from Supplement Book 1 through Supplement Book 25.

For keeping this expanded edition up to date, you are advised to subscribe to *TROPICAL FISH HOBBYIST MAGAZINE* (supplements are issued monthly as part of the magazine) or to maintain contact with your tropical fish supplier, who will have new supplement books as they are issued. If you have the looseleaf edition (either the Original Edition or the Expanded 1980 Edition), new supplements can be inserted by using one of the two page numbers which appear on the first page of each supplement; one page number is for the Original Edition and one is for the Expanded Edition. If you have the hardcover edition, merely keep the supplement book alongside your hardcover edition and refer to the cumulative index to supplements which is issued regularly (once a year) in *Tropical Fish Hobbyist* magazine.

You can subscribe to *Tropical Fish Hobbyist* magazine by using the subscription form on the back

FAMILIARITY
BREEDS
CONTENT

TROPICAL FISH HOBBYIST magazine has been. . . and still is. . . the largest-selling aquarium magazine in the world. A subscription is your KEY to all the newest, most desirable of aquarium fishes. Its issues contain information that is not found in any aquarium book. As a matter of fact, that's our editorial policy: TO PROVIDE NEWS ABOUT AQUARIUM FISHES THAT IS NOT FOUND IN BOOKS.

SUBSCRIBE NOW TO THE WORLD'S LARGEST-SELLING AQUARIUM MAGAZINE. Send your check, cash or money order to:

TROPICAL FISH HOBBYIST MAGAZINE
P.O. BOX 27, NEPTUNE, N.J. 07753

☐ Sample copy, $1; ☐ 12 issues, 1 year, $7.50; ☐ 24 issues, 2 years, $13; ☐ 36 issues, 3 years, $20.00

YOUR NAME _____

STREET _____

CITY _____ STATE _____ ZIP _____

Subscribers receive every issue of TROPICAL FISH HOBBYIST without fail.

Subscribers are kept informed about every important development in the aquarium hobby. . . the new fish, the new people, the new products, the new techniques. . . every month.

They also know that they'll always be up-to-date with their free supplements to EXOTIC TROPICAL FISHES.

Subscribe NOW to TROPICAL FISH HOBBYIST, the biggest (more pages, more pictures, more information, more readers), most colorful (a minimum of 32 color pages in each issue), most interesting aquarium magazine in the world.

IMPORTANT NOTICE

In 1980 an expanded edition of *EXOTIC TROPICAL FISHES* was published in both a looseleaf form and in the usual hardcover form. This 1980 edition contains all the supplements issued from Supplement Book 1 through Supplement Book 25.

For keeping this expanded edition up to date, you are advised to subscribe to *TROPICAL FISH HOBBYIST MAGAZINE* (supplements are issued monthly as part of the magazine) or to maintain contact with your tropical fish supplier, who will have new supplement books as they are issued. If you have the looseleaf edition (either the Original Edition or the Expanded 1980 Edition), new supplements can be inserted by using one of the two page numbers which appear on the first page of each supplement; one page number is for the Original Edition and one is for the Expanded Edition. If you have the hardcover edition, merely keep the supplement book alongside your hardcover edition and refer to the cumulative index to supplements which is issued regularly (once a year) in *Tropical Fish Hobbyist* magazine.

You can subscribe to *Tropical Fish Hobbyist* magazine by using the subscription form on the back

MOST THOUGHT
AFTER MAGAZINE

TROPICAL FISH HOBBYIST magazine has been. . . and still is. . . the largest-selling aquarium magazine in the world. A subscription is your KEY to all the newest, most desirable of aquarium fishes. Its issues contain information that is not found in any aquarium book. As a matter of fact, that's our editorial policy: **TO PROVIDE NEWS ABOUT AQUARIUM FISHES THAT IS NOT FOUND IN BOOKS.**

SUBSCRIBE NOW TO THE WORLD'S LARGEST-SELLING AQUARIUM MAGAZINE. Send your check, cash or money order to:

TROPICAL FISH HOBBYIST MAGAZINE
P.O. BOX 27, NEPTUNE, N.J. 07753

☐ Sample copy, $1; ☐ 12 issues, 1 year, $7.50; ☐ 24 issues, 2 years, $13; ☐ 36 issues, 3 years, $20.00

YOUR NAME _____

STREET _____

CITY _____ STATE _____ ZIP _____

Subscribers receive every issue of TROPICAL FISH HOBBYIST without fail.

Subscribers are kept informed about every important development in the aquarium hobby. . . the new fish, the new people, the new products, the new techniques. . . every month.

They also know that they'll always be up-to-date with their free supplements to EXOTIC TROPICAL FISHES.

Subscribe NOW to TROPICAL FISH HOBBYIST, the biggest (more pages, more pictures, more information, more readers), most colorful (a minimum of 32 color pages in each issue), most interesting aquarium magazine in the world.

IMPORTANT NOTICE

In 1980 an expanded edition of *EXOTIC TROPICAL FISHES* was published in both a looseleaf form and in the usual hardcover form. This 1980 edition contains all the supplements issued from Supplement Book 1 through Supplement Book 25.

For keeping this expanded edition up to date, you are advised to subscribe to *TROPICAL FISH HOBBYIST MAGAZINE* (supplements are issued monthly as part of the magazine) or to maintain contact with your tropical fish supplier, who will have new supplement books as they are issued. If you have the looseleaf edition (either the Original Edition or the Expanded 1980 Edition), new supplements can be inserted by using one of the two page numbers which appear on the first page of each supplement; one page number is for the Original Edition and one is for the Expanded Edition. If you have the hardcover edition, merely keep the supplement book alongside your hardcover edition and refer to the cumulative index to supplements which is issued regularly (once a year) in *Tropical Fish Hobbyist* magazine.

You can subscribe to *Tropical Fish Hobbyist* magazine by using the subscription form on the back